MW00857010

THE MAHĀ-VAIROCANA-ABHISAMBODHI TANTRA

THE MAHĀ-VAIROCANA-ABHISAṂBODHI TANTRA

WITH BUDDHAGUHYA'S COMMENTARY

Translated by

STEPHEN HODGE

Routledge
Taylor & Francis Group
LONDON AND NEW YORK

First Published in 2003
by RoutledgeCurzon

Published 2015 by Routledge
2 Park Square, Milton Park, Abingdon, Oxfordshire OX14 4RN
711 Third Avenue, New York, NY 10017

First issued in paperback 2015

Routledge is an imprint of the Taylor and Francis Group, an informa business

Typeset in Baskerville by LaserScript Ltd, Mitcham, Surrey

British Library Cataloguing in Publication Data
A catalogue record of this book is available from the British Library

Library of Congress Cataloging in Publication Data
A catalog record for this book has been requested

ISBN 13: 978-1-138-98015-0 (pbk)
ISBN 13: 978-0-7007-1183-3 (hbk)

CONTENTS

Part I
INTRODUCTION

I GENERAL INTRODUCTION

During the last thirty years there has been a revolution in the understanding and appreciation of the Buddhist tantras in the West. Whereas they had been regarded in the past with suspicion and disdain by those who saw them as the hybrid products of a degenerate form of late Indian Buddhism, they are now the focus of great interest among both the growing band of Western Buddhists following the Tibetan tradition and the smaller number of Western academics specializing in Buddhist and related studies, as will be evident from even a cursory glance at bibliographies of works on Buddhism now in print. However, this new interest in the Buddhist tantras still has many limitations and unfortunately a detailed description of the development of tantric thought and practices is far from being complete. This situation will not be remedied until much more textual work has been done by the few scholars who have access to the original materials surviving in the various Asian languages. Moreover, almost without exception, present-day scholars in the West have relied solely on Tibetan materials and such Indic texts as have survived the ravages of time for their studies on the tantras. While much valuable work has thus been produced by these scholars, they do present a somewhat one-sided view of Tantric Buddhism as they have tended to concentrate on the more spectacular Anuttara-yoga tantras. For apart from these, there is also a wealth of other tantric literature preserved in Tibetan sources, dealing with the Kriyā, Caryā and Yoga tantras, that awaits detailed exploration and translation. Additionally, the neglect of the vast amount of literature related to Tantric Buddhism available in Chinese translation is quite regrettable, although this is understandable in view of the quite daunting range of linguistic skills which is needed to make full use of these texts. It would not be surprising to find that most Western scholars working on Buddhist tantras from the Indo-Tibetan side are largely unaware of the enormous volume of translated tantric texts preserved in Chinese. We can better understand the sheer bulk of available material if we relate it to the present work. The Chinese text of the *Mahāvairocana Tantra* covers just forty four pages in the standard Taishō Edition and my translation of this covers about 200 pages. However there are another 3,554 pages of texts related to Tantric Buddhism in Chinese, which at the above rate would amount to over 16,150 pages in English. And that is before we start on the native Chinese and Japanese commentarial works, manuals and so forth! A comprehensive study of this material is vital for an understanding of the origins of Tantric Buddhism, for while the Tibetan tradition is strong on later tantric works and less so on earlier ones, the situation with the Chinese materials is the reverse – they have preserved many of the earlier Indian texts which were never translated into Tibetan. This is not only true of 'tantric' style texts, but also can be said of all Buddhist works in general. It must be remembered that the bulk of Chinese translations had been completed before the Tibetans had really begun their work on the canon. Chinese translation activities began in the middle of the 2nd century CE and continued until at least the first half of the 11th century, a period of over nine hundred years! Moreover, in stark contrast to the paucity of relevant materials providing reliable dates in Indology, documents from the Chinese tradition often record various historical data with great accuracy. It is noteworthy that the dates when Buddhist texts were translated into Chinese during this nine hundred year period are known in the majority of cases, thereby providing us with a loose framework for the chronology of the development of Buddhist texts. It should therefore not surprise us if the insights we can derive from Chinese sources cast a different light on the development of Tantric Buddhism.

For example, it is normal to classify the tantras into four categories – Kriyā, Caryā, Yoga and Anuttara-yoga – following the normal Tibetan practice and this system of classification is now treated by modern Western scholars as though it were in some way definitive. But it is clear from a study of earlier tantric materials, especially of those preserved in the Chinese tradition, that this system of classification, useful though it was to very late Indian exegetes and their Tibetan successors, was gradually developed to make sense of the mass of tantric materials that they were faced with. Nevertheless, it may be said that this system of classification also represents, in a general manner, the historical sequence in which the tantras were developed. In other words, the majority of the texts that came to be classified as Kriyā tantras derive from the earliest proto-tantric phase, leading on through Caryā tantras to the Yoga and later the Anuttara-yoga tantras. This will be seen most clearly later when we briefly examine the contents of tantric-style texts surviving in Chinese, together with their dates of translation.

But before proceeding any further, it might be useful to attempt a definition for the reader of exactly what kind of texts we may legitimately call tantras, for the situation is not as straightforward as some might wish to believe. I remember asking someone who has specialized in the Indian tantric tradition how can one identify tantric texts as being such and was given the rather ingenuous answer that this is easy because tantras have the word 'tantra' in their titles. But this is clearly not the case, because a number of texts that one would formally classify as tantras are in fact called *sūtras*, such as the *Maha-vairocana-abhisambodhi*[1] itself, the *Sarva-tathāgata-tattva-saṃgraha* and several of the early rNying-ma tantras, such as the *dGongs-'dus* (T 829), the *rNgam-glog* (T 830), the *Kun-'dus* (T 831) and so forth. In fact, the word 'tantra' itself does not even appear anywhere in some of these texts, including the present text itself.

Definitions of the term do appear in some later tantric texts, such as the famous lines in the Continuation Tantra of the *Guhya-samāja*, which state '*"Tantra" is continuity and that continuity is threefold: the ground, the intrinsic nature and the indestructible. The intrinsic nature is the immanent cause, the indestructible is the result and the ground is the means. The meaning of "tantra" is summarized by these three*[2]'. However, important as these definitions are, they tend to be somewhat doctrinal or soteriological in nature, so we should try to isolate the key constituent elements which go to make up what one might call Tantric Buddhism in its widest sense, to get a better grasp of what we are dealing with. There are a number of such elements, some of which were derived from earlier trends within Buddhism itself and others which were adopted and adapted from non-Buddhist sources. Obviously it is beyond the scope of this book to present a full-scale study and documentation of all these elements, desirable though that may be, but instead I shall confine myself to a summary of those features which characterize the spirit of Buddhist tantric thought[3]:

1 Tantric Buddhism offers an alternative path to Enlightenment in addition to the standard Mahāyāna one.

2 Its teachings are aimed at lay practitioners in particular, rather than monks and nuns.
3 As a consequence of this, it recognizes mundane aims and attainments, and often deals with practices which are more magical in character than spiritual.
4 It teaches special types of meditation (*sādhana*) as the path to realization, aimed at transforming the individual into an embodiment of the divine in this lifetime or after a short span of time.
5 Such kinds of meditation make extensive use of various kinds of mandalas, *mudrās*, mantras and *dhāranīs* as concrete expressions of the nature of reality.
6 The formation of images of the various deities during meditation by means of creative imagination plays a key role in the process of realization. These images may be viewed as being present externally or internally.
7 There is an exuberant proliferation in the number and types of Buddhas and other deities.
8 Great stress is laid upon the importance of the guru and the necessity of receiving the instructions and appropriate initiations for the *sādhanas* from him.
9 Speculations on the nature and power of speech are prominent, especially with regards the letters of the Sanskrit alphabet.
10 Various customs and rituals, often of non-Buddhist origins, such as the *homa* rituals, are incorporated and adapted to Buddhist ends.
11 A spiritual physiology is taught as part of the process of transformation.
12 It stresses the importance of the feminine and utilizes various forms of sexual yoga.

Though by no means exhaustive, this list incorporates the main elements and preoccupations of the tantras. During the proto-tantric and early tantric phase only a few of these elements may occur together in any given text, but as we enter the middle and late phases, we find that an increasing number of them, in one form or another, are incorporated into the texts. This process of synthesis and development extended over several centuries, from the earliest proto-tantric texts down to the elaborate *Kālacakra Tantra*, which was possibly the last tantra to be developed in India. While it would be foolhardy to make any definitive statements about the early development of the tantras at the present stage of our knowledge, it might be of interest to briefly examine this process, particularly from the evidence available to us from Chinese sources.

First, the general trend may be seen if we examine a simple listing of the main translations (Table 1) containing any of the above elements down to the early Tang period. Other texts could be added to this list with some justification, such as the Pure Land cycle of texts. What immediately strikes one is the sudden increase of these texts from the Sui to Tang Dynasty, an indication of the increasing popularity of 'tantric' practice in India. Those translated after Xuan-zang during the Tang and early Song periods run into hundreds and so are far too numerous to list. Looking at their contents, we can see a gradual progression from external 'mundane' rituals and objectives to the internal and the 'spiritual', from the unsystematic to the systematic. Hence, as their titles indicate, the majority of the earlier texts are connected with *dhāraṇīs* and they deal with various kinds of prayers or requests for

Table 1: Chinese Translations of Sutras with 'Tantric' Elements

Wu	**Zhi-qian** (220-230 CE): *Ananta-mukha-dhāraṇī-sūtra* (T1011) *Mātaṅga-sūtra* (= *Śārdula-karṇāvadāna*) (T1300) *Dhāraṇī of Supreme Illuminator* (T1351) *Puṣpakūṭa-dhāraṇī-sūtra* (T1356)
E. Chin (317-420)	**Dharmarakṣa:** *Dhāraṇī for Relieving Toothache* (T1327) *Ārṣa-praśamanī-sūtra* (T1325) *Māyā-kāra-bhadra-dhāraṇī-sūtra* (T1378) **Daṇḍala-māyā Dhāraṇī* (T1391) *Maṇi-ratna-sūtra* (T1393) **Nanda:** *Sūtra of Avalokiteśvara's Dhāraṇī for Overcoming Poisoning* (T1043) **Śrī-mitra:** *Abhiṣeka-sūtra* (T1331) **Kumarajīva:** *Mahā-māyurī-vidyā-rājñī* (T988) **Buddhabhadra:** *Avataṃsaka-sūtra-hṛdaya-dhāraṇī* (T1021) **Unknown:** *Puṣpakūṭa-dhāraṇī* (T1357) (T1358)
W. Chin	**Dharmapāla** (385-400): *Mātaṅga-sūtra* (T1301) **Sheng-jian:** *Sūtra on the Dhāraṇī Against Perversities* (T1342)
N. Liang (397-439)	**Fa-zhong:** *Mahā-vaipulya-dhāraṇī* (T1339)
Liu Sung (420-478)	**Guṇabhadra:** *Ananta-mukha-dhāraṇī-sūtra* (T1013) ***Punyaśīla & Xuan-chang:** *Ananta-mukha-dhāraṇī-sūtra* (T1014) **Kālayaśa:** *Amitābha-dhyāna-sūtra* (T365) *Bhaisajya-rāja-bhaisajya-samudgati-sūtra* (T1161)
Qi (479-502)	**Wan-tian-yi:** *Infinite Dhāraṇī of Entry into all Dharmas* (T1343)
Liang (505-556)	**Saṅghapala:** *Mahā-māyurī-sūtra* (T984) *Ananta-mukha-dhāraṇī-sūtra* (T1016)
N. Wei (534-550)	**Buddhaśānta:** *Ananta-mukha-dhāraṇī-sūtra* (T1015) *Vajra-maṇḍa-dhāraṇī-sūtra* (T1344) **Tan-yao:** *Dhāraṇī for Great Benefit* (T1335) **Bodhiruci:** *Sarva-bala-rakṣa-dhāraṇī-sūtra* (T1028)
N. Chou (557-581)	**Jñānayaśa:** *Mahā-megha-sūtra* (T992) (T993) **Yaśogupta:** *Avalokiteśvaraika-daśa-mukha-dhāraṇī-sūtra* (T1070)

Table 1 (continued)

Sui (581-618)	**Narendrayaśa**:
	Mahā-megha-sūtra (T991)
	Jānagupta:
	Ananta-mukha-dhāraṇī-sūtra (T1017)
	Amoghapaśa-dhāraṇī-sūtra (T1093)
	Tathāgata-mahā-kauśalyopāya-dhāraṇī-sūtra (T1334)
	Dharmolka-dhāraṇī-sūtra (T1340)
	Mahā-bala-dhāraṇī-sūtra (T1341)
	Vajra-maṇḍa-dhāraṇī-sūtra (T1345)
	Dhāraṇī of the Twelve Buddhas (T1348)
	Dhāraṇī of Supreme Illuminator (T1353) (T1354)
T'ang	**Xuan-zang** (post 645):
	Sarva-buddha-hṛdaya-dhāraṇī (T918)
	Five Dhāraṇīs (T1034)
	Avalokiteśvaraika-daśa-mukha-dhāraṇī-sūtra (T1071)
	Amoghapaśa-hṛdaya-sūtra (T1094)
	Vasudhārā-dhāraṇī-sutra (T1162)
	Ṣaṇ-mukha-dhāraṇī (T1360) (T1361)
	Subāhu-mudrā-dhāraṇī-sūtra (T1363)
	Sūtra of Most Secret Dhāraṇī of Eight Names (T1365)
	Dhāraṇī that Saves from Adversities (T1395)

liberation from sufferings, adversities or disasters. Such texts probably have their roots in the early *paritta* type of sutras. But we are unable to detect any fusion in a systematic manner of Buddhist thought with these prayers and practices. So though a few of these texts, such as the *Sutra on the Dhāraṇī Against Perversities* (T 1342) and the *Infinite Dhāraṇī of Entry into all Dharmas* (T 1343) refer to emptiness (*śūnyatā*) and others such as the *Ṣaṇ-mukha-dhāraṇī* (T 1360 & T 1361) mention 'awareness-only' (*vijñapti-mātra*), the general feeling one gets from looking at these texts is that they were for the benefit of unsophisticated ordinary people beyond the confines of the great monasteries such as Nālandā. Hence the aims of the practices are often quite modest and do not entail a radical course of self-development using the complex types of meditation (*bhāvanā*) and the mandalas or *mudrās* that are so characteristic of fully developed tantras. On the other hand, as one might expect to find in a popular devotional form of Buddhism, we can note the existence of various kinds of worship and offering (*pūja*) to the Buddhas which later form a part of tantric practice. It is noteworthy that some texts describe types of worship that employ visualization of various Buddhas and Bodhisattvas, especially those associated with the Pure Land group of texts. For example, the *Amitāyur-dhyāna-sūtra* (T 365), translated into Chinese by Kālayaśa around 430 CE, gives vivid descriptions of Amitābha, Avalokiteśvara and Mahā-sthāma-prāpta and also of the mandala-like Pure Land of Amitābha itself. It can easily be seen how similar such meditative visualizations are to those prescribed in tantric texts both for worship and for *sādhana*. The visualizations of the Pure Land parallel to a remarkable extent those of mandalas, as for example, that in Chapter 16 herein of the *Mahā-vairocana Tantra*.

Other texts in the above list are important as they give some indication of the introduction and use of rituals. For example, the well-known *Mātaṅga Sutra* (T551, T552, T1300, T1301), first translated by Zhi-qian in 230 CE and re-translated several times down to the late 5th century CE, speaks of a magical ritual used for subjugation. The earliest versions tell of a low-caste (*caṇḍalī*) woman who was infatuated with Ānanda. Her mother tries to entice him in the following manner. She magically creates flowers in eight jars of water and then taking these up, she casts them back into the jars while reciting spells. Later versions of the text contain a prototype of the Buddhist *homa* ritual. The sorceress mother smears the floor of her house with cow-dung and spreads white rushes (*kuśa*?) upon it. She then lights a large fire there and casts a hundred and eight flowers into it while reciting the necessary spell with each flower. These texts also contain six *dhāraṇīs* and the instructions for performing the associated ceremonies.

We see other ritual elements in the *Mahā-māyūri-vidyā-rāja Sūtra*. The several versions of this text in Chinese bear witness to its continuing popularity. In an appendix to it, translated by Śrī-mitra (T 1331) around 340 CE, there are instructions for the delimitation of the ritual area (*sīma-bandha*), which is then to be decorated with five swords, five banners, five mirrors, twenty-one arrows and twenty-one lamps. This site is to be anointed with perfumes and mustard seeds are to be burnt to expel obstructing demons.

Further developments may be seen in the *Dhāraṇī for Great Benefit* (T1335) translated by Tan-yao in 462 CE. In addition to the burning of mustard seeds and such like, this text also prescribes the recitation of mantras before the images of various deities to bring about their appearance in order to fulfil the wishes of the practitioner. Again, it describes the making of a ritual area, but now with Buddha images arranged in circle to receive offerings.

Mandalas, which figure so much in tantras, can be formally divided into two main categories according to Buddhaguhya – the intrinsically existent mandala and the representational mandalas. The first of these is the 'real' mandala formed by the Buddha and the emanations of his qualities as Bodhisattvas and so forth. The second type is the graphic or plastic representation of the first. These two types seem to derive from different, though not entirely unrelated sources. As mentioned above, one might see the origin of the intrinsically existent mandala in the descriptions of the various pure lands, so striking is the similarity. On the other hand, the origins of the representational mandala may well lie in the arrangement of Buddha and Bodhisattva images upon altars for worship. As images of the Buddha and Bodhisattvas became acceptable to people in India, we often find representations of the Buddha flanked by Avalokiteśvara and Vajrapāṇi. With the proliferation of Buddhas and Bodhisattvas, one can understand how these would have come to resemble the basic pattern of a mandala when arranged geometrically. Hence the arrangement of such images in a circle, described in the *Dhāraṇī for Great Benefit*, can be seen as a rudimentary mandala. This same text also teaches various attainments (*siddhi*) to stop storms, to make rain, to become invisible and so forth.

I have only been able to select a few of the most noteworthy texts for mention here, but all of these works bear witness to the steady increase of tantric elements in Buddhism, leading on to the flowering of sophisticated tantric texts in the seventh and eighth centuries.

In addition to the evolutionary process indicated by the chronological sequence of these texts preserved in Chinese, there are other indications we may note that speak of the spread and acceptance of tantric practices. For example, Śāntideva (fl.

700–750 CE) compiled the *Śikṣā-samuccaya*, a valuable selection of quotations from various Mahāyāna texts, dealing with the practices a Bodhisattva was expected to engage in. There are several interesting features to be found in this work relevant to the development of Tantric Buddhism in India. One is Śāntideva's acceptance and use as a textual authority (*āmnāya*) of the *Trisamaya-rāja*, one of the sources of the *Mahā-vairocana Tantra*. The other is the evidence for the growing importance of internal visualization, similar to that in tantric practices. These are the relevant passages:

1 '*You should recite this* vidyā *mentioned in the* ***Tri-samaya-rāja*** *for the mandala* samaya: Namaḥ sarva-buddha-bodhisattvānām. Oṃ viraji viraji mahā-cakra-viraji. Sata sata sārata sārata trapi trapi vidhamani. Sabhajani saṃbhajani, taramati, siddha agre tvaṃ svāhā. *With that you may enter all mandalas. Or else you should recite Essence of the Tathāgata eight thousand times and then enter into both mundane and supra-mundane mandalas ...*'

2 '*Focusing upon the Buddhas and Bodhisattvas, you should also recite [the mantras] following the Rite of Good Conduct, with a mind that longs to benefit all beings. This prescribed rite* (vidhi) *should be observed at the conclusion of this ceremony. What is prescribed in the* ***Tri-samaya-rāja*** *is authoritative* (āmnāya), *so there is no fault [in doing this].*'

3 '*According to the* ***Tri-samaya-rāja***, *the prescribed ritual is to close your eyes and recite the Hundred Lettered [Mantra] eight thousand times, with your mind focused upon the Buddhas and Bodhisattvas. As soon as you have shut your eyes, you will behold the Buddhas and Bodhisattvas and be freed from sins. Or else circumambulating a stūpa, you should recite it eight thousand times and also place books of the holy Dharma in front of the image in the shrine.*'

4 '*The Bodhisattva who is endowed with eight qualities will constantly meet Buddhas. What are those eight? He urges people to visualize the body-form of the Buddha, he worships* (upasthāna) *the Tathāgatas, he expounds the eternal form of the Tathāgata* ....' (From the *Bṛhat-sāgara-nāga-rāja-paripṛcchā*).

5 '*Nobly born sons or daughters should visualize the Buddha depicted in paintings or described in books.*' (From the *Śraddha-balādhānāvatāra-mudrā*).

From this we can see that the kind of 'tantric' practice generally accepted around that time already included use of mandalas, the recitation of *dhāraṇīs*, ritual worship (*pūja*) and visualization.

Xuan-zang, the great Chinese traveller, was also in India until 645 CE. He has left us a detailed account of his travels in the *Da-tang-xi-yu-ji*, yet he makes no mention of anything which would clearly indicate the wide-spread existence of tantric practices or texts, apart from the use of *dhāraṇīs*. It has been argued that this could be due to his lack of interest in such matters, yet as he was a keen observer of the state of Buddhism as he found it throughout India at that time, it would not be unreasonable to expect him to have mentioned such practices in passing had he actually witnessed them. It is likely that any specifically tantric texts and practices that were already in existence at that time had not yet gained general acceptance in the main centres of Buddhism he visited, such as Nālandā.

However this situation seems to have changed thirty years later when Yi-jing arrived in India in 673 CE. We find a number of references in his 'Record of Eminent Monks who Sought the Dharma in the West' (*Xi-yu-qiu-fa-gao-seng-zhuan*) to tantric practices, where there is the very suggestive remark that people '*seek the secret books from the* nāga *palaces in the oceans and search for mantras from stone-chambers in the mountains*'. Even more noteworthy is what he has to say in the section dealing with Dao-lin, who also had spent many years in India. It seems that Dao-lin was very interested in tantric practices. He resided for a number of years at Nālandā and then set out first to Lāṭa in Western India where he '*stood before the divine altar and received the* vidyās *once again*'. Regarding the *vidyās*, Yi-jing says,

> '*It is said that the* Vidyādhara *Collection comprises a hundred thousand verses in Sanskrit, which in Chinese would amount to over three hundred rolls. But if one inspects these texts nowadays, it will be seen that many have been lost and few are complete. After the death of the Great Sage, Nāgārjuna in particular studied the main parts of this Collection. Then one of his disciples called Nanda, who was both intelligent and learned, turned his attention to this text. He spent twelve years in the west of India, applying himself solely to the study of the* dhāraṇīs. *At length he achieved success. Whenever it was time for him to eat, his meals descended from the sky. Furthermore, one day while he was reciting the* vidyās, *he wanted to get a wish-fulfilling jar, which he obtained after a short while. He was overjoyed to find that there was a book within this jar, but as he did not bind the jar with a* vidyā, *it suddenly vanished. Then, fearing that the* vidyās *might be scattered and lost, the Dharma Master Nanda gathered them together into a single collection of about twelve thousand verses, forming a single corpus. In each verse he matched up the text of the* vidyās *with* mudrās. *Although the words and the letters are similar [to those in normal use], in fact their meanings and usages are different. Truly, there is no way of comprehending them without an oral transmission. Later, the Master Dignāga saw that the merit of this work surpassed the intelligence of ordinary people and its thought pushed reason to its limits. He put his hand upon the book and said sighing, "If this sage had applied his mind to logic, what honour would have remained for me?". One can see by this the wise know their own value though fools are blind to the worth of others. This* Vidyā *Collection of Prayers is not yet available in China, hence Dao-lin applied his mind to these subtleties, for it is said in this Collection that 'one will only succeed in walking in the sky, riding* nāgas, *commanding the hundred spirits or being a benefactor of beings, by means of these* vidyās*'. When I, Yi-jing, was staying at Nālandā, I went several times to the altar place, but as I was not successful in either my application to the essence of this teaching or in gaining merit, in the end I gave up my hopes. I have touched on the main points of these new teachings here, in order to make them known.*'

The Chinese word *tán* (壇), which I have translated in the above passages as 'altar' is ambivalent, as it was also used to translate the word '*maṇḍala*'. In view of the quotations given above from Śāntideva's *Śikṣā-samuccaya*, there is a strong likelihood that Yi-jing is referring to the use of mandalas at Nālandā while he was there. It should also be remembered that Śubhakara-siṃha, who translated the *Mahā-vairocana Tantra* into Chinese, and his teacher Dharmagupta would have been at Nālandā exactly at the same time as Yi-jing was, which gives rise to the intriguing possibility that they may have actually met!

Yi-jing mentions at length another monk, the Dhyāna Master Wu-xing, who was in India around the same time as himself. He had been there since 667 and died as he began his journey back to China in 674. Upon his death, the large number of texts he had collected, together with his travelogue-report were forwarded to China. In the part of this report which survives, Wu-xing states that '*recently the Mantra Method has come to be venerated throughout the land*'[4]. More will be spoken of Wu-xing's importance later.

It is this period onwards to the end of the eighth century which saw the most rapid development in tantric thought and practice. Though strictly outside the scope of this book, some observations regarding the probable sequence of events may not be out of place, especially as our commentator Buddhaguhya was active in the middle years of this period. Although there are scholars who seem to speak with great confidence about the dating and chronological relationship of the texts and people who figure in this process, my following suggestions are of a tentative and hypothetical nature. I make no apology for this, as it merely reflects the uncertainty surrounding the whole subject. One only has to take into consideration the enormous amount of available historical and documental evidence, much of which is ambiguous or contradictory, to understand the daunting task awaiting anyone attempting even an outline history of Tantric Buddhism. For example, one may present a reasonably plausible account of the relationship of the eighty four tantric *siddhas*, as has been done by several scholars, only to find that this does not fit in with evidence derived from other sources. Also, as I have stressed elsewhere, one ignores the information preserved in Chinese works at one's peril. The *only* reliable and datable eye-witness accounts that we have for the whole of the period in question are those provided for us by the Chinese monks who travelled in India – nothing comparable is available from Indian or Tibetan sources.

For reasons that I give below in the next section, I believe it is likely that the *Mahā-vairocana Tantra* (hereafter MVT) was composed or 'revealed' some time during the first half of the seventh century, perhaps around 640 CE or a little earlier. If we examine its contents in comparison with other tantric works, it clearly belongs to the earliest phase of true tantras, and must precede all Yoga and Anuttara-yoga tantras on both doctrinal and iconographical grounds. Although we can identify several other works that would have been composed immediately following the MVT, the next major work in the development of tantric Buddhism must be the *Sarva-tathāgata-tattva-saṃgraha* (STTS). This work is of seminal importance, as it heralds a number of innovations such as the adoption of a five Buddha family pattern in contrast to the three Buddha family pattern which is predominant in the MVT. We are fortunate in possessing the Sanskrit text of this work, its Tibetan translation, as well as several Chinese versions. The earliest evidence we have for the existence of this tantra again comes from Chinese sources. The Indian *ācārya* Vajrabodhi introduced elements derived from it (which he had obtained around 700) into China with his *Recitation Sūtra Extracted from the Vajra-śekhara Yoga* (T 866), which gives in a summarized form the basic meditational practices now found in the first section of the STTS. It is thought by Japanese scholars that this summary is based on material pre-dating the more elaborate version of the STTS (T 865) translated by Amoghavajra in 753. A certain amount of circumstantial evidence points to south India as the area of its origin. For example, according to its Chinese commentary, a certain *bhadanta*

(Nāgārjuna?) took the *Tattva-saṃgraha* from the Iron Stupa in south India. It is also stated in Vajrabodhi's biography that he received teachings on the *Tattva-saṃgraha* in southern India when he was thirty one (700 CE) from Nāgabodhi (Nāgabodhi is said to have been the disciple of Nāgārjuna, according to Sino-Japanese traditions). This is the first datable reference to it, so we may therefore assume that it had come into existence by the last quarter of the seventh century, though this was unlikely to have been in the full form we now have. Furthermore, Śākyamitra, one of the later eighth century Indian commentators on the STTS, relates in the introductory salutation verses where and by whom he was instructed and initiated into the STTS in his commentary on it. From the places named, we can see that the southern area of India was the home of the majority of his teachers. Especially important seems to have been the coastal region in the present-day Bombay – Goa area, known then as Koṅkana and Sahya. Moreover, his commentary on the STTS is entitled 'The Adornment of Kośala' (*Kośala-alaṃkāra*). There were two Kośalas in India: the old Kośala centred on Śrāvastī, and another one further to the south, straddling a wide area across India from east to west. Śākyamitra's Kośala is likely to have been the latter. We know from Xuanzang's travelogue that this Kośala was the country in which the famous stūpa of Nāgārjuna-koṇḍa was located, which is significant in view of the tradition that it was Nagarjuna who removed the STTS from the Iron Stūpa. Finally, Amoghavajra, who translated the first section of the STTS, obtained his copy during his trip to southern India between 743-746.

The next text of major importance is the *Guhya-samāja Tantra*. Again, the first datable reference to this text is to be found in Chinese sources. When he returned from his trip to India, Amoghavajra wrote a summary of the eighteen parts of the *Vajra-śekhara* (understood by the Sino-Japanese tradition as another name for the STTS), the *Shi-ba-hui-zhi-gui* (T 869). This work gives titles and brief descriptions of the contents of eighteen tantras, though it is unfortunately not possible to identify all of those which he describes with extant tantras[5]. However, he clearly does include a description of a prototype *Guhya-samāja Tantra* (GST) as the fifteenth item, but the information he gives shows that the version which we have now in Tibetan and Sanskrit was still to be finalized when he returned to India in 743–746 CE. In fact, a detailed examination of the text of the GST, in conjunction with the oldest commentaries, indicates that the GST, like many other Buddhist texts, underwent several stages of development before the final form was reached. We can see from a comparison of the contents of its eighteenth chapter, the Continuation Tantra (*uttara-tantra*) with the preceding portion of the GST, that the GST originally comprised just the first twelve chapters of the version we now have, because all the fifty two questions and answers contained in the Continuation Tantra relate to topics mentioned only in those first twelve chapters of the GST. This is further borne out by an examination of the Explanatory Tantra, the *Sandhi-vyākaraṇa*, which also deals only with matters arising from the first twelve chapters. This, therefore, is likely to have been the form of the GST around the time when Amoghavajra was in India – a short version of twelve chapters, with perhaps the Continuation Tantra (the now eighteenth chapter) already having been composed but still existing as an independent work. Following this, we may posit a further development into a version with seventeen chapters, for the earliest commentaries by teachers such as Vajrahāsa do not deal with chapter eighteen, the Continuation Tantra. In view of the general chronology of people connected with him, Vajrahāsa's commentary seems to have been written c.750. It is noteworthy that Vajrahāsa is also named by the rNying-ma Tantric Collection (*rNying-ma'i rGyud-'bum*) as a translator of the first seventeen chapters of GST with rMa Rin-chen mChog, which were later re-translated by Śraddhākaravarma and Rin-chen bZang-po. Finally, the eighteenth chapter would have been appended to the Root Tantra shortly after this time. The rNying-ma Tantric Collection states, probably spuriously, that this was translated by Buddhaguhya and 'Brog-mi dPal Ye-shes.

Yet the GST did not spring into being out of a vacuum. As we have seen, it must have taken several decades to evolve from the prototype described by Amoghavajra to the full length version we now have. But we can additionally identify several stepping-stones in the process of evolution of tantras from the *Tattva-saṃgraha Tantra* to the *Guhya-samāja Tantra*, especially the *Guhya-garbha* and the *Māyā-jāla Tantra*. Although the exact relationship between these two texts is uncertain, it seems from iconographical considerations for example, that the sequence of development was *Tattva-saṃgraha* → *Guhya-garbha* → *Māyā-jāla* → *Guhya-samāja*.

Apart from these tantras, several other important works also belong to this early period, such as the *Buddha-sama-yoga Tantra* and the *Śrī-paramādya Tantra*. The former is of interest because Amoghavajra mentions it as the ninth item in his *Shi-ba-hui-zhi-gui*, which is an indication of its age, while parts of the latter are especially venerated in the Japanese Shingon tradition. However, I must now conclude this brief survey of the evolution of tantric literature as we are in danger of losing sight of the main theme of this introduction, the *Mahā-vairocana-abhisaṃbodhi Tantra*.

II HISTORICAL BACKGROUND

i. Date of Compilation

Following the above outline of the development of tantric Buddhism, it might be asked where the MVT itself fits in. Once again we may arrive at a tentative date for its composition by making use of evidence available from the Chinese tradition in particular. As we know, the MVT was translated by Śubhakara-siṃha into Chinese in 724. However, it seems certain that he was unable to make use of his own version of the text, if in fact he had brought one with him. Instead, he had to use a copy he and Yi-xing found at the Hua-yan Temple in Chang-an. As will be mentioned later, there are good grounds for believing this copy of the MVT was one of the texts gathered by Wu-xing, who was in India for eight years until his death there in 674. Of course, we do not know when he obtained a copy of the MVT during his stay in India, but let us assume that it would have been some time around 672 CE when he was beginning to think of returning to China. When we take into consideration the other evidence mentioned above regarding the increasing popularity of tantric practices around this time, it seems likely that the MVT was composed and gaining acceptance some time shortly before Wu-xing's arrival in India, perhaps about the middle of the seventh century. This is corroborated to a certain extent by the lineage given for the MVT according to Chinese sources: Mahā-vairocana → Vajrapāṇi → Dharmagupta → Śubhakara-siṃha. We see from this that Dharmagupta is the first human in the chain of transmission of the MVT, so it is not unreasonable to assume that the first version of MVT was compiled sometime during Dharmagupta's lifetime, which if we discount the stories in the Chinese records about his age as a pious fiction, would have been during the hundred years from around 615 CE to 715 CE[6]. It may even be the case that Dharmagupta himself was actually involved in the composition of the MVT. It is also difficult to imagine that MVT was compiled much earlier than this, since none of the Indian monks (Zhi-tong, Bhagavad-dharma, Atikūṭa, Divakara, Śikṣānanda, Maṇicinta) arriving in China from India at the end of the seventh century, who were involved in the translation of the tantric type of texts, are known to have brought a copy of the MVT with them.

As with all such texts, the MVT underwent several stages of development. As there is no known Sanskrit version of the MVT surviving[7], unless there is one hidden somewhere in Tibet or locked away among the Sanskrit texts 'rescued' from Tibet in recent decades and kept in Beijing, we must depend upon the Tibetan and Chinese translations for our understanding of this process. According to both the Chinese and the Tibetan traditions, the MVT we now have is said to have been an extract of an enormous original version – Śubhakara-siṃha says that it had 100,000 verses. This may in fact imply that the MVT is a compilation from a more amorphous set of materials or even a cycle of texts. Certainly, even a cursory glance through the MVT suggests that it was assembled from a variety of sources, some of which can still be identified. It has long been recognized in the Sino-Japanese tradition that Chapter I forms an entity in itself and is distinct from the remainder of the text. The traditional explanation is that this chapter contains the doctrinal basis for the practical matters discussed in later chapters. However, given the fact that it is almost entirely written in prose and its contents seem stylistically so different to the rest of the work, one has the feeling that it orginally was likely to have been an independent Mahāyāna work that was suitably modified and placed at the beginning of the MVT. Likewise, the prose Chapters VIII (The Samādhi Without Perceptual Forms) and XX (The Bodhisattva's Training Accompanied by Expedient Means) seem to deal with more standard Mahāyāna topics and were added to the MVT from others sources at the time of compilation. The early prose segment of Chapter VI (The True Nature of Siddhi Accomplishment) is based on a parallel passage in the *Tri-samaya-vyūha*, as I have noted at that point. One also has the feeling that the block of chapters dealing with the Hundred Letters (XXI–XXV), the three chapters, VII–IX, which the standard canonical Tibetan version has transposed from the end of the text where they were originally located, and also Chapter XXIX (The *Homa* Rituals) were later added to the MVT as it was developed and expanded. The earliest core of the MVT most probably comprised the three blocks of chapters dealing with the Body Mandala (II–VI), the Speech Mandala (X–XII), and the Mind Mandala (XIII–XVI), together with some of the remaining chapters which cover related general topics.

Whatever the truth of the matter is, the earliest version we now have is that preserved in the Chinese translation of the text and its commentary based on an oral exegesis given by Śubhakara-siṃha, probably using Wu-xing's Sanskrit copy which he obtained in India prior to 674. For the following stages in its evolution, we have to turn to the materials preserved in Tibetan, which include four documents we must consider. These are the Tibetan translation of the MVT itself, the unrevised and the revised versions of Buddhaguhya's commentary and his summary guide to the MVT, the *Piṇḍārtha*. The version embedded in the unrevised commentary is closer to the Chinese in order of chapters and phrasing than the Tibetan translation of the MVT itself. This can be seen from the accompanying chart (Table 2). Therefore, the version of MVT used by Buddhaguhya as the basis for his commentaries represents the second known stage in the development of the MVT. To what extent the differences in phrasing are due to Tibetan stylistics is not clear, but the text contained in the unrevised commentary often makes better sense than the 'official' translation of the MVT itself. The Tibetan translation of the MVT itself was based on a text which had undergone further re-organization and so gives us the third and final version available[8]. It is conceivable that this re-organization was done by the translators Śīlendrabodhi and dPal brTsegs themselves, or else by later redactors of the Kanjur. Later, gZhon-nu dPal incorporated this translation into Buddhaguhya's commentary when he revised it in 1461 CE. The situation is explained in the supplementary colophon to the revised commentary thus:

> 'When the available Tibetan translations of commentorial literature (*bstan-bcos*) were assembled at sNar-thang, it was apparent that the recent exemplars of this running commentary on the *Vairocana-abhisaṃbodhi-[tantra]* available in all the *bTan-'gyurs* are unfortunately corrupt and not redacted against the Tantra and the new standards of language (*skad gsar-bcad*), being based on a copy that was corrupt, with portions out of place, and slightly incomplete. Hence, in 1461 at the rTse-thang monastery, the central Tibetan *bande* gZhon-nu-dpal complied this revision by comparing the text with the words of the Tantra as translated by sKa-ba dPal-brtsegs who had mastery of both languages and by amending the language to the new standards.'

Table 2: Comparative Chart of MVT Chapters

T		B		V		C
1	->	1	->	1	->	1
2		2		2		2
3		3		3		3
4		4		4		4
5		–		–		5
6		5		5		6 + 7
7		6		24		28
8		7		25		29
9		8		26		30
10		9		6		8
11		10		7		9
12		11		8		10
13		12		9		11
14		13		10		12
15		14		11		14
16		15		12		13
17		16		13		15
18		17		14		16
19		18		15		17
20		19		16		18
21		20		17		19
22		21		18		20
23		22		19		21
24		23		20		22
25		–		–		23
26		24		21		24
27		25		22		25
28		26		23		26
29		27		27		27 + 31

This shows the sequence of chapters in each version relative to the standard Tibetan version (T) of the MVT. The chapter numbers are those of each translation of the MVT. The main difference is the placing of Chapters 7/8/9 of the standard Tibetan version towards the end of the Unrevised Commentary (V) and the Chinese MVT (C), which must be the earlier arrangement. The earlier location of these chapters suggests that they might not have formed part of the initial compilation of the MVT. Note also that the Chinese version makes two chapters out of both Chapters 6 and 29 of the Tibetan version. some text

This chronology may be summarized as follows:

Wu-xing's copy of MVT	pre	674
Uttara-tantra	714?	
Śubhakara-siṃha's translation of MVT		724
Śubhakara-siṃha's commentary on MVT		724
Buddhaguhya's copy of MVT	pre	760
Buddhaguhya's Piṇḍārtha	c.	760
Buddhaguhya's Commentary	c.	760
MVT translated by Śīlendrabodhi & dPal brTsegs	pre	812[A]
Buddhaguhya's Commentary revised by gZhon-nu dPal		1461

ii. Place of Compilation

Over the years, scholars in Japan and elsewhere have suggested a variety of locations for the composition of the MVT, ranging from Valabhī in western India, Ajaṇṭā in central India and Orissa in the east. But, although there is actually no clear evidence regarding the place of compilation, I feel everything points to somewhere in north eastern India, especially the region between Nālandā and the Himalayan foothills a hundred miles or so to its north, though there are some grounds to favour northern Orissa as a second choice. The great university-monastery of Nālandā flourished as one of the main centres of Mahāyāna Buddhist learning from the 5th century CE onwards. During the centuries of its existence, many of the greatest Buddhist teachers lived and taught there. All the people who we know were connected with the transmission of the MVT resided there. Śubhakara-siṃha received teachings on the MVT at Nālandā from Dharmagupta and later carried on his teaching career in that area. Wu-xing was based there during his stay in India and so it is probable that he also obtained his copy of the MVT there. Later Buddhaguhya also resided at Nālandā, where he was visited by the Tibetan delegation bringing an invitation from King Khri-srong lde-bstan to go to Tibet. A powerful piece of additional evidence is provided by the area of distribution of plants and trees mentioned in the MVT and its Continuation Tantra. These are identified as far as possible in the endnotes. Although these are individually found in several different regions, it is interesting to note that the only area where the majority of them are found together is in the foothills of the eastern Himalayas. If we accept that such texts as the MVT were composed by humans, albeit under divine inspiration, we might posit the following scenario. Nālandā itself would have been bustling with the large numbers of students and teachers resident there, so I think it is hardly likely that the initial compiler or compilers of the MVT sat in a back room at the monastery writing it. Actually, there is no particular reason why we should even assume that the originator of this text was even a monk: on the contrary, as it seems to have been written with lay devotees in mind, the compiler may also have been a well-educated lay-person. It is more reasonable to suppose that people particularly

A This translation is listed in the Den-kar-ma Catalogue which is thought to have been compiled in 812 CE or perhaps 800 CE according to how one interprets the Tibetan dating cycle.

interested in meditation went on retreats to remote areas of the forest and mountains to engage in their practice, as they have always done throughout the history of Buddhism. Indeed, the MVT itself recommends secluded places for the rituals connected with the mandalas and subsequent meditational practices. These people may well have gone up to the southern slopes of the Himalayas and were inspired to compose such texts as the MVT while there. After all, these practices reflect the kinds of meditational techniques they had evolved against an intellectual and devotional background which at this time was undergoing considerable ferment. Once these texts had been composed, they would have been brought back to places like Nālandā as new revelations, rather like the *gTer-ma* discoveries of later Tibetan tradition, to be promulgated, practised, expanded and commented upon by a larger audience.

iii. People involved in the transmission of the MVT

We have already mentioned most of the key figures connected with the transmission of the MVT. However, it may be of interest to give lengthier biographical details ofsome of these people as they are not as well known as they ought to be. Of these, some mention should first be made of Wu-xing, although he does not directly figure in the lineages of the MVT. As I have previously related, there are strong grounds for believing that the Sanskrit text of the MVT used by Śubhakara-siṃha was one of those collected by Wu-xing in India and forwarded to China upon his death around 674 CE. There is a biography of him in Yi-jing's 'Record of Eminent Monks', from which we learn the following details. In 667, Wu-xing went to India via the southern sea route, like Yi-jing. After residing a while in Sri Lanka and Harikela in Bengal, he made his way to Nālandā. There he studied Yogācāra, Mādhyamika and the *Abhidharma-kośa*, and the works on logic by Dignāga and Dharmakīrti at the nearby Tiladhāka monastery. He translated parts of the Sarvāstivādin Āgama dealing with the Buddha's Parinirvāṇa and sent these back to China. After a further period of residence at Nālandā during which time he and Yi-jing became friends, he decided to start the journey back to China via northern India and so in 674, at the age of fifty-six, he parted from Yi-jing. We know from the 'Song Biographies of Notable Monks' (*Song-gao-seng-zhuan*) that sadly he never completed the journey, but died in India soon afterwards. (In passing, we might also pay tribute to the many other courageous and talented Chinese monks who perished in India – of the fifty six monks mentioned by Yi-jing in his Record, over fifty died of sickness before they could return to China!) It is recorded that the books he had collected were forwarded to China where they were stored in the Hua-yan Temple. Among these were the *Mahā-vairocana Tantra*, the *Subāhu-paripṛcchā* and the *Susiddhi-kāra Tantra*, which were all translated later by Śubhakara-siṃha.

Śubhakara-siṃha, who translated the MVT into Chinese, is said by Chinese sources to have been born as a prince in Oḍra in 636 CE. Because of his outstanding abilities and popularity, he was named successor to the throne by his father, but when he ascended to the throne at the age of thirteen, his disgruntled brothers organized an armed rebellion. Śubhakara-siṃha defeated them, but was so dismayed by the misery of the war that he decided to transfer the throne to his eldest brother instead of punishing his brothers and to become a monk himself.

Based on his name, is commonly assumed by scholars that he had familial connections to early representatives of the Bhauma-kāras[9] who migrated from Assam (*Kāmarūpa*) to northern Orissa. However, there are some problems with this theory. It is not certain when the Bhauma-kāras arrived in Orissa but their emergence as dynastic rulers of Orissa is normally dated much later, probably around 736 with the accession of Kṣemaṅkaradeva. Moreover, although some of the early Bhauma-kāra kings were called Śubhākara, it should be remembered that in Śubhakara-siṃha's case the name is monastic rather than personal and therefore makes a connection with the Bhauma-kāra dynasty less likely. Apart from this, one should also bear in mind that the area known during Śubhakara-siṃha's youth and thereafter as Oḍra (corresponding to much of present-day Orissa) was the name of a region rather than a specific kingdom. At that time, the region was divided up into a number of smaller kingdoms, satrapies and principalities. Hence, though the region known as Oḍra would have been familiar to the Chinese in the eighth century since is was described by Xuanzang, it only gives a somewhat vague indication of Śubhakara-siṃha's true birthplace. It may therefore be useful to consider political situation in that region during the latter half of the seventh century CE.

At this time the northern portion of present-day Orissa was divided up into Uttara-Toṣali, Dakṣiṇa-Toṣali and Utkala while much of southern Orissa was known as Koṅg oḍa. At beginning of 7th century, both Utkala and Uttara-Toṣali formed part of Oḍra-viṣaya under the rule of the Datta dynasty founded by Somadatta. His successor Bhanudatta ruled over Utkala and Daṇḍabhukti as suzerain of Śaśāṅka during first quarter of 6th century, and his descendants seem to have ruled after death of Śaśāṅka around 625 CE. The conquest of Orissa by Harṣavardhana in 642 brought downfall of Datta dynasty. The subsequent rulership of Uttara-Toṣali is unclear though its kings were probably feudatory of the later Guptas. Their rule ended in 725 due to invasion by Yaśovarman of Kaunaj. Thereafter, the Bhauma-kāras rose to power, established a kingdom in Toṣali around 736 CE. The region of Dakṣiṇa-Toṣali which lay to the south of the Mahānāḍī River was ruled by Śailodbhavas as part of Koṅgoḍa until they were ousted by the Bhauma-kāras around 744 CE. Similarly, shortly after the fall of the Datta dynasty in 642, Utkala is thought to have been incorporated in the kingdom of South Kośala which was ruled by Tivaradeva of Mekala, founder of the Pāṇḍuvaṃśi dynasty. Finally, the kingdom of Koṅgoḍa occupied much of southern Orissa was ruled by Śailodbhava dynasty during the sixth and seventh centuries.

With this brief overview of the political situation of the region around the time of Śubhakara-siṃha's birth and youth, we may wonder where he was actually born as there is no obvious candidate for his homeland. However, if we assume that his Chinese biography is merely using the place-name Oḍra since it was well known to them, then it is possible that he was born in one of the component kingdoms of the region mentioned above. Bearing in mind the story related about the power struggle which occurred during Śubhakara-siṃha's youth, we should look for somewhere in the region where such events as described took place. Remarkably, a series of epigraphical inscriptions on copper plates[A] surviving from Koṅgoḍa do describe

A The *Kondenda Grant* Ep. Ind. XIX pp 265-270, the *Nivina Grant* Ep. Ind. XIX pp 265-70 and the *Puri Grant* JBORS XVI pp 176.

events, although from a different perspective, very similar to those leading to Śubhakara-siṃha's abdication, though there are possible difficulties in reconciling dates derived from these copper plates and those derived from Śubhakara-siṃha's biography. According to the epigraphical inscriptions, Madhyamarāja II, also known as Yaśobhita II, of the Śailodbhava dynasty ruled Koṅgoḍa during the third quarter of the seventh century. After his death, the throne was usurped by Mādhavarāja III from the elder son. Although not the eldest son, Mādhavarāja was the son of Madhyamarāja's chief queen and apparently based his claim to the throne on that relationship to the late king. It is not known for how long he reigned but his elder brothers did not accept the situation. This led to a bitter war in which the elder son Mānabhīta (said by some scholars to have eventually reigned from around 695 to 730) defeated Mādhava in the battle of Phasika. Mādhava took flight and was sheltered by King Tivaradeva in neighbouring South Kośala. Though these two united forces against Mānabhīta, they were decisively defeated in a battle near the Vindhyas. It is known that Mādhavarāja was not killed in this battle and is generally assumed to have passed his remaining years in the court of Tivaradeva.

The parallels with the version given by Śubhakara-siṃha's biographers is striking. We know from this that he was the son of the queen mother, that he had elder brothers who rebelled against his kingship and that he ceded the throne to one of his elder brothers. It is also mentioned in passing that later in his life, when he was a monk, he visited a certain unnamed king of central India who was married to one of his sisters. This king of central India may well have been Tivaradeva himself. Unless identical dynastic struggles were commonplace in Orissa during the later half of the seventh century, we have strong grounds for assuming that the monk Śubhakara-siṃha was in fact Mādhavarāja III, though further research will be needed to resolve the dating difficulties – according to the Chinese sources Śubhakara-siṃha was born in 636 and became a monk in 654 after ceding the throne. If this was the case, one wonders whether Śubhakara-siṃha's Chinese colleagues were aware of his true identity or whether Śubhakara-siṃha himself engaged in a degree of obfuscation. It is interesting to note in this connection that although he met Vajrabodhi who was also resident in Chang-an at the time of his arrival, one has the impression that they did not establish cordial relations. Among other reasons. it may have been that Vajrabodhi, who was a native of south-eastern India, was well aware of Śubhakara-siṃha's identity which led to problems.

Whatever the truth of this matter, his Chinese biographers state that he studied and travelled widely during his youth, until he finally arrived at Nālandā. There he became the disciple of the Master (*ācārya*) Dharmagupta. Not much is known about Dharmagupta, but it is said that he was an expert in meditation and mantra practice. According to Chinese biographical records, he appeared to be only about forty years of age but was actually over eight hundred. Xuan-zang is also said to have met him while he was in India, when he looked about thirty, but was actually over seven hundred. Nobody of that name is known from Tibetan sources, although there was a Śrī-gupta at Nālandā at the beginning of the eighth century. It is just possible that they were the same person. Śubhakara-siṃha was taught the mantras, *mudrās*, mandalas and *samādhis* connected with the MVT lineage by Dharmagupta and was given the initiations (*abhiṣeka*) by him. Afterwards, Śubhakara-siṃha travelled around the central Indian area, teaching and debating with non-Buddhists, and generally working for the benefit of the populace. Eventually, he was told by his teacher Dharmagupta that he had a profound karmic link with China, so he should go there and spread the teachings. This exhortation need not surprise us too much when we remember that there were a considerable number of Chinese monks at Nālandā around this time, including Yi-jing, as well as an imperial ambassador.

Śubhakara-siṃha set out from Nālandā and began the long overland journey to China. He travelled through Kashmir and then went on to Udyāna, where he taught at the court of the ruler of the region[10]. After he left Udyāna, he did not take the normal route through Central Asia along the Silk Road as he probably found his way blocked by Arab military activities in the region. Instead he went through Tibet and reached China that way. When he finally reached the borders of China he found an official reception party sent to meet him by the Emperor Rui-zang, as his fame had preceded him. It was in 716 CE that Śubhakara-siṃha finally arrived at the Chinese capital, Chang An. It is noteworthy that he was already eighty years of age when he arrived there. He busied himself visiting famous monks in Chang An and familiarized himself with the problems that he would face in translating Sanskrit texts into Chinese. The following year, having taken up residence at the Xi-ming Temple, he received an imperial command to begin translating. After he had translated a first short text, his reputation increased but unfortunately he was ordered to hand over all the Sanskrit texts he had brought from India to the imperial court, possibly for political reasons: the new Emperor, Xuan-zang, may have been under pressure from the Taoists who had lost prestige with the increasing influence of Buddhism. Whatever the reason, Śubhakara-siṃha was left without anything to work on, so he went with the Chinese monk and mathematician Yi-xing who had become his disciple, to the Hua-yan Temple where the texts collected by Wu-xing before his death some thirty years earlier were stored. Here he obtained several texts including a copy of the MVT. In 724, the Emperor went to Lo Yang and Śubhakara-siṃha was settled in the Fa-xian Temple in that city where he began his translation of the MVT. By the next year, he and Yi-xing had completed the MVT and the appendix volume[11]. While work was progressing on the translation of the MVT, he also lectured simultaneously on the text itself and a record of these lectures was kept by Yi-xing, which forms the basis of the main Chinese commentary on the MVT, the *Da-ri-jing-shu*. Following the MVT, Śubhakara-siṃha also translated the *Subāhu-paripṛcchā*, the *Susiddhi-kāra* and some works connected with the *Tattva-saṃgraha*. In 732 he petitioned the Emperor to permit him to return home to India, but permission was refused. Finally, at the age of ninety nine, on 7th November 735, Śubhakara-siṃha died in the meditation room and was buried with great honour, mourned by all up to the Emperor himself. He had been a monk for eighty years.

Of his character, it is said that he was a quiet and gentle person, fond of meditation and simplicity in his life. When people saw his face they said it was as though they were seeing a lotus open before their eyes and when they heard him speak it was as though their hearts were bathed in nectar. His biographies indicate that he was a man of many talents and had such compassion that he is said to have treated even plants as though they were his children. He was also skilled in rain-making, which he is said reluctantly to have done at the insistence of the Emperor in his presence on one occasion.

Following the deaths of Yi-xing and Śubhakara-siṃha, the lineage of the MVT in China was passed by one of Śubhakara-siṃha's disciples, the Korean monk Hyun-cho, on to Hui-guo (746–805). Hui-guo was probably responsible for much of the unique Sino-Japanese synthesis of the MVT and the *Sarva-tathāgata-tattva-saṃgraha Tantra*. Moreover, like so many of the early tantric masters, he must have been an Master of great ability as his fame spread to many East Asian countries. Not only did he have several Koreans among his disciples, but some even came from as far away as Java. However, the most noteworthy of his followers must be the Japanese monk Kūkai (775–834). Although the MVT had arrived in Japan within ten years of being translated into Chinese, it was little understood there. The young Kūkai, who realized its importance, set out to China with the intention of studying it there. He met Hui-guo within a year of arriving in Chang An. After having received complete instructions and initiations in the MVT as well as many other tantric scriptures, he was appointed by the dying Hui-guo as his successor. Despite his original plan to stay in China for twenty years, Kūkai was instructed by Hui-guo to return home to Japan and spread the teaching there. Though only in China for less than three years, the sights and people he encountered in Chang An must have made a profound impression on the young man. Apart from receiving teachings from Hui-guo, he also met the Indian monks Prajñā[12] and Muniśrī from whom he learnt some Sanskrit. Indeed, he was honoured by Prajñā with the gift of his new translation of the *Avataṃsaka Sūtra*. Additionally, it must be remembered that Chang An was an extremely cosmopolitan city at that time, with representatives of many countries living there. As well as Buddhist temples, there were also Nestorian Christian, Manichaean and possibly Muslim establishments there which certainly would have attracted the attention of the inquisitive Kūkai. Following his return to Japan, Kūkai was responsible for the establishment of the Shingon School, with its head-quarters on Mount Koya where it blossomed and has flourished to the present day. However in China itself, Hui-guo's tantric lineage unfortunately did not prosper for long and had probably died out by the time of the Northern Song Dynasty.

The one major figure we should consider on the Indo-Tibetan side of the tradition is Buddhaguhya. In stark contrast to the detailed biography we have of Śubhakara-siṃha, we know next to nothing about Buddhaguhya. Apart from his authorship of commentaries on the MVT and other tantric texts, we have only one piece of reliable information about him. We do not even know the precise dates of his birth and death. There are a few inconsequential details about him given by such Tibetan sources as Bu-ston, Tārānātha and the Blue Annals, mainly of interest to the hagiographer rather than the historian.

However, putting together these fragments we can form the following outline biography. Buddhaguhya was probably born in about 700 CE or a little before then and he lived mainly in the Vārāṇasī area. He seems to have been a somewhat senior contemporary of Buddhajñānapāda who is believed to have been deeply involved in the early development of the *Guhya-samāja Tantra*, since Buddhaguhya is said to have received some teachings and initiations from him — though given the disparity in their ages, this seems a trifle unlikely. He is also said to have received teachings from Līlavajra on the *Māyā-jāla* cycle of texts, especially the *Guhya-garbha Tantra*. The teachings of this lineage were passed on to Vimalamitra, who went to Tibet and passed them on there. Later in his life, when he was an established and respected teacher,

King Khri-srong-lde-bstan sent a delegation, which included dPal-brTsegs and others, to Buddhaguhya to invite him to Tibet to teach. This invitation is thought to have been made early in the reign of Khri-srong-lde-bstan, around 760. He declined the invitation, telling the Tibetans that his protector, the Bodhisattva Mañjuśrī, had warned him that he would die if he went to Tibet, hence it is likely that he felt unable to undertake the journey because of his advanced age. Instead, he wrote a letter addressed to the Tibetan King and people (*Bhoṭa-svāmi-daśa-guru-lekha* Q5693). Most of this letter is taken up with teachings and admonitions to the Tibetans in the tradition of Nāgārjuna's '*Precious Garland*' (*Ratnāvalī*), but Buddhaguhya mentions in passing that he instructed the visiting Tibetans on the MVT and other texts. It is presumably then that these texts were taken to Tibet to be translated later by dPal brTsegs himself, aided by Śīlendra-bodhi.

Looking at the commentaries and other works ascribed to Buddhaguhya in the Tanjur[13], it will be seen that he mainly specialized in the Kriyā and Yoga tantras. However, a number of other works are attributed to him in the Kang-xi Edition of the Tanjur, all connected with various aspects of the *Guhya-garbha-tantra*, and we also know from other sources that Buddhaguhya figures importantly in the transmission of the rNying-ma tantras, especially the *Guhya-garbha* cycle. Whether these works are genuinely his or not must await further study, though certainly there is no intrinsic reason why they should not be so. Nevertheless, the works belonging to this group which I have briefly examined do seem stylistically different to Buddhaguhya's other writings on the Kriyā and Yoga tantras in which one cannot find any reference at all to the *Guhya-garbha-tantra*, even where this might have been appropriate. It is also noteworthy that in his general discussion of tantras at the beginning of his commentary on the MVT and in his related summary (*piṇḍārtha*) of the same text, he speaks only of Kriyā and Yoga tantras, putting the MVT in a special category that bridges these two groups, which he calls by his term '*ubhaya*' (dual). This implies that any tantras in existence at that time, now treated as Anuttara-yoga tantras, were not yet considered to be a separate class of works. He lists such texts as *Susiddhi-kāra*, the *Guhya-sāmānya*, the *Tri-samaya-rāja*, the *Tri-kāya-uṣṇīṣa*, the *Vajrapāṇy-abhiṣeka* and the *Vidyādhara Collection* as representative of the Kriyā tantras, while he speaks of the *Sarva-tathāgata-tattva-saṃgraha* and the *Śrī-paramādya* as representative of the Yoga tantras. It is strange that he makes no mention of the *Guhya-garbha-tantra* at this point. One possible solution is that he became involved in the *Guhya-garbha-tantra* later in his life, some time after having written those commentaries. This would also make sense if we accept the tentative sequence and chronology of tantric texts given above, in which case it is quite likely that the *Guhya-garbha-tantra* had not been widely disseminated outside its place of origin prior to the middle of the eighth century. However, a detailed study of all the works attributed to Buddhaguhya would be necessary in order to make a definitive statement regarding his involvement with texts like the *Guhya-garbha-tantra*.

Beyond this, there is little we can say with certainty about Buddhaguhya himself, but we may however get some idea of Buddhaguhya's intellectual milieu, if not of the man himself, by considering in passing other teachers active around that time, some of whose names are linked with Buddhaguhya. It is clear from many of Buddhaguhya's comments to the MVT that he was strongly influenced by Yogācāra concepts. Given the period of his teaching life, he was perhaps affiliated to the synthesis of Yogācāra and Mādhyamika thought of the type that Tibetans would later dub Svātantrika-Yogācāra. Several people connected with him show such tendencies in their writings. For example, Jñānagarbha (700-770?) wrote a number of commentorial works and other writings of Yogācāra-Mādhyamika inspiration, in which his debt to MVT concepts are quite clear[14]. He is also said to have been taught by a Śrīgupta[15], who Tārānātha says was likewise a Yogācāra-Mādhyamika. Jñānagarbha in his turn was the teacher of Śāntarakṣita (710-779?) who is also well-known for his Yogācāra-Mādhyamika position. We have already mentioned Vimalamitra who, according to the rNying-ma tradition, was also a pupil of Buddhaguhya and Līlavajra, as was Vairocana (the teacher of Haribhadra?) who received the Mahāyoga (*Māyā-jāla* Cycle) transmission from Buddhaguhya. Unfortunately, if we are ever to know the precise relationship of these various teachers who were active in the revolutionary period which was the eighth century, an enormous amount of research still needs to be done on their writings and tantric texts produced then, so I can only offer here a translation of the MVT and Buddhaguhya's commentary on it, which may be used as a starting point for further study.

III ABOUT THIS TRANSLATION

I am presenting here a complete English translation of the *Mahā-vairocanābhisaṃbodhi-vikurvitādhiṣṭhāna-vaipulya-sūtrendra-rāja nāma dharma-paryāya*, its Continuation Tantra (*uttara-tantra*), together with the Commentaries by Buddhaguhya. Now, it might not be out of place to review briefly the problem of translating Buddhist works in general. 'Translation' has been usefully defined as 'a process of expression in another language, systematically retaining the original sense or meaning'[16]. I take 'meaning' here to imply the conceptual content of the original rather than the literal meaning of its words. This presents any prospective translator with a task of great complexity, especially when dealing with religious or philosophical texts, for a detailed knowledge of the conceptual range of the vocabulary in both the source and the target language is required. The difficulties are multiplied when, for example, we are obliged to use Tibetan and/or Chinese translations of Sanskrit texts, for then we often have to take into consideration the semantic decisions made by the translators of those works, should we wish to convey the likely intentions of the original compilers!

Surveying the translations of Buddhist texts now available, it immediately becomes evident that several contrasting techniques have been adopted, with greater and lesser degrees of success. In the case of Tibetan texts, I feel the results are generally unsatisfactory apart from a few honourable exceptions. More often than not,such translations are almost incomprehensible or unreadable, each in their own way. On one hand we have the 'literalists' who try to translate all words in a text based on the strict etymological meaning of the Tibetan words, apparently forgetting that the sum is greater than the whole. Or else there is the other camp which interprets and translates Buddhist texts utilizing the terminology of the latest philosophical fashions, be it phenomenology or Teutonic existentialism, and so produces impenetrable gobbledegook of another kind[17]. The concepts in Buddhist texts, especially the tantras, are difficult, but what is the advantage in making them more difficult than they really are? Apart from this, it is regrettable that the value of an elegant and concise style seldom seems to be given much consideration.

Like it or not, apart from fairly basic works, many Buddhist texts are difficult to understand and were clearly written for people of the highest acumen. Some texts parallel the most recondite modern works on nuclear physics or bio-chemistry in their complexity and subtlety. Unfortunately, this presumes the effort of constant study and possibly practice on the part of the reader. Bearing all this in mind, I have tried to produce a balanced translation which is reasonably accurate, avoiding the extremes of paraphrasing and metaphrasing, which does not mislead the reader by the use of concepts alien to the original and which is readable though perhaps requiring some effort. The reader will note that I have used a certain number of Sanskrit words, instead of attempting to translate them. This is not very fashionable at present in some circles, but my experience in teaching Buddhism for a number of years suggests that this approach is acceptable if people are prepared to make a little effort to learn the connotations of such words. A simple literal translation of such words would usually be inadequate, while a full interpretative translation to do them justice would be too prolix. For the benefit of the non-specialist reader, I have included a glossary of my terminology, giving glosses that in many cases use the words of Buddhaguhya himself. It should also be noted that although I have found it more natural to use the pronoun 'he' in reference to the Master and the practitioner to avoid awkward circumlocutions, this should be understood as shorthand for 'he or she'. Whatever might be said of the Sanskrit original, neither the Tibetan nor the Chinese versions specify a sex for these people. Indeed, the MVT itself makes clear that it is addressed to both 'sons and daughters' of the Buddha and values both sexes equally.

As already mentioned, no Sanskrit manuscript of the MVT has come to light, apart from a few dozen lines quoted in other works, so in preparing my translation, I have used the Tibetan and Chinese versions, in the following editions:

T: *rNam-par-snang-mdzad chen-po mngon-par-rdzogs-par-byang-chub-pa rnam-par-sprul-pa byin-gyis-rlob-pa shin-tu-rgyas-pa mdo-sde'i dbang-po'i rgyal-po zhes-bya-ba'i chos-kyi rnam-grangs* Qian-long 126, Narthang *Ta* 301a-455a, British Museum Ms OR 6724.73, sTog Palace 454

C: *Da-bi-lu-zhe-na cheng-fo shen bian jia-chi jing* Taishō 848

Apart from their intrinsic value, the commentaries preserved in Tibetan and Chinese proved invaluable for understanding the often obscure text of the MVT itself, so constant reference was made to them in the course of preparing the initial translation of the MVT. Those used were:

Buddhaguhya's Commentary (Tib. text)
V: a. Unrevised version Q 3487, Narthang *Ngu* 73–302
B: b. Revised version Q 3490, Narthang *Gu* 1–233, Derge *Nyu* 65a - 351a

P: Buddhaguhya's *Piṇḍārtha* (Tib. text) Q 3486, Narthang *Ngu* 1–73, Derge *Nyu* 1b-65a

CC: Śubhakara-siṃha's Oral Commentary as recorded by Yi-xing: Unrevised version[18] (大疏) 20 *juan*, Manji-zoku Vol 36, 27–253

As is often the case, this book is the result of many years of research. If I were to be starting afresh, it is quite likely that a different strategy would be adopted. In particular, the landscape of Tibetan textual studies has changed radically over the last few years, thanks to the efforts of Dr Helmut Eimer, Dr Paul Harrsion and others. In contrast to the present work, which can be seen as a kind of 'critical translation', I now think it would be highly desirable to first compile a fully collated edition of the Tibetan version using the much larger range of Tibetan Kanjur editions now available, possibly also linking this with the various divergent readings that exist in the Chinese MVT and its commentaries. The bifurcation of the Old Narthang Kanjur into the Them-spangs-ma and the Tshal-pa lineages with their derivatives is now fairly well understood in general terms. However, old manuscript editions such as the newly available Phug-brag Kanjur and the Tawang Kanjur, which preserve a textual tradition divorced from the Old Narthang Kanjur and all its subsequent editorial amendments, are of especial interest for texts such as the MVT with its transmissional problems[19]. Such Tibetan manuscript editions are often the sole witnesses to very old and more accurate readings, which can be confirmed by reference to parallel Chinese versions, despite the welter of scribal errors usually found in them.

However, for better or worse, this book contains a complete translation of the MVT itself, together with Buddhaguhya's Commentary and his *Piṇḍārtha* based on the above mentioned editions. I have also included the Continuation Tantra, which survives only in Tibetan and lacks any kind of commentary. As mentioned above, my translation of the MVT is slightly hybrid, for though I have used the above Tibetan version of the MVT as the basic text, variant readings have been adopted from the Chinese version or the lemmata in the various commentaries where there are reasonable grounds for supposing that these are closer to the original sense. There are several probable reasons for these variants. First, some must have arisen as intentional amendments to the original text as it developed, while others will have come about due to undetectable scribal errors as the manuscripts were copied. In such cases, it is difficult to decide which version is the more authentic as often each one fits the context quite well. For example, *bīja* (seed) regularly occurs in the Chinese text where the Tibetan has *jīva* (life) and either of these would be acceptable. What we seem to have here is merely a reversal of the syllables of the two words (*b* and *v* being virtually indistinguishable in many Indian scripts). Another fertile breeding ground for many apparently variant readings in the Tibetan and Chinese texts must have been the often considerable range of meanings contained in a single Sanskrit word. If we examine the Tibetan and the Chinese equivalents, we frequently find that they are likely to have had the same underlying Sanskrit original word which has been interpreted differently by the commentators and translators. A good example of this is the Sanskrit word *saṃjñā*, which has been interpreted both as 'perfect awareness' and as 'idea' at the same place by the different translators[20]. I have noted the occurrence of such cases where they seem important.

Obviously it will often be impossible to reconstitute many of the key words and their intended meanings that were found in the original Sanskrit text with any great certainty and indeed there will be those who question the value of any attempt to do so, but as some interesting results can be achieved by a careful comparison of the available materials, I have tried to convey in the translation given here what seems likely to have been the original intention of the compilers of the MVT. So while using the Tibetan version noted above as the basis for my work, I have sometimes given priority to the readings contained in the Chinese version (C) and to the Tibetan text embedded in the unrevised commentary (V) by Buddhaguhya, when these have the same reading of a line which differs to that given by the standard Tibetan translation (T) and the revised commentary (B).

As very few translations are available in English of commentorial literature, especially of that concerning Tantric Buddhism, I felt it would also be most desirable to include both of Buddhaguhya's commentaries on the MVT in this book – the main Commentary and the *Piṇḍārtha* – to present the general reader with an authentic explanation of the meaning of the MVT, though this is naturally dependent upon Buddhaguhya's understanding of the text. The translation of the Commentary given here represents about ninety percent of the complete text, as I have cut out a certain amount of material which either is repetitious or merely duplicates the words of the MVT itself[21]. Such omissions occur almost entirely in the first two chapters of the Commentary and although I do not specifically draw the reader's attention to such cases, these can be detected by a close scrutiny of the page numbers incorporated in the translation – a particularly short run of text between two numbers indicating that something has been cut out. However, the reader may rest assured that nothing of import has been omitted. Also, because of the way this edition is arranged, it has not been necessary to repeat all the passages from the MVT which Buddhaguhya cites for comment.

Ideally, an accompanying translation of the Chinese commentary to complement that of Buddhaguhya should have been included, but this has not proved possible as it would have added at least another seven or eight hundred pages to an already lengthy book. Therefore, although frequent use was made of it during the process of translation, only brief extracts from it could be given in the notes. It should also be remembered that quite apart from containing the kind of alternative readings mentioned above, a considerable divergence in interpretation of many passages of the MVT is reflected in these two commentaries, which would often necessitate separate translation to fit the comments.

IV THE THEMES AND SIGNIFICANCE OF THE MVT

In considering the textual history of the MVT, we have seen that it is an product of the early tantric phase of Buddhism in India. In fact, I believe it is likely to have been one of the first, if not actually the first *fully* developed tantra to be compiled, that has survived in some form to the present day. Nevertheless, it appears to be a very sophisticated text both doctrinally and practically. As I have suggested earlier in this Introduction, there are a number of elements that are characteristic of all tantras. All of these elements are present in the MVT, with the exception of an overt interest in the feminine *per se* as in later tantras, although a large number of female deities are mentioned[22]. As we have also seen, these elements were at first fairly disparate and are encountered separately in texts that date several centuries before the MVT itself. Indeed some of them, such as the *homa* fire sacrifices, have their roots in the pre-Buddhist Vedic culture. Furthermore, apart from the specifically tantric elements which I have mentioned, there are many echoes in the MVT of earlier Mahāyāna teachings, which place it well within the mainstream of Buddhist tradition. Hence we can see clear links between the MVT and the *Sad-dharma-puṇḍarīka Sūtra*, the *Avataṃsaka Sūtra*, the *Buddha-bhūmi Sūtra*, as well as Yogācāra works such as the *Mahāyāna-sūtrālaṃkāra* and the *Dharma-dharmatā-vibhāga*. Unfortunately a full length treatment of all the sources of the MVT would probably require a book to itself, so for lack of space I must leave this for another occasion.

Now, we might ask ourselves why the tantras were developed and ultimately achieved such popularity. Although certain social conditions prevailing in India around that time could be identified as contributory causes, I belief that the main reason is to be found in a particular characteristic of Buddhism. As the reader will be aware, Buddhism as a whole has always lacked a centralized authority which imposes its views upon the faithful, dictating what is or is not acceptable. So within certain general limitations, Buddhism was able over the centuries to undergo constant change, adaptation and renewal without hindrance, both in India and in the many countries to which it was transmitted[23]. It is for this reason that we see a variety of schools in Buddhism quite unparalleled in any other religion, though an underlying common core is always evident. Indeed, the MVT itself speaks of this, when it repeatedly states that Buddhas teach the Dharma to *all* beings throughout the universe in whatever manner is most suited to their needs. It is therefore likely that the tantras were first developed unconsciously as a part of this process of renewal. The early centuries of Mahāyāna were overshadowed by the *Prajñā-pāramitā Sūtras* and the Mādhyamika school of Nāgārjuna which derived from them. One can imagine the impact of these teachings when they were first taught – just read the Heart Sutra and consider what a shock it must have been to the Abhidharma-orientated monks of the time to be told that all their cherished categories and systems did not really exist! Yet as time went by, many must have felt unsatisfied by the austere teachings of the Mādhyamikas which seemed to cut away everything from under one's feet and not replace it with anything. As though in answer to this discomfort, the complex Yogācāra system was established around the fourth century CE by Maitreya, Asaṅga and Vasubandhu. This system has unfortunately been badly misunderstood by later Buddhist scholars both in Tibet and in the West. It attempted to retain the basic insight of the *Prajñā-pāramitā Sūtras* concerning emptiness (*śūnyatā*), while combining it with a new analysis of the nature of the universe and a structured path to liberation, which was designed to insure the practitioner against naive realism and the dangers of nihilism present in Mādhyamika teachings. As time went by, the Mādhyamikas and the Yogācārins became established as the two rival camps within Mahāyāna, each no doubt claiming that *theirs* was the correct viewpoint. While their respective scholars engaged in polemics that became more and more abstruse, especially with the emergence of the Buddhist schools of logic, the desire for a new approach must have been felt by the majority of people who were no doubt by then thoroughly confused. There was evidently a need for a kind of Buddhism that was inspiring, not so difficult to understand or practice, and which got you liberated quickly. Judging by the rapidity of its development once it had gained general acceptance in the main centres of Buddhism, it would seem that Tantric Buddhism answered this need very well. Yet despite its popular appeal, Tantric Buddhism was also remarkably sophisticated in its theories and practices, as will be seen from the MVT itself. All religions have been faced with a similar contradiction: how to explain the relationship between the infinite and the finite, and express that which is inherently inexpressible. Each have attempted to answer this problem in their own way. The Buddhist tantras do this brilliantly with their use of innovative theories and techniques of meditation. To understand something of this, let us look in outline at the main themes and aims of the MVT.

First, the central theme of the MVT is quite simple – what is Perfect Enlightenment and how does one achieve it? Throughout the MVT, Perfect Enlightenment is personified as Mahā-vairocana, so actually the aim of the practices prescribed is to become Mahā-vairocana. This central idea is said to have three interconnected aspects – the causal basis, the nature and the result of Perfect Enlightenment. Of these, the causal basis is twofold: the immediate cause and the indirect cause. The immediate cause is understood to be the fact that Enlightenment (*bodhicitta*) is inherent in all beings and so guarantees the attainment of Perfect Enlightenment by them. Naturally this concept does not originate with the MVT, for it first occurs several centuries before in such writings as the Lotus *Sūtra* and reaches its full flowering in the *Tathāgata-garbha* (Buddha Matrix) cycle of texts. The indirect cause is the aspiration to become enlightened together with the path, from the first glimmerings of spirituality onwards, which includes the eight mundane minds, the sixty types of mind and the supra-mundane levels of the Śrāvakas, Pratyekabuddhas and Bodhisattvas, described in Chapter One. Though the mantra path is singled out as being the most effective method, it is noteworthy here that the MVT adopts an extremely conciliatory attitude to all religious beliefs. The shortcomings of some are criticized, yet as Buddhaguhya says '*through relying upon the self of ordinary foolish people and upon the gods, people seek liberation and even the bliss they seek as liberation should be viewed as a cause linking them with the Bhagavat Vairocana*' (ad I.20). This is because the MVT considers *all* spiritual teachers who lead us towards reality to be manifestations and embodiments of the great compassion of Mahā-vairocana himself, present in all places at all times.

The nature of Perfect Enlightenment is succinctly defined in the MVT thus: '*It is to know your mind as it really is. That is the supreme, full and perfect Enlightenment*' (I.7). This definition is noteworthy because it highlights the importance of the mind in this text, so we ought to spend some time considering its various implications. In keeping with Buddhism in general, the MVT and its commentators have a sophisticated conceptual apparatus for describing various aspects of what we loosely call the mind. In particular we should note the use of the terms *citta* and *manas*. I have normally translated *citta* as 'mind', as in the above quotation, while reluctantly leaving *manas* untranslated due to the range and complexity of its meaning. Of these two, let us first examine the term *citta*. This word is derived from the verbal root √ *cit* which means 'to recognize / observe / perceive', 'to be bright, to shine' and 'to amass, to accumulate'. Although there are different usages of the word *citta* which reflect these meanings, the basic sense of *citta* in the MVT seems to refer to the general and comprehensive cognitive ground underlying the dynamic system of psychological operations. In its natural state it is said to be primordially existent and free from the artificial division into a perceiving subject and perceived objects, which characterizes the mind of a being still involved in *saṃsāra*. When in this natural state, *citta* is often described as being luminous and pure by nature (*prakṛti-prabhāsvara*). Though it has not generally been noted, this view of the mind has a long history in Buddhism, for the term *prakṛti-prabhāsvara-citta* (mind which is luminous by nature) is already found in a number of Pali *suttas* belonging to the earliest phase of Buddhism, such as the striking passage in the *Aṅguttara Nikāya* I.10: '*The mind is luminous, but it is defiled by adventitious defilements. Ordinary people who are unaware of it do not know it as it really is* (*yathā-bhūtaṃ*)'[24]. The mind is also said to be like gold which is intrinsically pure yet has become adulterated with impurities such as iron, copper, lead and so forth. This concept of the intrinsic purity or luminosity of the mind can be traced down the centuries as it makes its appearance in many major sutras, especially those associated with the *Tathāgata-garbha* theory. For our purposes we may also note the passage which occurs in the *Aṣṭasahāsrika-prajñā-pāramitā Sūtra* where the Buddha says '*Moreover, when a Bodhisattva Mahāsattva engages in the Perfection of Insight and cultivates it, he should train himself so that he does not take pride in that* bodhicitta. *Why is that? Because that mind is actually non-mind and is luminous in its intrinsic nature*'. In his commentary which deals with this Sūtra, the *Abhisamaya-āloka*, Haribhadra tells us that the mind is non-mind because it is intrinsically free from all attachments and conceptualizing and hence is luminous. *Citta* may therefore be understood as an abbreviation for, or equivalent to, the intrinsic *bodhicitta* (the *citta* which is *bodhi*). This view is confirmed by the discussion centring on the nature of the mind in Chapter One of the MVT itself, as well as in many Mahāyāna sutras which describe the mind (*citta*) as being without dualistic concepts (*nirvikalpa*), pure, radiant and mirror-like.

However, this inherently pure mind is usually obscured by adventitious defilements arising from a dualistic split imposed upon it, just as the sun is obscured by clouds in the sky, so we also see the term *citta* used in the MVT in the sense of our normal everyday mind. Due to this dualistic split and all that arises from it, the mind which is intrinsically unbounded like space becomes limited to a particular viewpoint or attitude. It is these attitudes that are described at length in sections 18 – 23 of Chapter I. Yet, although they are limited fragments of the primordial mind, they are also seen as possible causes for regaining that natural state of mind due to the nature of their relationship with it, just as the fragments of a broken mirror still have something in common with the whole mirror[25]. So when the MVT speaks of knowing your mind as it truly is, it means that you are to know this inherent natural state of the mind by eliminating the split into a perceiving subject and perceived objects which normally occurs in the world and is wrongly thought to be real. This also corresponds to the Yogācāra definition adopted by Buddhaguhya, that emptiness (*śūnyatā*) is the absence of this imaginary split. In other words, Enlightenment, which is the natural state of the mind, is characterized by non-duality and emptiness, for as the MVT states '*there is neither that which becomes enlightened nor that to which one is enlightened*' (I.7).

We may further elucidate the meaning of Perfect Enlightenment, and hence of the intrinsic nature of the mind, by correlating terms Buddhaguhya treats as synonyms. For example, he defines emptiness (*śūnyatā*) as suchness (*tathatā*) and says that suchness is the intrinsic nature (*svabhāva*) of the mind which is Enlightenment (*bodhicitta*). Moreover he frequently uses the terms suchness (*tathatā*) and Suchness-Awareness (*tathatā-jñāna*) interchangeably. But since Awareness (*jñāna*) is non-dual, Suchness-Awareness is not so much the Awareness of Suchness, but the Awareness which *is* suchness. In other words, the term Suchness-Awareness is functionally equivalent to Enlightenment. Finally, it must not be forgotten that this Suchness-Awareness or Perfect Enlightenment *is* Mahā-vairocana. In other words, the mind in its intrinsic nature is Mahā-vairocana, whom one 'becomes' (or vice versa) when one is perfectly enlightened. We shall return to this later.

Apart from *citta* (mind), the other key psychological term used in the MVT is *manas*. Although the *manas* was not always clearly distinguished from *citta* or *vijñāna* (consciousness) in some Buddhist schools, its main function is generally to distinguish and experience both sensory and non-sensory data, in the form of phenomena (*dharma*). Here we may possibly consider the term '*dharma*' to mean 'image'. In fact, it is the function of the *manas* to synthesize the input of bare sensory data, in conjunction with the images held in memory, into fresh perceptual images (*ākāra*)[26]. Hence the conscious perception of an object is not the object in itself but a synthetic image of it. Indeed, it should be noted that early Buddhist texts often did not make any distinction between internal images and external objects, to the extent that they were frequently confused. This no doubt paved the way for the insight of later Yogācāra thinkers who saw that one actually cannot distinguish objects of perception from the internal perceptual images[27]. For to say that the *manas* perceives objects is equivalent to saying that it creates them, for all perception is a synthetic creation[28]. In this sense we can understand the *manas* to indicate an image-making process similar to the Sufi term *himma*, creative imagination, discussed by Henri Corbin[29].

The relationship between *citta* and *manas* is indicated by Buddhaguhya who regularly defines *manas* as the mind having, or being associated with, perceptual images (*sākāra-citta*). The term *citta* in this context could be interpreted in several ways, but I think it makes most sense if we take it to mean the fragmented mode of *citta* which has become so because it is associated with perceptual images. As the reader will recollect, the mind in its natural state is pure and luminous, free from the dualistic split (*vikalpa*) into a perceiving subject and perceived objects. In fact, Buddhaguhya explicitly states that the perceptual images (*ākāra*) are synonymous with and symptomatic of this falsely imagined dualistic split. As we have already seen, these perceptual images are synthetic creations of the *manas* that are substituted for, or superimposed upon, the pure sensory data, which is precisely what is implied by the dualistic split (*vikalpa*) into a perceiving subject and perceived objects[30]. We should also remember here that when the MVT says the primordial mind is *śūnyatā* (emptiness) in nature, it makes use of the Yogācāra definition which states that *śūnyatā* is the absence of the falsely imagined duality.

Finally there is the result of Perfect Enlightenment. This is mentioned several times with specific reference to Mahā-vairocana. Basing himself on the MVT, Buddhaguhya states that '*at the moment of his Perfect Enlightenment, [Mahā-vairocana] spontaneously pervaded all of the Three Realms .... with the Adornments of his Inexhaustible Body [Speech and Mind]*' (3a) and acted for the benefit of all beings by revealing the Dharma. These Adornments are the self-revelation of the qualities or 'content' of Perfect Enlightenment on the physical, verbal and mental levels in structured patterns throughout the universe. It is because of their meaningful configuration in this way that these Adornments are also termed '*cakras*' or '*maṇḍalas*'. This revelation of the Dharma is said to occur spontaneously at the moment of Vairocana's Perfect Enlightenment by virtue of his compassion and so the three mandalas described in the MVT are collectively said to be '*arisen from the matrix of compassion (karuṇā-garbodaya)*'. However in keeping with the general Mahāyāna concept of a Buddha's three modes of being or embodiment (*tri-kāya*), this expression of the 'content' of Perfect Enlightenment operates on two levels according to the ability of the beings to be assisted. The first of the three modes of being is the *dharmakāya* which forms the ground for the other two and is equivalent to Perfect Enlightenment itself or Vairocana's Mind. Not only does it transcend all perceptual forms and so cannot be directly manifested or perceived, it is also said to be primordially existent. From the *dharmakāya*, two other modes of being arise, the *saṃbhoga-kāya* and the *nirmāṇa-kāya* which are equivalent to Vairocana's Speech and Body respectively. According to the MVT, these two modes of being form the intrinsically existent mandala and as such are the Inexhaustible Adornments of Body, Speech and Mind mentioned above. The *saṃbhoga-kāya*, as Vairocana's Speech aspect, is especially concerned with communication of the Dharma and appears in the form of various Buddhas and Bodhisattvas, though these are beyond the perceptual range of ordinary beings. To cater for their needs and abilities, Vairocana further creates various *nirmāṇa-kāyas*, a lower order of manifestation, in the physical form of Śākyamuni and other spiritual teachers. Moreover, those manifestations of the qualities of Perfect Enlightenment, the Inexhaustible Adornments of Vairocana's Body, Speech and Mind, are transformed by Vairocana into what we normally think of as mandalas, mantras and *mudrās*. These transformations act as a bridge between ourselves and Vairocana by which we may identify ourselves with and indeed actually become Vairocana. It is noteworthy that the title itself of the MVT summarizes these three modes of Perfect Enlightenment: *abhisambodhi*, *adhiṣṭhāna* and *vikurvita*.

It is noteworthy that the cause, nature and result of Perfect Enlightenment we have just examined implies a three stage process. Vairocana goes through the normal career of a Bodhisattva gradually dissolving the obscurations (*āvaraṇas*), achieves Enlightenment, and then in the instant following this, spontaneously manifests all his qualities as the tripartite, intrinsically existent mandala (*svabhāva-maṇḍala*) and its transformation into forms accessible to ordinary beings. However, this process conceals an interesting problem regarding the nature of Vairocana. As we know, the 'content' of Perfect Enlightenment is suchness. In several places in his commentary,

Buddhaguhya indicates that suchness is synonymous with the continuum of reality (*dharmadhātu*). This complex term basically implies the universal 'matrix' which is space-like or emptiness (*śūnyatā*) in nature, from which all phenomena arise. This is elaborated by Buddhaguhya when he says that the continuum of reality has two aspects, the Profound which is the core of Enlightenment (*bodhi-maṇḍa*), the 'beholding' of reality, and the Extensive which is the intrinsically existent mandalas formed by the Inexhaustible Adornments of Vairocana's Body, Speech and Mind. Presumably, Buddhaguhya is referring to the second aspect of the continuum of reality when he also states that it is the universe with all its world systems and societies of beings. But the continuum of reality must also be identical to Perfect Enlightenment, for as we have already seen, the 'content' of Perfect Enlightenment is identical to Perfect Enlightenment itself, because it transcends all duality. This is confirmed when Buddhaguhya says that the Profound aspect of the continuum of reality is the core of Enlightenment (*bodhi-maṇḍa*). In this case, our universe and ourselves must in some way form part of Perfect Enlightenment. This is borne out by passages in the MVT where it is said that the Buddha realm or mandala which Vairocana manifests (actually he *is* the mandala) is the 'Universe of World-systems Adorned with a Lotus-base Matrix' (*Kusuma-tala-garbha-alaṃkāra-lokadhātu*), which includes our part of the universe known as the *Sahā* world system. This realm is mentioned in several earlier Mahāyāna texts such as the *Avataṃsaka Sūtra* and the *Brahma-jāla Sūtra*, but unfortunately there does not seem to be a consistent definition of its nature. That is to say, at times it is thought to be just one of a number of vast Buddha realms, while at other times it seems to be the entirety of all Buddha realms. These interpretations depend upon the status of Vairocana. According to the Sino-Japanese tradition derived from Śubhakara-siṃha and the views of some Indian exegetes mentioned by Buddhaguhya in his *Piṇḍārtha* (57a), Mahā-vairocana is considered to be the primordial Buddha (*ādi-buddha*). In my view, this is clearly implied by many passages in the MVT, so we can assume that the term 'Universe of World-systems Adorned with a Lotus-base Matrix' in the MVT actually indicates the entirety of all Buddha realms. Consequently, we seem to reach the interesting conclusion that we and our universe are a manifestation or 'theophany' of Vairocana!

If this is indeed the case, then we encounter a further complication. For if the universe arose as a manifestation of Vairocana's Perfect Enlightenment, then where was he when he was still a Bodhisattva? In other words, some place must have existed for Vairocana to engage in the Bodhisattva practices during the vast amount of time needed to reach Enlightenment. Though this situation is puzzling, I think a tentative solution can be suggested which has quite profound implications for our conventional ways of understanding later Buddhism. First, it must be remembered that 'Vairocana' is really a symbol, a personification of Perfect Enlightenment, and that Perfect Enlightenment is the all-pervading cognitive state which is identical to its content. In other words, Perfect Enlightenment is the totality of the *dharmadhātu* and *vice versa*. If we also consider Mahā-vairocana as the sum total of Perfect Enlightenment "attained" by beings at the end of time when all beings have in fact become enlightened, then though Mahā-vairocana may be thought of as eternally existing outside of time, he only truly becomes an actuality at the end of space and time. This is reminiscent of Schelling's concept of God evolving and becoming enhanced as the universe proceeds through time. Additionally, this final point of the universe must also be its beginning, the point where it witnesses itself, as Mahā-vairocana, coming into being. Surely this is what is meant by the MVT when it uses the phrases '*the billowing forth of emptiness*' (XXIV.10)[31] and '*the billowing forth of the continuum of reality*' (XIII.1), or when it says that Mahā-vairocana manifested the intrinsically existent mandala the moment he became enlightened. In effect, he projects the beginning of the universe back into time and in a circular process begins the task of becoming perfectly enlightened again. If a large piece of glass that has been imprinted with a hologram is broken, each fragment of the glass stills retains the complete holographic image, though in a somewhat less distinct and clear form. Could this be a modern way of understanding the potentiality for Enlightenment or Buddha nature (*tathāgata-garbha*) which inheres in all beings? In other words, does Mahā-vairocana (Perfect Enlightenment) become fragmented when he returns to the beginning of time as the universe itself and all its inhabitants?

Moreover, the yogin's tantric practice parallels, or perhaps we might even say partakes in this threefold process by means of the three phases of *bodhicitta* known as the 'three minds' – the entering phase in which the yogin dissolves all beliefs in the substantiality of phenomena and the subject-object polarity, the abiding phase in which he abides in emptiness (*śūnyatā*) and then the arising phase in which he spontaneously generates the mandala and acts for the benefit of beings. At that moment, he remains in the emptiness of all phenomena (= *dharmakāya*) on the absolute level and at the same time he operates in the world, treating all phenomena as illusions (= *saṃbhoga-kāya* and *nirmāṇa-kāya*) on the relative level. In fact ,the MVT stresses that the yogin achieves complete identity with Vairocana through this process.

It now remains for us to look briefly at the variety of methods prescribed in the MVT for attaining Perfect Enlightenment. These fall into two separate groups: those described in the first chapter and those in the remaining chapters. According to the Sino-Japanese tradition, three main techniques are taught in the first chapter: i) The meditative observation in order to know the mind as it really is, ii) the meditative observation of the mind's lack of perceptual images and iii) the meditative observation of the three types of deluded mind. One can engage in any one of these three, though the meditation to '*know the mind as it really is*' contains all the others.

The first technique is the meditative observation in order to know the mind as it really is (I.7). This technique utilizes the process described by Vasubandhu in his *Trimśika* to eliminate the false idea of a perceiving subject and perceived objects:

> '*As long as consciousness does not abide in the state of representation-only, the tendency towards the twofold grasping will not cease to operate.* (26)
> *Though one may think 'This is representation-only', one is still regarding it as something placed before one. One is therefore still not abiding in the state of representation-only.* (27)
> *However, when consciousness no longer perceives objects* (ālambana), *one is then abiding in the state of representation-only, because where there is nothing to be perceived [as an object] there is also nothing perceiving it.*' (28)

The aim of the second technique (I. 9–13) is to make it clear that the mind in its natural state cannot be found in any of the perceptual images with which it is mistakenly identified. At the end of this process, it should be realized that the mind is unborn, unceasing and primordially pure. Because it is unborn, the mind cannot be found in any phenomenon, yet because it is unceasing, the mind is not separate from all phenomena. This is like space which is unconnected with all things and their perceptual images and yet pervades all things, acting as their 'location'. According to Śubhakara-siṃha, this technique is the most profound and is called the 'Dharma Gate to Swift Realization'.

The third technique is the meditative observation of the three types of deluded mind. This differs from the previous two techniques as it is more elaborate and requires a greater span of time to accomplish, since one can only embark upon it after the different types of mundane mind have been transcended. Moreover, this technique involves three stages: i) The analysis of the person into the five skandhas and so forth, by which it is seen that one cannot identify these with a self (*pudgala-nairātmya*). As there is a danger of concretizing these as really existing, one must also understand that these are relative and illusory by interdependent arising (*pratītya-samutpāda*) and also realize emptiness (*śūnyatā*) with regards the individual (I.23). ii) As this is not yet true emptiness, one must establish the absence of autonomous existence in phenomena (*dharma-nairātmya*). The MVT again utilizes a Yogācāra method to do this. By meditating on the six similes of magical illusions and so forth, one understands that phenomena do not really exist but just appear to do so. This leads one to the realization of consciousness-only, which then in its turn is also abandoned (I.24-25). iii) Finally, though one has realized the true emptiness of the individual and phenomena, one does not yet realize that the natural state of mind is the Tathāgata's inherent Awareness and that it is the all-pervasive Body of Vairocana with all the manifested Buddha realms. Therefore one must transcend even emptiness with the emptiness of emptiness (*śūnyatā-śūnyatā*), when it is seen that the mind is primordially unborn and unarisen[32] (I.26).

The second group of techniques are taught in Chapter II onwards and are more specifically 'tantric' in nature. Buddhaguhya summarizes the subject matter of these chapters into the twenty one topics which may be seen in Table 3, but following the standard sequence for tantric practice, we may divide these topics into three sections: the preliminary practices, the application practices and the effectuation practices. In turn, these practices are each sub-divided into two parts. Although each of these are dealt with by Buddhaguhya in his commentary, it may be helpful to the reader if I give an outline guide to them here.

The preliminary practices are divided into outer and inner practices. As their name suggests, the intention of these practices is to prepare the yogin physically and mentally for the main practices. The outer practices comprise all the rituals required to purify the yogin and to enable him to engage in the subsequent stages, such as the initiations into the three mandalas and the acceptance of the *samaya* commitments. These are mainly covered by Chapters II, X, XIII, XIV, XV and XVI, with some supplementary material in other chapters.

The inner preliminary practice is also twofold – with perceptual forms and without perceptual forms. The yogin must first engage in the preliminary practice without perceptual forms. This involves the repeated cultivation of emptiness (*śūnyatā*) or bodhicitta, which is understood here to mean the purity of mind in its natural state. Various methods can be employed, such as the processes described in Chapter VI.47

Table 3: Summary of Topics in MVT

1 Indication of the mandala Master's attributes.
2 Specification of trainees' attributes.
3 The attributes of the mandala site, its purification and taking hold of it.
4 Description of the ritual for the preparation of the trainees.
5 The specifications for the marking-out of the mandala, the attributes of its sections and of its gateways.
6 Description of the transformation of the Inexhaustible Array of the Bhagavat's Body by the arrayed bodies of the mandala deities in the *Mahā-karunodaya* Mandala.
7 Arrangement of the mandala deities with the letters of their seed-syllables which are transformations of the Inexhaustible Array of the Bhagavat's Speech in the Mandala of the Revolving Wheel of Letters.
8 The distinct arrangements of the deities of the mandalas of earth etc. by the different types of *mudrās* which reside in earth, water, fire and wind mandalas which are transformations of the Inexhaustible Array of the Bhagavat Vairocana's Mind, in the Secret Mandala.
9 The different types of pigments to be used.
10 The practice of transformation of the mandala deities after having drawn the mandalas.
11 The branches of worship (internal and external).
12 Description of the ritual to accept the trainees.
13 The ritual to make the *samaya* known to them.
14 The ritual to initiate them.
15 The ritual to cause them to uphold the *vidyās*.
16 Detailed description of the different types of *vidyās*, mantras and *mudrās*.
17 The specifications for the branches of *sādhana*.
18 The branches of *sādhana* such as the mandalas for the accomplishment of the *vidyās* and mantras.
19 The signs of accomplishment (internal and external attainments).
20 The ritual to be done with fire (*homa*).
21 The specifications for the branches of *sādhana*.

and Chapter VIII, but the aim is for the yogin's mind to achieve stability and be able to rest equipoised in a *samādhi* from which all perceptual forms are absent. Unless one-pointedness of mind is attained in this way, the yogin will find it impossible to engage in the practices involving creative imagination and recitation.

When the yogin has attained some skill in this practice without perceptual forms, he is then able to engage in the four-branched recitation. Normally at this stage of his development, the yogin will use the so-called 'external' version of the four-branched recitation in which the Buddha or any other deity is imagined to be outside and separate from himself. This corresponds to what is now generally known as front-generation, in contrast to the 'internal' recitation in which the deity is imagined seated within the yogin's own heart. The basic technique for this 'external' kind of meditative recitation is described at length in Chapter V and can be used in conjunction with any mantra and deity. In general terms, the yogin should imagine a moon-disc which is the manifestation of *bodhicitta* on the relative level. The mantra letter should be placed upon that moon-disc sounding forth its own sound. This is the first ground which the yogin should use to generate a divine body for himself, transforming himself into that deity by means of the appropriate mantras and *mudrās*. Then he should imagine the body-image of the deity before him and contemplate the mantra in a moon in the deity's heart. This forms the second ground. When this has been done, the yogin should train himself by controlling his breath and one-pointed recitation in silence until he reaches the stage when that deity appears with clarity and stability.

When the yogin has prepared himself sufficiently, he is ready to embark on the application practice to achieve union with the deity. Once again we find the twofold division into practice with perceptual forms and practice without perceptual forms. For the first, the yogin should use the 'internal' four-branched recitation. A typical example of this is described in VII.23 and may be summarized as follows. The yogin transforms himself into the body-image of Śākyamuni and then generates Vairocana within the moon-disc in Śākyamuni's heart. Next he places the mantra within a second moon-disc located in Vairocana's heart and then does the recitation after having regulated his breath. In the application practice without perceptual forms, the yogin should transform himself into the *dharmakāya* mode of his tutelary deity and then do the recitation. This is summarized by Buddhaguhya in his *Piṇḍārtha* (66a) as follows: '*First you should actualize all the four branches of [external] recitation for a while as before and then analyze the manifestation of the imagined* (parikalpita) *colour, shape and so on of your tutelary deity who is identical to yourself, breaking them down into atoms. Or it is also acceptable to do this by way of the reasoning that [the mind] is unborn and unarising from the very beginning, or likewise by way of the technique of re-uniting the vital-energy* (prāṇa) *through the yoga of turning your mind inside, or by way of not focusing on its appearance [as colour and shape]. In accordance with that realization, you should actualize the mind which is just self-aware, free from the body-image of your tutelary deity and without appearance [as subject and objects] and mentally recite your* vidyā *mantra as appropriate. In order to teach this, the text says:*

> *'The supramundane is that done mentally.*
> *Having completely left off drawing-in and so on,*
> *you should make yourself one with the deity,*
> *perceiving both to be identical,*
> *it should be inseparable from the nature of your* manas.
> *In no other way should it be done.'*

Finally when he has concluded the application practice, the yogin may engage in the practice for the application or effectuation of the power gained through union with the deity. The manifestations of this power are the ordinary and the special attainments. Generally speaking, these are the various kinds of mundane attainments described in detail in the MVT, especially in Section 43 onwards of Chapter VI, and the supramundane attainments which are the Five Supernatural Cognitions and ultimately Enlightenment itself. These two types of attainments are respectively attained by way of the practices with perceptual forms and without perceptual forms.

The MVT recommends that the yogin should devote his efforts to achieving the special attainments which arise from the *samādhi* with perceptual forms, because this will also give him access to the ordinary attainments.

Having concluded this brief survey of the wide range of practices taught in the MVT, it would probably be best to bring this introduction to a close and let the reader turn to the MVT itself. However as a footnote, I should like to mention the role of the *manas* and creative imagination in the MVT. We have already had occasion to examine the nature of the *manas*, but in the MVT it has another aspect of crucial importance in tantric practice which should be noted. For despite the suspect nature of the *manas* and the perceptual images it constructs, many passages in the MVT indicate that they may also be put to use in a positive way by those unable to break through to reality in the more direct manner described in Chapter I. For although our normal view of the world is unsatisfactory, the image-making function of the *manas* can also be used to construct a liberating alternative view of things by which we approximate ourselves to the structure of reality which is manifested by Vairocana as the intrinsically existent mandala. First the ordinary world of *saṃsāra* and its structures are dissolved into non-dual emptiness – the slate is wiped clean. Then, emerging from that *samādhi*, a new world is generated by the use of creative imagination, using the images of the deities, the mantra sounds and so forth as the blue-print. The validity of such images is vouchsafed by the transformational power (*adhiṣṭhāna*) of Vairocana. Vairocana continually interpenetrates the universe with his Body, Speech and Mind in order to reveal the true nature of things to beings, who for their part must reciprocate and reach out to make contact with the illuminating power of Vairocana. All the mandalas, mantras and *mudrās* taught in the MVT were revealed in order to act as bridges between ourselves and Vairocana.

This view that the *manas* can play a valuable role in reshaping one's spiritual life had a long history in India. For example, we can find echoes or even the origins of many 'tantric' ideas and practices in the Vedas. There, such terms as *manas* and other related words derived from the root √ *man* are used with great frequency to indicate the process by which the Vedic seers achieved illumination. For example, *manīṣā* is used to indicate the visionary perception which may be roused by Soma and finds its expression in sacred speech (= *mantra*). Thus according to Jeanine Miller (1985), revelation comes through the heart as the seat of synthesis, where the power of intelligence resides which combines awareness, understanding and intuitive perception and yields higher vision. It is interesting to note here the importance of the heart as the centre for creating the illuminating vision. In the MVT it is clearly stated that the *manas* is located in the heart. Here the term 'heart' should probably be understood as the core of man's inner dimension. Of course this idea is not unique to the MVT even in Buddhism, for the Theravādin school posited a 'heart-base' (*hadaya-vatthu*) as the location of the *manas*. While the great commentator Buddhaghosa in his Path of Purity (*Visuddhi-magga*) understands this quite literally as the physical heart, other Theravādins understood it as the interior core of the person.

There is also a very striking passage in the Ṛg Veda which states that Agni sits in the secret place (*guhā niṣīdan*), '*where men find him whilst meditating and reciting their mantras which they fashion in their hearts*' [RV I.67.2]. The secret place is the interior of the heart, which is also like a cave[33]. Indeed, this is made explicit in the Upaniṣads where the heart is the hidden cave in which abides the unborn *ātman,* the essence of the whole universe. Such statements can be compared with the words of the MVT such as: '*The second ground is the perfect Buddha who sits upon a great royal lotus within that same mirror disc, abiding in* samādhi, *[as though] within in a cave*' [VI.23]. The similarity of idea is even more remarkable when we realize that Agni symbolizes the immortal light of spiritual illumination in the Vedas and so is equivalent to Vairocana whose own name means 'illuminating'. Of course, this would not seem at all surprising for the compilers of the MVT, because to them Mahā-vairocana is the source of all that is valuable!

Part II

THE MAHĀ-VAIROCANA-ABHISAṂBODHI TANTRA WITH BUDDHAGUHYA'S COMMENTARY

INTRODUCTION

Having first attained All-knowing Awareness, the Bhagavat then saw with it that there are two types of trainees: those who are mainly orientated to teachings involving cognitive objects and those who are mainly orientated to the Profound and Extensive teachings. There are also two types of practice for those trainees: they can engage in practice with the Perfection Method or they can engage in practice with the Mantra Method. There are also two ways of engaging in practice with the Perfection Method: that of those beings who are mainly orientated to practice involving cognitive objects and that of those beings who are mainly orientated to the Profound and Extensive. The Vinaya, the Sutras, the Abhidharma and likewise Mahāyāna Sutras such as the *Vīradatta-gṛhapati* and so on, were taught for the sake of those trainees who engage in practice by way of the Perfection Method, and who are mainly orientated to that involving cognitive objects. On the other hand, the Profound and Extensive Sutras such as the *Gaṇḍavyūha*, the *Daśabhūmi*, the *Samādhirāja* and so forth, (2b) were taught for those trainees who are orientated to the Profound and Extensive.

In the same way, there are also two types of trainees who engage in practice with the Mantra Method: those beings who are mainly orientated to that involving cognitive objects and those beings who are mainly orientated to that which is Profound and Extensive. Such Kriyā Tantras as the *Susiddhikāra Tantra* and the *Vidyādhara Collection* were taught for the sake of those who are mainly orientated to engaging in practice with cognitive objects. On the other hand, such Tantras as the *Sarva-tathāgata-tattva-saṃgraha* and so on, were taught for the sake of those beings to be trained by the Profound and the Extensive.

Although we speak of 'beings who are mainly orientated to practices involving cognitive objects', it is not that they are uninterested in the Profound and Extensive and do not engage in it, but it means that a greater part of their interest is to engage in the practice which relies on cognitive objects. In the same way, it is not the case that those who are mainly orientated to the Profound and Extensive do not engage in practice which relies on cognitive objects, but that a greater part of their practice relates to the Profound and Extensive.

In this way, although the *Tattvasaṃgraha* and so on are mainly about inner yoga, outer practice also is not lacking. Likewise, although the Kriyā Tantras are mainly concerned with outer practice, they also do not lack inner practice. In the *Vidyādhara Collection*, immersion in the Three Gates of Liberation and so forth is spoken of, and you should understand this in a similar manner for those who engage in practice by way of the Perfections, according to the circumstances.

Thus, although the *Mahā-vairocana-abhisaṃbodhi-vikurvati-adhiṣṭhāna-tantra* is a Yoga Tantra which deals mainly with expedient means (*upāya*) and insight (*prajñā*), it also teaches practices which accord with the *Kriyā* Tantras (3a) so that those trainees who are orientated towards rituals may also be attracted. Hence it can be considered as a *Kriyā* Tantra or as a Dual (*ubhaya*) Tantra.

The Bhagavat also taught this Tantra for the sake of superior, middling and inferior types of beings to be guided: those who comprehend it by mention of the title (*udghaṭita-jña*), those who comprehend it by analysis into topics (*vipañcita-jña*) and those who refer to the words of the text.

Of these, those who comprehend it by mention of the title are those whose intelligence is extremely sharp and who have heard much, who understand the entire meaning of this Tantra by just hearing the words '*Vairocana-abhisaṃbodhi-vikurvita-adhiṣṭhāna*' following the meaning of the words.

By the word '***Vairocana***', they know that the Bhagavat Vairocana is the *saṃbhoga-kāya*, the perfect accumulation of merit and awareness, all-knowing in nature.

'***Abhisaṃbodhi***' is to know one's mind as it is in reality. It is also to realize that emptiness (*śūnyatā*) is the attribute (*lakṣaṇa*) of all phenomena, just as it is of space.

Vikurvita (manifested/displayed): They understand that at the moment of his Perfect Enlightenment, he spontaneously pervaded all of the Three Realms, unsurpassed by anyone, with the Adornments of his Inexhaustible Body which he naturally attained by the power of his previous aspirations and, with whatever embodiment of *saṃbhoga-kāya* or *nirmāṇa-kāya* needed to train suitable beings, acted for their benefit. So to beings to be guided by the Body of a Buddha, he manifested himself in the Body of a Buddha and to those to be guided by the form of a Śrāvaka, a Pratyekabuddha, Śakra, Brahmā and so on, he manifested in those forms and benefited them. (3b) Likewise the Adornments of his Inexhaustible Speech also pervaded all of the Three Realms with the sacred Speech of the Buddha and taught the Dharma. And in the same way, the Adornments of his Inexhaustible Mind manifested as the various *cakras* of earth, water and so on, which arise from the mind with perceptual images.

In the same way, they understand by the word '***adhiṣṭhāna***' (transformation) that the manifestations of the Adornments of the [Bhagavat's] Inexhaustible Body, Speech and Mind pervading all of the Three Realms are within the perceptual range (*gocara*) of the completely pure Bodhisattvas such as Samantabhadra and so on. But they are not within the perceptual range of trainees, so those same Adornments of his Inexhaustible Body and so on are revealed for the sake of trainees as physical, verbal and mental attributes, by means of the mandalas, mantras and *mudrās* in the Tantra. '***Adhiṣṭhāna***' means he caused them to be present in the nature and the guise of body, speech and mind, by means of mandalas, mantras and *mudrās*.

Thus, those trainees who understand just by mention of the title, understand the meaning in this way by just the words and corresponding meanings of the title '***Vairocana-abhisaṃbodhi-vikurvita-adhiṣṭhāna***'. You should understand that just the name of this Tantra was mentioned for their sakes. And they do not only understand it in that manner, but furthermore they will know that it reveals the causal relationship (*saṃbandha*), the subject matter (*abhidheya*) and the purpose (*prayojana*) of this Tantra. They will see that this Tantra is connected with the Bhagavat's intrinsically existent mandala, the causal Inexhaustible Body and so on. It should be understood that this intrinsically existent mandala is the causal basis of this Tantra and this Tantra is the result. That is the causal relationship (*saṃbandha*). Likewise they will know that this Tantra (4a) indicates the manner of existence of the intrinsically existent mandala by revealing his Body, Speech and Mind as they actually are, by means of the mandalas, mantras and *mudrās* in this Tantra. Therefore, this Tantra is the discourse (*abhidhāna*) and the subject matter (*abhidheya*) is the intrinsically existent mandala. As for its purpose, one propitiates one's tutelary deity (*adhidevatā*) by the practice of the *sādhana* according to the process explained in this Tantra and then one accomplishes the signs of success such as divine and human pleasures, the attainments of the sword, *vidyādhara* and so forth. This is the purpose (*prayojana*). Then following on from that, the purpose should also be understood as the attainment of supreme All-knowing by the excellent Awareness of the Bhagavat Vairocana.

Those trainees who comprehend it by analysis into topics: they are able to understand all the topics of the Tantra merely by mention of the headings corresponding to the topics, so the analysis and explanation of the topics of the Tantra is for their sake. This is the explanation of the causal basis, nature and result of Vairocana, and the causal basis, nature and result of his Enlightenment and so forth. Now with regards the explanation of Vairocana, the causal basis of Vairocana is explained by the eight stages of mundane minds and so on, and the stages of the supra-mundane Levels, such as the Level of Practice with Devoted Interest and so on, up until the Level of Perfect Enlightenment. The nature of the Bhagavat Vairocana is explained by the attributes of his four Bodies, with the explanation of the reason for considering the *nirmāṇa-kāya* as two, so resulting in four Bodies. (4b) The result is explained as the pervading of all the Three Realms by the manifestation of the Adornments of his Inexhaustible Body, Speech and Mind, and the appearance in the bodies of beings and non-beings, in accord with their suitability. Furthermore, the causal basis of his *abhisaṃbodhi* (Perfect Enlightenment) is stated by the words '***The cause is* bodhicitta, *the root is compassion and the completion is expedient means***' and so on. Its nature is spoken of with '***What is Enlightenment? It is to know your mind as it really is***' and so forth. Likewise its manifestation and transformation [as the result] are what is described [in the Tantra]. This has all been explained in detail in my *Piṇḍārtha*, so I shall not deal with them here.

Those trainees who refer to the words of the text do not understand the words and their significance, though they have been analyzed and explained here as cause, nature and result and so forth. In order to explain each word extensively for their sakes, I shall now comment in detail upon the entire Tantra from start to finish.

This Tantra teaches eleven perfections (*saṃpat*) of the Bhagavat Vairocana and these are i) the perfection of abandonment, ii) the perfection of place, iii) the perfection of entourage, iv) the perfection of revelation, v) the perfection of power, vi) the perfection of expedient means to benefit others, vii) the perfection of the causal basis of the Bhagavat Vairocana, viii) the perfection of his nature, ix) the perfection of the causal basis of Enlightenment, x) the perfection of its nature and xi) the perfection of the manifestation and transformation of Enlightenment. (5a)

The perfection of abandonment is indicated by the word '***Bhagavat***', because he is characterized by having abandoned all the obscurations of emotional afflictions and wrong understanding.

The perfection of place has eight qualities (*guṇa*) and these are as follows: i) the perfection of being the abode of all the Tathāgatas, ii) the perfection of being solid and extensive, iii) the perfection of being the place where the Great Enlightenment is realized, iv) the perfection of being the assembly of the Vajradhara Bodhisattva Mahāsattvas, v) the perfection of the extensiveness of the pinnacle, vi) the perfection of colour, vii) the perfection of shape, and viii) the perfection of the throne.

Of those, '***the abode of all Tathāgatas***' indicates the perfection of being the abode of all the Tathāgatas. '***Great and extensive vajra***' shows the perfection of being solid and extensive. '***The mansion of the continuum of reality***' is the perfection of being the place where the Great Enlightenment is realized. '***The assembly of all the Vajradharas***' is the perfection of being the assembly of the Vajradhara Bodhisattva Mahāsattvas. '***A [domed] pinnacle with neither boundary nor centre, manifested with playful ease by the Tathāgata's inclinations***' is the perfection of the extensiveness of the pinnacle. '***Most splendidly adorned with royal jewels***' is the perfection of colour. '***Regally jewelled great residence***' is the perfection of shape. '***Seated upon a lion-throne formed from the bodies of Bodhisattvas***' is the perfection of the throne. These eight aspects form the second perfection [of place].

The perfection of the entourage should be known by the words '***Those Vajradharas were Vimala-ākāśa***' down to '***Mañjuśrī and Sarva-nīvaraṇa-viṣkambhin***'. The entourage is headed by them.

The perfection of the revelation is the revelation of the Dharma as scripture and as realization, and that is indicated by the words '***The Sun of the Tathāgata, which transcends the three times, was transformed and manifested thus [as Vairocana], expounded the teachings of the Dharma Gate known as "The Ground of the Sameness of Body, Speech and Mind"***'.

The perfection of power is the perception by the chief mundane and supramundane yogins of the yoga emanations (*nirmāṇa*) they had not hitherto perceived and this is shown in this section by '***Then those Bodhisattvas, Samantabhadra and so on, and those Vajradharas such as Vajrapāṇi and so on, through empowerment by the Bhagavat, entered into the display of the treasury of the manifestations of the sameness of his Inexhaustible Body, and likewise they entered the display of the treasury of the array of the sameness of his Inexhaustible Speech and Mind.***'

The perfection of the expedient means to benefit others is shown in this section by the words from '***all the activities of his Body, all the activities of his Speech and all the activities of his Mind were seen by all of them to reveal the Dharma with the words of the secret Mantra Method continually throughout all realms of beings***' down to '***likewise the All-knowing Awareness also refreshes the world of men and gods***'. (4)

Moreover all the things explained in this Tantra are, as appropriate, the perfection of the causal basis of the Bhagavat Vairocana, the perfection of his nature, the perfection of the causal basis of Enlightenment, the perfection of its nature and the perfection of the manifestation and transformation of Enlightenment, but as these have already been explained, they will not be explained again. Therefore, you should understand that the whole of this Tantra is summarized by these eleven perfections of the Bhagavat Vairocana.

I
THE ELUCIDATION OF THE TYPES OF MINDS

1. [Thus I have heard. At one time][1] the Bhagavat was in the regally jewelled great residence, which is most splendidly adorned with royal gems, a domed pinnacle with neither boundary nor centre, manifested with playful ease by the Tathāgata's inclination, the assembly of all the Vajradharas, the mansion of the continuum of reality, a great and extensive vajra, and the abode of all Tathāgatas, seated upon a lion-throne formed from the bodies of Bodhisattvas.

In other sutras and tantras the words '***thus I have heard***' appear, but they are not mentioned in this Tantra because of the fixed nature of the teacher, time and place, and because the audience and compilers are such Bodhisattvas as Samantabhadra, Vajrapāṇi and so on who are mainly realization [orientated]. As for the teacher of this Tantra, it was expounded by the Bhagavat Vairocana as the *saṃbhoga-kāya* which is a transformation of the *abhisaṃbodhi-kāya* since that [aspect] perpetually dwells in the core of Enlightenment (*bodhimaṇḍa*), and because he was definitely present there at that very time and place, the words '***at one time***' are not even mentioned[2]. Furthermore those who formed the audience such as Samantabhadra and so on are not essentially listeners [to scriptural Dharma] but are mainly [orientated to] realization, so the words '***thus I have heard***' are not mentioned. Furthermore the *saṃbhoga-kāya* of the Bhagavat does not reside in a fixed time and place in other sutras and tantras, for in some of them he resides in the Akaniṣṭha Heaven and expounds the Dharma, or in others he resides on the summit of Mount Sumeru and expounds the Dharma, or likewise some *nirmāṇa-kāyas* reside at Rājagṛha or others reside in such place as Śrāvastī and teach the Dharma. (6b) In this way, such sutras have the words '***at one time***' because the time and place are not fixed. They also have the words '***thus I have heard***' because the audiences also are composed of the Noble Śrāvakas and so forth who are essentially listeners and not mainly orientated towards realization.

The eleven perfections of the Bhagavat Vairocana can be summarized into four aspects. What are those four? The individual, the place, the entourage and the purpose. Of those, the nature of the Great Being is indicated by the word '***Bhagavat***' for he has conclusively destroyed and brought to nothing the tendencies towards the obscurations of the emotional afflictions and wrong understanding with insight. Secondly, it also refers to one who has defeated the Māras. In brief, the *abhisaṃbodhi-kāya* refers to one who is devoid of the obscurations of emotional afflictions and wrong understanding. Also, the manifestation of the Great Being is for the two kinds of beings who listen to the Dharma: for followers through Dharma (*dharma-anusārin*) and for followers through faith (*śraddhā-anusārin*). Of those, the followers through the Dharma are those who just distinguish good and bad Dharma, without judging the individual who gives the teaching, while the followers through faith only have trust in the teachings in dependence upon an eminent individual, therefore that eminent individual who is necessary for them, is manifested. The perfection of the place also is in order to attract beings who follow through faith, for by residing in such a place, the greatness or the eminence of the Bhagavat is shown. The perfection of the entourage means that he does not reside there alone, but resides surrounded by an entourage and that also shows the greatness or eminence of the Bhagavat. When manifesting as an eminent individual, he manifests in order to attract the beings who follow through faith by encouraging them to listen without apprehension to such an individual. (7a) The description of the place is also for three reasons – because if the practitioner (*sādhaka*) has recollected the virtues of that kind of eminent individual and the place, he will be successful and because those places where Buddhas and Bodhisattvas have trod become a stūpa. The eminent individual has been explained above. The perfection of the entourage is also threefold: to show the eminent individual, the excellence of the Bodhisattvas and Vajradharas such as Vimala-ākāśa and so on who listen to the Dharma and retain it, and to show that it is witnessed by those Bodhisattvas whom he has gathered together, since those most excellent of listeners are present. The individual has already been explained. As for the purpose, this Tantra is intended for the attainment of the bliss of prosperity and beatitude (*abhyudaya-niḥśreya-sukha*) when one has accomplished the causal basis and intrinsic nature of the Perfect Enlightenment of Vairocana according to the sequence in which the mandalas of earth, water and so forth and the actions are explained. In that way the eleven perfections are summarized in these four.

Now, '***the abode of all Tathāgatas***' refers to all the Tathāgatas of the past, present and future who are present in the core of Enlightenment. The word 'abode' (*adhiṣṭhāna*) means 'residence'[3]. To clear away the doubt that so many Buddhas could be present on this occasion since all the Buddhas of the past, present and future reside in the core of Enlightenment, I have explained the matter in detail in my *Piṇḍārtha*[4], so I shall not deal with this here. The'***great vajra***: That vajra is not an ordinary one, but one which is most excellent or supreme, so it is called '***great***'. ***Extensive***: This means either that the vajra-palace is broad and extensive, (7b) or else that those vajras are without number. The ***mansion of the continuum of reality*** (*dharmadhātu*): ***Dharma*** (phenomena): The psycho-physical constituents (*skandha*), the perceptual sources (*āyatanas*) and elements (*dhātu*). ***Dhātu***: Intrinsic nature (*prakṛti*). Such phenomena as the psycho-physical constituents which belong to the relative level in character, cannot logically be maintained, for their intrinsic nature is emptiness (*śūnyatā*). The direct experience of that intrinsic nature which is emptiness is the '***mansion***', or source. The ***assembly of all the Vajradharas***: '***Vajra***' is the insight which destroys incorrect views. The Bodhisattva who has that insight is a Vajradhara. The word '***assembly***' has already been explained in the section on the perfection of the place. It is not the case that Bodhisattvas who are not Vajradharas were not assembled there, but since this is an occasion when mantras are explained, the Vajradharas are emphasized. Moreover the Vajradharas are '***dhara***' (√ *dhṛ*)[5] for three reasons: because of '***revealing***' the Gate of the Pratimokṣa, '***upholding***' the observances of spiritual learning and '***maintaining***' the branches of offering. You should also know that such symbols as *utpalas* and lotuses held by the Bodhisattvas who arise through the Perfections indicate their individual gates of liberation. ***Manifested with playful ease by the Tathāgata's inclination***: ***Playful ease***: He attained and carried out whatever he aspired to, through having aspired and wished for such a place and so on as this while he was engaged in the practices of a Bodhisattva. ***A [domed] pinnacle with neither boundary nor centre***: Because the two extremes cannot be perceived, there is also no objective basis to a centre. ***A [domed] pinnacle***: It is like the *uṣṇīṣa* on the Tathāgata's head and does not appear like a point. ***Most splendidly***

adorned with royal jewels: The perfection of colour refers to that palace which is constructed from jewels. (8a) '***The regally jewelled great residence***' describes the form. ***Seated upon a lion-throne formed from the bodies of Bodhisattvas***: This means either that the Bodhisattvas changed into the bodies of lions by their previous aspirations and formed a lion-throne, or that the bodies of the Bodhisattvas themselves formed the throne of the Bhagavat and acted as lions.

2. Those Vajradharas were Vimala-ākāśa, Ākāśa-vicaraṇa, Ākāśa-saṃbhava, Vicitra-vastra, Vicitra-caraṇa, Sarva-dharma-samatā-sthita, Pramāṇa-sattva-dhātv-anukampana, Nārāyaṇa-bala, Mahā-nārāyaṇa-bala, Suvajra, Parama-vega, Vimala, Parama-vajra, Tathāgata-varma, Tathāgata-padodbhava, Niḥprapañca-pratiṣṭha, Tathāgata-daśa-balodbhava, Vimala-netra and Vajrapāṇi, the Lord of the Secret Ones, (116a) **and so forth. They were present together with other Vajradharas equal in number to all the atoms in the ten Buddha Fields. Also there were the great Bodhisattvas assembled around, headed by Samantabhadra, Maitreya, Mañjuśrī and Sarva-nīvaraṇa-viṣkambhin.**

As well as the Bhagavat residing in such a place, these Bodhisattva Vajradharas of the entourage such as Vimala-ākāśa and so on also reside there. He teaches the Dharma to these Bodhisattvas who encircled him, headed by those mentioned in the text whose names accord with their functions.

3. The Sun[6] of the Tathāgata, that transcends the three times, was transformed and manifested thus [as Vairocana] and revealed the teachings of the Dharma Gate known as 'The Ground of the Sameness of Body, Speech and Mind'. Then those Bodhisattvas headed by Samantabhadra and those Vajradharas headed by Vajrapāṇi, being empowered by the Bhagavat, entered into the display of the treasury of the manifestations of the sameness of his Inexhaustible Body and likewise they entered into the display of the treasury of the array of the sameness of his Inexhaustible Speech and Mind, and yet they could not discern[A] any engagement [in activities] or disengagement on the part of the Body, Speech and Mind of the Bhagavat Vairocana. All the activities of his Body, all the activities of his Speech and all the activities of his Mind were seen by all of them to reveal the Dharma with the words of the Mantra Method continually throughout all realms of beings. Thus, teachers were seen resembling the bodies of the Vajradharas, the Bodhisattvas Samantabhadra, Padmapāṇi and so on, who taught the Dharma with the pure words (116b) **of the Mantra Method in the ten directions. They taught it in order to perfect completely those beings who have nurtured lives of action, from the first generation of *bodhicitta* up to those who dwell in each of the Ten Levels, and to bring about the acquirement of the sprout of existence in those who have suppressed lives of action.**

A C has 一切處起滅邊際不可得 '*they could not discern any limit to the arising and disappearing in all places*'.

There are two types of Dharma: the scriptural Dharma and the Dharma as realization. There are also two types of Dharma as realization: the absolute and the relative. Absolute Dharma as realization is defined as Suchness and is emptiness in nature. Relative Dharma as realization is manifested throughout all of the Three Realms by the Adornments of the Inexhaustible Body, Speech and Mind of the Tathāgata. The scriptural Dharma is the twelvefold set of scriptures such as the Sutras, the *Udānas* and so forth. Which of these does he expound? In this case, he expounds scriptural Dharma, this very Tantra. He teaches the Dharma Gate known as '***The Ground of the Sameness of Body, Speech and Mind***'. Here, '***Sameness***' should be understood in three ways: i) Because the configurations (*cakra*) of the Bhagavat's Body, Speech, (8b) and Mind pervade the body, speech and mind of all beings. ii) When applied to the task of benefitting beings, the Bhagavat's Body, Speech and Mind each equally do the work of the other two. iii) The Bhagavat's Body, Speech and Mind and the body, speech and mind of beings are without distinction through both being empty in nature and being of one taste. ***Dharma Gate***: It is a gate because it is the way of entry to the Dharma as realization, since it explains that ground of the Sameness of Body, Speech and Mind. Likewise, you should understand that other scriptural Dharmas are also ways of entry to the Dharma as realization. By which of the four embodiments (*kāya*) does the Bhagavat expound the Dharma? Because the *dharmakāya* and the embodiment which resides in the core of Enlightenment (*Bodhi-maṇḍa-kāya*) are unchanging and transcend words, they do not expound with words, but the Bhagavat expounds the Dharma through their transformational power (*adhiṣṭhāna*) with the *saṃbhoga-kāya* and the *nirmāṇa-kāya*. Now in this case, the *saṃbhoga-kāya*, the Bhagavat Vairocana, expounds the Dharma Gate known as 'The Ground of the Sameness of Body, Speech and Mind'.

Thus the Bhagavat [Vairocana] expounds the Dharma after the Sun of the Tathāgata which transcends the three times had been transformed. Because his *dharmakāya* shines like the sun in nature it is called '***the Sun of the Tathāgata***'. It '***transcends the three times***' because the *dharmakāya* transcends time as measured by the sun and moon. (9a) The '***three times***' are the past, present and future times. This indicates the perfection of the Teacher.

Then those Bodhisattvas headed by Samantabhadra ... throughout all realms of beings: This shows the perfection of power. Upon attaining the Tenth Level, such Bodhisattvas as Samantabhadra and so on, because of their *samādhis*, the power from their gates of liberation, the granting of supernatural power and the adornment of Buddha fields and so forth, joyfully think that there is nothing other than this to be done. Then they are struck on the heads by the excellent rays of light from the *Śrīvatsa* mark of the Bhagavat Vairocana. By that transformational power, Samantabhadra and those Bodhisattvas entered into the '***display of the treasury of the inexhaustible array of the sameness of his Body***' and likewise they entered into that of his Speech and Mind. '***Sameness***' has already been explained. ***Array***: It appeared in many different forms. ***Inexhaustible***: Through the transformational power of the *dharmakāya*, his Body, Speech and Mind will always abide as long as there is *saṃsāra*. (9b) ***Treasury***: This refers to the Body of the Bhagavat Vairocana. There arise from that Body, *cakras* of his Body, Speech and Mind without end, which correspond to whatever being is to be guided. So, because those same *cakras* of his Body and so on carry out their specific actions without being surpassed by anyone, it is the '***display***'.

Yet they could not discern any engagement [in activities] or disengagement on the part of the Body, Speech and Mind of the Bhagavat Vairocana: There are four categories of beings to be guided: Those Bodhisattvas who have abandoned the obscurations of both the emotional afflictions and wrong understanding, but in whom just a small amount of obscuration due to selective concepts remain; those who have actualized the pure Level of Practice with Devoted Interest; the Śrāvakas and Pratyekabuddhas who have abandoned the obscurations of the emotional afflictions, but who have not yet abandoned the obscurations of wrong understanding; and the various beings who have neither abandoned the obscurations of the emotional afflictions, nor those of wrong understanding. Therefore if you should wonder whether the Bhagavat's Body and so on are accessible to the pure Bodhisattvas or not, since no '***engagement [in activities] or disengagement***' can be discerned or perceived in the Bhagavat's Body and so on, then in reply it should be said that at the moment of his perfect Enlightenment, the Bhagavat Vairocana by the power of his previous aspirations, naturally and spontaneously acted without any deliberation (*nirvikalpa*) in all places with the *saṃbhoga-kāya* and the *nirmāṇa-kāya* for the benefit of suitable beings, and so the text says, '***All the activities of the Bhagavat Vairocana's*** (10a) ***Body, Speech and Mind were seen by all of them to reveal the Dharma***' and so on. ***Were seen***: These activities were accessible to Samantabhadra and so on, though they do not see them in all aspects. However, in measure with their vision and perceptual range, they are able to see or directly know the configurations of the Bhagavat's Body and so on. ***The activities of the Bhagavat's Body, Speech and Mind***: (10b) The endeavours or functions of the Bhagavat's Body, Speech and Mind which cause the perfection of the Levels and the Perfections and which are thus the causal basis of the attainment of Enlightenment. The special types of power accumulated by them in the Bhagavat's Awareness are called '***activities***'. The actions characterized by that power are the practices embodied as deities in the Mandala.

Taught the Dharma with the words of the Mantra Method: The word '*mantra*' refers to the Buddhas and Bodhisattvas, because they are endowed with knowledge (*man-*) and protection (*-tra*). '*Mantra*' also refers to the words[7] of their gates of liberation and to the letters[8] and syllables which transform into the Buddhas and Bodhisattvas. The technique of achieving the causal basis, the intrinsic nature and the result of those mantras is the '***Method***'. The '***words***' are the words of the Dharma which bring about the knowledge and realization of that. It also refer to the words of the mantras. The Bodhisattvas Samantabhadra and so forth saw the activities of the Bhagavat, which appear as the mantra deities and so on, revealing the Dharma which expounds the characteristics of the Mantra Method. (11a) This has three facets : the embodiment as the deities of the Mandala of the activities of the Tathāgata; the correspondence of the ability to guide to the suitability of those to be guided; and the words of the Dharma and mantras which teach that.

Thus teachers were seen ... (11b) ... ***those who have suppressed lives of action***: Through abiding in the Level of Devoted Interest, one comes to definitely know what sort of virtues there are in the practice of the Three Minds[9] and the Ten Levels and so on, and have devoted interest in them, so one strives to abandon the obscurations of the emotional afflictions, and by the power of such wholesome deeds as purification of the mind, one is born as whoever one desires, such as Indra, Brahmā and so forth, according to one's inclination. This is the '***nurturing of lives of action***'. This is also the time from the first generation of *bodhicitta* up until the Tenth Level. The first generation of *bodhicitta* refers to the First Level, the Joyful One.

Those who have suppressed lives of action: The Śrāvakas who have abandoned the obscurations of the emotional afflictions at the moment of Nirvāṇa without remainder, reside for eighty eons (*kalpa*) in the heart of the sacred lotus; then Bodhisattvas cause those who have [thus] suppressed life to reject that suppression of life, and after the sprout of existence has been produced in them, they are made to enter and perfect the Ten Levels.

4. Then Vajrapāṇi, the Lord of the Secret Ones, who was seated in that assembly of Vajradharas said to the Bhagavat, 'Bhagavat! How do the Tathāgata Arhat Samyak-saṃbuddhas, having achieved the All-knowing Awareness themselves, reveal that All-knowing Awareness to beings[A] and teach [it to them] with various methods, intentions and expedient means. For they teach the Dharma to some beings with the Śrāvaka-yāna method, to some with the Pratyekabuddha-yāna method, to some with the Mahāyāna method, to some with the method of the Five Supernatural Cognitions, to some with activities in the shape of gods, to some in human shape, or in the shape of *mahoragas, nāgas, yakṣas, gandharvas, asuras, garuḍas* and *kinnaras?*

'How is it that each of those beings to be guided sees them in the shape of a Buddha, or in the shape of a Śrāvaka, or in the shape of a Pratyekabuddha, or in the shape of a Bodhisattva, or in the shape of Maheśvara, or in the shape of Brahmā, or in the shape of Nārāyaṇa, or in the shape of Vaiśravaṇa, or in the shape of mahoragas, kinnaras *and so on?*

'How is it that they use the modes of speech appropriate to each being and are seen behaving in various ways, and yet the All-knowing Awareness has the sole taste of the Tathāgata's liberation[10]?'

Having achieved All-knowing Awareness: They fully abide in the core of Enlightenment.
All-knowing Awareness: There are two types, the relative and the absolute. The relative type is to know in all forms the Ten Strengths, the Four Fearlessnesses, (13b) the Eighteen Uncommon Qualities of a Buddha and so forth. The absolute type is to know emptiness.

Reveal: Means to expound individually. The attributes of oneness of taste and perfection of All-knowing Awareness will be expounded below. Even those born as gods or men who have accomplished the ten mundane wholesome actions and the Śrāvakas and so forth, they are all aspects of All-knowing Awareness. Why? You should know that even the merits of mundane beings are the indirect causal basis of becoming All-knowing. They are the causal basis since they have a portion of All-knowing, and furthermore you should understand that of the two types of cause, direct and indirect, they are the indirect cause. (14a)

The sole taste of the Tathāgata's liberation: Thus, many different body-images are projected through various methods, intentions and expedient means. Yet they all have in common the Tathāgata's liberation, which is characterized by the abandonment of the obscurations of the emotional afflictions and wrong understanding and the

A C: 無量衆生 '*countless beings*'.

complete transcendence of the basis of the habitual tendencies to selective conceptualization. They are all of one taste. For example, if you make sugar from the sap of many sugar-canes, there is no difference in the taste of each sugar cane. This is like the '***sole taste***'.

5. 'Bhagavat! Just as space is free from all selective thoughts and concepts[A] and is not subject to thinking and conceptualizing[B], (117a) **likewise All-knowing Awareness is free from all selective thoughts and concepts[C] and is not subject to thinking and conceptualizing[D]. Bhagavat! Just as this great earth sustains all beings, likewise All-knowing Awareness also provides sustenance for the world of gods, humans and asuras. Bhagavat! Just as the element of fire burns all fuel and yet is never exhausted, likewise All-knowing Awareness also burns all the fuel of ignorance and yet is never exhausted. Bhagavat! Just as the element of wind clears away all dust, likewise All-knowing Awareness also clears away all the dust of ignorance[E]. Bhagavat! Just as the element of water refreshes the bodies of all beings, likewise All-knowing Awareness also refreshes the world of men and gods. Bhagavat! What is the cause of this Awareness? What is its root? What is its completion?'**

These examples show the attainment of the perfection of the intrinsic nature of All-knowing Awareness, the perfection of the successful benefitting of others, the perfection of abandoning and the perfection of the benefitting of others which brings about happiness. These examples also show that All-knowing Awareness spontaneously functions to benefit beings by the power of the Bhagavat's previous aspirations, (14b) through various methods and so on, without any conceptualization or deliberation.

Space: The example of space shows the perfection of its intrinsic nature.

Earth: If All-knowing Awareness is thus devoid of deliberation and thinking, then how does it put forth a stream of embodiments and act for the benefit of beings, without any thought? The example of the earth shows the functioning of the perfection of successfully benefiting beings though without deliberation. So, though being without any thoughts or ideas, the earth provides sustenance for all beings with roots, fruits, flowers and so forth. Likewise that All-knowing Awareness, although without thoughts and concepts, manifests itself through the mantra deities and so forth, and makes beings happy by causing them to attend to and recite those mantra deities and to attain the attributes of success, the wealth of men and gods.

Fire: The perfection of abandonment is shown by the example of fire. Just as when fire burns up all vegetation, it nevertheless retains its potential to burn. Likewise, All-knowing Awareness also burns up all the fuel of ignorance. During the causal phase, the inimical factors, the emotional afflictions such as ignorance and so forth, (15a)

A C omits '*concepts*'.

B C: 無分別無無分別 '*is devoid of concepts and non-concepts*'.

C C omits '*concepts*'.

D C: 無分別無無分別 '*is devoid of conceptualizing and non-conceptualizing*'.

E C: 一切諸煩惱塵 '*all the dust of the conflicting emotions*'.

are cleared away and brought to nought by the stages of the Levels and the Perfections. Secondly, during the resultant phase, All-knowing Awareness has the inherent nature of burning up the fuel of ignorance since it is characterized by the absence of ignorance.

Wind: Therefore, the following example of the wind shows that all habitual tendencies which remain are abandoned through the above perfection of abandoning. So the text says '***the wind clears away all dust***'. Dust is characterized by fineness, so in the same way, the final traces of habitual tendencies to ignorance are abandoned by All-knowing Awareness.

Water: The perfection of the benefitting of others which brings about happiness is shown by the example of water. Just as water is used to refresh the bodies of beings who are tormented by heat and so on, in the same way, that All-knowing Awareness is characterized by cooling all beings who are afflicted by suffering and such emotional afflictions as attachment and so forth. By uniting them with Nirvāṇa, it causes them to become perfected, and so it '***refreshes the worlds of men and gods***'.

Although the Bhagavat has spoken of the methods of All-knowing Awareness on other occasions, Vajrapāṇi is stating, 'This is the way I have understood it', with these examples. (15b) Now, you may be wondering whether Vajrapāṇi understands the various methods and so on and the sole taste of the Tathāgata's liberation with the insight derived from realization or the insight derived from what has been heard, If it is by the insight derived from realization, there would be no difference between him and the Tathāgata, and if it is by the insight derived from what he has heard, then he would be like ordinary beings. So in reply, it should be said that it is acceptable for him to comprehend them by both of those types of insight, for when he entered into the Adornments of the Bhagavat's Inexhaustible Body, his range of comprehension was in accordance with his capability. But since he did not comprehend it in all aspects like the Bhagavat, he is not the same as a Tathāgata. Since what he has heard is predominantly what he has realized and not just what has been heard alone, he is not like ordinary beings. Secondly, even if he was aware of all aspects by the insight derived from realization, this would still be acceptable, for just as one may know the thoughts of others through the Bhagavat's empowerment, so also would he be able to know all the aspects of the range of All-knowing Awareness.

6. Then the Bhagavat said to Vajrapāṇi, 'Vajrapāṇi! Excellent, excellent! Vajrapāṇi, it is good that you have asked me about this matter. So listen carefully to what I shall explain and retain it carefully in your mind! The causal basis is *bodhicitta,* the root is compassion and the completion is expedient means[11].'

(16a) ***The causal basis is* bodhicitta, *the root is compassion and the completion is expedient means*:** There are two aspects to '***bodhicitta***': the mind (*citta*) directed towards Enlightenment (*bodhi*) and the mind whose intrinsic nature is Enlightenment. Although the mind directed towards Enlightenment also includes the minds of aspiration and of application, in this case it refers to the mind directed towards Enlightenment at the First Level, because that First Level mind is what unites you with the Mind of Perfect Enlightenment. As for the mind whose intrinsic nature is Enlightenment, because the mind directed towards Enlightenment at the First Level consists of realizing the sameness of all phenomena, it has the same intrinsic nature as the Mind of Perfect Enlightenment (*abhisaṃbodhi-citta*). You should understand that that kind of mind directed towards Enlightenment is the main cause of All-knowing Awareness. ***The root is compassion***: In order to remove the afflictions of suffering from beings by means of compassion, you should generate the mind directed towards Enlightenment of aspiration (*praṇidhāna-bodhicitta*) and so forth. Therefore, that compassion should be regarded as the cause of the cause, since it arises as the root of *bodhicitta*. Secondly, it is called '*root*' because it causes the firm abiding of All-knowing Awareness. Through being sustained by compassion, you will abide in the Nirvāṇa without (16b) localization (*apratiṣṭhā-nirvāṇa*) at all times, not entering the Nirvāṇa without remainder (*nirupadhiśeṣa-nirvāṇa*), and have firm relative and absolute Awareness. Since it makes it firm like the roots of a plant stem, it is the root of All-knowing Awareness. ***The completion is expedient means***: '***Expedient means***' are the Perfection of Generosity and so forth. They are considered as its completion because it is fostered by them until the completion which is perfect union with All-knowing Awareness.

7. 'Lord of the Secret Ones! What is Enlightenment? (117b) **It is to know your mind as it really is. That is the supreme, full and perfect Enlightenment. Therein neither exists nor can be perceived any phenomenon whatsoever[A]. Why is that? Because Enlightenment has the same attribute as space. Therein there is neither that which becomes enlightened nor that to which one is enlightened. Why is that? Because Enlightenment is without attributes. Lord of the Secret Ones! All phenomena are also without attributes, just as space is.'**

Bodhicitta has been explained as the causal basis of All-knowing Awareness, so now the intrinsic nature of his Enlightenment will be explained. ***It is to know your mind as it really is***: A yogin's mind sees something with the perceptual image of a jar and so on, then in the following instant he refutes that perceptual image of a jar and so on as it is without any real existence. Having thus refuted the part which is perceived, the portion which perceives will also not exist in the absence of that[12]. To know that your mind is devoid of an intrinsic perceiving subject and perceived objects and is utterly pure, without perceptual images, and pure by nature is '***to know your mind as it really is***'. Furthermore, you should understand that Enlightenment is explained in other texts as the Awareness of Sameness, while All-knowing Awareness is explained as (17a) the Mirror-like Awareness, the Investigating Awareness and the Awareness of Accomplishing Activities.

It is also the supreme, true and perfect Enlightenment: ***Supreme*** (*anuttara*): Because there is no other Enlightenment superior to that one. ***True*** (*samyak*): This refers to the Enlightenment which is free from error. Although Śrāvakas and Pratyekabuddhas have abandoned the obscurations of emotional afflictions, but not those of wrong understanding, they are only partially free from error, but this is true Enlightenment because both the obscurations of emotional afflictions and wrong understanding have been abandoned. ***Perfect Enlightenment*** (*saṃbodhi*): This refers to complete

A C also links this negation with Enlightenment.

Enlightenment, since the last traces of the habitual tendencies of the obscurations of emotional afflictions and wrong understanding have been abandoned without remainder. So in the second place, to know your mind as it really is refers to knowing the emptiness in all aspects of both absolute and relative phenomena.

Why? Because Enlightenment has the same attribute as space*:** Even though it is characterized by purity, immutability, emptiness and so on, the 'attribute***' of space here refers to the non-existence in it of anything with the nature of a perceiving subject and perceived objects. Therefore, in order to show this, it says '***Therein there is neither that which becomes enlightened not that to which one becomes enlightened***'. (17b) That which becomes enlightened is that which perceives and that to which one becomes enlightened is the perceived, and so Enlightenment is devoid of any perceiving subject or perceived objects.

***Why is that? Because Enlightenment is without any attributes*:** Because Enlightenment lacks the perceptual forms of images such as colours like blue and yellow, and shapes[13].

All phenomena are also without attributes*:** If Enlightenment is said to be the knowledge of your mind as it really is, then is it not also knowledge of phenomena apart from the mind, as they really are? Just as Enlightenment is said to be full knowledge of one's mind as it really is, and to be without attributes and so forth, it is also said that phenomena are without attributes, like space. Moreover it is taught that that lack of attributes to all phenomena, that attribute of space, is Enlightenment, which is also without attributes. Here 'phenomena***' refers to the psycho-physical constituents and so forth, apart from one's mind. (18a)

8. Then Vajrapāṇi said to the Bhagavat, 'Bhagavat! Where should one seek that All-knowing Awareness? By what is Enlightenment perfectly awakened[A]

9. The Bhagavat replied, 'Lord of the Secret Ones! Enlightenment and All-knowing Awareness should be sought in one's mind. Why is that? Because the mind is utterly pure by nature. It is neither internal nor is it external. Nor is it to be found between the two. Lord of the Secret Ones! The mind has not been seen, is not seen, nor will be seen by any of the Tathāgata Arhat Samyak-saṃbuddhas[B]. It is not blue, not yellow, not red, not white, not purple, not transparent, not short, not long, not round, not square, not bright, not dark, not male, not female and not neuter.'

***Enlightenment and All-knowing Awareness should be sought in one's mind*:** If one's mind itself has become free from the habitual tendencies which cause the proliferation of selective concepts which have the nature of a perceiving subject and perceived objects and has become utterly pure, it will be Enlightenment in nature, characterized by natural radiance, immediate experience, immutability and luminosity of

A C adds 維發起彼一切智智 '*what gives rise to that All-knowing Awareness?*'.

B C omits '*The mind has not been seen, is not seen, nor will be seen* [*by any of*]' at this point (inserting it after '*nor in the intellect*' in section 11 omitting '*the mind*') and then has 入來應正等覺非青非黃 ... '*the Tathāgata* [*does not see or reveal*] *perfect Enlightenment to be blue or yellow* ...'.

Awareness. By what kind of investigation of the mind will one come to know this matter? Here there are two types of individuals who investigate it: the Buddhas and Bodhisattvas who are endowed with the Awareness which transcends the faculties, and ordinary beings who have the lower levels of vision. Regarding the investigation by ordinary beings, the text says '***It is neither internal nor external, nor is it to be found between the two***'. '***External***' is the perceived object, '***internal***' is the perceiving subject and '***between***' is a combination of the two. The mind cannot be found in any of these. Furthermore, those who have the Awareness which transcends the faculties will not find the mind in any of the five categories of colour, form, the realms, the streams of consciousness and location. Therefore, the text says '***it is not blue, not yellow***' and so on. (18b)

10. 'Lord of the Secret Ones! The mind does not have the nature of the Realm of Desire, nor the nature of the Realm of Form, nor the nature of the Realm of Formlessness. It does not have any nature corresponding to any beings, whether they are gods, *nāgas*, *yakṣas*, *gandharvas*, *asuras*, *garuḍas*, *kinnaras*, (118a) *mahoragas*, humans or non-humans.'

11. 'Lord of the Secret Ones! The mind does not reside in the eye, nor in the ear, nor in the nose, nor in the tongue, nor in the body, nor in the intellect. Why? Because the mind has the same attribute as space and so it is free from all thought and conceptualization. Why? Because the nature of space is the nature of the mind. The nature of mind is the nature of Enlightenment. Lord of the Secret Ones! Therefore the mind, the realm of space and Enlightenment are without duality and cannot be separated. It also has compassion as its root and is fulfilled by the expedient means which are the Perfections. Lord of the Secret Ones! It should therefore be understood that whatever Dharma I teach in this assembly is for the complete purification of *bodhicitta* and the full knowledge of the mind.'

If the mind were to appear with such perceptual images as colour, form and so on, it would not be free from the attributes of a perceiving subject and perceived objects and so would be sullied. Being sullied, it would not be the All-knowing Awareness. Therefore the mind which is purified of all these impurities is All-knowing. Because of that, it says '***Why? Because the mind has the same attribute as space***'. The attribute of space is to be without thought and conceptualization, so the attribute of the mind is similar to that of space, hence the text says '***it is free from all thought and conceptualization***'. (19a)

The complete purification of* bodhicitta**: Because the *bodhicitta* attained at the First Level is free from perceiving subject and perceived objects, it is 'purified***'. ***The full knowledge of the mind***: This refers to that knowledge of the natural state of mind, by virtue of which the First Level is attained, and is the generation of *bodhicitta* at the time of practice with devoted interest.

12. 'Lord of the Secret Ones! Therefore if a son or daughter of good family wishes to fully know Enlightenment, they should know their own minds. Lord of the Secret Ones! How is one to fully know one's mind? Even though one

searches, one will not find it in any percepts, colours, shapes, sense objects, form, feeling, ideation, motivation, or consciousness, nor in any I and mine, nor in any perceiving subject nor in perceived objects, nor in the pure or the impure, nor in the perceptual elements, nor in the perceptual sources, nor in any other perceptual data.'

13. 'Lord of the Secret Ones! This is the first method of beholding reality, called the "Gate to Pure *Bodhicitta*". If they abide in it[A], (118b) Bodhisattvas will attain a *samādhi* by which all obscurations will be abandoned with little hardship, and having attained it, Bodhisattvas will become associated with all Buddhas. They will also obtain the Five Supernatural Cognitions; they will acquire *dhāraṇīs* in unlimited languages, sounds and tones; they will know the inclinations of all beings; through being empowered[B] by all Tathāgatas, they will be endowed with qualities that are unimpaired by *saṃsāra*; they will not tire in their deeds to benefit beings; they will abide in the unconditioned morality, completely abandon perverse opinions and directly experience the true vision.'

(20a) That kind of full knowledge of the mind on the Level of Practice with Devoted Interest (*adhimukti-caryā-bhūmi*) is explained as a threefold cause, of the First Level *bodhicitta*, of actual Enlightenment and of All-knowing Awareness. Now, it is called the '***Gate of Pure* Bodhicitta**' because it is the means of entry to the attributes of the pure First Level *bodhicitta*. ***Method of beholding reality***: '***Reality***' is Nirvāṇa free from a perceiving subject and perceived objects. '***Beholding***' (*√ālok*) means knowing and is the core of Enlightenment itself and the cause or '***method***' of attaining it is the mind. Regarding this method of beholding reality, in the first instant of Enlightenment one is perfectly enlightened to the attributes of the Awareness of Sameness. Then in the second instant one obtains the attributes of All-knowing, which are Mirror-like Awareness, Investigating Awareness and the Awareness of Accomplishing Activities. It is the complete knowledge of the reality of Nirvāṇa on both the absolute and the relative levels. (20b) '***First***' refers to the attainment of Enlightenment at the first instant.

The five supernatural cognitions: With the divine eye, distant forms can be seen, without being obstructed even by mountains and walls and so on. With the divine ear, distant sounds can be heard without being obstructed by mountains and walls and so on. One will know whether the minds of others have attachments or are free from attachments and so forth. One will recollect what one did and where one dwelt in former lives. One will attain the bases of supernatural powers (*ṛddhi-pāda*). (21a)

Unconditioned morality: This refers to that which is emptiness in character, since those Bodhisattvas abide in the realization of emptiness, but not to such relative moralities such as the morality which benefits beings, the morality of wholesome actions and the moral restraints (*saṃvara*). (21b)

A C has 住此修學 '[*If they*] *abide in this training, ...*'.
B C: 護持 '*protected and upheld*'.

14. 'Lord of the Secret Ones! Furthermore, the Bodhisattva who resides in this *samādhi* by which all obscurations are abandoned, will completely perfect all Dharmas of the Buddha with little effort by having generated the power of devoted interest. Lord of the Secret Ones! In brief, that son or daughter of good family will be endowed with immeasurable virtues.'

By the accumulation of the power of devoted interest in that mind which is devoid of a perceiving subject and perceived objects and which is radiant by nature and Enlightenment in character, one will also obtain the Dharmas of the Buddha, such as the Dharma which is realization and scripture in character, the Perfections and so forth, and the configurations of the Body and so forth, which one has not yet accomplished. If one were to enumerate each one of the virtues of a son or daughter of good family who is endowed with that *samādhi*, one would not finish in an eon (*kalpa*).

15. Then Vajrapāṇi asked the Buddha,
'Bhagavat! How is the mind
directed towards Enlightenment engendered?
How should one know the attributes
of the arising of the mind
from which Enlightenment emerges?
Great Hero who has arisen from Awareness,
Best of those who understand the mind!
Please teach us the number of stages
after which it will arise!
Lord! Please explain in detail
the attributes and time-scale of this mind.
What will its merits be like?
What will its practices be like?
I also entreat the great Sage to teach about
the various types of minds relating to that mind.'

The causal basis of All-knowing Awareness and the attributes of Enlightenment have been explained above in detail. The Bhagavat has also said that the virtues of one who has attained the *samādhi* which abides in that *bodhicitta* are immeasurable, so now Vajrapāṇi asks about the generation of that *bodhicitta* and so on. (22a) ***How does* bodhicitta *arise?***: Generally speaking there is 'engendering' (*utpāda*) and 'arising' (*utpatti*). To be engendered refers to the mere declaration, which is like a child in the womb. The meaning of 'arising' designates the birth, like the actual birth of the child. Hence, Vajrapāṇi does not merely ask about the engendering of *bodhicitta*, but also about the complete arising of the First Level mind which is Enlightenment (*bodhi*) in character. ***Enlightenment*** (*bodhi*): This means that it is generated for the sake of supreme Enlightenment. This is also the attribute of the mind (*citta*) at the First Level, which is one in nature with supreme Enlightenment. This mind is perfected in stages by the higher Levels, however though these have the same nature, they are given different names due to the means of renunciation, such as the contrary actions and their antidotes. For example, when one makes various ornaments and so on from gold, they are given many different names, although their nature is the same. In the same way, this refers to the *bodhicitta* of the First Level which is Enlightenment in nature, but not to the aspiration and application minds, because they are not one in nature with supreme Enlightenment in the way that the First Level *bodhicitta* is, although they are also called *bodhicitta.* (22b) ***The various types of minds relating to that mind***: Here '***mind***' refers to *bodhicitta* in general.

16. When he had been asked that, the Bhagavat Vairocana replied to Vajrapāṇi,

> **Son of the Buddhas!** (119a)
> **The attributes of the stream of mind,**
> **which is the most excellent rank of the Mahāyāna,**
> **are most fortunate and excellent.**
> **It is the greatest secret of the perfect Buddhas,**
> **and is unknown to all logicians**[A]**.**
> **Listen with concentrated attention,**
> **for I shall explain everything to you!**
> **Having gone beyond the one hundred and sixty types of mind,**
> **the mind which produces Enlightenment will arise,**
> **the core formed by great merit**[B]**.**
> **Like space, it is immeasurable,**
> **without impurities, it abides thus.**
> **It is undisturbed by any phenomenon,**
> **primordially calm and without attributes,**
> **and is accomplished by immeasurable Awareness.**
> **Because it is accomplished**
> **through offerings and practice,**
> **the Fully Enlightened Teacher regards it**
> **as the first directed towards Enlightenment.'**

(23a) The Bhagavat Vairocana now replies to Vajrapāṇi's questions. ***Most fortunate***: this refers to the attributes of the stream of mind, because Enlightenment and the Great All-knowing Awareness arise from the stream of mind. It is '***the greatest secret of perfect Buddhas***' because a pure mind like that, which is All-knowing Awareness and Perfect Enlightenment in nature, is beyond the perceptual range of ordinary beings and it is not revealed to those who are unsuitable. Hence it is '***secret***'. It is '***unknown to logicians***' because the mind which is empty in character cannot be understood as it really is, either by direct or inferential reasoning.

Having gone beyond the one hundred and sixty types of minds: When you have passed beyond the one hundred and sixty mundane minds, you will realize that phenomena lack any autonomous existence and will cultivate the Three Minds of practice with devoted interest, engage in the Perfections and carry out the Four Methods of

---

A T *rtog-ge* implies an underlying Sanskrit *tārkika*, while 外道 in C implies *tīrthika*.

B C: 越百六十心 生廣大功德 其性常堅固 知彼菩提生 '*After transcending the hundred and sixty minds, one will generate vast merit which is constantly stable in nature: this should be known as the arising of* bodhicitta.'

Attracting Beings. Then you will pass beyond the Level of Practice with Devoted Interest and enter (23b) the mind of the Level of the Joyful One, the Level of Awareness.

Core (*maṇḍa*): That which is faultlessly perfect, the most excellent part of something, for example like the essence of sandalwood or acacia wood. ***The first directed towards Enlightenment***: This refers to the *bodhicitta* of the First Level. These explain the causal basis and intrinsic nature of *bodhicitta*.

17. 'Lord of the Secret Ones! In beginningless *saṃsāra*, foolish ordinary people are attached to egotism and self-interest, and so they imagine countless types of self. Lord of the Secret Ones! Without investigating the nature of such selves, they give rise to egotism, saying "I am". There are others who imagine that the self is something that has arisen from time, or that it is a transformation of the supporter[A], or else that it is emancipation, or that it is Īśvara, Brahmā, the cosmic law, the Supreme Being, the Creator or not the Creator, the self of the Yoga School or of the Logicians, or that it is purity, impurity, the inner self, the *puruṣa*[14], the soul, the individual, consciousness, the substratum, the knower, the seer, perceived objects or the perceiving subject, knowing or the known, that which is to be realized, that which is born or descended from Manu, the expressible or the inexpressible. Lord of the Secret Ones! Such types of self have been imagined in the past by yogins who esteem yoga[B] in the hope of liberation.

(24a) The following sections explain the causal basis of becoming the Bhagavat Vairocana. That causal basis is twofold: The one hundred and sixty mundane minds are the immediate cause (*upadāna-hetu*) and the other minds of the Levels and the Perfections are the co-operating cause (*sahakāri-hetu*)[15]. Therefore there are also two types of ordinary beings: those who know the mundane scriptures and those who do not. The stupid speak, act and think maladroitly, and do not even know their own scriptures. The remainder of beings are those who know their own scriptures and who have reached the Noble Path. After having been tormented by the three kinds of suffering of *saṃsāra*, they practise generosity and so on, hoping for liberation, based on these imagined concepts of me (*ātman*) and mine (*ātmanīna*), in order to be freed from those sufferings. The stupid people who do not know their own scriptures are those who having become attached to a self, then also cling to those concepts about the countless types of beliefs in a self, without even investigating what is the nature of the so-called self. But even those who know their own scriptures base themselves upon those various concepts about a self, thus the text says, '***There are also those who imagine the self is something that has arisen from time ... the expressible or the inexpressible***'. These are the various different theories about a self among mundane people. They imagine that we creatures are brought into being by those selves and what belongs to it, which they believe in, and that we are also destroyed by them. (24b)

A C: 地 '*the earth*'

B C: 順理 implies '*yoga*' or '*yukti*'. This could be translated as '*who esteem such inferences*'.

Yogins who esteem union: Union or yoga is to withdraw the body, speech and mind from their objects and concentrate or fix the mind one-pointedly upon whatever point of reference is before oneself, in the manner of mundane people. It refers to the yogins who esteem the state of union wherein body, speech and mind are suppressed without getting involved with their objects, and who falsely imagine those types of self.

18. 'Lord of the Secret Ones! Furthermore, it sometimes happens that someone among the animal-like foolish people has a virtuous idea, namely, they think: (119b) "I shall undertake a fast[16]." And just having that idea, they feel glad and they then gradually accustom themselves to doing it. Lord of the Secret Ones! This is the first mind, which is like a seed from which wholesome actions will be born.

'Then because of that, they make offerings to their parents, sons and daughters, relatives and friends, on each of the auspicious days. This is the second mind, which is like a sprout.

'Others give gifts to strangers. This is the third mind, which is like a stalk.

'Others seek out those who are especially worthy of gifts and give gifts to them. This is the fourth mind, which is like leaves.

'Others give those gifts joyfully to teachers and musicians. This is the fifth mind, which is like the flowers.

'Others give those gifts to those who have need and delight in them. This is the sixth mind, which is like the fruit,

'Lord of the Secret Ones! Others keep the moral observances, in order to be born into heaven. This is the seventh mind, which is like the harvest of the fruit.'

The animal-like foolish common people: This refers to those who do not even know their own scriptures. The phrase '***animal-like***' is used as a simile for their maladroit thoughts, speech and actions, because nothing stimulates animals apart from eating, sex and fear. As foolish people have these attributes they are said to be animal-like.

This is the first mind, which is like a seed from which wholesome actions will be born: It is the seed which produces the wholesome deeds that safeguard the moral discipline at the time of the seventh mind. Should anyone be concerned that fasting has the attributes of ritualism and so forms part of the emotionally afflicted, (25a) and wonder how it can be the seed of wholesomeness, then to dispel this worry it should be known that the mind related to generosity, worship and so on, arises subsequent to having fasted and that fasting functions as the immediate causal factor (*samanantara-pratyaya*) for the wholesomeness of generosity and so on. Therefore there is no problem. Furthermore, generosity here refers to the sullied wholesomeness. (25b)

19. 'Lord of the Secret Ones! There are others who wander through *saṃsāra* with such minds and they will hear these words from some spiritual friend:

> **"These gods are great gods:**
> **they bestow happiness upon all.**

If you respectfully make offerings to them,
you will become fortunate in all things.
They are as follows:
Īśvara and Brahmā,
Viṣṇu[A], Śaṅkāra, Rudra[B],
Skanda, Āditya, Candra and Varuṇa[C],
Kubera, Dhanada[D], Śakra,
Virūpākṣa and Viśva-karma,
Yama, Kālarātrī[E], Nirṛti[F],
Loka-guru, Agni, Vinatāka-putra[G],
and likewise the goddess Umā,
the *Nāgas* Padma, Takṣaka,
Vasūki and Śaṅkha,
Karkoṭaka, Mahā-padma,
Kulika, Mahā-phaṇaka,
Sadānanda and Ādideva[H].
As well as these gods,
there are the most excellent sages, (120a)
the Vedas and their followers.
The wise person should make offerings to them!"

'Then when they have heard such words, they feel great joy in their hearts, and then with reverence, they apply themselves earnestly to those gods.

'Lord of the Secret Ones! This is the most excellent refuge of the foolish common folk who wander lost in *saṃsāra*, and the Jinas have explained this as the eighth mind, which is like the digestion of the fruit.'

Some learned person who knows the mundane scriptures will act as a spiritual friend to those who practise generosity and keep the moral observances in the above manner and will cause them to turn to his own teacher-god for support. That spiritual friend will also teach them the nature of the gods with the words '***these gods are great gods***' and so forth. (26a)

20. 'Lord of the Secret Ones! There are others who understand the different types of self and adhere to one of these types as they have been propounded. They arrive at the idea of "isolation" and claim that this is real, thinking that mere emptiness is an actual entity. But, Lord of the Secret Ones, they are completely ignorant of emptiness. Emptiness is neither an actual entity nor is it not an actual entity. It neither exists nor does

A C: 那羅延 '*Nārāyaṇa*'.
B C: 黑天 '*Kāla-deva*' = '*Rudra*'.
C C: 龍尊 '*Nāga Lord*'.
D C: 毗沙門 '*Vaiśavaṇa*'.
E C: 閻魔后 '*Yama's consort*'.
F C: 梵后 '*Brahmā's consort*'.
G C: 迦樓羅子天 '*Garuḍaputra-deva*'.
H C places Ādideva before Sadānanda and then reads 薩陀難陀等龍 '*Sadānanda and other nāgas*'.

not exist and is not both. If there is neither conceptualization nor non-conceptualization of it, how can one say "This is emptiness"?

> **'Whoever does not know emptiness**
> **does not know Nirvāṇa.**
> **Therefore emptiness should be known**
> **by the destruction of both existence and non-existence[A].'**

There are those who know the types of self previously mentioned and the nature of the teacher-gods as described, who then rely upon an imagined self and those gods. With the scriptures revealed by these gods, they abandon karmic actions and the emotionally afflicted and believe the self has been purified. They think that that purity is emptiness or Nirvāṇa, and they imagine that in that emptiness there is a minute entity (26b) the size of a grain of rice or a hair, which they call the self, with the nature of experiencing pleasure or pain.

People seek liberation through relying upon the self of ordinary foolish beings and upon the gods, and that bliss of liberation they seek should be viewed as a cause linking them with the Bhagavat Vairocana. Regarding such gods as Īśvara, Brahmā and so forth, generally speaking, there are two types: those beings arising subject to karmic actions and those that are Awareness Beings (*jñāna-sattva*). In this case, those gods are also teachers of the path to ordinary Nirvāṇa to ordinary foolish people who wander lost. Since the path which they teach is a cause for the knowledge and attainment of the Bhagavat Vairocana, you should view those gods such as Īśvara and Brahmā as Awareness Beings, emanated from the Body of Vairocana.

But they are completely ignorant of emptiness: Because they imagine emptiness to be a type of self they call 'aloneness', it is not truly empty. As long as they imagine it to be an entity, then they believe in the extreme of existence and so will not truly know emptiness. (27a)

Whoever does not know emptiness: Those who do not correctly know the intrinsic nature of emptiness, but imagine emptiness to be a thing. They will also be unable to know the continuum of reality (*dharmadhātu*), peace, or Nirvāṇa. How is emptiness to be known? By not thinking of emptiness as a thing, since it neither exists nor does not exists.

21. Then Vajrapāṇi spoke again to the Bhagavat and asked, 'Please explain those types of mind, Bhagavat!'

Then the Bhagavat said to Vajrapāṇi, the Lord of the Secret Ones, 'Lord of the Secret Ones, listen carefully to the attributes of the types of minds! Lord of the Secret Ones, there is the mind of attachment, the mind of non-attachment, the mind of hatred, the mind of friendliness, the mind of stupidity, the mind of intelligence, the mind of decisiveness, the mind of doubt, the mind of darkness, the mind of clarity, (120b) the mind of gathering together, the mind of disputation, the mind of dissent, the mind of agreement, the mind of a god, the mind of an *asura*, the mind of a *nāga*, the mind of a man, the mind of a woman, the mind of Īśvara, the mind of a merchant, the mind of a farmer, the mind of a river, the mind of a pond, the

A C: 離於斷常 '*to be devoid of cessation and permanence*'.

mind of a well, the mind of a guard, the mind of avarice, the mind of a cat, the mind of a dog, the mind of a *garuḍa*, the mind of a rat, the mind of a song, the mind of a dance, the mind of music, the mind of a house, the mind of a lion, the mind of an owl, the mind of a crow, the mind of a *rākṣasa*, the mind of a thorn, the mind of the underground realm, the mind of wind, the mind of water, the mind of fire, the mind of mud, the mind of dirt[A], the mind of paint, the mind of a shield, the mind of confusion, the mind of poison, the mind of a noose, the mind of shackles, the mind of a cloud, the mind of a field, the mind of salt, the mind of a razor, the mind of Mount Sumeru, the mind like an ocean, the mind like a cavern and the mind of kinship[B].'

Vajrapāṇi asks the Bhagavat to explain the attributes of the one hundred and sixty types of minds that are to be transcended for *bodhicitta* to arise. (27b) You should know that the explanation of these minds deals with them by means of their names, attributes, abandonment and path. Also the nature of these minds is of four types: the emotionally afflicted, the wholesome, the unwholesome and the neutral. Also, in order to transcend these minds, there are generally speaking two types of practice by means of mantras: that of those who are accomplished and those who are bound by conventional practice. Of these, those who are accomplished advance to whichever level they wish with a mind-formed body, from the Level of Practice with Devoted Interest , so their [practice] has neither a sequence nor interval of eons. Regarding those who are bound by conventional practice, there are again two types: those with dull faculties and those with sharp ones. Those with dull faculties proceed first from the mundane path, the idea that emptiness is 'aloneness', and then they understand that there is no self in the individual. They also realize that these minds are suffering, impermanent, nothing [in themselves] and without a self. When they repeatedly practise renunciation, they cultivate the understanding that an individual lacks autonomous existence over three eons, starting on the mundane path. Then, when they have also rejected the idea that the psycho-physical constituents have autonomous existence, they then realize that phenomena such as the psycho-physical constituents and so on, which are like magical illusions and mirages, also lack autonomous existence. They then enter the Level of Practice with Devoted Interest, which is characterized by the practice of the Perfections and the cultivation of the Three Minds.

Those with sharp faculties understand from the beginning that both the individual and phenomena are without autonomous existence, so they abandon those minds by means of the similes of illusion and mirage. (28a) By practising in sequence the Perfections and the cultivation of the Three Minds, they perfect that Level of Practice with Devoted Interest in one eon and enter into the Level of Awareness in a quarter of an eon. However, those with dull faculties and sharp ones are similar in perfecting that Level of Practice with Devoted Interest in one eon when they have entered it and entering the Level of Awareness in a quarter of an eon.

A This is omitted in C.

B Because the list in C is short by one mind, Śubhakara-siṃha added '*the mind of a monkey*' in his oral comments to Yi-xing.

Furthermore, the increase from the sixty types of minds to one hundred and sixty is because they are divided into three according to the degree of obscuration and each of those three is further divided into three, making nine in all for each. Thus for the major major obscuration, one mind is abandoned, for the medium major type two are abandoned, for the minor major type three are abandoned, for the major medium type four are abandoned, for the medium medium type five are abandoned. For the minor medium type six are abandoned. For the major minor type seven are abandoned. For the medium minor type eight are abandoned. Starting from the bottom, those one hundred and sixty minds are purified through the Level of Practice with Devoted Interest and so one perfects that Level. You should know that the last of the nine, the minor minor type is abandoned after advancing from the Level of Practice with Devoted Interest, at entry into the Level of Awareness.

22. 'Lord of the Secret Ones! What is the mind of attachment? It is that which has recourse to religion with desire. What is the mind of non-attachment? It is that which has recourse to religion devoid of desire. What is the mind of hatred? It is that which has recourse to religion with aversion. What is the mind of friendliness? It is that which has recourse to religion with friendliness. What is the mind of stupidity? It is that which has recourse to religion lacking reflection. What is the mind of intelligence? It is that which has recourse to religion with greater and greater understanding. What is the mind of decisiveness? It is that which acts in accordance with orders and injunctions. What is the mind of doubt? It is that which has recourse to religion with doubt regarding whatever is definitely reliable. (121a) **What is the mind of darkness? It is that which has thoughts of uncertainty about that which is incontrovertible. What is the mind of clarity? It is that which acts with certainty about that which is incontrovertible. What is the mind of gathering together? It is that which makes the many one. What is the mind of disputation? It is that which is mutually antagonistic [to others]. What is the mind of dissent? It is that which is at odds with oneself. What is the mind of agreement? It is that which considers oneself allied because of similarity. What is the mind of a god? It is that which gives rise to arrogant thoughts about oneself according to one's inclination. What is the mind of an *asura*? It is that which delights in *saṃsāra*. What is the mind of a *nāga*? It is that which thinks about getting great wealth. What is the mind of a man? It is that which thinks about one's own advantage[A]. What is the mind of a woman? It is that which has recourse to religion just for pleasure. What is the mind of Īśvara? It is that which arrogantly thinks that everything is as imagined by oneself. What is the mind of a merchant? It is that which hoards and increases the value of things and then later uses them. What is the mind of a farmer? It is that which seeks to hear many things and to attend to them later. What is the mind of a river? It is that which has recourse to religion [not][17] relying on the two extremes. What is the mind of a pond? It is that which has recourse to religion with greed. What is the mind of a well? It is**

A C: 思念利他 '*which thinks of benefitting others*'.

that which thinks that what is shallow is profound. What is the mind of a guard? It is that which thinks that oneself is correct and others are wrong. What is the mind of avarice? It is that which uses things for oneself and not to give to others. What is the mind of a cat? It is that which has recourse to religion advancing in leaps. What is the mind of a dog? It is that which is joyful about things even though they are meagre. What is the mind of a *garuḍa*? It is that which has recourse to religion with partiality. What is the mind of a rat? It is that which thinks about cutting all restraints. What is the mind of a song? It is that which thinks one will attract beings by songs of various melodies. What is the mind of a dance? (121b) It is that which thinks one will cause others to be aroused by one's various accomplishments. What is the mind of music? It is that which thinks one shall beat the drum of the Dharma. What is the mind of a house? It is that which has recourse to religion in order to protect one's body. What is the mind of a lion? It is that which has recourse [to religion] by excelling over all. What is the mind of an owl? It is that which always thinks of the night. What is the mind of a crow? It is that which thinks of everything with fear. What is the mind of a *rākṣasa*? It is that which brings about evil from good. What is the mind of a thorn? It is that which has regrets about everything. What is the mind of the underground realm? It is that which thinks of benefits under the ground. What is the mind of wind? It is that which roams about everywhere in everything. What is the mind of water? It is that which practises in order to wash away all evil attitudes. What is the mind of fire? It is that which causes oneself torment with asceticism. What is the mind of mud? It is that which smears others with one's own faults. What is the mind of dirt? It is that which dirties one's mind by contact with the evils of others[A]. What is the mind of paint? It is that which has recourse [to religion] while being attached to it. What is the mind of a shield? It is that which has recourse [to one religion] and rejects other wholesome ones. What is the mind of confusion? It is that which perceives one thing and thinks that it is something else. What is the mind of poison? It is that which thinks of the complete non-existence of something. What is the mind of a noose? It is that which binds and immobilizes oneself in everything. What is the mind of shackles? It is that which thinks that one's two legs are held. What is the mind of a cloud? It is that which thinks like rain. What is the mind of a field? It is that which devotes all its attention to one's body. What is the mind of salt? It is that which considers again whatever it has already considered. What is the mind of a razor? It is that which thinks it is enough just to become a monk. What is the mind that is like Sumeru? It is to think that one is lofty. What is the mind that is like an ocean? It is that which reflects upon one's body. (122a) What is the mind that is like a cavern? It is that which differs later about that which was previously fixed. What is the mind of kinship? It is that which accompanies, with a like nature, any mind which has arisen.'

A C omits this mind.

(1) ***What is the mind of attachment*** (*rāga*) ***? It is to have recourse to religion with desire***: This refers to the mind endowed with attachment. You should know that it is to be attached to and indulge in religion[18] (*dharma*) with any one of the four types of qualities: wholesome, unwholesome, emotionally afflicted or neutral, as appropriate. (28b) If one is attracted to the gods in whom one should believe and worship, and then goes on to do those acts of worship and so on, this is recourse to religion, having desire which is wholesome. Likewise if one lusts after women and so on, and performs those actions, then that is recourse to religion having desire which is emotionally afflicted. If one is attracted to stealing and lying, and goes on to do those deeds, then this is recourse to religion having desire which is unwholesome. If one is attracted to such things as technology and so on, and performs such actions, then this is recourse to religion having desire which is neutral. In this same manner you should also link the wholesome, unwholesome, emotionally afflicted or neutral qualities to the other minds as appropriate.

(2) ***Non-attachment*** (*virāga*): This is to conduct oneself naturally or without coercion, with regards those four types of qualities mentioned above, without attachment or without interest, and to perform those actions.

(3) ***Hatred*** (*dveṣa*): This refers to the mind having aversion, that functions in the above manner, as wholesome, unwholesome and so on[19].

(4) ***Friendliness*** (*maitrī*): This is the friendly mind which functions as above, as wholesome, unwholesome and so on.

(5) ***Stupidity*** (*moha*): [The mind that which lacks reflection.]

(6) ***Intelligence*** (*prajñā*): '***Greater and greater***' (29a) refers to the acquisition of insight which one did not have before, and from having that insight one gains a better insight and special understanding.

(7) ***Decisiveness*** (*nirṇaya*): It is inappropriate that one should not obey the king's orders or the teacher's injunctions, so one acts with resolution.

(8) ***Doubt*** (*saṃśaya*): It is to question and have doubts in oneself about something that had previously been grasped correctly.

(9) ***Darkness*** (*tamas*): This is the mind which is like darkness. Just as one cannot see clearly whether there is a vase and so on in the dark, one is not sure if it is there or not. In the same way because something which is incontrovertible is obscured by the darkness of ignorance, one has this mind which is like darkness, giving rise to doubt.

(10) ***Clarity*** (*āloka*): Just as material phenomena are easily visible in the clear sky, in the same way with regards to colour-form which also has the nature of visibility, one realizes without any doubt that it is a knowable phenomenon with this mind and acts upon it without any doubt.

(11) ***Gathering together*** (*saṃgraha*): (29b) This is to gather together into one general attribute such as emptiness or the absence of autonomous existence, all the individual separate attributes of the psycho-physical constituents, the perceptual elements and sources and so forth.

(12) ***Disputation*** (*vivāda*): This is to take mutually opposing extremes and to have recourse to religion with contention.

(13) ***Agreement*** (*nirvivāda*): This is to act together in harmony with the views of another with regards any particular thing and to have recourse to religion with agreement.

(14) ***God*** (*deva*): This is either the mind of a god, in which one [arrogantly] thinks 'I am that' about whatever one is, just as a god thinks 'I am a god', or else it is the mind of one who would be a god, with which one thinks 'I must become a god'.

(15) ***Asura*** (*asura*): Just as *asuras* take delight in such things, so this mind has recourse to religion, delighting in *saṃsāra*.

(16) ***Nāga*** (*nāga*): (30a) Just as an opulent *nāga* has many heads which experience great enjoyments, likewise this mind also has recourse to religion, indulging in great enjoyments. In Sanskrit, the word '*bhoga*' means both 'enjoyment' and also the 'head' of a *nāga*. So since that mind causes one to have recourse to religion associated with great enjoyments, it is said to be a *nāga*-like attitude.

(17) ***Man*** (*nara*): This mind is what makes one indulge in the five kinds of sensuous pleasures of human enjoyment.

(18) ***Woman*** (*nārī*): Women perform the actions of those religious practices in order to acquire the things which are the objects of their desire. In the same way this mind has recourse to such religious practices in order to gain the desired objects.

(19) ***Īśvara***: Īśvara thinks that he is responsible for the creation and destruction of all worlds. In the same way this mind has recourse to religion, thinking one has done and undone things by oneself. ***Īśvara*** refers to the Great God.

(20) ***Merchant*** (*vāṇija*): (30b) A merchant hoards up the things that he deals in when prices are low, and when the price has risen he trades them all, increasing his profit. In the same way, this mind has the attribute of renouncing, when appropriate, the things one previously had such as the psycho-physical constituents and so forth, due to the factors of impermanence, suffering and so forth.

(21) ***Farmer*** (*kārṣika*): The farmer first gathers together his harvest, and then he later turns that same harvest into his food and drink. In the same way, with this mind one listens to and accumulates many teachings, and then one later turns oneself to the consideration and practice of those teachings that one has heard.

(22) ***River*** (*ogha*): A river flows down the centre of its channel without rising over its two banks. In the same way, this mind functions in rejecting the two extremes of eternalism and nihilism. Furthermore, this can mean that just as a river flows along dependent upon its two banks, likewise this mind adheres to the extremes of eternalism or nihilism and has recourse to religion in that way.

(23) ***Pond*** (*vilva*): A pond accumulates water flowing from elsewhere within itself and does not let it run from itself. In the same way, this mind gathers everything from elsewhere (31a) and does not give out anything from itself.

(24) ***Well*** (*kūpa*): A well full of water appears to be deep even if it is not, because its depth is not clear. In the same way, this mind behaves as though it is profound, even though it is intellectually shallow.

(25) ***Guard*** (*rakṣaṇa*): With this mind one firmly holds onto whatever one has heard and grasped, thinking that it is not to be spoilt and that it is not to be grasped or comprehended by others.

(26) ***Avarice*** (*mātsarya*): [No additional comment.]

(27) ***Cat*** (*mārjara*): When a cat catches a bird or something, it leaps and bounds and seizes it. In the same way this mind also leaps from the time of entry, bounding along the sequence, when one reaches the Noble Path and so on.

(28) ***Dog*** (*śvāna*): Dogs are delighted even by small things, and in the same way this mind has recourse to religious practice which makes one delight in small things.

(29) ***Garuḍa***: (31b) When a *garuḍa* catches a *nāga*, it seizes it, flapping its wings. In the same way, this mind has recourse to religion adhering with partiality to whatever is one's own. In Sanskrit, the word '*pakṣa*' means both 'wings' and 'a faction'. Thus there is a similarity in the meanings of the one word, for as the *garuḍa* seizes the *nāga* in order to make it its own, likewise partiality is adhering with partiality to whatever thing one would make one's own.

(30) ***Rat*** (*mūṣa*): Rats sever all restraints and free themselves. In the same way, this mind has recourse to religious practice which frees it from the bonds of attachment, hatred and stupidity.

(31) ***Song*** (*gīta*): Just as people are delighted by a song and gather together, in the same way this mind has recourse to religion considering that beings will have faith and be attracted to one's pleasing words by their melodiousness.

(32) ***Dance*** (*taṇḍava*): 'Dance' means movements of the body, and all the countless magical creations of the body in a single dance, such as walking in the sky and so forth, are movements of the body. (32a) Therefore, this mind has recourse to religion causing beings to fix their attention upon various magical creations by those physical creations.

(33) ***Music*** (*tūrya*): It is the mind which has recourse to religion causing one to sound the drum of the Dharma and proclaim it.

(34) ***House*** (*gṛha*): A house guards and protects one's furniture and so on without fail, and in the same way, this mind has recourse to religion to guard one's body.

(35) ***Lion*** (*siṃha*): Just as a lion excels over all animals in its skill, in the same way, this mind has recourse to religion to make one excel over others by all that one knows and is famed for.

(36) ***Owl*** (*ulūka*): Owls carry out all their activities such as hunting for food and so on by night. Likewise, this mind has recourse to religious practice in which one carries out one's activities at night.

(37) ***Crow*** (*kāka*): Crows carry out their activities in fear and apprehension of everything. In the same way, this mind has recourse to religion in anxiety and fear about everything one should carry out.

(38) ***Rākṣasa***: (32b) *Rākṣasas* have become powerful due to the good that they previously performed, but with that power they indulge in unwholesome deeds such as killing and so on. This mind is like that.

(39) ***Thorn*** (*kaṇṭaka*): Thorns prick and cause pain. In the same way, this mind has recourse to religion giving rise to regret for things that one has done. By bringing that regret to mind again and again, one is tormented by it.

(40) ***Underground*** (*paṭala*): This mind is directed towards the underground [realms]. It has recourse to religious practices causing one to do one's actions when one has gone underground.

(41) ***Wind*** (*vāyu*): The wind at times enters into people and at times it enters into the water and so forth. In the same way, this mind has recourse to religious practice sometimes commencing by being wholesome. Becoming agitated, it then does what is unwholesome. At other times it commences by being unwholesome and then does what is wholesome. In a word, it enters into everything, yet does not rest anywhere.

(42) ***Water*** (*udaka*): [Missing from Commentary]

(43) ***Fire*** (*agni*): Just as fire is scorched by its own heat, (33a) in the same way this mind has recourse to religious practices which cause one to torment and humiliate one's body and mind by one's own asceticism. In Sanskrit, the word '*tapas* means both 'heat' and 'ascetic practices'.

(44) ***Mud*** (*paṅka*): Mud sticks its dirtiness to other things and soils them. In the same way this mind has recourse to religion staining others with one's own evil.

(45) ***Dirt*** (*āvila*): This is the mind which is like dirt. It is when others cause one's mind to be troubled by their evil.

(46) ***Paint*** (*raṅga*): When one paints something with white or red coloured paint, then it becomes the same in nature as the paint. In the same way, this mind has recourse to religious practices, adhering to whatever one is thinking of, changing whatever one was thinking of into its nature.

(47) ***Shield*** (*phalaka*): A shield has the function of protecting one from the sword-thrusts and so on of others. In the same way, this mind has recourse to religion obscuring other wholesome qualities by the practice of one wholesome quality.

(48) ***Confusion*** (*viparyāsa*): (33b) It is to become confused about something when one has comprehended it, thinking that it is something else.

(49) ***Poison*** (*viṣa*): If one has taken poison, one will die and cease to exist. In the same way, with this mind one abandons such emotional afflictions as opinionatedness and so forth, and not giving rise to them again, one makes them cease to exist.

(50) ***Noose*** (*pāśa*): A noose has the function of binding. In the same way, this mind has recourse to religious practices which cause oneself to be bound.

(51) ***Shackles*** (*nigaḍa*): Shackles restrain the two legs, and in the same way this mind has recourse to the religious practices which restrain the two extremes of the words 'existence' and 'non-existence'. In Sanskrit, the word *pada* means both 'leg' and 'word'.

(52) ***Cloud*** (*megha*): A cloud has the function of gathering up water and causing rain to fall. In the same way, this mind has recourse to religious practices that function as rain-fall.

(53) ***Field*** (*kṣetra*): (34a) In order to produce grain and so on, a field has to be made ready by ploughing and so forth. In the same way, this mind has recourse to the religious practice that makes one adorn one's body through washing, perfuming and ornamenting, in order to make oneself beautiful.

(54) ***Salt*** (*lavaṇa*): If you put salt into a metal jar or some other container, the container will be eaten away and scoured by the salt, and both the salt and the rust will taste the same. In the same way, this mind has recourse to religious practice in which it perceives and conceptualizes something, and then in the following instant of that conceptualizing mind, refutes and negates that concept.

(55) ***Razor*** (*kṣura*): A razor only has the function of shaving a monk's head and contributes no other work to renunciation. In the same way, with this mind one just remains in a state of renunciation, with one's head shaven, but does not engage in any efforts to train as a monk or keep the moral observances.

(56) ***Mount Sumeru***: Mount Sumeru soars up loftily thousands of yards, and in the same way this mind has recourse to religion proudly considering oneself to be great, thinking that one's merits are superior to all others.

(57) ***Ocean*** (*sāgara*): (34b) The ocean billows and strikes itself with its own waves. In the same way, this mind realizes that one's body is impermanent and nothing in itself.

(58) ***Cavern*** (*guha*): While the entrance to a cavern is defined and small, inside it is large and of irregular shape. It is likewise with this mind, for although one previously lived in a restrained way with the moral observances and merits, one becomes proud because of those same moral observances and merits, and because of that one changes and acts arrogantly.

(59) ***Kinship*** (*upapatti*): Because one has habitual tendencies from previous behaviour, whether wholesome or unwholesome, one is born together with those tendencies wherever one is reborn. Even though one has obtained a birth dissimilar to the matured results of previous actions whether wholesome or unwholesome, one is still reborn with them. For example, because one habitually and frequently killed in a previous lifetime, in a later lifetime one will have many illnesses and a short life. You should modify and apply this as appropriate for wholesome actions.

23. 'Lord of the Secret Ones! By doubling [them] five consecutive times[20], one arrives at the one hundred and sixty mundane minds, and after the elapse of three eons these are transcended and the supramundane mind arises[A]. That is to say,

> **'This is just the psycho-physical constituents,**
> **and there has never existed a self.**
> **Through the faculties, perceptual sources and elements,**
> **the mundane world is understood to be valueless.**
> **This twelve-fold chain of dependent origination**
> **is produced by emotional afflictions and karmic action**
> **that arise from the seeds of ignorance,**
> **without the need for a creator and so forth.**
> **Such a calm and tranquil attitude**
> **is difficult for logicians to comprehend,**
> **yet it is devoid of all faults,**
> **and has been taught previously by the Buddhas.'**

After the elapse of three eons, these one hundred and sixty mundane minds are transcended and the supramundane mind arises: There are two kinds of supramundane mind: the mind which realizes the absence of autonomous existence of the individual, and which is without impurities although it has perceptual images (*ākāra*), and the mind which realizes the absence of autonomous existence of all phenomena, (35a) which is without impurities and perceptual images, and which is radiantly clear by nature.

24. 'Lord of the Secret Ones! There also arises in those who abide in this supramundane mind, the idea that the psycho-physical constituents really exist. Then they give rise to the mind which is devoid of attachment to the psycho-physical constituents, and because they dissolve them by considering them to be like froth, bubbles, a plantain tree, a mirage or a phantom, they become free from that notion.

A C: 越世間三妄執出世間心生 '*after the three mundane false concepts* (kalpa) *have been transcended, the supramundane mind will arise*'.

'Thus, whoever has abandoned the psycho-physical constituents, the perceptual elements, the perceptual sources, the perceiving subject and perceived objects, will directly realize the continuum of tranquility, the intrinsic nature of reality.

'Lord of the Secret Ones! This supramundane mind which is free from the net of emotional afflictions and karmic actions associated with the sequence of eight complete and incomplete minds[21], will be transcended by yogins with the elapse of one eon.'

When you abide in the profound and peaceful supramundane mind which has perceptual images, but lacks the idea of autonomous existence of the individual, you will think in the way mentioned above that the psycho-physical constituents alone exist, while realizing that there is no autonomous existence of the individual. This mind is completely perfected in three eons.

Then they give rise to the mind which is devoid of attachment to the psycho-physical constituents ... (35b) ***... transcended by yogins with the elapse of one eon***: In this way they investigate the psycho-physical constituents in general, and when they have investigated them, they come to think that they are real. But when they analyze each of the psycho-physical constituents and refute them, colour-form is seen to be like froth, for just as when each bubble of froth bursts, the froth is seen to be insubstantial. In the same way, when they have broken down that psycho-physical constituent and investigated each part of it, they know that there are only the specific attributes of each phenomenon, such as its colour, form and so on, and that there is no such reality called a 'psycho-physical constituent'. Likewise feeling is like bubbles on water. They know that there is no such thing to be considered as that psycho-physical constituent in something which has no abiding location, because that which perishes as soon as it arises is impermanent. Likewise consciousness is seen to be like a phantom when analyzed, for a phantom ox is not a really existent ox, but just a product of drugs or props by nature. Consciousness is also like that, for there is no such thing to be considered as that psycho-physical constituent, but it merely has the nature of consciousness. Likewise ideation when analyzed is seen to be like a mirage, for just as a mirage is seen as water by a person tormented by thirst, and yet there is no real water, but only that which has the nature of a mirage. Ideation is also like that, for there is no such thing to be considered as that psycho-physical constituent, but only that which has the nature of grasping perceptual images. Likewise motivation is seen to be like a plantain tree. This example is well known so I shall not mention it here.

Thus when the psycho-physical constituents have been refuted with the examples of froth and so on, (36a) nothing real will remain [for you] to conceive as being a psycho-physical constituent, for they are merely their specific individual attributes. If the psycho-physical constituents cannot be established in that way, there is also nothing real for you to conceive of as the perceptual elements and the perceptual sources, since they are no different to the psycho-physical constituents, and merely have the individual natures of the phenomena involved.

The perceiving subject and the perceived objects are also thus. Colour-form is conceived to be the perceived objects, and the other four psycho-physical constituents are conceived to be the perceiving subject, but no such things exist, just the individual nature of the phenomena involved.

When they have arrived at such a mind which is free from attachment to the psycho-physical constituents, by analyzing them into their froth-like natures and so forth, they are also liberated from the idea which perceives the psycho-physical constituents to be really existent. When they have thus been liberated from the psycho-physical constituents, they will realize that the attributes linked with psycho-physical constituents only exist as the intrinsic nature of phenomena.

Thus, whoever has abandoned the psycho-physical constituents ... the intrinsic nature of reality : By the above means of refuting anything that is conceived to be a psycho-physical constituent, they will completely abandon them because the intrinsic nature of reality does not exist as anything conceived in the perceptual image of blue and so forth. (36b)

Lord of the Secret Ones! This supramundane mind ... by yogins with the elapse of one eon: Having freed themselves from the belief in the existence of things conceived to be the psycho-physical constituents, they have the tranquil mind which realizes that there is only the individual natures of phenomena. Beginning with the realization that things corresponding to the psycho-physical constituents do not exist, they then enter into the realization that there are just the individual natures of phenomena, such as blue and so on. They then transcend that mind with the elapse of one eon, and enter the Level of Practice with Devoted Interest which is the realization of the absence of autonomous existence of phenomena.

The eight incomplete and complete minds: These refer to the eight minds from Śrotāpanna to Arhat. (37a) They are incomplete because they believe the psycho-physical constituents to be the things they are conceived to be. Yet, because of the abandonment of the emotional afflictions, they are complete. But because they still have the habitual tendencies of the emotional afflictions, they are incomplete.

These are the stages in which intelligent Bodhisattvas who engage in mantra practice abandon the one hundred and sixty emotionally afflicted minds, with the sequence of realizing the absence of autonomous existence of the individual and so forth.

25. 'Lord of the Secret Ones! Moreover, there are those who fare in the Mahāyāna and have no regard for the other Ways, and who give rise to the thought that phenomena lack autonomous existence. Why is that? Because when they break down the basis of the psycho-physical constituents by practising those previous practices, they fully comprehend the intrinsic nature of phenomena (122b) **and give rise to the idea that they are like magical illusions, mirages, shadows, echoes, a wheel of fire or a *gandharvas'* city.**

'Lord of the Secret Ones! Therefore, since they have come to be dominated by these ideas, even the notion of the lack of autonomous existence of phenomena must be abandoned, for the mind itself has not arisen from the very beginning. How? Lord of the Secret Ones! Because they fully know the essential nature of mind, they are unable to perceive either a past point [of arising] or a future point [of extinction] to mind. Yogins complete all this after the elapse of a second eon.'

Now the text describes the stages in which those Bodhisattvas of acute intelligence and much learning, who fare in the Mahāyāna without regard for the other Ways, meditatively observe the lack of autonomous existence of individuals and phenomena and enter the Level of Practice with Devoted Interest. (37b)

***Why is that? Because they dissolve ... or a* gandharvas' *city*:** At first, while doing the entry practice, striving with faith, they know that the nature of the psycho-physical constituents is like that of magical illusions and so forth, and they repeatedly practise this, so even though they have not engaged in the stages of the realization that the individual is without any autonomous existence, they realize the absence of any autonomous existence to phenomena.

***Magical illusions*:** They arrive at the idea that phenomena are like magical illusions and so forth. Although magical cows and horses can be projected upon stones and wood, and do not appear to be stones and wood, but in the forms of cows and horses, there is nothing there really existing as a cow or horse, just the stones and wood. Likewise, even though such phenomena as the psycho-physical constituents are visible, they appear in the consciousness through the power of delusive error. In reality, the intrinsic nature of the psycho-physical constituents is like that of the magical cows and horses: although they appear, they do not really exist. Consciousness is like the stones and wood, and although it is not obvious, the phenomena which appear as colour-form and so on, do not really exist, but are just perceptual images within the deluded consciousness[22].

Likewise with '***mirages***': a person sees mirages as water in lonely deserts because he is tormented by thirst, but the water has no reality. It is just a mirage. In the same way, although the psycho-physical constituents appear, they have no real existence, but are just perceptual images within the deluded consciousness.

In the same way, '***shadows, echoes,*** (38a) ***a wheel of fire***' and the '**gandharvas' *castle***' should also be understood following the above explanation of illusion. In brief, the appearance of such phenomena as the psycho-physical constituents is nothing other than appearance in a deluded consciousness. If it is possible for one to see such things as colour-form in dreams which carry out their functions, even though there are no colour-form objects in dreams, it is obvious that colour-form and so on do not really exist when dreaming, but are all merely generated by the power of consciousness.

Having reflected thus and entered the Level of Practice with Devoted Interest, these yogins who have directly realized that such phenomena as the psycho-physical constituents and so on are without autonomous existence, arrive at the idea that they are like magical illusions, reflections and so on, and that though phenomena do not really exist, they are perceived to exist just in the consciousness. Yogins who directly realize the lack of autonomous existence to phenomena in this way, by the cultivation of the Three Minds which enter, abide and arise respectively, will come to fully know the Levels and Perfections which they did not know completely, and make them a reality. These three are the mind which dissolves and comprehends phenomena in this way with the examples of magical illusion and so on, the mind which resides in the non-conceptualizing *samādhi*, having thus dissolved the phenomena, and the mind which engages in the Perfections and so on, and knowing the virtues of the Ten Levels by the insight born of hearing, considering and cultivation, has great trust in them. By the insight born of what they have heard, considered and cultivated, these yogins will realize the absence of any autonomous existence in phenomena and will perceive them to exist merely in consciousness.

These are the attributes of the Level of Practice with Devoted Interest, which will be completed in one eon.

Then after a quarter of an eon, they will rise above this Level of Practice with Devoted Interest and enter into the Level of Awareness. (38b) Concerning this process, the text says, '***Lord of the Secret Ones! Therefore on account of these minds ... elapse of a second eon***'. Regarding the passage '***Therefore, since they have come to be dominated by those ideas, even the notion of the lack of autonomous existence of phenomena must be abandoned, for the mind itself has not arisen from the very beginning***', having previously realized that phenomena do not have autonomous existence, they become dominated by the thought that there is only consciousness in the form of a perceiving subject and perceived objects. Therefore by realizing that that consciousness is unarisen from the very beginning, they abandon even that idea that there is just consciousness, and so they abandon even the idea itself that phenomena lack autonomous existence.

How do they abandon even that idea that there is just consciousness? ***How? Because they fully know ... or future point to mind***: If one thus seeks a point at some time in the past when one's mind first arose, that point cannot be found. Because there is no point of origin, one will also not find a future point of perishing, so neither past nor future points can be found. Because there is thus no starting point, (39a) the mind has obviously not arisen, and if it has not arisen from the very beginning, then one will abandon the idea that there is just consciousness, that whatever exists in any place is just consciousness appearing in the form of the perceiving subject and perceived objects. So one also abandons even the [idea of] the autonomous existence of phenomena. Meditating in this manner, they perfect the abandoning of [the idea of] autonomous existence of phenomena in a second eon.

26. 'Lord of the Secret Ones! Moreover, there are Bodhisattvas who engage in the practice of Bodhisattvas by means of the secret mantra path, who have accumulated an immeasurable mass of merits and awareness in countless hundreds of thousands of millions of eons. They will gain possession of immeasurable insight and expedient means, and they will be saluted by the worlds of gods and asuras, they will surpass all Śrāvakas and Pratyekabuddhas, and also will be saluted by Indra, Brahmā, Viṣṇu and others. Furthermore, there arises the mind whose essential nature is emptiness, without substance, which is without attributes, without perceptual forms, which transcends all proliferations, which is limitless like space, which is the ground of all phenomena[A], which is separate from the conditioned and the unconditioned realms, which is free from actions and activities[23], separate from eye, ear, nose, tongue and body, and is without any self-existent nature whatsoever. Lord of the Secret Ones! This is spoken of by the Jinas as the first [level] of *bodhicitta*.'

Now the sequence of the arising of *bodhicitta* at the Joyful Level. You should understand that this section explains the perfection (*saṃpad*) of the causal basis of

A C: 一切佛法 '*all Buddha qualities*'.

that *bodhicitta* of the First Level, the perfection of its nature, the perfection of its attributes and the perfection of the accomplishment of those attributes.

Perfection of its causal basis is taught with the words '***Accumulated an immeasurable mass of merits and awareness in countless hundreds of thousands of millions of eons***'. Perfection of its nature is taught with the words '***They will gain possession of immeasurable insight and expedient means ... saluted by Indra, Brahmā and Viṣṇu***'. This perfection of nature also includes the perfection of abandonment and of strength. The perfection of abandonment is taught with the words '***gain possession of immeasurable insight and expedient means***' and '***they will surpass all Śrāvakas and Pratyekabuddhas***'. (39b) The perfection of strength is taught with the words '***will be saluted by the worlds of gods and asuras***' and '***will be saluted by Indra***' and so forth. The perfection of attributes is taught with the words '***there arises the mind whose essential nature is emptiness***'. The perfection of the accomplishment of the attributes is taught with the words '***is without attributes ... without any self-existent nature whatsoever***'.

Insight (*prajñā*): This is the total understanding of the intrinsic nature of all phenomena. ***Expedient means*** (*upāya*): To mature and liberate beings by the power of compassion. (40a) ***Proliferation*** (*prapañca*): This refers to conceptualization (*vikalpa*). (40b) ***The ground of all phenomena***: '***All phenomena***' refers to the conditioned phenomena. If the [belief in] existence of these phenomena is dissolved by means of [arguments based on] the directions of atoms[24], or by means of the examples of magical illusions, mirages and so forth, they will be [understood to be] devoid of self-existence, and since emptiness and *bodhicitta* are of one single taste, it becomes the ground of all those phenomena. Secondly, '***all phenomena***' refers to the phenomena which are the virtues of the Buddha, such as the Ten Strengths, the Four Fearlessnesses, the Eighteen Uncommon Qualities and so forth, so it is the ground of all such qualities. ***Separate from the conditioned and the unconditioned realms***: It is separate from the conditioned because it is the antidote to the inimical, which is attained by the mind of the First Level. It is separate from the unconditioned because they do not abide in the realm of Nirvāṇa, not having abandoned the habitual tendencies of the obscurations of emotional afflictions and wrong understanding.

Arises: The attributes of the mind which is without any self-existence, for you should know that that mind directed towards supreme Enlightenment arises following the perfection of the virtues of the First Level, whose causal basis is the mass of merit and awareness which was accumulated in the above mentioned number of eons.

27. **'They will be free from emotional afflictions and action,**
even though they have emotional afflictions and action.
They are the object of the world's gifts,
and should always receive offerings and respect.
Furthermore, Lord of the Secret Ones,
the Level of Practice with Devoted Interest
is the cultivation of the Three Minds.
Through the practice of the Perfections
and the Four Methods of Attracting, (123a)
the Level of Devoted Interest is unequalled,
immeasurable and inconceivable.

The emergence of immeasurable Awareness
will come about by the ten minds.
Everything that I have spoken a little about
will be attained through this [Level].
Therefore the All-knowing One
calls this "devoted interest"[A].
The intelligent person will perfect
this Level with the elapse of one eon,
Moreover, he will transcend devoted interest
after just a quarter [of an eon].'

(41a) ***Free from emotional afflictions and karmic action*:** They are separated from karmic actions which lead to the unfortunate states of existence, and from the elements inimical to the First Level. ***Even though they have emotional afflictions and karmic action*:** Though they do have the karmic actions which cause the attainment of the higher levels of existence and the obscuring emotional afflictions associated with them.

This section now recapitulates the attributes and virtues of the Level of Practice with Devoted Interest. ***With devoted interest*:** They know the virtues of the Buddha, the Levels and Perfections by the insight born of hearing, pondering and cultivation, and generate extremely devoted interest, thinking that this really is it and no other. ***The cultivation of the Three Minds*:** These are the three minds of entry, abiding and arising, and the method of cultivating them has already been explained above in the section dealing with the lack of autonomous existence in phenomena. ***Practice with Devoted Interest*:** This is not only to have devoted interest with regards those factors, but it is also to make diligent efforts with regards their qualities which are to be repeatedly practised, so it says '***Through the practice of the Perfections and the Four Methods of Attracting***'. ***The practice of the Perfections*:** Each of the Perfections such as Generosity and so on are practised at the time of each Level, from the First Level up to the Tenth Level, (41b) and just as they engage in the Perfections for themselves, they also attract other beings by means of the Four Methods of Attracting in order to make them engage in the Perfections. Thus while delighting in the virtues of the First Level, the Joyful One, they engage with devoted interest in the practice of the Perfection of Generosity with the Dharma and material provisions. While they themselves engage in this when abiding on this Level, they also gather other beings to them and cause them to engage in it, by means of the Four Methods of Attracting. On the Second Level, the Stainless One, they also engage with devoted interest in the stainless Perfection of Morality, both engaging in it themselves and also causing others to engage in it, by means of the Four Methods of Attracting. On the Third Level, the Illuminating One, they accept the non-arising of phenomena, and while engaging with devoted interest in the practice of the Perfection Of Patient Acceptance, they both engage in it themselves and cause others to engage in it. On the Fourth Level, the Flaming One, they engage in the Perfection of Strenuousness with the radiant light of Awareness. On the Fifth

A C: 是故智者當思惟此一切智信解地 '*therefore the wise one should reflect upon this level of devoted interest concerning All-knowing [Awareness]*'.

Level, the One Difficult to Conquer, they engage in the Perfection of Meditative Concentration which is very difficult for demons to overcome. On the Sixth Level, the One Which Is Present, they engage in the Perfection of Insight, with the actualization of insight. On the Seventh Level, the One Which Goes Far, they engage in the Perfection of Expedient Means, by which they cause beings to be liberated. On the Eighth Level, the Unshakable One, they engage in the Perfection of Devoted Interest, by which they aspire to attain what is higher, through the attainment of the mastery of aspiration. On the Ninth Level, the One With Good Discrimination, they engage in the Perfection of Strength. On the Tenth Level, the Cloud of the Dharma, they engage in the Perfection of Awareness which brings them into contact with the Dharma, so it becomes accessible to them by Awareness, in the presence of all the Tathāgatas of the ten directions. When they engage in these Levels, they repeatedly accustom themselves to their practice and they also gather beings to them by means of the Four Methods of Attracting, making those beings also engage in them.

What are the Four Methods of Attracting? They are i) to cause others to engage in the Perfections by means of generosity, ii) by means of kind words, iii) by means of beneficial acts, (42a) and iv) by means of appropriate benefitting. You should refer to the Dasabhumi-sutra and so forth for the detailed attributes and virtues of these Levels.

Therefore the Level of All-knowing is explained as "devoted interest": Because they will thus attain all the qualities of a Tathāgata by devoted interest, that Level of Practice with Devoted Interest is the cause of the Level of All-knowing, and so the result is figuratively referred to by the cause.

Moreover, he will transcend devoted interest after a quarter [of an eon]: They will rise above the Level of Practice with Devoted Interest, the Level where they realize the lack of autonomous existence to phenomena, in one quarter of an eon. Having abandoned even [the idea of] the absence of autonomous existence to phenomena, which is the bridge of entry into the Level of Awareness, they undertake the meditative observation that their minds are unborn and unarisen from the very beginning. (42b)

If you should wonder why these states and virtues of the Level of Practice with Devoted Interest are explained after the explanation of the First Level, the Joyful One, and not in the previous section about that Level of Practice with Devoted Interest which is the entry into the absence of autonomous existence to phenomena, it is because the Joyful One is the result of the Level of Practice with Devoted Interest, for when one wishes to know what a cause is, one should first investigate what its result is. Therefore the Level of Practice with Devoted Interest is explained after it. Those stages have been explained in detail as the cause of Vairocana: the eight minds of generosity and so forth; the recourse to the various concepts concerning a self and the subsequent idea that arises of 'aloneness'; the subsequent arising of the supramundane minds; the realization that there is no autonomous existence to the individual, just the perception of the psycho-physical constituents, following the realization that the imagined selves do not exist; the primordial non-arising, the emptiness of one's mind following the realization that phenomena lack autonomous existence; and the realization that the mind of the First Level is emptiness in nature and that it is without intrinsic existence, being just sameness.

28. Then Vajrapāṇi said to the Bhagavat,
'O Lord and Saviour! If you would teach
the attributes of the minds,
these Excellent-born Ones will be encouraged,
having received much relief.'
The Bhagavat Mahā-vairocana then replied to Vajrapāṇi, 'Pay attention and listen carefully, Lord of the Secret Ones! When foolish common people abandon unwholesome actions and do what is wholesome, they will be relieved by the wholesome. When they fully know the truth of the self as it is in reality, they will be relieved, through relying on the self. When they have accepted the psycho-physical constituents and examined their essential nature, having completely abandoned dependence upon a self, they will be relieved by the lack of a self. When they have abandoned the psycho-physical constituents and abide in the perception of phenomena, they will be relieved by phenomena. When they have abandoned phenomena and abide in non-arising, they will be relieved by the lack of autonomous existence to phenomena. When they have produced the Awareness of emptiness, wherein it is known that there is nothing self-existent in the intrinsic nature of emptiness, nor in the psycho-physical constituents, the perceptual sources and elements, the perceiving subject, the perceived objects, the self, life and so forth, the phenomena and non-arising, they will be relieved by the sameness which is the intrinsic nature of all phenomena.'

Now these will be summarized by means of ***relief*** (*āśvāsa*). ***Having received much relief***: Just as one is relieved in ordinary life when one is free from the danger of bandits in fearful places on precipitous roads, likewise beings who wander here in the desolation of *saṃsāra* feel relieved when they are freed from the fear of the danger from the bandits that are emotional afflictions and karmic actions. (43a)

They fully know the truth of the self as it is in reality: This does not refer to the knowledge by insight of its real nature of emptiness, but to the correct knowledge of the nature of self as found in the mundane scriptures.

These stages refer to the perfection of the causal basis of Vairocana. But this is not the entire explanation of the perfection of cause, for in the other sections on the causal basis, the text says, '***Enlightenment has the attribute of space: it is devoid of all selective concepts. Whoever desires to realize that is called a "Bodhisattva"***' [28.3]. (44b) Those who desire that supreme Enlightenment are not only those on the First Level and so on, but also the Bodhisattvas who dwell on the Tenth level and the All Good Level who desire to realize the supreme Enlightenment. Therefore the practices of those Bodhisattvas should also be understood as the causal basis of Vairocana.

29. 'Lord of the Secret Ones! At that time, the Bodhisattva who engages in the practice of Bodhisattvas by means of the secret mantra path (123b) **will meditatively observe the chain of interdependent origination with ten similes and comprehend the secret Mantra Method. What are the ten? They are phantoms, mirages, dreams, reflections, *gandharvas'* cities, echoes, the moon in water, bubbles, magical illusions and a wheel of whirling fire.**

'Lord of the Secret Ones! Bodhisattvas who engage in the practice of Bodhisattvas by means of the secret mantra path should investigate as

follows: What is a phantom? Through the use of drugs and spells by magicians, various different things are made to appear which delight the mind and the eye, even though they have not been seen before and yet those things do not go to and fro in the ten directions. Why? Because phantoms are by nature nothing and likewise all things arise from the endeavours of those who practise the secret mantra path.

'Lord of the Secret Ones! Moreover, mirages are by nature nothing and yet they are established by the action of ideas and can be spoken about. Likewise these mantras are established merely by the action of ideas and are said to be performed.

'Lord of the Secret Ones! Moreover, in dreams one appears to abide there for a day, an hour, a minute, a second or a year and may experience many types of pleasures and pain, and yet when one awakens, nothing of it remains to be seen. Likewise this secret Mantra Method should be understood to be like a dream.

'Lord of the Secret Ones! Moreover, the arising of the attainments of the secret Mantra Method should be known to be like a reflection. For example, just as the reflection of a face arises in conjunction with a mirror and a head, so also should the accomplishment of the secret Mantra Method be understood.

'Lord of the Secret Ones! Moreover, the supernaturally produced places which occur should be viewed as a city of the *gandharvas*.

'Lord of the Secret Ones! Moreover, the sound of the secret mantras should be understood to be like an echo. (124a) **For example, just as an echo arises in dependence upon a sound, so also should this secret Mantra Method be understood.**

'Lord of the Secret Ones! Moreover, when the moon shines, its reflection is seen in water and that is called a "water-moon". Likewise, the *mantrin* is called a "knowledge-holder" (*vidyādhara*).

'Lord of the Secret Ones! Moreover, just as when rain falls, bubbles are produced, likewise one should consider the various emantions of the secret mantra attainments.

'Lord of the Secret Ones! Moreover, there are no sentient beings, no life and no creator: all things are nothing and are no more than the appearance of mere magical illusion.

'Lord of the Secret Ones! Moreover, just as when somebody holds a burning torch in his hand and whirls it around, it seems like a wheel, likewise all things arise from emptiness.'

Now this matter will be examined: It says in the text that the general attribute of the mantras is Enlightenment. Enlightenment is without self-existence, having the nature of emptiness, and is free from such perceptual images as the psycho-physical constituents, perceptual sources and elements, the perceiving subjects, perceived objects, action and activity, and yet the mantras are the Buddhas and Bodhisattvas and the sounds and letters which reveal them. They also bring about activities such as the superior, medium and inferior attainments, and the rites of Pacifying, Enriching and Destroying. So how are we to understand them, if they are thus at variance [with the attributes of Enlightenment]? The text therefore says '***Lord of the Secret Ones! At that time, the Bodhisattva who engages ... arise from emptiness***'. Though they appear to exist, phenomena on the relative level cannot withstand reasoning by logic and on the absolute level they are empty in nature. However, on the relative level, the effects of the certainty of the relationship of individual causes and results do occur, so it would be inadmissible to say that they do not exist. Thus their appearance on the relative level through the nature of emptiness is like a phantom and so forth. Likewise, although the nature of mantras, which is Enlightenment, is also emptiness on the absolute level, various results of accomplishment appear and are experienced on the relative level, by the transformational power (*adhiṣṭhāna*) of the continuum of reality and by the power of the yogin's practice. These are also explained by the examples of the phantom and so on.

30. 'Lord of the Secret Ones! This is the ground of the Mahāyāna[A], the ground of equality to that without equal, the ground of certainty, the ground of Perfect Buddhahood, the ground of entry by stages into the Mahāyāna.

'If you know this treasure,
from which various great Awarenesses arise,
you will fully know the different types
of minds of all as they really are.'

(46b) This section teaches the praises of that realization of sameness by Bodhisattvas. ***The ground of Mahāyāna***: It is the knowledge of that *bodhicitta*. The Mahāyāna is the path of the Bodhisattva, together with the result. If you know that *bodhicitta*, you will also know the sequence of the eight mundane minds and so on, up to the Level of the Joyful One, therefore it is its '***ground***'. '***That without equal***' is space, for space is without limits and so is not equal to anything whatsoever. '***The ground of equality***' is emptiness, the continuum of reality. The knowledge of intrinsic emptiness is the ground of equality with the unequal. (47a) ***The ground of certainty***: The definite and correct knowledge that phenomena are empty in nature. '***The ground of Perfect Buddhahood***' refers to the realization by the First Level *bodhicitta* that all phenomena are the same. This is not different to supreme Enlightenment and is of one taste [with it], so it is Perfect Buddhahood. ***The ground of entry by stages into the Mahāyāna***: Both the mundane minds and the higher supramundane minds, which are the causal basis of Vairocana, are contained within this First Level *bodhicitta*, and also the minds from the First Level up to the All Good Level are not different to this, so it is their ground.

A C adds: 心句 '*the ground of the mind*'.

II
THE LAYING-OUT OF THE MANDALA

1. Then Vajrapāṇi, the Lord of the Secret Ones, said to the Bhagavat, 'It is most wonderful that the Bhagavat should reveal to beings with various means and methods, in accordance with their inclinations and interest, the inconceivable continuum of reality that utterly transcends all mind levels, which the Bhagavat himself has fully realized[A]. I beg you, Bhagavat, to explain the method of the mantra practice which completely perfects the Great Mandala King Arising From the Matrix of Great Compassion, (124b) **for in future times it will bring benefit, welfare and happiness to many beings.'**

Now, having attained All-knowing Awareness, the Bhagavat Vairocana pervaded all of the Three Realms spontaneously with the configurations (*cakra)* of the Adornments of the Inexhaustible Sameness of his Body and so forth, by the power of his previous aspirations, in order to supremely liberate limitless realms of beings with that All-knowing Awareness, by various means and various methods. While that intrinsically existent Mandala (47b) is actually seen by such pure Bodhisattvas as Samantabhadra, Vajrapāṇi and so on, and is accessible to them, those configurations of the Bhagavat's Body and so on are not accessible to lower creatures. So Vajrapāṇi asks the Bhagavat to explain the transformation of those configurations of his Body and so on into the mandalas, mantras and *mudrās* for the sake of those beings.

2. Then the Bhagavat Vairocana gazed upon the assembly of all those around him and said to Vajrapāṇi, the Lord of the Secret Ones, 'Listen to this discourse which teaches the method for practising the Mandala which causes All-knowing Awareness to be fully perfected!' Then, because the Bhagavat Vairocana had not completed[B] his task with regards to the continuum of reality and because he had vowed to liberate all realms of beings without exception, all the Tathāgatas gathered together in consultation [with him], and he then entered into the *samādhi* called 'The Arising of the Matrix of Great Compassion'. As soon as the Bhagavat had entered it, Tathāgatas emerged from all parts of his Body who performed acts benefitting beings, from those at the first arousing of the intention up to those on the Tenth Level. Having come forth, they encompassed the ten directions and then they returned to take up their places within the Body of the Bhagavat.

Having become perfectly enlightened, the Bhagavat himself directly experienced the continuum of reality which is inconceivable and transcends all the levels of minds. (48a) He then manifested himself throughout all realms of beings with the configurations of his Body and so on, which cause the individual inclinations of

A C adds: 三菩提 '*the perfect Enlightenment* [*which the Bhagavat* ...]'

B C omits '*not*' and reads: 本昔誓願成就無量盡法界.... 故 '*because of his former vow to accomplish unlimited continuums of reality*'.

beings to be fulfilled according to their individual faith. Once again Vajrapāṇi asks the Bhagavat about what he sees and experiences. (48b)

The Bhagavat replies: '***Listen to this discourse which teaches the method for practising the Mandala which causes All-knowing Awareness to be fully perfected!***'. He is going to explain the practice in sixteen parts for propitiating the deities by means of the Mandala. Thus gradually, by way of the *sādhana*, the deities are to be propitiated by the practice which generates the deities, the four-membered recitation, and the purification of one's mind, and then, when one has actually accomplished the *vidyādhara* attainments and so forth, (49a) one will fully perfect All-knowing Awareness.

Practising the Mandala: The sixteen acts of drawing the Mandala and so forth.

Then because the Bhagavat Vairocana had not completed ... their places within the Body of the Bhagavat: The Bhagavat revealed the *samādhi* from which the intrinsically existent Mandala arises, for the sake of future beings, so that the Mandala Arising From Great Compassion may be drawn. The *samādhi* which he revealed was also revealed to show the way in which the Master who is to draw the Mandala Arising from Great Compassion should actualize such a *samādhi* and then draw the Mandala which depicts the details of his Body and so on, with colours upon the ground.

Continuum of reality: Suchness (*tathatā*), emptiness (*śūnyatā*), or the limits of reality (*bhūṭakoṭi*). The Bhagavat's '***task***' is to completely pervade all realms of beings with the Adornments of his Inexhaustible Body and so on, and liberate those beings into supreme Enlightenment. Yet since there still remains beings to be liberated, his task is not yet completed. ***Because he vowed to liberate all realms of beings***: (49b) As the completion of his task regarding the continuum of reality remains unfinished, for when the Bhagavat was previously engaged in the Bodhisattva practice he made a vow to liberate all beings without remainder upon his attainment of Enlightenment. ***All the Tathāgatas gathered together in consultation***: The Buddhas of the past, present and future, are identical in their accumulations[1], *dharmakāyas* and benefitting of beings[2], so this shows that all the Buddhas teach with one voice. Secondly, '***all the Tathāgatas gathered together in consultation***' means that they all had actualized the continuum of reality, Suchness. Thirdly, this is also mentioned in order to humble arrogant beings in the future, and to prompt beings who have not made enquiries to question and enquire of gurus and spiritual friends. If even the All-knowing Tathāgatas deliberate with others and then teach the Dharma, then we ourselves should consult with others when we are attempting something. ***The* samādhi *called 'The Arising of the Matrix of Great Compassion'*** (*Mahā-karuṇā-garbhodbhava*): This can be interpreted either as the Matrix of Great Compassion arising from that *samādhi*, or as the *samādhi* which arises from that Matrix of Great Compassion. (50a)

3. Then the Bhagavat said to the Bodhisattva Vajrapāṇi, 'Vajrapāṇi! Listen carefully to the laying out of the Mandala! To begin with, the Master should have his mind fixed upon *bodhicitta*, be endowed with insight, be firm[A], be compassionate, be skilled in the arts, be ever wise in the methods of the Perfection of Insight, know the differences between the Three Ways, be skilled in the true nature of mantras, know the inclinations of beings, have

A C omits 'be firm'.

trust in the Buddhas and Bodhisattvas, have the initiation and permission to perform the task of drawing the Mandala[A], be strenuous and decisive in the practice of the mantras, be well born, be skilled in practice, have attained the union of opposites and be established in *bodhicitta*. (125a) **Lord of the Secret Ones! Such a Master is a son of the Jina, and is praised by Buddhas and Bodhisattvas. Lord of the Secret Ones, it is fitting for others to call him a Master.'**

After emerging from that *samādhi*, the Bhagavat begins to explain the Mandala to Vajrapāṇi. The explanation of the drawing of the Mandala should be considered in three parts – the cause, its nature and the result. The cause is the Master, its nature is the actual marking out and the drawing of the Mandala, and the result is the entry of the trainees and their initiation. Now as the main cause of the drawing of the Mandala is the Master, the Master's attributes will first be explained. In the explanation of his attributes there are the attributes of the qualities which make him a Master, those which accomplish him as a Master, and his special attribute.

The attributes which make him a Master are '***having his mind fixed upon* bodhicitta**' and so on, the attributes which accomplish him as a Master are '***having the initiation and permission to perform the rites of drawing the Mandala***' and so on, and his special attribute is to be '***established in* bodhicitta**'. These also comprise the qualities of body, speech and mind, and should be linked with them as appropriate.

His mind is fixed upon* bodhicitta**: He has dissolved all phenomena such as the psycho-physical constituents, perceptual elements and sources into emptiness. ***Endowed with insight: There are two types of insight: innate insight, and the insight born of hearing, pondering and cultivation. He has either one of these as appropriate. (50b) ***Compassionate***: Compassion is the desire to extricate beings from suffering. There is also innate compassion and created compassion. He has both of these. ***Skilled in the arts***: Although there are, generally speaking, many mundane crafts, reference is being made in this section to skill in drawing the Mandala and in the branches of the offerings. ***Ever wise in the methods of the Perfection of Insight***: He is skilled in both absolute and relative methods. The absolute one refers to skill in the method of the Perfection of Insight, the meditative observation of the intrinsic emptiness of all phenomena, which are from the very beginning unborn and unarisen. The relative one refers to skill in engaging in the Perfection of Generosity and so on, in a manner wherein the three elements of the deed[3] are completely pure, without attachment, when one engages in the Perfections following that meditative observation of emptiness. ***Know the differences between the Three Ways***: This refers to his skill in distinguishing the attributes of the Śrāvaka Way, which is the realization of the impermanence, suffering and the absence of autonomous existence in the psycho-physical constituents, perceptual elements and sources, following the realization of the absence of autonomous existence in the individual; the Pratyekabuddha Way which is the realization that these psycho-physical constituents, perceptual elements and sources have also the nature of interdependent origination; and the Mahāyāna which is the realization that all phenomena are from

A C reads this as '*have the permission and initiation, be conversant with the drawing of the mandala*'.

the very beginning unborn and unarisen. ***Be skilled in the true nature of mantras***: The general definition of the true nature of mantras is *bodhicitta*, and to be skilled in that is to be skilled in the mantras, the seed-syllables and the *samādhis*. To be skilled in the mantras is to be skilled in uttering the words of the mantras, and in distinguishing the nature of the various *mudrās*. To be skilled in the seed-syllables is to be knowledgable about the individual seed-syllable essences of the deities, and about their *samādhi* gates and functions. (51a) To be skilled in the *samādhis* is to be skilled in entering *samādhi* and laying out the mandalas of earth, water and so on, and the accomplishment of their rites. ***Know the inclinations of beings***: This refers to the inclinations of the trainees, but it does not mean knowing them through knowledge of the minds of others[4]. Instead he is wise in [ascertaining] what the trainees ought to do in service of the wrathful and peaceful deities, and what they ought to do for the superior, medium or inferior attainments, by ascertaining the [appropriate] practice and method for the trainees by means of distinguishing their group of mantra [deities]. ***Have the initiation and permission to perform the task of drawing the Mandala: Initiation***: This refers to the bestowal of power with the water from a jar adorned with perfumes, flowers, medicines and jewels, in the Initiation Mandala. ***Permission***: The permission given verbally after that initiation with the words 'You may draw the Mandala and engage in the *sādhana*'. ***Skilled in practice***: Skilled in the practices of the *sādhana* and the rites of pacification and so forth. ***Established in* bodhicitta**: He is able to abide in the non-conceptualizing *samādhi* of emptiness. (51b) ***A son of the Jina***: He is born from the very nature of the Jina. The Jina is the Buddha, whose very nature is the continuum of reality. One who is born from the very nature of the Jina is one who has arisen through devoted interest in emptiness, which is the continuum of reality.

4. 'Furthermore, he may see beings who are suitable to become receptacles for the teachings and who are free from faults, who have much trust and firm faith, and who rejoice in benefitting others, so upon making the acquaintance of such a trainee, the Master should call him, without having been asked, out of a desire to benefit him, saying:

> **"You are a receptacle for the great method,**
> **therefore, child, I shall reveal to you**
> **the ritual of the Mahāyāna Mantra Method!**
> **The Perfect Buddhas of the past,**
> **likewise of the future, and the Lords**
> **who have appeared in the present,**
> **who abide for the welfare of creatures,**
> **they have all been acquainted**
> **with this excellent and good mantra ritual.**
> **Like the Hero under the Bodhi-tree[A],**
> **they have attained the All-knowing Awareness**
> **which is without perceptual form.**
> **The mantra practice[B] is unequalled:**

A C: 坐無相菩提 '*seated in Enlightenment devoid of attributes*'

B C: 勢 '*the energy* [*of mantras is* ...]'.

With it, the Protector Śākyasiṃha
overcame the great host
of the inexhaustible army of Māra.
Therefore, to attain All-knowing Awareness,
child, you should do it with understanding[5]!"
With a compassionate heart,
he should praise it many times.'

Now, such a Master should investigate which trainees should be introduced into the Mandala. The investigation of those trainees is done by means of their intrinsic qualities and their created qualities. (52a) ***Free from faults***: Without any evil. How is the Master to see whether there is any evil in the mental stream of the trainee? This does not mean that he actually sees whether evil is absent from the mental stream of the trainee, but that he sees whether the trainee engages in the path of the ten unwholesome deeds which are the cause of evil, and thereby he can see whether evil is present or absent. ***Much trust***: It is to have much trust that this is thus and no other is, regarding the qualities of the Buddha's virtues such as the Levels and the Perfections, by means of hearing, pondering and cultivation, even though he has not yet directly understood them and brought them into being himself. ***Firm faith***: To believe in the reliability of the Three Jewels and the Mantra Method.

5. **'When he knows the trainee is firm,**
the Master should search out a good site.
Pure and pleasing places[A] with water,
having fruit and flowers,
these are praised by all Buddhas
for the task of drawing the Mandala.
Wherever there is much running water
enlivened by geese and swans,
there should the discerning *mantrin*
draw the Mandala Arising From Compassion.
Whatever areas were frequented
by Buddhas, Pratyekabuddhas,
and the victorious Śrāvakas:
these are always praised by the Sage.
Or in various other places:
fine temples and hermitages,
elegant houses and towers,
ponds, (125b) **and beautiful groves,**
stūpas, palaces[B], cow-pens,
valleys where running water gathers,
and all holy places,
or even in a deserted house[C].

A C: 山林 '*mountains and woods*' instead of '*places*'.
B C: 火神祠 '*shrines for Agni*' instead of '*palaces*'.
C C: 仙得道處 '*places where hermits attain the path*' instead of '*deserted houses*'.

In such places he should carefully
draw the Mandala,
out of a desire to benefit the trainees,
or in any other pleasing place
wherever it is suitable, he should draw it.'

6. 'Lord of the Secret Ones! Then, in order to purify the site, he should clear away stones, broken pottery, pebbles[A], hair, chaff, cinders, ashes, thorns, bones, bits of wood and splinters. He should remove ants, worms and insects. Such a place from which all impediments have been removed is pleasing to the deities.'

Having ascertained the suitability of the trainees in the above manner, the Master should investigate places where he can draw the Mandala for them. These can be pleasing because of the qualities of the place itself, because they have been frequented by the Noble Ones, because they are enjoyed by gods and men, or because the *mantrin* himself is inspired by it.

(53b) ***In order to purify the site***: The purification is twofold: the inner and the outer. Therefore there are also two types of Master: those who have interest in the Profound and Extensive, and those who rely on cognitive objects. The Master who has interest in the Profound and Extensive has cultivated *bodhicitta*, so he realizes that the phenomena of external imperfections are unborn and unarisen from the very beginning, so they are cleansed by the inner purification of his mind. Therefore, although it is not necessary for him to clear away external impediments, he should investigate the sites without being attached to them, in order to accommodate the minds of the trainees. Therefore, the Master who has interest in the Profound and the Extensive should purify the site both internally and externally. The Master who relies on cognitive objects should purify the external site because he has not repeatedly cultivated *bodhicitta*. Internal purification is to repeatedly cultivate *bodhicitta*, and the external purification is to '***clear away stones, broken pottery***' and so forth.

7. 'Then on a day when the calendar, constellations, planets, hours and minutes are auspicious, at a time with good omens early in the morning[B], the Master should make salutations to all the Tathāgatas, and recite these two verses calling on the Earth Goddess, Pṛthivī:
"O Goddess! You are a witness
to the Levels and Perfections,
the special methods of practice
of all the Protector Buddhas.
Just as the Protector Śākyasiṃha
overcame the armies of Māra,
Likewise I shall be victorious over Māra
and draw a mandala here[6]!"

A C: 碎瓦破器髑髏 '[*stones*], *smashed tiles, broken pottery, skulls*, [*hair* ...].
B C: 於食前時 '*before breakfast*'

Then touching the ground with his hand,
he should call on her many times;
kneeling on the ground
he should offer flowers and perfumes.
When he made these offerings, the *mantrin*
should then salute all the Tathāgatas,
and then with these rituals
the wise one should purify the ground.'

8. Then Vajrapāṇi bowed at the feet of the Bhagavat and asked him:
'Buddhas[A] are without perceptual forms,
and reside in the *dharmakāya*;
If the Dharma they reveal is
without attributes, unconditioned, unequalled,
then why, O Great Hero, is
this ritual with perceptual form
taught for the mantra practice?
It does not accord with reality!' (126a)

***Buddhas are without perceptual form*:** They are without the perceptual forms of a perceiving subject and perceived objects.

9. When he had spoken thus,
the Bhagavat Vairocana
replied to Vajrapāṇi:
'Listen to the attributes of the Dharma:
the Dharma is free from concepts,
and devoid of all imagining;
All workings of the mind and its contents
are abandoned in it[B].
The Dharma which I have realized
has arisen[C] from space,
but this is unknown to the stupid
who wrongly conceive of their environments.
Objects, time, perceptual forms and so on
are asserted by those who are enveloped in darkness.
So in order for them to be helped,
I teach this ritual.
But there are no objects, no time,
no doer nor done,
all phenomena are without existence,
phenomena are just ephemeral[D]!

A C: 佛法 '*Buddhas and the Dharma*'.
B C: 若淨 '... *if it is purified*'.
C C: 究竟如 '*its limits are like space*'.
D C: 彼一切諸法唯住於實相 '*all these phenomena merely abide in their true aspect*' instead of '*all phenomena are without existence, phenomena are just ephemeral*'.

Moreover, Lord of the Secret Ones,
in future ages, there will appear
beings who have weak minds,
who are confused by mere actions[A],
and who are attached to material things[B].
Since they do not understand this method,
these confused beings expect results
with wholesome and unwholesome attributes,
from objects, time and activities.
O Great Being! For their sakes
expound this ritual.'

Though the Buddha explains these omens of the calendar, constellations and so forth, the intrinsic nature of the mantras, which on the absolute level is *bodhicitta*, is without perceptual forms and hence transcends them. However, although the mandalas, the *sādhana* and the members of the mantra practice have perceptual forms on the relative level, they do bring about beneficial effects. But these perceptual forms of the calendar, constellations and so forth are at variance with the absolute level and also they do not even bring about beneficial effects even on the relative level. So why does the Bhagavat explain these things with perceptual forms? In reply, the Bhagavat indicates what the attributes of the Dharma are on the absolute level and then explains that although its attributes are like that on the absolute level, it is also appropriate to describe things with perceptual forms in order to guide beings in the future, since they will not comprehend the absolute method. Moreover, those beings are of two types: those who are attached to the existence of things, and those who are attached to the non-existence of things. Those who are attached to the existence of things are taught and instructed with such things as calendars, time, environment and so on, and those who are attached to the non-existence of things will also be dissuaded from that through being instructed by means of such things. (55a)

10. 'Lord of the Secret Ones! Having firmly trodden down the site at one of the suitable places that have been mentioned, the Master should smear it with clean cow's urine mixed with cow's dung that has not fallen to the ground. Then this mantra should be recited while sprinkling water : *NAMAḤ SAMANTA-BUDDHĀNĀM APRATISAME GAGANASAME*[C] *SAMANTĀNUGATE PRAKṚTI-VIŚUDDHE DHARMADHĀTU-VIŚODHANE SVĀHĀ.* (Salutations to all the Buddhas! O that which is unequalled! That which is the same as space! That which is present everywhere! That which is naturally pure! That which purifies the continuum of reality! Svāhā!)

'Then the *mantrin* should arise,
and in the middle, imagine
myself upon a white lotus throne,

A C: 以癡愛自蔽 '*who envelop themselves with confused infatuation*'.
B C adds 恒樂諸斷常 '*forever delighting in the permanent and the impermanent*'.
C T: '*gagana*', omitting '*same*'.

with topknot and crown[A],
spreading out in all directions
light rays of various colours.
Then the wise one should imagine
the four perfect Buddhas in their places.
The Tathāgata Ratnaketu
should be imagined like the rising sun.
In the south, the Victorious Hero
called Saṃkusuma-rāja,
who shines golden in colour, (126b)
he is in the *samādhi* that overcomes evils[B],
In the north, there is Akṣobhya,
who resides in the *samādhi* free from ills.
In the west, there is Amitābha[C].
These five Jinas should thus
be imagined, and then the *mantrin*
seated in the central place of the Jinas,
should completely take possession of the site,
with the all-accomplishing mantra
of the great Lord Acala,
or else of Trailokya-vijaya.
In the centre, five circles
should be made with pure sandalwood.
The first is mine[D],
the second is that of all the Protectors,
the third should be made the same as that,
without hesitation, and is that of the Mother,
the fourth is that of Padmapāṇi,
and the fifth is for Vajrapāṇi.
The sixth, that of the Lord Acala,
should be carefully laid out immediately outside.
Having brought the Tathāgatas to mind,
the *mantrin* should offer them flowers and incense,
and entering into *samādhi*,
he should reverently utter these words:
"Pay heed to me, all you Lords
who have compassionate natures!
Please take possession of this site
with your sons, after noon tomorrow!"
Having uttered these words,
he should recite this mantra:

A C: 髮髻以爲冠 '*with a crown formed from his topknot*'.
B C: 垢 '*impurities*' (*mala*).
C C: 西方仁勝者是名無量壽 '*In the west, there is the benevolent Jina called Amitāyus*'.
D C: 中第一我身第二諸救世 '*The first in the centre is my body, the second is that of the Protectors*'.

***NAMAḤ SAMANTA-BUDDHĀNĀṂ SARVA-TATHĀGATĀDHIṢṬHĀNĀDHIṢṬHITE ACALE VIMALE SMARAṆI PRAKṚTI-PARIŚUDDHE SVĀHĀ.* (Salutations to all the Buddhas! O She who is transformed by the empowerment of all the Tathāgatas! She who is unmoving! She who is unsullied! She who remembers! She who is pure by nature! Svāhā!)'**

Seven days beforehand, the site where the Mandala is to be drawn should be requested from the visible and the invisible ones. Here, the visible ones are such people as the king and so on, and the invisible ones are the mundane gods, *yakṣas, rākṣasas* and so forth. If one goes ahead and draws the Mandala without requesting the site from the gods and so on, then such mundane gods will be harmed by the radiant glare of the wrathful deities of the Mandala, and if they are thus harmed, they will be a great obstruction to the *sādhana*. Secondly, if the Master draws the Mandala while harming them, he is not being compassionate. Therefore, in order that he might be given the site by them, he first announces this and requests the gods for it, and then those gods will take heed and go elsewhere, so no fault will be incurred. If he also requests the site from such people as the king and so on, disputations will not arise later.

Having first requested them for the site, he should investigate the site, in the appropriate way as mentioned above, three days before the subsequent drawing of the Mandala, and then he should follow the procedure for seizing the site thus: first a disc should be made on the site with pure [cow's] urine mixed with cow's dung that has not fallen to the ground. Next the site should be safeguarded with the mantra. Then all obstacles should be cleared from the precincts. Following that, a perfumed mandala should be made there, twelve inches square. Then standing, the *mantrin* should imagine the Buddhas in the sky in the centre of that mandala. Furthermore, he should make the *Mudrā* of the Three Samayas, imagining [the deities of] the intrinsically existent Mandala who have been gathered together. (55b) The *mantrin* who stands and imagines is the one who reveals what is not present, because he imagines the Five Buddhas in the sky. Then making offerings to them with perfumes and flowers, he should take possession of the site with the Mantra of Acala, or of Trailokya-vijaya, or any other one that is suitable, in the presence of the Buddhas. He then entreats the Buddhas to come with their Children, on the evening when the trainees are to be lead into the Mandala.

Then the *mantrin* should lie down to sleep on the west side, with his mind directed towards Enlightenment and with compassion, so that he may have a dream. There are three types of dreams: superior, middling and inferior. If he sees Bodhisattvas, that is inferior; if he sees Buddhas, that is middling; and if he dreams of those Buddhas joyfully exhorting him, saying 'Son! This is excellent! Draw the Mandala without delay!', this should be known as the superior type of dream.

This procedure is also mentioned in the Tantra itself, but I have laid it out here in the sequence of acts because they are out of order in the Tantra.

11. **'Then having arisen, the *mantrin***
with a compassionate heart,
should place himself on the west side,
and with a pure inner nature,

he should think of *bodhicitta*,
and like that he should go to sleep.
Then the *mantrin* will see a dream,
either of renowned Bodhisattvas,
or of Buddhas and the Blessed Ones,
who exhort him to undertake
the task of drawing the Mandala,
in order to benefit beings;
or else they say to him:
"O Great Being! It is excellent!
You should quickly draw the Mandala!"
or anything else suitable to encourage him.'

12. **'Then on the next day,**
he should gather together
faithful trainees of noble families.
They should have trust (127a) **in the Three Jewels,**
and have profound understanding[A]**,**
great enthusiasm, keep the moral code,
be patient and be without jealousy,
be steadfast and firm in their vows.
They are suitable whether they have ten
or eight, or seven, or five,
or one, two, four or more [of these],
so there is no need to investigate [further],
but they should be accepted.'

This section deals with the investigative selection of the trainees. For this there are the special (*viśeṣa-lakṣaṇa*) attributes, the attributes of the different types (*prabheda*) and the ordinary (*sāmānya*) attributes. Of these, the special attributes are those described with the words, '***faithful disciples of noble families***' and so on. The attributes of the different types will be explained later[7], and the ordinary attributes are all the others apart from those mentioned and listed above.

Below, the text says, '***Furthermore, the Master who has great compassion, should just vow to liberate all realms of beings without remainder, and he should accept countless beings in order that it may become the cause of* bodhicitta**'. (56a) Regarding those trainees, when the Master has introduced into the Mandala those who are skilled in the Tantra and who have repeatedly cultivated *bodhicitta*, he should initiate them for the *sādhana*. Those who are skilled in the Tantra, but have not yet repeatedly cultivated *bodhicitta*, should be made to cultivate *bodhicitta* and then be initiated. As for those who neither know the Tantra to begin with, nor have repeatedly cultivated *bodhicitta* and who will not comprehend the Tantra or cultivate *bodhicitta*, they are the ordinary trainees. They should not be initiated either time, but they can be accepted into the Mandala so that it may become a seed for *bodhicitta* in them.

A C: 以嚴身 '*adorn their bodies* [*with profound understanding*]'.

13. Then Vajrapāṇi asked the Bhagavat: 'What is the name of this mandala? Why is it called a mandala?'

The Bhagavat replied: 'Lord of the Secret Ones! This mandala is the source of the Buddhas. "*Maṇḍa*" means essence and "*la*" means perfect. Because there is nothing higher than this essence, it is therefore called a "*maṇḍala*". Lord of the Secret Ones! Moreover, this extensive mandala is called "That which Arises from the Matrix of Great Compassion", because indefinite realms of beings will be fully protected by it. It is the transformation of the supreme and perfect Enlightenment fully accomplished by Tathāgatas through countless eons. Lord of the Secret Ones, therefore you should understand likewise concerning this discourse. Tathāgatas do not become perfectly awakened to Enlightenment for the sake of one being, or for the sake of two beings, or for the sake of three, but these Masters of Great Compassion become perfectly awakened to Enlightenment in order to completely save unlimited realms of beings. They teach the Dharma according to the inclinations of the many different realms of beings. Lord of the Secret Ones! While those who have not repeatedly practised the Mahāyāna will not have the least bit of joy or faith arise in their hearts if they see or hear this method of the mantra practice, Lord of the Secret Ones, whosoever has repeatedly practised the accomplishment of the limitless gates of the method of the Mahāyāna mantra practice previously is a Vajrasattva, (127b) **and it is for his sake that this number [of qualifications] has been made.'**

Now Vajrapāṇi questions the Bhagavat about the name of the Mandala and why it is called a '*maṇḍala*'. (56b) The first question is about the Mandala, so that it may be revealed in a perceptible form, and the second question concerns the etymology of the word '*maṇḍala*'.

***This Mandala is the source of the Buddhas*:** Because it is like the birthplace of the Buddhas, for when Buddhas arise then the qualities of the Buddha's virtues also arise and the benefitting of beings will come about. In the same way, the qualities of the Buddhas arise from this Mandala and the benefitting of beings will also come about, because immediately *bodhicitta* is generated, one will have in stages the superior attainments and so forth and carry out the rites of Pacifying and so on, and finally it causes one to become a Buddha.

"Maṇḍa" ***means essence and*** **"la"** ***means perfect*:** This is like the essence (*maṇḍa*) of butter or the core of sandalwood, which are the most excellent or best parts. Just as it is possible that some of the essence of butter or core of sandalwood is not perfect or is deficient, so is it thus not possible that it could be the same in this case? Although it is indeed like those essential parts, the word 'perfect' (*la*) shows that it is superior to them. 'Perfect' means sufficient or completely perfect. In what way is the essence of this Mandala sufficient or perfect? Having accumulated a mass of merit and awareness during countless eons, the Bhagavat fully perfected such Buddha qualities as the Ten Strengths, the Ten Fearlessnesses and so on, and was directly enlightened to the supreme Enlightenment. That is the most excellent essence. That excellence is fully accomplished and unchanging because it need not be sought elsewhere but is fulfilled by that. That perfect awakening to supreme Enlightenment, the unchanging complete accomplishment, became the configurations of the Adornments of his Inexhaustible Body, Speech and Mind by the power of his previous aspirations and so on, and they were transformed into this Mandala. Therefore this Mandala is said to be fulfilled by this essence. (57a)

Moreover, this extensive Mandala is called "That which Arises from the Matrix of Great Compassion", because indefinite realms of beings will be fully protected by it*:** The introduction of countless realms of beings into this Mandala by the power of his Great Compassion is the cause of supreme Enlightenment, so it says they will be fully protected by it. ***"That which Arises from the Matrix of Great Compassion"[8]: This Mandala arises from his Great Compassion, for after the Bhagavat attained All-knowing Awareness, this Mandala of the Adornments of the Inexhaustible Body and so on, arose by the power of his Great Compassion. ***Matrix*:** The source. That Great Compassion is the source of the Mandala. Furthermore, it can also mean that Great Compassion arises from this Mandala, because the qualities of the Buddha virtues such as Great Compassion arise from it, leading to the attainment of All-knowing Awareness. ***It is the transformation of the supreme and perfect Enlightenment, fully accomplished by the Tathāgata through countless eons*:** This shows that this Mandala and no other is the array and transformation of that same supreme Enlightenment attained by the Bhagavat after accumulating a mass of merit and awareness through countless eons into the mantra deities, the *mudrās* and the mantra letters. (57b)

Lord of the Secret Ones! While those who have not repeatedly practised the Mahāyāna ... of the Mahāyāna mantra practice*:** There are two types of Bodhisattvas: (58a) those who engage in the practice of the Perfections, and those who engage in the practice of the Mantra Method. The Bodhisattvas who follow the practice of the Perfections also engage in the Mantra Method, and the Bodhisattvas who follow the practice of Mantra Method also engage in the Perfections. So there some who mainly engage in the practice of the Mantra Method with the Perfections as a subsidiary, and others who mainly engage in the Perfections with the Mantra Method as a subsidiary. But even though there are thus two modes of practice, they are one in having the attributes of the Mahāyāna. Any beings who have not entered into the Mahāyāna in a previous life, by means of hearing, pondering and cultivation and have not exerted themselves, will not have any faith or be joyful, even if they do hear the teachings of the practice of the Mantra Method or see the mandalas and so forth. Those who have previously accustomed themselves to the practice of the Perfections and the practice of the Mantra Method, will have faith in both of them, so one who has accustomed himself to the practice of the Mantra Method will be joyful and have faith if he hears about or sees the Perfections. Also one who has accustomed himself to the practice of the Perfections will be joyful and have faith if he sees or hears about the mantra practice. Therefore, the text says, 'whoever has repeatedly practised the sādhana of accomplishment of the limitless gates of the methods of the Mahāyāna mantra practice***'. Hence those who have accustomed themselves thus to the methods of the Mahāyāna mantra practice will have faith in this method of mantra practice and will be suitable receptacles for it, but the others will not. ***They are Vajrasattvas*:** The minds of those beings who have repeatedly practised this kind of Mahāyāna are very stable, (58b) and not distracted by heretics and demons, so their minds are vajra-like[9] and they are therefore Vajrasattvas.

14. 'Furthermore, the Master who has great compassion should just vow to liberate all realms of beings without remainder and he should accept beings without limits, in order that that may become the cause of *bodhicitta*.'

15. 'Then calling them, he should make the trainees take refuge in the Three Jewels. He should also explain to them the evils which should not be committed. Then he should give them incense, flowers and so forth. He should also make them accept the Discipline of the Awareness without Obscurations in the three times[A].

'After they have been made to accept this,
the *mantrin* then gives them tooth-sticks,
Equipoised with one-pointed minds,
they should be made to face the east or the north.
Then they should bite the tooth-sticks
made of good quality *udumbara* or *aśvattha*
protected and smeared with flowers, perfume and so on.
Those who are suitable or unsuitable as recipients
should be distinguished from the cast down tooth-sticks.
Then with equipoised mind,
he should carefully tie a thrice-knotted thread
onto the left arms of the trainees.
Then, so that these faultless trainees,
who have thus been received,
should have firm intentions,
the Master should encourage them thus:
"Illustrious Ones! Today you will acquire
an unequalled acquisition,
because, O Great Ones,
all the Jinas with their Sons
have received and borne
you all into this teaching.
Therefore tomorrow
you will be born into the Mahāyāna[10]!"
If in dreams they see
temples, fine groves,
various kinds of beautiful houses,
likewise pinnacles,
swords, wish-fulfilling gems,
parasols and various flowers,
beautiful women dressed in white,
comely relatives and children[B],
books, (128a) and also brahmins[C],
Buddhas, Pratyekabuddhas,
and the victorious Śrāvakas,

A C has this portion in verse.
B C inserts 群牛豐犉乳 '*herds of cattle and bounteous milch cows*'.
C C omits '*brahmins*' and reads: 淨無垢 '*pure without taints*'.

mighty Bodhisattvas,
or of the attainment of results,
the crossing of lakes and seas,
or else auspicious pleasing words
from the sky, announcing
the arising of the desired results,
then such dreams as these
are divined to be auspicious.
The wise one should know that
dreams opposite to these are bad.
"O you fine trainees! In the morning,
you should recount all to me!"
Having commanded them thus,
the Master should also explain the Dharma.
"This most excellent and glorious Path
is the great source of the Mahāyāna:
Since you are progressing along it,
you will become Tathāgatas,
self-arisen, endowed with great fortune[A],
shrines for all the world[B].
It transcends existence and non-existence,
and is pure like space.
Its[C] profundity is beyond the ken
of all logicians and it is unlocalized[D].
It is free from all proliferations
though it is elaborated by proliferations;
If you abide in this method,
you will attain this most excellent Way
which is devoid of actions and activities[E]
and does not rely upon the two Truths[11]." '

This section explains the procedure for accepting the trainees the evening before the Mandala is to be drawn, and there are nine parts to this: the confession of failings, the taking of refuge, causing them to accept the Discipline of the Awareness without Obscurations in the three times, the offering of flowers and incense, causing them to bite the tooth-sticks, the binding of the thread on their arms and protecting them, the generation of enthusiasm, having them see dreams, and the explaining of the Dharma to them. Although these topics also appear later in the Tantra, you should understand in this way the actual sequence of actions to be done.

They should be made to '***take refuge***', for some of them may by chance have taken refuge previously by means of the *Pratimokṣa* Code[12] and so on, (59a) but they should be made to take refuge again. If they have already taken refuge before, they would

A C: 大龍 '*great nāgā*' (*mahā-nāga*), error for '*mahā-bhāga*'?
B Reading taken from C and Skt. T has '*who know all worlds*'.
C C: 諸法 '[*The profundity*] *of all phenomena*'.
D C: 無含藏 '*without any substratum*' (**anālaya*)
E C: 作業妙無比 '*whose actions and activities are quite without equal*'.

have only taken refuge with eight venerable persons of the Saṅgha. Although the Buddha and the Dharma in which they take refuge here are the same as when they took refuge before, the Saṅgha is not the same, because one should especially take refuge with the noble irreversible Bodhisattvas. Also it is because the others, who have not yet taken refuge must be made to take refuge for the first time, and also those who have previously taken refuge, should be made to take refuge again here in order to make them steadfast.

***He should also explain to them the evils which should not be committed*:** Because they should undertake not to do again now, or in the future, those evils previously committed which they have confessed. If it is acceptable for them to undertake not to do such things again now or in the future, what is the point of confessing those that they have already done? Because if they can see that there is no virtue in the evils previously done by them and confess them, then at the time of their death, the phenomena related to the evils they have done will not be actualized. Here the confession of faults should be done before taking refuge in the Three Jewels. Why? Because one who has confessed his faults and made himself pure is suitable to take refuge.

***He should give them flowers, incense and so forth*:** This should be done after the Discipline of the Awareness without Obscurations in the three times has been accepted. Why? By accepting that Discipline after having confessed his faults and having taken refuge, the trainee will become a suitable receptacle and an appropriate recipient for offerings, so he should then be offered flowers and incense.

***He should make them accept the Discipline of the Awareness without Obscurations in the three times*:** The Awareness without Obscurations in the three times is the All-knowing Awareness. Since All-knowing Awareness has the attribute of being devoid of the obscurations of the emotional afflictions and wrong understanding, one sees the real object without any obscuration or obstruction, in all times past, present and future. (59b) The discipline by which one abandons the path of the ten unwholesome actions in order to attain that Awareness is called 'The Discipline of the Awareness without Obscurations in the three times'. That Discipline will also be explained in detail below, with the distinctions of the relative and absolute types.

***After they have been made to accept this, the* mantrin *then gives them tooth-sticks ... from the cast down tooth-sticks*:** This is done in order to purify them, in order to accept and accommodate trainees when they are to fast from the next day in the manner of the mundane [practices] and should bite the tooth-sticks[13] that evening, and also in order to see the omens concerning which attainments the trainees are suitable receptacles for according to the direction in which the tooth-sticks point when they are cast down. As for the directions in which the tooth-sticks point, if its tip points towards the trainee, then he is a suitable receptacle for the swift attainment of the most excellent attainment. If the tip of the tooth-stick points to the west, he will be a suitable receptacle for the rite of Subduing. If the tip points to the east, he will be a suitable receptacle for the most excellent attainment and the rite of Enriching. If the tip of the tooth-stick points to the south, he will be a suitable receptacle for the accomplishment of the rite of Destroying. If he is facing north and the tooth-stick points towards him, he will be a suitable receptacle for the swift attainment of medium attainments. If the tip of the tooth-stick points northwards, he will accomplish the rite of Pacifying. If it points north-east, he will accomplish both Pacifying and Enriching. (60a) If it points south-east, he will accomplish Destroying. If it points south-west, he will accomplish the rites of driving away, drying up and so on. If it points north-west, he will accomplish the rites concerning *yakṣiṇī*[14] and so on. If the bottom of the tooth-stick sticks in the ground and the tip points up to the sky, he will accomplish sky-travelling. If it points upwards, he will become accomplished as a *vidyādhara*, and if it points downwards, he will be a suitable receptacle for the accomplishment of travelling below the ground. This is all explained in detail in the *Guhya-sāmānya-tantra* and so forth.

Although the trainees with the attributes previously explained should see the omens of the tooth-sticks, it is not necessary to distinguish what the omens are in the case of the ordinary trainees because even if they do have such omens from the tooth-sticks, they will not be able to apply themselves to those attainments and so forth.

***He should carefully tie a thrice-knotted thread onto the left arms of the trainees*:** The Master should empower each knot of each thread with the Mantra of Acala or Trailokya-vijaya as appropriate, and he ties them himself onto the left forearm of the trainees in order to protect them.

If in dreams you see ... he should also explain the Dharma*:** Having thus encouraged them [with the above verse], the Master should indicate these dream omens to the trainees, and they should be made to relate to the Master later which of these they saw. Also among these omens there are three types: those coming from the ground below, those coming from the sky, and those coming from the Noble ones. These should be viewed as indicating superior, medium and inferior attainment. Moreover, these three should also each be divided into three parts: upper, middle and lower. From 'temples***' to '***brahmins***' arise from the ground. From '***Buddhas***' to '***Bodhisattvas***' are the Noble Ones. From '***the attainment of results***' to '***the arising of the desired results***' are the omens that arise from the sky. Of those, the inferior omens arising from the ground are '***temples***' to '***pinnacles***', the medium ones arising from the ground are '***parasols***' to '***brahmins***', and the superior ones arising from the ground are '***swords and wish-fulfilling gems***'. The superior omen of the Noble Ones is '***Buddhas***', the medium ones are '***Bodhisattvas***' and '***Pratyekabuddhas***', and the inferior one is '***Śrāvakas***'. The inferior omen from the sky is '***attainment of results***', the medium ones are '***crossing lakes and seas***', and the superior ones are '***auspicious, pleasing words***'.

So that they may see dreams, it is fitting that the special trainees should be made to sleep near the place where the Mandala is to be drawn. (61b)

16. Then the Vajradhara Niḥprapañca-pratiṣṭha said to the Bhagavat, 'Bhagavat! Please explain the Discipline of the Awareness without Obscurations in the three times, which makes the Buddhas and Bodhisattvas joyful if a being dwells therein.'

Then the Bhagavat replied to the Vajradhara Niḥprapañca-pratiṣṭha, 'Well-born son! Listen carefully concerning this discipline which unites body, speech and mind, which is unconcerned with all phenomena and free from activity. What is it? It is to completely give oneself to the Buddhas and Bodhisattvas. (128b) Why is that? Because whoever completely gives himself, gives three things. What are those three things that he gives? His body, speech and mind. Therefore, well-born son, the Bodhisattva should uphold the discipline of body, speech and mind. Why is that? Because Bodhisattvas

do not uphold the training without completely giving their bodies, speech and minds.'

Now the Discipline of the Awareness without Obscurations in the three times that was mentioned previously will be explained in detail. The Vajradhara Niḥprapañca-pratiṣṭha asks the Bhagavat to explain about that Discipline, which causes the Buddhas (62a) and Bodhisattvas to become joyful and you to attain prosperity and happiness, if you abide therein.

Unites body, speech and mind: The body, speech and mind enter into emptiness at the same time, and having thus become empty in nature, they are no longer perceived as objects. Therefore attachment, that to which one is attached and that which becomes attached, also cannot be perceived as objects. Because they lack reality in this manner, the body, speech and mind are unable to do evil, and that is the Discipline. ***Unconcerned with all phenomena:*** Body, speech and mind do not act as the generative causes of all such phenomena as the psycho-physical constituents, the perceptual elements and sources, and so they are said to be disciplined because they do not function as those generative causes. This shows the absolute Discipline. Whoever gives his body, speech and mind to the Buddhas must also act in accordance with the Dharma, that is, not follow the path of the ten unwholesome deeds. [This is the relative Discipline.] (62b)

17. 'Then, the next day, after having made salutations to the Bhagavat Vairocana, the Master transforms himself into Vajrasattva, empowers a jar filled with perfumed water with the Mantra of Trailokya-vijaya and places it at the first gate. The wise one should then sprinkle all persons with it, and in order to purify their minds, he should pour out perfumed water for them[A].'

This section explains what the Master who is going to draw the Mandala should do the following morning. If he examines the rising sun in the morning, he will be able to ascertain clearly the north, south, east and west. Therefore, having washed and so on, he should go to the middle of the place where the Mandala is to be drawn and bring to mind the Bhagavat Vairocana and make obeisances to him. Then making the *Mudrā* of the Three Samayas, he should transform himself into emptiness with the Continuum of Reality *Mudrā*. Then, making the Dharma Wheel *Mudrā*, he should transform himself into Vajrasattva. Then he should armour himself, making the Vajra Armour *Mudrā*. This is the transformation into Vajrasattva. '*Vajrasattva*' refers to one whose mind is extremely firm, (63a) like a vajra. What is that mind? It is the mind of the core of Enlightenment, which is authentically consummate in character (*aviparyāsa-pariniṣpanna-lakṣaṇa*). This is the transformation into the Bodhisattva Body of the Noble Vajrasattva. Then the Master who has transformed himself into Vajrasattva, should calculate and fix the north, south, east and west of the Mandala, and he should also mentally decide the places where the deities are to be located.

He empowers a jar ... sprinkle all persons with it: He should put five types of precious things, five types of medicines, five types of grains[15] and so on into a jar filled with

A C: 與令飲 '*and make them drink it*'.

water with the qualities mentioned in the text and place it at the entrance to the Mandala house. When the trainees enter within, he should sprinkle them with it to dispel obstacles. As for the empowerment of that jar with the Mantra of Trailokya-vijaya, he should recite one hundred and eight times if empowering with the essence mantra, and seven or twenty one times if empowering with the root mantra.

Then, '***in order to purify their minds, he should pour out pure perfumed water for them***', he should pour out pure perfumed water for them so that they may be cleansed of ideas about having eaten something which infringes the mantra practice. '***Pure***' means without parts of animals and so on. Even if they do not have ideas about having eaten something that infringes the mantra practice, they should think that their minds will be purified by drinking that pure water, so that they may become free of worries about impurity and so forth. For these reasons the water should be given to them. (63b)

18. Then Vajrapāṇi said to the Bhagavat:
'Would the All-knowing One, Best of Speakers,
tell us the time and hour
at which the Great Beings
will empower the Mandala,
when the mandala Masters exert
themselves in mantra *sādhana*?'
Then the Bhagavat replied to Vajrapāṇi, 'Those who aim to make the Mandala should always draw it at night.'

In this section, '***Great Beings***' refers not to the Buddhas, but to the Bodhisattvas who engage in the practice of the Perfections. Why? As Buddhas can empower at all times, it is not necessary to ask about the time, but Bodhisattvas cannot empower at all times, because when they arise from *samādhi*, they go giving priority to their perception of the benefitting of beings. Secondly, the Buddha Bhagavats are never called 'Great Beings' (*mahā-sattvas*), but Bodhisattvas are, so the words '***Great Beings***' refers here to the Bodhisattvas.

The Bhagavat prescribes the night-time for drawing all the mandalas for all occasions to those who wish to draw them, and says that those Bodhisattvas will go there in the night-time. Therefore you should know that both the *samaya* mandalas and the *sādhana* mandalas should be drawn in the night on all occasions. Regarding that, it is mentioned in the *Guhya Tantra* and elsewhere that all mandalas, apart from the *sādhana* mandalas, should be drawn in the night, so it says that the *sādhana* mandala should be drawn during the daytime. Why is that? The *sādhana* should be accomplished during the whole of the night from the evening watch to the next morning, therefore, as there will be no chance to draw the *sādhana* mandala in the night, it should be drawn in the daytime. But here it is said that both should be drawn at night, so the *samaya* mandala should be drawn that same night, and the *sādhana* mandala also should be drawn at night, and not during the daytime as mentioned in the *Guhya Tantra*. But since there will be no opportunity for one to draw it during the night of the actual *sādhana*, and if one draws it that same evening, it will take one a whole three hour period to draw the mandala, making it impossible for one to do the *sādhana* for the whole night. Therefore you should know that the mandala should be drawn the previous evening and the *sādhana* should be done from the next evening.

You should follow this rule also in the case of the large mandalas which cannot be completed in one evening.

19. 'Vajrapāṇi! The Master should make prostrations to all the Buddhas and then taking a thread of five different colours, he should transform himself into the Bhagavat Vairocana.

'To mark out a line to the east,
the cord should be held in the air,
level with his navel.
Then going to the south,
it should be marked out to the north[A].
Then taking up a second cord
and recollecting the Tathāgatas there,
he should face east and mark the line.
Then going to the south,
he should mark the line to the north.
Then the wise one turns around, (129a)
and standing in the south-west,
he should mark a line northwards.
Then he should turn around to the right,
and having done so, he should stand there,
and mark a line to the south.
Then leaving that place,
he should go and stand in the south-east,
then the *mantrin* who abides in the mantra ritual
should mark a line eastwards.
Then likewise going to the north-east,
he should face westwards,
he should mark a line northwards
to the north-western quarter.
In that way the *mantrin*
should make a complete square[B].'

A C: 如是南及西終竟於北方 '[*it should be marked out*] *in this manner from the south, the west, and finally the northern direction*'.

B The process described by C in this important passage has significant differences in the procedure: 第二安立界亦從初方起憶念諸如來所行如上說右方及後方復周於勝方阿闍梨次迴依於涅哩底受覺對持者漸次以南行從此右施邊轉依於風方師位移本處而居於火方持眞言行者復修如是法弟子在西南師居伊舍尼學者復施邊轉依於火方師位移本處而住於風方如是眞言者普作四方相 '*In the case of the second cord which is for establishing the realm, he should again begin from the east. Recollecting the Tathāgatas, he does what has been described above. He should go around to the south, then to the west and to the north. The Master next goes around, taking his position in the south-west. The recipient trainees should gradually move around to the south, then going around to the right, they should transfer to the north-west. The Master moves from where he is and goes to the south-east, The mantra practitioners should also act in accordance with this rule. The trainees should be in the south-west, and the Master stays in the north-east. The trainees should again move around and transfer their position to the south-east, while the Master moves from where he is and takes up position in the north-west. In this manner, the* mantrin *should make it entirely square.*'

Now the marking out with a cord in order to draw the Mandala will be explained. The [description of the] drawing of the Mandala is finished by six things. What are they? i) The explanation of the *samādhi* for the marking-out of the Mandala, ii) the explanation of the actual marking-out with a cord, iii) the explanation of the dimensions of the Mandala, iv) the divisions of the sections of the surface area, v) the divisions of the gates and arches, and vi) the explanation about allocating the deities to their places.

The Master should make prostrations to all the Buddhas ... transform himself into the Bhagavat Vairocana: This explains the *samādhi* of the marking cord. ***A cord of five colours***: Imagining it to be the Five Awarenesses in nature, he should transform himself into the Body of Vairocana, endowed with the Five Awarenesses. ***Transforming himself into Vairocana***: As there are three types of Mandalas, (64b) there is also a division into three types of *samādhi* in which he should abide. In the case of the Great Compassion Mandala, the Master should transform himself into the Body of Vairocana and carry out the various rites of the Mandala[16]. In the case of the Mandala of the Revolving Wheel of Letters, he should transform himself into the *dharmakāya* and carry out the rites of the Mandala[17]. In the case of the Secret Mandala, the Master should transform himself into the Body which has the five mandalas of earth and so on[18] and carry out the rites of the Mandala. These are explained in the *Piṇḍārtha* and will also be explained in the various individual chapters of the Tantra itself.

The imagining of the cord of five colours to be the Five Awarenesses should be linked to the imagining of the five pigments to be the five Buddhas which is mentioned below.

To mark out a line to the east ... marked out to the north: First there is the manner in which the Master should position himself to the west of the Mandala, stand facing the east and imagine the intrinsically existent Mandala in the sky. He should clearly imagine the configuration of the Adornments of the Inexhaustible Body and so forth of Vairocana, and then making an assistant hold the end of the cord, he should stretch it out to the east. Likewise he should stretch it out from the south to the north. This is the imagining of the intrinsically existent Mandala in the sky. When he has thus imagined the intrinsically existent Mandala in the sky, he should draw the Mandala which is thought of as a representation of the intrinsically existent Mandala. Why is it necessary to imagine mentally this intrinsically existent Mandala in the sky and then to draw the Mandala? In order to ascertain the perceptual form of the intrinsically existent Mandala in the sky.

Then with a second cord, having taken it up himself: Because the first cord has already been used, it is not fitting to use it for the marking-out, so he should mark out the second Mandala with another cord of five colours.

Recollecting the Tathāgatas there, he should face east and mark out the line: (65a) In order to fix the Mandala without error, he should mark out the lines crosswise from the centre and stick a peg (*kīla*) into the centre of the Mandala. Then, lining up the cord, he should determine the four corners with it, from the peg in the centre. When he has thus determined them, he should also insert four pegs as markers for the four corners. Also he should not untie the knots on the cord, but leave them on as markers for the cord. ***Standing in the south-west, he should mark a line northwards***: The Master should stand in the south-western area facing towards the north side and mark the line of the western side. ***Then he should turn to the right ... a line southwards***:

Staying in the same south-western area, the Master should turn his gaze from the north to the east, and then making an assistant hold the end of the cord and go around the Mandala to the south-eastern corner, he should mark out the line of the eastern side. ***The* mantrin *who abides in the mantra ritual*:** This means one who abides in the *samādhi* of Vairocana. ***Then likewise going to the north-east ... a line northwards*:** (65b) Positioning himself in the north-eastern corner, the Master should mark out the line of the northern side. ***In that way the* mantrin *should complete the four corners*:** The Master should make the Mandala completely square according to the specifications mentioned above.

Why is it that the Master should first do the west, then the south, then the east, and finally the north when he is thus marking out the Mandala? The western side is thought of as the Investigating Awareness, the southern side as the Awareness of Sameness, the eastern side as the Mirror-like Awareness, and the northern side as the Awareness of Accomplishing Activities. So first there is the Investigating Awareness, and when that has been perfected, the Awareness of Sameness will be perfected. When that has been perfected the Mirror-like Awareness will be perfected. When that has been perfected, the Awareness of Accomplishing Activities, which is characterized by *nirmāṇa-kāyas*, material wealth and location, will arise from it. Therefore the sequence is mentioned in that way. Also the cognitive object (*ālambana*) of the Four Awarenesses is the pure continuum of reality, so the lines which are drawn crosswise by the cord coming from each side, meet in the centre, which is the Awareness of the Continuum of Reality. The meeting at the one point of the cross is the symbol of the continuum of reality. When he has thus marked out the lines and divided up the surface, he should go over the lines with a wet cord made of one colour[19]. This should be done to make the lines clear without any erasures.

20. 'Then having gone into the interior,
he should divide it into three.
Having divided into three parts
the whole of the site,
then each one of those parts also
should be divided into three parts;
the outer part is made into the courtyard,
and the other two parts should be fixed
as the abode of the deities.'

Having gone into the interior, the Master should mark out the whole area into three, and then he should divide the third area into three parts, joining each part to each side. He should do likewise for the two [other] areas. '***Having divided into three parts the whole of the site***' means that he should divide that Mandala into three sections running all around. ***Each one of those parts should again be divided into three parts*:** Each of the three areas should again be divided into three [strips], with one third established as the courtyard (*aṅgana*) and the other two thirds made into the abode of the deities[20].

21. 'In the four directions, the wise one
should make portals in each portion,

with care and restraint,
as the places of the Lords of the deities.'

This section deals with the setting-off of the portals (*niryūha*). The size of the portals should be made one ninth the surface area of the Mandala. The *Dharmakāya Mudrā* should be placed in the eastern portal of those of the inner matrix Mandala. Avalokiteśvara should be placed within the northern portal, and Vajrapāṇi should placed within the southern portal. The *nirmāṇa-kāya* of Śākyamuni should be placed within the eastern portal of the portals in the middle section, Yama in the south and Indra in the north. Although Yama and Indra are also located within the portals of the middle area of the Mandala, they are to be understood as *nirmāṇa-kāyas* of the Bhagavat. Because Yama guides beings who are to be guided, the image of Yama who is the ruler of the hungry ghosts, is treated as their Lord and located in that portal. Likewise, Śākyamuni as the Lord of humans resides in a portal.

You should know the Lords who reside in the matrix of the Mandala are the four Awarenesses in nature. The attribute of the Bhagavat Vairocana who is perfectly enlightened, resting in the centre, is to be the Awareness of Sameness in nature. The *Dharmakāya Mudrā* which is located in the east is the Mirror-like Awareness in nature. Avalokiteśvara who resides in the north is the Investigating Awareness in nature. (66b) Vajrapāṇi who resides in the south is the Awareness of Accomplishing Activities in nature.

Manjuśrī resides in the form of the Lord of the eastern portal of the outer section of the Mandala, the Bodhisattva Sarva-nīvaraṇa-viṣkambhin resides in the southern portal, and in the same way, Ākāśa-garbha and Kṣiti-garbha reside in the western and the northern portals.

22. **'When he has finished all this**
careful division into sections,
he should draw an excellent
white lotus in the centre,
and this is called the matrix.
The Mandala entirely arisen from Compassion
is therefore said to have a matrix.
As for its size, it is taught that
it should be sixteen inches[21] or more.
It is complete with eight petals,
and has very beautiful stamens.
In between all the petals,
he should draw vajras[A].'

The white lotus in the centre represents the accumulation of merits that are the cause of the Bhagavat Vairocana. The whiteness is the purity of that accumulation. The '***matrix***' is the source, the accumulation of merit, and that is the source of the Bhagavat's compassionate nature. This Mandala arises from that great compassion, therefore it is said to have a matrix.

A C: 金剛之智印 '*vajra awareness* mudrās'.

As for its size … sixteen inches or more: The central lotus should be sixteen inches in size. '***Or more***' means that it is acceptable even to make it larger than that. The significance of that is as follows: Sixteen is the [total of] the Ten Levels together with the Six Perfections. '***Or more***' refers to the All Good Level which surpasses them. In brief, you should consider that lotus to be a symbol of the accumulations of merit and awareness which are the cause of the Bhagavat.

Complete with eight petals: Because that accumulation of merit is endowed with eight Awarenesses, it says '***eight petals***'. Here the eight Awarenesses are as follows: Since the Mirror-like Awareness, the Awareness of Sameness, (67a) the Investigating Awareness and the Awareness of Accomplishing Activities have evolved from the five gates of consciousness, they are divided into five types[22]. Since that [accumulation] is endowed with those eight Awarenesses, it has eight petals. Moreover, the Awarenesses are the direct realization that phenomena lack any objective reality, and since it is thus realized that everything lacks objective reality, it is also realized that the three elements of giver, gift and recipient also lack objective reality. Hence the accumulation of merit through Generosity and so forth is endowed with such Awarenesses, and therefore you should understand them as the completely pure nature of the three elements of Generosity and so on.

It has very beautiful stamens: The stamens are thought of as the symbols of the causal qualities of the Bhagavat such as the *Samādhis*, the *Dhāraṇīs*, the Liberations, the Strengths, the Fearlessnesses and so forth, for that accumulation of merit is endowed with those qualities. ***In between all the petals he should draw vajras***: The vajras symbolize the Awarenesses, for it is endowed with the eight Awarenesses as mentioned above.

23. **'In the centre of the matrix, he should draw**
the most excellent Lord of the Jinas,
golden in colour, blazing in light,
with his topknot and crown.
He is completely surrounded by pure light.
The Lord free from all ills
should be depicted residing in *samādhi*.'

VAIROCANA. ***Blazing in light***: Blazing and burning in nature, for he has the Awareness whose nature is to burn up the obscurations of emotional afflictions and wrong understanding. ***Golden in colour***: This indicates that he is rich in nature. ***Topknot***: He has a topknot because he is residing in the Akaniṣṭha Heaven, where the gods there have topknots. As his actions are similar to theirs, he also has a topknot. ***With a crown***: Because he is a Dharma King or else because he is crowned as a Lord, (67b) he wears a jewelled crown. ***Completely surrounded by pure light***: This means that he is surrounded by light which is his utterly pure Awareness in nature and also by that which emanates from the circle of light. ***Free from all ills***: Free from the faults of the obscurations of emotional afflictions and wrong understanding. ***Residing in* samādhi**: That is to reside one-pointedly in the unmoving self-aware Awareness. His appearance is also of one who abides as though in *samādhi*.

24. **'In the east, the wise one**
should carefully draw

the sign of the Buddhas[A]**.**
It is triangular, completely white
and rests upon a lotus, its circumference
encircled by white rays of light.'

DHARMAKĀYA MUDRĀ. To the east of the Bhagavat Vairocana, he should draw a triangular sign which symbolizes the earlier perfectly enlightened Tathāgatas of the past. It is placed in the east because the Sanskrit word for 'east' (*pūrva*) also means 'previous'. ***Triangular, resting on a lotus:*** It is the symbol of the completely perfected Three Gates of Liberation – emptiness (*śūnyatā*), the absence of perceptual forms (*animitta*) and the absence of purpose (*apraṇidhi*). In the chapter on the Secret Mandala, it says that the Master should place a five-pointed vajra in the centre of that symbol, and from two of its sides rays of light shine forth. The five-pointed vajra is the symbol of the Five Awarenesses, and the two rays of light which shine forth are the symbols of the *saṃbhoga-kāya* and the *nirmāṇa-kāya*, which emerge from the *dharmakāya* of which that *Mudrā* is a symbol.

25. **'To its north, the wise one should draw**
the Mother of all the Protectors. (129b)
She shines brightly the colour of gold,
and wears a white robe.
She illuminates all directions
and should be depicted in *samādhi*[B]**.'**

GAGANA-LOCANĀ (Sky Eye). (68a) To the north of the triangular symbol, he should draw the Blessed Lady Gagana-locanā, whose nature is the Perfection of Insight, the Insight associated with Perfect Enlightenment (*abhisaṃbodhi*). '***The Protectors***' are the Buddhas, and since they arise from that Insight, it is called the Mother of the Protectors. ***She shines brightly:*** She shines brightly due to her nature of having consumed the obscurations of the emotional afflictions and wrong understanding. ***The colour of gold:*** Indicates her rich nature. ***She illumines all directions:*** She pervades [everywhere] with her intrinsic nature of the Awareness which is extremely pure and radiantly clear by nature.

26. **'To the north of the Lord,**
there is the heroic Avalokiteśvara.
He should be drawn
seated upon a white lotus,
and he is white himself
like a conch, jasmine, or the moon.
His face is smiling and
on his head there is Amitābha.'

AVALOKITEŚVARA. To the north of Vairocana on his right, the Master should draw Avalokiteśvara, Lord of the Lotus Family. Being the Investigating Awareness in nature,

---

A C: 一切遍知印 '*the* Mudrā *of All-pervading Knowledge*'.
B C transposes Section 33 to follow on here after Section 25.

Avalokiteśvara gazes upon (*avalokita*) beings in order to completely mature them and he also gazes upon the utterly pure continuum of reality. '***Īśvara***' refers to the Hero who overcomes the thieves that are the obscurations of the emotional afflictions and wrong understanding. ***Seated on a white lotus***: It is the completely pure accumulation of merit and awareness in nature. In the Yoga Tantras, a red lotus is spoken of, but here it is said to be a white lotus. The Yoga Tantras deal mainly with expedient means, so it is red there to show involvement in the aim of liberating and maturing beings by expedient means. (68b) Since this Tantra mainly deals with Insight, it is said to be white here, to symbolize the realization of the utter purity of all phenomena by Insight. ***On his head is Amitābha***: Amitābha is the Investigating Awareness in nature, so this is shown as a symbol of that. Secondly, it is because in the Yoga Tantras there are various initiations into the various Families, and the initiation into the Lotus Family is through Amitābha. ***His face is smiling***: This means that he is smiling with open eyes and not abiding in *samādhi*, in order to explain the Dharma for the sake of beings.

27. **'On his right there is the Goddess**
known as the great Tārā.
She is virtuous and removes fear,
light green in colour, with various forms.
She has the proportions of a young woman;
in her clasped hands she also holds a blue lotus,
she is encircled with rays of light,
and is wearing garments of white[A].'

TĀRĀ (Saviouress). Avalokiteśvara gazed upon realms of beings and he saw that even if he were to transfer all his accumulation of merit and awareness in order to benefit all the countless beings and save them, he would still not be able to free them all from *saṃsāra*. Then from his tears which arose from the power of his great compassion, many Tārā goddesses emerged and took on the forms of saviours for all beings. Therefore she is called the Goddess Tārā (Saviouress). Moreover, her many forms may be known from other Tantras.

Virtuous and removes fear: She is peaceful and clears away the eight fearful things, such as kings, robbers and so on[23]. ***Light green in colour***: Light green is a mixture of white, blue and yellow. (69a) The symbolism of these colours is as follows: White signifies pacifying, yellow signifies enriching and blue signifies subduing, and their mixture into one colour signifies the performance of all these activities. ***Various forms***: She changes into many different forms for the sake of the many different types of beings, so to some she appears in a male form, to others in a female form and so on. ***The proportions of a young woman***: She is youthful, for although her qualities are not incomplete, she is also not aged in the sense of having entered Nirvāṇa, the Enlightenment which transcends those qualities. The proportions that she has symbolize her extensive accumulation of merit and awareness. ***In her clasped hands she holds a blue lotus***: She has various means of liberating, so you should understand that the sword-like petals of the blue lotus are like the Insight method of liberation.

A C adds: 微笑 '*and is smiling*'.

Wearing garments of white: These symbolize her decorum. Just as one's body is covered and made modest by clothes, so also is decorum a sign of modesty, so she is decorous. White symbolizes the purity of that decorum. Why is she decorous? Because decorum is a quality of Bodhisattvas, as will be explained later.

28. 'To his left, the Goddess Bhṛkuṭī
should be drawn.
She holds a rosary in her hand,
has three eyes and plaited locks of hair.
The colour of her body is white,
and she is encircled with
rays of white, yellow and red light.'

BHṚKUṬĪ (Wrinkle-brows). He should draw Bhṛkuṭī on the left of Avalokiteśvara. Her name is derived from reference to the frown wrinkles (*kuṭi*) on Avalokiteśvara's brow (*bhru*), that is, she emerged from anger as her origin, so she is called '***Bhṛkuṭī***'. ***She holds a rosary***: This shows that the goddess does not only have a wrathful nature, but is also endowed with the Perfections and so on. (69b) The rosary symbolizes the Perfections. '***Three eyes***' show her wrathful nature. ***Plaited locks of hair***: In accordance with the Akaniṣṭha gods.

29. 'Near to the Goddess Bhṛkuṭī,
Mahā-sthāma-prāpta should be drawn,
holding an unopened lotus in his hand;
he is very merciful and is dressed in white.
This heroic being is encircled with light rays.'

MAHĀ-STHĀMA-PRĀPTA (He who has Obtained Great Strength). He should be drawn near to Bhṛkuṭī, because he has assembled together great power. He '***holds an unopened lotus***' in order to distinguish him from Avalokiteśvara.

30. 'In front of him, the wise one should draw
the *vidyā* Goddess Yaśodharā;
she is the colour of gold,
and fully adorned with ornaments;
in her left hand, she holds
a bunch of pleasing *priyaṅgu* flowers[24].'

YAŚODHARA. She is called '***Yaśodhara***' (Glory-holder) because she holds the glories of the qualities of the Buddha. Her golden colour is a symbol of her richness. The '**priyaṅgu *flowers***' she holds are the sign of this goddess.

31. 'Nearby to Tārā,
the wise one should draw
Pāṇḍara-vāsinī.
She has braided locks and wears white;
in her hand she holds a lotus.'

PĀṆḌARA-VASĪNĪ. Her name means 'She who dwells in whiteness' or 'She who is dressed in white', (70a) because she dwells in the purity of the continuum of reality. She is drawn near Tārā in order to show that the Goddess Tārā does not only perform all actions in saving beings, but that she also resorts to the pure continuum of reality.

32. 'Below her, the *mantrin* should draw
the Vidyā-king of great strength,
who is the colour of the dawn sun.
He is adorned with white lotuses,
has a blazing aura and is wrathful;
his hair is like a lion's mane[A]:
he is renowned as Haya-grīva.
Thus the wise one draws
[the domain] of Avalokiteśvara[B].'

HAYA-GRĪVA (Horse-necked One). ***Vidyā-king***: He is the Vidyā-king of the Lotus Family. ***The colour of the dawn sun***: This shows that his body is red in colour. ***He is adorned with white lotuses***: He is adorned with the pure white accumulation of merit and awareness. *Has a blazing aura*: He has the Awareness that consumes the obscurations of the emotional afflictions and wrong understanding, and when they have been burnt up, the pure continuum of reality will be obtained. Therefore you should know that he is drawn below the Goddess Pāṇḍara-vasīnī who is the utterly pure continuum of reality in nature, to show that he is the Immediate Path to that in nature. ***His hair is like a lion's mane***: This is a sign that he cannot be overcome by anybody, like a lion. ***He is renowned as Haya-grīva***: He is called Hayagrīva because the Awareness which penetrates the Dharma is swift and speedy like a horse, (70b) and because he is swift in doing deeds to benefit beings, like a horse.

The domain of Avalokiteśvara: These deities are to be known as the circle of Avalokiteśvara, and they are drawn as representations of the Lotus Family in the intrinsically existent Mandala. All the intrinsically existent Mandalas are limitless and cannot be encompassed in a drawing, so all these [drawn] Mandalas should be understood as a means of condensing the intrinsically existent Mandalas.

33. 'In the south of the Buddhas,
there is the one called Wish-fulfilling Gem,
the symbol of the protector Bodhisattvas;
It is endowed with great fortune,
and perfects all wishes.
It should be drawn upon a white lotus.'

WISH-FULFILLING GEM. To the south of the triangular sign of the Buddhas of the past, he should draw a symbol of the Bodhisattvas, like a Wish-fulfilling

A C reads: 吼怒牙出現利瓜... '*he howls wrathfully, baring his fangs; he has sharp claws [and his hair ...]*'.

B T: *spyan-ras-gzigs-dbang blo-ldan-gyi* | *rta-mgrin-can zhes grags-pa bri* , V: *rta-mgrin zhes-su bsgrags-pa ste* | *blo-ldan spyan-ras-gzigs-kyi'o* , C: 如是三摩地觀音諸眷屬 '*These are the* samādhis *of Avalokiteśvara and his retinue*'. T seems corrupt, so translation based on V and C.

Gem (*cintāmaṇi*). If you were to actually draw all the Bodhisattvas, they would be countless and without end, so you should know that by drawing a symbol as a means of including them all together, you draw them all. ***Great fortune***: This refers to their possession of the accumulation of merit and awareness. It also means that they are greatly revered by many beings. ***Perfects all wishes***: It is called a Wish-fulfilling Gem because [the Bodhisattvas] are like wish-fulfilling gems that completely fulfil all wishes, by acting for the benefit of all beings according to their inclinations. Moreover, the symbol itself should be drawn like a Wish-fulfilling Gem. ***Upon a white lotus***: They arise from the pure white accumulation of merit and awareness.

34. 'To the south of the Lord Vairocana, (130a)
Vajradhara should be drawn;
he fulfils all wishes,
and in colour he is like a *priyaṅgu* flower,
greenish-yellow, or like an emerald.
This Lord has a crown and is adorned
with all the ornaments of a Great Being;
he holds a vast vajra which penetrates all places,
and he is encircled with rays of light.'

VAJRAPĀṆI. (71a) Vajrapāṇi is drawn to the south of the Bhagavat Vairocana, and he also signifies the Awareness of Accomplishing Activities. As he abides majestically, adorned with various ornaments, he is similar to the tranquil Bhagavat and so is to be drawn on the left of the Bhagavat. ***Holds a vajra***: He holds a vajra which is the Five Awarenesses in nature.

35. 'To his right[A], the *mantrin* should draw
the Goddess called Māmakī;
she is adorned with vajra ornaments,
and holds a vajra[B] in her hand.'

MĀMAKĪ. She is the consort of Vajrapāṇi and she is the Perfection of Insight, endowed with the Awareness of Accomplishing Activities in nature. ***She holds a vajra in her hand***: She holds a three-pointed vajra, the symbol that she is Awareness in nature.

36. 'Below her, the *mantrin* should draw
the Goddess, the mighty Vajra-sūcī.
She is completely surrounded by her assistants,
and is smiling slightly.'

VAJRASŪCĪ (Vajra Needle). Because she is the Immediate Path of the Mother Perfection of Insight in nature, she is drawn below her. She is called '***Vajrasūcī***' because it is her disposition to pierce through to reality. (71b) ***Completely surrounded by her assistants***: She has the branches of the Immediate Path, and since this is a royal entourage, it is possible for there to be servants and so on.

A C: 金剛藏 '[*to the rght of*] *Vajragarbha*'
B C: 堅慧 '[*the vajra of*] *stable insight*'

37. **'To the left of Vajrapāṇi,**
the *mantrin* should draw Vajra-śṛṅkhalā,
who carries a chain of vajras in her hand.
She is encircled by her assistants,
and she is greenish-yellow in colour,
like a *priyaṅgu* flower,
and should be well adorned with vajra symbols.'

VAJRA-ŚṚṄKHALĀ (Vajra-chain). The nature of Vajra-śṛṅkhalā is the Noble Path. She holds a symbol of leading beings to that Path and causing them to enter it. Also, since she is the summoner[25] of the royal entourage, she symbolizes the seizing and binding of the malicious and harmful.

38. **'In the region below Vajrapāṇi,**
he should draw the wrathful Candra-tilaka;
he pacifies great obstructors and enemies:
his wrath is known throughout the Three Worlds.
He has three eyes and four fangs,
his colour is like summer rain-clouds,
and he gives out a peal of laughter;
he is adorned with vajra ornaments,
and is encircled by
limitless wrathful lords[A].
His hundred thousand hands
brandish various kinds of weapons.
This great wrathful being
should be drawn seated upon a lotus.'

CANDRA-TILAKA (Moon-marked). ***In the region below***: Since he is the path of unhindered practice leading to the Awareness of Accomplishing Activities in nature, he has not surpassed the level of that Awareness and so he is drawn below Vajrapāṇi. ***Candra-tilaka***: He is completely pure like the moon, and it is his nature to satisfy the existential streams of all beings. ***Tilaka***: He has a *tilaka* mark[26]. In Sanskrit, the word *tilaka* also means the 'chief' of something. ***Obstructors and enemies***: He clears away gods and *yakṣas* (72a) who are obstructors and human enemies. ***Three eyes***: These either symbolize his possession of the Eye of Awareness, or his wrath. ***Four fangs***: These show that he possesses the Four Gates of Liberation: Emptiness, the absence of perceptual forms, the absence of purpose and luminosity by nature. ***Like summer rain-clouds***: Since summer rain-clouds are a turbid mass of rain and wind, this symbolizes that he performs all the activities which they do. ***His hundred thousand hands***: These symbolize that he causes beings to enter the Noble Path by the many hundreds of thousands of branches of the Path, or else that he clears away the many obscurations to the Path by those branches. ***Various kinds of weapons***: Those qualities of the branches of the Path turn into such weapons as vajras and so on. He should be drawn as described above, but his many arms and his entourage should be drawn as wished, and one can draw less of them as appropriate.

A C adds: 攝護衆生故 '*in order to regulate and protect beings*'.

39. **'Going around to his west,**
the *mantrin* should draw many Vajradharas,
who hold various weapons in their hands;
they are of various colours and very powerful,
completely surrounded by rays of light;
they benefit all beings.'

VAJRADHARAS. He should draw the Vajradharas who are the entourage of Vajrapāṇi, and their names and appearances should correspond to those given in the Chapter on the Secret Mandala.

40. **'In the area behind the Lord of Mantras,**
in the south-western region,
the *mantrin* should draw Acala[A].
He holds a sword and a noose,
his plaited hair hangs from the left of his head,
he is well adorned and one of his eyes squints[B].
He abides amidst his own light,
wrathfully seated upon a rock.
His face is creased in anger,
and he has a robust youthful form.'

ACALA (Unshakable). (72b) This section describes the special features of the Noble Lord Acala who is drawn immediately behind the Bhagavat. He is the Immediate Path to the Awareness of Sameness in nature. ***He holds a sword***: This is the symbol of the Path, for he leads beings to and causes them to enter that Path. ***One eye squints***: Because he is the Immediate Path in nature, this symbolizes that his realization of all aspects of the continuum of reality and the Awareness of Sameness, is incomplete. ***Seated on a rock***: Because his nature is the Path which is fully accomplished and without distortion, he is firm and unchanging. ***Youthful form***: Since he has newly entered the Immediate Path, this symbolizes the undeveloped Path. Consequently, Trailokya-vijaya who symbolizes the developed Path, is placed in the north-west.

41. **'Having drawn him, the wise one** (130b)
goes to the north-west and carefully draws
the wrathful Trailokya-vijaya of the Bhagavat,
with an inexhaustible blazing aura;
in his hand he has a vajra and he wears a crown,
and he is seated as though receiving commands[C].
He is the colour of the end of time.'

TRAILOKYA-VIJAYA (Victorious over the Three Realms). This describes the special features of the depiction of Trailokya-vijaya, who is the perfected Immediate Path to

---

A C adds: 如來使 '*the Tathāgata's servant*'.
B C adds: 諦觀 '*gazing at truth*'.
C C: 不顧自身命專請而受教 '*he receives commands with no regard for his own life*'.

the Awareness of Sameness of Vairocana in nature. ***The colour of the end of time*:** At the end of time there will be no sun or moon, (73a) so all will be murky black. Hence he should be depicted black in colour, like the dark colour of wrath.

42. 'Thus the drawing of the interior
with the Jinas has been explained[A].'

Thus the symbols of the Five Awarenesses together with their entourages within the matrix mandala, which is an abbreviated depiction of the intrinsically existent Mandala, the Adornments of the Inexhaustible Body and so on, have been explained.

43. 'Then the *mantrin* moves outwards,
and within the eastern region,
in the second division, with certainty,
the area is divided into two,
and on the innerside of the portal,
the *mantrin* should draw Śākyamuni.
He shines golden in colour,
and has the thirty two excellent marks.
The Lord wears saffron-coloured robes,
and is seated upon a white lotus,
in the Dharma-expounding posture,
in order to cause the teaching to spread.'

Now, the text will describe the drawing in the second area of the Mandala of those who manifest in the forms of the *Nirmana-kāya* Śākyamuni, Indra and Yama together with their entourages and so on, who are included among the Adornments of the Inexhaustible Body and so on.

ŚĀKYAMUNI. Śākyamuni is drawn in the '***eastern region***' to show that Vairocana had previously become perfectly enlightened under the Bodhi Tree. ***The saffron-coloured robes*:** These show that he is not attached to *saṃsāra*, yet by the power of his compassion, he is attached to sentient beings. The coloured robes show his attachment to beings by his compassion, and these are of an unclear saffron colour, not pure red which would indicate attachment to *saṃsāra*.

44. 'To his right, the *mantrin* should draw
the Goddess called Buddha-locanā.
Her face is smiling slightly,
and her aura of light extends six feet outwards;
her unequalled body is very gracious,
and she is the mother of Śākyamuni.'

BUDDHA-LOCANĀ (Buddha-eye). The embodiment of the Mother Insight of the Buddhas should be drawn on the right-hand side of Śākyamuni. She is called

A T reads '*rgyas*' or '*rgyan*' in error for '*rgyal*' (*jina*). This is confirmed by C which reads: 諸尊方位等 '*the locations of the lords*'.

the Mother of the Buddhas because the Buddha Śākyamuni arose from that Insight. She is called '***Buddha-locanā***' (Buddha-eye) since the nature of the eye is to see, so it refers to the Insight. ***Unequalled***: Since she is the Awareness without perceptual images in nature, she cannot be grasped or measured as a limited size.

45. **'The Goddess to her right**
is the *vidyā* Ūrṇā.
She is seated upon a white lotus,
and in colour she is like
a conch, jasmine, or the moon.
In her hand she holds a wish-fulfilling Gem
and she fulfils all wishes.'

ŪRṆĀ. Ūrṇā is the goddess who embodies the *samādhi* of the spot-like mark of a Great Being between the eyebrows of the Buddha.

46. **'Then to the left, the *mantrin***
should draw the Protector Śākyamuni's
five brilliant and energetic *uṣṇīṣas*:
Sitāta-patroṣṇīṣa, Jayoṣṇīṣa,
Vijayoṣṇīṣa, Tejorāśy-uṣṇīṣa,
and Vikiraṇoṣṇīṣa.
He should carefully draw those five Uṣṇīṣas
of Śākyamuni, the powerful one,
in their five places.'

THE FIVE UṢṆĪṢAS. (74a) They arise from the top of the Bhagavat's head and they are the results named by their origins. Their symbols and so on are mentioned in detail in the Secret Mandala, so they will not be described here.

47. **'Going to their north,**
he should draw the Gods of the Pure Abode:
Īśvara, Saṃkusumita,
Prabhāmālin, Manobhava,
and Vighuṣṭa should be drawn as well.'

THE GODS OF THE PURE ABODE. Although the text says '***north***', they should be drawn to the south of the Five Uṣṇīṣas. Why? Because Śākyamuni and so on are located to the north of the Five Uṣṇīṣas, so there is no room to draw them there. Hence they are actually drawn to the south.

48. **'On the left side of Ūrṇā,**
there should also be carefully drawn
three more Uṣṇīṣas: the great Uṣṇīṣa Mahodaya,
Abhyudgata and Ananta-svara-ghoṣa.

The five powerful Uṣṇīṣas
are white, pale yellow and golden;
the other three are white, yellow and red.
All of them have rays of light,
and they are completely adorned with ornaments.
They are endowed with the power of resolve
and they bring all wishes to fulfilment.'

49. 'Then in the south-east, the *mantrin*
should draw Agni, seated within fire,
with the great sages (*ṛṣi*),
he is marked with three spots of ash,
and this hero is completely red.
On his breast he has a triangle,
he sits within flickering tongues of fire
and holds a rosary and a water-pot.'

50. 'Then in the southern portion
the Lord Yama should be drawn.
He holds a club and rides a buffalo,
his colour is that of summer rain-clouds.
He is accompanied by the wrathful Mothers,
Kālarātrī and the Lord of Death[A].'

YAMA. (74b) ***Rides a buffalo***: Since this is the mount of a mundane god, it is not white like an ordinary buffalo. ***Holds a club***: This is a symbol of Insight, but the club is one with a round head, for he reveals the results of good and evil actions in the stream of *saṃsāra*, but does not sever its flow.

51. 'To the south-west, the *mantrin*
should draw Nirṛti.
He is fearsome, with sword in hand.'

NIRṚTI. In order to train the *yakṣas*, the Inexhaustible Adornments of his Body take on the form of Nirṛti, the king of the *yakṣas*, in the south-west.

52. 'Then the wise one also
should promptly go to the north,
and draw the King of the Gods,
seated upon Mount Sumeru,
and encircled by the gods.
He has a vajra and a crown,
and is completely adorned with ornaments.'

INDRA. In order to train the gods of the Realm of Desire, the Adornments of his Inexhaustible Body take on the form of Indra, the King of the Gods. He should be

A C omits '*Lord of Death*'.

drawn seated on the peak of Mount Sumeru, surrounded by his entourage of gods. (75a) ***He has a crown***: He holds it in the manner of a king. ***Vajra***: This is the symbol of his Awareness. He holds both of these royal insignia in his hands.

53. **'To his east, he should then draw**
Varuṇa, holding a noose[A].
Next to him should be drawn
Āditya, seated on a carriage,
and on his left and right
should be drawn Jayā and Vijayā.'

VARUṆA (Water). He is drawn in the east because in Sanskrit the word '*pūrva*' (east) also means 'before', and after the emergence of a new eon, the foundation of the world is first established with water.

ĀDITYA (Sun). He is also drawn in the east because of the meaning 'before' [of *pūrva*], for after the emergence of a new eon, the sun and the moon are the first to arise among the worlds. ***Jayā and Vijayā***: The two consorts of Āditya.

54. **'To his right, Brahmā should be drawn**
with four faces and braided hair.
He utters the sound "Oṃ"[B],
and sits upon a lotus[C] upon a goose.
To his west should also be drawn
the goddess Pṛthivī and Sarasvatī,
Viṣṇu, Skanda and Vāyu,
Śaṅkāra and Candra.
These should be carefully drawn
abiding in the west.'

BRAHMĀ. ***Four faces***: The one of four Vedas arises from each of these. He sits upon a lotus placed upon a goose, which is his mount.

The goddess Pṛthivī and so forth should be drawn on the western side, according to the sequence given, from the south. They are drawn '***in the west***', because the gate faces west. They are drawn in the portal for those gods, Brahmā, Viṣṇu and so on are the gates leading to the supramundane Path. (75b) They are also the Adornments of the Bhagavat's Inexhaustible Body which have taken on their appearance to train the gods. Although the Adornments of his Inexhaustible Body have taken on the appearance of gods like Indra and are similar to them in form, you should know that their great power and magical abilities are superior to those of such gods. The same principle should be applied in connection with the others such as Yama.

55. **'When he has drawn them,**
without any confusion, the *mantrin*

A C inserts this portion dealing with Varuṇa at the end of Section 51.
B C: 唵字相爲印 '*his mudrā is the letter Oṃ*'
C C: 執蓮 '*he holds a lotus*'.

should draw below the Lord of Mantras
the wrathful one called Aparājita
and the Goddess Aparājitā;
Pṛthivi holding a water-pot in his hand
should also be drawn respectfully kneeling.'

APARĀJITA & APARĀJITĀ. (Not defeated by others). Aparājita is Śākyamuni's Immediate Path in nature. The Goddess Aparājitā reveals the power of Śākyamuni.

56. **'He should carefully draw**
the great Nāgas, Nanda and Upananda,
on each side of the gate (131b)
of Śākya-siṃha, the Protector.
Also the wise one should draw
the *mudrās* and mantras of the mandalas
which are explained
in all the tantras of Śākyamuni.'

57. **'Then stepping back, the *mantrin***
should draw Mañjuśrī in the third section.
He is the colour of saffron,
and his head has five braided locks of hair,
and is like a young boy in appearance.
In his left hand, he holds
a blue lotus with a vajra,
and he sits upon a white lotus seat;
he has a smiling face,
and is completely encircled
with splendid rays of light.'

Now the way in which one should draw the great Bodhisattvas such as Mañjughoṣa, who are seated to listen to the Dharma, will be explained. Here, the Dharma to which they listen is both the scriptural Dharma and the Dharma as realization. The scriptural Dharma is that spoken by the mouth. The Dharma as realization (76a) is the four Bodies with their entourages within the second inner mandala that are the Adornments of the Inexhaustible Body. Therefore, so that they may experience those Dharmas, those Bodhisattvas are drawn encircling them, placed in attendance upon them. Also you should know that those Bodhisattvas are born just from the Perfections.

MAÑJUGHOṢA (Beautiful Voiced). Mañjughoṣa should be drawn within the portal of the eastern side. He is the Insight connected with speech in nature. Having intellectually investigated and examined the general and specific attributes of all phenomena, that Insight brings about the direct realization of them. Therefore, the Bodhisattva who brings about the abandonment of all obscurations after such direct realization, [Sarva-nīvaraṇa-viṣkambhin], should be subsequently drawn in the south. When obscurations have thus been abandoned, Kṣiti-garbha, whose nature is patience and joyfulness, should be drawn in the north. After having thus attained patience and joyfulness, you should draw Ākāśa-garbha whose nature is the realization of the space-like emptiness of all phenomena, in the west. Since this is the sequence of liberation, one should first draw in the east Mañjughoṣa, whose nature is Insight.

Five locks of hair: They are the Five Awarenesses in nature. ***A blue lotus with a vajra***: He holds in his left hand a vajra symbolizing the Five Awarenesses, (76b) and this is placed upon a blue lotus. The lotus symbolizes the Sword of Insight. ***He has a smiling face***: This is a sign that he teaches the Dharma of Insight.

58. **'To his north, he should draw**
the youth Jālinī-prabha,
who holds a jewel net in his hand,
and sits upon a white lotus seat,
gazing at the Buddha's Son.'

59. **'He should also draw the five female servants**
on the left of Mañjuśrī:
Keśinī, Upakeśinī, Citrā,
Vasumati and also Ākarṣaṇī.
These are the Wise One's female servants.
In front of them, there should be drawn
the two entourages of the youth Jālinī-prabha
and the five female attendants.'

60. **'Then in the south, the *mantrin***
should draw the greatly renowned Bodhisattva
Sarva-nīvaraṇa-viṣkambhin,
who holds a Wish-fulfilling Gem.
Ignoring a division into two parts here,
the wise one should draw the eight Heroes:
Kautuhala, Sarvābhayaṃdada,
Sarvāpāya-jaha, Paritrāṇāśaya-mati,
Karuṇā-mṛdita-mati, Maitry-abhyudgata,
Sarva-dāha-praśamita and Acintya-mati.'

SARVA-NĪVARAṆA-VIṢKAMBHIN & ENTOURAGE (He who clears away all obscurations). (77a) ***The wise one should draw the Eight Heroes***: He should draw the eight attendants of the Lord in sequence, four on the left and four on the right. ***Ignoring the division into two parts here***: Because of the absence of a demarcation between master and attendants.

61. **'Then going to the north side,**
he should draw Kṣiti-garbha.
He shines with blazing light,
and has patience and [excellent] joy.
The wise one should draw
this renowned Bodhisattva sitting
upon an inconceivably pleasing (132a)

lotus made of four types of jewels,
placed upon the ground which produces all,
and is adorned with every kind of jewel.'

KṢITI-GARBHA (Earth Treasury). (77b) ***Has patience***: He has the three kinds of patient acceptance with regards to the profound Dharma, suffering and the harm done by others. ***Excellent joy***: Joy and delight due to his method of liberation. He is called '***Kṣiti-garbha***' because he has such patience, like the earth. ***A lotus made of four types of jewels***: These symbolize the three kinds of patience and the joyfulness which are the Bodhisattva Kṣiti-garbha's qualities.

62. 'His attendants are countless
Lords of unlimited virtues;
among them are the Bodhisattvas
Ratnākara[A], Ratnapāṇi,
Dharaṇiṃdhara, Ratna-mudrā-hasta,
and Dṛḍhādhyāśaya:
these Great Ones should be drawn.'

63. 'Likewise in the west,
the *mantrin* should draw
the Hero Ākāśa-garbha;
he is very majestic and is dressed in white,
he should be visualized holding a sword[B],
and this Son of the Buddha is seated upon a lotus.'

ĀKĀŚA-GARBHA (Sky Treasury). ***Holding a sword***: The symbol of the Insight of his liberation.

64. 'Around this Great Being,
there should also be drawn other glorious ones.
These Great Beings in his entourage are:
Gaganāmala, Gagana-mati,
Visuddha-mati, Caritra-mati,
and Sthira-buddhi.
These should be carefully drawn.'

65. 'The Heroic One should always be visualized
accompanied by these beings in sequence.'

For the colour of those Bodhisattvas and their symbols which are not clearly mentioned here, (78a) you should refer to the Secret Mandala.

66. Then Vajrapāṇi, the Lord of the Secret Ones, looked at the entire assembly and then looked at the Bhagavat for a long time with unwavering eyes. Then he recited this verse:

A C: 寶掌 '*Ratnakara*' ('Ratna [palm of the] hand')
B C adds: 生焰光 '*which gives out flaming rays*'

'Like *Udumbara* flowers[27],
so the All-knowing Ones:
they rarely appear in the world,
anywhere or at any time.
Even rarer than that is the appearance
of the method of the mantra practice.
If any evils one has done
throughout many millions of eons
will all be cleansed away
merely by seeing such a mandala as this,
then what can be said when one abides
in this most glorious method of mantra practice?
If one recites the mantras of the Protectors,
one will reach the supreme state.
Whoever follows with unwavering resolution
this most excellent practice,
will completely sever all arising
of suffering and birth in the evil states of being!' [28]

After Vajrapāṇi had understood the above description of the Mandala and the arrangement of the deities, his mind became serenely clear with regards to their appearance and qualities. By virtue of that clarity, he spoke these verses which show the rarity and great power of the Mantra Method, the great power of seeing the Mandala, the great power of reciting the mantras, and the great power of faith through hearing and seeing the mantras. Now there are three types of serene clarity of mind: that gone to the skin, that gone to the bones, and that gone to the feet. That gone to the skin is horripilation and so on. That gone to the bones is the flow of tears and so on. That gone to the feet is the outburst of speech. Therefore since the mind of Vajrapāṇi was very serenely clear, having gone to his feet, he spoke out in words. (78b)

If any evils one has done ... by seeing such a Mandala as this: (79a) This says that any evil which one has accumulated, by doing the ten unwholesome actions through many eons, will all be cleansed away by seeing this Mandala, which is the transformation of the Adornments of the Inexhaustible Body of the Tathāgata. Although they will indeed be cleansed away, that does not happen just by seeing the Mandala, but they will be cleansed away if one has carried out the preliminaries, the main part and the supplements. The preliminary section is the confession of faults, the taking of refuge in the Three Jewels, and accepting the Discipline of the Awareness without Obscurations in the three times, in order to enter the Mandala. The main part is the generation of *bodhicitta* at the time of entry. Then after having entered the Mandala, there is the seeing of the Buddhas' and Bodhisattvas' appearances and symbols , as well as the ornaments and streamers of the Mandala, and the arising of serene clarity. The supplementary section is the consideration of the commitment not to abandon the sacred Dharma and *bodhicitta* and so on. If you see the Mandala with all these aspects, then all the evil you have accumulated over many eons will be cleansed away, just as darkness that has been present [in a room] for many years will be dispelled instantly by the shining of a lamp there. (79b)

67. Then the entire assembly, together with those Vajradharas, said with one voice: (132b)

'Excellent! Excellent! O Great Hero
who has mastered the mantra practice!
Ask the unequalled All-knowing One
of the matters you are thinking about!
Then the other Bodhisattvas
who know the tantras with understanding,
and we who abide in the fruits of mantra practice,
will also master everything.'

68. Then Vajrapāṇi asked the Bhagavat the following:

'What are the colours?
Why are they called "colours"?
How should the colours be applied?
Which of them should be applied first?
What is the size of the archways,
the portals and the gates?
I ask the Lord to explain this!
Please speak in detail about
the foodstuffs for offering,
flowers, perfumes, jars and so forth.
Please tell me also
how the trainees should be received,
and how they should be initiated,
and about the gifts to the guru,
and the place for the fire offering.
What are the attributes of mantras,
and what is entry into *samādhi*?'

69. Then the Bhagavat,
who has attained mastery of all qualities,
replied thus to the Vajradhara:
'Listen carefully with a one-pointed mind!
O Great Being, I shall explain
all that you have asked
about the excellent method of mantra practice
from which the fruit of Mahāyāna arises.
Although beings are attached to the realms by them,
the Buddhas have previously taught
that they have the taste of the continuum of reality,
therefore they are called "colours".
Colour should be applied from inside,
and not from the outside[29]**.**
First white should be applied,
and then red and then yellow.
Next green should be applied.

All the inner parts are black.
Thus the colour method is explained.'

(80b4) This section deals with the significance of the word 'colour'[30]. The intrinsic nature of colour is to cause attachment. Thus in this case also, the interest of beings is aroused by the appearance of the colours and attributes of the Buddhas and Bodhisattvas and the drawing of the Mandala, and since they cause delight and involvement, they are said to be 'colours'. ***They have the taste of the continuum of reality:*** Since these colours are empowered by the letters whose intrinsic nature is the Body of the Buddha which is associated with the continuum of reality, the continuum of reality is indicated by these colours, and since they are of one taste, it is the taste of the continuum of reality. Furthermore, you should refer to the chapter dealing with the Mandala of the Revolving Wheel of Letters for details about their empowerment with the letters. (81a)

The intrinsic nature of '***white***' is the continuum of reality. Having thus become the continuum of reality, '***red***' should be applied next, for its intrinsic nature is involvement with beings by virtue of the compassion which benefits beings through expedient means. Following that, this benefitting of beings should also be enriched, so '***yellow***' is applied, which is the attribute of enrichment. Having thus been enriched, one becomes capable of carrying out everything, therefore '***green***' which does everything should be applied[31]. When one is thus able to carry out all activities, the colour '***black***' should be applied, for black is the attribute of the subduing which trains harm-doers and evil ones. It is applied to all the '***inner parts***' because it is secret.

70. **'Also the size of the archways**
should be the same as the central mandala,
and the portals are also the same;
the lotus is said to be sixteen inches.
The first gate is the same [size]
as the matrix mandala,
and the wise one should know that
the others should be gradually larger.
Within each of the gates, (133a)
he should place the gate-keepers.'

71. **'In brief, *samādhi* is explained**
as the complete satisfaction of mind[A]**.**
Great Being, listen attentively
to the explanation of the distinctions:
The *samādhi* of all the Buddhas
is said to be emptiness by the Jina.
It is attained through complete knowledge of the mind,
and from nothing else.
The complete abandonment of both

A C: 一心住於緣 '*single-mindedly abiding on a perceptual object*'.

is said to be the *samādhi* of Perfect Buddhas:
It is called the Great Emptiness,
and perfects the All-knowing Awareness.
Therefore you should always recollect
emptiness in all situations.'

'***Samādhi***'[32] is defined as the one-pointedness of mind. There is also one-pointedness on the relative and the absolute levels. One-pointedness on the relative level is when the mind rests one-pointedly upon the earth or water mandalas and so on. The absolute level is one-pointedness of mind upon the intrinsically empty, the abandonment of perceiving subject and perceived objects. The mind which is involved and contented without turning aside, by becoming one-pointed upon either of these is called the satisfied mind. That is the general definition of *samādhi*.

O Great Being! Listen attentively and so forth: This explains the qualities of the *samādhi* of the absolute level. (82a) That is the *samādhi* of the Buddhas and the *samādhi* of the Perfect Buddhas. Regarding the *samādhi* of the Buddhas, the text says, '***The* samādhi *of all the Buddhas is said to be emptiness by the Jina***'. ***Emptiness***: If one dissolves such phenomena as the psycho-physical constituents, and the perceptual elements and sources by virtue of their not having been born or arisen from the very beginning, or if one dissolves them by means of the absurdity of [the idea of] atoms and so forth, they will not exist, and even their appearance as perceptual images will cease to exist. The direct realization in that way of the non-existence of the attributes of a perceiving subject and perceived objects is '***emptiness***'. When one has realized that the intrinsic nature of the attributes of each phenomenon is emptiness, the mind remains one-pointedly there, without moving from that intrinsic nature of emptiness to anything else. This is the *samādhi* attained by the Bodhisattvas who have completed the Ten Levels, at which time they are called 'Buddhas'.

Though it is not the case that the emptiness in which the forms of a perceiving subject and perceived objects are abandoned completely, is not also attained at the time of the Level of the Joyous One, such Bodhisattvas have not yet entered into spontaneity since the inimical and its antidotes have not yet been completely abandoned from the First Level (the Joyous One) up to the Eighth Level. Therefore this does not refer to them, but since the inimical and its antidotes are abandoned from the Eighth Level onwards and a start is made with spontaneity, it is linked with the Eighth, Ninth and Tenth Levels. When the Ten Levels have been perfected, this *samādhi* will be fully attained. This *samādhi* which is fully attained by them will not be attained by anything else but through the complete knowledge of one's mind.

(82b) ***The complete abandonment of both ... the All-knowing Awareness***: This refers to the *samādhi* of Perfect Buddhas. '***The complete abandonment of both***' is the abandonment of both the idea of the abandonment of a perceiving subject and perceived objects, and of the intrinsic nature of emptiness. When one abides in the Eleventh All Good Level, one abandons even the idea of emptiness after having understood that the intrinsic nature of all phenomena is emptiness, and one abides in just the idea that even the intrinsic nature of emptiness does not exist. Therefore, even the idea of emptiness is abandoned, so this is called the '***Great Emptiness***'. ***It perfects the All-knowing Awareness***: Immediately one is perfectly enlightened, one will attain the All-knowing Awareness which is defined as the abandonment of even the idea [of emptiness]. Because that Perfect Enlightenment causes one to be united with the All-knowing Awareness, it is said to perfect the All-knowing Awareness.

Therefore you should always recollect emptiness in all situations: Because All-knowing Awareness is thus perfected by that *samādhi* of emptiness, you should always cultivate this kind of emptiness in all types of *samādhis*, such as those for the four-membered recitation, the practice of your own tutelary deity (*adhidevatā*), or the earth, water and other mandalas.

72. Then the Bhagavat Vairocana and all the Buddhas, being of like mind, spoke of the various methods of the Śrāvaka, the Pratyekabuddha and the Bodhisattva *samādhis*. And at that time, he entered into the *samādhi* called 'The Swift Power of the Unity[A] of All Buddhas'.

(83a) Now in order to teach the various individual *samādhis* of the Bodhisattvas, Śrāvakas and Pratyekabuddhas, the Bhagavat entered a *samādhi* and when he emerged from that *samādhi*, he taught the *samādhis* of the Bodhisattvas and so on.

Being of like mind: This shows the unity of their activities, since the intentions of all the Buddhas are in agreement, because of the sameness of their accumulations of merit and awareness, their *dharmakāyas* and their benefitting of beings. ***The* samādhi *called 'The Swift Power of the Unity of all Buddhas'***: Though various kinds of activities occur for the sake of beings, all Buddhas arise from a single unity, they arise from the single taste of the *dharmakāya*. For example, just as when the light from many lamps is mingled, it is one and the same, without distinction. ***Power***: Unimpeded energy. ***Swift***: That energy is quick to act for the sake of beings.

73. Then the Bhagavat said to the Bodhisattva Vajrapāṇi:

Because I sat in the core of Enlightenment
and overcame the Four Māras,
I am called the Great Hero:
This was joyfully proclaimed
with voices free from all fear
by the crowds of gods such as Brahmā.
Thereafter, I who am mighty,
have been renowned as the Great Hero.
I directly realized that there is no arising,
and abandoned the perceptual range of words;
I became free from all faults,
and separated from causes and conditions.
There arose in me, as it really is,
the Awareness which is empty, like space,
the utterly pure reality,
which is devoid of all darkness.
To abide in the mode of "idea alone"[B]:

A C: — 體 '*the single substance of* ... '

B T has '*kun-mkhyen tsam*' which should be amended to ' '*du-shes tsam*' in view of context and Buddhaguhya's comments. Presumably the confusion arose because the underlying Sanskrit, **saṃjñā-mātra*, can be translated as either of these.

this is the attribute of Perfect Enlightenment.
Hence I revealed this reality
in the form of letters,
by the power of transformation,
to illumine the world,
and out of pity for beings
I teach everything to them.'

***The Four Māras*:** He overcame the Māra of the Psycho-physical Constituents (*skandha-māra*), the Māra of the Emotional Afflictions, the Māra of Death and the Māra Demigods. You should understand that there is also both a relative and an absolute level here. The relative overcoming of Māra (83b) is the overcoming of the Māra Demigods and the Māra of the Emotional Afflictions at the Great Enlightenment, and following that, the overcoming of the Māras of the Psycho-physical Constituents and Death, which are well known from the Hīnayāna School. As for the absolute overcoming, here it is the overcoming of the Four Māras through knowing that they do not exist even though they appear, having realized the unarisen and unborn nature of all phenomena.

***I directly understood that there is no arising*:** He overcame the Māra of the Psycho-physical Constituents, because he understood that even the psycho-physical constituents are lacking any objective basis, by the direct realization that all phenomena have really not arisen from the very beginning. ***Completely abandoning the perceptual range of words*:** Devoid of dualistic conceptualization. By transcending the perceptual range of dualistic conceptualization, he overcame the Māra Demigods. ***Devoid of all faults*:** By liberation from emotional afflictions, he actually overcame the Māra of Emotional Afflictions. ***Free from causes and conditions*:** Because of the non-existence of causes and conditions, he is unborn. Because of being unborn, he is without death, so he actually overcame the Māra of Death.

The Awareness which is empty, like space*:** Because of his liberation following the emergence of those four aspects, there arose the Awareness devoid of perceptual images, which is luminous by nature, (84a) characterized by emptiness and unborn, like space. ***Arose in me as it really is*:** That empty Awareness was attained by him without any error. ***Reality*:** Because it is authentic consummacy in character, it is not possible to refute it either by scriptures or logic. Therefore' 'reality***' refers to that empty Awareness. ***To abide in the mode of "idea alone": this is the attribute of Perfect Enlightenment*:** That Perfect Enlightenment is to abandon the idea of the intrinsic emptiness of phenomena and to abide in just the idea which knows that even intrinsic emptiness does not exist.

***Hence I revealed this reality ... I teach it all to them*:** Although he thus realized that all phenomena are from the very beginning unarisen and unborn, out of his pity for beings, he transforms the real Dharma into letters so that it may be spoken of in words. You should refer to the section on the Great Hero *Samādhi* about those letters. (84b)

74. **Then the glorious Vajradhara,** (133b)
amazed, with wide open eyes,
saluted the All-knowing One

with his head and said:
'The inconceivable Insight and Means
of all Buddhas are a great wonder.
Having realized the Dharma
which is devoid of all proliferations,
the Self-arisen Ones reveal
the complete perfection
of all the hopes of all worlds.
So also the attributes of mantras
abide well in the two Truths;
any being would be revered[A]
by people of the world
if he were to know just that.'

Then, after having offered these verses, Vajrapāṇi, the Lord of the Secret Ones, gazed with unwavering eyes at the Bhagavat Vairocana in silence.

'***Insight***' (*prajñā*) is the direct realization of the emptiness of phenomena, and '***expedient means***' (*upāya*) are the revelation of that Dharma of emptiness in letters and so on. Then beings are led to it by way of superior, medium and inferior attainments, and the carrying-out of the rites of Pacifying and so on.

So also the attribute of mantras: The teaching in that way of the Dharma with proliferations after the realization of the Dharma without proliferations is the attribute of mantras. This attribute of mantras also conforms to both relative and absolute levels of truth. On the absolute level they are intrinsically empty in nature and on the relative level they are the superior attainments and so on, and the performance of the rites of Pacifying and so on.

Any being would be revered by people of the world if he were to know just that: (85a) Even if one does not become accomplished and so on, but just knows that Mantra Method by hearing and thinking of it, one will still become an object of reverence for the people of the world.

75. Then the Bhagavat said to Vajrapāṇi, the Lord of the Secret Ones: 'Moreover, Lord of the Secret Ones, as for the *samādhi* method of those Bodhisattvas with one remaining rebirth, who abide in the Buddha Level:

'Having known the nature of the world,
free from all purposeful activity,
those on the level of purposeful activity
dwell on the Buddha Level.'

This explains the *samādhi* of the Bodhisattva who has perfected the Tenth Level and abides on the Buddha Level, who then abides on the level where things are done by expedient means for the benefit of beings, having directly realized the intrinsic emptiness of all phenomena.

Though they have directly realized that the worlds are unarisen from the very beginning since they are not the result of anything, nor have they arisen from any

A C adds: 猶如敬制底 '*just as a* caitya *is revered*'.

cause, those Bodhisattvas stay on the level of purposeful acts and adorn the Buddha fields in various forms. There they exert themselves for the sake of beings, so those Bodhisattvas who dwell on the Buddha Level are said to dwell on the level of purposeful acts. This is the *samādhi* method of those Tenth Level Bodhisattvas who dwell on the Buddha Level.

76. 'Moreover, Lord of the Secret Ones, as for the *samādhi* method of the Bodhisattvas who are masters of the Eighth Level:

> **'Not perceiving any phenomena as objects,**
> **and having abandoned existence and arising,**
> **and knowing that the world is like an illusion:**
> **people call them Masters of the World.'**

77. 'Moreover, Lord of the Secret Ones, the Śrāvakas who abide on the level with cognitive objects have destroyed the two extremes through a direct understanding of arising and perishing. But they do not practise the Awareness which concerns the utter non-existence of things, since they do not perceive any basis for it. This is the *samādhi* method of the Śrāvakas.'

The Śrāvakas view such phenomena as the psycho-physical constituents and so on as causative and resultant phenomena (*kārya-kāraṇa-bhāva*) which arise and perish, so they have cognitive objects. Since they thus [understand] there is arising and perishing, they have dissolved the two extremes of eternalism and nihilism. They dissolve the extreme of nihilism since they perceive the fact there is arising, and they dissolve the extreme of eternalism since they perceive the fact that there is perishing. But since they thus perceive the existence of arising and perishing, they do not generate the Awareness which sees the utter non-existence of phenomena, because they do not perceive any cause which would generate Awareness in the utter absence of all phenomena.

78. 'Lord of the Secret Ones, those Pratyekabuddhas who abide in the method of the inexpressibility of phenomena after having dissolved [the idea of] cause and result, enter into the Awareness in which phenomena are inexpressible. (134a) **This involvement in the *samādhi* in which speech is extinguished is the *samādhi* method of the Pratyekabuddhas.'**

(86a) The *samādhi* of the Pratyekabuddhas. They have dissolved [the idea of] cause and effect by refutation, for the existence of the causes and conditions of phenomena is only present without duration for the space of a moment, just as a mustard seed cannot rest on the tip of a needle. Since [the idea of] permanence does not stand up, they realize the non-existence of causative and resultant phenomena. Since phenomena thus do not exist, the Pratyekabuddhas generate the Awareness which sees that they are inexpressible with words, and so they thus also bring an end to verbalization. In brief, although the Pratyekabuddhas have dissolved [the idea of] causative and resultant phenomena, and have realized that phenomena are without self-existence, they abide in mere silence. Hence they do not abide, as Bodhisattvas do, in the Radiance of Awareness (*jñāna-āloka*) *samādhi* which is without perceptual images, although they have not merely realized the absence of a self in the individual like the Śrāvakas.

79. 'Moreover, Lord of the Secret Ones, while mundane people understand results coming from causes, the arising and perishing due to karmic action, they generate a *samādhi* of emptiness dependent on the power of others. This is the *samādhi* method of mundane people.

'Lord of the Secret Ones!
This is the *samādhi* method,
the method of the ritual of mantra practice,
in which dwell the Buddhas, Pratyekabuddhas,
the protector Bodhisattvas,
the Śrāvakas who are famed
as having overcome evil,
and even the mundane gods.
Wishing that beings might be benefitted,
the Hero therefore expounds it.'

Although there are mundane people who realize that karmic actions and results arise from causes, they believe that these are produced by Indra or Brahmā, who they call their Lord. Even their perception of the unreality and emptiness of phenomena is not the intrinsic emptiness, for they think that these are made empty by Indra and so on, and hence are made to abide in a *samādhi* of emptiness by them.

80. Then the Bhagavat also said to Vajrapāṇi, the Lord of the Secret Ones: 'Lord of the Secret ones! Listen to the attributes of mantras!' And Vajrapāṇi said: 'Bhagavat, please let it be so!', and he listened to the Bhagavat who said:

'Lord of the Secret Ones!
The mantras of the perfect Buddhas
are characterized by words, names and symbols.
By mastery of the words[A],
the mantras accomplish all aims.
Some have words of exhortation,
and some their names spoken at the beginning.
Those with *hūṃ* and *phaṭ*
are those of the Uṣṇīṣas[B].
As for those with "Hold!", "Devour!",
"Destroy!", "Afflict!",
"Kill!" or "Tear asunder!",
the Guide says that these are the mantras
for the attendants and the wrathful ones.
Those with *namaḥ* and *svāhā* and so on,
are associated with those who are in *samādhi*.
Mantras with the words

A C adds: 如因陀羅宗 '*like the treatise of Indra*'.

B C: 若唵字許字及與發磔迦 '*Those with* Om *and* Hūṃ, *and well as* Phaṭ [*are those …*]'.

**Śānta and *viśuddha*,
which perfect all wishes,
are those of all Buddhas
and the protector Bodhisattvas.
Mantras of the Śrāvakas** (134b)
**are single, as they abide in one base.
Those of Pratyekabuddhas are likewise,
but their special features to be mentioned
are the purification of karmic action and life
through their type of *samādhi*.'**

This section explains the attributes of the individual mantras of the Tathāgatas, the Perfect Buddhas, the Buddhas, the Bodhisattvas, the Śrāvakas and the Pratyekabuddhas. Furthermore, you should understand the attributes of the mantras in three categories: the mantras as deities, the meanings of mantras and the nature of mantras.

Of these, the mantras as deities were explained in the Mandala Arising from Great Compassion, and they are the very Tathāgatas, the Perfect Buddhas, the Buddhas, the Bodhisattvas, Śrāvakas, Pratyekabuddhas and so on themselves. (87a) The Three Families arranged in the matrix mandala are the Tathāgatas. The Perfect Buddhas are Śākyamuni and his entourage residing in the middle section of the Mandala. The Buddhas are the chief Bodhisattvas such as Ratnapāṇi and so on. Although the Śrāvakas and Pratyekabuddhas are not actually mentioned, they are counted among those to be guided by the *nirmāṇa-kāya*, so you should understand them to be included in the middle section of the Mandala. The mundane gods are also included there as well.

The meanings of the mantras are the *samādhis* of the Tathāgatas and so on, down to those of the mundane gods, previously mentioned, and you should know that this is also of two types, the absolute and the relative. The absolute is the intrinsic nature of emptiness, their mode of liberation. The relative is the expounding of the Dharma for the sake of beings mentioned above with the words '***those who are on the level of purposeful activity***' and so on, and the qualities of the Bhagavat such as the Ten Strengths, the Ten Fearlessnesses and so on.

The nature of mantras should be known under four categories: words, syllables, vowels and local languages. Of these, words are the verbal utterances composed of many syllables joined together. Syllables are each individual syllable of a mantra, such as the letter *Ka* and so on. Vowels are those connected with the group of vowel signs for *A*, *I* and so on. Local language refers to those that are spoken in accordance with whatever language is used in each region. (87b)

***The mantras of Perfect Buddhas are characterized by words, names and symbols*:** By uttering such words as *jina jik* , that are the symbols of the Buddha's name, they function as the mantras of the Buddhas.

***By mastery of the words, the mantras accomplish all aims*:** Also the uttering of words of the mantras of the Perfect Buddhas, which are the symbols of the *samādhi* of earth, brings about the accomplishment of all enriching aims.

***Some have words of exhortation, and some have their names spoken at the beginning*:** By mentioning the power and qualities of the deity of the mantra through the words of the mantra, or by mentioning an exhortation regarding [various] rites such as '*śānti kuru!*' (Pacify!), or by mentioning the name of the deity with '*jina jik*' and so on, you will know to which deity it belongs. You should know that those with the words '*hūṃ*' and '*phaṭ*' are the mantras of the eight Uṣṇīṣas mentioned above. In other texts the mantras of the Uṣṇīṣas appear without *hūṃ* or *phaṭ*, and the mantras of deities who are not Uṣṇīṣas do appear with '*hūṃ*' or '*phaṭ*', so you should know that the mantras of the Uṣṇīṣas with '*hūṃ*' and '*phaṭ*' are the mantras of those Uṣṇīṣas mentioned in this text. (88a)

Mantras of the Śrāvakas are single, as they abide in one base*:** There are no mantras for such members as the crown of the head, the *uṣṇīṣa* and so on, among the mantras of the Śrāvakas, so they are 'single***'. Because the Śrāvakas do not turn into various forms like the Bodhisattvas, but maintain just the appearance of a monk, or because they just realize the absence of a self in the individual, '***they abide in one base***' only. (88b)

81. 'Moreover, Lord of the Secret Ones, the properties of mantras are not created by all the Buddhas, nor caused to be created by them, and nor are they sanctioned by them. Why is that? Because this is the intrinsic nature of phenomena, for whether Tathāgatas appear or not, their intrinsic nature has always been present, and so that is also the intrinsic nature of the mantras of *mantrins*.'

This section explains the nature of mantras. The nature of mantras, which are characterized as words, names and symbols, is the power to bring about whatever is commanded by the words of exhortation and so forth. Yet even if the Tathāgatas were to bring about that nature of mantras, saying 'Let this thing be done by this power!', or were to cause others to bring it about, or to sanction others to bring it about, it still would not be brought about by them, nor caused to be brought about by them, nor sanctioned by them, as Tathāgatas are devoid of perceptual forms. Why? If that nature of mantras was brought about by the Tathāgatas, then the work of all beings would be carried out by the Tathāgatas, and so any *sādhana* undertaken would definitely become accomplished by everybody. But *sādhanas* are not thus accomplished by everybody, and so it is not brought about by the Tathāgatas. If the meaning of the mantra and its power were both permanently joined together, then that meaning would be accomplished merely by uttering the word. (89a) For example, when one says the word 'fire', one's mouth is not destroyed, even though the nature of fire is to burn.

Why is that? Because this is the intrinsic nature of phenomena and so forth: Even though mantras, which are characterized by words, names and symbols, have words of exhortation and so forth, and have meanings, any aim that is commanded is not carried out by anybody, but that property has been present from the very beginning, without reference to another cause. For example, the sweetness of sugar and the bitterness of salt have not been created by any cause, but that sweetness or bitterness has been present from the very beginning. For if it had been brought about by the Tathāgatas, then when the Tathāgatas appear, the nature of mantras would also come about, and when they do not appear, it also would not come about. Therefore, regardless of whether the Tathāgatas appear or not, that intrinsic nature of phenomena is present from the beginning, and this is the same with the intrinsic nature of the mantras of the *mantrin*.

82. 'Lord of the Secret Ones! Whenever a Perfect Buddha, who is all-knowing and all-seeing, appears in the world, he expounds the Mantra Method by transforming that intrinsic nature, with various methods and intentions, in accordance with the different inclinations of beings, into various words, various letters and various languages for those who understand them.'

83. 'In what way do Tathāgatas transform the Mantra Method into letters[A]? Lord of the Secret Ones! They are the words of truth, the Four Noble Truths, the Four Recollections, the Four Bases of Supernatural Power, the Ten Strengths of a Tathāgata, the Seven Precious Limbs of Enlightenment, the Four Divine States and the Eighteen Uncommon Qualities of a Buddha, which were accomplished by the Tathāgatas over many billions of eons. In brief, Lord of the Secret Ones, all that which is the All-knowing Awareness of the Tathāgatas is transformed through the power of the Tathāgatas' merit and awareness, through the power of the awareness of their previous aspirations, (135a) **and through the transformational power of the continuum of reality, and then the mantra ritual is fully revealed by them to beings in accordance with their lot.'**

(90a) This section explains how the intrinsic nature of the mantras is transformed into letters and manifested, and also how the Qualities, Strengths, Fearlessnesses and so forth of the Tathāgata are transformed into the letters of the mantras. You should know that this transformation into words and letters is both relative and absolute. Of these, the relative is the transformation and manifestation of the Strengths, Fearlessnesses and so on, as words and letters. The absolute is the manifestation of the intrinsic emptiness of all phenomena, which are unborn and unarisen from the very beginning, as letters. (90b)

84. 'What is that mantra technique? *A* is a gate to all phenomena, because they are unarisen from the beginning. *Ka* is a gate to all phenomena, because they are without purpose. *Kha* is a gate to all phenomena, because they cannot be perceived as objects, like the sky. *Ga* is a gate to all phenomena, because no movement whatsoever can be perceived in them. *Gha* is a gate to all phenomena, because their solidity cannot be perceived. *Ca* is a gate to all phenomena, because they are devoid of all perishing. *Cha* is a gate to all phenomena, because they are the same as shadows. *Ja* is a gate to all phenomena, because birth cannot be perceived in them. *Jha* is a gate to all phenomena, because no impurities can be perceived in them. *Ta* is a gate to all phenomena, because pride cannot be perceived in them. *Tha* is a gate to all phenomena, because creation cannot be perceived in them. *Da* is a gate to all phenomena, because disorder cannot be perceived in

A C: 謂加持此書寫文字 '*that is to say, transformed into written letters*'.

them. *Dha* is a gate to all phenomena, because they are devoid of deception. *Ta* is a gate to all phenomena, because Suchness cannot be perceived in them. *Tha* is a gate to all phenomena, because no abode can be perceived in them. *Da* is a gate to all phenomena, because subjugation cannot be perceived in them. *Dha* is a gate to all phenomena, because the realms cannot be perceived in them. *Pa* is a gate to all phenomena, because ultimate truth cannot be perceived in them. *Pha* is a gate to all phenomena, because they are without substantiality, like bubbles. *Ba* is a gate to all phenomena, because they are devoid of modes of speech. *Bha* is a gate to all phenomena, because no existence cannot be perceived in them. *Ya* is a gate to all phenomena, because all Ways cannot be perceived in them. (135b) *Ra* is a gate to all phenomena, because they are devoid of all pollution. *La* is a gate to all phenomena, because no attributes can be perceived in them. *Sa* is a gate to all phenomena, because they are tranquil by nature. *Sa* is a gate to all phenomena, because they are dull by nature. *Sa* is a gate to all phenomena, because no truths whatsoever can be perceived in them. *Ha* is a gate to all phenomena, because causes cannot be perceived in them.'

Those words and letters mentioned by the Bhagavat with the words ***mantras are characterized by words, names and symbols*** are also explained as being *samādhi* gates. Also that transformation of each of these words and letters into the *samādhi* gates is both relative and absolute. (91a) Of these, the relative is the manifestation of the Buddha's qualities such as the Strengths and the Fearlessnesses, through letters and words. The absolute is the manifestation [of the fact] that all phenomena are unborn from the very beginning and are intrinsically empty, by means of those same letters. Therefore, since both the relative and the absolute meanings are revealed by means of the words and letters, the Bhagavat has revealed the attributes of the mantras as words, names and symbols, by means of *mudrās* and so on. That is, they are transformed and revealed as letters and words. Therefore the text here explains the revelation of the intrinsic emptiness of all phenomena by means of such letters as *A*. Also the thirty-two letters beginning with *Ka* and so on are *samādhi* gates to emptiness. As appropriate, you should consider some as *samādhi* gates revealing the emptiness of all phenomena, other as revealing partial emptiness, or others as revealing emptiness by means of entry into emptiness. (91b)

A (*anutpada*) He who has realized directly the emptiness of all phenomena, since they are unborn from the beginning, is a Tathāgata. Therefore the letter *A* is transformed into and established as the *samādhi* gate to the realization of emptiness. Therefore by means of the letter *A*, it is revealed that all phenomena are unborn and unarisen from the beginning.

Ka (*kārya*). *Kārya* (purpose) means 'result'. It is said: 'If there is no process of generation, the cause itself is inadmissable. If the cause itself is inadmissable, what becomes of the result?' So although the result does not exist because it is not generated by a cause, does that cause exist in the nature of the result generated? [No, for in that case] the cause itself would be formed by the result! Therefore you should understand the fact that all phenomena are unborn and unarisen.

Kha (*kha-sama* 'like the sky') [No comment]

Ga (*gati*). In Sanskrit, *gati* means 'movement', 'mode of existence' and 'understanding'. If you treat it as 'movement', then this means that there is no going or goer to the east, west and so on that can be perceived. (92a) If you treat it as 'mode of existence', then it means that the six states of existence, such as those of the gods, humans and so on cannot be perceived. If you treat it as 'understanding', then it means that no understanding nor one who understands can be perceived with regards all phenomena which are unborn from the very beginning.
Gha (*ghana*). In Sanskrit, *ghana* means 'solid'. There is nothing to perceive which is a solid mass of atoms.
Ca (*cyuti*). In Sanskrit, *cyuti* means 'perishing'. Because all phenomena are unborn, perishing also cannot be perceived.
Cha (*chāyā*). In Sanskrit, *chāyā* means 'shadow'. If a shadow was independent of the body, then a shadow would be seen even if there was no body present. On the other hand, if a shadow is not independent of the body, it would seem inadmissable for a shadow to appear in any direction. Hence as they do appear in that way, they are not absolutely real, but are delusory, like a magical illusion. Delusions or magical illusions are without real existence, so all phenomena are likewise, since they are like shadows.
Ja (*jāti*). In Sanskrit, *jāti* means 'birth'. Since there is nothing to be born or being born, birth cannot be perceived in them.
Jha (*jhamara*). In Sanskrit, *jhamara* means 'impurity'. No phenomena which can become impure can be perceived. (92b)
Ṭa (*ṭakara*): In Sanskrit, *ṭakara* means 'pride'.
Ṭha (*viṭhana*): In Sanskrit, *viṭhana* means 'creation'.
Ḍa (*ḍamara*): In Sanskrit, *ḍamara* means 'disorder'.
Ḍha (*ḍhaṅga*): In Sanskrit, *ḍhaṅga* means 'deception'.
Ta (*tathatā*): In Sanskrit, *tathatā* means 'Suchness'. Suchness, the limits of existence and emptiness are all synonyms.
Tha (*sthāna*): In Sanskrit, *sthāna* means 'abode'.
Da (*damana*): In Sanskrit, *damana* means 'subjugation'.
Dha (*dhātu*): In Sanskrit, *dhātu* means 'realm', that is, the Realms of Desire, Form and the Formless.
Pa (*paramārtha*): In Sanskrit, *paramārtha* means 'absolute truth'. (93a)
Pha (*phena*): In Sanskrit, *phena* means 'bubble'.
Ba (*vāk-patha*): In Sanskrit, *vākpatha* means 'mode of speech'.
Bha (*bhāva*): In Sanskrit, *bhāva* means 'existence'. It refers to the five psycho-physical constituents, for they arise in the Three Realms.
Ya (*yāna*): In Sanskrit, *yāna* means 'way'. If you know the significance of the Teachings, you will leave behind even the Teachings, like a raft. Therefore because of the realization of the emptiness of all phenomena, that very Way which one has entered and realized cannot be perceived.
Ra (*rajas*): In Sanskrit, *rajas* means 'dust'. The word *rajas* refers both to atoms and to the emotional afflictions, neither of which has any objective basis. (93b)
La (*lakṣaṇa*): In Sanskrit, *lakṣaṇa* means 'attribute'.
Śa (*śānti*): In Sanskrit, *prakṛti-śānti* means 'tranquil by nature'.
Ṣa (*ṣaṭa*): In Sanskrit, *ṣaṭa* means 'dull'. Phenomena perceived by the faculties such as the eyes, ears and so on, are not truly perceived because such faculties as the eyes

are not trustworthy, due to their dullness, and so the phenomena perceived by them do not really exist.
Sa (*satya*): In Sanskrit, *satya* means 'truth'. Neither the relative nor the absolute truth can be perceived in them.
Ha (*hetu*): In Sanskrit, *hetu* means 'cause'.
In brief, you should understand that these letters reveal the *samādhi* gates to emptiness.

85. 'Lord of the Secret Ones! *Ṅa, Ña, Ṇa, Na* and *Ma* cause the mastery of all *samādhis* and are endowed with all power. They will cause the purpose of the undertaking to be quickly accomplished.'

By attaching the *anusvāra* to those letters, because it is the symbol of emptiness, ***Ṅa*** gives mastery over the whole *Ka* group of letters, ***Ña*** relates to the whole *Ca* group, ***Ṇa*** relates to the whole *Ṭa* group, (94a) ***Na*** relates to the whole *Ta* group and ***Ma*** relates to the whole *Pa* group. Likewise those letters should also be linked to the emptiness of the letters *Ya, Ra* and so on. Since they are the signs (*lakṣaṇa*) of the emptiness of everything, they are endowed with all powers, and even the aims of attainments on the relative level will be quickly accomplished with them.

86. 'Lord of the Secret Ones! This *samādhi* Gate, the Mantra Method which completely perfects all hopes, is the inconceivable result of the maturation of the Tathāgatas; it is endowed with the most excellent attributes; it is the definite meaning of the truth of mantras; it transcends the three times and is unsullied like space.

> **'While abiding on the inconceivable mind level,**
> **it appears through actions and activities,**
> **and after the level of practice has been attained,**
> **it bestows inconceivable results.**
> **This is the supreme truth,**
> **revealed by all the Buddhas.**
> **If he knows this mantra technique,**
> **the *mantrin* will acquire attainments.**
> **Sound, the most excellent truth,**
> **is the mantra attribute of mantras.**
> **If the *mantrin* bears this in mind,**
> **he will attain the immortal state.'**

Having explained the Mantra Method, the letters *Ka* and so on, as being the gates of the *samādhis* to the experience of reality, there now follows praises of it and teachings about its nature. (94b) ***If he knows this Mantra Method, the* mantrin *will acquire attainments*:** This refers to the cultivation of emptiness and *bodhicitta*, which are the intrinsic nature of mantras. If the *mantrin* knows such mantra techniques as uniting himself with the body-image of the deity through the mantra letters, and doing the four-membered recitation, he will accomplish the attainments.

87. Then Vajrapāṇi, the Lord of the Secret Ones, said to the Bhagavat: 'The revelation by the Bhagavat of the discourse on the inconceivable method of the attributes of mantras is a great wonder. It is not shared by any of the Śrāvakas, or Pratyekabuddhas[A]. (93b) Bhagavat! Whosoever believes in that Mantra Method will also become endowed with uncommon virtues. I now request the Bhagavat to explain the rules for the requisite articles for the Mandala!' (136a)

(95a) ***The rules for the requisite articles for the Mandala***: After completing the drawing of the Mandala, it is fitting for offerings and so on to be made. So one has the *samādhi* of the offerings, mentally-formed offerings, offerings with joined palms, offerings of loving-kindness and compassion, and the mundane offerings of flowers and fragrances. Vajrapāṇi asks the Bhagavat to explain these four types of offerings, the protection of the Mandala, (95b) and the entreaty to the deities of the Mandala to enter it. Of these, some are dealt with in the Chapter on the Mandala Arising from Great Compassion, some in the Chapter on the Mandala of the Revolving Wheel of Letters and others in the Chapter on the Secret Mandala. Whatever is not mentioned here but appears in the two later Chapters should be appended to this Chapter and likewise what is mentioned here, but not in the two later Chapters should also be appended to them.

88. The Bhagavat replied to Vajrapāṇi, the Lord of the Secret Ones:
'Then the *mantrin* should earnestly make offerings
to the deities, with pleasing yellow,
white and red flowers.
Such flowers as white and blue lotuses,
***keśaras, punnāgas,* jasmine[B],**
campakas, aśokas, tilakas
or else *patalā* and *śala* flowers.[33]
Such flowers as those are fragrant,
pleasing to look at and auspicious.
The wise *mantrin* should carefully offer those.
He should offer various fine, excellent,
and pleasing perfumes, such as sandalwood,
tagara, spṛkkā,* crocus and *kuṣṭha.
The *mantrin* should also offer to the deities,
according to the rules, various incenses
that are auspicious, world-famed and pleasing,
such as *agaru,* pine, camphor, sandalwood,
the gum of the *śala* tree, or else the *śrīvāsaka.*
Furthermore, Great Being, listen carefully
to the rules concerning foodstuffs for offering:
creamed rice, boiled rice with yoghurt,
spiced cakes and wafer biscuits,

A C adds: 非普爲一切衆生 '*nor are they at all widespread among all beings*'.
B C adds: 末利 'jasmine' (*mallikā*)

delicious fried honey cakes,
indescribable fine drinks,
flat bread, doughnuts,
and sweet pancakes, sugar puffs,
spiral cakes and dumplings.
Such foods as these, together with
sugar lumps, various fruits,
molasses, honey and ghee,
and various drinks such as
yoghurt and milk,
should be extensively offered.
Also various kinds of lamps
should be filled with fragrant oil
that is very pure and fine,
and then offered.
Parasols and pennants should be set up,
along the sides, in various colours.
The beautiful archways also
should be decorated with bells.
Furthermore, the mental offerings (136b)
should all be diligently produced and offered.
Then eight, sixteen, or more jars
should be procured and filled up
with perfumed water.
The necks should be adorned with cut flowers,
and likewise the mouths filled with fruit,
and adorned with flower perfumes and so on.
When they have been made very beautiful
and had their necks bound with scarves,
the wise one should set them out.
Cotton scarves should be offered,
one to each of the main deities,
and one per group for the ordinary Great Beings.'

This explains the external offerings, such as perfumes and so on. Although the noble deities will not be displeased even if the *mantrin* does not make the external offerings correctly with actual objects, their entourages of lower beings will be annoyed, and although they may not do any harm immediately, it says in other Tantras that they will not bring about the accomplishment of whatever aims you are hoping for and will not assist you. Therefore the *mantrin* should earnestly make those offerings. Although the Master who has devoted interest in the profound and extensive should mainly make mental offerings, he should also make these external offerings at all times, in order to gain the attention of those trainees who rely on actual objects. You should refer to the [Chapters on] the Mandala of the Revolving Wheel of Letters and the Secret Mandala for the offering *samādhi* and the mentally formed offerings. (96a)

89. **'After the offerings have thus been made,
the trainees are led before the Mandala,
and are sprinkled with water by the *mantrin.*
He should give them perfumes and flowers,
and when they have called upon the Tathāgatas,
they should be made to accept *bodhicitta.*
Because of this, they will all be born
into the wholesome Family of the Jinas.
He makes for them the *Mudrā*
which arises from the continuum of reality,
and the Dharma Wheel *Mudrā* also,
then they are transformed into Vajrasattvas.
He should then firmly make
the *samaya* of all the Buddhas,
at the same time reciting aloud three times
over the scarves, in accordance with the mantra ritual.
Then with a compassionate mind,
he should blindfold them.
Having recited the *samaya* three times,
he should place upon their heads
the letter *Ra* with an *anusvāra.*
It shines like the risen moon,
white in colour and radiates
a flaming garland.
In the presence of all the Protectors,
he then makes them throw their flower,
and wherever their flower falls,
that deity should be given to them.
The trainees should be held
in front of the outer mandala gate,
in between the two gates,
in the central area of the portal[A].
With them abiding there, all the rituals
should be done well, following the sequence.'**

(97a) This explains the ritual for the acceptance of the trainees into the Mandala. First of all, the Master should sprinkle the trainees with water from a jar empowered with the mantra of Trailokya-vijaya, at the gate of the outer wall of the Mandala, in order to clear away their impediments. Then making the *Mudrā* of the Three *Samayas* over the blindfold scarves of the trainees and reciting the mantra of the Three *Samayas* three times, the Master should blindfold the trainees. Then placing a flower in their hands, they should be made to generate *bodhicitta.* Then with the *mudrā* and mantra of the continuum of reality, he transforms them into the continuum of reality. Then with the *mudrā* and mantra of the Dharma Wheel, and the mantra of the Vajra Armour, (97b) the trainees should be transformed into

A C: 大龍廂衛處 '*the sentry post of the great* Nāgas'.

Vajrasattvas. Imagining the letter of the continuum of reality, a blazing white *Ra* with an *anusvāra* upon the top of their heads, he should cause them to make the *Mudrā* of the Three *Samayas* and to recite its mantra, and then to throw their flowers. The Master should give to the trainees whichever deity upon whom their flower falls. He should then make them circumambulate the Mandala three times. These in brief are the stages of the ritual for introducing them into the Mandala.

Now each will be explained. ***They should be made to accept* bodhicitta**: They should be made to accept the aspiration *bodhicitta*. ***Having called upon the Tathāgatas***: They should request the Buddhas and Bodhisattvas to think of them. Even though they have generated the aspiration *bodhicitta*, they should say 'O, all you Buddhas and Bodhisattvas! I ask you to think of me! I, (name) from this time until I reach the core of Enlightenment, will aspire to Enlightenment just as the blessed Buddhas and Bodhisattvas who have abandoned the psycho-physical constituents, perceptual elements and sources, perceiving subject and perceived objects, whose minds are unborn from the very beginning, just as they aspired to Enlightenment whose intrinsic nature is emptiness!'. ***Because of this, they will be born into the wholesome Family of the Jinas***: By thus planting seeds through the generation of *bodhicitta*, they will be born into the wholesome Family of the Jinas. The Family of the Jinas is endowed with insight and expedient means. Insight is the Mother Perfection of Insight, the intrinsic nothingness of all phenomena. (98a) Expedient means are the Perfection of Generosity and so on. Even the Tathāgatas arise from these, so it is called the Family of the Jinas.

He makes for them the* Mudrā *which arises from the continuum of reality: This is the generation of the aspirational *bodhicitta* and the application *bodhicitta*. With the mantra and *mudrā* of the continuum of reality which is emptiness, the trainees are transformed into emptiness.

Having also made the Dharma Wheel Mudrā, they are transformed into Vajrasattvas: Having thus realized the intrinsic emptiness, the trainees are changed into Vajrasattas by the mantra and *mudrā* of the Dharma Wheel, so that they may turn the Wheel of the Dharma for beings by means of returning again to the relative level. '***Vajrasattva***' is one whose mind is firm, vajra-like and cannot be overpowered by anybody. His body is crowned and adorned with various ornaments and he resides within a moon disc which itself is encircled with light. You should imagine a five-pointed vajra, whose nature is the Five Awarenesses, resting on the moon disc in his heart.

He should firmly make ... in accordance with the mantra ritual: He should empower the blindfolds of the trainees with the mantra and *mudrā* of the Three *Samayas*. Although it is not mentioned here, this should be the first of these actions. ***He should blindfold them***: With the scarves that have been empowered with the *Samayas*. The blindfolding is also done so that although the trainees had ordinary sight before, it is suspended by transforming them with the *Samaya* Mantra and *Mudrā*, (98b) and then transforming their sight into Awareness Sight. With the opening of those Awareness Eyes, the Mandala of the Vajra Adornments of the Inexhaustible Body of the Bhagavat will be revealed.

'***The Three Samayas***' are the Mandalas of the Vajra Adornments of the Inexhaustible Body, Speech and Mind of the Bhagavat, and the mantras and *mudrās* into which they are transformed. If you make the *mudrā* and recite the mantra [of the Three *Samayas*] three times, the Vajra Adornments of the Inexhaustible Body and so forth will be revealed. Therefore it is for that reason that whenever the Master recites the mantra, he should always make the *mudrā* of the Three *Samayas.* If he recites the mantra three times while making the *mudrā* of the Three *Samayas,* failings in the *samaya* commitments will also be repaired.

He should place on their heads the letter Ra ... a flaming garland: He visualizes the letter ***Ra,*** the Awareness of the Continuum of Reality, on the heads of the trainees. The intrinsic nature of '***Ra***' is the absence of the obscurations of emotional afflictions and wrong understanding. ***With an* anusvāra**: That is emptiness in nature. ***Like the risen moon:*** When the moon has arisen it is white by nature, but has a little red in it. The white shows purity in nature and the red shows desire for the benefit of beings. (99a)

90. **'Having thus made all the trainees,**
who are free from faults, enter the Mandala,
fire offerings should be made according to the ritual,
in order to make them calm.
Within the third outer section (137a)
of the middle area of the Mandala,
in front[34] **of the matrix mandala,**
with unwavering mind,
the Master should make a hearth,
fifteen inches in size.
The rim should be made four inches in size,
and a vajra should be marked within.
Then the materials for the burnt offerings
should be placed on the right of the *mantrin.*
On the left are the trainees
who should be made to squat in attendance.
The officiant himself sits on the ground,
upon a seat spread with *kuśa*[35] **grass.**
Furthermore, obtaining fine red pigment,
the *mantrin,* in brief, draws
all of the fire area with it.
***Kuśa* grass should be spread all round**
the circumference, going from the right,
spreading it by going around many times.
It should be sprinkled with perfumed water.
Then he should imagine Agni in the hearth,
in order to benefit the beings present.
The good officiant should make offerings
with an excellent ladle, using this mantra:
NAMAḤ SAMANTA-BUDDHĀNĀM AGNAYE SVĀHĀ.
(NSB. For Agni! Svāhā!)
Then going from each trainee,
the wise one should grasp
the right thumb of each with his left hand.

Then equipoised, he should make the burnt offerings.
He should make twenty-one offerings for each disciple,
reciting, according to the mantra ritual, for each oblation:
***NAMAḤ SAMATA-BUDDHĀNĀM ĀḤ MAHĀ-ŚĀNTI-GATA ŚĀNTI-KARA PRAŚAMA DHARMA-NIRJĀTA ABHĀVA-SVABHĀVA-DHARMA-SAMATĀ-PRĀPTA SVĀHĀ* (NSB. Āḥ! O that which has reached great peace! That which pacifies! That which arises from the tranquil Dharma! That which has completely realized the Dharma which is without objective existence in nature! Svāhā!).'**

(99b) In order to put at peace the trainees who have been made to enter the Mandala, the Pacifying Fire Offering should be made. Although the trainees have been cleansed of faults and have had their mind-streams purified by entering into the Mandala, their merit will increase if the Master offers materials to the Vajra Adornments of the Inexhaustible Body and so forth of the Bhagavat. By means of burning the offerings and by having their faults cleansed, the trainees will become tranquil.

The sequence of the rite is as follows: First a hearth fifteen inches in size should be made within the third outer section of the gate of the middle mandala in front of the matrix mandala. If there is no room for it inside because the Mandala is too small, it should be made in the gateway of the outer section of the Mandala. If it is not possible to dig it, in such cases as when the Mandala is on a rooftop and so on, the hearth should be marked with red pigment. Then on the outside of the hearth, *kuśa* grass should be spread around it, going around to the right, beginning in the south, pressing down the tips of each stalk. Then he should sprinkle it with perfumed water empowered with the mantra of Trailokya-vijaya. Then the Master sets into that hearth the all-accomplishing mundane Fire God called '*Mṛda*' who is long-necked, hairy and tawny-coloured, casting a flower into that hearth and transforming it into that Fire. Then giving to the Fire God mouth-washing water and ladles full of offerings (*pūrṇa-huti*) such as are mentioned in the text, he should be just left there blazing. Then casting a flower into the hearth, it should be transformed into the supramundane Pacifying Fire, and as before mouth-washing water and ladles full of offerings should be given. Then for each of the trainees, twenty-one offerings should be made. These should be done with the Master holding the right thumb of the trainee in his left hand. This is the process in summary. (100a)

Free from faults: If the trainees take refuge in the Three Jewels when they are preparing to enter the Mandala and then generate *bodhicitta* when they enter it, and subsequently do the mantra practice even after they have entered it, the preliminaries, the main part and the supplementary part will be wholesome, and they will be free from faults.

The size and shape of the hearth: The text only says fifteen inches in size and does not state whether it should be round or square, but it should be made as prescribed for the Pacifying or Enriching hearths. On this occasion, it ought to be round since this is a Pacifying ritual. However, there is no harm if it is square, if the same site is used for both Enrichment and Pacifying.

91. 'Following the burnt offerings, the *mantrin*
should receive gifts from the trainees:

gold, silver, jewels, horses and elephants,
camels[A], cows, buffaloes[B], clothes,
or whatever suitable things they have.
Full of faith and respect,
the trainees should be glad of heart,
and offer the gifts to the guru.
The guru should thus be made delighted.
When this has been done, he protects himself,
and calling the trainees, he instructs them thus:
"All the Protectors say that
this is a field of merit
for the benefit of all beings, (137b)
so give of everything to the Saṅgha,
who have extensive pure virtues.
Giving to the Saṅgha has great results:
if any wise people offer gifts to the Saṅgha,
they will be born in agreeable surroundings,
and have unlimited great wealth."
Therefore, when they have been made glad,
in agreement with all of this,
he should teach them to offer what they can
to the Saṅgha praised by the Buddha.'

92. Then the Bhagavat Vairocana said to the Bodhisattva Great Being Vajrapāṇi :

'O Great Being! I shall now explain in detail
the initiation explained by previous Buddhas.
Listen carefully with attentiveness!

'Lord of the Secret Ones! The *mantrin* should draw a second mandala, square with one gate, in front of the main mandala, two cubits apart. In the four corners he should allocate four Vajradharas. Which are the four? Niḥprapañca-pratiṣṭha, Vimala-ākāśa, Vimala-netra and Vicitra-vastra. In the centre a great lotus with eight petals and stamens should be placed. On four of the petals he should draw the four associated Bodhisattvas who are endowed with power from their previous aspirations: Dhāraṇīśvara-rāja, Smṛtiprajanyin, Hitādhyāśayin and Kāruṇya. On the other four petals, he should draw their four attendants: He Who Acts According to Different Attitudes[C], He Who Fulfils What is Desired, He Who is Unattached and He Who is Liberated. In the centre he places the form of the inconceivable continuum of reality. Then having empowered four precious jars filled with jewels and medicines, with [the mantras of] Samantabhadra, Maitreya, Sarvanīvaraṇa-viṣkambhin and Sarvāpāyajaha, (138b) he should consecrate the trainees on their heads.

A C: 車乘 '*vehicles*'.
B C: 羊 '*sheep*'. Probably '*meṣa*' read for '*mahiṣa*'.
C C: 雜色衣 '*citra-vastra*', possibly a scribal error for '*citta-viśeṣa*'.

'The *mantrin* should place him
in that holy lotus,
and then he should make offerings
with incense and flowers,
lamps and food offerings should also be given.
He should propitiate the deities
with parasols, banners, pennants,
pleasing drum beats,
auspicious and extensive melodious words.
In the presence of the Protectors,
he prepares the trainee and consecrates him.
With fine incense and flowers,
he should also make offerings to him.
Then taking a golden stylet,
and sitting in front of him,
he should recite these words
to stir the heart of the trainee:
"Just as the great physicians of the past
cleared away the world's blindness,
so the Jinas also remove
your blinding film of ignorance."
Then taking up a mirror,
he should explain the attributes of phenomena:
"Phenomena are like reflections:
pellucid, pure and without turbidity,
they cannot be perceived or expressed.
Arising from causes and action,
they are without inherent reality or duration.
When you have thus understood these phenomena,
act for the unequalled benefit of beings,
and you will be born as a son of the Buddha!"
Then he should place a Dharma-wheel
between his legs and also give him
a very fine conch in his right hand:
"This day forth you will turn
the Wheel of the Protectors in the world
and blow the supreme Dharma-conch
throughout all places.
Do not have any doubt about this,
but with a fearless attitude
expound to all the world
the excellent method of mantra practice.
One who has acted thus is praised
as an assistant of the Buddhas.
Also all the Vajradharas
will protect you in all things[36]!" '

(101a) This section explains the occasion when the trainees are initiated. ***Initiation*** (*abhiṣeka*): One is sprinkled with water from a precious jar in the presence of the transformation of the Adornments of the Inexhaustible Sameness of the Bhagavat's Body, Speech and Mind, the intrinsically existent Mandala, hence the basic meaning of the word which is 'sprinkling'.

Furthermore it should be investigated under three headings: What is the name of the initiation, who is to be initiated and why are they to be initiated? Of these, what is the name of the initiation? In general there are many kinds of initiation, [such as] the initiation to bestow the knowledge which makes one a *mantrin*, the initiation for the rites, which is the initiation needed in order to carry out the rites of Pacifying, Enriching and Destroying, and the initiation in order to clear away trouble and so on. Of these, it is called the 'Master Initiation' in this section, so that is its name.

Who is to be initiated? Initiation is not to be given to all trainees in common, but as it says in the section dealing with the five *samaya*-holders:

> ***'Those who have seen the mandalas and* mudrās,**
> ***and who have also applied themselves***
> ***to the actions and activities'*** [XIII.44].

So the special trainees who have heard the mantra tantra and are able to request the Mandala, as well as the perfected trainees, should be initiated.

Why is the initiation given? So that the Eye of the Dharma will not be blind. In the ordinary world also, after a student has completely learnt the mundane sciences of grammar, logic, medicine and so on, the teacher may perform an initiation ritual as far as it is possible for mundane people [to do so] and then give them a certificate allowing them to explain those sciences and so on. Because if those students give explanations of those various sciences (101b) without perfectly knowing them and without having been initiated, they will not be able to explain those sciences as they actually are, as their eyes are blind. In the same way in this case also, the trainees should know the Tantra and so forth completely. When they have recited it in the presence of the Master, the Master will be confident that they know the explanation of the Tantra, the drawing of the Mandala and so on as they actually are, and if he gives the initiation to those who are able to benefit beings, their Dharma Eyes will not be blind. Secondly, if the trainee who has thus been consecrated becomes a Master himself, even the mundane people will have confidence in a teacher who has arisen from such a source and will revere him.

If you were precipitously to explain the Tantra and draw the Mandala without having been initiated according to the sequence and without knowing the Tantra, you would not know how it really is. Because the rites would be incorrect, the mantra deities would not empower it and therefore whatever aim you wish for would not be accomplished. Those beings who are to be guided will be hostile and not trust you, and hence the Dharma Eye will be blind. This is the reason for giving the initiation.

Furthermore, just as a king in the world who promulgates laws based on the path of the ten wholesome actions and who brings about prosperity, should be consecrated into such regal behaviour, so likewise in this case also the initiation is given in order to consecrate one as a Dharma King who brings about prosperity and happiness.

This should be done as follows: first, in front of the basic Mandala, the Master should mark out an area two cubits apart and draw there the Initiation Mandala, with one section and one gate. In the middle of this, he should draw an eight-petalled lotus. (102a) Drawing the four Vajradharas in the four corners of the Mandala, he should also draw the four Bodhisattvas and the four Attendants on the eight petals. In the centre of the lotus he should write the continuum of reality letter, *Raṃ*, and place the trainees there [in turn]. Offering flowers and incense, and reciting auspicious verses and melodious discourses, he should circumambulate the Great Mandala once, with each of the jewelled jars [containing water] empowered with the Bodhisattvas Samantabhadra and so on, and then sprinkle water over the head of the trainee. Following that, although it is not actually mentioned here, he should also transform the trainee who is on the lotus, with the mantras and *mudrās* of the Uṣṇīṣa, the Eye, Tongue and Armour of the Tathāgata. Then leading him from that place, he should set him upon a fine seat in the vicinity of that Mandala. The trainee should change into new clothes and wear them for a period of twenty four hours, and then he should be set upon the seat. Having offered flowers, incense and so on, the Master should take the eye-opening stylet (*śalākā*) and sit in front of the trainees. He should recite the verse beginning '***Just as the great physicians of the past***'. Then taking a mirror, he should recite the verse beginning '***Phenomena are like reflections***'. Then having fully perfected his self-benefit, he places a golden wheel between the trainee's legs in order to perfect the benefit of others and says '***Turn the Wheel of the Dharma!***'. Then the Wheel of the Dharma should be turned by the excellent speech of the Buddha which is famed throughout all world systems. (102b) He places the symbol of that excellent speech, a fine conch, into the trainee's right hand and says '***May you blow the Conch of the Dharma!***'. Having thus benefitted those beings, he should recite the words '***One who has done thus is praised as an assistant of the Buddhas***' and so on. This is a summary and explanation of the process of carrying out the initiation. Now each section will be explained.

***The* mantrin *should draw a second mandala, square with one gate, in front of the main Mandala, thirty-six inches apart*.** The other rites have already been explained and although the rite [for this] is not actually mentioned here, if it is done according to the general rule, then when the inner Mandala faces east, the Initiation Mandala should be drawn to the north. When the inner Mandala faces north, the Initiation Mandala should be drawn to the west. Here it just says draw the Initiation Mandala in front of the inner Mandala. So, in order for the initiation water not to flow onto the inner Mandala, it should face the north of the inner Mandala, or if it does face east, the space between them should be divided with a ridge.

In the four corners, he should allocate the Vajradharas*.** These four Vajradharas and also the four Bodhisattvas with their four Attendants (103a) who appear later, are formed from the qualities of the Tathāgata. ***Niḥprapañca-pratiṣtha*:** Because he is without dualistic conceptualization. ***Vimala-ākāśa*:** Because the range of emptiness is like that of space, and is devoid of the impurities of the emotional afflictions and wrong understanding. ***Vimala-netra*:** He has the Insight devoid of the obscurations of the emotional afflictions and wrong understanding, or the perceiving subject and perceived objects. ***Vicitra-vastra*: *Clothes (*vastra*): Because he is concealed by decorum. Whoever has decorum will not do what is not to done, but will do what it is fitting to do and is praised by the Holy Ones. He has that sort of decorum.

The four Bodhisattvas are formed from qualities of Suchness. Two [of them] are the excellent self-benefit in nature, and the other two are the excellent benefit of others in nature. By the power of their aspirations, they become the supports of the lotus throne of that Dharma King Initiation Mandala. ***Dhāraṇīśvara-rāja*** (Dhāraṇī Lord King): That Dhāraṇī is Insight and he is its king. ***Smṛtiprajanyin*** (he who has mindfulness): That Insight is non-localized Nirvāṇa in nature, constantly recollecting beings. ***Hitādhyāśayin*** (he who is resolved to help): He who thinks of helping beings. ***Kāruṇya*** (he who has compassion): He who thinks of helping others by virtue of his compassion. The nature of these last two is the excellent benefit of others, and the nature of the first two is the excellent self-benefit. (103b)

The four Attendants are qualities of Suchness. ***He who Acts According to Different Wishes***: His nature is the knowledge of the minds of others. ***He who Fulfils what is Desired***: He who completely fulfils the hopes of beings. ***He who is Unattached*** and ***Liberation*** are the qualities of the result. Emptiness is the absence of attachment in nature, and because of the absence of attachment, it is liberation. The nature of the first two is the cause.

The form of the inconceivable continuum of reality: A white *Raṃ*, the letter of the continuum of reality, should be placed in the heart of the lotus.

Precious jars: This refers to the jars made of gold, silver, ruby and [green] copper, adorned with gold and silver. If you do not possess such jars as these, you should use earthenware jars with similar colours. If you do not use the equipment mentioned even though you do possess it, you are being mean-spirited, and there is a text which says that if your mind is impure, the deities will not even grant their empowerment (*adhiṣṭhāna*). If you really do not have them, should you lose confidence and not do [the ritual], thinking that it is not fitting to be without them? [No, for] if you have not gathered together all the necessities of life and medicines for illnesses you intend to, or if you feel dissatisfied, [then you get them] and then when you have got a sufficient amount of the necessities of life and medicines for illnesses, if you are not generous with the excess you have, this would be like the situation mentioned above. So in brief, you should be pure in spirit and without guile.

As for the empowerment of the jars with the Bodhisattva Samantabhadra and so forth, in order to show that the trainee will abandon the miserable states of existence, (104a) first of all he should be washed with the water from the jar empowered by the mantra of the Bodhisattva Sarva-durgati-pariśodhana. When he has abandoned the miserable states of existence, he should be washed with water from the jar empowered by the mantra of Sarva-nīvaraṇa-viṣkambhin so that he may be free from the obscurations of the emotional afflictions and wrong understanding. Then he should be washed with water from the jar empowered by the mantra of Samantabhadra so that he may reach the All Good Level. Then he should be washed with water from the jar empowered by the mantra of Maitreya so that he may become a Dharma Regent.

The* mantrin *should place him ... he should also make offerings to him: The other matters have already been explained above, but when the initiation is to be given to a trainee, he should be transformed into the Body of Vajrasattva, although that is not actually mentioned here. Since the text does not say he should be transformed into the Body of anyone else, the initiation should be given after changing him into the Body of Vajrasattva. Also regarding the way he is to be set upon the lotus seat, he should be placed in the style of a Wheel-turning King – his left leg is placed upon the seat, and his right leg is placed upon the ground. His left hand rests upon the seat and his right hand is placed upon his knee. His face should neither look up nor down, but straight ahead.

93. **'Then taking those trainees**
the *mantrin* should instil
a compassionate frame of mind in them,
and teach the *samaya* commitments to them:
"From this day forward, you should never abandon
the holy Dharma and *bodhicitta*, (138b)
even for the sake of your life.
You should not be parsimonious[A]**,**
nor do what harms beings.
All the Buddhas prescribe
these *samaya* commitments
to you, well-disciplined one.
You should guard them
just as you guard your life!"
With faith and devotion, the trainees
should bow at the guru's feet,
and then with very certain minds
they should accept all of that.'[37]

(105a) The *samaya* commitments should be taught to the trainees. They should be taught both to those who have previously accepted the *samaya* commitments and to those who have not yet accepted them. There are four and five *samaya* commitments for the trainee which are related to actions and activities. Why is it necessary to teach these to those who already know and have accepted the Tantra and the *samaya* commitments? Even mundane kings may have previously known and maintained the kingly duties, yet at the time of their inauguration as kings[38], they are instructed and trained by the teachers. Likewise here also, even though one has previously maintained these *samaya* commitments, they should be taught according to custom at the time of initiation as a Dharma King. Secondly, (105b) it is because if they are repeatedly taught thus, they will be strengthened.

Making him leave the place where he was shown the mirror, conch and so on, the Master should take the trainee's parasol and lead him inside the portal of the first Mandala, and placing him there, the Master should then teach him the following *samaya* commitments.

The holy Dharma may be abandoned in three ways: If you wrongly view the Mahāyāna, if you slander and revile one who speaks the Dharma, and if you do not daily do any one of the activities such as listening to the holy Dharma, pondering on it, cultivating it, reading it or making offerings to it, you have abandoned the holy Dharma. You should not abandon it even for the sake of your life. You should not abandon any of the four aspects of *bodhicitta*, that is you should not abandon the

A C adds: 一切法 '*with all things/Dharma*'.

aspiration *bodhicitta* but instead always think: 'May I become enlightened in order to help beings!', and you should not abandon the application *bodhicitta*, but instead meditate upon the intrinsic emptiness of all phenomena.

You should not be parsimonious: You must give whatever is suitable to others of the Dharma and possessions you own. ***Nor do what harms beings***: You should not do anything by body, speech and mind, that will immediately or subsequently harm beings. (106a)

94. Then Vajrapāṇi, the Lord of the Secret Ones, said to the Bhagavat: 'Bhagavat! How much merit will be accumulated by the sons or daughters of good family who have undertaken the *samaya* commitments of this Great Mandala King that has arisen from great compassion?' The Bhagavat replied to Vajrapāṇi, the Lord of the Secret Ones: 'O Lord of the Secret Ones! You should know that the amount of merit that is accumulated, beginning with the first generation of *bodhicitta* up until Tathāgatahood, is equivalent to the amount of merit accumulated by these sons or daughters of good family.

'Lord of the Secret Ones! You should also consider likewise concerning this discourse. And you should understand that those sons and daughters of good family are children born from the mouth and heart of the Tathāgatas[A]. In whatever place those sons and daughters of good family abide, it will become unnecessary for Tathāgatas to concern themselves about great acts for beings in such places. Lord of the Secret Ones! Therefore if there is anybody who wishes to make offerings to the Tathāgata, they should make offerings to those sons and daughters of good family. Those who wish to see the Tathāgata should look at them.'

Then Vajrapāṇi and the other Vajradharas, and Samantabhadra and the great Bodhisattvas, speaking in one voice said: (139a) **'Bhagavat! From today onwards we shall honour and make offerings to those sons and daughters of good family. Why is that? Because those sons and daughters of good family should be regarded as Tathāgatas.'**

(106b) Now the explanation of the praise given to those who have entered into that Mandala Arising From Great Compassion. ***Born from the mouth***[39] ***of the Tathāgata***: They are born from the gate of entry. '***Mouth***' refers to the Level of Practice with Devoted Interest and so on, because they have entered the Level of Practice with Devoted Interest. To be '***born***' is to enter into the [Family of] the Tathāgata. They are born from the '***heart***' of the Tathāgata because they behave in accordance with the behaviour of the Tathāgata. (107a)

95. Then the Bhagavat Vairocana gazed at the entire assembly and said to Vajrapāṇi with those Vajradharas and the whole assembly: 'O Sons of Good Family! There is a mantra phrase which arises from the Mandala of the Configuration of the Tathāgata's Speech which is vast and penetrates into infinity; it is like a multi-formed gem, it completely perfects all aspirations, it is an accumulation of an immeasurable mass of merits, it abides in

A C: 從如來口生佛心之子 '[*they are*] *children of the Buddha's heart born from the Tathāgata's mouth*'.

unimpeded realization and it is endowed with the power that is independent[A] of the three times.'

Now the mantras for the protection and so forth of the Mandala will be explained. Those mantras are also the transformations of the configuration of the Tathāgata's Speech which pervades the Three Realms.

It is vast and penetrates into infinity: It penetrates and encompasses all realms of beings. ***It is like a multi-formed gem***: The Wish-fulfilling Gem appears in various forms and carries out various actions so that beings may obtain what they desire. Likewise this *Vidyā* Queen also manifests in various forms for the sake of beings and carries out various activities for them. ***It is an accumulation of an immeasurable mass of merits***: Because the Speech of the Tathāgata arose from the accumulation of a measureless mass of merits. ***It abides in unimpeded realization***: This refers to the unimpeded Knowledge by Awareness of all realms of beings.

96. Then Vajrapāṇi, the Lord of the Secret Ones, with the Vajradharas and the entire assembly, spoke as with one voice: 'Bhagavat! That time has arrived! Sugata! That hour has come!'

97. Then the Tathāgata manifested his tongue faculty which completely perfects all desires and it covered all the Buddha fields in their entirety. Then he entered the *samādhi* called 'The View from the Peak of the Completely Pure Vast Emblem of the Dharma Banner'. As soon as the Bhagavat had entered it, all the Tathāgatas uttered a sound that permeated the continuum of reality and completely protected all the realms of beings without remainder, and spoke this powerful protector Queen of *Vidyā*-mantras: *NAMAḤ SARVA-TATHĀGATEBHYAḤ* (139B) *SARVA-BHAYA-VIGATEBHYO VIŚVA-MUKHEBHYAḤ SARVATHĀ HAṂ KHAṂ RAKṢA MAHĀ-BALE SARVA-TATHĀGATE PUṆYA-NIRJĀTE HŪṂ HŪṂ TRAṬ TRAṬ APRATIHATE SVĀHĀ* (Salutations to all the Tathāgatas who remove all fear, who are multi-faceted! Omnipresent! *Haṃ khaṃ*! Most powerful protectoress! She who has arisen from the merit of all the Tathāgatas! *Hūṃ hūṃ traṭ traṭ*! She who is unimpeded! *Svāhā*!).'

The Tathāgata entered the *samādhi* in order to fully proclaim the *Vidyā* Queen. Because he entered that *samādhi*, he encompassed all the Buddha fields with his vast, narrow, copper-coloured tongue, the Tathāgata's mark of a Great Being, which arose from the mass of truth accumulated by the Tathāgata through many eons.

The View from the Peak of the Completely Pure Vast Emblem of the Dharma Banner: ***The View from the Peak***: Because all of the Three Realms are seen, it is lofty like a peak. ***Completely pure***: Because it is without the obscurations of the emotional afflictions and wrong understanding. ***Vast***: This qualifies that *samādhi* because it pervades all of the Three Realms. ***Emblem***: That *samādhi* itself is the sign which reveals the word of the Mantra. ***Dharma Banner***: Like a royal banner, it proclaims and reveals the Dharma which is superior to all others. These are the special features of this *samādhi*. (107b6)

A C: 無比力 '*power that is incomparable*'.

98. When all the wise Buddhas
spoke this *Vidyā*-mantra,
all these Buddha fields
shook in six ways.
All those Bodhisattvas
had their eyes wide open in wonder,
then in the presence of all the Buddhas,
they spoke these pleasing words:
'Ah! All the Buddhas
utter this very powerful protection
to guard all beings,
to be a refuge for them, to envelope them.
In whoever's heart this protection abides,
they will ever be without fear.
When this great powerful Mantra is remembered,
all obstacles and gremlins,
***rākṣasas* in fearful shapes,**
they will all be destroyed.'

99. Then having transformed the extensive continuum of reality, the Bhagavat entered a *samādhi* called 'The Matrix of the Treasury of the Continuum of Reality'. No sooner had the Bhagavat entered this *samādhi* than this *vidyā*-mantra of Entry into *Samaya* emerged: *NAMAḤ SAMANTA-BUDDHĀNĀṂ ASAME TRISAME SAMAYE SVĀHĀ* (NSB O *Samaya* of the three samenesses, without equal!) Then the sound of the *Vidyā*-mantra of entry into *samaya* arose immediately in all the Buddha fields and in all the entire assembly of Bodhisattvas, and those who heard it and became wise did not fall back from any of the Dharma.

(108a) This section explains the mantras necessary for the Mandala. ***Then having transformed the extensive continuum of reality***: There are two aspects to the Continuum of reality, the Profound and the Extensive. The intrinsic nature of the Profound is the core of Enlightenment, and the Extensive is the configurations of the Vajra Adornments of the Inexhaustible Body and so forth. So it means 'Having transformed those configurations of the Inexhaustible Body and so forth'.

A* samādhi *called 'The Matrix of the Treasury of the Continuum of Reality': This name shows the distinctive features of that *samādhi*. It is the '***Treasury of the Continuum of Reality***' because the *Samaya* Mantra and so forth emerge from it. ***Matrix***: Because it is the source of those mantras.

The* vidyā*-mantra of Entry into Samaya arose: '***Samaya***' means going everywhere or realizing everything. It is also the Vajra Adornments of the Inexhaustible Body and so forth, and this *vidyā* is the entry into the direct realization of that. As for entry, there are two types: Entry without having attained, and entry after having attained. Of these, entry without having attained is to first receive this *vidyā* and enter [into the *samaya*], without having seen the Mandala. Even such Bodhisattvas as Samantabhadra will perceive the intrinsically existent Mandala as soon as that *vidyā* is uttered. (108b) Entry after having attained refers to those who have entered the Mandala and are obstructed by something else, so they recite the *Samaya* Mantra. Also one recites that Mantra to utter and hear the qualities of the three configurations of the Tathāgata's Body, Speech and Mind.

Those who heard it and became wise did not fall back from any of the Dharma: When those who did not know this *samaya* heard it, they did not fall back from either the scriptural Dharma nor from the Dharma as realization. Not to fall back from the scriptural Dharma is not to be separated from the *samaya* commitment, not to abandon the holy Dharma and so on. Not to fall back from the Dharma as realization is not to abandon one's orientation towards the intrinsically existent Mandala.

100. Then the Bhagavat uttered the mantra which produces the continuum of reality: *NAMAḤ SAMANTA-BUDDHĀNĀM DHARMADHĀTU-SVABHĀVAKO 'HAM* (NSB. I am the continuum of reality in nature!). The transformation into Vajrasattva: *NAMAḤ SAMANTA-VAJRĀNĀM VAJRĀTMAKO 'HAM* (Salutations to all the Vajras! I am a vajra in nature!). The Vajra Armour: *NSV*[40] *VAJRA-KAVACA HŪṂ* (NSV Vajra Armour Hūṃ!). The Eye of the Tathāgata: *NSB*[41] *TATHĀGATA-CAKṢU-VYAVALOKĀYA SVĀHĀ* (NSB. To that which sees with the Tathāgata's Eye! Svāhā!). (140a) **The Perfume Mantra: *NSB VIŚUDDHA-GANDHODBHAVĀYA SVĀHĀ* (NSB. That which arises from pure perfume! Svāhā!). The Flower Mantra: *NSB MAHĀ-MAITRY-ABHYUDGATE SVĀHĀ* (NSB. That which is born from Great Kindness! Svāhā!). The Incense mantra: *NSB DHARMA-DHĀTV-ANUGATE SVĀHĀ* (NSB. That which accompanies the continuum of reality! Svāhā!). The Lamp Mantra: *NSB TATHĀGATĀRCI-SPHURAṆĀVABHĀSANA-GAGANODĀRYA SVĀHĀ* (NSB Radiance of the shining rays of light of the Tathāgata, which is as vast as space! Svāhā!). The Food Offerings: *NSB ARARA-KARARA BALIṂ DADĀMI BALIṂ-DADE MAHĀ-BALIḤ SVĀHĀ* (NSB. I give you arara and karara food offerings! Give food offerings! Great food offerings! Svāhā!)[A]. The Oblation Mantra: *NSB GAGANA-SAMĀSAMA SVĀHĀ* (NSB. That which is unequalled equal to space! Svāhā!). The *Uṣṇīṣa* Mantra: *NSB GAGANĀNANTA-SPHARAṆA VIŚUDDHA-DHARMA-NIRJĀTA SVĀHĀ* (NSB. That which pervades limitless space! That which is born from the pure Dharma! Svāhā!). The Armour of the Tathāgata: *NSB VAJRA-JVALA*[B] *VISPHURE HŪṂ SVĀHĀ* (NSB. Shining vajra! Shine forth! Hūṃ! Svāhā!). The Illumination Mantra: *NSB JVALA-MĀLINI TATHĀGATĀRCI SVĀHĀ* (NSB. Garland of light! Radiant light of the Tathāgata! Svāhā!). The Tongue of the Tathāgata: *NSB MAHĀ-MAHĀ-TATHĀGATA-JIHVA SATYA-DHARMA-PRATIṢṬHITA SVĀHĀ* (NSB. Most great tongue of the Tathāgata! That which abides in the true Dharma! Svāhā!).**

The Mantra producing the continuum of reality: This is for the entering [phase], and transforms either the trainee or oneself into emptiness. ***Transformation into Vajrasattva***: This is for the abiding [phase], and is to abide as the Body of Vajrasattva himself, or as the Five Awarenesses in nature. ***The Vajra Armour***: This is for the arising [phase],

A This mantra is not included in T.

B T adds *pracaṇḍa* before *vajra*.

and is the wearing of the armour of the great blissful kindness to all beings. ***The Eye of the Tathāgata***: To cause the trainee to see the Mandala after undoing his blindfold. ***Perfume***: Formed from the qualities of the Tathāgata's pure morality. ***Flowers***: Formed from the qualities of his great kindness. ***Incense***: Formed from the qualities of his Awareness which accords with the continuum of reality, (109a) and burns up the emotional afflictions. ***Lamps***: Formed from the shining lamp of the Tathāgata's Awareness which illumines as vastly as space. ***Food Offerings***: Arising from the pure continuum of reality which is the same as space yet dissimilar. ***Uṣṇīṣa***: Arises from the Tathāgata's *Uṣṇīṣa* which is invisible to sight and limitless like space. ***The Armour of the Tathāgata***: Arises from the Awareness of the Path which brings about the attainment of reality, by the blazing flames of which the obscurations of the emotional afflictions and wrong understanding are burnt up. ***The Illumination Mantra***: This also arises from the Insight of the Path which causes the obscurations of the emotional afflictions and wrong understanding to be burnt up by its blazing flames. ***The Tongue of the Tathāgata***: Arises from abiding in the Dharma of the words of truth.

These Mantras of the Tathāgata's Eye, *Uṣṇīṣa* and so on should be recited with the *mudrās* that appear later in the text. Also when the Master transforms himself into the Body of the Tathāgata, he should transform himself with those mantras, but when he transforms himself with a single essence syllable, they are not necessary. Also these mantras, together with the *mudrās*, should be used when initiating the trainees, after they have been washed with the water from the jars.

III
THE OVERCOMING OF OBSTACLES

1. Then Vajrapāṇi asked the Bhagavat Vairocana:
'What should be done to overcome obstacles
when drawing the Mandala,
or when accomplishing the mantras
so that gremlins[1] will not appear[A]?
How should one accomplish the mantras,
and what will their results be like?'

First the Mandala is to be drawn, but what should be done if obstacles arise either at the time of doing that, or after having drawn it, when performing the ceremony of accepting the trainees into it and so on, or after having introduced the trainees into it? ***Or when accomplishing the mantras, so that gremlins will not appear***. Or else if obstacles arise during the mantra *sādhana* in general when you are not even drawing the Mandala, how are they to be quelled? (109b) ***How should one accomplish the mantras?***: How are the four members of recitation, the mantra *sādhana*, done? ***What will their results be like?***: When the mantras have been accomplished, what will their results be like?

2. Having been asked this,
Mahā-Vairocana replied:
'O Great Being, excellent, excellent!
I shall reveal to you
everything you have asked about.
Obstacles arise from your own mind,
due to previous indulgence in avarice[B].
In order to destroy their cause
I teach[C] *bodhicitta*.'

Here the Bhagavat teaches how the obstacles are to be quelled, and this is both without and with perceptual forms. That without perceptual forms is the cultivation of *bodhicitta*. That with perceptual forms is the transformation [of oneself] into the appearance of the Noble Acala and the practice accompanied by the mantras, *mudrās* and mandalas. Obstacles are formed from the habitual tendencies accumulated in your mind, which are based upon meanness in not having given the Dharma and material goods, [hence] the cause of those obstacles is avarice. The cultivation of *bodhicitta* in order to destroy that is the repeated practice of that which is the core of Enlightenment (*bodhimaṇḍa*) in nature. Thus, these obstacles will be quelled through [the realization of] the absence of any objective basis to both the phenomena of avarice and the obstacles, when you have repeatedly practised emptiness.

A C: 云何道場時　淨除諸障者　修眞言行人　無能爲惱害 '*When [engaged] in the mandala, how is one to eliminate obstacles so that they are unable to trouble the practitioner who cultivates the mantras?*'

B C: 慳悋 '*miserliness*', '*meanness*'.

C C: 念 '*you should recollect*'.

3. **'It is devoid of all thoughts[A]**
that arise from the mind and mental states,
and wherein all proliferations arising
from conceptualization have been extinguished[B].'

This section refers to the distinctive qualities of *bodhicitta* itself, [signifying that] the intrinsic nature of that *bodhicitta* is the abandonment and extinction of conceptualization and so forth.

4. **'Recollecting *bodhicitta*, the *mantrin***
should mentally recite [the mantra of] Acala,
and make his *mudrā*, (140b)
and he will destroy all obstacles.'

This is the second technique of clearing obstacles away. Having recollected *bodhicitta*, (110a) the *mantrin* should mentally recite the mantra of the Noble Acala. Imagining the letter *Hāṃ* located within the wind mandala in his heart and not perceiving an objective basis to causes or effects in any phenomenon with the sound of that letter *Hāṃ*, is the recollection of *bodhicitta*. The recitation of the mantra is to recite the [mantra of] Acala mentally. If you threaten an obstacle, having recited that mantra with the *mudrā*, it will take flight.

5. **'Lord of the Secret Ones!**
Listen to this, the binding of the wind:
Transform yourself with *A*,
and mentally recite *Hāṃ*[C].
Having positioned yourself in the north-west[2],
make seven spots[D] of perfume on the ground!
They should be covered with a dish.
You should repeatedly imagine
that that dish is great Sumeru.
On top of it, fully imagine
A with an *anusvāra*.
This kind of great wind-binding
was taught by the Jinas of the past.'

This section teaches the ritual for binding the wind. Having transformed yourself into Vairocana with the letter *A*, you should mentally imagine the essence of the Noble Acala, *Hāṃ* and make seven spots of perfume [on the ground] in the north west, which are the Lord of the Wind and his entourage. Having put his entourage of six around the circumference, the King himself should be set in the centre. They should all be imagined as being blue, riding on the backs of deer. They should be covered

A C: 妄分別 '*false concepts*'.
B C reads: 憶念菩提心 行者離諸害 '*recollecting* bodhicitta, *the yogin will eliminate all faults*' instead of '*and wherein … have been extinguished*'.
C C: 訶 '*ha*'.
D C: 大空點 '*a great* anusvāra'.

over with a dish, which should then be imagined as Mount Sumeru. Above it the letter *Aṃ* should be imagined and you should imagine that *Aṃ* becoming a very fierce earth[3] mandala, like gold in colour.

6. **'O Great Being! Listen attentively**
concerning that of rain also.
Imagining a letter *Raṃ*[A],
the *mantrin* transforms himself
into a completely red, very powerful,
terrifying [Acala] with a flaming aura.
The Wrathful One holds a sword[B] in hand,
and should draw a picture of clouds on the ground[C];
then he should strike them with the Sword *Mudrā*.
Clouds arising from all directions will be dispersed.'

The dispelling of rain obstacles. Having imagined yourself as a red Noble Acala with the letter *Raṃ*, you should draw a picture of rainclouds on the ground and if you strike them with the Sword *Mudrā*, they will disperse.

7. **'Or to strike them with a dagger[D],**
the unwavering *mantrin*
should become Vajrapāṇi,
and stab them all with a Vajra Dagger.'

Another way of dispelling that rain obstacle: you should transform yourself into Vajrapāṇi and if having made a five-pointed vajra *mudrā*, you stick the point of the *mudrā* into an image of the clouds, (110b) as though striking them with a dagger, they will disperse.

8. **'I shall also explain**
the purifying of all obstacles:
Sitting in the centre of the Mandala,
the *mantrin* should imagine
the mantra of most powerful Acala
located in the Mandala
of the terrifying Lord himself.
Having made an image of [the obstacle],
he should crush its head with his left foot,
and then it will be pacified,
or else destroyed, without a doubt[E].'

This explains another technique of pacifying obstacles. Having transformed himself into the appearance of the Noble Acala, the *mantrin* should recite the mantra.

A C: 囉 '*Ra*'.
B C: 渴伽 '*khagḍa*'.
C C: 隨所起方分 '*according to the direction from which they have arisen*'.
D C: 蒯 羅 劍 '*peg*', '*pin*' (*śalākā*).
E C: 息滅而不生 '[*or else*] *destroyed and not arise again*'.

Imagining a wind mandala in the heart of Acala into whom he has transformed himself, he should imagine his mantra located there, the *mantrin* himself sitting in the archway of the Great Mandala. If he draws an image of the obstacle there and crushes its head with his left foot, the obstacle will be pacified.

9. **'[Or] having made an image of it,**
he should smear it with
a mixture of black mustard and poison.
Then, when it has been scorched by the *mantrin*,
that harm-doer will quickly be destroyed[A].
If one were to smear them with poison
and scorch them on a fire,
even Brahmā or else Śakra[B]
would be speedily destroyed that instant[C].'

This also explains another technique for clearing away obstacles. If the *mantrin* makes an image of the obstacle, smears it with a mixture of black mustard and poison and then scorches it in a fire, the obstacle will be pacified.

10. Then Vajrapāṇi said to the Bhagavat: 'When I consider what the Bhagavat has said, I understand it to be as follows: Bhagavat! When they are located in their specific mandala [abodes], (141a) **the deities are caused to exert their transformational power. If they are located there, the Tathāgata's words will not be contradicted. For to abide in their specific type [of mandala] is the *samaya* of all mantras. The Bodhisattvas who engage in the bodhisattva practice by means of mantras should also abide in the specific [mandala] abodes and accomplish all aims.'**

This concerns Vajrapāṇi's understanding of the significance of the description of abiding as the wind-coloured Noble Acala and expelling [obstacles], transforming yourself into the fire-coloured [Acala] and expelling obstacles, and the binding of the wind through imagining an earth mandala upon a dish, in the previous section describing the dispelling of obstacles. He understands that the rites of Pacifying and so on are done after locating the deities on their respective mandalas during the performance of the rites of Pacifying and Enriching, for then they carry out the actions of Pacifying and so on. Why is that? It is thus by way of *samaya*, for if you use the deities who abide in their specific mandalas, then they will exert their transformational power towards whatever you have imagined, (111a) and also whatever actions are to be done, they will be carried out just as the Tathāgata has said. Therefore he understands that *mantrins* should also transform themselves into whatever is the colour of the deity and perform the rite.

A C reads: 彼諸根熾然 勿生疑惑心 '*all of his organs will be burnt up, of that have no doubt*' instead of '*that harm-doer … destroyed*'.
B C adds: 不順我教故 '*if they had not followed my teachings*'.
C C adds: 況復餘衆生 '*what need be said of other beings*'.

11. The Bhagavat replied, 'It is so, Lord of the Secret Ones, it is just as you have said. Lord of the Secret Ones! Moreover, it was revealed by previous Buddhas that whatever colour has been mentioned for any [deity], that is also [the colour of] its mandala and likewise of the body-image of the deity.'

What Vajrapāṇi has understood is correctly understood. The meaning of what the Bhagavat says is that the specific colour of a deity should also be that [of the mandala]. In other words, a yellow coloured deity should be connected with an earth mandala. A white coloured deity should be connected with a water mandala. A red coloured deity should be connected with a fire mandala. Blue and black colours should be connected with a wind mandala. This is prescribed only for their individual mandalas. If you change them to something else out of necessity, due to the [colour of the] offering materials and so on, then you should know that it is acceptable to change an Enriching deity to a Pacifying deity, or for a Pacifying one to be Wrathful and so forth. Some deities have all the colours, for example like the Noble Tārā who is green in colour, hence you should know they can be used in all mandalas and all rites.[4] Likewise if out of necessity you have to change the offering materials, you should know that they can be used in all rites, though they each have their own specific rites.

12. 'Lord of the Secret Ones! In the future there will appear faithless beings with little intelligence, who not believing this teaching will have great misgivings and doubt, and who will just hear it, neither retaining it in their hearts nor accomplishing it. They themselves are unsuitable and they corrupt others. They will say "This is not what was spoken by the Buddhas, but it belongs to the non-Buddhists!". But those foolish people do not know that the Bhagavat, the All-knowing One who has attained mastery over all phenomena, who has directly understood what benefits beings, has said "I shall explain all of these things", having previously [vowed to] help beings.

> **'Those foolish people do not know**
> **the intrinsic nature of phenomena.**
> **The nature of all phenomena**
> **is said [by the Buddhas] to be emptiness.'**

When the Bhagavat states that whatever colours the deities are, (111b) so also are their mandalas, it may be said [by some people] that while the mandalas of earth, fire and so on are found in the mundane [non-Buddhist] tantras, they do not appear in any of the supramundane Kriyā and Yoga Tantras, therefore they were not taught by the Buddha. But this is because they do not know that even the mundane tantras were taught by the All-knowing Bhagavat Buddha in accordance with the individual faith of beings. Why do they not know that? Because this eon is one with people who have such defects as weak intelligence and little faith. They themselves are unsuitable and they corrupt others.

13. 'Ever abiding thus, with certitude,
the *mantrin* should carry out the rites.'

This means that the *mantrin* should abide in emptiness and perform the rites of Pacifying and so forth. Also regarding the performance of the rites while abiding in emptiness, one [person] may accomplish attainments through abiding in the *samādhi* without perceptual forms, and another [person] may accomplish those attainments by actualizing the *samādhi* of emptiness and then doing the recitation after having arisen from it.

IV
THE GENERAL MANTRA TREASURY

1. Then those Vajradharas, Vajrapāṇi and so on, and those Bodhisattvas, Samantabhadra and so on, bowed down to the Bhagavat Vairocana and because they desired to utter, in this great Mandala Arisen from Great Compassion, the mantras which indicate in each one of their syllables how they each realized the Gates of the pure continuum of reality, (141b) **they requested the Bhagavat [to let them do so].**

Now, those Bodhisattvas such as Samantabhadra desired to utter the mantras which reveal how they realized their respective Gates of Liberation when they completely perfected the Tenth and Eleventh Levels through having repeatedly practised those Gates of Liberation revealed by the mantra syllables when they first entered into the Level of Practice with Devoted Interest, in order to arrange them in the Mandala Arising from Great Compassion, and so they requested the Bhagavat [to allow them to do this]. (112a)

2. Then the Bhagavat Vairocana empowered those Bodhisattvas and Vajradharas into a state of steadfastness and then he said, 'Noble children, speak the words of the mantras which correspond to your realization of the continuum of reality which will purify the realms of beings!'

He empowered those Bodhisattvas so they would not be sluggish, or else to make them confident.

3. Then at that moment, the Bodhisattva Samantabhadra entered into the *samādhi* called 'The Realm of the Buddha Adornments' and he spoke the mantra of unimpeded strength: *NSB SAMANTĀNUGATE VIRAJA-DHARMA-NIRJĀTA MAHĀ MAHĀ SVĀHĀ* (NSB. All-pervading one! Born from the unsullied Dharma! Greatest of great ones! *Svāhā*!).

Buddha Adornments*:** After the Bodhisattva Samantabhadra entered into *samādhi*, each of the Buddhas emerged from each of his pores, and those Buddhas who thus emerged without number from his body are called 'adornments***'. You should know in this way that the *samādhis* correspond to the respective qualities of the Bodhisattvas, and you should also know in this way that the mantras arise from the Tathāgata's qualities and are the respective Gates of Liberation of those Bodhisattvas, transformed into the syllables of the mantras.

4. Then the Bodhisattva Maitreya entered into the *samādhi* called 'The Arising of Great Kindness' and spoke his own essence: *NSB AJITAṂ-JAYA SARVA-SATTVA-ĀŚĀYĀNUGATA SVĀHĀ* (NSB. Vanquisher of the unvanquished! Fulfiller of the wishes of all beings! *Svāhā*!

5. Then the Bodhisattva Ākāśa-garbha entered into the *samādhi* called 'The Pure Realm' and spoke his mantra: *NSB ĀKĀŚA-SAMANTĀNUGATA*

VICITRĀMBARA-DHARA SVĀHĀ (NSB Pervader of all places like space! Wearer of multi-coloured garments! *Svāhā*!).

6. Then the Bodhisattva Sarva-nīvaraṇa-viṣkambhin entered the *samādhi* called 'The Courage of Great Compassion' and spoke his mantra: *NSB ĀḤ SATTVA-HITA-ABHYUDGATA TRAṂ TRAṂ RAṂ RAṂ SVĀHĀ* (NSB. *Āḥ*! Manifester of benefit for beings! *Traṃ traṃ raṃ raṃ*! *Svāhā*!).

7. Then the Bodhisattva Avalokiteśvara entered the *samādhi* called 'Gazing Everywhere' and spoke his own mantra and those of his entourage: (142a) *NSB SARVA-TATHĀGATĀVALOKITA-KARUṆĀ-MAYA RA RA RA HŪṂ JAḤ SVĀHĀ* (NSB. You who are formed from the sight and compassion of all the Tathāgatas! *Ra ra ra hūṃ jaḥ*! *Svāhā*!). Mahā-sthāma-prāpta's: *NSB JAṂ JAṂ SAḤ SVĀHĀ*. Tārā's: *NSB KARUṆODBHAVE TĀRE TĀRIṆI SVĀHĀ* (NSB. You who have arisen from compassion! Tārā! Saviouress! *Svāhā*!). Bhṛkuṭī's: *NSB SARVA-BHAYA-TRĀSANI HŪṂ SPHOṬAYA SVĀHĀ* (NSB. Terrifier of all fears! *Hūṃ*! Smash asunder! *Svāhā*!). Pāṇḍara-vāsinī's: *NSB TATHĀGATA-VIṢAYA-SAMBHAVE PADMA-MĀLINI SVĀHĀ* (NSB. Born from the realm of the Tathāgatas! Garland of lotuses! *Svāhā*!). Haya-grīva's: *NSB HŪṂ KHĀDA BHAÑJA SPHOṬAYA SVĀHĀ* (NSB. *Hūṃ*! Devour! Shatter! Smash asunder! *Svāhā*!).

8. Then the Bodhisattva Kṣiti-garbha entered the *samādhi* called 'The Realm of the Realization[A] of the Indestructible Vajra' and spoke his mantra: *NSB HA HA HA SUTANU SVĀHĀ* (NSB. *Ha ha ha*! You with a beautiful body! *Svāhā*!).

9. Then the Bodhisattva Mañjuśrī entered the *samādhi* called 'The Emanation of the Buddha's Transformational Power' and spoke his own essence: *NSB HE HE KUMĀRAKA VIMUKTI-PATHA-STHITA SMARA SMARA PRATIJÑĀṂ SVĀHĀ* (NSB. *He he*! Child! You who abide on the path of liberation! Remember, remember your vow! *Svāhā*!).

10. Then Vajrapāṇi, the Lord of the Secret Ones, entered the *samādhi* called 'The Invincible Vajra' and spoke his own essence, together with those of his entourage: *NSV CAṆḌA MAHĀ-ROṢAṆA HŪṂ* (NSV. Fierce most wrathful one! *Hūṃ*!). Māmakī's: *NSV TRIṬ TRIṬ JAYANTI SVĀHĀ* (NSV. *Triṭ triṭ*! Victorious one! *Svāhā*!). Vajra-śṛṅkhalā's: *NSV HŪṂ BANDHA BANDHAYA MOṬA MOṬAYA VAJRODBHAVE SARVATRĀPRATIHATE SVĀHĀ* (NSV. *Hūṃ*! Bind, bind! Pulverise, pulverise! Vajra-born one! Invincible in all places! *Svāhā*!). Candra-tilaka's: *NSV HRĪḤ HŪṂ PHAṬ SVĀHĀ*. Vajra-sūcī's: *NSV SARVA-DHARMA-NIRVEDHANI VAJRA-SŪCI VARADE SVĀHĀ* (NSV. Vajra-needle who penetrates all dharmas! Bestower of favours! *Svāhā*!). All the Vajradharas': *NSV HŪṂ HŪṂ HŪṂ PHAṬ PHAṬ PHAṬ JAṂ JAṂ SVĀHĀ*. The Servants': *NSV HE HE KIṄ CIRĀYASI GṚHṆA GṚHṆA KHĀDA KHĀDA*

A C reads 行境 '*range of activity*' instead of '*realization*'.

PARIPŪRAYA SVA-PRATIJÑĀṂ SVĀHĀ (NSV. *He he he*! Why do you delay? Seize, seize! Devour, devour! Fulfil your vow! *Svāhā*!).

11. (142b) Then at that moment, Śākyamuni entered the *samādhi* called the 'Source of Treasures' and then spoke his own essence and those of his entourage: *NSB SARVA-KLEŚA-NIṢŪDANA SARVA-DHARMA-VAŚITA-PRĀPTA GAGANA-SAMĀSAMA SVĀHĀ* (*NSB* Destroyer of all emotional afflictions! You who have attained mastery of all dharmas! You who are unequalled like space! *Svāhā*!). Ūrṇā's: *NSB VARADE VARA-PRĀPTE HŪṂ SVĀHĀ* (NSB. Bestower of favours! You who bring about what is desired! *Hūṃ*! *Svāhā*!). All the Uṣṇīṣas': *NSB VAṂ VAṂ VAṂ HŪṂ HŪṂ PHAṬ SVĀHĀ*. Aparājita's: *NSB DHRIṂ DHRIṂ RIṂ RIṂ JRIṂ JRIṂ SVĀHĀ*. Aparājitā's: *NSB APARĀJITE JAYANTI*[A] *TAḌITE SVĀHĀ* (NSB. You who are undefeated by others! Victorious one! You who strike! *Svāhā*!). Pṛthivī's: *NSB PṚTHIVYE SVĀHĀ*. Viṣṇu's: *NSB VIṢṆAVE SVĀHĀ*. Rudra's: *NSB RUDRĀYA SVĀHĀ*. Vāyu's: *NSB VĀYAVE SVĀHĀ*. Sarasvatī's: *NSB SARASVĀTYAI SVAHA*. Nirṛti's: *NSB RĀKṢASĀDHIPATAYE SVĀHĀ*. Yama's: *NSB VAIVAŚVATĀYA SVĀHĀ*. The Lord of Death's: *NSB MṚTYAVE SVĀHĀ*. Kālarātrī's: *NSB KĀLARĀTRIYE SVĀHĀ*. The Seven Mothers': *NSB MĀTṚBHYAḤ SVĀHĀ*. Śakra's: *NSB ŚAKRĀYA SVĀHĀ*. Varuṇa's: *NSB APĀṂ-PATAYE SVĀHĀ* (*NSB* To the Lord of the Waters! *Svāhā*!). Āditya's: *NSB ĀDITYĀYA SVĀHĀ*. Brahmā's: *NSB PRAJĀPATAYE SVĀHĀ*. Candra's: *NSB CANDRĀYA SVĀHĀ*. The Nāgas: *NSB MEGHA-AŚĀNĪYE SVĀHĀ* (*NSB* To the clouds and lightning! *Svāhā*!). Nanda and Upananda's: *NSB NANDOPANANDAYE SVĀHĀ*[B].

12. Then the Bhagavat Vairocana, desiring that the teachings might be successfully accomplished, spoke the (143a) *Vidyā* Queen, the Mother of all the Buddhas and Bodhisattvas[C] (Buddha-locanā): *NSB GAGANA-VARA-LAKṢAṆE GAGANA-SAME SARVODGATĀBHIḤ SĀRA-SAMBHAVE JVALA NAMO 'MOGHĀNĀṂ SVĀHĀ* (NSB. You who have the best of attributes like space! You who are equal to space! You who appear in all places! You who are born from the quintessence! Shining one! Salutations to the unfailing one! *Svāhā*!).

13. Then the Bhagavat Vairocana entered into the *samādhi* called 'The Arising of Majestic Radiance', in order to purify all hindrances, and he spoke this mantra of the Destroyer of Great Hindrances[D] (Acala-nātha): *NSV CAṆḌA MAHĀ-ROṢAṆA SPHOṬAYA HŪṂ TRAṬ HĀṂ MĀṂ* (MSV. Fierce most wrathful one! Smash asunder! *Hūṃ traṭ hāṃ māṃ*!). Trailokya-vijaya's: *NSV HA HA HA VISMAYE SARVA-TATHĀGATA-VIṢAYA-SAMBHAVA-TRAILOKYA-VIJAYA HŪṂ JAḤ SVĀHĀ* (NSV. *Ha ha ha*! Miraculous one! Conqueror of the Three Worlds, born from the realm of all the Tathāgatas! *Hūṃ jaḥ! Svāhā*!).

A T: *jvalanti*.
B This mantra omitted in T.
C C adds: 虛空眼 '*Gagana-locanā*'.
D C adds: 不動主 '*Acala-nātha*'.

14. The Śrāvakas': *NSB HETU-PRATYAYA-VIGATA-KARMA-NIRJĀTA HŪṂ* (NSB. O You born from karma free from causes and conditions! *Hūṃ*!). The Pratyekabuddhas': *NSB VAḤ*. The essence of all the Buddhas and Bodhisattvas: *NSB SARVA-BUDDHA-BODHISATTVA-HṚDAYĀNY-ĀVEŚĀNI NAMAḤ SARVA-VIDE SVĀHĀ* (NSB Salutations to you who have entered the essences of all the Buddhas and Bodhisattvas! O All-knowing One! *Svāhā*!). The general essence of the gods and so on: *NSB LOKĀLOKA-KARĀYA SARVA-DEVA-NĀGA-YAKṢA-GANDHARVA-ASURA-GARUḌA-KINNARA-MAHORAGĀDI-HṚDAYĀNY ĀKARṢAYA VICITRA-GATI SVĀHĀ* (NSB. [Salutations] to you who carry out the mundane and the supramundane! You who gather in the essences of all the gods, *nāgas, yakṣas, gandharvas, asuras, garuḍas, kinnaras, mahoragas* and so forth! You who move in various ways! *Svāhā*!). All the Bodhisattvas: *NSB SARVATHĀ-VIMATI-VIKIRAṆA-DHARMADHĀTU-NIRJĀTA SAṂ SAṂ HA SVĀHĀ* (NSB. O You who scatter confusion in all places, born from the continuum of reality! *Saṃ saṃ ha*! *Svāhā*!). The Gatekeeper Durdharṣa's: *NSB DURDHARṢA-MAHĀ-ROṢAṆA KHĀDAYA SARVĀN TATHĀGATĀJÑĀṂ KURU SVĀHĀ* (NSB. O great wrathful one who is difficult to assail! Devour! Carry out all the Tathāgata's commands! *Svāhā*!). The Gatekeeper Abhimukha's: *NSB HE MAHĀ-PRACAṆḌĀBHIMUKHA GṚHṆA KHĀDAYA KIÑ CIRĀYASI SAMAYAM ANUSMARA SVĀHĀ* (NSB *He!* O most fierce one who is close at hand! Seize! Devour! Why do you delay? Remember your vow! *Svāhā*!). For Binding the Great Area: *NSB SARVATRĀNUGATE BANDHAYA SĪMĀṂ MAHĀ-SAMAYA-NIRJĀTE SMARAṆE 'PRATIHATE DHĀKA DHĀKA CARA CARA BANDHA BANDHA DAŚA-DIŚAṂ* (143B) *SARVA-TATHĀGATĀNUJÑĀTE PRAVARA-DHARMA-LABDHA-VIJAYE BHAGAVATI VIKURU VIKURE LE LU PURI VIKURI SVĀHĀ* (NSB. You who accompany in all places! Bind the boundary! O you born from a great vow, remember! O you who are unimpeded! Break, break, move, move, bind, bind the ten directions! You who are authorized by all the Tathāgatas! Victorious blessed lady who has obtained the most excellent Dharma! *Vikuru vikure le lu puri vikuri! Svāhā*!).

15. For Enlightenment: *A*. For practice: *Ā*. For Perfect Enlightenment: *AṂ*. For Nirvāṇa: *AḤ*.

16. Trailokya-vijaya's: *NSV HAḤ*. Acala's: *NSV HĀṂ*. Sarva-nīvaraṇa-viṣkambhin's: *NSB AḤ*. Avalokiteśvara's: *NSB SAḤ*. Vajrapāṇi's: *NSV VAḤ*. Mañjuśrī's: *NSB MAṂ*. Gagana-locanā's: *NSB GAṂ*. The Continuum of Reality: *NSB RAṂ*. Mahā-vīra's: *NSB KHAṂ*. Jaleśvara's: *NSB JAṂ*. Tārā's: *NSB TAṂ*. Bhṛkuṭī's: *NSB BHṚH*. Mahā-sthāma-prāpta's: *NSB SAṂ*. Pāṇḍara-vāsinī's: *NSB PAṂ*. Haya-grīva's: *NSB HAṂ*. Yaśodharā's: *NSB YAṂ*. Ratna-pāṇi's: *NSB SAṂ*. Jālinī-prabha's: *NSB JĀṂ*. Śākyamuni's: *NSB BHAḤ*. The Three Uṣṇīṣas': *NSB HŪṂ TRŪṂ*. Sitāta-patroṣṇīṣa's: *NSB LAṂ*. Jayoṣṇīṣa's: *NSB ŚAṂ*. Vijayoṣṇīṣa's: *NSB SAṂ*. Tejorāśy-uṣṇīṣa's: *NSB TRIṂ*. Vikiraṇoṣṇīṣa's: *NSB HRUṂ*. Aparājita's: *NSB HŪṂ*. Aparājitā's: *NSB TAṂ HAṂ PAṂ HAṂ YAṂ*[A]. Pṛthivī's: *NSB BI*. Keśinī's: *NSB KILI*. Upakeśinī's:

A T omits Aparājitā's name and mantra.

NSB DILI. **Citrā's:** ***NSB MILI.*** (144a) **Vasu-mati's:** ***NSB HILI.*** **Kautuhala:** ***NSB HA SA NAṂ.*** **Sarva-sattva-abhayaṃdada's:** ***NSB RA SA NAṂ.*** **Sarvāpāya-jaha's:** ***NSB DHVAṂ SA NAṂ.*** **Karuṇā-mṛdita-mati's:** ***NSB VI HA SA NAṂ.*** **Maitry-abhyudgata's:** ***NSB ṬHAṂ.*** **Paritrāṇāśaya-mati's:** ***NSB YAṂ.*** **Sarva-dāha-praśamita's:** ***NSB Ī.*** **Acintya-mati-datta's:** ***NSB U.*** **Ratnākara's:** ***NSB DAṂ*** **[A]. Ratna-pāṇi's:** ***ṢAṂ.*** **Dharaṇīṃdhara's:** ***NSB ṄAṂ.*** **Dhāraṇī-pratilabha's:** ***JAṂ.*** **Ratna-mudrā-hasta's:** ***PAṂ*** **[B]. Dṛḍhādhyāśaya's:** ***NSB ṆAṂ.*** **Gaganāmala's:** ***NSB HAṂ.*** **Gagana-mati's:** ***NSB RIṂ*** **[C]. Visuddha-mati's:** ***NSB GATAṂ.*** **Caritra-mati's:** ***NSB DHIRAṂ.*** **Sthira-buddhi's:** ***NSB HŪṂ.*** **The Servants':** ***NSB DHI ŚRĪ HAṂ BRAṂ*** **[D]. That spoken by all the Bodhisattvas: NSB KṢAḤ ḌAḤ RA YAṂ KAṂ[E]. The Gods of the Pure Abodes:** ***NSB MANO-RAMA DHARMA-SAMBHAVA VIBHAVA-KATHANA SAṂ SAṂ SVĀHĀ*** **(NSB O delightful one born from the Dharma! You who speak with prowess!** ***Saṃ saṃ! Svāhā!*****). The Rākṣasas':** ***NSB KRAṂ KERI.*** **The Ḍākinīs':** ***NSB HRĪ HAḤ.*** **The Yakṣas':** ***NSB YAKṢA-VIDYĀ-DHARI.*** **The Piśācas':** ***NSB PICI PICI.*** **The Bhūtas': NSB** ***GUṂ I GUṂ I MAṂ SA NE.*** (144b) **The Asuras':** ***NSB RAṬA RAṬA DHVĀNTAṂ VRA VRA.*** **The Mahoragas':** ***NSB GARALAṂ VIRALAṂ.*** **The Kinnaras':** ***NSB HASANAṂ VIHASANAṂ.*** **The Humans':** ***NSB ICCHĀ-PARAṂ MANO-MAYE ME SVĀHĀ*** **(NSB. Let there be the best mind-born wishes for me!** ***Svāhā!*****).**

17. **'Lord of the Secret Ones, I have taught all these mantras and so forth,**
'Now, Noble One, listen
to the Essence of all mantras.
I have taught that ***A***
is the Essence of all mantras:
all mantras reside within it,
and thus mantras are reliable.'

A T: *traṃ.*
B T: *thaṃ.*
C T: *raṃ.*
D T: *dhiṃ śriṃ haṃ braṃ.*
E T: *kṣadatara.*

V
THE ACCOMPLISHMENT OF MUNDANE *SIDDHI*

1. Then the Bhagavat said to Vajrapāṇi, 'Lord of the Secret Ones! Listen to how mantras are to be accomplished and what the result of their accomplishment is!

2. 'Letter should be joined to letter[1],
likewise ground becomes ground[A].
You should recite 100,000 times
mentally, with restraint.'

3. 'The [first] letter is *bodhicitta*,
the second is said to be sound.
[One] ground is your tutelary deity,
which should be created in your body.'

4. 'The second ground should be known as
the perfect Buddha, the most excellent of men[B].
The *mantrin* should imagine him
located in a pure moon disc.'

5. 'He should carefully arrange
the letters within that in sequence.
Suppressed by the drawn-in syllables[2],
life and exertion will be purified.'

6. 'Life is said to be "breath"[3],
exertion[4] is "recollection".
After he has restrained both of them,
he should do the preliminary service.'

7. 'Then, well restrained, the mantrin
should recite for one month.
The preliminary practice of the mantras
is entry from one ground to the other.
This is called preliminary practice
by all the renowned Buddhas.'

8. 'After that he should offer (145a)
just a few flowers, perfume and so on.
So that he may become a Buddha
he should also dedicate [to others] his *bodhicitta*.
Thus, without fear, the *mantrin*
should recite for a second month[5].'

A C: 句句 '*position* [*becomes*] *position*'. C normally has 句 (**pada*) where T has *gzhi.*
B C: 勝句 '*the most excellent rank*'.

9. **'Then at the time of the full moon**
that person should start the accomplishment.
He should confidently draw a mandala,
making all of it as a vajra palace,
on a mountain top, or in a cow-pen,
or else in river valleys,
at cross-roads, or in a isolated room,
or in a place of the Mothers, or a quiet place[A6].
He should stay there and protect himself,
and then resolutely carry out the *sādhana*.'

10. **'The following signs will arise there**
at midnight, or else at sunrise,
which should be known by the intelligent one:
***Hūṃ*, or the sound of a drum,**
likewise earth-shaking,
or else pleasant words are suitable
if they sound out from the sky,
then by these signs he should know
the material will be transmuted as wished[7].'

11. **'The Buddhas, most excellent of men,**
describe this as its result.
He who abides thus in the Mantra Method
will certainly become a Buddha.
Therefore in all respects
you should always recollect the mantra;
the powerful Buddhas in the past also
taught that one should recollect that.'[B]

A C reads: 神室大天室 '*a shrine or a temple*' for this line and then adds 彼漫荼羅處悉如金剛宮 '*That mandala site should completely resemble a vajra palace*'.
B No commentary is available for this chapter. It may have been lost at some time or else Buddhaguhya himself did not comment on this chapter as the same practice is given in greater detail in Chapter VI . 22 onwards.

VI
THE TRUE NATURE OF *SIDDHI* ACCOMPLISHMENT

Previously the four aspects of the letter *A*, the *samādhi* gates of Enlightenment, Practice, Perfect Enlightenment and Nirvāṇa, were mentioned[1]. Also their significance, that is, their being Enlightenment, Practice, Perfect Enlightenment and Nirvāṇa in nature was taught. The teaching of them causes some of the beings who are to be guided to engage in practice by means of the letters *A* and so on, and others to engage in practice by means of their significance. Therefore, they are taught by way of the significance of the letters so that the intrinsic nature of Enlightenment and so forth may be understood.

1. Then the Bhagavat Vairocana gazed at the entire assembled entourage and spoke these Dharma words which completely perfect the definitive Awareness, [which is diversified as] the gates of the three times that are without limit, and which causes all hopes to be completely fulfilled[A]:

The definitive Awareness [which is diversified as] the gates of the three times that are without limit, which completely fulfils all hopes, refers to the Awareness of Suchness (*tathatā-jñāna*). (112b) ***Which causes all hopes to be completely fulfilled***: Though the Bhagavat's Awareness does not form judgmental concepts, by the power of his previous aspirations he acts beneficially in accordance with all beings, with the Vajra Adornments of his Inexhaustible Body and so forth throughout all of the Three Realms. ***The gates of the three times that are without limit***: They enter into emptiness by the many *samādhi* gates of the Śrāvakas, Pratyekabuddhas and Bodhisattvas and attain specific Awarenesses. ***He spoke [these] Dharma words which completely perfect Awareness***: They are the words that completely perfect that same Awareness and they refer to the verses beginning '***Like space, it is stainless and without intrinsic properties***'. Because if you directly realize their meaning, that Awareness will be completely fulfilled.

2. 'Like space, it is stainless[2]
and without intrinsic properties,
it bestows many diverse kinds of Awareness;
By nature it is ever emptiness,
dependent on conditions,
profound and difficult to see.
In particular, it always bestows upon beings
the excellent results which they wish for[B].'

Like space it is stainless and without intrinsic properties: This is the intrinsic nature of Enlightenment. Just as space is devoid of obscuring impurities such as dust and cannot be perceived to have such intrinsic properties as blue and so on, likewise the intrinsic nature of Enlightenment is devoid of the obscuring impurities of the

---

A C: 爲欲滿足一切願故 '*out of a desire that all hopes might be fulfilled*'.
B C reads: 於長恒時殊勝進 隨念施與無上果 '*it is perpetually active in special ways, and bestows the supreme result according to one's aspirations*'.

emotional afflictions and so forth, and its perceptual image cannot by perceived by Awareness. ***It bestows many diverse kinds of Awareness***: This is the intrinsic nature of Practice. At the very moment of perfect Enlightenment, by the power of his previous aspirations, the Vajra Adornments of his Inexhaustible Body and so on reveal the scriptural and experiential Dharma to many types of beings in accordance with their condition. (113a) For those various kinds of beings will attain Awareness where those Dharmas are taught. Secondly, it also refers to practice in the causal phase, because it brings about the attainment of relative and absolute Awareness at the time of entry into that pure Dharma. ***By nature it is ever emptiness***: This refers to the intrinsic nature of Perfect Enlightenment. If even the external, perceived phenomena, are without intrinsic existence, then the perceiving awareness also does not exist. Its nature, which is thus freedom from both perceiving subject and perceived object, refers to its authentically consummate character (*aviparyāsa-pariniṣpanna-lakṣaṇa*). ***Dependent on conditions, profound and difficult to see***: This refers to the intrinsic nature of Nirvāṇa. ***Dependent on conditions***: This means that the Awareness which is relative in character (*paratantra-lakṣaṇa*) interdependently arises in an uninterrupted continuity of instants by nature, which is like the continuity of lamps. ***Profound and difficult to see***: The profound is the abandonment of perceiving subject and perceived objects, emptiness in nature. Therefore, since there are no such perceptual images as blue and so on in that emptiness, it is difficult to see. ***In particular, it always bestows upon beings the excellent results which they wish for***: When you have heard, pondered and cultivated the intrinsic nature of Enlightenment, that pure reality (*dharmatā*), you will attain blissful excellent [results] such as kingship and possessions in the world.

3. 'Just as space which has an unhindered range
becomes the dwelling of all creatures, (145b)
likewise this pure reality provides
the unlimited wealth[A] of the Three Realms.'[3]

(113b) If you have repeatedly cultivated that pure reality (*dharmatā*), having abided on the Level of Practice with Devoted Interest, you will attain the attribute of successful mastery of the Three Realms. Though that pure reality does not deliberate, it produces such results. It is pure: for example, though space does not deliberate, it functions as the dwelling-place (*bhavana*) of all creatures, likewise that pure reality also provides the wealth of the Three Realms though it does not deliberate.

4. 'If a wise one, most excellent of people,
engages in this, his perceptual range
will become one with all the Jinas.'[4]

When those who attain the Joyous Level have repeatedly cultivated it, its result is oneness of perceptual range (*gocara*) with the Buddhas.

5. 'There is no other state more difficult to attain
than the pure reality which illumines[B],
of which the Jina has thus spoken.'[5]

A C: 清淨 '*purification*'.
B C adds: 世 '*the world*'; probably a mis-reading of '*sakalāloka*'.

The result is the attainment of Buddhahood. ***Difficult to attain***: Because there is nothing more difficult to acquire than Buddhahood, and because it illumines throughout all world systems with All-knowing Awareness. ***The pure reality of which the Jina has thus spoken***: These are words of summary meaning that the pure reality was taught by the Bhagavat Vairocana.

6. 'Engage in the vast reality
which is profound without deficiency,
without equal and helps the world,
abandoning concepts about it!' [6]

This means that you should abandon concepts concerning that reality endowed with such an intrinsic nature and engage in it! ***The vast reality which is profound without deficiency***: (114a) This refers to the pure reality. Because it is defined as being vast and unchanging consummacy, both cessation and non-cessation are taught as the general nature of that reality.[A]

7. Then having spoken these verses, the Bhagavat Mahā-Vairocana gazed upon the entire entourage and then said to Vajrapāṇi and such Vajradharas, 'Nobly-born Ones! Let the words which accomplish attainment and which are each the outflowing power of the continuum of reality, by which beings will attain delight and joy in just the present world and then reach bliss, be revealed.'

8. When he had spoken thus, all the Vajradharas prostrated to the Bhagavat Vairocana and said, 'May it be done as the Dharma Lord has commanded!' And they asked the Bhagavat himself, 'We beg you to teach the words which accomplish attainment, out of pity for us! Why? O Bhagavat, it is most rare to have described in the presence of the Bhagavat what we ourselves have realized, so we ask the Bhagavat to explain it for the benefit, help and happiness of future beings!'

9. When they had thus asked him, the Bhagavat Vairocana said to all the Vajradharas, 'O Nobly-born Ones, excellent, excellent! There is one factor of great benefit in this Vinaya Dharma taught by the Tathāgata, and that is modesty. A son or daughter of good family who has modesty will quickly achieve two factors in this very world: (146a) they will not do what should not be done and they will be praised by the Holy Ones. There are a further two: they will realize what they have not yet realized and they will gain companionship with the Bodhisattvas and Buddhas. There are a further two: they will abide in the moral discipline and they will attain birth as humans and gods. Therefore retain this most carefully in your minds.

'I shall explain the words for engagement in the *sādhana* of secret mantras, by which words the Bodhisattvas who engage in the Bodhisattva practice by means of mantras will speedily attain the mantra attainment from the mantras.'

A The Commentary breaks off here and resumes at Section 12.

10. 'First of all, one who has seen the mandala, who has been permitted by the guru to accomplish the mantras, who has generated *bodhicitta*, who has trust, who is without avarice, who is compassionate, who has self-control, who is skilled in the analysis of interdependent arising, who maintains the discipline and who abides in his training:

11. 'He is wise in expedient means, very firm,
he knows the suitability of the occasion,
he is without fear, he is hospitable[A],
he is tolerant and has a friendly disposition[B],
he exerts himself in the mantra practice,
he is skilled in the significance of those mantras,
he delights in practising meditation:
that practitioner is blessed for accomplishment.'

12. 'Lord of the Secret Ones! The Lords (*īśvara*) of the Desire Realm have a *vidyā*-mantra called "Intoxication". By it, all the gods who indulge in the sensual, faint with intoxication. They also manifest delightful places with many varieties of flowers, and they emanate various different kinds of pleasures and sensuous enjoyments, and bestow these to the Paranirmita-vaśa-vartin gods[7] and they also enjoy these themselves.'

Now, the Bhagavat explains the cause, the nature, the power and the results of mantras. The cause and the nature of mantras were dealt with earlier in the [section on] the letters [I.80-85]. In the following section he gives teachings about the power of mantras. Also, the doubts of *sādhakas*, who are sceptical about the *sādhana* and wonder whether they will accomplish attainments or not, will be cleared away by teaching the power of the mantras mentioned below. First, he says that the best power is that arising from the two *vidyā*-mantras called the 'Intoxication' of the Lords of the Desire Realm and the 'Creating at Will' *vidyā*-mantra of the Great Lords. The power of the mantra 'Material Possession' of Indra and the mantra 'Illusion' of the Asuras are explained as being middling. The counteracting of poison and diseases, causing death with the mantras of the Mothers and the cooling of fire and so on are said to be the inferior powers.

Thus, Lord of the Secret Ones, the Lords of the Desire Realm have a vidyā-mantra called "Intoxication"*: *'Desire' is indulgence in colour-form, sound, taste, smell and touch. ***The Great Lords* (maheśvara) *of the Desire Realm***: (114b) The Lords of the six levels of the heaven of the gods of the Desire Realm have a *vidyā* called 'Intoxication'. Since those born in that realm naturally possess that *vidyā*, just by thinking or uttering it, they will have the enjoyment of the five sensual objects. ***Who indulge... faint with intoxication***: It is not that they become forgetful with their faculties clouded, but by the power of that *vidyā* those gods become attached to the enjoyment of the five sensual objects and are enthralled by desire, hence it means that they are intoxicated with desire. ***They also manifest delightful lands with many varieties of flowers*: *Varieties of flowers*:**

A C: 好行惠捨 '*engages well in generosity*'.
B C omits '*he is tolerant and has a friendly disposition*'.

These orchards, flower gardens, pleasing parks, flowers and groves are adorned with sweet fragrances and beautiful colours. ***Delightful places***: They manifest groves and bowers decorated with various jewels and so on. ***They emanate various kinds of pleasures and sensuous enjoyments***: The pleasures and enjoyments of the five sensual objects, food to eat, beautiful soft divine clothing and so on. ***Emanate***: By the power of the vidyās of each of the gods in that place, the enjoyment of the five sensual objects arise. ***And bestow these on the Paranirmita-vaśa-vartin gods.... enjoy these themselves: Paranirmita-vaśa-vartin gods***: They give the enjoyments of the five sensual objects that have arisen through their power to those gods and they also enjoy them themselves. In the same way, though Bodhisattvas also engage at will in [producing] offerings and so forth for the Tathāgatas, they also use these themselves without attachment.

13. 'Then the Great Lords have a *vidyā*-mantra called "Creating at Will". With it they carry out the needs of beings in the triple thousand great thousand worlds, (146b) and they also emanate all pleasures and sensuous enjoyments. Giving them to the gods of the Pure Abodes, they also enjoy these themselves.'

(115a) Their *vidyā* is called 'Creating at Will' (*mano-bhava*) because by just thinking of it, they create whatever benefits beings and go to whatever places they wish in the space of an instant. ***The triple thousand great thousand worlds***: This refers to everything above and below, or else the triple thousand great thousand worlds of the Realm of Form. The triple thousand are well known from the scriptures. ***The needs of beings***: They benefit the beings in the Realm of Form with the pleasures mentioned below, by the power of that *vidyā*. ***They also emanate all pleasures and sensuous enjoyments***: Specifically, they do not indulge in fragrant morsels of food, but in the other pleasures, similar to the rest [mentioned above]. ***Giving them to ... enjoy these themselves***: They also give these to the gods of the Pure Abodes in the Realm of Form and they themselves also indulge in the pleasures produced by the power of this *vidyā*. The above teaches the superior power of *vidyās*.

14. 'Then, Indra manifests with mantras various kinds of things such as parks, lakes, streams and people.'

This shows the power of the mantra of Indra. When Indra and the gods fight with the Asuras, they emanate countless Indra gods with mantras and deceive the Asuras, (115b) and they act with the power of illusion without being opposed anywhere. Through the power of Indra's mantra, groves, lakes, rivers and people are conjured up and manifested.

15. 'Then, for example, the Asuras manifest illusions with mantras. Or, for example, there are [mundane] mantras which counteract poison and fevers. Or else there are the mantras with which the Mothers send sickness[A] upon

A C: 災癘 '*pestilence*'.

people. Or else[A], the heat of a fire can be extinguished and made cold with mantras. Nobly-born Ones! By these examples you should have faith in the power of mantras.'

***Then, for example, the Asuras manifest illusions with mantras*:** This explains the power of the mantra of the Asuras. What is that? When the Asuras fight with Indra and the gods, they emanate countless Asuras, Rahula comes from the abode of the Asuras and takes on a body higher than the King of Mountains Sumeru and terrifies the gods, and they manifest magical illusions with its power. These two, the power of the illusion-making mantra of the Asuras and the power of the mantra of Indra mentioned above, are explained as the middling power.

***Or, for example, there are [mundane] mantras which counteract poison and diseases*:** This explains the power of the mantras of men. What is that? With the power of those mantras, they remove all poison and such diseases as fever and so forth.

***Or else there is the mantra with which the Mothers send sickness upon people*:** This explains the power of the mantra of the Seven Mothers. What is that? When Indra and the gods fight with the Asuras, if the gods are unable to defeat the Asuras, seven goddesses called the Mothers emerge from Indra, Brahmā and so on and these seven goddesses drink the blood drawn by swords before it falls to the ground and they also quell the harmful Asuras. When doing malevolent rites with the mantra of the Seven Mothers, if you have acted according to the words of the mantra of the Mothers, you will cause people to die. (116a) If, when the gods and Asuras are fighting, beings in the world are very virtuous and do much good, the gods will be victorious, while if beings do little good and have little power, then the Asuras will be victorious. If the gods are victorious, the attainments for eclipsing the sun and moon can also be accomplished, but if the Asuras are victorious, pestilences which will kill beings in the world can be brought about through the power of this mantra.

***Or else the heat of a fire can be extinguished and made cold with mantras*:** With the power of mantras, even though you have entered into blazing fire, the burning and the heat will be nullified and you will be as cool as though walking in water.

***Nobly-born Ones! By these words you should have faith in the power of mantras*:** When those who do not believe in the teachings above concerning the superior, middling and inferior powers of mantras, do come to believe in them and the doubt of those who are sceptical and dubious has been cleared away, the Bhagavat exhorts them to have faith in the power of the mantras.

16. 'What is that power of mantras? It does not arise from the mantras and it does not enter into the materials[B], nor can it be perceived to inhere in the yogin.'

This section explains the nature of mantras. ***What is that power of mantras? It does not arise from the mantras*:** That power of mantras does not arise from the letters of mantras, for if it were in the letters of mantras, then it would never be possible for

A C adds: 及世間咒術攝除衆毒及寒熱等 '*and there are mundane spells which can eliminate poisons and cool fevers*'.

B C reads: 衆生 '[*into*] *beings*'.

books of mantras to be stolen by thieves or burnt by fire. Therefore the power does not arise from the letters of the mantras. ***It does not enter into the materials*** (*dravya*): This refers to such objects (116b) as swords, wheels, balls and so on. It means that the transmutation does not arise when the power of the mantra has entered into those objects. ***Nor can it be perceived to inhere in the yogin***: Nor does the power of mantras come from the yogin who undertakes the *sādhana*. For if it came from the person who undertakes the *sādhana*, he would already be accomplished and hence there would be no need for the *sādhana*.

17. 'Yet, Nobly-born Ones, [that power] arises from the intrinsic nature of mantras by their transformational power and then does not pass away, because [their intrinsic nature] transcends the three times and because [its effects] are formed through inconceivable and profound interdependent arising. Therefore, Nobly-born Ones, one who has directly realized the Dharma, which is inconceivable in its essential mode of being, should constantly adhere to it by the Mantra Method.'

This explains that the intrinsic nature (*dharmatā*) of mantras is present everywhere regardless of whether Tathāgatas appear in the world or not. ***Because [their intrinsic nature] transcends the three times***: If its nature had already been accomplished in the past in nature, it would not be accomplished in the present or in the future; and if its nature was to be accomplished in the present or in the future, it would not have been accomplished in the past. Therefore, the nature of mantras to accomplish is not located in any of the three times and so it transcends the three times. ***Because [its effects] are formed through inconceivable and profound interdependent arising***: For example, it is like various plants – when there are seeds, shoots and leaves, they are green, and when there are flowers, they change colours. And though a cow eats green and rough roots, they are changed into smooth and white milk. Accordingly, although the mantra attainments do not inhere in anything, when there is the concurrence of causes and conditions, (117a) and the inconceivable and profound intrinsic nature [of mantras], one will obtain superior, middling and inferior attainments through the intrinsic nature of the transformational power of mantras. ***[That power] arises from the intrinsic nature of mantras by their transformational power and then does not pass away***: This explains that their transformational power is constant. ***Transformational power*** (*adhiṣṭhāna*): By their intrinsic nature, they transform whatever is to be accomplished, and moreover the attainments which are obtained are stable and unchanging. Hence, it says '***Therefore, Nobly-born Ones, one who has directly realized the Dharma, which is inconceivable in its essential mode of being, should constantly adhere to it by the Mantra Method***'.

18. Then the Bhagavat Vairocana entered a *samādhi* endowed with the matrix of the pure adornments of the inconceivable embodiment of the Tathāgata, the transformation of the ground of the power that is unimpeded in the three times.

If the four aspects of *A* uttered by the Buddha, which reveal the ground endowed with four members that are Enlightenment in nature, have already been mentioned, why are they to be repeated here? The previous explanation was a general description each of the letters which form *samādhi* gates on the absolute level, and what is repeated here is the specific description, so that you will meditatively observe their significance and recite them by the mantra *sādhana*.

In order to utter those four aspects of *A*, the Bhagavat entered a *samādhi*. It reveals meaning on both the absolute and the relative levels. On the absolute level it reveals Suchness by way of that letter *A*. (117b) On the relative level it indicates that the Thirty Two Marks of a Great Being arise from that letter *A*. Hence, in the chapter on the Hundred Letters there is the explanation of the emanation of the thirty two letters beginning with *Ka* from that letter *A*, and it says that those thirty-two letters should also be regarded as the Thirty-Two Marks of a Great Being. [So] through this *samādhi* two aspects of meaning are revealed.

The ground (pada) ***of the power that is unimpeded in the three times***: On the absolute level, that Suchness should be revealed as the support of the *A* letters. Since the nature of Suchness is unchangingly consummate in character, it is like space; and it has the power which is unobstructed in the three times. '***The ground***' is Suchness in nature, it is what empowers the letter of the letter *A*, and this means that it supports the *A* letters until the ending of samsara. That is what is indicated on the absolute level.

The pure adornments of the inconceivable embodiment of the Tathāgata: This indicates that the Thirty-Two Marks of a Great Being arise from the letter *A* on the relative level. '***The inconceivable embodiment*** *(āśraya)* ***of the Tathāgata***' is the inconceivable Body of the Tathāgata, because inconceivable different types of magical displays arise from the Tathāgata's Body. ***Adornments***: These are the Thirty-Two Marks of a Great Being and since these have also arisen from the four aspects of *A*, the word 'adornments' also applies to these aspects of *A*. ***Pure***: Those Thirty-Two Marks are also said to be pure because they abide clearly in their respective places and are completely perfected. (118a) ***The matrix***: This means the *samādhi* is a source. Because the four aspects of the letter *A*, by which the absolute and relative meanings are thus revealed and produced, emerge from this *samādhi*, it is said to be '***endowed with the matrix***' and so forth.

19. Immediately after he had entered it, there arose the four modes from a single sound, the sounds which make known the entire continuum of reality without remainder, whose strength abides in the continuum of reality, whose strength is equal to the unequalled, (147a) which arise from the fervent inclination of the perfect Buddha and which having pervaded all of the continuum of reality became space-like: *NAMAḤ SARVA-TATHĀGATEBHYO VIŚVA-MUKHEBHYAḤ SARVATHĀ A Ā AṂ AḤ*. (Salutations to all the Tathāgatas, who are multifaceted, omnipresent! *A Ā Aṃ Aḥ*)

The sounds which make known the entire continuum of reality without remainder: The words ***continuum of reality*** should be understood as meaning the receptacle world and the realms of beings. [These sounds are the words which make known such things as pots, sheets of cloth, carriages and so on. The syllables which are the reverse of those words are these four *A*s which arise from the unborn sound[A].] Since they make

A These two sentences only occur in V.

those things known through these four *A*s which arise from the unborn sound, all the words for such things as pots and on, are also included within the unborn word. This indicates the attributes of the four aspects which form those words. ***Whose strength abides in the continuum of reality***: Since those four aspects of *A* are the words of the continuum of reality, they are said to abide in the continuum of reality. ***Strength***: Because they have power, as they do not change into anything else apart from words of the continuum of reality. ***Whose strength is equal to the unequalled***: This indicates the perfection of their power. ***Which arise from the fervent inclination (adhimokṣa) of the perfect Buddha***: Because these four *A* letters arise from the coming to perfection at the moment of perfect Enlightenment of whatever qualities of a fully perfect Buddha to which the Tathāgata was fervently inclined during his causal phase. (118b) ***The four modes which arise from one sound***: Because the various individual words such as 'pot' and so on, arise from the single unborn sound. ***Which having pervaded all of the continuum of reality, became space-like***: This either means that the unborn sound functioned like space which pervades all of the continuum of reality, or that it pervaded all of the continuum of reality, equal to the limits of space. ***Continuum of reality***: This should be understood as [referring to] the world systems. The letter *A* is Enlightenment in nature, and its four aspects are that Enlightenment with its four members, which should be viewed in sequence as Enlightenment, Practice, Perfect Enlightenment and Nirvāṇa.

20. As soon as these essences of the perfect Buddha had arisen, then the sounds which make things known, characterized by the words of the essence of the perfect Buddha, sounded forth from each one of the gates which communicate the entire continuum of reality.

With the utterance of those essences, the unarisen, unborn sound characterized by the words of the Tathāgata arose from the sounds of the mundane phenomena.

21. When all the Bodhisattvas heard it, they opened their eyes in wonder and spoke these praises to the All-knowing One who is devoid of affliction:

'Ah! Through the mantra practice
the Buddhas, most excellent of humans,
produce the vast great Awareness
which pervades all of this!
Therefore in all of its aspects,
you should always exert yourself
in the essence praised by Buddhas,
with a pure inner self[A].'

When the Bodhisattvas thus heard the unborn sound which pervades all world systems, they were amazed. They then uttered words of praise to the Bhagavat.

A C: 是故勤精進 於諸佛語心 常作無間修 淨心離於我 '*Therefore you should exert yourself in the Buddha speech essences, continually cultivating it with a pure mind devoid of a self*'. V: '*... you should always do it most assiduously, with a pure mind*'.

22. '[A]Then if one of these essences of the perfect Buddha is to be accomplished, you should stay in a grove, a monastery, a cave, or wherever there is mental solitude, cultivating bodhicitta until signs appear[B].'

This explains that *bodhicitta* should be cultivated prior to the *sādhana*. Also such places as groves, monasteries and so on (119a) are mentioned, but you can cultivate it residing in any other place that you find pleasing. Groves and caves are places where you will be physically isolated. Monasteries are places for mental solitude, and it is better that you have mental solitude even if you do not have it physically. ***Or wherever there is mental solitude***: Places other than those mentioned are permissable. The main thing is to stay where you have mental solitude, and this should be linked up with the words '***until signs appear***'. In this case, the word '***signs***' does not refer to the occurrence of freedom from sickness, hunger and so on through the recitation of mantras, but to the mind becoming stable and unchanging in meditative absorption (*dhyāna*).

23. 'Then starting with any one of those essences, you should accomplish the ground until it becomes definite. Placing the essence in [your] heart, you should accomplish your mind, until it appears to be very pure, unsullied, stable without wavering, free from conceptualization, like a mirror, and very subtle. You should do it with continual application to the practice until you see your body as the body of the deity. The second ground is the perfect Buddha who sits upon a great royal lotus within that same mirror disc, abiding in *samādhi*, [as though] within a cave. He has a top-knot and (147b) a crown, and is surrounded by infinite rays of light. He is devoid of all thoughts and concepts (*kalpa-vikalpa*) and is peaceful from the very beginning, like space.

> **'Imagining that the sound abides in him,**
> **you should recite in equipoise.**
> **It is taught that the preliminary service**
> **should be done a hundred thousand times[C].'**

Bodhicitta should be continuously cultivated in the above manner and when the signs have appeared, you should repeatedly cultivate the practice of the body-image of your tutelary deity (*adhidevatā*), imagine the Buddha's Body in the mirror mandala in your heart, and also imagine a moon disc and the mantra you are going to recite within the heart of the Buddha's Body. This is the sequence.

You should imagine any one of the four aspects of *A* as appropriate in the moon disc in your heart. Perceiving that the sound of this *A* signifies that all phenomena are unborn from the very beginning, you should dissolve your psycho-physical constituents into emptiness, with the technique (*yoga*) [of realizing that] they are unarisen and unborn from the very beginning, or with the technique of reducing them to

---

A C inserts: 爾時薄伽梵 復說此法句 '*Then the Bhagavat spoke these Dharma verses*'.
B C: 觀彼菩提心 乃至初安住 不生疑慮意 '... *Visualizing that* bodhicitta *until it starts to become stable and confused thoughts do not arise*'.
C C: 一月修等引 持滿一洛叉 '*You should cultivate it for one month in equipoise, reciting it a hundred thousand times*'.

atoms. Having imagined that there is only the *A* present in the moon disc, you should then, following the above method, dissolve both the moon disc and the *A* itself, which are without any objective basis, and maintain the *samādhi* of emptiness for as long as you wish. (119b) Then arising out of that *samādhi* by virtue of your compassion, you should imagine that *A* in the area of your heart, with the conviction that it is like a magical illusion. With the technique of radiating light forth from that *A* and then drawing it back, you should transform yourself into the appearance of your tutelary deity. That should be done until you appear with certitude in the body-image of your tutelary deity. Now, in general there are three ways of changing yourself into the appearance of a deity. The first is just the conviction that 'I have that divine appearance!', by use of the *mudrā* and mantra. The second is your vivid appearance, without doubt, in the body-image of your tutelary deity through repeated practice of it. The third is to change into the divine body, forgetting your own body, by virtue of union. On this occasion the text is referring to the vivid appearance of your own body as the body-image of the deity through repeated practice. Having thus transformed your own body into the body-image of the deity, you should imagine an *A* in your heart, and following that *A* you should imagine a moon disc, the *bodhicitta* symbol, which is like a mirror. It should be very radiant and unsullied. You should then imagine that the letter *A* in its centre becomes the Bhagavat Vairocana. Hence, the text says '***The second ground is the perfect Buddha who sits upon a great royal lotus within that same mirror disc, abiding in* samādhi**'.

[As though] within a cave: This means you should imagine him seated within it, like the reflection of a face within a mirror. Then you imagine a moon disc in the heart of the Tathāgata and within that you should imagine the mantra you are going to recite. You should do a hundred thousand recitations as the preliminary service. Therefore, the text says, '***It is taught that the preliminary service should be done a hundred thousand times***'.

24. 'Then in the second month,
you should offer flowers, perfume and so on,
acting helpfully towards beings
in many different ways,
regardless of profit and loss,
you should recite for another month.'

(120a) The time is specified by application to a prior recitation of a hundred thousand times, then during the second month, recitation in each [three hour] period of morning and afternoon and half a midday period. During the preliminary hundred thousand recitations and the recitation in the first month, one should recite without making offerings of perfumes, flowers and so forth, because the mind of one who is cultivating *bodhicitta* for the first time will be disturbed by making external offerings. But during the second subsequent month, since *bodhicitta* will have been cultivated and stabilized, one's mind will not be disturbed by making external offerings.

Acting helpfully towards beings, in many different ways:...[A]

A V and B break off here in mid-sentence in all editions and do not resume until Section 45.

25. ' "By the power of my merits
may all beings be happy!
May they be free from all ills!
May they also perfect all wishes
praised by the Tathāgatas!
May the fulfillment of all hopes
of all beings also
come about without hindrance,
in a way free from obscurations!
May the torments never arise
of one animal eating another!
May food and drink arise
without hindrance for the hungry ghosts!
May the various unendurable torments
of the beings in the hells
be quickly calmed
by the power of my merits!" '

26. 'Having generated great compassion
for all suffering beings,
he should repeatedly think
of this and other things to be done.'

27. 'In order to accomplish whatever they desire,
he should empower them all
with the three bases of transformation,
and also mentally recite the mantras.'

28. ' "By the power of my merit,
by the power of the Tathāgatas,
and by the power of the continuum of reality,
may beings be helped by this!
May all aims whatsoever that are wished for
in these realms of beings without exception,
arise without hindrances,
all of them, as appropriate!" '

29. Then the Bhagavat spoke the *Vidyā* Queen, whose power is equivalent to space, which gives rise to a sky treasury: (148a) *NAMAḤ SARVA-TATHĀGATEBHYO VIŚVA-MUKHEBHYAḤ SARVATHĀ KHAṂ UDGATE SPHARA HE MAṂ GAGANA-KHAṂ SVĀHĀ* (Salutations to all the Tathāgatas, who are multi-faceted, omnipresent! You who are sky-born, spread forth! *He!* [Reveal] to me the realm of space! *Svāhā*!). If this is recited three times, all aims will occur as wished for, without hindrance.

30. 'Then at the time of the full moon,
that person should commence the accomplishment,

on a mountain peak, or in a cow-pen,
or at a confluence of rivers, in a cemetery,
at crossroads, or under a single tree,
in an abode of the Mothers, or in a tranquil place.'

31. **'Listen carefully about the mandala**
which will intoxicate all obstacle-makers:
Draw an excellent vajra mandala,
which is completely square,
one-gated, with a perimeter,
completely coloured in gold.
The vajras should be joined to each other,
in the manner of a vajra mesh.'

32. **'In the gate two guards should be drawn:**
Durdharṣa and Abhimukha.
They should be drawn red-eyed and angry,
wrathful and making menaces.'

33. **'Three-pointed spears[A] in each corner**
should carefully be drawn.
In the centre a pleasing vajra throne
should be drawn, facing all directions.'

34. **'Upon it a great lotus**
with eight petals and stamens[B].
You should prostrate to all the Jinas,
and declare your resolutions;
then having safeguarded the place, stay there.'

35. **'Having obtained cleansed material,**
with a pure inner self,
you should recite the whole night long.'

36. **'Then, at midnight or else at sunrise,**
the material will be transmuted
as though brilliant with a flaming aura.'

37. **'If the *mantrin* takes hold of it himself,**
he will travel through the sky;
he will abide for an eon, most brilliantly;
if he wishes, that Buddha-child can die[C]

A C adds: 焰光 '*blazing with light*'.

B C adds: 當結金剛手 金剛之慧印 '*You should make the vajra insight mudrā of Vajrapāṇi*'.

C C: 於生死自在 '*he will have mastery over life and death*'.

and go to other realms,
assuming the forms of various Lords.
He should make noble offerings
with the material arising
from this mantra accomplishment.
This is explained as the attainment of the material,
which does not perish[A].'

38. 'Lord of the Secret Ones! (148b) Though they know all these contrived things to be empty by nature, the Tathāgata Arhat Samyak-saṃbuddhas who dwell in all world systems and who have directly realized the Perfection of Expedient Means, treat those same contrived things as the causal attribute and figuratively designate them as the unconditioned, by the power of their Perfection of Expedient Means. They reveal the great power of the continuum of reality by means of transmutation to beings so that they may abide happily in the present world. By that they will be joyful and attain long life, then enjoy the acme of joy with the five sensual objects, making offerings to the Buddha Bhagavats, and this path which is different to all the mundane [ones] will be accomplished[B].'

39. 'Also the Tathāgatas and Bodhisattvas[C], having seen the power of its use, joyfully expound this ritual of the method of mantra practice[D]. Why is that? That which cannot be attained even though one were to strive diligently over many eons, undertaking deeds of asceticism, will be attained in just this one lifetime by those Bodhisattvas who engage in the Bodhisattva practice by way of mantras. Lord of the Secret Ones! Moreover, if the Bodhisattva who engages in the Bodhisattva practice by way of mantras, obtains banners of the Tathāgatas[E], or swords, parasols, sandals, wish-fulfilling gems, antimony or bezoar (*gorocana*), and transmutes them in that manner, performing three hundred thousand recitations, they will be transmuted thus.'

40. 'Furthermore, Lord of the Secret Ones, if sons or daughters of good family skilfully transmute the objects they desire, these will be transmuted just by the power of their minds. Lord of the Secret Ones! Those foolish people who look for the result in the cause (149a) do not know the mantra nature (*lakṣaṇa*) of mantras at all. Why is that?'

41. 'I have said that the cause is not the agent,
nor does it have a result.

A C: 具德吉祥者 展轉而供養 眞言所成物 是名爲悉地 以分別藥物 成就無分別 '*The virtuous noble one should repeatedly make offerings of the materials transmuted by the mantra. This is called attainment. With conceptually reified materials he will accomplish the non-conceptual*'.

B C: 證如是句一切世人不能信 '*they will realize this rank* (pada) *which all mundane people are unable to believe*'.

C C omits '*and Bodhisattvas*'.

D C adds: 菩薩 '[*of*] *Bodhisattvas*'.

E C omits '*of the Tathāgatas*'.

If the cause is devoid of causality,
how can it be a cause[A]?
Therefore one should know the results of mantras
are devoid of cause and action.
When he experiences the *samādhi*
without attributes, as it really is,
then the *mantrin* will accomplish
the attainment arising from the *manas*.'

42. Then Vajrapāṇi said this to Bhagavat, 'Bhagavat! Please explain the ground of the perfect Buddhas, with whose attainment-accomplishing words the sons and daughters of good family abide in this very world, experiencing joy and happiness, without being out of tune with the continuum of reality. Bhagavat! Why is that? The continuum of reality is an inconceivable realm, yet it is revealed by the Tathāgata Arhat Samyak-saṃbuddhas. Bhagavat since that is so, the Bodhisattvas who engage in the Bodhisattva practice by means of mantras desire to directly realize the indivisible continuum of reality.'

43. When he had spoken thus, the Bhagavat replied to Vajrapāṇi, 'Lord of the Secret Ones! Excellent, excellent! Lord of the Secret Ones, it is excellent that you have thought of asking the Tathāgata about this matter! Therefore listen carefully and bear this in mind, for I shall explain it to you.' Vajrapāṇi said, 'Yes, indeed!', to the Bhagavat who then spoke as follows, 'Lord of the Secret Ones, for the accomplishment of A, (149b) [the *mantrin* should reside] in a temple, cave or any suitable place and place *A* in all the members of his body and make three hundred thousand recitations. Then at the time of the full moon, he should make offerings with whatever he possesses and recite until the Bodhisattva Samantabhadra, Manjuśrī, Vajrapāṇi or any other suitable one, comes and caresses his head, or says "Excellent!". Then having prostrated to them, if he offers them oblations (*argha*), he will attain the *samādhi* of not forgetting *bodhicitta*. When he has repeatedly cultivated lightness of body and mind and has recited it, both his body and mind will become purified[B]. When he has united *A* with his breath (*prāṇa*) and cultivated this at the three [specified] times [of the day], desiring that his life-energy (*prāṇa*) be maintained, he will live for a long time. If he places the *anusvāra* on top of it, he will draw out all abiding and moving poisons[C].'

A C: 果 '[*how can there be*] *a result?*'.

B C adds 置於耳上持之當得耳根清淨 '*If he places it on his ear and recites, then he will attain purity of the faculty of hearing*'.

C C omits '*he will draw out ... poisons*', yet we can assume this was mentioned in its base text since CC (156a5 – 9) mentions this benefit, stating that the abiding poisons are drugs and so forth, and the moving poisons are such insects as mosquitoes.

44. 'Then if he wishes to control a lover[A], he should make himself into an *A* and likewise the person to be controlled into a *Va*[B]. He should place a lotus in himself and in the other he should place a conch, with each looking at the other, then at that instant he will gain control.'

45. Then gazing at the entire assembled entourage, the Bhagavat Vairocana said to Vajrapāṇi, the Lord of the Secret Ones, 'Vajrapāṇi! There is a mantra called "Arising from the Minds of the Tathāgatas" which disports by actions and activities, which is the bursting forth of the dance of practice, which is extensive, which is the reservoir of the four elements, which abides in the king of minds, which like space pervades everything, which has many results both visible and invisible, which is directly available to all Śrāvakas, Pratyekabuddhas and Bodhisattvas, which completely fulfils all the hopes of those who engage in the practice of Bodhisattvas by means of mantras, which is endowed with various functions, (150a) and which brings help to all beings. Listen carefully to this and bear it in mind, for I shall explain it to you!'

Now the *sādhana* and levels of the five essence syllables of the Great Hero will be explained. Generally speaking, the aspects which include whatever causal and resultant qualities of the Tathāgata that have been accumulated from the Level of Practice with Devoted Interest up to Sambuddhahood are *Nirvāṇa* with remainder (*sopadhiśeṣa-nirvāṇa*) and Nirvāṇa without remainder (*nirupadhiśeṣa-nirvāṇa*). Of those, Nirvāṇa without remainder is the attribute of Tathāgatahood, which is to become perfectly enlightened in Akaniṣṭha, devoid of even the subtle idea of emptiness. Nirvāṇa with remainder is the attribute of Perfect Buddhahood, which is to become perfectly enlightened under the Bodhi-tree in the Realm of Desire and to overcome the Four Māras, while there remains the subtlest of traces of just the idea that phenomena are empty since they do not exist even in the nature of illusions. The essence of the Nirvāṇa without remainder is the four aspects of *A*. Their *sādhana* has been explained already.

(120b) Here the *sādhana* and the levels of the *samādhi* gates which conquer the Four Māras, the essence of Nirvāṇa with remainder will be explained, and that is with the words '***Then gazing at the entire assembled entourage***' and so forth. Now, the sequence for overcoming the Four Māras through the *samādhi* gates of *A* and so on and the transformation of these *samādhis* into the *mahendra* (earth) mandala and so forth is as follows: The letter *A* reveals the *samādhi* gate of the realization that all phenomena are unborn and unarisen from the very beginning. Through that gate you will realize that such phenomena as the psycho-physical constituents, the perceptual elements and sources are unborn and are without objective basis, so the Māra of the Psycho-physical Constituents is overcome. The letter *Va* is the *samādhi* gate which reveals that all phenomena are separate from modes of speech (*vākpatha*), because modes of speech are conceptualization (*vikalpa*). Realizing that there is nothing to be conceptualized, you will overcome the Māra demi-gods through the

A C: 願囉闍等之所愛敬 '*If he desires* [*a person*] *beloved by kings and so on*'.

B C reverses the lotus and conch, and gives *Ha* instead of *Va*.

absence of conceptualization. If there are thus no phenomena such as the psycho-physical constituents and no concepts which refer to them, then the emotional afflictions such as attachment and so on which adhere to them will not exist. This is revealed by the gate of the letter *Ra*, and you will realize that all phenomena are devoid of dust. 'Dust' (*rajas*) refers to the emotional afflictions, and by that you will overcome the Māra of Emotional Afflictions. The letter *Ha* is the *samādhi* gate to the realization that all phenomena are devoid of causes. Karmic action and rebirth occur through the emotional afflictions, but if there is nothing which is emotionally afflicted, then karmic action and rebirth will not occur. If there is no birth, then you will not die, and by that realization you will overcome the Death Māra. (121a) The letter *Kha* is the gate to the realization that phenomena are empty in nature, due to their being unborn from the very beginning, and it reveals that all phenomena are like space.

Thus each of those letters beginning with *A* should also be linked with the mandala of the earth mandala and so on in those *samādhis*, on the relative level. With the *samādhi* entered through the letter *A*, the Māra of the Psycho-physical Constituents is overcome. The psycho-physical constituents are firm and able to bear a burden. Thus in accordance with that, the letter *A* forms the earth mandala, for the earth is also said to be firm and burden-bearing. The letter *Va* becomes the *samādhi* gate of separation from concepts, and it cleans away impurities which are thoughts (*kalpa*) and so on. Thus that letter *Va* forms the water mandala, and in accordance with that, it cleans away impurities. The letter *Ra* becomes the *samādhi* of all phenomena being free from dust. It consumes the emotional afflictions of attachment and so on. Thus, in accordance with that, the letter *Ra* becomes the fire mandala, for fire burns up and destroys everything. Likewise the letter *Ha* becomes the *samādhi* gate of all phenomena being free from causes. It scatters the karmic actions which arise from emotionally afflicted causes. In that way the letter *Ha* becomes the wind mandala in accordance with that. The nature of wind is to scatter or destroy. The letter *Kha* becomes the *samādhi* gate to the realization that all phenomena are empty, with the nature of space. Thus the letter *Kha* which becomes the wind mandala, is in accordance with the nature of wind. That is their general significance.

"Arising from the Minds of the Tathāgatas": This means arising from the Awareness of Suchness, and refers to the emptiness of the *A* and so forth. (121b) ***Which disports by actions and activities***: It carries out the superior attainments and so on, and the actions of Pacifying and so on. ***The dance***[8] ***of practice***: It resembles a dancer, because dancers display various kinds of dance such as dance-drama (*nāṭya*) and so on, and in the same way these essences also manifest various accomplishments and actions. ***The reservoir*** (saṃgraha) ***of the four elements***: Because the mandalas of earth, water, fire and wind arise from these essences[A]. ***Which like spaces pervades everything***: Just as space pervades everything, in the same way these essences also pervade everything. These [epithets] teach the nature of those essences.

Which has many results both visible and invisible: This teaches its power. The '***visible***' refers to the actualization of the *vidyādhara* attainments and so on, and the '***invisible***'

A There is no extant explanation of '*which abides in the king of minds*' which should occur here.

refers to those attained through the result itself which is Buddhahood. It bestows such excellent results. ***Which is directly available to all Śravakas and Bodhisattvas*:** This means that it is accessible to them. Even the Śrāvakas have immediate experience of the *samādhis* of the earth device (*pṛthivi-kṛtsna*), the water device (*ap-kṛtsna*) and so on, because they also have the nature of these mandalas. Also Bodhisattvas fill all sites with jewels and so forth, and offer them to the Tathāgatas, because they also have the nature of these mandalas. ***Which completely fulfils all the hopes of those who engage in the Bodhisattva practice by means of mantras*:** Because all hopes will be completely fulfilled through the accomplishment of attainments by those who have embarked upon this teaching. ***Endowed with various functions*:** It has various functions such as clearing away demonic possession[9] and poison. (122a) ***Brings help to all beings*:** It assists those beings who have embarked on this teaching and also those who have not.

46. 'Vajrapāṇi! What is this dance of practice, which accomplishes extensive results through actions and activities, which can be actualized by all beings[A]?'

47. 'He who knows the ritual should first
in sequence carry out the true nature of self.
The *mantrin* sits as before[B],
and having recollected the Tathāgatas,
he should make himself into an *A*
augmented with an *anusvāra.*
All is quite yellow and beautiful,
square and marked with vajras.
The *mantrin* should imagine
the Lord of all perfect Buddhas dwelling there.
This is called the true nature of self
by all the Buddhas.'

This section explains the practice of the true nature of self (*ātma-tattva*) by the *mantrin* and its praises [in the following sections]. After the *mantrin* has done the preliminary yoga of the true nature of the self, he arranges (√*nyās*) the letters in their specific places in his body and changes them into the earth mandala and so on, and then he undertakes their *sādhana* and their actions. Also the undertaking of the process in that way was taught by previous Buddha Tathāgatas who perfectly understood the intrinsic nature of phenomena, that is, emptiness, and who subsequently by the power of their previous aspirations pervaded all worlds in a perfect manner with the Adornments of their Inexhaustible Bodies and so on. Therefore the *mantrin* should also first perceive emptiness which is the true nature of self and thereafter arrange and recite the letters.

The above section describes the yoga of the true nature of self. ***The true nature of self*:** This is [the process] by which the *mantrin* dissolves even his own body into

---

A C: 持眞言者一切親證 '*which* mantrins *directly realize in totality*' instead of '*which can be actualized by all beings*'.

B C: 如前依法住 '*he abides as before in accordance with the method*'.

emptiness as it is unborn and unarisen from the very beginning, by means of the letter *A*, and then he imagines the *A* becoming a bright yellow solid earth mandala, (122b) and then a Buddha seated upon it. In that way he imagines his own body.

He should carry out in sequence the true nature of self: This means that he should cultivate *bodhicitta* and then carry out the process in accordance with the *sādhana* of the body-image of the deity and so forth.

The* mantrin *sits as before: This means that he should sit in a manner similar to that described in the section above which explains the essences of the Tathāgata. ***Having recollected the Tathāgatas***: When he carries out the actions of recitation and so on, he should do them after having imagined himself to be in the presence of the Tathāgatas, because it is to them that the mantras and *vidyās* refer. Secondly, if he imagines himself to be in the presence of the Tathāgatas, there will be no obstacles. ***He should make himself into an A, augmented with an anusvāra***: He should imagine himself to be emptiness in nature through the letter ***A***. ***With anusvāra***: This shows that the perceiving Awareness is also emptiness, meaning that he should become empty in nature, without the existence of a perceiving subject and perceived objects.

All is quite yellow and beautiful, square and marked with vajras: Having become empty in nature, he then imagines a square earth mandala, bright yellow in colour, marked with a vajra symbol[10].

The* mantrin *should imagine the Lord of all perfect Buddhas dwelling there: He should imagine the Body of the Bhagavat Vairocana upon that mandala, and furthermore he should understand that it is his own body which is imagined to be thus.

48. **'When the *mantrin* has become free of doubts**
concerning the true nature of self[A]**,**
then he will indeed be a benefactor
of all those in the world.
He will be endowed with various wonders
and will live like a magician.'

That is, when he has no doubts about perceiving the true nature of the self as emptiness (123a) and the vivid appearance of [himself] in the body-image of the deity. One has certitude concerning emptiness when one's *samādhi* is pure and is devoid of perceptual images and devoid of all conceptualization. Then one will have no doubts about the way things really are. When the *mantrin* has become free of any doubts through a firmly convinced (*adhimukta*) mind, he will attain the things that are praised here.

Then he will indeed become a benefactor of all those in the world: By means of the accomplishment of attainments and so forth, he will be able to benefit beings. That is the perfection of benefitting others. ***He will be endowed with various wonders and live like a magician***: This means that having accomplished the attainments of the *vidyādharas* and so forth, he will be able to perform various wonders of magical feats like a magician. That is the perfection of power.

A C: 修行不疑慮 自眞實相生 '*When the* mantrin *practises with certitude, the true nature of self will arise.*'

49. 'When the *mantrin* is equipoised
he will eliminate all karmic actions
accumulated by ignorance from beginningless time
in the confines of samsaric existence.'

This means that when he is equipoised in that type of yoga, all those unwholesome and emotionally afflicted karmic actions, accumulated within the confines of samsara by the power of ignorance from time without beginning, will become cleansed away. That is the perfection of abandonment.

50. 'If the *mantrin* visualizes his mind
as the supreme *bodhicitta*,
he will always be unsullied by the results
arising from wholesome and unwholesome actions,
as a lotus is unaffected by the water,
and then how much more so
if he transforms himself
into the most excellent Jina!'

Since that *bodhicitta* is characterized by being empty, one will not be sullied by the results of wholesome or unwholesome actions because it is the antidote to the resultant phenomena which are wholesome and so forth. (123b) Now, though it makes sense for one to be unsullied by the results of the unwholesome, yet if one is unaffected by the results of the wholesome, will not the effects of maintaining the morality (*śīla*) and so on also be lost? Although the wholesome also lacks any objective basis because the intrinsic nature of *bodhicitta* is emptiness, after he has arisen from that [*samādhi*] the yogin then makes the following resolution: 'May I be endowed with the body and material goods that are the cause of becoming awakened!', so that the dispositions (*vāsanā*) for the results of wholesome actions may once again be developed. ***Then how much more so if he transforms himself into the most excellent Jina***: If he becomes as described by just cultivating *bodhicitta*, then if the yogin who has cultivated *bodhicitta* transforms himself into the Body of the Buddha, how much more so will he be unsullied by unwholesome actions and so forth.

51. Then the Bhagavat Vairocana entered a *samādhi* called 'The Vajra Play, the Conqueror of the Four Māras' and then he spoke these words of vajra letters which conquer the Four Māras, which cause liberation from the six streams of existence, which completely perfect All-knowing Awareness: *NAMAḤ SAMANTA-BUDDHĀNĀṂ AḤ VI RA HŪṂ KHAṂ.*

Then the Bhagavat Vairocana entered a* samādhi *called 'The Vajra Play, the Conqueror of the Four Māras': After the Bhagavat entered that *samādhi* there arose the mantra which conquers the Four Māras and which is vajra play, so that *samādhi* is also called 'The Vajra Play, the Conqueror of the Four Māras'. ***The Conqueror of the Four Māras***: This is its perfection of abandonment. ***Vajra Play***: Manifestation which is not impaired by anything, like a vajra. This is the perfection of its power. Hence the words '***Conqueror of the Four Māras***' and so on are linked with the words below, '***then he spoke these words of vajra letters***'.

Which cause liberation from the six streams of existence: When you have entered the *samādhi* of emptiness you will be liberated from the six streams of existence by means of the letters, through the realization that all of the six streams of existence are without any objective basis. Secondly, (124a) when you have done the practice of the mandala of earth and so on by means of those letters and have accomplished the *vidyādhara* attainments, you will proceed up to the higher levels in sequence, therefore the words '***which cause liberation from the six streams of existence***' reveal its perfection of benefitting others. ***Which completely perfects All-knowing Awareness***: This refers to the perfection of its Awareness. Because when you have entered the higher levels in sequence, the All-knowing Awareness will be completely perfected.

The process of changing the letters of the mantra into the *samādhis* which conquer the Four Māras and into the earth mandala and so on have already been explained.

52. Then Vajrapāṇi, the Lord of the Secret Ones, with those Vajradharas, and Samantabhadra and the Bodhisattvas, (150b) together with the entire assembly were astonished, and with wide-opened eyes they prostrated to the All-knowing One and spoke these words:

'By this treasure of all the Buddhas
and the saviour Bodhisattvas,
those Buddhas and saviour Bodhisattvas,
Pratyekabuddhas and Śrāvakas[A],
such wise beings as those attain
the supreme Buddha Awareness,
the unequalled Awareness,
in this world, and then
by manifesting various supernatural powers,
they roam over all the land.'

When the Bhagavat had uttered the mantra, the Bodhisattvas Vajrapāṇi and so forth directly understood the power and qualities of that mantra and were amazed, and understood its blessings. ***By this treasure*** and so on: These essences are the treasure jewels of the Buddhas and Bodhisattvas. By them ***those Buddhas ... roam over all the land***: By the power of these essences, (124b) the Buddhas and Bodhisattvas perform various kinds of magical deeds, and also the Śrāvakas and Pratyekabuddhas imagine the earth [element] and so forth in the empty sky by *samādhi* and abide there in the four physical postures (*īryā-patha*), perform various kinds of magical deeds such as making water flow from the upper part of their bodies and fire blaze from the lower part, or with the wind mandala they even destroy mountains.

The supreme Buddha Awareness, the unequalled Awareness: Also after having performed such kinds of magical deeds by the power of those essences, they will attain by stages the All-knowing Awareness.

53. 'Therefore we ask you to explain individually
their extensive rituals and various actions,
and also the arrangement of them all.'

A C adds: 害煩惱 '*who have destroyed the conflicting emotions*'.

They ask him to expound now the teachings about the rituals for changing those essences into the earth mandala and so on, their arrangement (*pratiṣṭhā*) and the engagement in their actions.

54. **'By this, beings will delight**
in the Supreme Mahāyāna
of the secret mantra practice,
while dwelling in the present world.'

Furthermore, they request the Bhagavat to expound them because the explanation of these things will cause beings to attain the happiness of success in the present world. This indicates the purpose of the explanation.

55. **When they had spoken thus, the Bhagavat**
replied in a gentle voice:
'You should all listen to this,
equipoised, one-pointedly.'
At that time, he transformed
the site into a great vajra,
and he spoke, desiring to reveal
the core of Enlightenment through his body[A].

Now the individual rites of those mantras mentioned above will be explained. For those rites also, the *mantrin* should imagine himself to be empty through the letter *A* as explained previously, and then he should imagine himself [as] the Body of the Bhagavat Vairocana sitting on an earth [mandala], and also imagine within his body an earth mandala, and then the letters there according to the sequence. Therefore it says, '***at that time he transformed the site into a great vajra***' and so on. (125a)

He transformed the site into a great vajra: His Body was transformed into an earth mandala. ***To reveal the core of Enlightenment through his Body***: To reveal the arrangement of the letters *A* and so on, having thus changed [himself] into the earth mandala. It is called '***the core of Enlightenment***' because those letters are the *samādhi* gates to perfect Enlightenment. Thus, the fact that the Bhagavat first transformed himself into an earth mandala and then revealed the arrangement of the letters also teaches future beings to act in the same manner.

56. **'You should know that the excellent *A***
has a *mahendra* mandala;
both inside and outside
it is a vajra mandala.
Imagine all of them abiding thus.
This is explained as the yoga-posture.'

Following the sequence explained above, you should imagine your body becoming the Buddha's Body, accompanied by an earth mandala. '***Vajra mandala***' is an earth

A T: *nyid kyi sku* (**ātma-kāya*) 'his body', C: 下身 = (**adha-kāya*) 'lower body'.

mandala which is marked with a vajra symbol. ***Imagine all of them abiding thus*.** Thereafter, you should imagine the letters beginning with *A* in sequence. ***Yoga-posture*** (*yoga-āsana*): Because that Body which abides on an earth mandala is the mode of sitting for yoga, it is called the yoga-posture.

57. '*A* is the supreme life-energy,
and is called the most excellent magnet[11].'

After having seated himself on the earth mandala, the *mantrin* should imagine that letter *A*, like refined gold in colour, being drawn up in the inner mandala by his breath and then emerging from his nostrils it enters into the nostrils of another person who is sick and penetrates all throughout their interior. He should imagine this happening like a cloth being dipped into water or a yak-tail [whisk] spreading out in water. (125b) Then once again he should imagine in his mind that *A* being drawn back with his breath, imagining it to be like the cloth or yak-tail [whisk] immersed in water becoming limp after it has been drawn out of it. All the sickness is gathered together by that into the intrinsic nature of the *A*. He should imagine it emerging from the nose of the sick person and entering into himself. When he has repeatedly done this many times, all [the sickness] will be drawn out.

Also when you guide your mind thus, imagining that *A* going from your body as before with the breath and entering the body of another, if you imagine in particular that your breath and the breath of the other person mingle and become one, and then draw back your breath as before, you will gain control over them.

Likewise if you imagine that *A* pervading the stream of any faculty such as the eyes [of the person] you are going to control (*sādhya*) and then guide it back again, they will come to you on foot.

Also if you do as before and imagine that *A* penetrating the entire interior of the body [of the person] to be controlled and then draw it back, they will be attracted to you.

58. 'When you surmount it with an *anusvāra*,
it will become the attracter of all beings[A].'

This is the summary.

59. 'When the *mantrin* has recited at the three times,
for one month, while making the vajra-like[B] *mudrā*,
the fortress of ignorance will be destroyed,
and he will become firm,
unshakable even by gods and asuras.'

A T: *lus-can kun-gyi sel-bar 'gyur* , '*It becomes the cleanser of all beings*'; V: *sems-can kun-gyi sdud-par 'gyur* , '*It becomes the attracter of all beings*'; C: 能攝授諸果 '*It is able to attract and bestow all results*'. In view of V and C, it seems that the reading in T is unreliable.

B T has *rdo-rje-can* and C has 金剛慧 '*vajra-insight*'. It would seem from this that the Sanskrit for T probably read *vajra-mat*, and for C *vajra-mati*. It is hard to decide which would have been the original, so I have adopted T, although C has parallel examples elsewhere.

This explains the attainment arising from the recitation. If he recites for one period in the early morning and late night, and a half period at midday, for a whole month, transforming his body as before, then he will clear away ignorance and will also be unharmed by gods and asuras.

60. 'In order to obtain possessions
or for some degree of enriching action,
all these should always be done
by the *mantrin* in the centre of the mandala.'

This means that he should also carry out the *sādhana* [to obtain] possessions (*bhoga*) and the rite of Enriching while residing in the mandala.

61. 'A perfect Buddha dwelling in *samādhi*,
shining, golden in colour,
with top-knot and crown, (151a)
is called the *mahendra* ground[A].'

(126a) You should imagine the Bhagavat's Body dwelling in that way on the *mahendra* (earth) mandala.

62. 'You should meditate and transmute
in the *mahendra* mandala [such things as]
a vajra, a lotus, a sword,
or else a goose, pure gold or earth
or else a wish-fulfilling gem, as appropriate.'

The *mantrin* should transmute such materials as vajras and so forth while residing in the *mahendra* (earth) mandala, according to the process mentioned in other Tantras.

63. 'Now I shall also explain subduing,
so you should listen one-pointedly!
In brief, the *mantrin* should imagine
an eight-peaked Sumeru, on top of which
he should place a lotus,
and subsequently a vajra[B];
on top of that the chief holy letter[C].
If the yogin presses that on the head,
he will remain motionless.'

In order to subdue false teachers (*para-pravādin*), the *mantrin* should imagine himself abiding in an earth mandala as before, and he should then imagine a bright yellow, heavy eight-peaked Sumeru mountain on the head of the one to be suppressed and

A C: 大金剛句 **mahā-vajra-pada*, 'great vajra ground'.
B C: 立金剛智印 '*and erects the vajra awareness mudrā*'.
C C reads: 字門威焰光 '*the letter-gate majestic with blazing light*'.

a lotus upon that, and then a *viśva-vajra* upon that. On top of all that he should imagine that *A*, upon which is the Body of the Bhagavat. If he imagines that this presses down on the head of all those to be crushed, they will become completely motionless.

64. **'If it is recited one hundred times**
over medicine to be drunk by someone,
his illnesses which arise from
previous actions will be cured.'

If he imagines himself as before and recites the mantra over medicine a hundred times, administering it to a sick person, their illness will be cured.

65. **'Then furthermore, listen carefully**
about the excellent *Va*,
which is [white] like snow, milk or a conch,
and arises in the middle of the navel,
It rests in the middle
of a fine white lotus.
The excellent Lord is tranquil,
like the light of the autumn moon.
That mandala is said to be
wonderful by the perfect Buddhas.
It should be imagined completely white,
and also encircled with nine swirls.
That which calms all torments
rests within dew-drops.'

(126b) The [following sections] explain the *sādhana* of *Va*. The imagining of the letter *Va* should also be done in an earth mandala, as before, and thereafter it should be specifically imagined in the navel region of the inner earth mandala. This section describes the rite of *Va*. Having transformed himself into the earth mandala, the *mantrin* should imagine a *Va* in the navel region of the inner vajra mandala. He should imagine a lotus, white like snow, milk or a conch, emerging from within the navel and resting there. Upon the lotus there is the letter *Va*, the colour of the autumn moon, and the *Va* should be surrounded by nine swirls of water, and a water mandala like moon light should also be imagined as its base. Moreover, that letter *Va* should be imagined as though resting in a mass of white dew drops in a jar-like container. If he imagines it penetrating right throughout the interior of his body, all poisons and fevers will be purged. In the same way, if he imagines his own body resting on an earth mandala and then similarly imagines that [*Va*] in the body of another, they will also be purged of poisons, fevers and so forth.

66. **'If the *mantrin* imagines it in his mind,**
with streams of water flowing all round
like milk, strings of pearls,
crystal or moonlight,
then he will be freed from all torments.'

This describes another rite for the letter *Va*. He should imagine that letter *Va* as before, and then imagine the white streams of water arising from that *Va*, without dew drops, and that those streams of water encircle the *Va* and then rest in a swirl around it. If he imagines that it is put into motion by his breath and pervades the whole of his body, it will soothe all such ailments as fevers and so on. Likewise, if he imagines it in another, then their ailments such as fevers will be soothed in that same way.

67. **'These things should be transmuted**
in this mandala, while equipoised:
such materials as clarified butter,
milk, strings of pearls,
likewise lotus-root[A], crystal,
yoghurt, or even water, as are appropriate,
should be transmuted for the accomplishment
of various attainments.
Your life will be long,
your appearance will be very wonderful,
you will be free from all illnesses,
you will have excellent good fortune[B],
your intelligence will be sharp and retentive,
your vision will be free from impediments:
with these transmuted materials, (151b)
all these things will quickly come about.
This noble mandala is called the "pacifier".'

(127a) If you abide in the yoga of the *Va* mandala, and then transmute vajras and such materials (*dravya*) as named, you will attain such attainments as long-life and so on and will be endowed with the others as listed.

68. **'If done with an *anusvāra*,**
it will be the most excellent purifier.'

When you imagine that *Va* with an *anusvāra* in the body of a sick person, the *Va* makes all the perceived phenomena empty, and the *anusvāra* reveals the emptiness of all perceiving subjects, and so that person's body will thus become empty, devoid of perceiving subject and perceived objects, and the sickness will also be absorbed into the intrinsic nature of emptiness and become non-existent.

A T has *khyu-mchog* which usually translates the Sanskrit *vṛṣa* 'bull'. C has 藕 'lotus-root', which would correspond to the Sanskrit *bisa*. As the latter fits the context better, one can assume that '*bisa*' was the word originally used, and had been amended to or misread as '*vṛṣa*' in the Tibetan base Sanskrit text. It should be noted that there is some evidence of Prakrit forms in this text, which can be seen in some of the surviving Sanskrit passages. A Prakrit form of '*vṛṣa*' would be identical to *bisa*, so one can easily imagine how an over-enthusiastic scribe might have Sanskritized what he thought was a Prakrit word. Some of differences elsewhere between T and C can be explained in the same way.

B C reads: 天人咸恭敬 '*you will be totally respected by gods and humans*'.

**69. '*Ra*, most excellent truth,
is called the best of the luminous ones.'**

The following describes the *sādhana* of *Ra* and its rites. ***Ra, most excellent reality***: Since that letter *Ra* reveals the most excellent true meaning and its intrinsic nature reveals the *samādhi* in which all phenomena are devoid of dust (*rajas*), it is called '***most excellent truth***'. This is its attribute on the absolute level (*paramārtha-lakṣaṇa*). ***It is called the best of the luminous***: ***The luminous ones*** refers to the sun, moon and stars, and amongst these luminaries, the light of fire is the best. Since the letter *Ra* is the seed syllable of fire, it is called the '***best of the luminous ones***', and this shows its nature on the relative level.

**70. 'By it, whatever arises from actions,
even from the five heinous deeds,
will all be destroyed,
if the yogin imagines it, while equipoised.'**

This shows the results of having cultivated it. When you have meditatively observed the intrinsic emptiness of all phenomena which are devoid of dust, the ten unwholesome actions and the heinous deeds[12] will also be found to lack any objective basis, so their effects will be destroyed and not arise.

**71. 'He should place it in his heart,
where it abides in the form of a triangle,
pleasing and completely red,
and marked with a triangular sign,
tranquil yet encircled with a flaming aura.'**

(127b) This describes the attributes of the fire mandala. It means that he should imagine a brilliant red triangle, like the [Sanskrit] letter *E* (▽), resting upon the vajra mandala within his heart, marked with a triangular sign.

**72. 'Placed therein, the yogin
should imagine Ra with an *anusvāra*.'**

This means that within the symbol of the fire mandala, he should imagine a red letter *Ra* with an *anusvāra*, resting upon an *E* (▽) shape. ***With* anusvāra**: This indicates that the essence of Perfect Enlightenment is devoid of both perceiving subject and perceived objects.

Likewise it should be seen that even if the letter *Va* is without an *anusvāra*, it is still the essence of Perfect Enlightenment, for the hole in *Va* (व), which is like the *anusvāra* (o), shows that there is no perceiving subject.

**73. 'Fearlessly he should transmute
these things as appropriate with it:
If the sun and all the planets,
and likewise fire,
all things to be controlled,**

and furthermore making angry,
parching, killing[A],
and also confining and harming[B],
are done in conjunction with fire here,
they will all be carried out.'

This describes the accomplishments of *Ra* and its functions. If having abided in the *Ra* mandala, the *mantrin* transmutes the things to be transmuted which are mentioned by name, with the rituals appearing in other Tantras and Kalpas that are either with or without perceptual forms, he will gain control of the sun[13] and so forth, and whatever he commands will be heeded.

74. '*Ha*, the most excellent truth,
arising from the wind:'

The following describes the *sādhana* for the letter *Ha*, its qualities, mandala and so forth. ***Ha is the most excellent truth***: Since all phenomena are emptiness in nature and are devoid of causes, it is the most excellent truth. ***Arising from the wind***[14]: Since it arises from the wind mandala, or since the wind mandala arises from it.

75. 'Causes, karmic actions, results,
by which seeds are produced,
all these will be destroyed
if you unite this with an *anusvāra*.'

(128a) This shows the results of having cultivated its intrinsic nature. By having imagined *Ha* with an *anusvāra* there will be no objective basis for either a perceiving subject or perceived objects, due to the absence of causes in all phenomena. '***Causes***' refers to emotional afflictions such as ignorance. '***Karmic action***' refers to the wholesome or unwholesome deeds one has carried out by body, speech, or mind. '***Results***' refers to the miserable or fortunate states of existence which are the fruition of those actions. ***By which seeds are produced***: This means that the psycho-physical constituents are recreated by those causes and actions, but because they are all empty, without any objective basis, it (*Haṃ*) destroys them.

76. 'To describe its appearance also,
it is black in colour, with great light
and is encircled with a fierce flaming aura
which also flows out in all [directions].
The wise one should imagine it
on the disc located between his eyebrows;
Indigo, like a crescent moon [in shape],
it ripples like the emblem on a flag,

A C: 消枯衆支分 '*parching all the limbs*' and omit '*killing*'.
B C omits '*and also confining and harming*'.

the supreme letter, which is unchanging[A],
should be imagined located there by the *mantrin*.'

The following indicates the appearance of the letter *Ha*. It should also be imagined located on top of a wind mandala, and concerning this wind mandala, the text says '***the wise one should imagine it on the disc located between his eyebrows***' and so forth. ***It ripples***: The mandala should be imagined to ripple because the nature of wind is movement. ***The supreme letter which is unchanging, should be imagined located there by the*** **mantrin**: Although the nature of the letter (*akṣara*) is as previously described based on the word '*akṣara*' (letter, unchanging), the text also means that it is to be recited without its changing, which means that you should imagine the letter to be unchanging, by the power of repeated practice.

77. **'Whosoever just sees them**
in the middle of that mandala
will then transmute the objects
which benefit beings.
Travelling in the sky,
also the magical powers,
the divine sight and hearing,
will likewise be attained by the *mantrin*.
The equipoised *mantrin* will carry out
all [these] things if he abides in the mandala:
both the general and the specific things (152a)
that have been spoken of, such as invisibility[B].'

This means that when the *mantrin* has abided in the wind mandala, (128b) he should transmute the things mentioned by name, according to the rites appearing in other Tantras.

Any one of these four letters can be the starting point for counting and should be imagined in the centre of an earth mandala. The transformation of yourself into the Perfect Buddha's Body, the transference of the letter *Va* and so on from the inner vajra mandala to whatever location you intend, the making of a five-pointed vajra *mudrā* over the things to be transmuted regardless of the intentions and purposes, the performance of the preliminary service for one month at the three times, and

---

A It is evident from a comparison of the various versions that the original text literally read something like C: 最勝訶字門 '*The supreme Ha letter* (akṣara) *gate*'. However, to accommodate Buddhaguhya's comments, the Tibetan versions translate the word *akṣara* twice, once in its sense of 'letter' (T: *yi-ge*), and then again in the sense of 'unchanging' (T: *mi-'gyur-ba*).

B C is somewhat different for this section: 住彼漫荼羅 成就所應事 作一切義利 應現諸衆生 不捨於此身 逮得神境通 游步大空位 而成身秘密 天耳眼根淨 能開沈密處 住此一心壇 而成衆事業 [*If*] *he places them in that mandala, he will accomplish whatever is to be done: he will bring about all things which benefit, and manifest them to beings; Without abandoning his present body, he will quickly attain magical powers: the ability to walk in the air, and to make his body invisible, pure faculties of divine sight and hearing, and he will have access to secret places.* [*For these*] *he should abide in this single heart mandala, and accomplish a multitude of tasks*'.

the rites of accomplishment which are either with or without perceptual forms should be carried out with regards all of them.

78. 'By this [letter], the renowned Bodhisattvas
will be victorious over demons,
[dwelling] in this Enlightenment Essence,
through the absence of any objective basis to all causes.'

This teaches the power of the letter [*Ha*]. It means that Bodhisattvas also will overcome the Four Māras and attain perfect Enlightenment by the realization that all phenomena are devoid of causes, by means of this letter.

79. 'Since there are no causes,
there are also no results,
and even actions do not exist.
As those three phenomena do not exist[A],
the Awareness of emptiness will be attained.'

The following sections describe the nature of the letter *Khaṃ* and its *sādhana*. By means of the letter *Khaṃ* which reveals the absence of a perceiving subject and perceived objects, [one realizes that] there is no objective basis to such emotionally afflicted causes as ignorance and so on, nor to such actions as the wholesome and unwholesome ones, nor to such results as the fortunate and miserable states of existence.

80. 'The perfect Buddha, of great power,
has fully described its appearance:
With an *anusvāra*, *Khaṃ* is called
the most excellent of space[B].'

This speaks of the nature of that letter. Because the letter *Khaṃ* reveals the absence of both perceiving subject and perceived objects, it is called the '***most excellent space***'.

81. 'He who has the sword[C] *mudrā*,
will definitely transmute
that which is to be transmuted.
If you have such articles as
swords, nooses, wheels,
iron arrows and hammers
you will accomplish the best state[D].'

A C: 彼三無性故 '*because of these three non-existent natures*'.

B Based on V: *nam-mkha'i mchog*, T has: *stong-pa'i mchog ces-bya, while* C has: 尊勝虛空空 '*the most excellent emptiness of space*'. C has evidently read '*khaṃ*' in the sense of 'space'.

C C adds: 慧 '*insight* [*sword* mudrā]'.

D C: 不久成斯句 '*speedily attain this state*'. Could there have been some confusion here between **varaṃ* (Tib: *dam-pa*) 'best' and **satvaraṃ* 'speedily'?

(129a) After arranging themselves in the yoga-posture, *mantrins* should imagine the letter *Khaṃ* on the crown of their heads, then imagine everything as being space in nature. Then when they have imagined just the letter *Khaṃ*, like the sky in colour, and made the Sword *Mudrā* and recited as previously, those things mentioned by name will be transmuted.

82. Then the Bhagavat Vairocana said to Vajrapāṇi, the Lord of the Secret Ones, 'Lord of the Secret Ones! When the Bodhisattva who engages in the practice of a Bodhisattva by means of mantras has transformed himself into the nature of *A*, and without perceiving any thing related to the external or the internal, [views] both gravel, stones and gold in the same way, and abandons negative actions and such faults as attachment, hatred and so forth[A],

'Then he will become pure
like the perfect Buddha Sage,
he will be capable of all deeds
and will be free from all faults.'

This section explains that when the *mantrin* has repeatedly cultivated the true nature of self, which is empty, following the cultivation of the yoga-posture as before, specifically until he is able to stop the arising of emotional afflictions such as attachment and so forth, he will accomplish the essences beginning with *A* and their rites without regard for external substances (*dravya*).

[When he] has transformed himself into the nature of A and without perceiving any thing related to the external or internal*:** He transforms himself into the nature of A and so on, and then not giving rise to external phenomena such as colour-form (*rūpa*), or internal representational (*rūpaṇa*) thoughts, he becomes unattached to phenomena. If he has accomplished that *A*, then as a result he will cease to make any distinctions between gravel, stones and gold, for just as one feels no attachment towards stones and gravel, likewise he will also feel no attachment even to gold. Attachment and aversion will not arise, and he will not be subject to the effects of failings done through the ten unwholesome actions. Therefore, it says '[he] abandons negative actions***' and so on. ***He will be capable of all deeds*:** This means that he will accomplish the superior, (129b) medium, or inferior attainments, and be capable of the rites of Pacification and so on. ***[He] will be free from all faults*:** For if he does engage in those rituals, he will be able do them without such faults as impurity or confusion.

83. 'Then furthermore, he who is devoted
to the mantra yoga and knows the ritual
should carry out the actions of *Va*,
desiring to aid all beings.
Perceiving the sufferings of the world
with a compassionate mind,
his body will be completely filled
by that Lord, with a white stream of water,

A The above is verse in C.

like snow or cow's milk.
Then when he has become certain about it,
an extremely pure flow of water
will come forth from all the follicles
on all parts of his body, (152b)
and all these realms without exception[A]
will be completely filled with that water[B].
Whosoever drinks that water
or else even touches it with their hands
will all definitely become Enlightened,
of this there is no doubt!'

This is the yoga of the letter *Va.* Arranging himself in the yoga-posture, the *mantrin* should imagine the letter *Va* becoming a water mandala and so forth, as before, and in particular he should imagine streams of water flowing from the *Va,* and his whole body from head to toe is pervaded and filled with the water mandala. When he is firmly convinced of this, he should imagine water flowing out of his pores and filling up all the area surrounding his body, his room and so forth. Then if he imagines it gradually filling the entire monastery, the country and so on, whatever is drunk or touched by fortunate beings will be that water. Since they are directly blessed unlike ordinary people, they will definitely become enlightened.

84. **'[Or else,] equipoised , he should imagine**
***Ra* in all parts of his body,**
surrounded with a peaceful lustrous aura,
which flows out to all places.
Then if the yogin releases outwards
the all-illuminating radiance,
the *mantrin* will do as he wishes
by manifestations with *Ra*[C].'

This teaches the yoga of *Ra.* Arrranging himself in the yoga-posture as before, the *mantrin* should imagine the letter *Ra* resting upon a fire mandala in his heart, (130a) and in particular he should imagine that the inside of his whole body is filled with rays of blazing light. When he has become convinced of this, he should imagine it issuing out of all his pores and gradually filling the entire town and region with the illumination from the rays of light of the fire. When he has done that yoga, the *mantrin* will be able to do whatever he wishes with that fire issuing from the *Ra.*

85. **'When he has *Ra* in his upper body,**
and *Va* in his navel,
then lustrous radiance and flowing water
will be manifested at the same time.'

A C adds: 悲愍 '[*of*] *kindness*'.

B C adds: 觀世苦衆生 '[*as he*] *gazes upon the suffering beings in the world*'.

C C: 利世隨樂欲 行者起神通 '*benefitting people according to their desires, the* mantrin *will attain the supernatural powers*' and omits '*the* mantrin *will … with* Ra'.

This is the contraction and uniting of the *Ra* and *Va*. If the *mantrin* arranges himself in the yoga-posture as before, and imagines the letter *Ra* resting on a fire mandala in his heart, and the letter *Va* in his navel, as before, the miracle of fire issuing from the *Ra* and water flowing from the *Va* will occur.

86. 'With *Ra*, those who suffer in cold hells
will be made to feel soothed.'

When he has established just the *Ra* on a fire mandala as described above and carried out its *sādhana* diligently, he should abide in the sky above beings in the cold hells, and then that fire which has been accomplished will issue forth from his body, penetrating all such hell-beings who are enveloped in coldness, and he will be able to soothe those suffering beings with that fire.

87. 'The *mantrin* who abides in the mantra method
will also soothe the hot ones with *Va*.'

If the *mantrin* arranges himself in the yoga-posture as before and also imagines the letter *Va* as before, resting upon a water mandala, and then also imagines water flowing out from the *Va*, all those hell-beings who are tormented by heat will be cooled by that nectar water. (130b) The process for cooling is similar to that of the fire yoga.

88. 'A pennant-like *Ha*
should be placed below *Ra*,
and then even sinful people
will quickly bring about its action[A].'

If when you use that fire for a rite, it does not blaze and is not suitable for use, you should imagine the letter *Ha* resting on a wind mandala below that fire mandala. If you imagine it being fanned by that wind, you will definitely be able to perform whatever ritual in which you use that fire. ***Even sinful people***: If it can be accomplished even when undertaken by sinful people, how much more so by others! This teaches the certainty of the action that is performed. Because a yogin cultivates that without distinguishing inner and outer things, free from the arising of emotional afflictions and so forth, he will not act negatively.

89. 'When the *mantrin* resides in the *mahendra* [mandala],
should he apply himself to the actions of water[B],
he will do all such deeds as cleansing,
of that there is no doubt!'

This explains that it is appropriate to do the water rites while abiding in the earth mandala. This means that while seated in the yoga-posture as before, the *mantrin*

A C: 作業速成就 救重罪衆生 '*the action will be swiftly accomplished and he will save beings who have committed heinous crimes*'.
B C: 水龍 '*water serpents*' (*nāga*).

should imagine the letter *A* resting on an earth mandala as before and then he should perform the rite to be accomplished by the letter *Va*. Here, the rite of *Va* disregards the filling of everything with water, because if you were to fill everything with water, even the earth mandala would become water and would cease to be an earth mandala. ***He will do all such deeds as cleansing*:** This means that if he imagines that letter *A* on the heads of sick people, with their bodies being filled and washed inside and out, from head to toe, with its rays of yellow light which are peaceful by nature, even sicknesses will thus become purified. Likewise when he does the practice of the letter *Va*, (131a) he also imagines the water mandala of the *Va* as before, on top of the sick person's head, with white nectar water flowing from an upturned jar. If he imagines that sick person to be washed gradually from head to toe, both inside and out, all his sicknesses will be cured. That practice is the general ritual and should be used in connection with the other ones.

90. 'Wind is said to be all-pervasive,
and also it forms all things[A].
The various actions of the diverse images
which arise from [their] distinctions,
should be carried out with this ritual
within the colour-form mandala.'

This describes how the letter *Ha* performs the functions of all the mandalas of earth and so on, so wind is said to be '***all-pervasive***' (*sarvatraga*). The intrinsic nature of the letter *Ha* is the wind and it accompanies (*samanvāgata*) all the mandalas of earth and so on. It is because of the wind that they are individually distinguished in shape, such as the squareness of the earth mandala, the roundness of the water mandala and so on, therefore it is also said to '***form all things***'. This is connected with '***The various actions of the diverse images which arise from the distinctions***'. ***The diverse images which arise from the distinctions*:** The various different perceptual images (*ākāra*) of the earth mandala and so forth, which are yellow, white, red and so on. The '***various actions***' refers to the various individual functions (*karma*) of those mandalas. ***Arise from the distinctions (prabheda)*:** This refers to the individual mandalas of earth, water and so on. ***Should be done with this ritual*:** They should be done with the ritual of the letter *Ha*. ***Within the colour-form mandala*:** The *mantrin* should transform himself into the body-image of the deity and abide in the earth mandala yoga-posture. In brief this means that if you imagine the letter *Ha* in the individual mandalas of earth, water and so forth, and have performed the practice, the actions of *A* and so on will be carried out.

91. 'If you have recited it,
having cleansed the *manas*
your *manas* will become clear[B].'

A T: *'jig-par-byed-pa* and C: 開壞 both imply 'destroy', but Buddhaguya's comments require 'form' or 'create'. It is likely that the text originally had a form of the verb √ *rūp*, interpreted in the Buddhist sense of 'destroy' by T and C, while Buddhaguhya understood it according to the standard Sanskrit meaning of this root.

B Prose in T, verse in C and V.

(131b) The *manas* is the mind (*citta*) with perceptual images. You should imagine a mirror disc in your heart, and if you have recited that letter *Ha*, imagining it within that, as though it were a reflection in the mirror, you will know the minds of others.

92. 'If you recite while walking along,
having cultivated lightness of the body,
you will attain magical powers.'

If you recite the letter *Ha* mentally while walking along, thinking that your body is light like cotton, or that you are flying along in the sky, you will attain magical powers and travel in the air.

93. 'If while sitting, you place *A*
in your ear and quietly recite
it for one full month,
you will attain divine hearing!'

This means that if the *mantrin* makes himself quiet, places the letter *A* in his ears and recites it for one month, he will attain divine hearing.

94. 'Lord of the Secret Ones! Such levels of attainments arise from one's *manas*.'

Those attainments mentioned above arise from the *manas* of one who has practised without making any distinction between interior or exterior.

95. 'Lord of the Secret Ones, you should see that the various different formations [arise] from immaterial entities by just having imagined them, and the results of the seed-syllables of all actions[A] arise by just having uttered them.'

This teaches that mantra attainments, generally speaking, arise from imagining with the *manas*, the utterance [of the seed-syllables], and the transformational power of the Tathāgata. ***From immaterial entities***: From the immaterial entities of mind and mental states (*citta-caitta*). (132a) ***The various different formations***: The attributes (*lakṣaṇa*) which appear as the mandalas of earth, water and so forth. In brief, this means that the many different kinds of attainments which have colour-form are produced from mental imagining alone without any external phenomena.

The results of the seed-syllables of all actions arise by just having uttered them: The mere utterance of the sounds of the letters *Ha* and so on, changes them into the letters such as *Ha* and so on, which are the seed-syllables (*bīja*) of the earth mandala and so forth, yet it happens that they bring about the superior, medium and inferior attainments and rites of Pacifying and so on.

A C: 善 '*wholesome* [*actions*]'.

96. 'Lord of the Secret Ones! Furthermore, the Tathāgata who is in tune with all (153a) and who pleases all beings in accordance with their wishes, appears before the Bodhisattvas who engage in all actions and mantra practice, like a reflection.'

This describes the Tathāgata's transformation in all [places]. Also that transformation of the Tathāgata is the bringing to fulfilment of the hopes of all beings, in accordance with the individual faith of those to be guided, by the power of his previous aspirations, and he comes into the presence of each being like a reflection, just as the moon's reflection appears in all lakes, ponds and reservoirs, although [the moon itself] is located in the sky. This means that you should consider the many different types of attainments to arise just from the mental imagination, the utterance of the sounds and the transformational power of the Tathāgata.

97. 'A Tathāgata does not conceptualize and is inaccessible to the *manas*, and transcends time, place, actions, activities, right and wrong[A].'

Although the Tathāgata abides thus in the presence of all beings, he is free from those phenomena such as conceptualizing and so on. Here '***does not conceptualize***' means that the Tathāgata does not entertain any judgements such as 'I shall work for the benefit of this [particular] being'. ***He is inaccessible to the* manas**: (132b) The *manas* is the mind with perceptual images, and he transcends that. ***Actions and activities***: He is free from the actions and effects carried out by means of body, speech or mind. ***Right and wrong***: 'Right' is the path of the ten wholesome actions, and 'wrong' is the path of the ten unwholesome actions, and it says that he has transcended those phenomena.

98. 'Yet he grants the rank of All-knowing,
that arises from mantra practice;
hence All-knowing, attainment,
and the best state will be accomplished.' [B]

Even though he has abandoned such categories as those, he brings about the attainment of such phenomena as the Five Supernatural Cognitions and forth, by means of mantra practice. Because of that, the Five Supernatural Cognitions and even the most excellent state of Buddhahood will be accomplished.

99. Then the Noble Vajrapāṇi
opened his eyes in amazement,
and brandishing his vajra,
its light like a flashing spark of fire,
illuminating entirely
all these Buddha fields,
he spoke these pleasing words
to the Sage who is master of all Dharmas:

A Verse in C.

B C has a chapter break here and goes on with its Chapter VII.

However, regarding the previous explanations about the four members of the outer and inner recitation, the four members of the inner recitation and the three members of recitation of the five essences of the Great Hero, the text just mentioned briefly that you should arrange the mantra to be recited on a moon disc in the Tathāgata's heart, and that the mantras to be recited should be allocated on a earth mandala and so forth and recited. Although the technique of imagining the vivid appearance of the moon disc and the mantras to be recited at the time of the actual recitation, has not been dealt with in detail, the text briefly gave an explanation of them with reference to the purification for their vivid appearance, and the imagining of the Tathāgata's Body located in a mirror[-like] disc in your heart during the practice of the four members of recitation. However, they have not been clearly explained, (133a) so [the text now] explains how the mantra should be made vivid in the mind (*citta*) at the time of the actual recitation.

Then the Noble Vajrapāṇi opened his eyes in amazement: When he had heard and understood the above descriptions of the essences of the Great Hero, he became amazed. ***Brandishing his vajra, its light like a flashing spark of fire***: Due to the energy of his being thus amazed and joyful, he brandished his vajra, and the spark-like flashes of light coming from his vajra pervaded all the Buddha fields and illumined them. Secondly, such vajra-brandishing also causes future beings to have confidence in the mantra practice, because if they see that all the Buddha fields were pervaded with light from the brandished vajra, the symbol of mantras, they will feel confident.

100. 'You have described the movement of the mantras,
however I do not comprehend that movement,
so I ask you, Lord, to explain to me
from where mantras come,
and to where they go.'

When Vajrapāṇi imagines the mantras in his heart, which were prescribed to be arranged in the moon disc when the Bhagavat spoke of the four members of recitation, as his breath flowing from his heart to the Tathāgata's heart and then being drawn back in again from the Tathāgata's heart, he perceives his own heart while doing the recitation, but he does not clearly perceive the place from which they come, so he asks the Bhagavat to explain how he is to perceive those places.

101. 'There is no better state than yours:
you are the source of all Dharma,
just as the ocean is of water[A].'

Words of praise for the Bhagavat. ***The source of all Dharma***: He is the source of all scriptural Dharma and Dharma as realization. ***Just as the ocean is of water***: (133b) This is an example of that, meaning that he is like the ocean which is the source of all water.

102. When he asked that, the Bhagavat said to the Bodhisattva Vajrapāṇi, in reply,

A C: 流 'flowing water, rivers'.

'O Great Being! I teach that *manas*
is the site of the mandalas.
If you know that the heart is the mantra abode,
you will attain the results.
White, yellow, or red,
are imagined by the *manas*;
for whatever is distinguished there,
that is a function of mind[A].'

Concerning the point Vajrapāṇi asked about above, the Bhagavat explains that it is the *manas*, although he had said that the mandalas are the abodes of the mantras. The *manas* is the mind (*citta*) with perceptual images (*ākāra*), so this means that when your *manas* appears in the image of a moon disc, it is called the 'abode'. In brief, your mind (*citta*) itself should appear in the perceptual image of a moon disc at the time of doing the mantra recitation by the power of repeated practice. Hence it says '***If you know that the heart is the mantra abode, you will attain the results***'. If you know that your mind is the abode of the mantras, you will attain whatever you wish to accomplish, since that is the sign *samādhi* has been accomplished and the mind has been purified. ***White, yellow, or red are imagined by the* manas; *for whatever is distinguished there, that is a function of mind*:** These words are an explanation of '***O Great Being! I teach that* manas *is the abode of the mandalas***', and shows in what way the *manas* is an abode and what the mandalas are. The mandalas of earth, water and so on, which are such colours as white, yellow and red are what the *manas* imagines. It is that aspect of mind which distinguishes (*vyava-√ cchid*) and precisely delimits (*pari-√ cchid*) them. When you imagine any one of these mental mandalas and your mind changes into the perceptual image of that mandala by the power of repeated practice, then that mind is called the '*abode*'.

103. 'The mind which is satisfied and fixed
is what I describe as the heart.'

(134a) This comments on the explanation above, '***If you know that the heart is the mantra abode you will attain the result***'. Your mind is grasped in the perceptual image of the mandala, and if it becomes one-pointed without shifting from that, then the mind is definitely contented, and you should know that the mind which has become contented in that manner is the abode of the mantras, that is, the heart.

104. 'The mantras which are located there
will bestow vast results.'

Thus your mind itself takes on the perceptual image of a moon disc and so forth, and if the mantras also appear located there and are known to be just mind, then those mantras will bestow vast results.

105. 'Imagine a lotus there,
with eight petals and stamens.

A T: *sems* (Skt. *citta*). C: 意 (*manas*).

The *A* that is located there,
with a beautiful radiant aura[A],
as though pulsating everywhere[B].
[It is] the Lord who has various forms, (153b)
like the flashing of a thousand lightning bolts,
manifesting his appearance everywhere,
like a mirror in a cave[C],
present before all [beings]
like the images of the moon in water.
The *mantrin* who abides in the mantra place
should know his manas to be thus[D].'

This explains in detail the process of imagining the Body of the Tathāgata dwelling within the mirror mandala, in the heart of your body transformed into a deity, during the four members of inner recitation which were previously explained. ***Imagine a lotus there with eight petals and stamens; the A that is located there*:** This means that you should imagine the lotus and the *A* in your mind which has taken on the perceptual image of a moon mandala. That *A* which is imagined to change into the Body of the Tathāgata, is '***with a beautiful radiant aura***' and so on.

As though pulsating everywhere*:** You should imagine it as though it has life-energy (*prāṇa*). ***The Lord who has various forms*:** The Adornments of the Inexhaustible Body and so on have the nature of arising in many different perceptual images. ***Manifests his appearance everywhere*:** He manifests in the presence of all beings. ***Like a mirror in a cave*:** This has already been explained. ***Like the images of the moon in water*:** This is an example. He is like the moon which causes its form (134b) to appear upon the water. ***[He should] know the* manas *to be thus*:** The *mantrin* should know that it is his own *manas* which takes on the perceptual image of that Body of the Tathāgata. Also those descriptions of the attributes of the Tathāgata's Body thus show that the yogin should cultivate it in that way, and secondarily they also show the praise of the three aspects of the Tathāgata's Body. 'The A that is located there***' indicates and praises the intrinsic nature of the *dharmakāya*. ***With a beautiful aura and pulsating everywhere, the Lord who has various forms, like the flashing of a thousand lightning bolts*:** This praises the intrinsic nature of the *saṃbhoga-kāya*. ***And is present before all [beings] like the images of the moon in water*:** This praises the intrinsic nature of the *nirmāṇa-kāya*.

106. 'Then the *mantrin* should imagine
within the expanse of his cranium
an *A*, marked with an *anusvāra*,
stainless, pure and beautiful,
like crystal, the moon, or snow;
it is the tranquil *dharmakāya*
and the ground of all.

A T also has '*is tranquil*'. But this is omitted in V and C.

B C: 照明衆生故 '*since it illumines beings* [*everywhere*]'.

C C: 深居圓鏡中 '*abiding profoundly in the centre of a round mirror*'.

D C: 知心性如是 得住眞言行 '*he who knows the nature of his mind to be thus will abide in the mantra practice*'.

Through it the mantra attainment
will be accomplished in various forms
When you see that abode of the Tathāgata,
you will attain paradise and beatitude.
Having placed a *Ra* in your eyes,
which shines like a lamp,
bend your neck a little
and press your tongue on your palate,
then gazing within your heart,
equipoised, look at your *manas*.
It is unsullied and extremely pure,
always present like a mirror.
That is the true nature of *manas*
spoken of by the Buddhas of the past.
The consciousnesses will become radiant
when one is on the path illumined by *manas*.
Then the *mantrin* will see
the Lord of humans, the perfect Buddha.
The *mantrin* who sees him will always
accomplish the supreme attainment.
Then having previously transformed it,
the letter you should imagine
is a *La* with an *anusvāra*.
It should be imagined in your eye sockets;
If you see this as the emptiness of everything,
you will attain the imperishable state
If you desire to attain the splendid Awareness
or else the Five Supernatural Cognitions,
or the attainments of the *vidyādharas*,
or to be long-lived and youthful,
you will not attain them
as long as you do not engage in this,
This Awareness arising from the mantra
is the most excellent true Awareness.
It is the treasury of the saviour Bodhisattvas,
and of all the Buddhas,
the most excellent Awareness
of Buddhas, Bodhisattvas, (154a)
and Śrāvakas with certitude.
Having attained that unparalleled Awareness,
they reside in all lands with it,
telling of it those places[A].'

A C: 由是諸正覺 菩薩救世者 及諸聲聞等 遊涉他方所 一切佛剎中 皆作如是說 故得無上智 佛無過上智 *'with that, the Buddhas, the saviour Bodhisattvas, Śrāvakas and so on, wander through other regions in all the Buddha fields, and they all act as I have described. Hence they attain the supreme Awareness, the unsurpassed Awareness of Buddhas'.*

The above section describes i) the imagining of an extremely white letter *Aṃ* within the yogin's cranium and the letter *Ra* in his eyes, after he has established himself in the yoga-posture, the imagining of the Body of the Tathāgata in his heart with the light [rays] of that letter, and its [vivid] appearance; ii) then having imagined them, the imagining of the letter *La* in both his eyes, the site of the letter *Ra*, and the imagining of the intrinsic emptiness of all things through focussing his attention upon the true meaning of the letter *La* which reveals that all phenomena are devoid of attributes; the arising of attainments from having repeatedly imagined the letters *A* and so on; and iv) their praise, because attainments will be accomplished through having imagined those letters, having purified the mind and having done their yoga.

Of those, as for the process of the purification of mind, you should first dissolve your body into emptiness, which is unborn and unarisen, through the letter *A*. Then once again imagining the letter *A*, you should transform your body into the divine body-image which has the inner and outer vajra earth mandalas, through that letter *A*, (135a) according to the process which has already been explained, and imagine the Bhagavat Vairocana within the inner mandala according to the technique previously described. Then imagining an extremely white letter *A* inside your cranium and *Ra* in both your eyes, the light of that very white continuum of reality letter should also cause the vivid appearance of the Body of the Bhagavat which abides in your heart, as though within a mirror. When you have once more imagined it [as being empty] through its light, that letter *A* should be made to appear vividly. When it has become steadily vivid, once again you should imagine a letter *La* with an *anusvāra* in both of your eyes, the site of the letter *Ra*, and by perceiving that all phenomena are devoid of attributes, which is the true meaning of its sound, you should imagine that the letters *A* and so on, which you have previously imagined, are emptiness. When that imagining of emptiness has also become steady, you should also form the yoga-posture and imagine the Body of the Bhagavat in your heart and the *A* in your cranium, in accordance with the previous process, in order to gain control of your mind. In that way you should repeatedly practise many times again and again, so that you can imagine the letter *La* and make it empty, and then once again imagine the body-image of the Bhagavat, the *A* and so forth, and make those empty. Therefore, the text says '***Then the* mantrin *should imagine within the expanse of his cranium an A marked with an* anusvāra**' and concerning its qualities it says it is '***stainless, pure, and beautiful, like crystal, the moon, or snow; the tranquil, the* dharmakāya*, the ground of all***'.

The method of imagining this has all been explained above. As for the significance of the letter, (135b) the letter *A* should be imagined white, like crystal or the moon, with an *anusvāra*, for you should know that it is the *dharmakāya* in nature. Therefore, it says '***the ground of all***', for the *dharmakāya* is the ground of everything, because everything arises by virtue of the *dharmakāya*. Secondly, it is called '***the ground of all***' because that *A* is the essence of everything.

When you have thus purified the mind and imagined that *A* within your cranium, you will accomplish such attainments as those of *vidyādhara* and so forth[A].

A The Commentary breaks off here without giving a line for line explanation of the remainder of the above section of the text.

VII
THE DEITY *SAMĀDHI*

1. Then Vajrapāṇi, the Lord of the Secret Ones, asked the Bhagavat, 'Bhagavat! Please explain the transformation into the various forms of the deity, by which the Bodhisattvas who engage in the Bodhisattva practice by means of mantras may perceive the body-image of the deity and change themselves into the body-image of their tutelary deities, and without doubt accomplish attainments!'

Now the *samādhis* of the intrinsic nature of the deity (*devatā*) will be explained. It should be understood that the intrinsic nature of the deity has six aspects according to the modes appearing below. These six aspects are the body-image, the *mudrā* and so forth[1], and those [six aspects of] the intrinsic nature of the deity are those which have already been explained with the four members previously described. Thus, the intrinsic nature of the body-image deity is the perception of the Body of the Tathāgata externally[2], and the changing of yourself into the body-image of the deity[3]. The moon mandala is the intrinsic nature of the deity which has become the symbol (*mudrā*) of *bodhicitta*[4]. The letter arranged upon the moon mandala is the intrinsic nature of the sound deity[5]. The symbols of liberation such as the lotus, when you have changed yourself into the deity, are the intrinsic nature of the *mudrā* deity with form. The action of changing that same symbol into a hand *mudrā*, and transforming yourself into the Body of the deity and doing the [rituals of] protection and so on, is the intrinsic nature of the *mudrā* deity without form. The sixth is the intrinsic nature of the utterly pure deity, which resides in the *samādhi* without perceptual form. (136a) Since the intrinsic natures of these deities has not yet been explained, they will be explained in this section, for although the five intrinsic natures described above are known just as the members of recitation, they are not known as the intrinsic natures of the deity. So in order to show that those *mudrās* and so on are also the intrinsic natures of the deities, the text says '*Then Vajrapāṇi, the Lord of the Secret Ones, asked the Bhagavat*' and so forth. This means that Vajrapāṇi requests the Bhagavat to explain that process of transformation into the forms of the deity to be mentioned below. The word '*form*' means the intrinsic natures of the deity. Why is it necessary for him to ask for those intrinsic natures to be explained? It says, '*by which the Bodhisattvas ... accomplish attainments*'. There, '*may perceive the body-image of the deity*' means so that they may perceive the Body of the Tathāgata externally and the intrinsic nature of the deity of the moon disc with the mantra internally. *And change themselves into the body-image of their tutelary deities*: By changing themselves into the body-image of the deity for the superior, medium or inferior attainments, and the rites of Pacifying, Enriching and so forth. *Without doubt accomplish attainments*: If they understand that by the explanation of those intrinsic natures of the deities, whatever they wish for will be accomplished without doubt. This is the reason for Vajrapāṇi's request for these intrinsic natures to be explained.

2. When he had asked this, the Bhagavat Vairocana said to Vajrapāṇi, the Lord of the Secret Ones, 'Lord of the Secret Ones, excellent! What you have asked me about this matter is excellent! Therefore, pay attention and I shall explain it to you!'

3. Vajrapāṇi, the Lord of the Secret Ones said, 'Bhagavat! I do so desire!', and the Bhagavat then said, 'Lord of the Secret Ones! The form of the deity is of three types – the letter, *mudrā* and natural form[A]. Of these, there are also two types of letters – sound and *bodhicitta*. There are also two types of *mudrā* – that with form and that without form. Lord of the Secret Ones, the natural form of the deity is of two types – the completely pure and the impure. Of these, the completely pure is realization in nature, which is devoid of all perceptual forms. (154b) The impure is the body-image with perceptual forms, [with] colour and shape. By these two natural states of the deity, two types of aims may be accomplished: attainments with perceptual forms will arise through that with perceptual forms and those without perceptual forms will arise through that without perceptual forms[6].'

The form of the deity is of three types – letter (*akṣara*), ***symbol*** (*mudrā*) ***and natural state*** (*rūpa*): The three types of the form of the deity are the three types of intrinsic nature of the deity. The word ***letter*** (*akṣara*) (136b) means 'unchanging intrinsic nature'. What is it? ***There are also two types of letter – sound and* bodhicitta**. Of these, '***sound***' refers to the letters of the mantra. They are unchanging because their intrinsic nature does not change to anything other than revealing liberations of the relative and absolute deities by their sounds. Thus this nature of phenomena remains present from the very beginning, regardless of whether Tathāgatas appear or not[7]. That is also referred to with the words 'The mantraness of mantras'. '***Bodhicitta***' refers to the moon mandala. *Bodhicitta*, which is Suchness in intrinsic nature, is transformed into the moon mandala, because that moon mandala is sealed with the symbol (*mudrā*) of *bodhicitta*. That *bodhicitta* is said to be 'unchanging'.

There are also two types of* mudrā *– those with form and those without form: Those with form are the symbols (*mudrā*) such as the lotus or *utpala* of the individual liberations of the various deities. Those without form are those same symbols which have been changed into the hand *mudrās*.

The natural state (*rūpa*) ***of the deity is also of two types – the completely pure and the impure***: '***The natural state of the deity***' refers to its intrinsic nature. What are its two types? ***The completely pure is realization in nature*** (*adhigata-rūpa*) ***which is devoid of perceptual forms***: The *samādhi* of emptiness which is devoid of all perceptual forms of images such as colour, shape and so on, is the intrinsic nature of the deity of Awareness of Suchness. ***The impure is the body-image*** (*rūpa*) ***with perceptual forms [such as] colour and shape***: (137a) These are the body-images of Mañjuśrī, Avalokiteśvara and so on. These are impure because one perceives them with such perceptual forms as colour, shape and so on, but from the viewpoint of the function they perform, they are not impure.

By these two natural states of the deity, two types of aims may be accomplished: By these two aspects of the deity's natural state, the pure and the impure, two types of aims may be accomplished. ***The attainments with perceptual forms arise through that with perceptual forms***: The materials with perceptual forms for the attainments of the sword, vajra and so on, are accomplished by the *samādhi* with perceptual forms that has colour and shape, and transformation into the body-image of the deity. ***Those without***

A C: 形像 '*form*', '*appearance*'

perceptual forms will also arise from that without perceptual forms: By the *samādhi* which is without perceptual forms, the intrinsic nature of the emptiness deity, such attainments as the Five Supernatural Cognitions, the *Dhāraṇīs*, the Liberations and so on, unrelated to such materials as swords, vajras will be obtained. In this instance, although '***those without perceptual forms***' refers to those without the perceptual forms of such materials to be transmuted like swords and so on, it does not refer to that without perceptual forms in the sense of not having referential objects (*anālambana*), because the Five Supernatural Cognitions and so forth which are accomplished have referential objects.

4. 'The Jinas say that attainments with forms
come from that with perceptual forms;
but you will also accomplish those with forms
by abiding in that without perceptual forms[A].
Hence, you should, in all cases,
rely on that without perceptual forms[8].'

This explains that although both the attainments with perceptual forms and attainments without perceptual forms, each come about through the impure and the pure *samādhis* [respectively], and the attainments with perceptual forms will indeed arise from the intrinsic nature of the deity with perceptual forms, it is also certain that the attainments without perceptual forms will not arise [from that]. (137b) You should rely on that which is without perceptual forms in all cases, because both [the attainments] with forms and those without forms will be accomplished through the *samādhi* which is without perceptual forms.

A C: 以住無想故 獲無相悉地 '*by abiding in that without concepts, you will accomplish the attainments without perceptual forms*'.

VIII
THE *SAMĀDHI* WITHOUT PERCEPTUAL FORMS

1. Then the Bhagavat also said to Vajrapāṇi, the Lord of the Secret Ones, 'Lord of the Secret Ones! A Bodhisattva who engages in the Bodhisattva practice by means of mantras, who desires to accomplish the *samādhi* without perceptual forms should think as follows: "From whence do perceptual forms arise? Is it from my body, or from my mind, or from my *manas*[1]?" '

Although the technique of cultivating the *samādhis* of the two types of deities, the pure and impure – the four members of recitation and so on – have already been explained in the previous chapter, the process of cultivating the *samādhi* of the intrinsic nature of the pure deity has not yet been taught, so now the Bhagavat teaches the process of stopping perceptual forms from arising by first dissolving and then refuting in turn [the idea] of the arising of the perceptual forms from the body, mind and *manas*, when you are cultivating that *samādhi* which is without perceptual forms.

From whence do perceptual forms arise? Is it from my body, or from my mind, or from my* manas?**: First the question concerning where the perceptual forms might arise from. ***From my body? (138a) You should investigate whether such perceptual forms (*nimitta*) as blue and yellow arise from your body which has the nature of the great elements, unconnected with both the mind and *manas*. ***From my mind?*** You should investigate whether the perceptual forms arise from the consciousnesses related to the six gates [of perception][2]. ***Or from my* manas?**: '***Manas***' refers to the mental processes associated with perceptual images (*ākāra*), that is, with the perceptual images of colour-form (*rūpa*) and so forth which are generated from the consciousnesses of the six gates of perception[3].

2. 'With regards to these, he should ascertain that the body is produced from [previous] karmic actions and by nature lacks creative power [of its own], like grass, trees and pebbles, and is insensate and resembles external things (*ākāra*), as though it were a statue. Though some person gets angry[A] with such a statue, or destroys, burns or cuts it with fire, poison, swords, water or vajras, it is not the least bit discomforted[B]. Even if one makes offerings to that statue of various different kinds of divine and human articles, such as food, drink, baths, incense, garlands, clothing, sandalwood or camphor and so forth, it will not become joyful. Why is that? For whoever makes offerings or does harm to that figure, which lacks any inherent reality, due to perverse delusive ideas generated by his arrogance, is a fool in nature. (155a) Lord of the Secret Ones! In that way you should meditate on the lack of self-existence in the body, by the recollection which attends to the body.'

Of these, there is first the investigation of whether they arise from the body or not. In brief, that body which is produced through [previous] karmic actions is inherently

A C adds: 麁語 '[*speaking*] *harsh words*'.
B C: 能少分令其動作 '[*one will not*] *be able to make it move in the slightest*'.

insensate (*jaḍa*) like grass, trees and pebbles. This means that just as grass, trees, and pebbles do not carry out the creative activities from which perceptual forms such as blue, yellow and so on might arise [in them], so also the body does not carry out the creative activities from which perceptual forms arise. Furthermore, to give an example, the text says you should ascertain that it '***resembles external things, as though it were a statue***'. Just as when somebody gets angry with a statue made by a craftsman with stone or clay in the form of a god or man, and destroys it, burns it or cuts it with fire, poison, swords, water or vajras, it is not the least bit discomforted. In the same way, even if somebody with a friendly attitude were to make offerings to it, with such divine or human things as mentioned, such as food, drink or ornaments, no feelings of gratitude and friendliness will arise in that figure. Likewise, having dissolved the body [with the idea] that your body also is inherently insensate and is not an instigator of the creative activities which generate perceptual forms, (138b) you should enter into the *samādhi* which is without perceptual images.

3. 'Moreover, Lord of the Secret Ones, the mind should be considered to be without inherent reality, devoid of all perceptual forms and lacking in self-existence. Lord of the Secret Ones, the three times[4] cannot be found in the mind. You should consider that that which is devoid of the three times is also inherently devoid of perceptual forms.'

This is the teaching about the technique of meditation to stop the arising of perceptual forms [supposedly] arisen from the mind. Because the mind, which on the absolute level, is devoid of the inherent reality of a perceiving subject or perceived objects, lacks self-existence and is separate from all such attributes as blue, yellow and so on, it completely transcends the three times. Having understood that that which is beyond the three times and lacks self-existence is non-conceptualizing, Suchness in character, and so is not a source of perceptual forms (*nimitta*), you should abide in the *samādhi* which is without perceptual forms.

4. 'Furthermore, Lord of the Secret Ones, foolish ordinary people imagine that the *manas* has perceptual forms. But this is just a designation (*adhivacana*) for what is falsely imagined. They do not know that that which is not real is unarisen.'

This teaches the investigation into the non-arising of perceptual forms from the *manas*. It is an erroneous concept of foolish people that the six consciousnesses related to the six gates such as the eyes and so on give rise to the appearance of the perceptual images of colour-form and so on, and those foolish people do not know that this is erroneous. ***That which is not real is unarisen.*** This means that since the above consciousnesses related to the six gates also do not really exist, they are not, on the absolute level, the cause which gives rise to the perceptual forms.

5. 'Lord Of the Secret Ones! If a Bodhisattva who engages in the Bodhisattva practice by means of mantras, has thought in that way, he will attain the *samādhi* without perceptual forms.'

Just as when you have changed your body into the impure deity, (139a) you have changed to resemble the colour and shape of that deity, so also when you have changed yourself into the intrinsic nature of the deity without perceptual forms, you change yourself into the intrinsic nature of the pure deity, if you have entered the *samādhi* which is without perceptual forms. ***He will attain the* samādhi *which is without perceptual forms*:** He will reside in the intrinsic nature of the pure deity.

6. 'Lord of the Secret Ones, when he abides in the *samādhi* without perceptual forms, the mantra deities uttered by the Tathāgatas will draw near and come into his presence.'

When he abides in the intrinsic nature of the pure deity, the deities of the techniques spoken of by the Tathāgata will be accomplished. '***Come into his presence***' means that those deities will come face to face with that *mantrin*.

IX
THE TRUE NATURE OF MUNDANE AND SUPRAMUNDANE RECITATION

'Futhermore, Lord of the Secret Ones,
I shall explain the secret recitation.
Alone with one or one with one,
you should always do the recitation
either mentally or else in a whisper,
with the most excellent yoga[A].
Do not recite the mantras in any other way[B],
with a deficiency in the members!
I have explained the four members [of recitation]
which combine the inner and outer:
that is the mundane [recitation],
best of those with cognitive objects[C].
The excellent whispered recitation
engrossed in the drawing-in of the syllables,
with your *manas* focussed on the deity,
I have prescribed for that with cognitive objects. (155b)
The supramundane is that done mentally,
ceasing to do the drawing-in and so on[D].
You should make yourself one with the deity,
perceiving both to be identical,
it should be inseparable from the nature of your *manas*[E].
In no other way should it be done.
The number of mantras, three hundred thousand,
which I have generally prescribed,
is the number of recitations stipulated
for the pure *mantrins*,
beings who are free from failings.
In no other way should it be done.'

This is the explanation of the Chapter on the True Nature of Recitation. Moreover, that recitation is the recitation abiding in the twofold deity yoga, that is, abiding in the pure and impure nature of the deity as explained above. Furthermore the four-membered recitation while abiding in the impure nature of the deity which has already been explained, but which will also be explained here in order to describe the

---

A C: 一一諸眞言 作心意念誦 出入息爲二 常第一相應 '*For each of the mantras, you should perform the recitation* [*either*] *mentally, or secondly with your breathing in and out: these are always the foremost of yogas.*'

B This is based on C. T: '*The* mantrin *should not recite in any other way*'.

C C: 有所緣相續 '*which you should do successively with cognitive objects*'. There seems to have been some textual confusion between *parama* (*bla-med*) 'supreme' and *paraṃpara* (相續) 'successively'.

D C: 遠離於諸字 '*devoid of any syllables*'.

E C: 不壞意色像 '*not separating your* manas *and the image*'.

inner recitation without perceptual forms, and to distinguish the mundane and the supramundane [recitations].

Of these, '***alone with one***' (*ekaikaṃ*) refers to just mental recitation abiding in the pure deity yoga alone. '***Or one with one***' refers to the mental recitation with the impure deity yoga also[1]. '***Or else in a whisper***' means you should do the whispered recitation with both the yoga of the pure and impure deities. (139b) Therefore it says '***You should always do the recitation with the most excellent yoga***'. You should always apply yourself to the yoga of the pure and of the impure deities.

Do not recite the mantras in any other way with a deficiency in its members: Apart from the four-membered inner and outer recitation, and these two inner absolute (*paramārtha*) recitations, you should not do any other [type of] recitation which is deficient in the ritual, or with incomplete members.

I have explained the four members [of recitation] with the union* (yoga) *of the inner and the outer: that is the mundane [recitation], best of those with cognitive objects: Of the absolute and the relative intrinsic natures taught briefly above, the relative recitation which has been explained as fourfold – the three external members and the one inner one – is the mundane recitation. That is the most excellent of the recitations with cognitive objects.

Engrossed in the drawing-in of the syllables: As before. ***Your* manas *focussed on the deity***: You should focus your attention on it with one-pointed mind.

The supramundane is that done mentally ... in no other way should it be done: A detailed commentary on that absolute recitation was given above. ***Ceasing to do the drawing-in and so on***: This means that there is no drawing-in to the inner member from the external members of recitation because that supramundane recitation is not focussed upon the intrinsic nature of the impure deity. ***You should make yourself one with the deity***: You should make your own form one with that of the deity. ***Perceiving both to be identical***: (140a) Since it is possible to make both yourself and the deity as one, yet with different forms occupying the same place, this says that it should not be so, but that you should make both yourself and the deity identical (*abhinna*). Because it is possible for there to be a difference in the intrinsic nature of the form, though there is no difference between yourself and the deity, so it says '***it should be inseparable in nature from your* manas**'. It is not that you should make your form and so forth one, but you should make your *manas* inseparable from the other in the intrinsic nature of emptiness. ***In no other way should it be done***: That supernatural recitation should not be done in any other way apart from this method. In brief, when you have focussed your attention upon the true meaning of the sound of whatever essence you have chosen, you should dissolve your form into emptiness. When you have dissolved it, you should understand that just as your form is empty, all internal and external phenomena are also the same, in being empty in nature. Since you are thus inseparable from all phenomena in having emptiness as your intrinsic nature, you should realize that the intrinsic nature of yourself and the deity are inseparable in being characterized by emptiness, and then abiding in the one-pointed *samādhi* of emptiness, you should do the recitation mentally.

The number of mantras ... should it be done: It is for the *mantrins* who are without failings that the Bhagavat has generally prescribed that the *sādhana* should be done after having performed the preliminary service of three hundred thousand in number. Those without failings refers either to those who have already accumulated the mass of merits and awareness in former existences, or to those in whom the signs have arisen after they have practised the technique of cultivating *bodhicitta* in this life, according to the process which has previously been explained[2].

X
THE WHEEL OF LETTERS

1. Then the Bhagavat Vairocana gazed upon the entire assembly and then also gazed upon all realms of beings with his eyes of kindness and compassion, and then entered the *samādhi* called 'Arising from the Deathless'. No sooner had he entered it than there arose from all his members the Queen of *Vidyās* which has strength unhindered in the three times: *GAGANA-SAME 'PRATISAME SARVA-TATHĀGATA-SAMANTĀNUGATE GAGANA-SAMA-VARA-LAKṢAṆE SVĀHĀ.* (Unequalled one who is equal to space, who accompanies everywhere all Tathāgatas, who has the best of attributes like space! √ *Svāhā*!)

(140b) Among the three Mandalas which are transformations of the configurations of the Body, Speech and Mind of the Enlightened Vairocana, the Mandala of Great Compassion, which is the transformed configuration of his Body, has been explained. Now the Revolving Wheel of Letters, the transformed configuration of his Speech should be explained here. Although the configurations of his Body, Speech and Mind are included herein, since the Speech configuration is the main topic, it is the transformed Speech configuration, yet it is not the case that the others are absent.

Now, when first undertaking to draw the Mandala, the Master should focus his attention upon whichever of the types of the self-*samādhis* that have been explained is appropriate[1], and in order to protect himself and all of the gathering, he should recite this *Vidyā* three, seven or twenty-one times. The Bhagavat focussed his attention upon the meaning of that *Vidyā* in a *samādhi* of liberation (*vimokṣa-samādhi*) and then uttered the mantra. This is dealt with by '***Then the Bhagavat gazed ... Unhindered in the three times***'.

And then also gazed upon all realms of beings with his eyes of kindness and compassion: Since the Bhagavat has entered the unlocalized Nirvāṇa which is free from all thoughts (*kalpanā*), (141a) the thought of gazing does not occur to him, but due to the power of his previous aspirations, he gazed at all realms of beings with the Mother Great Compassion and the Lord Great Kindness, and desired to utter the *Vidyā* in order to liberate the unliberated and mature the immature.

[He] entered the* samādhi *called 'Arising From the Deathless' (*amṛtodaya*): '***Amṛta***' signifies 'deathless' and also the *dharmakāya*, emptiness. This *samādhi* arose after he focussed his attention upon that, so it is called 'Arising from the Deathless'. Or else this could mean 'Source of the Deathless' since the Deathless arises from this *samādhi*. This means that the *dharmakāya* Awareness arises from Enlightenment. Having entered that *samādhi*, he spoke the *Vidyā*.

No sooner had he entered it than there arose from all his limbs the* Vidyā *Queen which has the strength unhindered in the three times. From all his members: This means that it arose from all the members of the *saṃbhoga-kāya*, the *nirmāṇa-kāya* and the embodiment of the core of Enlightenment (*bodhimaṇḍa-kāya*), and the text says '***from his members***' as it was impossible for the words to be uttered verbally as he was abiding in a non-conceptualizing *samādhi* of emptiness. ***Which has the strength unhindered in the three times***: That which is unhindered in the past, present and future is emptiness, in other words, the continuum of reality. The strength to generate perception of that relates to the absolute level, and the strength to be unharmed by obstructions caused by all demons and opponents, through the power of this *Vidyā*, relates to the relative level. '***Vidyā***' means knowledge and here it refers to the Insight (*prajñā*) of Enlightenment. ***Queen***: Because the Insight of Enlightenment is the most excellent of all insights, it is a queen. (141b) Therefore this *Vidyā* is also the transformed intrinsic nature of Enlightenment Awareness itself.

2. 'Noble Son! This *Vidyā* Queen has the same experiential range as the Body of all the Tathāgatas.'

Here the Bhagavat teaches the nature and form of the *Vidyā*. In this case, the '***Body of all the Tathāgatas***' refers to the *dharmakāya*, and the experiential range of the *dharmakāya* and this *Vidyā* are not different, because of their similarity in perceiving the true nature [of things].

3. **'The Buddhas and renowned Bodhisattvas**
who are empowered by this[A],
will attain the unhindered reality
which extinguishes suffering everywhere.'

He says this in order to teach the great power of this *Vidyā*. This means that because all the Buddhas and Bodhisattvas are empowered by this *Vidyā*, those Buddhas and Bodhisattvas will attain the unhindered reality of the unlocalized Nirvāṇa which extinguishes suffering everywhere. Here '***Buddhas***' does not refer to the supreme Buddhas, but to the Bodhisattvas who have reached the Tenth Level, the Buddhas who have attained the Ten Masteries[2]. '***Bodhisattvas***' refers to the other ones apart from those Buddhas, who abide on the noble Levels. '***The unhindered reality***' is the nature of the unlocalized Nirvāṇa and it is said to be unhindered because it is free from the obscurations of the emotional afflictions and wrong understanding. And what is it like? It '***extinguishes suffering everywhere***' because that reality, Nirvāṇa, is free from the sufferings of the psycho-physical constituents.

4. Then having brought to mind all the Tathāgatas, the Bhagavat Vairocana transformed both himself and Vajrapāṇi into the primordial state of unbornness[B], and said to Vajrapāṇi and the other Vajradharas, 'O Nobly-born Ones! Listen to this extensive section (*paṭala*) that concerns what should be practised for the Mandala called the "Revolving Wheel of Letters", which waits in attendance with Buddha deeds (156a) for those who engage in the Bodhisattva practice[C].'

A C: 由是佛加持 菩薩大名稱 '*With this the Buddhas empower the renowned Bodhisattvas*'.
B C: 尋念諸佛本初不生加持自身及與持金剛者 '*Then having recollected that Buddhas are primordially unborn,* [*Vairocana*] *transformed himself and Vajrapāṇi*'.
C C: 眞言門修行諸菩薩能作佛事普現其身 '[*with which*] *bodhisattvas who cultivate the mantra method will be able to perform Buddha activities and manifest their bodies everywhere.*'

Then the Bhagavat declares that he will explain to the entourage what should be practised for the Mandala of the Wheel of Letters. ***Having brought to mind all the Tathāgatas*:** (142a) This instructs other and future beings first to recollect the Tathāgatas whenever they begin to do something. He ***transformed both himself and Vajrapāṇi into the primordial state of unbornness*:** This teaches the ritual for the mandala. This is the mode of explaining and listening after both the one who explains and listener entered *samādhi*, therefore the text indicates that both Vairocana, the one who explains, and Vajrapāṇi, the listener, entered into the *samādhi* of the unborn phenomena, emptiness, and that is also because it is not accessible to those who have not entered that *samādhi*. Therefore it tells us that when the Master is first embarking upon making the Mandala, he should transform himself and also his assistants with [the mantra of] Vajra-varada[3]. They should also be transformed into emptiness by themselves, or by the Master.

The extensive section that concerns what should be practised for the Mandala called the "Revolving Wheel of Letters". The Revolving Wheel of Letters*:** First this means 'the revolving of letters, like a wheel', because the letter *A* is placed in the centre, and the other letters beginning with *Ka* encircle it. Secondly, it is 'the [r]evolving wheel of letters' because the letters are changed into the wheel of the Mandala, for their substance is transformed into the syllables and arranged in that Mandala. 'That which should be practised***' refers to the things that should be done for the ritual of the mandala. '*Section*' means that chapter of the text. ***Extensive*:** The accumulation of merit and wisdom of the trainees is augmented in that Mandala.

What is that Mandala like? In order to indicate its nature, the Bhagavat says it ***waits in attendance with Buddha deeds*** *(buddha-kṛtyena pratyupasthā)* ***for those who engage in the Bodhisattva practice***. The '***Buddha deeds***' are deeds that cause the attainment of the results which are success and welfare in this life and henceforth. (142b) This means that this Mandala, likewise, is in attendance with Buddha deeds in order to make those who engage in the mantra practice by means of this Mandala attain mundane and supramundane results in this lifetime and in the future. The Bhagavat is going to explain it, so he tells them to listen.

5. Then Vajrapāṇi saluted the Bhagavat Vairocana and descending from his vajra lotus seat like a bolt of lightning[A], he praised the Bhagavat:

> **'I salute you who are *bodhicitta*!**
> **I salute you who are the source of Enlightenment!**
> **I salute you who are the embodiment of practice**
> **which is the Levels and Perfections!**
> **I salute you who were the first to do it[B]!**
> **I bow to you who reside[C] in emptiness!'**

Vajrapāṇi is very delighted and he praises the Bhagavat by reference to his virtues (*guṇa*), because the Bhagavat is going to explain what should be practised for the

---

A C omits '*like a bolt of lightning*'.

B T: *thog-mar byed-pa*, C: 先造作 which suggest **ādya-kāra*. However, Buddhaguhya's comments on this line seem to indicate he read this as a negative: * *ādy-akāra*, to give the reading '*You who are primordially unacting / unformed*'.

C C: 證 '*have realized*'.

Mandala of the Revolving Wheel of Letters, and also because he feels respect for the Bhagavat. Therefore he '***saluted the Bhagavat Vairocana and descended from his Vajra lotus seat like a bolt of lightning***'. This means that he descended steadily, without wavering or trembling. First, because Vajrapāṇi praised the Bhagavat by means of his causal and resultant virtues which arise from within this Mandala, it adds '***and then Vajrapāṇi praised the Bhagavat***'. He praised the Bhagavat by means of five kinds of virtues: by means of *bodhicitta*, by means of the causal and resultant practice, by means of the Immediate Path of the Tathāgata, by means of the virtues of complete Buddhahood and by means of the virtues of Nirvāṇa. Although this is the logical sequence of the virtues, the verse mixes them up for the sake of style.

I salute you who are* bodhicitta**: Although the word 'bodhicitta***' really applies from the First Bodhisattva Level onwards, it does not refer to that here, since Vajrapāṇi will also praise him by means of the First Level and so forth and the Perfections, but to the *bodhicitta* of the Level of Practice with Devoted Interest. It is also the cause of Tathāgatahood, so the term for the result, Tathāgatahood, is linked to that cause. (143a)

I salute you who are the source of Enlightenment: This praises him by means of the virtues of the Immediate Path of the Tathāgata. The Immediate Path is the period from after leaving the Tenth Level up until the attainment of Enlightenment. Since Enlightenment arises from that, he is called the '***source of Enlightenment***'.

I salute you who are the embodiment of practice: [Praise] by means of the causal and the resultant practice. The resultant practice is to teach throughout the Three Realms by the practice of the configurations of Body, Speech and Mind, and the embodiment of the causal practice consists of the Levels and the Perfections.

I salute you who were the first to do it: Praise by means of the virtues of Perfect Buddhahood. Since phenomena are utterly devoid of a perceiving subject and perceived objects, that is, they are empty from the very beginning, Vajrapāṇi salutes that[4].

I bow to you who resides in emptiness: The praise by means of the intrinsic nature of Nirvāṇa. In other words, he salutes the unlocalized Nirvāṇa, whose essential nature is that all phenomena are unborn and unarisen.

6. When Vajrapāṇi, the Lord of the Secret Ones, had praised the Bhagavat with those words, he spoke the following request to the Bhagavat, 'O Bhagavat, Lord of the Dharma! Please explain them out of pity for us, so that by having them we may act for the benefit of beings, and that the mantra practice of which you have spoken may be fully perfected!'

Vajrapāṇi requests the Bhagavat to explain that Mandala. ***If we have them***: That is, those methods of the Mandala of which the Bhagavat will speak. It is contrary to reason for one to say that since Vajrapāṇi is endowed with the Dharma as realization, he should act for the benefit of beings and perfect the mantra method after he heard that scriptural Dharma. Why is that? Is it because it is unreasonable for one who abides in the very Dharma as realization to listen to scriptural Dharma and then act for the benefit of beings? That is not so, because on the one hand he praised the Dharma expounded by the Bhagavat as precious and noble, (143b) and so if even one such as Vajrapāṇi who has understanding when the Bhagavat expounds the Dharma, can listen to it and gain special virtues, how much more so with others! On the other hand, even though Vajrapāṇi is endowed with the Dharma as realization, there is no defect for him to listen to the scriptural Dharmas [spoken by] the Bhagavat and benefit beings with them.

7. When he had made this request, the Bhagavat Vairocana said to Vajrapāṇi, the Lord of the Secret Ones:

> **'I shall expound the Dharma which is unequalled,**
> **primordially tranquil and supreme**
> **to the first in the world**
> **by whom I am called the Protector of the World[A].'**

Then, so that there cannot be any criticism of this, such as the idea that it is contrary to reason for words communicating the Dharma to arise from the Bhagavat because he does not make any reflective selection, as he abides in the unlocalized Nirvāṇa, or else that words without reflective selection are confused, the Bhagavat says '***I shall expound the Dharma … the Protector of the World***', because he expounds the Dharma with the *saṃbhoga-kāya* and the *nirmāṇa-kāya*, and also reveals it without confusion from non-conceptualizing *samādhi*. Here the words '***I shall expound the supreme Dharma***' and '***to the first in the world***' show that the teaching of the Dharma does indeed arise from a non-conceptualizing state. Regarding that, '*the first in the world*' (*laukika-prathama*) are of two types, the pure and the impure. The pure are the Bodhisattvas of the First Level onwards, and this shows that it is not the case that beings who expound the Dharma appeared in the past and do not appear subsequently in the present. Because they became Buddhas in previous worlds, they are called '***first in the world***'. The impure ones are Brahmā, Śakra and so on, who arose first of all, when the first realm evolved following the great eon of destruction, so they are '***first in the world***'. Because the Bhagavat expounds the Dharma which has three aspects to them, (144a) they call the Bhagavat the '***Protector of the World***' (*loka-nātha*). What are the three aspects of the Dharma expounded by him? These are the Dharma which is unequalled, which is primordially tranquil and which is supreme. These can also be viewed by way of the categories of entry, practice and result. '***Unequalled***' is the Dharma for entry into the supreme [state], the wholesome Dharma such as the ten wholesome actions, Generosity and so forth. It is unequalled because it is dissimilar to the teachings (*dharma*) of the non-Buddhists. The '***primordially tranquil***' is the process of practice towards Buddhahood, and this indicates that it is primordially tranquil because no phenomena are generated by causes and conditions. '***Supreme***' is the result of entry and practice and indicates the unlocalized Nirvāṇa.

8. Then, when the Bhagavat had spoken these verses, he performed an empowerment, such that when the Bodhisattvas and Vajradharas were empowered by it, they saw the Bhagavat who had entered the most excellent

---

A C: 我一切本初 號名世所依 說法無等比 本寂無有上 '*I am the very first of all [Buddhas] and I am called the support of the world. I expound the Dharma which is unequalled, primordially tranquil and supreme*'.

core of Enlightenment, which is devoid of proliferations like space, in non-dual union with practice and is like the fruition of karmic action.

In order to show that the Dharma can be taught and expounded thus, yet be without confusion due to the absence of reflective selection (*avikalpa*), the text says '***He performed an empowerment** (adhiṣṭhāna), **such that when the Bodhisattvas and Vajradharas***' and so forth. ***Such an empowerment***: This shows that the Bodhisattvas such as Samantabhadra, who have pure motives were empowered by the Bhagavat, who inspires them with rays of light and so on, and then they saw his embodiment that resides in the core of Enlightenment. How does that embodiment of the core of Enlightenment, which they see, appear? It is '***devoid of proliferations, like space***' and so forth. ***Like space***: Its intrinsic nature is emptiness, luminous by nature and without impurities. ***Without proliferations*** (*niṣprapañca*): This means it is free from all internal selective concepts (*vikalpa*) of the intellect (*mano-vijñāna*). ***In non-dual union with practice***: It is the non-dual union of practice by the configurations of his Body, Speech and Mind, and the embodiment of the core of Enlightenment (*bodhimaṇḍa-kāya*), because the two are inseparable in nature. The embodiment of the core of Enlightenment is '***like the fruition of karmic action***'. It is similar to the fruition of karmic action, (144b) which indicates that although it is not fruition itself, it resembles it. Why is that? Because beings with pellucid minds are dependent upon the fruition of karmic action and that becomes exhausted, but Buddhahood is a result which flows naturally from his great accumulation of merit and wisdom, and does not become exhausted. Since that embodiment of the core of Enlightenment is a result naturally flowing from the great accumulation of merit and wisdom, it is like the fruition[5].

9. Then at that moment, from the Bhagavat's limbs and all the Bodies of the Tathāgatas, there emerged this letter which is like the life-energy of all mundane and supramundane beings, (156b) of Śrāvakas and Pratyekabuddhas who exert themselves in meditative absorption and the object of meditative absorption and the accomplishment of attainments, which is the vital-force[A], the life-energy, the refuge and the protector of all letters: *NAMAḤ SAMANTA-BUDDHĀNĀṂ A.*

The letter *A* is established as the Lord of the Mandala of the Revolving Wheel of Letters, and the virtues of that *A* are spoken of with these epithets. ***From the Bhagavat's limbs and all the Bodies of the Tathāgatas***: That letter *A* emerged from all the Bodies, the configurations of the Tathāgata's Body. ***The mundane and the supramundane*** and so on indicates the great power of the letter *A*. Of these, the '***mundane***' refers to the non-Buddhist sages (*ṛṣi*) who are able to perceive a partial emptiness. The '***supramundane***' refers to the Bodhisattvas, but since the Śrāvakas are mentioned next, they are not included herein. The '***Śrāvakas and Pratyekabuddhas***' also abide in a partial emptiness, which is their specific type of liberation. They also have the two types of entry to it – entry through mantra *sādhana* and entry by way of meditative absorption (*dhyāna*), and *A* is like the life-energy of both of them. Why is that? On the absolute level they

A T: *'tsho ba* 'life-force' (**jīva*), C: 種子 'seed' (**bīja*); probably the result of syllabic reversal but either could correspond to the original reading.

all perceive emptiness: some of them the emptiness which is authentically consummate emptiness, and some of them only a partial emptiness. But since in general they all depend upon the fact (*artha*) of emptiness, the meaning of the letter *A*, the unborn reality (*dharmatā*), it is like the life-energy of them all. (145a) On the relative level, all phenomena which depend upon letters come from *A*, so it is like their life-energy.

Meditative absorption (*dhyāna*) is thought (√*dhyai*), being [in] union (*yoga*). '***The object of meditative absorption***' (*dhyeya*) is the result of that thought. That is entry by way of that meditative absorption.

The accomplishment of attainments: These are superior, medium and inferior, and they undertake to accomplish them through the mantra *sādhana*.

Both on the relative and the absolute levels it is like the vital-energy and so forth of those letters. Of those, it is the '***vital-energy***' (*jīva*) of all letters because they depend upon *A*, through its Enlightenment aspect. For the meaning of *A* is 'unborn' and likewise the meaning of the letter *Ka* is the absence of all purpose (*kārya*), that is, it is unborn. Therefore the letter *Ka*, also depends upon *A*, the vital-energy of the seed of Enlightenment, so it is called '***vital-energy***'. You should know that this is the same for the other letters. It is the '***life-force***' (*prāṇa*) of all letters because all letters depend upon it, through its Practice aspect. It is the '***refuge***' of all letters because it is the support of letters, through its Perfect Buddha aspect. '***Source***' (*trāṇa*) means that it is the source of all letters, because it produces all letters through its Nirvāṇa aspect.

10. 'Nobly-born Ones! This has been empowered by all the Tathāgatas and it waits in attendance with Buddha deeds for the Bodhisattvas who engage in the Bodhisattva practice by means of mantras. All Dharma evolves from this *A* gate.'

This has been empowered (*adhiṣṭhita*) ***by all the Tathāgatas***: It has been empowered by the entire configuration of the Body of the Buddha. ***It waits in attendance with Buddha deeds for the Bodhisattvas who engage in the Bodhisattva practice by means of mantras***: This shows the great power of that letter *A*. The ***Buddha deeds*** are the twofold revelation of the Dharma when a Buddha appears in the world. These two are i) the revelation of the Dharma as realization to those of pure motive and ii) the revelation of the scriptural Dharma to those of impure motive. (145b) Likewise the letter *A* is also the cause of the revelation of those Dharmas, therefore '***it waits in attendance with Buddha deeds***'. In what way? Because the Dharma as realization arises from that *A* in its meaning of 'unborn', and the scriptural Dharma is explained by means of words, and all words evolve from the letter *A*. How do we know it performs Buddha deeds? Because '***all Dharma evolves from this A gate***'. How is that? Because all of the Dharma as realization and the scriptural Dharma arises from the causal *A* letter, thus that letter *A* performs Buddha deeds and is the gate through which all Dharma arises. Therefore the Bodhisattvas who are engaged in mantra [practice] should view that letter *A* as the Tathāgata. This is to be linked with the next section.

11. 'Therefore, Lord of the Secret Ones, those Bodhisattvas who engage in the Bodhisattva practice by means of mantras, who desire to see [and to

make offerings to][A] the Tathāgatas, who desire to actualize *bodhicitta*, who desire to associate with Bodhisattvas, who desire to benefit beings, who desire attainments, who desire to attain All-knowing [Awareness] of all aspects, they should exert themselves in this essence of the Tathāgata.'

Because the meaning of the letter *A* is none other than the intrinsic nature of the Tathāgata, it is the essence of the core of Enlightenment – that is the absolute [meaning]. And on the relative level, when you have meditated on the letter *A*, countless Tathāgatas will appear, by its power. '***Those who desire to see [and to make offerings to] the Tathāgatas***' should also meditate on this letter. You should understand offerings to be of two types: the *sādhana* offerings and the material offerings. Offering by the *sādhana* because the meaning (*artha*) of that letter comes about by meditating on it, and the offerings with material things because vast offerings which fill space arise through the power of having meditated on that letter *A*. ***Who desire to actualize* bodhicitta**: This refers to the *bodhicitta* of Bodhisattvas from the First level onwards, and it means that those who desire to actualize it should directly engage in the accomplishment of the meaning of the letter *A*. (146a) Why? Because as *bodhicitta* is also unborn it is in harmony with the meaning 'unborn' of the letter *A*. ***Who desire to associate with Bodhisattvas***: Those who so desire should meditate on the letter *A* gate, because Bodhisattvas focus their attention on the significance of the 'unborn', and the meaning of the letter *A* is also 'unborn'. Therefore, as their experiential range coincides, they will be born together with them. Then to show the ordinary virtues of both cultivation by means of meditation and entry through *sādhana* by means of the mantra *A* itself, the text says '***who desire to actualize attainments***', referring to the superior, medium and inferior attainments through entry by means of mantras.

These [phrases] express [the matter] in parts and in summary it says that those '*who desire to attain the All-knowing Awareness of all aspects*' should cultivate it.

12. Then the Bhagavat Vairocana spoke of the ritual of this King of Mandalas which arises from the Matrix of Great Compassion, regarding its layout and the specifications for the residence of the deities, that which is to be manifested with *samādhi*, the mantras to be used and that which is to be imagined[B].

This section indicates the three parts of the ritual of drawing the Mandala. Here the phrase '***which arises from the Matrix of Great Compassion***' is applied to both the Mandala which is the transformation of his Body configuration and to this Speech Mandala. Why is that? Because the threefold Mandala arises from Great Compassion. That name (*karuṇodbhava*) is given to them in reference to the power (*śakti*) and the causal basis (*hetu*) of the Mandala. ***The specifications for the residence*** (*avasthā*) ***of the deities***: What should be done to fix the residence where the deities abide, who are to be arranged around the circumference and in the centre. ***That which is to be manifested with* samādhi** (*samādhi-vikurvita*): The protection *vidyā*, the mantras and

A Added from C and B.

B C: 不思議法 '*and the inconceivable methods*'.

so forth, [manifested] after having entered that *samādhi*. ***The mantras to be used***: Those to be used in the rite on the occasion of entering into the Mandala. (146b) ***That which is to be imagined*** (*cintya*): This refers to the special parts such as the imagining of *bodhicitta* by the trainees, the Master's abiding in his own *samādhi* and so forth, when entering the Mandala. The individual explanations of these will be given below.

13. 'Abiding in *A*, the gate to the All-knowing [Awareness], the Master should take a cord, and making salutations to all the Buddhas, he should extend it to the east and then go around to the right and facing the north, he should again extend it.'

The Bhagavat says this in order to explain the topic of the layout for the ritual of this King of Mandalas. This deals with each of the *samādhis* of the Master for each of the areas of the Mandala when he is extending the cord for the Mandala. Since the Bodhisattvas such as Mañjuśrī born from the Perfections reside in the external section of the Mandala, it says regarding the *samādhi* of the Master who marks out the Mandala, that he should abide in the letter *A*, the essence of the causal ground of All-knowing, and extend the cord for the Mandala. When first stretching the cord, it mentions that he should extend the sky-cord thus: ***making salutations to all the Buddhas, he should extend it to the east and then go around to the right and facing the north, he should again extend it.***

14. 'Changing to the west, he should mark it out with the cord. He should then transform himself into Vajrasattva with the *mudrā* of Vajrapāṇi, or with the letter *Va*, (157a) and entering within, he should draw the matrix mandala.'

Then in order to extend the cord for the Mandala on the ground, it says '***changing to the west, he should mark it out with the cord***'. The other [things] not mentioned here have already been explained in detail with the marking-out of the Mandala of Great Compassion, so the remainder should also be done in the same way.

Then in order to explain the *samādhi* of the Master who marks out the matrix mandala, it says '***he should transform himself into Vajrasattva with the mudrā of Vajrapāṇi, or with the letter Va, and entering within, he should draw the matrix mandala***'. As for the *samādhi* of the Master for that, (147a) he should transform himself into Vajrasattva who is generated by the letter *A*, the seed of Enlightenment. The name '***Vajrasattva***' also indicates those such as Karma-vajrasattva and so on, but in this chapter and not elsewhere, '***Vajrasattva***' refers to Vajrapāṇi.

15. 'Likewise he should also transform himself for the second [portion of] the mandala thus: into the primordially tranquil, the form of the non-dual yoga, the form of the Tathāgata, the form of the essential nature of emptiness[A].'

A T: *snying-po-nyid* 'quintessence', corrected to *stong-pa-nyid* 'emptiness' by C 空性 and V *stong-pa-nyid*.

The Bhagavat then says this in order to teach the *samādhi* for the marking-out of the middle portion of the Mandala. Because the *saṃbhoga-kāya* and the *nirmāṇa-kāya* reside within the middle area of the Mandala, the Master should transform himself with the fourfold causal *samādhi* of those two Bodies when he is marking out that part of the Mandala. It means that the Master should act with his attention focussed upon those *samādhis*. '***The primordially pure***' is Enlightenment. '***The form of non-dual yoga***' is Practice. '***The form of the Tathāgata***' is Sambuddhahood. '***The form of intrinsic nature of emptiness***' is Nirvāṇa.

16. 'Then to form the residence of the Tathāgatas, he should mark it out with the cord. He should establish two thirds of the exterior mandala as the residence of the deities and one third as the courtyard. The remaining two [sections] of the mandala should be divided likewise, and that is prescribed as the residence of the deities.'

These are the specifications for the residence prescribed in this Tantra, which will be explained later. For that, the whole area is divided into three, meaning that one third should be made into the courtyard and two thirds for the figures of the deities. ***Then to form the residence of the Tathāgatas, he should mark it out with the cord***: The division of the residence of the deities and the courtyard should be done carefully, marking them out with the cord, and not in haste. It also means that at that time, the residence of the Tathāgatas should be made while one's attention is focussed upon emptiness.

17. 'Then transforming himself into the Bhagavat Vairocana with his *mudrā*, he should imagine [the pigments] to be the vast continuum of reality. He should first take up the white pigment, which should be transformed thus:

> **'"This is the pure continuum of reality**
> **which purifies the realms of beings.**
> **This itself is[A] the Tathāgata,**
> **devoid of all faults."**
> **When he has thus reflected, the wise one**
> **should also imagine a *Ra* there,**
> **peaceful, with a flaming aura,**
> **like a conch, moon, or jasmine in colour.**
> **Then taking red, the second pigment,**
> **he should earnestly imagine**
> **a blazing letter *A* with an *anusvāra*.**
> **It is the holy Jina, Durdharṣa,**
> **like the shining first sun.**
> **Then the *mantrin* should take**
> **the third colour, yellow:**
> **according to the ritual,**
> **the wise one should imagine a *Ka*.**
> **[It is] like Kanaka-muni,**

A C adds: 如 '*like* [*the Tathāgata*]'.

who shines with the colour of gold,
abides in *samādhi*, overcomes failings
and illumines everywhere.
Then he should place *Va* there,
[with] the pigment resembling emeralds,
which liberates one from *saṃsāra*.
It is Mahā-bodhimaṇḍa-muni,
the Hero who is green in colour[A],
and causes all to be fearless.
Then taking up the black pigment,
the wise one should visualize there
a *Ha*, [Trailokya-vijaya]
who radiates a blazing aura, (157b)
inexhaustible, like the fire at the end of time,
a vajra in his hand, adorned with a crown,
he threatens in every way
all the hostile demon armies.'

(147b) This section teaches the ritual for the transformation of the mandala pigments. ***Then transforming himself into the Bhagavat Vairocana with his mudrā***: When transforming the pigments, the Master should transform himself into the Body of Vairocana with the vajra *mudrā*. Since the vajra is the symbol of Awareness, it means that he transforms them with the Five Awarenesses. The transformation of the pigments is twofold, absolute and relative. Of these, for the absolute transformation, it says '***he should imagine [the pigments] to be the vast continuum of reality***'. This shows that he transforms the five pigments into the vast continuum of reality, which is emptiness. ***He should first take up the white pigment*** and so on: This indicates that on therelative level, he should transform each of the pigments with each of the deities. Of these, the white pigment is said to be the transformation of the continuum of reality, and in order to show the intrinsic nature and power of that continuum of reality it says '***This is the pure continuum of reality which purifies the realms of beings. This itself is the Tathāgata, devoid of all faults***'. Having thus considered the meaning of the continuum of reality, he should transform it with the letter *Ra* which is described as having such qualities as a flaming aura and so on. Then to transform the red pigment, it says '***Then taking red, the second pigment***' and so forth. This indicates that it is transformed by the Buddha Durdharṣa who is generated by his seed-syllable, the letter *A*. Then for the yellow pigment, it says '***Then the* mantrin *should take the third colour, yellow***' and so forth. It is transformed by the Buddha Kanaka-muni who is generated by the seed-syllable, the letter *Ka*. In order to transform the green pigment with Bodhimaṇḍa-muni, it says: (148a) '***Then he should place Va there***' and so forth. The green pigment should be like the colour of emeralds. In order to transform the black pigment with Trailokya-vijaya, it says '***Then taking up the black pigment***' and so forth. And what is the figure of the Wrathful One like, who is generated with the letter *Ha*? It says: '***He radiates a blazing aura, inexhaustible, like the fire at the end of time***' and so forth.

A C: 虹霓 '[*like a rainbow* [*in colour*]'.

Furthermore, those five pigments should be considered as having the nature of the Five Awarenesses. White is the [the Awareness of] Continuum of Reality in nature, red is the Buddha Durdharṣa, the Mirror-like Awareness in nature, yellow is the Awareness of Sameness in nature, green is the Investigating Awareness, and black is the Awareness of Accomplishing Activities. As for the sequence in which they are described, first you should enter into the continuum of reality, and then because it is not appropriate for one's attention to be focussed upon emptiness alone, you should then focus it upon beings by virtue of compassion and become involved [with them], so next the red pigment is applied. By having embarked upon the benefitting of beings, you will become a Buddha, therefore the yellow pigment is applied next. Because you have become enriched and have power, you become capable of all actions, and you are capable of benefitting both yourself and others, so next the green pigment is applied. You should teach gently those who are to be trained with gentleness and wrathfully teach those who are wicked. If there are no other means to train those wicked ones, then finally they should be trained with ferocity. Therefore black should be applied next and you should do the wrathful rites.

18. Then emerging from that *samādhi*, the Bhagavat Vairocana entered the *samādhi* called 'Infinite Victory'. No sooner had the Bhagavat entered that *samādhi* than there emerged the *Vidyā* Queen called 'Universally Unimpeded Power' which arises from the sphere of all the Tathāgatas: *NAMAḤ SARVA-TATHĀGATEBHYAḤ SARVA-MUKHEBHYAḤ ASAME PARAME 'CALE GAGANE SMARAṆE SARVATRĀNUGATE SVĀHĀ* (Salutations to all the Tathāgatas, who are multi-faceted! Unequalled one! Supreme one! Unmoving one! You who remember space! You who penetrate all places! *Svāhā*!).

That which is manifested with *samādhi* (*samādhi-vikurvita*) mentioned above, is explained in this section. ***Then emerging from that* samādhi**: Arising from the *samādhi* which he had previously entered, (148b) the Bhagavat entered the *samādhi* called 'Infinite Victory'. ***Infinite Victory*** (*ananta-vijaya*): This means that it overcomes countless numbers, since it is not harmed by countless numbers of hostile beings. ***There emerged the* Vidyā *Queen called 'Universally Unimpeded Power'***: That power is both relative and absolute, and it is not harmed by the Māra of Emotional Afflictions and the Māra demigods and so forth.

19. 'Having done the ritual to transform the colours, he should make the *mudrā* or mantra of the Blessed Lady Prajñā-pāramitā[A] and recite this *Vidyā* Queen eight times. Then arising from [that *samādhi*], he should circumambulate the Mandala and enter within. With the power of great kindness and compassion, he should focus his attention upon the trainee practitioners (*sādhaka*) and transform himself into the Action Vajra-sattva with *Va*, together with Varada-vajra[6], and then he should draw the Mandala which Arises from Great Compassion. For that, the specifications of the inner

A C: 頂禮世尊及般若波羅蜜 '[*he should*] *make prostrations to the Bhagavat and Prajñāpāramitā*'.

mandala are as follows: In the centre there is the Bhagavat Mahā-Vairocana, seated upon a white lotus, with topknot and crown, wearing a lower garment of cotton or silk and an upper garment of embroidered silk. He is encircled by an aura which shines like gold in colour. He should draw either his *mudrā* [A], his body-image[B], or his syllable. Of these, his syllable is *A*. In the east, the letter *A* with an *anusvāra*, the essence of the dharmakāya of all the Buddhas: *AṂ*. In the north-east, he should draw the Mother of all the Buddhas, the Blessed Lady Gagana-locanā, or else her syllable *GA*. (158a) In the south-east, he should draw the symbol of all the Bodhisattvas, the Wish-fulfilling Gem, or its syllable *KA*. In the north, he should draw a lotus symbol or the syllable *SA* for the Bodhisattva Padmapāṇi together with all the Bodhisattvas who are held back by one birth. In the south there are three sections. He should draw a vajra symbol[C] or the syllable *VA* for the Lord of the Secret Ones together with his vajra entourage. In those three sections he should draw the symbol of all the Vajradharas or the letter *HŪṂ*. Below the Bhagavat Vairocana he should draw either the symbol or syllable of Acala who is seated upon a crag, holding a sword and a noose in his hands, and who is encircled with a blazing aura, threatening all obstructors. His syllable is *HĀṂ*. In the north-west he should draw either the symbol or the syllable of the destroyer of great obstructors, Trailokya-vijaya. He has a flaming aura above, which is like the fire at the time of the Great Destruction. He causes absolute terror. In his hand he holds a vajra that radiates light. His syllable is *HA*.

'Then in the four directions, the four great Guardians should be arranged. In the east he should draw either the symbol or the syllable of the great guardian Abhaya, like gold in colour, wearing white garments, with a slightly fierce face and holding a staff in hand. His seed syllable is *CA*[7]. In the north he should draw the symbol or the syllable of Sarva-trāsa-vinaśa, coloured white, holding a sword in his hand, wearing white garments, with a blazing aura, who destroys all fear. His syllable is *GA*[8]. In the west he should draw the symbol or syllable of Durdharṣa, coloured like a red *aśoka* flower, wearing red garments, with a smiling face, looking at the mandala of the entire assembly. His syllable is *SAḤ*. (158b) In the south he should draw the symbol or syllable of Vajrādanta-damaka, the great guardian, black in colour, with a face wrinkled in wrath, wearing a black lower garment, with a crown and topknot, who causes all world systems to be illumined with his lustre, holding a club in his hand and destroying the great obstructors. His syllable is *KṢA*. They also should be drawn accompanied by their entourages and their servants, all seated upon white lotuses.

'When the wise one has thus laid them out,
the *mantrin* who cleaves to the mantras
moves outwards according to the ritual,
then he should draw with certitude

A C: 頂印 '[*with his*] *Uṣṇīṣa mudrā*'.
B C omits '*his body-image*'
C C: 金剛慧印 '*vajra insight* mudrā'.

the King of Sages, who delights the Śākya clan.
The Lord wears the robes of a monk,
and has the thirty-two excellent marks,
the divine one who benefits by teachings
and bestows fearlessness upon all beings.
The symbols to be arranged by the *mantrin*
are the bowl, the Dharma robes and so on,
or else the wise one should put down his syllable, *BHA*.
This is his sacred ritual.'

'Then transforming himself into the essential nature of the continuum of reality in the outer mandala, the Master should divide it into three parts with his thoughts imbued with *bodhicitta*, and recollecting the Bhagavat Vairocana[A], he should then take upon that [specific] colour.

'In the east of the third section, he should draw the symbol or syllable of Vajra-varada (Mañjuśrī) who has the appearance of a youth and who holds an indigo *utpala* in his left hand, upon which there is a vajra. He is adorned with all ornaments, is dressed in a silk or cotton lower garment and an embroidered upper garment of silk. His colour is like saffron and upon his head he has five plaited braids of hair. This is his mantra: *NAMAḤ SAMATA-BUDDHĀNĀṂ MAṂ*. On his right the Master should draw the symbol or the syllable of the body-image of Jālinī-prabha, who is most excellent in all respects. In his hand he holds a jewel-net or a hook[B]. (159a) This is his syllable: *CHA*.

'Then in the south he should draw the symbol or syllable of the Bodhisattva Sarva-nīvaraṇa-viṣkambhin, who is golden in colour, with a topknot and crown. In his hand he holds a Wish-fulfilling Gem. This is his syllable: *Ā*[C].

'Then in the north he should draw the symbol or syllable of the Bodhisattva Kṣiti-garbha, who is green in colour[D], holding a lotus in his hand, and adorned with all ornaments. His syllable is *I*.

'In the west he should draw the symbol or syllable of the Bodhisattva Ākāśa-garbha, who is excellent in all respects, wearing white garments, with a radiant lustre. In his hand he holds a sword. This is his syllable: *Ī*.'

20. 'Then the *mantrin* who cleaves to the continuum of reality
should be seated[E] and then
abide facing towards the east,
his thoughts imbued with *bodhicitta*,
that is the continuum of reality in nature[F],
then making the vajra *mudrā*[G],

A C adds: 當三作禮 '[*he should*] *make three prostrations*'.
B C adds that the jewel-net is to held in his left hand and the hook in his right hand.
C C: *Āḥ*
D C: 色如鉢孕遇華 '*like a* priyaṅgu *flower in colour*'.
E C: 宴坐安住於法界 '[*The* mantrin *should be seated comfortably and establish himself in the continuum of reality*'.
F C: 我即法界性 '[*Thinking*] *"I am the continuum of reality in nature"* '.
G C: 金剛慧印 '*the vajra insight* mudrā '.

he should become the Action Vajra[sattva]
and diligently make offerings.'

21. 'Then in an all-encompassing spirit,
he should show the *mudrā* called
The *Samaya* of All the Saviour Buddhas,
and recite the mantra three times[9].'

22. 'Calling the pure trainees, according to the ritual,
they should take refuge in the Three [Jewels]
in the presence of the Mandala.
They should then also generate *bodhicitta*,
and the Master should make for them the *Mudrā*
which is the continuum of reality in nature.
Then making the Dharma Wheel [*Mudrā*]
he should mentally transform their appearance[A10]
and blindfold them with cotton [scarves];
then with a compassionate mind,
he should not let them be empty-handed[11],
so that they may perfect
the accumulations of Enlightenment.
He whispers into their ears:
"This is the best of *Samayas*".
He should then make for them
the *Samaya* [*Mudrā*] of the Buddhas,
and then with a compassionate mind[B]
he should make them cast flowers.
Wherever the flower falls,
that deity is given to them by the mantrin.
For the sake of *samaya* with all the beings (159b)
he should perform the ritual thus[C].'

23. Then the Noble Vajradhara
also asked the Lord:
'Would the Lord, the Best Of Speakers,
tell of the Initiation ritual!'
When he asked that, the Bhagavat
who cleaves to the continuum of reality

A C: 一心同彼體 '*Mentally making them identical to that*'. 一心 is probably an error for 以心 corresponding to T: *yid-kyis*.

B C: 令發菩提意 '*he should make them generate the aspiration for Enlightenment*'.

C T: *lus-can kun-la dam-tshig phyir | cho-ga de-ltar rab-tu-bya*, but C: 作如是要誓 一切應傳授 '*He should perform it thus and the commitments should be given to all*'. This is one of several occurrences in the text where T has '*lus-can*' = *dehin*, while C consistently has 應傳 or similar, which suggests an underlying Sanskrit reading of '*deya*'. Though Buddhaguhya's comments are require the '*lus-can/dehin*', the reading derived from C usually seems more natural in the context.

said to the Vajradhara:
'Listen to the ritual with concentration,
because I shall explain the excellent ritual
for the mastery of all Dharmas[A]!'

'Lord of the Secret Ones! For that, the Master should transform himself into the body-image of the Tathāgata with his mantra or *mudrā*. He should then call the trainees and establish them in the Great King of Lotuses whose substance is the continuum of reality[12]. He should make the *Mudrā* which Produces All the Members[13], and he should then sprinkle then sprinkle water on their heads from four jewelled jars empowered by the four great Bodhisattvas.

'The wise one should place on their heads
an *A* with an *anusvāra*,
and then he should place *A* in their hearts,
and place *Ra* on their breasts.
Or else he should place *A* in all places,
golden coloured with radiant light,
with topknot and crown,
seated upon a white lotus throne,
the excellent Jina who resides in *samādhi*.'[14]

A C: 勝自在攝持 '[*the rituals I explain*] *are a source of excellent mastery*'.

XI
THE *MUDRĀS*

1. Then the Bhagavat Vairocana gazed upon the entire assembly and spoke as follows to Vajrapāṇi, the Lord of the Secret Ones, 'Lord of the Secret Ones! If Bodhisattvas adorn themselves with the *mudrās* which are the symbols of realization of the continuum of reality, [which are] the Adornments of the Tathāgata, when they wander in *saṃsāra* through all levels of existence, gods, *nāgas*, *yakṣas*, *gandharvas*, *asuras*, *garuḍas*, (160a) *kinnaras*, *mahoragas*, humans and non-humans will accept them and also become their audiences, because they are marked with the symbols of the Great Enlightenment of all the Tathāgatas. Therefore you should listen carefully and bear them in mind, for I shall explain them to you!' When he had spoken thus, Vajrapāṇi said to the Bhagavat, 'Bhagavat, now is the time! Sugata, the hour has come!'

Now the chapter on the *mudrās* will be explained. The explanation of the *mudrās* is generally speaking twofold: for those beings to be trained who have devoted interest in the Profound and Extensive, and for those who have devoted interest in that with cognitive objects. Of these, those to be trained who have devoted interest in the Profound and Extensive through the mantra words which have been explained, focus their attention upon the true meaning of the sound of the mantra words, and practise the body-image of the deity, prior to the cultivation of *bodhicitta*. Moreover, that practice of the body-image of the deity is the practice of the pure *samādhi* which is devoid of all other concepts and the practice of perfect appearance in the body-image of the deity.

As for those beings to be trained with devoted interest in that with cognitive objects, they are incapable of focussing their attention on the true meaning of the sound of the mantras and so forth, and can only do the practice of the body-images of the deities after having made the *mudrās*. Therefore for their sakes the causal and resultant virtues of the Bhagavat were transformed into the form of the *mudrās*. Of these, the *mudrās* of the sword, vajra and so forth are the virtues of Mind. The conch *mudrā* and so forth are the virtues of Speech. The *mudrās* of the Uṣṇīṣas and so forth are the virtues of Body. This should be applied as appropriate.

(149a) Here, they are '***the adornments of a Tathāgata***' because the *mudrās* of the Uṣṇīṣas, the Eyes and so forth are the adornments of his Body. ***The symbols of the realization of the continuum of reality***: The continuum of reality is the Awareness of Suchness. The symbols of the realization and understanding of that are the *mudrās* of the sword, vajra and so forth. ***If Bodhisattvas adorn themselves with the* mudrās, *... will also become their audiences*:** This explains the purpose of the revelation of these *mudrās*. If any Bodhisattva is endowed with those *mudrās*, he will be marked by the symbols of the Great Enlightenment of all the Tathāgatas, and so he will not be harmed by any gods, asuras and so on, but those gods and asuras will even become audiences for that Bodhisattva. It is just as in the world, where a person who bears the king's seal will be untroubled by people, who on the contrary will obey his words. In brief, this teaches that beings to be guided will be helped in the present world and in future lifetimes by the explanation of these *mudrās*.

2. Then the Bhagavat entered into the *samādhi* called 'That which Transforms[A] the Embodiment of Unimpeded Strength', and no sooner had the Bhagavat entered that *samādhi*, than there emerged the *Vidyā* Queen endowed with three strengths: universally unimpeded strength, unequalled strength and the strength which causes entry into *samaya*[B]: *NSB ASAME TRISAME SAMAYE SVĀHĀ* (NSB. O *samaya* of the three samenesses, without equal! *Svāhā*!).

Those *mudrās* which appear below are the embodiment of unimpeded power. (149b) Since the Bhagavat will expound those *mudrās* after having entered that *samādhi*, the name of that *samādhi* is ***'That which Transforms the Embodiment of Unimpeded Power'***. There, '***unimpeded***' means that those Vajra Adornments of the Inexhaustible Body and so forth of the Bhagavat are unhindered by anything. ***Power***: That same unimpededness is power. '***Embodiment***' *(āśraya)* refers to the Body and so forth of the Bhagavat. ***That which Transforms***: The Vajra Adornments of the Inexhaustible Body and so forth of the Bhagavat, which are that unimpeded power itself, were transformed by it into the substance of the *mudrās*.

The* Vidyā *Queen endowed with three strengths – universally unimpeded strength, unequalled strength and the strength which causes entry into* samaya: *Unequalled strength: That unhindered strength is unequalled by anything. ***Which causes entry into* samaya**: The meaning of *samaya* has already been explained earlier. ***Which causes entry***: Because the intrinsically existent Mandala of the Inexhaustible Body and so forth is not accessible to the vision of lower beings, it will be as though they did see that intrinsically existent Mandala if they use this *Samaya Mudrā* and recite its Mantra, which cause its transformation, therefore it says it '***causes entry***'. Secondly, if you use this *Samaya Mudrā* and Mantra, when you have deviated from the *samaya* to be maintained, it will be as though you see the Mandala. Deviations from the *samaya* will be repaired just by making it and you will once again enter into the *samaya*, therefore it says it '***causes entry into* samaya**'. Thirdly, that is also said of it because when you are entering into the Mandala, you use this *Samaya Mudrā* and Mantra and then enter.

3. 'Lord of the Secret Ones, this *Vidyā* Queen reveals all the Tathāgatas, she does not let you depart from the confines of the path of the Three Dharmas and she causes you to perfect the Levels and Perfections. You should join your two hands with a hollow between the palms and lift up both hands.

> **'This sign is the great *mudrā***
> **of all the Saviour Buddhas.**
> **The *samaya* of all Buddhas**
> **resides in this *mudrā*.'**

(151a) It says she '***reveals all Tathāgatas***' since by reciting this *Vidyā*, it will be as though you were seeing the intrinsically existent Mandala, the residence of all the Tathāgatas. Secondly, because the representational Mandala which has been drawn is shown after

A C omits '*That which Transforms*'.
B C adds: 一切如來 '*of all the Tathāgatas*'.

reciting this *Vidyā*, or because that Mandala of all the Buddhas is seen after reciting it, it says she '***reveals all the Tathāgatas***'. ***She does not let you depart from the confines of the path of the Three Dharmas***: The Three Dharmas are the Vajra Adornments of the Inexhaustible Body, Speech and Mind of the Tathāgata, or else the Three Bodies (*tri-kāya*). The path is the activity of maintaining *samaya* and so forth, and she stops you from departing from that path. ***She causes you to perfect the Levels and the Perfections***: She causes you to perfect by stages the Perfections beginning with Generosity, by worship of the Bhagavat after you have entered that *samaya*, and by her power you will leap up the Levels stage by stage.

The* samaya *of all the Buddhas resides in this* mudrā**: The meanings of '*samaya*', such as 'not allowing you to depart from the *samaya* which is to be maintained', 'causing realization of the Inexhaustible Body' and so on, or 'the perfection of that Body' and so on, are denoted and understood by way of this *mudrā*, so it says it 'resides in this* mudrā**'.

4. 'Also the wise one should make
both of his hands into fists,
and insert both thumbs inside.
This symbol is the great *mudrā*
which purifies the continuum of reality[A].
'Its mantra is: *NSB DHARMADHĀTU-SVABHĀVAKO 'HAṂ* (NSB I have the nature of the continuum of reality!).'

This symbol is the great* mudrā *which purifies the continuum of reality: Since the continuum of reality, emptiness, is denoted and understood by this *mudrā*, it is said to '***purify the continuum of reality***'.

5. 'Likewise, joining together all the fingers of both your hands, you should interlace them and put your two thumbs together.
'This glorious *mudrā*
is renowned as the Dharma Wheel.
The Saviour Protectors of the world
all turn this Wheel. (160b)
'Its mantra is: *NSB VAJRĀTMAKO 'HAṂ* (NSB I am a vajra in nature!).'

(150b) You should be transformed into Vajrasattva after having been transformed into the continuum of reality, in order to turn the Wheel of the Dharma. '***Glorious***' refers to Vajrasattva himself, so it is Vajrasattva who turns the Wheel of the scriptural Dharma and the realized Dharma. When they have changed themselves into Vajrasattva with that *mudrā*, even the Bodhisattva Protectors of the World will be made to turn the wheel of the Dharma.

6. 'Likewise, join your two hands, the palms flat together and place your two forefingers on top of your two thumbs. This should be made like a sword.
'With this Sword *Mudrā* [B]
of all the Saviour Buddhas,

A This section is prose in C.
B C: 大慧刀印 '*great insight sword mudrā*'.

you will sever all beliefs
in the reality of the person[1].

'Its mantra is: *NSB MAHĀ-KHAḌGA VIRAJA-DHARMA-SAṂDARŚAKA SAHAJA-SATKĀYA-DṚṢṬI-CCHEDAKA TATHĀGATĀDHIMUKTI-NIRJĀTA VIRĀGA-DHARMA-NIRĪKṢITA HŪṂ* (NSB. O Great Sword! Manifester of the unsullied Dharma! That which severs innate beliefs in the reality of the person! That which is arisen from the fervent conviction of the Tathāgata! That which reveals the Dharma free from attachment! *Hūṃ*!).'

The Sword *Mudrā* is the symbol of the Awareness that realizes the absence of autonomous existence to both phenomena and the individual. By this Awareness, belief in an innately existing person (*sahaja-satkāya-dṛṣṭi*) will be severed.

7. 'Likewise, join together both your hands with a hollow between the palms and encircle your thumbs with both your forefingers, making it like a conch.

'This glorious *mudrā*
is called the Dharma Conch.
With it, the Buddhas and Bodhisattvas
expound the undefiled Dharma
which leads to the peace of Nirvana
in these worlds.

'Its mantra is: *NSB AṂ*.'

This Conch *Mudrā* is the symbol of the Buddha's Speech. It means that Buddhas and Bodhisattvas expound the undefiled Dharma which brings about the attainment of the tranquil Nirvāṇa, by this Buddha-speech.

8. 'Likewise, join all your fingers at the palms and stretch them out [hollowed] like a bell. Place both thumbs and little-fingers together in one point and place your forefingers and middle-fingers together.

'This glorious excellent lotus
is the indestructible vajra-seat
of all the Buddha Saviours;
There the Guide was enlightened,
and all the Jinas and their Children
are born from this and become enlightened.

'Its mantra is: *NSB AḤ*[A].'

This Lotus *Mudrā* is the seat of the Buddhas. Whenever they become enlightened, the Protector Buddhas sit upon this seat and become enlightened. (151a) Also the children of the Buddha, the Bodhisattvas, are born from this lotus.

9. 'Likewise, you should link together both your hands into a fist and raise up both your middle-fingers, then crooking both your forefingers, place them at their sides like a vajra. Raise both your thumbs and little-fingers and holding them thus, insert both of your ring-fingers within your hands.

A T: *A*

'[This] great *mudrā* is the vajra symbol
which destroys the citadel of ignorance,
it is the Awareness of the Buddhas
which cannot be harmed by gods or men[A].
'Its mantra is: *NSV HŪṂ.'*

That Awareness of the Immediate Path was transformed by the Bhagavat into the vajra *mudrā*. '***The destruction of the citadel of ignorance***' means that ignorance and its entourage of mental factors are overcome with that Awareness.

10. 'Likewise, link both of your hands together (161a) into a fist and raise up your middle-fingers, then crook both of your forefingers and place them at their sides, and join them together.
'This is the great *mudrā* of the *Uṣṇīṣa*[B]:
just by making it
you will become an excellent Jina.
'Its mantra is: *NSB HŪṂ HŪṂ.'*

The *Uṣṇīṣa* is [one of] the Bhagavat's marks of a Great Being, and it is transformed into a *mudrā*. ***Just by making it, you will become an excellent Jina***: One changes into the divine body-image by accumulating the many individual *mudrās*, yet by making this Uṣṇīṣa *mudrā* alone, it is possible to change yourself into the Body of a Buddha[C].

11. 'Likewise, make your right hand into a fist and place it at your eye-brows.
'This *mudrā* is called Ūrṇā
by the holy Jinas.
Just by making it
one becomes an excellent Jina[D].
'Its mantra is: *NSB ĀḤ HAṂ JAḤ.'*

There emerges from the Ūrṇā between the Bhagavat's eyebrows one single strand of hair, a mark of a Great Being, which if extended would encompass all the Three Worlds. It is coiled up and confined there, and that is transformed into the *mudrā*.

12. 'The wise one should do as for yoga,
and place both of his hands
at his navel, as though holding a bowl.
This is called the Bowl *Mudrā*[E].
'Its mantra is: *NSB BHAḤ.'*

A Both T and V agree with C for the first half of this verse, however all versions differ for the second half. T: *sangs-rgyas-rnams-kyi ye-shes 'di | nyid-kyis byin-du brlabs-te bstan* – '*this Awareness of the Buddhas is transformed and revealed by it* '; V: *sangs-rgyas-rnams-kyi ye-shes te | lha-min lha-yis [mi]-btsugs-pa'o* – '*it is the Awareness of the Buddhas and cannot be harmed by* asuras *or gods*'; C: 曉寤睡眠者 天人不能壞 '*it rouses those who sleep but it cannot be harmed by gods or men*'. Given the similarity of V and C, I have based the last line on C.

B C: 此印摩訶印 所謂入來頂 '*This* mudrā *is a great* mudrā *called the Tathāgata's Uṣṇīṣa*'.

C The translation of this comment is based upon V which makes better sense than B.

D C reads: 此名毫相藏 佛常滿願印 '*This is called the Treasury of the Ūrṇā attribute, the* mudrā *of the Buddha's constant fulfilment of wishes*'.

E This verse is prose in C.

The Bowl *Mudrā* is clearly described in this verse.

13. 'Likewise, you should raise your right hand up as though bestowing fearlessness.
'Fearlessness is bestowed by it to all beings.
When somebody makes that *mudrā*,
it is called the *Mudrā* of Fearlessness.
'Its mantra is: *NSB SARVATHĀ JINA JINA BHAYA-NAṢANA SVĀHĀ* (NSB. Most victorious one of the victorious in all places! Remover of fear! *Svāhā*!).'

(151b) This is the *mudrā* of bestowing fearlessness. If you or other beings are frightened by obstacle-makers, make this *mudrā*, show it and you will be freed from them.

14. 'Likewise, your right hand should be lowered as though bestowing favours.
'This is called the Bestower of Favours,
by the Protectors of the World,
just by making it,
the Jinas will bestow favour.
'Its mantra is: *NSB VARADA-VAJRĀTMAKA SVĀHĀ*. (NSB Bestower of favours! Vajra-formed! *Svāhā*!).'

This is the *mudrā* of the Bhagavat's bestowing of favours upon beings. When you receive such favours as the attainments and so on, you should make this *mudrā* and receive them.

15. 'Likewise, your right hand should be made into a fist and you should extend your forefinger like an angry brow-crease.
'This *mudrā*, which is a great *mudrā*,
should be known as the terrifier of demons
of all the Saviour Buddhas,
it destroys all that brings ruin.
Just by making it,
the unending armies of demons,
and other obstructors and gremlins
with be scattered, without a doubt.
'This is its mantra: *NSB MAHĀ-BALA-VATI* (161b) *DAŚA-BALODBHAVE*[A] *MAHĀ-MAITRY-ABHYUDGATE SVĀHĀ* (Possessor of Great Strength! That born from the ten strengths! That arisen from Great Kindness! *Svāhā*!).'

This is the *mudrā* for terrifying obstructors and so on. Just by making this *mudrā*, all obstructors will be terrified and flee. When the obstructors have thus fled, there will be no obstructions, so whatever you wish for will be accomplished. Therefore it fulfils all hopes.

A T: *daśa-bala-tejodbhave*.

16. 'Likewise, make your right hand into a fist and stretch out both its middle-finger and ring-finger and place the thumb below.

> **'This is the Eye which arises from**
> **the compassion of the Buddha Protectors.**
> **The wise one should place it over his eyes**
> **and then they will become Buddha Eyes.**

'Its mantra is: *NSB GAGANA-VARA-LAKṢAṆA KARUṆA-MAYA TATHĀGATA-CAKṢUḤ SVĀHĀ* (That with the best of attributes! That formed by Compassion! Eye of the Tathāgata! *Svāhā*!).'

'*The Eye which arises from compassion*' is the Eye of Insight which gazes upon all beings, by virtue of the Bhagavat's Great Compassion. Because that Eye has been transformed into this *mudrā*, if you make the *mudrā* and place over your eyes, they will turn into the Buddha's Eyes when you are changing yourself into the Body of the Buddha.

17. 'Likewise, join both your hands together and make a fist with the fingers interlaced, then raise up both your thumbs and crook them, putting them together in a circle.

> **'This is called the excellent Noose,**
> **which destroys all hostile ones.**
> **When the *mantrin* makes it**
> **the hostile ones will always be bound.**

'Its mantra is: *NSB HE HE MAHĀ-PĀŚA PRASARAUDARYA SATTVA-DHĀTU-VIMOHAKA TATHĀGATĀDHIMUKTI-NIRJĀTA SVĀHĀ* (NSB. *He he*! Great Noose! Vast and Extensive! Remover of stupidity from realms of beings! Born from the Tathāgata's fervent conviction! *Svāhā*!).'

(152a) The Awareness which consists of the eight members of the Noble Path, which extricates all beings, is transformed into the Noose *Mudrā*. By making this Noose *Mudrā* you will perform the rites to bind all harm-doers, such as obstructors and so forth.

18. 'Likewise, join both your hands together, making them into a fist, then raise up your fore-fingers and bend them at the third joint placing the others like a bracelet.

> **'This is called the Hook**
> **of all the Saviour Buddhas.**
> **It draws to you**
> **all the great Bodhisattvas**
> **who dwell on the Ten Levels,**
> **and also others who are hostile.**

'Its mantra is: *NSB ĀḤ SARVATRĀPRATIHATA TATHĀGATĀṄKUŚA BODHI-CARYĀ-PARIPŪRAKA SVĀHĀ* (NSB. *Āḥ*! Unimpeded in all places! Hook of the Tathāgata! Fulfiller of the practice of Enlightenment! *Svāhā*!).'

In connection with the causal and resultant practices of a Tathāgata, there is the gathering together and guiding of beings with the Four Methods of Attracting during the causal phase, and there is the gathering together and guiding of beings with the Vajra Adornments of the Inexhaustible Body and so on in the resultant phase. These practices were transformed into the hook *mudrā*. Also that Hook guides all, both harm-doers such as obstructors and Bodhisattvas who dwell on the Tenth level. So, if it is able to attract even Bodhisattvas who dwell on the Tenth Level, how much more so others!

19. 'From the Hook *Mudrā*, hook both your middle-fingers and join them together at the same time. This is the *mudrā* of the Tathāgata's heart. Its mantra is *NSB JÑĀNODBHAVA SVĀHĀ*. (NSB That which arises from Awareness! *Svāhā*!).'

20. 'From that *mudrā*, raise up both your ring-fingers and leave the others as they are. This is the *mudrā* of the Tathāgata's navel. Its mantra is *NSB AMṚTODBHAVA SVĀHĀ* (NSB That which arises from the nectar of immortality! *Svāhā*!).'

***From that* mudrā**: You should know that [your hands] should be straightened out from that hook *mudrā*, raising up both of your ring-fingers from the Hook *Mudrā*.

21. 'From that *mudrā*, (162a) raise up both your little-fingers and leave the others as they are. This is the *mudrā* of the [Tathāgata's] legs. Its mantra is *NSB TATHĀGATA-SAṂBHAVA SVĀHĀ* (NSB. That which is arisen from the Tathāgata! *Svāhā*!).'

22. 'Likewise, join both your hands with a hollow between them, then crook your forefingers and put them inside. Likewise, do the same with both your ring-fingers. Your thumbs and little-fingers should be slightly crooked and your middle-fingers should be raised up parallel. This is the *mudrā* of the Tathāgata's treasury. Its mantra is *NSB RAṂ RAṂ RAḤ RAḤ SVĀHĀ*.'

23. 'From that *mudrā*, remove your ring-fingers and leave them extended. This is the *mudrā* of delimiting the great boundary (*mahā-sīma-bandha*). Its mantra is *NSB LE LU PURI VIKULE SVĀHĀ*.'

24. 'From that *mudrā* crook both of your middle-fingers and raise up both of your thumbs. This is the *Mudrā* of Great Protection. Its mantra is *NAMAḤ SARVA-TATHĀGATEBHYAḤ SARVA-BHAYA-VIGATEBHYAḤ VIŚVA-MUKHEBHYAḤ SARVATHĀ HAṂ KHAṂ RAKṢA-MAHĀ-BALE SARVA-TATHĀGATA-PUṆYA NIRJĀTE HŪṂ HŪṂ TRAṬ TRAṬ APRATIHATE SVĀHĀ* (Salutations to all the Tathāgatas who remove all fear, who are multi-faceted! Omnipresent! *Haṃ khaṃ*! Most powerful protectress! She who has arisen from the merit of all the Tathāgatas! *Hūṃ hūṃ traṭ traṭ*! She who is unimpeded! *Svāhā*!). This is the Great Protectress called Unbearable.'

25. 'Likewise, insert your forefingers within. This is the *mudrā* called "Universally Shining". Its mantra is *NSB JVALA-MĀLINI TATHĀGATĀRCI SVĀHĀ* (NSB. Garland of light! Radiant light of the Tathāgata! *Svāhā*!).'

26. 'Likewise, join both your hands with a hollow at the palms and encircle their sides with both forefingers. This is the *mudrā* of the Tathāgata's armour. Its mantra is *NSB PRACAṆḌA-VAJRA-JVALA VISPHARA HŪṂ* (NSB. Fiercely Shining vajra! Shine forth! *Hūṃ*! *Svāhā*!).'

27. 'From that *mudrā*, join both your forefingers and thumbs together. This is the *mudrā* of the Tathāgata's tongue. Its mantra is *NSB TATHĀGATA-JIHVA SATYA-DHARMA-PRATIṢṬHITA SVĀHĀ* (NSB. Greatest of great tongue of the Tathāgata! O that which abides in the true Dharma! *Svāhā*!).'

28. 'From that *mudrā*, crook both your forefingers and ring-fingers and join them within. Extend the thumbs (162b) and crook them a little, with their tips facing your middle-fingers. Your little-fingers should be stretched out, like both thumbs above. This is the *mudrā* of the Tathāgata's great mouth[A]. Its mantra is *NSB TATHĀGATA-MAHĀ-VAKTRA VIŚVA-JÑĀNA-MAHODAYA SVĀHĀ* (NSB. Great mouth of the Tathāgata! Great source of manifold Awarenesses! *Svāhā*!).'

29. 'From that *mudrā*, release your forefingers and insert them within your palms. Hold them bent facing upwards. This is the *mudrā* of the Tathāgata's tooth. Its mantra is *NSB TATHĀGATA-DAṂṢṬRA RASA-RASĀGRA-SAṂPRĀPAKA SARVA-TATHĀGATA-VIṢAYA-SAṂBHAVA SVĀHĀ* (NSB. Tooth of the Tathāgata! That which has fully attained the highest essence of essences! That born from the realm of all the Tathāgatas! *Svāhā*!).'

30. 'From that *mudrā*, raise both your forefingers and hold them there, crooked at the third joint. This is the *mudrā* of the Tathāgata's eloquence. Its mantra is *NSB ACINTYĀDBHŪTA-RŪPA-VĀCAṂ SAMANTA-PRĀPTA VIŚUDDHA-SVARA SVĀHĀ* (NSB That which has completely attained the inconceivable miraculous speech! Pure voice! *Svāhā*!).'

31. 'Likewise, join both your hands together with a hollow at the palms and insert both your thumbs and little-fingers inside, putting them together as one. This is the *mudrā* of the Ten Strengths. Its mantra is *NSB DAŚA-BALĀṄGA-DHARA HŪṂ SAṂ JAṂ SVĀHĀ* (NSB. That which possesses the members of the Ten Strengths! *Hūṃ saṃ jaṃ*! *Svāhā*!).'

32. 'From that *mudrā*, crook both your forefingers to the tips of your thumbs and join them together. This is the *mudrā* of the application to recollection. Its mantra is *NSB TATHĀGATA-SMṚTI SATTVA-HITĀBHYUDGATA-GAGANA SAMĀSAMA SVĀHĀ* (NSB. Recollection of the Tathāgata! That which gives rise to benefit for beings! That which is without equal like space! *Svāhā*!).'

33. 'From that *mudrā*, both of your ring-fingers should be held on top of your thumbs. This is the *mudrā* of the realization of the sameness of all phenomena. Its mantra is *NSB SARVA-DHARMA-SAMATĀ-PRĀPTA-*

A C: 如來語 '*the Tathāgata's speech*'.

***TATHĀGATĀNUGATA SVĀHĀ* (NSB. That which has attained the sameness of all phenomena, which accompanies the Tathāgata! *Svāhā*!).'**

The *mudrā* of the Tathāgata's vajra is connected with perfect Enlightenment. The hook *mudrā* is connected with Practice. The *mudrās* of the Tathāgata's heart and Ten Strengths are connected with Perfect Buddhahood. The *mudrā* of the realization of the sameness of all phenomena is connected with Nirvāṇa. Likewise, the mantras [beginning] *NAMAḤ SAMANTA-BUDDHĀNĀṂ* should be linked with Perfect Buddhahood, those beginning *NAMAḤ SAMANTA-VAJRĀNĀṂ* with Enlightenment and those beginning *NAMAḤ SARVA-TATHAGATEBHYAḤ* (152b) with the Tathāgata.

34. 'Likewise, joining both your hands together, encircle both your middle-fingers with your forefingers and leave the remainder as they are. (163a) This is the *mudrā* of Samantabhadra's Wish-fulfilling Gem. His mantra is *NSB SAMANTĀNUGATE VIRAJA-DHARMA-NIRJĀTA MAHĀ MAHĀ SVĀHĀ* (NSB. That which pervades all places! That born from the pure Dharma! Greatest of the Great! *Svāhā*!).'

35. 'From that *mudrā*, crook and insert both of your forefingers into both the middle-fingers and leave the remainder as before. This is the *mudrā* of Maitreya. His mantra is *NSB AJITAṂ-JAYA SARVA-SATTVĀŚĀYĀNUGATA SVĀHĀ* (NSB. Vanquisher of the unvanquished! Fulfiller of the wishes of all beings! *Svāhā*!). '

36. 'From that *mudrā* insert both your thumbs within. This is the *mudrā* of Ākāśagarbha. His mantra is *NSB ĀKĀŚA-SAMANTĀNUGATA VICITRĀMBHARA-DHARA SVĀHĀ* (NSB. Pervader of all places like space! Wearer of multi-coloured garments! *Svāhā*!).'

37. 'From that *mudrā* insert your ring- and little-fingers within and join together as one both your forefingers and middle-fingers. This is the *mudrā* of Sarva-nīvaraṇa-viṣkambhin. His mantra is *NSB ĀḤ SATTVA-HITĀBHYUDGATA TRAṂ TRAṂ RAṂ RAṂ SVĀHĀ* (NSB. *Āḥ*! Manifester of benefit for beings! *Traṃ traṃ raṃ raṃ*! *Svāhā*!).'

38. 'Likewise, join both of your hands together and open out all your fingers like a bell. Join together both your thumbs and little-fingers and leave the others as before. This is the *mudrā* of Avalokiteśvara. His mantra is *NSB SARVA-TATHĀGATĀVALOKITA-KARUṆĀ-MAYA RA RA RA HŪṂ JAḤ SVĀHĀ* (NSB. You who are formed from the sight and compassion of all the Tathāgatas! *Ra ra ra hūṃ jaḥ*! *Svāhā*!).'

39. 'Likewise, join the hands together with a hollow within and make them like an opened lotus. This is the Lotus *Mudrā* of Mahā-sthāma-prāpta. His mantra is *NSB JAṂ JAṂ SAḤ SVĀHĀ*.'

40. 'Likewise, make both hands into fists and raise both your forefingers up into a peak, and place both of your thumbs in front of them. This is the *mudrā* of Tārā. Her mantra is *NSB TĀRE TĀRIṆI KARUṆODBHAVE SVĀHĀ* (NSB. You who have arisen from compassion! Tārā! Saviouress! *Svāhā*!).'

41. 'From that *mudrā*, extend and twist both of your forefingers. (163b) The others are as before. This is the *mudrā* of Bhṛkuṭī. Her mantra is *NSB SARVA-BHAYA-TRĀSANI HŪṂ SPHOṬAYA SVĀHĀ* (NSB. Terrifier of all fears! *Hūṃ*! Smash asunder! *Svāhā*!).'

42. 'Likewise, join both of your hands together with a hollow between the palms and insert both of your ring-fingers and thumbs inside. This is the *mudrā* of Pāṇḍara-vāsinī. Her mantra is *NSB TATHĀGATA-VIṢAYA-SAṂBHAVE PADMA-MĀLINI SVĀHĀ* (NSB. Born from the realm of the Tathāgatas! Garland of lotuses! *Svāhā*!).'

43. 'From that *mudrā*, raise up both of your thumbs and place the tips of your forefingers in front of them, with the space of a grain of wheat between them. This is the *mudrā* of Hayagrīva. His mantra is *NSB KHĀDAYA BHAÑJA SPHOṬAYA SVĀHĀ* (Devour! Shatter! Smash asunder! *Svāhā*!).'

44. 'From that *mudrā*, raise up both of your ring-fingers and little-fingers and leave the others in the form of fists. This is the *mudrā* of Kṣitigarbha. His mantra is *NSB HA HA HA SUTANU SVĀHĀ* (NSB. *Ha ha ha*! You with a beautiful body! *Svāhā*!).'

45. 'Likewise, join both of your hands together with a hollow between the palms and encircle both of your ring-fingers with your middle-fingers. Also both forefingers should be crooked and placed upon both thumbs. The others are as before. This is the *mudrā* of Mañjuśrī. His mantra is *NSB HE HE KUMĀRA VIMUKTI-PATHA-STHITA SMARA SMARA PRATIJÑĀṂ SVĀHĀ* (NSB. *He he*! Child! You who abide on the path of the liberation! Remember, remember your vow! *Svāhā*!).'

46. 'Make your left hand into a fist and crook your forefinger. This is the *mudrā* of Jālinī-prabha. His mantra is *NSB HE HE KUMĀRA MĀYĀ-GATA SVABHĀVA-STHITA SVĀHĀ* (NSB. *He he*! Child! You who have realized illusion! You who abide in the intrinsic nature! *Svāhā*!).'

47. 'From that *mudrā*, bend all your fingers. This is the *mudrā* of Vimala-prabha's Lotus. His mantra is *NSB HE KUMĀRA VICITRA-GATI-KUMĀRAM*[A] *ANUSMARA SVĀHĀ* (NSB. *He!* Child! Remember the child who realizes various things! *Svāhā*!).'

48. 'Likewise, make your right hand into a fist and raise up both your forefinger and middle-finger in parallel. This is the *mudrā*[B] of Keśinī. (164a)

A T: *kumāra pratijñānām anusmara*.

B C: 刀印 '*sword* mudrā'.

Her mantra is *NSB HE HE KUMĀRIKE DAYĀ-JÑĀNAṂ SMARA PRATIJÑĀṂ*[A] *SVĀHĀ* (NSB. *He he*! Girl! Remember compassion and awareness! And your vow! *Svāhā*!).'

49. 'Likewise, make your right hand into a fist and extend your middle-finger upwards, making it like the point of a halberd. This is the *mudrā* of Upakeśinī. Her mantra is *NSB BHINNAYĀJÑĀNAṂ HE KUMĀRIKE SVĀHĀ* (NSB. Cleave ignorance! *He*! Girl! *Svāhā*!).'

50. 'Make both your hands into fists and extend both of your middle-fingers and place your forefingers at their sides. This is the *mudrā* of Citrā's staff. Her mantra is *NSB HE KUMĀRIKE ĀJÑĀNA-PRAVIDVAṂSAṆI SVĀHĀ* (NSB. *He*! Girl! You who have realized complete knowledge of commands! *Svāhā*!)[B].'

51. 'Likewise, make your left hand into a fist and raise both your ring-finger and little-finger. This is the *mudrā* of Vasumati's banner. Her mantra is *NSB HE SMARA JÑĀNA-KETU SVĀHĀ* (NSB. *He*! Remember! Banner of Awareness! *Svāhā*!).'

52. 'Make your right hand into a fist, raise up your forefinger and crook its tip. This is the *mudrā* of Ākarṣaṇī's hook. Her mantra is *NSB ĀKARṢAYA SARVĀṂ KURU ĀJÑĀṂ KUMĀRASYA SVĀHĀ* (NSB. Draw in all [beings]! Carry out the commands of the Child! *Svāhā*!).'

53. 'Likewise, make both your hands into fists and raise up both forefingers and crook them at the third joint. This is the *mudrā* of the Female Servants. Their mantra is N*SB ĀḤ VISMAYA-NIYE SVĀHĀ* (NSB. Ah! O wonderful one! *Svāhā*!).

54. 'Likewise, make your right hand into a fist and extend the middle-finger, crooked at the third joint. This is the *mudrā* of Kautuhala's vajra. His mantra is *NSB VIMATI-CCHEDAKA SVĀHĀ* (NSB. Severer of doubts! *Svāhā*!).'

55. 'Likewise, raise your right hand to your shoulder and make it as though bestowing fearlessness. This is the *mudrā* of Abhayaṃdada. (164b) His mantra is *NSB ABHAYAṂ-DADA SVĀHĀ* (NSB. Bestower of fearlessness! *Svāhā*!).'

56. 'Likewise, make that same hand as though drawing upwards. This is the *mudrā* of Apāya-jaha. His mantra is *NSB ABHYUDDHĀRAṆI SATTVA-DHĀTUṂ SVĀHĀ* (NSB. Saviour of realms of beings! *Svāhā*!).'

57. 'Place the same hand on your chest. This is the *mudrā* of Paritrāṇāśayamati. His mantra is *NSB HE MAHĀ MAHĀ SMARA PRATIJÑĀṂ SVĀHĀ* (NSB. *He*! Greatest of the great! Remember your vow! *Svāhā*!).'

A T: *kumāri kleśa cchedayājñānaṃ smara pratijñāna*.

B C omits this *mudrā* and mantra.

58. 'Make the same hand as though holding a flower. This is the *mudrā* of Maitry-abhyudgata. His mantra is *NSB SVA-CITTODGATA*[A] *SVĀHĀ* (NSB Born from his own mind! *Svāhā*!).'

59. 'Place that same hand on your heart and crook your middle-finger inside. This is the *mudrā* of Karuṇā-mṛdita-mati. His mantra is *NSB KARUṆĀMṚDITA*[B] *SVĀHĀ* (NSB. You who are repeatedly compassionate! *Svāhā*!).'

60. 'Likewise, make your right hand as though bestowing flowers. This is the *mudrā* of Sarva-dāha-praśamita. His mantra is *NSB HE VARADA VARA-PRĀPTA SVĀHĀ* (NSB. *He*! Bestower of favours! You who have attained the most excellent! *Svāhā*!).'

61. 'Make that same hand as though holding a Wish-fulfilling Gem. This is the *mudrā* of Acintya-mati. His mantra is *NSB SARVĀŚĀ-PARIPŪRAṆA SVĀHĀ* (NSB. Fulfiller of all wishes! *Svāhā*!).'

62. 'Likewise, make both your hands into fists, put out both of your middle-fingers and extend them. This is the *mudrā* of Kṣitigarbha's banner. His mantra is *NSB HA HA HA VISMAYE SVĀHĀ* (NSB. *Ha ha ha*! Wondrous one! *Svāhā*!).'

63. 'Make your right hand into a fist and extend three fingers. This is the *mudrā* of Ratnākara. His mantra is *NSB HE MAHĀ MAHĀ SVĀHĀ*.'

64. 'Extend the ring-finger from the same hand and raise it upwards. This is the *mudrā* of Ratnapāṇi. (165a) His mantra is *NSB RATNODBHAVA SVĀHĀ* (NSB. You who have arisen from a jewel! *Svāhā*!).'

65. 'Likewise, interlace both hands back to back. Hook together your left thumb and right little-finger and likewise the right with the left. The remainder are like a vajra. This is the *mudrā* of Dharaṇīṃdhara. His mantra is *NSB DHARAṆI-DHARA*[C] *SVĀHĀ* (NSB. Supporter of the earth! *Svāhā*!).'

66. 'The *mudrā* of Ratna-mudrā-hasta is a five-pointed vajra as before. His mantra is *NSB RATNA-NIRJĀTA SVĀHĀ* (NSB. Born of a jewel! *Svāhā*!).'

67. 'From that *mudrā*, your fingers should be laid out. This is the *mudrā* of Dṛḍhādhyāśaya. His mantra is *NSB VAJRA-SAṂBHAVA SVĀHĀ* (NSB. Vajra-arisen! *Svāhā*!).'

68. 'Make both hands likewise. This is the Sword *Mudrā* of Ākāśagarbha. His mantra is *NSB GAGANĀNTA-GOCARA SVĀHĀ* (NSB. You who have a limitless realm like space! *Svāhā*!).'

A T: *sattve vajrodbhava.*

B T: *karuṇodbhava.*

C T: *dhāraṇi-prāpta.*

69. 'The *mudrā* of Gagana-mati is the wheel *mudrā* as made before. His mantra is *NSB CAKRA-VARTI SVĀHĀ* (NSB. Wheel-turner! *Svāhā*!).'

70. 'The *mudrā* of Viśuddha-mati is the Conch *Mudrā* as made before. His mantra is *NSB DHARMA-SAṂBHAVA SVĀHĀ* (NSB Dharma-born! *Svāhā*!).'

71. 'The *mudrā* of Caritra-mati is the Lotus *Mudrā* as made before. His mantra is *NSB PADMĀLĀYA SVĀHĀ* (NSB Lotus Treasury! *Svāhā*!).'

72. 'The *mudrā* of Gaganāmala is the *Utpala Mudrā* as made before, but without being opened out. His mantra is *NSB JÑĀNODBHAVA SVĀHĀ* (NSB. Arisen from Awareness! *Svāhā*!).' (165b)

73. 'The *mudrā* of Sthira-buddhi is a vajra made as before. His mantra is *NSB VAJRA-KĀRA SVĀHĀ* (NSB. Vajra Action! *Svāhā*!).'

74. 'Likewise, join both of your hands together and insert both ring-fingers inside, and raise up both of your thumbs and little-fingers. Crook the forefingers at the sides of your middle-fingers, leaving the space of a grain of barley. This is the *mudrā* of Vajrapāṇi. His mantra is *NSV CAṆḌA-MAHĀ-ROṢAṆA HŪṂ* (NSV. Fierce most wrathful one! *Hūṃ*!).'

75. 'From that *mudrā*, insert both you thumbs and little-fingers inside. This is the *mudrā* of Māmakī. Her mantra is *NSV TRIṬ TRIṬ JAYANTI SVĀHĀ*. (NSV. *Triṭ triṭ*! Victorious One! *Svāhā*!)'

76. 'Likewise, place together the backs of both hands and interlace your fingers and twist them. Press the right thumb with the left thumb. This is the *mudrā* of Vajra-śṛṅkhalā. Her mantra is *NSV HŪṂ BANDHA BANDHA MOṬAYA MOṬAYA VAJRODBHAVE SARVATRĀPRATIHATE SVĀHĀ* (NSV. *Hūṃ*! Bind, bind! Pulverise, pulverise! Vajra-born-one! Invincible in all places! *Svāhā*!).'

77. 'From that vajra *mudrā*, slightly crook your thumbs and also point your forefingers forward. This is the *mudrā* of Vajra Candra-tilaka. His mantra is *NSV HRIḤ HŪṂ PHAṬ SVĀHĀ*.'

78. 'Likewise, make both your hands into fists and raise up both forefingers parallel. This is the *mudrā* of Vajra-sūcī. Her mantra is *NSV SARVA-DHARMA-NIRVEDHANI VAJRA-SŪCI VARADE SVĀHĀ* (NSV. Vajra-needle who penetrates all Dharmas! Bestower of favours! *Svāhā*!).'

79. 'Likewise, make both your hands into fists and place them at your heart. This is the *mudrā* of the Vajra Fist. Its mantra is *NSV SPHOṬAYA VAJRA-SAṂBHAVE SVĀHĀ* (NSV. Smash asunder! Vajra-born! *Svāhā*!).'

80. 'Make your left hand into a fist and raise the forefinger and point threateningly as though angry. This is the *mudrā* of Durdharṣa. (166a) His

mantra is *NSV DURDHARṢA-MAHĀ-ROṢAṆA KHĀDAYA SARVĀṂ TATHĀGATĀJÑĀṂ KURU SVĀHĀ* (NSV. O great wrathful one who is difficult to assail! Devour! Carry out the Tathāgata's commands! *Svāhā*!).'

81. 'Make your right hand into a fist, as though about to strike. This is the Hammer *Mudrā* of Abhimukha. His mantra is *NSV HE ABHIMUKHA-MAHĀ-PRACAṆḌA KHĀDAYA KIÑ CIRĀYASI SAMAYAM ANUSMARA SVĀHĀ* (NSV. *He*! O most fierce one who is close at hand! Devour! Why do you delay! Remember your vow! *Svāhā*!).'

82. 'Śākyamuni's begging bowl *mudrā* is made like the previous begging bowl. His mantra is *NSB SARVA-KLEŚA-NIṢŪDANA SARVA-DHARMA-VAŚITA-PRĀPTA GAGANA-SAMĀSAMA SVĀHĀ* (NSB. Destroyer of all emotional afflictions! You who have attained mastery of all phenomena! You who are unequalled like space! *Svāhā*!).'

83. 'The Ūrṇā *mudrā* is as before.'

84. 'Join all the fingers of your right hand together into a point and place them on top of your head. This is the *mudrā* of all the Uṣṇīṣas. Their mantra is *NSB VAṂ VAṂ HŪṂ HŪṂ*[A] *PHAṬ SVĀHĀ*.'

85. 'Make your left hand into a fist and extend both your forefinger and middle-finger, and place your thumb at the tips of the ring- and little-fingers. Insert the forefinger and the middle-finger of your right hand into the left palm. The thumb should be as before. This is the sword of Acala sheathed in its scabbard.'

86. 'The *mudrā* of Trailokya-vijaya is as before[B].'

87. 'Likewise, join both your hands together and insert both your ring-fingers and little-fingers inside. Raise up both your middle-fingers and crook your forefingers, and place them at the third joint of your middle-fingers. Both your thumbs should be like eyes. This is the *mudrā* of the Mother of the Buddhas and Bodhisattvas.'

88. 'Extend your left hand, face down, and make your right hand into a fist with the forefinger extended to support it like a parasol. This is the *mudrā* of Sitāta-patroṣṇīṣa. *LAṂ*. A sword, as before, is that of Jayoṣṇīṣa. *ŚAṂ*. A wheel, as before, is that of Vijayoṣṇīṣa. *SAṂ*. (166b) A hook, as before, is that of Vikiraṇoṣṇīṣa, making your right hand into a fist and leaving the forefinger crooked. *HRŪṂ*. An *uṣṇīṣa*, as before, is that of Tejorāśy-uṣṇīṣa. *TRIṂ*.'

A C repeats '*hūṃ*' three times.
B Added from C.

89. 'The *mudrā* of Mahodaya is said to be a vajra *mudrā*. *UṂ*. The *mudrā* of Abhyudgata is a fine lotus, as before. *TUṂ*. The [*mudrā* of] Ananta-svara-ghoṣa is described as a conch. *RUṂ*[A].'

90. 'Make your right hand into a fist and place it at your eyebrows. That is the Wish-fulfilling Gem, the *mudrā* of Ūrṇā.'

91. 'That of Locanā is the *uṣṇīṣa* as before, specially marked with a vajra.'

92. 'Place your right hand at your heart as though holding a lotus and extend your left hand as though giving a slap with the palm. This is the *mudrā* of Aparājita. His mantra is *DHIṂ DHIṂ RIṂ RIṂ JRIṂ JRIṂ*.'

93. 'Make both your hands into fists, raise up both your thumbs and then crook them. This is the *mudrā* of the mouth of Aparājitā. [Her mantra is] *APARĀJITE JAYANTI TAḌITE SVĀHĀ* (You who are undefeated by others! Victorious one! You who strike! *Svāhā*!).'

94. 'The right hand placed on your cheek is the *mudrā* of Īśvara. From that *mudrā*, hold your middle-and forefingers as though twisted. This is the *mudrā* of Saṃkusumita. From that same *mudrā*, insert your thumb inside. This is the *mudrā* of Prabhamālin. From that same *mudrā*, make your forefinger and little-finger as though holding a flower. This is the *mudrā* of Manobhava. Place your thumb on top of your right finger and extend the forefinger, the middle- and little-fingers, and place them at your ear. Do likewise with your left hand. This is the *mudrā* of Vighuṣṭa. Join both your hands together and placing together the tips of your thumbs, crook the tips of the other fingers. This is the jar *mudrā* of Pṛthivi[B].'

95. 'Likewise, make your right hand as though bestowing fearlessness and place your thumb inside. This is the *mudrā* for inviting Agni. From that same *mudrā*, make your hand as though bestowing fearlessness, (167a) and place your thumb at the second joint of the little-finger. This is general *mudrā* for the Ṛṣis. These should be made as appropriate in sequence.'

96. 'Likewise, join both hands together and insert both your forefingers and little-fingers inside. Gather the others together, holding them upwards. This is the *mudrā* of the club of Yama. Make your right hand like a bell facing downwards. This is the *mudrā* of the bell of the Lord of Death. Likewise, make your left hand into a fist, with the forefinger and middle-finger raised. This is the *mudrā* of Kālarātrī. From that same *mudrā*, raise up your middle-finger. This is a trident, the *mudrā* of Raudrī. From that same *mudrā*, make it as though holding a lotus. This is the *mudrā* of Brahmī. From

---

A C omits the *mudrā* of Mahodaya, and then reads (without seed-syllables): 如前蓮華印是發生佛頂印,如前商佉印是無量音聲佛頂印 '*a lotus* mudrā *as before is the* mudrā *of Abhyudgata Uṣṇīṣa, and a conch* mudrā *as before is the* mudrā *of Anantasvaraghoṣa Uṣṇīṣa*'.

B Text possibly defective at this point: T omits '*Pṛthivi*' and C omits '*jar*'.

that same *mudrā*, place together your forefinger to the back of the third joint of the middle-finger. This is the *mudrā* of Kaumārī's trident. From that same *mudrā*, place your forefinger at the tip of your thumb. This is the *mudrā* of Vaiṣṇavī's wheel. From that same *mudrā*, raise your thumb up. This is a hammer, the *mudrā* of Camuṇḍā. From that same *mudrā*, make your hands as though cupped. This is a skull, the *mudrā* of Kauverī. The *mudrā* of Nirṛti is a sword, as before. The *mudrā* of Viṣṇu is a wheel as before.'

97. 'Likewise, raise both of your hands from the left side and make a circle. This is the *mudrā* of the clouds of Nanda and Upananda. From that same *mudrā*, raise up three fingers. This is the *mudrā* of Śiva's trident. From that same *mudrā*, make those fingers straight. This is the earth of Umāpati. The *mudrā* of Candra is a lotus, as before, and it should be especially white. Extend both hands in parallel and crook both forefingers and ring-fingers at the sides of both hands. This is a carriage, the *mudrā* of Āditya. Place together the palms of your hands and make both the middle-fingers and the ring-fingers like a bow. This is the *mudrā* of Jayā and Vijayā. The *mudrā* of Vāyu is a banner *mudrā*, as before.' (167b)

98. 'Likewise, placing your left hand in the region of your navel, hold it with two fingers raised. The right hand should be near it, made as though playing a *vīṇā*. This is the *vīṇā mudrā* of Sarasvatī. The *mudrā* of the *Nāgas* is a noose, as before. The *mudrā* of the *Asuras* is like the *mudrā* of Sarasvatī, but with the forefingers crooked. Their mantra is *NSB GARALAYAṂ SVĀHĀ*. From that *mudrā* extend the ring-fingers. This is the *mudrā* of the *Gandharvas*. Their mantra is *NSB VIŚUDDHA-SVARA-VAHINI SVĀHĀ*. From this *mudrā*, crook your forefingers. This is the *mudrā* of the *Yakṣas*. Their mantra is *NSB YAKṢEŚVARA SVĀHĀ*. From that same *mudrā*, join the tips of your thumbs and little-fingers. This is the *mudrā* of the *Yakṣiṇīs*. Their mantra is *NSB YAKṢA-VIDYA-DHARI SVĀHĀ*. From that same *mudrā* extend the middle-fingers. This is the *mudrā* of the *Piśācas*. Their mantra is *NSB PIŚĀCA-GATI SVĀHĀ*. Hold those middle-fingers crooked. This is the *mudrā* of the *Piśācinīs*. Their mantra is *NSB PICI PICI SVĀHĀ*.'

99. 'Likewise, join together both your hands and raise up both thumbs and hold them there. This is the *mudrā* of all the Planets. Their mantra is *NSB GRAHEŚVARYA-PRĀPTA JYOTIR-MAYA SVĀHĀ* (NSB. You who have attained mastery of the planets! Light-formed! *Svāhā*!). From that same *mudrā* reverse and join both your middle-fingers and thumbs. This is the *mudrā* of the Constellations. Their mantra is *NSB NAKṢATRA NIRNĀDANIYE SVĀHĀ* (NSB. O constellations! Silent ones! *Svāhā*!). From that same *mudrā*, crook both of your ring-fingers and place them on your palms. This is the *mudrā* of the *Rākṣasas*. Their mantra is *NSB RĀKṢASĀDHIPATĀYE SVĀHĀ* (NSB. To the Lord of the *Rākṣasas*! *Svāhā*!). Place your right hand to your mouth and touch it with your tongue. This is the *mudrā* of the *Ḍākinīs*. Their mantra is *NSB HRĪ HAḤ*.'

100. 'Lord of the Secret Ones, *mudrās* such as these which emerge through the fervent inclination of the Tathāgatas are extensive *mudrās* that become (168a) the symbols of the Bodhisattvas. Furthermore, Lord of the Secret Ones, you should understand that whatever way the limbs [of the Tathāgatas] move are all vast *mudrās*. You should understand that however their tongues move, that is all revelation of mantras. Therefore, Lord of the Secret Ones, the Bodhisattvas who engage in the bodhisattva practice by means of mantras, should abide at the Tathāgata Level with their *manas* endowed with *bodhicitta*[A], and draw the Mandala. To do otherwise is to be deceitful[B] towards the Buddhas and Bodhisattvas, and Enlightenment also, and by departing from the *samaya*, one will certainly fall into the miserable states of existence.'

Regarding the teaching of the mantras and *mudrās*, there is the general teaching and the individual teaching. Of these, the individual teaching is also twofold: the actual teaching and that occurring elsewhere. The actual teaching refers to those named above. Those occurring elsewhere are '**mudrās** ***such as these***' which occur in other Tantras.

The general teaching is '***Furthermore, you should know that whatever limbs they move***' and so on. Furthermore, how should bodhisattvas abide? '***They should abide at the Tathāgata Level with their*** **manas** ***endowed with*** **bodhicitta,** ***and draw the Mandala***'. If the *mantrin* has a *bodhicitta*-endowed *manas* and abides at the Tathāgata Level, however he moves his limbs, that will be a *mudrā*, however he moves his tongue, that will be mantra practice. '***The*** **manas** ***endowed with*** **bodhicitta**' is the mind which is focussed upon emptiness. To '***abide on the Tathāgata Level***' is both absolute and relative. To abide on the Tathāgata Level relatively is to do the practice of the body-image of the deity. To do so absolutely is to become the deity which is emptiness in nature. This is actually saying that if you engage in the *mudrās* and mantras or draw the mandala, without *bodhicitta* and without doing the practice of the body-image of a deity which has either absolute or relative attributes, you will be shunned by the Buddhas and Bodhisattvas.

A C: 已發菩提心應當住如來地 '*when they have generated* bodhicitta, *they should abide on the Tathāgata Level*'.

B C: 同謗 '*is the same as insulting [the Buddhas]*'.

XII
THE DHARMA LETTER METHOD, THE ALL-PENETRATING GATE

1. Then the Bhagavat said to Vajrapāṇi, the Lord of the Secret Ones, 'Furthermore, Lord of the Secret Ones, listen to this Dharma discourse regarding the all-encompassing gates! Lord of the Secret Ones, Bodhisattvas should abide in *A*[A] and accomplish all that is necessary.'

(153a) Now the *samādhi* gates formed by the syllables and letters of the mantras expounded in the chapter on Mantras, and the thirty-two consonants *Ka* and so forth, together with the sixteen vowels *A* and so forth, will be taught. Of those, the thirty-two consonants *Ka* and so forth are not enunciated without the letter *A*, so it should be known that they also all have *A*[1].

'***The all-encompassing gates***' are the letters with *A*, the all-encompassing gates of entry to the mantra practice and all the *samādhis* and so forth. Therefore, the Bhagavat says '***Bodhisattvas should abide in A and accomplish all that is necessary***'.

2. ***NAMAḤ SAMANTA-BUDDHĀNĀṂ A***
NAMAḤ SAMANTA-BUDDHĀNĀṂ SA
NAMAḤ SAMANTA-VAJRĀNĀṂ VA
KA KHA GA GHA
CA CHA JA JHA
ṬA ṬHA ḌA ḌHA
TA THA DA DHA
PA PHA BA BHA
YA RA LA VA
ŚA ṢA SA HA
ṄA ÑA ṆA MA
NAMAḤ SAMANTA-BUDDHĀNĀṂ A
NAMAḤ SAMANTA-BUDDHĀNĀṂ SA
NAMAḤ SAMANTA-VAJRĀNĀṂ VA
KA KHA GA GHA
CA CHA JA JHA
ṬA ṬHA ḌA ḌHA
TA THA DA DHA
PA PHA BA BHA
YA RA LA VA
ŚA ṢA SA HA
ṄA ÑA ṆA NA
NAMAḤ SAMANTA-BUDDHĀNĀṂ AṂ
NAMAḤ SAMANTA-BUDDHĀNĀṂ SAṂ
NAMAḤ SAMANTA-VAJRĀNĀṂ VAṂ
KAṂ KHAṂ GAṂ GHAṂ
CAṂ CHAṂ JAṂ JHAṂ

[A] C: 此字門 '*in these letter gates*'.

ṬAṂ ṬHAṂ ḌAṂ ḌHAṂ
TAṂ THAṂ DAṂ DHAṂ
PAṂ PHAṂ BAṂ BHAṂ
YAṂ RAṂ LAṂ VAṂ
ŚAṂ ṢAṂ SAṂ HAṂ
ṄAṂ ÑAṂ ṆAṂ NAṂ
NAMAḤ SAMANTA-BUDDHĀNĀṂ AḤ
NAMAḤ SAMANTA-BUDDHĀNĀṂ SAḤ
NAMAḤ SAMANTA-VAJRĀNĀṂ VAḤ
KAḤ KHAḤ GAḤ GHAḤ
CAḤ CHAḤ JAḤ JHAḤ
ṬAḤ ṬHAḤ ḌAḤ ḌHAḤ
TAḤ THAḤ DAḤ DHAḤ
PAḤ PHAḤ BAḤ BHAḤ
YAḤ RAḤ LAḤ VAḤ
ŚAḤ ṢAḤ SAḤ HAḤ
ṄAḤ ÑAḤ ṆAḤ NAḤ
I Ī U Ū E AI O AU **(168b)**

First, the three letters *A*, *Sa* and *Va* are mentioned, denoting the Three Families. With regards the fact that the simple (*prakṛta*) letter[2] *A* is mentioned first, and then the thirty-two consonants *Ka* and so on, you should know that the consonants *Ka* and so forth are also simple in nature. They all reveal the intrinsic nature of Enlightenment. Then the long *A* letter is mentioned first, followed by the long *Ka* and so forth. You should know that all of these are the intrinsic nature of Practice. Then the letter *Aṃ*, followed by all the thirty-two consonants which include *Aṃ*. You should know that all of these are the intrinsic nature of Perfect Buddhahood. Then the letter *A* with a *visarga*, followed by all the consonants which also have *visargas*. You should know that all of these are the intrinsic nature of Nirvāṇa. The thirty-two consonants beginning with *Ka*, conjoined (*saṃyukta*) with the vowels *I* and so on, should be known to reveal by nature the gates of those *samādhis*. (153b) There *Ṛ Ṝ* and *Ḷ Ḹ* are not mentioned because you should know that *Ṛ* and *Ṝ* are included within the letters *Ra* and *I* and so on above, and *Ḷ* and *Ḹ* are included within the letters *La* and *I* and so on.

3. 'Thus, Lord of the Secret Ones, this is the Dharma discourse regarding skill in the letter method, the process of abiding in the mantra method, that which is transformed by the transforming power of all the Tathāgatas, the process of upholding the deity[A], the skill in the method of all full and perfect Buddhas and the dance of Bodhisattva practice. It was, is and will be expounded by the Buddhas of the past, present and future. Lord of the Secret Ones, I do not see anywhere in the vast Buddha field where the Tathāgatas do not expound this Dharma discourse regarding the all-encompassing gate.'

A C omits '*the process of upholding the deity*'.

This section expounds the praises of the letters which have been explained, and shows the perfection of their nature, the perfection of their action[A], the perfection of their transformational influence and the perfection of their power. With regards the perfection of their nature, the nature of the letters is shown with the words '***the Dharma discourse of skill in the letter method***'. The perfection of their action is shown with the words '***the process of abiding in the mantra method***'. The perfection of their transformational influence, which is the transformation by the Tathāgatas when you recite the letters as the sounds of the mantras, or cultivate *samādhi* or practise the body-image of the deity, and this is shown by the words '***that which is transformed by the transformational power of all Tathāgatas***'. The perfection of their power is shown with the words '***It was, is and will be expounded by the Buddhas of the past, present and future***'. They have great power because they are expounded by all the Buddhas[B].

There are four actions in the perfection of their transformational influence – the practice of the mantras, the practice[C] of the body-image of the deity, the practice of *samādhi* and behaviour. (154a) Of those, the practice of the mantras is the practice of the method of the mantra words through those letters, and is [shown] with the previous words '***the process of abiding in the mantra method***'. The practice of the body-image of the deity is the practice of the body-image of the deity through any one of the letters that is appropriate, and this is [shown] by the words '***the process of upholding the deity***'. The practice of *samādhi* is the practice of the *dharmakāya* which is emptiness in nature, through those letters, and this is [shown] by the words '***skill in the method of perfect Buddhas***'. Behaviour is what one does to accomplish the rites of Pacifying, Enriching and so forth, and the superior, medium and inferior attainments, which is [shown] by the words '***the dance of Bodhisattva practice***'[3].

4. 'Lord of the Secret Ones, if Bodhisattvas who are engaged in the Bodhisattva practice by means of mantras wish to know the mantra ritual, they should zealously apply themselves to this Dharma discourse, the all-encompassing gate. When *Ka, Ca, Ṭa, Ta, Pa* and so forth are conjoined with initials, medials and finals, they cause the attainment of Enlightenment, Practice, Perfect Buddhahood and Nirvāṇa, by entry into their *samādhi* groups. Hence it should be known that those [letters] associated with the first mode of expression and so on, in the mantra ritual, are formed together with initials, medials and finals. *Mantrins* should apply themselves with certainty to each one of the mantra syllables as they wish. If understood by the intelligent ones, they bestow the supreme excellent state.'

When Ka, Ca, Ṭa, Ta, Pa and so forth are conjoined with initials, medials and finals and so on: When Bodhisattvas use those thirty-two consonants beginning with *Ka* conjoined with the pair *A* and *Ā* initially, the pair *Aṃ* and *Aḥ* finally and *I* and so on medially, if they practice the *samādhis* associated with them, they will attain Enlightenment and so forth since the intrinsic nature of those [letters] reveals the gates of Enlightenment, Practice, Perfect Buddhahood and Nirvāṇa. ***Hence it should be known that those***

A B reads *lus* 'body' here, but it seems preferable to adopt *las* 'action' from V.
B Added from V.
C V: 'transformation [into]'(*bsgyur-ba*).

***[letters] associated with the first mode of expression and so on, in the mantra ritual, are formed together with initials, medials and finals*:** If they recite *Ka* and so on with the initial *A* and *Ā*, the final *Aṃ* and *Aḥ*, and the medial *I* and so on, not only will Enlightenment and so forth be attained, but they will also form the mantra syllables. (154b) **Mantrins *should apply themselves with certainty to each one of the mantra syllables as they wish. If understood by the intelligent ones, they bestow the supreme excellent state*:** This means that the wise one should use each one of the syllables in the primary mantra as he wishes, and he will definitely become enlightened and be given the supreme excellent state. That is, if the wise one uses any one letter he desires from among those letters while practising any *samādhi* he wishes or any tutelary deity in the manner mentioned above, it will bring about the accomplishment of whatever aim he has wished for.

5. 'Thus this is a single wheel of letters, a single continuum, which revolves like a wheel. If the *mantrin* knows that wheel of letters, he will always illumine [the world][A], like the Bhagavat Vairocana who turned the wheel.'

Thus this is a single wheel of letters, a single continuum* (*cakra*), *which revolves like a wheel*:** The letters beginning with *Ka*, which are the intrinsic nature of many kinds of *samādhi*, encircle the single letter *A*, like a wheel. ***If the* mantrin *knows that wheel of letters, he will always illumine [the world], like the Bhagavat Vairocana who turned the wheel*:** If he knows that wheel of letters mentioned above, he will become capable of engaging in all rites and practices, like the Bhagavat Vairocana. 'Illumine***'[4] should be known as a term for 'engaging in action'.

A C adds: 世間 '*the world*', adopted here.

XIII
THE SECRET MANDALA

The Vajra Adornments of the Inexhaustible Body, Speech and Mind of the Bhagavat Buddha were transformed into Mandalas. That Mandala which is the transformation of his Inexhaustible Body is the Mandala Arising from the Matrix of Great Compassion, the transformation of his Inexhaustible Speech is the Mandala of the Revolving Wheel of Letters, and these have both been explained already above. Now the Mandala of the Inexhaustible Mind, which is the transformation of the *dharmakāya*, will be explained.

In conjunction with this, the remaining rituals for the two Mandalas previously explained, (155a) the characteristics of the Master and the trainees, and the articles needed for the Mandalas, which have been lacking as they were not explained in detail, will also be explained here at length, together with the *homa* ritual and so forth.

The *dharmakāya* transcends revelation through perceptual forms and is without substantive reality (*abhāva*), so though it cannot be directly revealed [in itself], it may be revealed through what resembles its qualities (*guṇa*). The qualities of the *dharmakāya* are authentic unchanging consummacy, freedom from all conceptualizing, liberation from all emotional afflictions and the intrinsic ability to perform all activities. If it is to be revealed through what resembles these [qualities], then it may be revealed by transformation into the mandalas of earth, water, fire and wind. Earth is stable and unchangingly perfect by definition, like a vajra, so that [quality] is transformed into the earth (*mahendra*) vajra mandala and revealed. Since the nature of water is to purify everything by washing, the *dharmakāya*'s nature of freedom from all concepts (*vikalpa*) is transformed into the water mandala and revealed[1]. Its attribute of liberation from all emotional afflictions is transformed into the fire mandala and revealed, because the nature of fire is to burn, and through its letter [*Ra*] it is indicated that all phenomena are free from dust. The ability to perform all activities is transformed into the wind mandala and revealed, because wind goes everywhere and does everything as has already been explained.

1. Then the Bhagavat Vairocana (169a) gazed upon all realms of beings[A] with the Eye of the Tathāgata and entered into a *samādhi* endowed with the matrix of the array of the sameness of the Tathāgatas, the billowing forth of the treasury of the continuum of reality, in order to complete his vow to elevate all realms of beings without remainder by this very manifestation of the inexhaustible array of the continuum of reality, and the accomplishment of mantra practice.

In order to describe that Secret Mandala which is thus the transformation of the *dharmakāya* and also the complete ritual for all three Mandalas, the Bhagavat entered into a *samādhi*. Furthermore, what did he do before he entered it? (155b) The text says '***Then the Bhagavat Vairocana gazed upon all realms of beings with the Eye of the Tathāgata***'. This means that he gazed with the Eye of the Tathāgata.

Endowed with the matrix of the array of the sameness of the Tathāgatas, the billowing forth of the treasury of the continuum of reality. The '***continuum of reality***' is Suchness (*tathatā*).

A C reads 法界 '*continuum of reality*' for '*realms of beings*'.

The attributes of the Vajra Adornments of the Bhagavat's Inexhaustible Body and so on which arise from that are the '***array of the sameness of the Tathāgatas***'. Since they arise from that continuum of reality, that same continuum of reality is called a '***treasury***'. '***Billowing forth***' (√ *vistṛ*) is 'magical manifestation' (*vikurvita*), meaning that the Tathāgatas who arise from it act in many different guises. ***Sameness***: Because those Bodies of the Tathāgata that arise are similar from the viewpoint of their accumulations, *dharmakāyas* and benefitting of beings. '***Array***' is a term for 'a multitude'. '***Endowed with the matrix***' refers to that *samādhi* itself which is the source, because such [beings] arose when he entered into that *samādhi*.

Having entered into that *samādhi*, what did he reveal? The text says '***in order to complete his vow to elevate all realms of beings without remainder by this very manifestation of the inexhaustible array of the continuum of reality***'. The words '***continuum of reality***' in this case refer to the realms of beings[2]. The ***manifestation*** of what arises from it is explained below with the words '***the results of karmic action, life and recompense***' and so on. (156a) Although the Mandala Arising from Great Compassion and the Mandala of the Revolving Wheel of Letters have been revealed, the five types of *samaya* and so forth will be deficient if the Secret Mandala is not revealed. For if the remainder of the rituals for the previous Mandalas which should be completely described are not taught in conjunction with it, the mantra practice will be incomplete and so the *samaya* will also be incomplete. Therefore, if they are all completely taught, his vow to elevate all realms of beings without remainder will be fulfilled.

2. No sooner had the Bhagavat entered it, than at that very moment there emerged from all his pores, which are gates that bring about the deliverance of the realms of beings, Bodies generated by the Dharma-dhātu with the form, colour, shape, voice, movement, behaviour and diction of the recipients and inflicters of karmic action, rebirth and the matured results, who satisfy all beings individually as they desire.

As soon as the Bhagavat entered that *samādhi*, Bodies of Tathāgatas resembling all [types of] beings, who appear as the recipients (*bhojaka*) and inflicters (*bhojayitṛ*) of karmic action, rebirth and matured results, emerged from all the pores of his Body. To appear as the recipient of karmic action, rebirth and matured results is to appear as each recipient of the happy and miserable results of any particular good or evil action that has been done. Inflicters are those like the king or guardians of the hell beings. By their power, others are made to experience happiness or misery. Their distinctive attributes (*viśeṣa*) are indicated with the words '***form, colour***' and so on, (156b) and these relate to the emergence of the Bodies who preach the Dharma, in accordance with the form, colour, wishes and so on of beings. Therefore, it is said that '***they satisfy all beings individually***'.

The gates that bring about the deliverance of all realms of beings without remainder: Because the pores of the Tathāgata's Body are the gates from which there emerge the Bodies that appear as those who experience karmic action, rebirth and matured results and also as those who cause them to be experienced, and as those who bring about the deliverance of all realms of beings without remainder.

3. After they had emerged, there sounded forth these verses in the vast expanse of worlds equivalent to space, by which Tathāgatas are produced, and which were proclaimed throughout the continuum of reality with one single sound[3]:

The uttering of the verses which appear below: because they all sounded forth as words, they were heard and understood in all realms of beings. Here '***continuum of reality***' should be understood as the realms of beings. Those verses which were thus proclaimed are the words which he reveals, having focussed his attention upon the continuum of reality. If you have understood and repeatedly practised the teaching of these verses, you will become a Tathāgata. Therefore they are the '***verses by which Tathāgatas are produced***'.

4. 'Everything there is emerges from
the intrinsic nature of phenomena:
the Protector Buddhas,
Śrāvakas and Pratyekabuddhas,
the heroic Bodhisattvas,
and likewise the excellent Jinas,
beings and the receptacle world,
emerge in a conventional sequence,
and the phenomena which arise and abide
are continually generated from that.
You should cultivate this Path,
which is taught by the Perfect Buddhas,
with insight and expedient means,
free from hesitation[A] and doubt.'

These are the verses which were mentioned earlier. They enumerate what emerges from that intrinsic nature, beginning with the Buddhas and Śrāvakas. In brief, all the Buddhas, Śrāvakas, Bodhisattvas, Perfect Buddhas, the realms of sentient beings, receptacle worlds (157a) and the phenomena which arise and are present, emerge from the intrinsic nature of phenomena, that is, from the continuum of reality, Suchness. Since they constantly arise, thus endowed with insight and expedient means, you should always cultivate this Path. That is what has been taught by the Perfect Buddhas.

'***In a conventional sequence***' refers to the relative level. In brief you should know the intrinsic nature of the continuum of reality, the emergence of the *nirmāṇa-kāyas* and so on from the Tathāgata's Body by its power, and the path by which it will be reached from Śrāvakahood, Pratyekabuddhahood and so on up to Buddhahood, having focussed your attention upon it. Thus after the Bhagavat had entered that *samādhi* both the mundane and the supramundane Dharma was revealed. The mundane Dharma is the experiencer and those who cause the experience of karmic action, rebirth and matured results. The supramundane is this verse itself.

A C: 無慧 '*ignorance*'.

5. Then having completely filled the entire continuum of reality with those Tathāgata Bodies generated by the continuum of reality, with a cloud of emanations which make known (169b) his Body, the Bhagavat Vairocana by the power of his mind alone, manifested Buddhas who emerged from all the pores of his body in succession[4] and they each entered their respective places in the continuum of reality[A].

Those Bodies generated by the continuum of reality, which emerged from all the Bhagavat's pores, filled all realms of beings with many *nirmāṇa-kāyas,* just by the power of the Bhagavat Vairocana's Mind. These *nirmāṇa-kāyas* made known his Body, were Buddha embodiments which became enlightened, turned the Wheel of the Dharma and so forth. Then, by the power of his Mind alone, (157b) they [re-]entered into their respective places in the continuum of reality. ***Just by the power of his Mind*:** The Bhagavat Vairocana is viewed as the accomplishing practitioner (*sādhaka*) and the *nirmāṇa-kāyas* which arise are viewed as the deities who are to be accomplished (*sādhya*). ***The Tathāgata Bodies generated by the continuum of reality*:** The *nirmāṇa-kāyas* of the Bhagavat Vairocana emerged through the transformational power of the continuum of reality. This also indicates to beings in the future who are to be guided, that they should make themselves appear in the body-image of their own deity by just the power of their minds as practitioners and the transformational power of the continuum of reality. ***They each re-entered their respective places in the continuum of reality*:** This does not refer to their re-entering into those pores, but it means that they became invisible in the continuum of reality which is emptiness in nature, at the same places from whence they had emerged.

6. Then the Bhagavat said to the Bodhisattva Vajrapāṇi, 'Lord of the Secret Ones, there is a secret mandala to be laid out, which is imagined as the assembly of the abodes of the deities, which are marked with their seed-syllables, so listen carefully and remember it, for I shall now explain it to you!'

Having then shown that the Bodies of the Tathāgatas which the Bhagavat produced from his own Body pervaded all the realms of beings and then became invisible again, the text next says '***Then the Bhagavat said to the Bodhisattva Vajrapāṇi***' and so on, and goes on to explain the Secret Mandala, the transformation of the Vajra of the Inexhaustible Mind and the remaining rituals for the three Mandalas.

Secret*:** It is not the nature of this Mandala to actually reveal the intrinsic nature of his Mind[B], the *dharmakāya,* because it is [only] the transformation of the *dharmakāya,* the intrinsic nature of his Mind, but since it is subtle, it is 'secret***'. Secondly, since the intrinsic nature of his Body and Speech have also been changed into the form of symbols (*mudrā*), it also refers indirectly to his Body and Speech. ***The abodes of the deities*:** Because those mandalas of earth and so on (158a) are the transformed abodes of the deities. ***Marked with the seed syllables*:** The mandalas of earth and so on are marked with their respective seed syllables, *A, Va* and so forth.

A C: 法界宫 '*the palace of the continuum of reality*'.

B B has *yid* (*manas*), but *sems* (*citta*) 'mind' seems more appropriate here.

7. When the Bhagavat had said that, Vajrapāṇi, the Lord of the Secret Ones, listened and the Bhagavat spoke the following to him.:

'First the *mantrin* should arrange
those mandalas in his own body:
from his feet up to his navel
he should imagine that of earth[A];
from above that to his heart
he should resolutely imagine that of water;
above that of water is that of fire,
and above that of fire is that of wind.
When he has imagined them [thus],
the wise one should establish
the representation upon the ground.'

Prior to spreading the pigments, the *mantrin* establishes himself in the yoga-posture as previously explained and establishes in due order the mandalas of earth and so forth in his body. ***Above that of water is that of fire***: Though it is clear that the fire [mandala] should be imagined from the heart upwards, the text does not clearly state from where the wind mandala starts, but since it has been stated [elsewhere] that the letter *Raṃ* should be imagined from the heart to the eyebrows, you should know that the portion above the eyebrows is to imagined as the wind mandala.

8. Then Vajrapāṇi entered[B] into the Level of the Bhagavat Vairocana's Body, Speech and Mind and perceived the sameness of all phenomena, and thinking of future beings, he uttered this *Vidyā* King which severs all doubts: *NSB ASAMĀPTA-DHARMADHĀTU-GATIṂ-GATĀNĀṂ SARVATHĀ AṂ KHAṂ AṂ AḤ SAṂ SAḤ HAṂ HAḤ RAṂ RAḤ VAṂ VAḤ SVĀHĀ HŪṂ RAṂ RAḤ HRA HAḤ SVĀHĀ RAṂ RAḤ SVĀHĀ*. (Salutations to all the Buddhas, to those who have gone beyond the inexhaustible continuum of reality, in all places! *Aṃ khaṃ aṃ aḥ saṃ saḥ haṃ haḥ raṃ raḥ vaṃ vaḥ svāhā! Hūṃ raṃ raḥ hra haḥ svāhā! Raṃ raḥ svāhā!*)

Then Vajrapāṇi entered in the Vajra Adornments of the Inexhaustible Body, Speech and Mind of the Bhagavat. ***And perceived the sameness of all phenomena***: This refers both to the sameness of all phenomena in their being empty in nature on the absolute level and to the sameness of the Body, Speech and Mind of the Bhagavat and the number of realms of beings on the relative level. ***Thinking of future beings***: (158b) He uttered this *Vidyā* King [which severs all doubts] for the sake of future beings. So in future times, the *mantrin* should attend to this Mantra King before drawing the Mandala, in order to request this Mandala, to comprehend the meaning (*artha*) of the mantra and to be protected by it.

9. As soon as Vajrapāṇi, the Lord of the Secret Ones, uttered this *Vidyā* King, all the Tathāgatas who reside in the world systems of the ten directions extended their right hands and placed them upon Vajrapāṇi's head and

A C: 大金剛輪 '*a great vajra disc*'.
B C: 昇 '*ascended to*'.

saying 'Excellent!', they spoke these words, 'O Nobly-born One! It is excellent, (170a) this Mantra King which you uttered after you entered[A] into the Level of the Bhagavat Vairocana's Body, Speech and Mind, out of a desire to illumine all places[B] for the Bodhisattvas who dwell in the sameness of the mantra method. Why is that? Because the Bhagavat Vairocana, Tathāgata Arhat Samyak-saṃbuddha, sat in the core of Enlightenment and contemplated the continuum of reality with these twelve syllables: he subdued the Four Māras and then these [syllables] which emerged from the continuum of reality flowed out from the three places of his Body and destroyed the hostile demons. Then the Bhagavat attained the sameness of Body, Speech and Mind, and his Body became measureless because space is measureless, and likewise his Speech and Mind also became measureless. Because he was thus endowed with measureless Awareness and had attained mastery of all phenomena, he expounded the Dharma, beginning with that twelve-syllabled Mantra King.

'Nobly-born One! Since you have also comprehended the sameness of the Bhagavat's Body, Speech and Mind, you appear[C] as a perfect Buddha.

'You should ask the Bhagavat Vairocana,
the All-knowing, perfect Buddha,
about the excellent mantra practice words[D],
and he will tell you in detail of the ritual.
In the past, we also realized
supreme Enlightenment with them
and expounded the unequalled[E] Dharma
which leads to Nirvāṇa,
and they are directly experienced
by all the perfect Buddhas
who dwell in the world systems.'

This section relates the praises [by the Tathāgatas] of this Mantra King which Vajrapāṇi uttered.

10. Then the glorious Vajrapāṇi
became most joyful in thought,
and being empowered by the perfect Buddhas
he spoke the following verses:
'These phenomena are without attributes[F],
without inherent reality, unlocalized,
liberated from karmic action and rebirth,

A C: 超昇 '*leapt up to*'.
B T adds '*the mantra method*' here, but I have deleted it on basis of C which puts it later.
C C: 衆所知識 '[*you*] *will be known by people as* ...'.
D C omits '*words*' (*pada*).
E C: 一切法 '*all phenomena*' (*sarva-dharmāḥ*), not '*unequalled phenomena*' (*asama-dharmāḥ*) as T.
F C: 是法無有盡 '*this Dharma is inexhaustible*'.

and are said to resemble ideas[A]. (170b)
After being encouraged by the expedient means
of the Protectors, Masters of Compassion,
I have understood this nature of phenomena[B]!'

Vajrapāṇi recounts to the Bhagavat the meaning of the instruction given by the Bhagavat earlier, '***you should cultivate this Path***' and so forth, according to his understanding of it. Moreover to show that his understanding was gained by the Bhagavat's empowerment, the text says '***Then the glorious Vajrapāṇi***' and so forth.

These phenomena are without attributes: Since such phenomena as the psycho-physical constituents, the perceptual elements and sources, lack self-existence, they are without attributes. ***Without inherent reality***: They lack any inherent existence of a self and what belongs to a self. ***Unlocalized***: (159a) Everything which the non-Buddhists (*tīrthikas*) imagine as abiding with parts does not exist. ***Liberated from karmic action and rebirth***: There is no inherent existence of causes and results for phenomena. Since there is no inherent existence of causes and results, there is also no karmic action and rebirth, and this should be linked to the words '***without attributes***' and so forth. ***Said to resemble ideas only***: All phenomena lack any objective reality, but are just ideas (*saṃjñā*). ***Having been encouraged*** and so forth: Vajrapāṇi says that he understands the nature of phenomena (*dharma-lakṣaṇa*) to be thus, having been empowered by way of the expedient means of the Bhagavat's Great Compassion.

11. Then, when Vajrapāṇi, the Lord of the Secret Ones, had spoken these verses, out of consideration for future beings, he asked the Bhagavat Vairocana [these questions] to remove confusion about this great Mandala arising from the matrix of Great Compassion:

'For the sake of all beings,
O All-knowing One, free from malady,
Guide who removes all doubts,
may you tell us about what I ask!
What should be done
in preparation for the Mandala?
Great Sage, please explain the types
of Master and trainees.
What sort of site should be sought out?
How should it be selected?
How should the site be purified?
How should it be made firm?
Would the Guide also speak of the tasks
that should be done to purify the trainees?

A Each version interprets this differently. T and V: *rdzogs-pa'i sangs-rgyas*, Skt. *saṃbuddha* 'Perfect Buddha'; B: *'du-shes*, Skt. *saṃjñā*; C: 正遍知, Skt. *saṃjñā* 'Perfect Awareness'. In view of C and Buddhaguhya's comments, we may assume an original *saṃjñā* in the sense of 'idea'.

B C: 諸救世方便 隨於悲願轉 開悟無生智 諸法如是相 '*after the expedient means of the Protectors had been transformed into compassionate aspirations, I came to understand* [*through*] *the unborn Awareness that the attributes of all phenomena are thus*'.

What are the signs of purity like[A]
and how are they to be protected[B]?
How should the site be transformed?
How should one first ascertain it there[C]?
What types of cords are to be sought
for marking out the sections of the site[D]?
How many types of offerings should one seek out?
Would the Guide tell us
what sort of flowers and incense [to use],
and how to offer the flowers, incense and so forth?
How should we perform such acts as
the food offerings and Homa rites?
Tell us with what and where
the seats of the deities should be made!
Would the Protector tell us in sequence
their colour, shapes and forms?
Please also explain the *mudrās* of the deities,
and the size of their seats!
From whence do the *mudrās* come?
Why are they called *mudrās*?
How many types of Initiation are there?
How many types of *samaya*-holders are there?
How does the *mantrin* who exerts himself
in the practice of mantras
become a Bodhisattva, an All-knowing One[E]?
How will he see truth[F]?
How many types of attainment are there?
When will they be accomplished?
When they are achieved, how will he walk in the sky,
or become invisible? (171a)
Lord, how will he attain a divine body,
without abandoning this one?
From where do various emanations arise?
How is he to avoid the arising
of all the bad omens
of the sun, moon, fire, directions,
planets, stars and constellations,
seconds and minutes, and also
old age, death or frailty?

A C: 云何已淨相 '*What are the signs that they have been purified?*'
B C: 以何而作護 '*With what is the protection to be done?*'
C C: 事業誰爲初 '*Which activities should be done first?*'
D C: 修多羅有幾 云何作地分 '*How many types of cords are there? How should the site be divided up?*'
E C: 眞言者幾時 勤修眞言行 當具菩薩道'*How long does it take for a* mantrin *who exerts himself to get the Bodhisattva path?*'.
F C: 云何見眞諦 '*How long does it take until he sees the truth?*'.

How is the *mantrin* to avoid separation
from the Lord of Men, the Buddha?
How should he satisfy
the fire and rites of Homa[A]?
Would the Guide also speak of
the individual natures[5] of the deities?
And the scale and number of results
of the mundane mantras,
likewise the supramundane ones?
And the special features of the *samādhis*?
Where will karmic actions mature
and how will they not mature?
When will the *mantrin* be liberated
from karmic action and rebirth?'

This section deals with questions about the drawing of the Secret Mandala and the remainder of the rituals for all three Mandalas. You should know that apart from the *samādhi* of the Master and the rituals of initiation, all these other rituals are the same [for each Mandala]. ***To remove confusion about this great Mandala which arises from the matrix of Great Compassion*:** Because all three Mandalas arise from Great Compassion, the Secret Mandala is also said to arise from the matrix of Great Compassion. ***The removal of confusion*:** If the topics mentioned below are not explained, the rituals will be incomplete, so future beings will be confused. (159b) Since the topics of the questions will be dealt with in detail by the answers below, they should be linked up with them.

12. **Then the All-knowing Perfect Buddha,**
the Bhagavat who is free from malady,
said this to Vajrapāṇi:
'Great Hero! What you have asked about
is most fortunate and excellent!
Most powerful Vajrapāṇi!
I shall explain to you in brief
the layout of the Secret Mandala
which arises from the root of Great Compassion,
the defining of the deities,
and the most excellent states[B] of the Mahāyāna
that are the great secret of the Perfect Buddhas!'

Now the Bhagavat will give Vajrapāṇi the answers to his forty questions in the following sections. Also the questions asked by Vajrapāṇi are grouped here into three general categories by the Bhagavat. i) ***The defining of the deities*:** This summarizes the questions about the specific qualities (*viśeṣa*) of the mundane and

---

A C: 幾種護摩火 幾事而增威 '*How many types of Homa rites are there? What things should be done to satisfy them?*'.

B C: 生 '*arising*', CC: 根源 or 根本 '*source, origin*'. Probably both T and C had *udaya* in their texts but have interpreted it differently. C reads '*the source of the Mahāyāna*'.

supramundane deities, their colours and so on and the abodes of those deities which are conceived to be the mandalas of earth and so forth. ii) With '***the most excellent states of the Mahāyāna***', he summarizes the questions '***How does the* mantrin *become a Bodhisattva and an All-knowing One? How will he see truth?***'. Since those conditions are the states which cleave to Enlightenment, they are '***the most excellent states of the Mahāyāna***', for although there are others which are conditions of the Mahāyāna, they are subsidiary and these are the main ones. iii) All the other questions apart from these two, such as those concerning the attributes of the Master, the spreading of the pigments and so forth should be understood as being included in '***the layout of the Secret Mandala***'. In this case, the term '***secret***' is used with regards to the Mandala because the topics of the questions about the general rituals of the Three Mandalas are not taught to those without the *samaya*. The remainder is as mentioned above. (160a)

Most fortunate (*mahodaya*): All these questions are simply causes for supreme Enlightenment, so the topics of these questions are termed 'the cause of great fortune'. ***Which arises from the root of Great Compassion***: Since those Mandalas arise from Great Compassion, even the matters about its materials and so on are said to arise from the root of Great Compassion. ***The great secret*** (*atiguhya*) ***of the Perfect Buddhas***: Because those excellent states of the Mahāyāna and so on are not explained to unsuitable beings, they are a ***great secret***.

13. **'Listen attentively to what should be done**
beforehand for the Mandala!
The most powerful *Vidyā* King
formed from the syllables of its twelve components
should be recited in due sequence,
abiding in your own *samādhi*.
Then knowing the appropriate method,
you should perform each action as wished.'

In the *Guhya Tantra*[6] it states that prior to drawing a mandala, the Master should attend for a while to the mantras which bring about such effects as the protection of himself and the trainees, and then apply himself to each of the actions. Therefore, prior to drawing the Mandala, the *Vidyā* King should be recited and if you recite it until signs appear, you will be able to attend to everything. Also these signs should be linked up with the words '***Then the* mantrin *will see a dream, either of renowned Bodhisattvas, or of Buddhas and the Blessed Ones, who exhort him to undertake the task of drawing the Mandala***'[7] and so forth.

Formed from the syllables of its twelve components: This refers to the twelve component letters which form the syllables of the Mantra, and secondly it refers to its nature on the absolute level (*paramārtha-lakṣaṇa*) which is realized through the twelve letters. The '***components***' are the letters. The '***syllables***' (*pada*) are what one is to comprehend. ***The most powerful Vidyā King***: It is most powerful because on the absolute level it reveals the intrinsic emptiness [of phenomena], and on the relative level it creates emanations and so on. ***Should be recited in due sequence***: This means that the root, the essence, (160b) and subsidiary essences[8] should be recited in sequence. ***Abiding in your own* samādhi**: The Master should recite it abiding in his own *samādhi*, that is, abiding in a *samādhi* in which he either places the essences of the Three Families in the three places, or lays out the essences of the Great Hero in the five places, or allocates the letters in all members [of his body]. ***Then knowing the appropriate method, you should perform each action as wished***: When you have done the preliminary service by that process, you should practise the Mantra in the appropriate way, to protect yourself, the place and the trainees. You should know that this *Vidyā* King which you must attend to beforehand, should be used with all three Mandalas.

14. 'There are two types of Masters
who comprehend the mantras and *mudrās*;
you should know their attributes through
the categories of profound and not-profound.
[The first] should know the Profound and Extensive,
and does not have recourse to beings[A],
he is a beloved child of the Buddhas,
and he has abandoned the present world. (171b)
The second type is intoxicated
by the present world and relies on supports.
He is given permission and empowerment
by the Best of Men, the Buddhas,
in order to draw all mundane mandalas[B].'

This describe the attributes and qualities of Masters. It also describes the general attributes and special qualities. The general attributes have already been described with the words '***he should have his mind fixed upon* bodhicitta**' and '***know the differences between the Three Ways***' and so forth. Here the special qualities of those who have devoted interest in the Profound and Extensive and of those who rely upon cognitive objects are explained, so the text says '***you should know their attributes through the categories of profound and not-profound***'.

[The first] should know the Profound and Extensive and so forth: These are the qualities of the Master who has devoted interest in the Profound and Extensive. The '***Profound***' means that the mental stream of one who has devoted interest in emptiness, in that which is without cognitive objects, cannot be comprehended and is difficult to measure. The '***Extensive***' is the realization that all phenomena are empty, (161a) like the nature of space on the absolute level, and the engagement in vast offerings, knowing that they are like illusions and mirages on the relative level. ***He pays no heed to [other] beings***: Since his behaviour is incompatible with that of [ordinary] beings, they do not heed each other. ***He is a beloved child of the Buddhas***: Because he conforms to the behavioural activities of Buddhas. In the ordinary world, one who acts in harmony with the behavioural activities of his elders is called a

A C: 可傳者方授 '*and he bestows [it] upon those who can receive*'. This is another case where the base text for C probably had '*deya*', while T read '*dehin*'. T has additionally read an negative where C has none.

B C: 第二求現法 深著癡攀緣 世間曼荼羅 一切爲斯作 '*The second type is interested in the present world and is deeply attached to foolish supports. All the mundane mandalas were created for him*'.

'beloved child'. ***He has abandoned the present world*** (*dṛṣṭa-dharma*): He is not attached to the worldly, relative phenomena.

The second type is intoxicated by the present world and so on: The qualities of the Master who relies upon cognitive objects. Although they have interest in the intrinsic emptiness [of phenomena] by the insight derived from hearing and pondering on the mantra tantras and so on, they are unable to cultivate it with the insight derived from meditation. Therefore they are empowered and permitted by the Bhagavat [only] to draw the mundane mandalas with pigments and so forth. The '***mundane mandalas***' are so called because when they have been drawn with pigments and so forth and they are accessible to the sight of mundane people. This does not refer to the mandalas of the non-Buddhists (*tīrthika*). Therefore, the Masters who rely upon cognitive objects are empowered to draw the mandalas with pigments and so forth, but they are not empowered to mentally depict the mandalas, because their minds are not capable of it. The Master who has devoted interest in the Profound and the Extensive is empowered to draw both the outer and the inner mandalas. He is empowered to depict the inner mandala because his mind is capable of it and he is unattached to external modes of behaviour, (161b) but he also draws external mandalas in order to make contact with the minds of the trainees.

15. **'There are four types of trainees[A]**
to be known through the categories
of their readiness or otherwise:
those to be accomplished on a single occasion,
those to be accomplished on two,
and those who are neither of those,
but he who has all attributes perfected
is the trainee dearest to the Jinas.'

This explains the qualities of the trainees. ***Through the categories of their readiness or otherwise***: Of the four types of trainees, there are some trainees who have heard and understood the mantra tantras and so forth and who have also cultivated *bodhicitta*. They should be initiated for the *sādhana* on the actual occasion of being introduced into the Mandala and if they have the attributes of the Master who relies upon cognitive objects in the initiation for the *sādhana*, they should be initiated as Masters at that time, even if they do not have *bodhicitta*. Of them, the text says '***those who will be accomplished on that single occasion***'. The others are not suitable to be initiated for the *sādhana* if they have not cultivated *bodhicitta*, even though they have heard and know the mantra tantras and so forth, but they should be taught the technique of cultivating *bodhicitta* after they have been introduced into the Mandala. Those who should be initiated for the *sādhana* when they have repeatedly cultivated *bodhicitta* are those who will be accomplished on the second occasion. Thus, even though they desire to be initiated as Masters, they should be made to study completely the mantra tantras and so on, if they do not know them, before being initiated as Masters. When they do have the attributes of a Master, they may be initiated as such.

A C: 諸佛二足尊 灌頂傳教者 '*Concerning those who are to be given instructions in the mandalas, the Buddhas, Best of Men.* [*say that there are four* ...]'.

They will also be accomplished on the second occasion. Of these, there are some who do not previously know the mantra tantras and have not even cultivated *bodhicitta*, nor subsequently do they study or cultivate them. After having merely been received into the Mandala, they are not to be initiated even on a second occasion as Masters or for the *sādhana*. They are '***those who are neither of those***'. ***But he who has all attributes perfected is the trainee dearest to the Jinas*:** (162a) The one who both knows perfectly the tantras and so on, has cultivated *bodhicitta* correctly and who has entered the Mandala to augment his merit, is also included in the number of trainees. Since such a person has already been initiated and so on, it is not necessary for him to be initiated for the first time here, and he is said to have '***all attributes perfected***'.

16. **'First you should know the site**
which is specified as the mind,
and it should be purified as taught before:
by that you should completely purify it.
When it is devoid of faults,
there will be nothing
to fear in the mental site,
and then it will be truly[A] **pure,**
and devoid of all impediments,
appearing as perfect Enlightenment,
so it is said to be stable.'

This describes the purification of the site. Of the two types of site, the external and the internal, the purification of the external has already been explained, so here it is the purification of the internal site which will be explained. ***It should be purified as taught before***: The impurities of mind are purified because the *samādhi* is pure, devoid of all perceptual images and free from all conceptualizing, in the manner that has previously been described with the words '**bodhicitta** ***is to know your mind as it really is***' and '***Even though you search, you will not find it in any percepts, colours, shapes***' and so forth. When it has thus been purified, you should draw either the external or the internal Mandala. ***By that you should completely purify it***: You should purify the mental site by that purification of mind which was previously mentioned. ***When it is free from impediments, there will be nothing to fear in the mental site***: If it is free from concepts and the emotional afflictions such as attachment, just as the external site is without such defects as bits of bone, stones and so forth, there will be no opportunity for obstructors and so on [to interfere], so the text says that there will be nothing to fear. Therefore it is said '***And then it will be pure and devoid of faults,*** (162b) ***appearing as perfect Enlightenment, so it is said to be stable***'.

17. **'If you act in any other way,**
you will be unable to purify the site.
Any *mantrin* who [tries] to carry out
the purification of the site,

A T omits '*truly*'.

abiding in conceptual thought,
while lacking in *bodhicitta*,
will not be able to purify it[A].
Hence you should abandon thoughts
and then purify the whole of the site.'

If you do the purification while dwelling in conceptual thought without *bodhicitta*, even when purifying the external site, it will be ineffectual. ***If you should act in any other way, you will be unable to purify the site*:** That is, in any way other than the way in which the internal site is purified, and this refers to the external site. ***Abiding in conceptual thought*:** Thinking that there are [really] such phenomena as the psycho-physical constituents and the perceptual elements and sources, that is, if the Master purifies the site thinking that there actually is something to be purified and that there really are such defects as bits of bone and so forth, it will not become pure because he lacks *bodhicitta*. Therefore the text says '***Hence you should abandon thoughts and then purify the whole of the site***'.

18. 'Of those mandala rituals
I have taught in detail,
these which I prescribe as preliminary
are not understood by the stupid.
Concepts are the cause of suffering,
and as long as they are not abandoned
you will not be enlightened in this world,
nor will you be called All-knowing[B].'

These are not understood by the stupid, because with regards to the prior cultivation of *bodhicitta*, the text specifies among the attributes of Masters, '***he should be ever wise in the methods of the Perfection of Insight and know the differences between the Three Ways***' and so forth. Therefore to be wise in the methods of the Perfection of Insight is clearly to be skilled in the intrinsic emptiness [of phenomena], so you should understand that *bodhicitta* should be cultivated beforehand. One also becomes skilled in emptiness by knowing the differences between the Three Ways, through being skilled in their specific qualities regarding the absence of autonomous existence to the individual and phenomena. The Master who has such attributes and who has performed all these activities which should be done for the Mandala, does not abide in conceptual thought at all but has *bodhicitta* when he purifies the site. So the Bhagavat's intention when describing in full the purification of external sites is to accommodate the minds of ordinary people, but '***the stupid do not understand them***'. These activities will not act as a cause for Buddhahoood and All-knowing in whoever has not abandoned such concepts (163a), therefore the text says, '***Concepts are the cause of suffering and as long as they are not abandoned you will not be enlightened in this world nor will you be called All-knowing***'.

A C: 非淨以離菩提心 '*will not purify it since he is lacking in* bodhicitta'.
B C: 非名世間覺 亦非一切智 乃至不能捨 分別諸苦因 '*They will not be called learned in the mundane sense and they will not [be called] All-knowing, nor will they even be able to abandon concepts that are the cause of all suffering*'.

19. 'The trainees should diligently be made pure with *bodhicitta*.'

This deals with the purification of the trainees. With regards to the two types of purification, aspiration *bodhicitta* and application *bodhicitta*[9], they will have been made pure if they have previously cultivated the application *bodhicitta*; so subsequently at the time of entry into the Mandala, the aspiration *bodhicitta* should be given and they will be purified by both of them. If the application *bodhicitta* has not been cultivated previously, then the aspiration *bodhicitta* should be given at the time of entry into the Mandala and then the cultivation of the application *bodhicitta* should be started. That is the purification of the trainees with *bodhicitta*.

20. 'The protection should be done with the Lord Acala or Trailokya-vijaya.'

This deals with the protection of the trainees. All the trainees who are to be protected when they first come inside and when they are being consecrated (*adhivāsana*), should be protected by either one of these two [mantras].

21. 'When a trainee is not swayed at all
by any objects of perception,
he will then be without impurities,
like space and become utterly pure[A].'

This deals with the attributes of the pure trainee. When he abides in yoga, the *samādhi* of that trainee will also be pure, devoid of conceptual thought and free from percepts. If he is unmoved by the perception of either the wholesome or the unwholesome, and if he is also unmoved by the perception of any object towards which he might become attached and so on, though he engages in the wholesome activities of worship and so on, even after he has arisen from the yoga, he is said to be characterized as pure. ***Then he will be without impurities, like space***: Just as space is pellucid by nature, as it is not constrained by anything, (163b) and does not degenerate from its intrinsic purity even when obscured by adventitious clouds and so on, in the same way when he abides in *samādhi*, he is free from the impurities of both the wholesome and the unwholesome. When he arises from *samādhi*, he is mindful of the intrinsic illusoriness and so forth [of phenomena], even though he performs the activities of worship and so forth, because he is unsullied by the impurity of imagining that such phenomena really exist.

22. 'The first transformation of the site
is said to be done by the Perfect Buddhas,
and the second by virtue of your mind;
here it should be done in no other way.'

A C: 當成最正覺 無垢喻虛空 '*then he will become fully enlightened, free from impurities like space*'.

To recapitulate here what was previously mentioned about imagining the five Buddhas in the purified mandala site, when taking possession of the site with great compassion, it is prescribed in the following sequence: First the Buddha Bhagavats should be imagined in that mandala site, then following that transformation, one should take possession of it internally with the mind[10] and then protect it with the mantra. One should take possession of it in these three [steps] and not in any other way[11].

**23. 'The cords are said to have four parts,
that is, white, yellow, red and black.
The fifth is described as being like space.'**

The cord which was previously described in a general way as being of five colours is here clearly described with the names of its five colours.

**24. 'Having held [one cord] in the air,
the mandala should be fixed there[12]. (172a)
With a second cord, the mandala
should be laid out upon the ground.'**

It was mentioned in a general way concerning the previous Mandalas that the cord should be held level with one's navel, but it was not explained that the mandala should be drawn there, so it is clearly stated that one should hold that cord in the air and draw that mandala in the air. ***With a second cord, the mandala should be laid out on the ground***: It was mentioned previously in a general way that you should take a second cord and face the east and so forth, but this clearly states where the mandala itself should be drawn, which was not specified before. Having drawn it in the air, the mandala should be drawn on the ground with the second cord which you have taken up.

**25. 'The seats of all the Buddhas
and their wise Sons
should be excellent mind-formed lotuses,
praised by the world as auspicious.'**

(164a) This means that their seats should be made of white lotuses. Previously, when the four members of recitation were described, it was stated that a white lotus should be imagined in your heart. Since it does not specify a white lotus here, the words '***excellent mind-formed lotuses***' mean that the seats should be like the white lotuses which have been imagined mentally.

**26. 'For the Pratyekabuddhas and Arhats
who are described as partial knowers,
petals coming from lotuses[A]
should be known as their seats.'**

A C: 青蓮 '*blue lotus*'.

The seats of the Śrāvakas and Pratyekabuddhas who partially have Awareness should be made of a petal of a white lotus.

27. 'For the mundane gods whom
the world call Brahmā and so forth[A]**:**
their seats are red lotuses,
which are praised by the Jinas.'

The mundane gods such as Brahmā and so on who have the appearance of kings, are said to have red lotuses as their seats because they have attachment[13].

28. 'From the remainder, you should imagine them
according to their specific level as appropriate.'

Since it is not fitting for the ordinary entourage to have lotus seats in the presence of those important beings as though they also were as important, so seats which are inferior to those should be made, as appropriate. Although the seats of the Śrāvakas, Pratyekabuddhas and mundane gods are described here, they are not mentioned in the [section on the] Mandala, so they should be known as described now. Also the mundane gods such as Yama and so on, who are mentioned in the middle portion of the Mandala, are just emanations from the Body of the Tathāgata, so it is appropriate for them to have lotus seats, but not for the ordinary mundane gods.

29. 'There are four types of worship
which should be presented to all Saviours:
salutations with joined palms,
likewise kindness and compassion,
mundane flowers and incense,
and flowers produced with the fingers.
Making the *Mudrā* which Produces All the Members[14]
and then cultivating *bodhicitta*,
they should be made diligently
for each one of the Protectors and their Children.
These are the faultless flowers,
sweet-smelling and splendid,
the trees of the continuum of reality which arise
to be offered to the Jinas;
they are created by mantras,
changed by virtue of *samādhi*;
excellent vast multitudes of clouds
arisen from the continuum of reality,
always pour [flowers] like rain
in the presence of the Buddhas.'

This section describes the worship (*pūja*), (164b) and in general there are four types of worship: with joined palms, with kindness and compassion, with flowers, incense

---

A C: 梵衆以爲初 '[*such as*] *Brahmā whom the world calls foremost*'.

and so on, and with mental offerings[15]. As for the worship by the *mantrin* who is interested in the Profound and Extensive, he will engage in these four types of worship and will do both the internal mental worship and the external worship. The *mantrin* who relies on cognitive objects will also do the external worship, but not the internal ones because his *samādhi* lacks that capability. Kindness and compassion are behavioural offerings (*pratipatti-pūja*). Having made either internal of external offerings, one should generate kindness and compassion towards beings and transfer those same offerings to beings. Of those, the external offerings have already been described.

Now the mental offerings will be described here, regarding which the text says '***flowers produced with the fingers***' and so forth. This means that those flowers and so on which are produced by joining the palms of the hands together should be presented to all the Saviours. In order to send them forth, it says '***making the* Mudrā *which Produces All the Members and then cultivating* bodhicitta**'. As for the mental offerings which are to be made, you first make this *Mudrā* yourself and then pray that clouds of offerings such as have been imagined may arise for the Buddhas and Bodhisattvas; then abiding in the *samādhi* of emptiness, that *bodhicitta* will be actualized. While abiding in *samādhi* thus, you should also recite the *Vidyā* of Gagana-gañja and imagine vast amounts of the offerings which are mentioned below, pouring out like rain from that *mudrā*. Having imagined thus, at that moment [offerings] will pour down like rain in the presence of the Buddhas, by the transformational power of the continuum of reality, by virtue of *samādhi* and the power of the mantra. (165a) These are extolled with the words '***these are faultless flowers***' and so forth.

30. 'For the other ordinary deities
these are the specified flowers[A],
they should be offered as appropriate,
with their specific mantras and *mudrās*.
Thus flowers, incense and perfumes,
should be imagined as appropriate.'

This indicates the process for presenting the external offerings, flowers and so forth, to the deities of the representational mandala drawn with pigments. Having pronounced the mantras of each one, you should first worship the Tathāgata Family, Vairocana and so on, then the Lotus Family and so forth. Hence the text says '***they should be offered as appropriate***'.

31. 'The thumb and ring finger joined together
is called the "Auspicious [*Mudrā*]".
The flowers should be taken with that
and presented from the area of your heart.
For the mundane deities, know that
it should be done from your navel.'

A C: 亦當散此華 '*Also these flowers should be scattered*'.

This section shows the method of presenting the offerings. ***The thumb and ring finger joined together*** and so forth, describes the presentation of the flowers. ***For the mundane deities, know that it should be done from your navel***: Here '***mundane***' refers to the deities of the representational mandala. The flowers should be presented to those deities from the navel and from the heart for the deities of the supramundane mental mandala.

32. **'The incense should be held up in the air**
with the Vajra Fist or the Lotus Garland [*Mudrā*],
and then presented to the mundane Protectors.
Do it in due order
for the other mundane deities[A].'

While offering the incense you should make the Vajra Fist or the Lotus *Mudrā*. A censer should be held with the Vajra Fist and a dish with the Lotus *Mudrā*. For the deities of the mental mandala, it should be held up in the air and praised, then offered to them. For the deities of the representational mandala, it should be offered as appropriate from the navel. (165b) Hence it says, '***Do it in due order for the other mundane deities***'.

33. **'Two types of Homa should be known (172b)**
by the categories of internal and external.
Freed from karmic action and rebirth,
and once again arising from the seed,
he who desires to do a rite should do [this] Homa[B].
[This is] said to be the internal Homa.'

This section describes both the internal and the external Homa. Of these, the external Homa is that which is burnt, and refers to external things such as the consuming fire and so forth. The internal Homa is that which is done mentally, without reference to external materials, hence it says, '***Freed from karmic action and rebirth***'. You should dissolve into emptiness such phenomena as the psycho-physical constituents, the perceptual elements and sources with the dissolving *bodhicitta*. You should realize with non-proliferating insight (*niḥprapañca-prajñā*) that karmic action and rebirth have no objective reality, and that neither causes and results can be perceived to exist in the *manas* with regards the psycho-physical constituents and so on, the mind and mental factors. That is termed liberation from karmic action and rebirth. That which burns is non-proliferating insight, and it is karmic action and rebirth that are to be burnt and the fire which burns is the *manas* free from perceptual images. ***Once again arising from the seed*** (*bīja*): This refers to the formation (*rūpaṇa*) of the deity by virtue of compassion, after having arisen from the *samādhi* of emptiness which is characterized by burning up karmic action and rebirth. That

---

A C: 或金剛拳印 若復蓮華鬘 而在空中獻 導師救世者 乃至諸世天 各如其次第 '*Or with the Vajra Fist or else the Lotus Garland, they should be held in the air and offered to the Protector Guides and so forth down to the mundane deities, each according to their prescribed rite*'. There is no mention here of '*incense*'.

B C reads: 以能燒業故 '*because it consumes karma* [*this is said to be* ...]'.

is, you transform yourself into the body-image of a deity by means of the process already spoken of, in which you change yourself into a deity through the seed-syllable (*bīja*) of the mantra which is your own deity. In that, the first *bodhicitta* which destroys the psycho-physical constituents and so on is the entering *bodhicitta*. The non-proliferating insight which has destroyed them and is devoid of the concept of them and which is characterized by not conceptualizing, by being the burner of karmic action and rebirth and by being self-aware (*pratyātma-adhigama*), is the abiding *bodhicitta*. (166a) The transformation again into the body-image of the deity with the seed-syllable, is the arising *bodhicitta*. ***He who desires to do a rite should do [this] Homa***: Anyone who desires to accomplish such rites as Pacifying, Enriching and so on, should do this internal Homa. This should be linked up with the words, '***The Jinas say that attainments with form come from that with form, but you will also accomplish those with form by abiding in that without form***'. This means that you can also accomplish those [Homas] with the perceptual forms of things such as wood and so, by that internal Homa which is devoid of perceptual forms, without regard to external materials.

34. 'The external one has the three aspects,
with the three abodes and is placed in three:
thus the path[A] of the three rites will be accomplished.
This is the most excellent mundane Homa.
Whosoever does otherwise,
not knowing the Homa rites,
is devoid of mantra knowledge:
that fool will not attain any results.'

The external one has the three aspects: When you do the external Homa, it should be done with three things: i) it should be done with the method and colour appropriate for Pacifying, Enriching, or Destroying, ii) the materials should also be imagined with that colour and iii) you yourself should be transformed into the deity which corresponds to that colour. Thus to do it with the fire, materials and yourself in accordance with the method and colour appropriate for the specific rites of Pacifying and so forth is to have the '***three aspects***'. ***With the three abodes***: Having the three abodes – the earth, water and fire mandalas for Pacifying, Enriching and Destroying. ***Placed in three***: The three types of hearth – round, square and triangular – for Pacifying, Enriching and Destroying are the places where the materials are to be burnt. '***The three rites***' are Pacifying, Enriching and Destroying. ***The path [of the three rites] will be accomplished***: This refers to the actions which are to be accomplished. If you should do any other Homa ritual than either the internal or the external one, their effects will not come about. Hence the text says, '***whosoever does otherwise***', with regards both types.

35. 'The mantras uttered by the Tathāgatas,
likewise those uttered by the perfect Buddhas,
should be known as white and yellow.
That of Vajrapāṇi is multi-coloured.

A Correct *las* 'action' in T to *lam* 'path' on the basis of B and C.

The mantra of Lokeśvara
is white due to his type of action.
The shapes are said to be
completely square in form,
according to the sequence, round,
triangular and like a half-moon.
Their bodies are of two types:
male and female.'

(166b) This section describes the colours, shapes and size of the mantra deities and so on. ***The mantras uttered by the Tathāgatas and likewise those uttered by the perfect Buddhas, should be known as white and yellow.*** Since the intrinsic nature of the Tathāgata Family is tranquillity, which is defined as the purity of all phenomena, you should know that its colour is white. The perfect Buddhas such as Śākyamuni and Bodhisattvas like Mañjuśrī and so on engage in actions for the benefit of beings, and since they are characterized as perfecting the accumulations and enriching them, you should know that their colour is yellow. ***That of Vajrapāṇi is multi-coloured:*** Since Vajrapāṇi, whose intrinsic nature is the Awareness of Accomplishing Activities, engages in all practices for the benefit of beings, you should know that his has all (*sarvaka*) colours. ***The mantra of Lokeśvara is white due to his type of action:*** Avalokiteśvara, whose intrinsic nature is Investigating Awareness, cleanses all phenomena, so you should know that white is his colour.

The shapes are said to be completely square in form, and according to the sequence, round, triangular and like a half-moon: This describes the shape of the mandalas of earth and so on associated with those deities and they should be known in sequence.

Their bodies are of two types: male and female: This describes the bodies of the deities. There are also three types of deities: those whose bodies are in recompense (*vipāka-rūpa*), those whose bodies are physical metamorphosis (*āśraya-parivṛtti*), and those whose bodies are emanations (*nirmāṇa-rūpa*). The bodies of deities which are in recompense are those generated by their actions and merits. The bodies of deities which are metamorphosis are the bodies accomplished by *sādhana*. (167a) The bodies of deities which are emanations are any one of those which are imagined in the *manas* by virtue of *samādhi*, and some of those deities appear as male and some as female.

36. **'Furthermore, in all places,**
in all colours, shapes and bodies,
they arise from inconceivable Awareness,
therefore they are also inconceivable.
The Awareness realized always becomes a diversity
of Awarenesses for the sake of beings[A].'

A Though the general sense is clear, it is not clear exactly how this couplet should be read as each version has a different rendering: *ye-shes mkhyen-gyi* [=*gyis?*] *ye-shes* | *sems-can don phyir tha-dad gyur* || (T+ B); *sems-can don-byed tha-dad-pas* [=*pa'i?*] | *ye-shes mkhas-pas rtag-tu mkhyen* || (V); 應物有殊異 智智證常一 '*Though things have a diversity of forms, the Awareness which comprehends them is always one*'. (C)

Furthermore, in all places, in all the colours, shapes and bodies: Furthermore, the colours white and so forth, the shapes square and so forth, and the male and female bodies mentioned above are not fixed, but all of them should also be known to be each colour, shape and body. Why is that? The text says, '***they arise from the inconceivable Awareness, therefore they are also inconceivable***': Since all of them arise solely from the inconceivable Awareness of Suchness, their colours, bodies and so forth are undivided [from it], so they are also inconceivable. Why is that so? ***The Awareness realized always becomes a diversity of awarenesses for the sake of beings***: For though their colours, bodies and so forth are undivided [from it], they manifest in the bodies and so forth adapted to the beings to be guided, with that Awareness which is skilled in the various ways of benefitting beings.

37. **'As much as the capacity of your *manas*,**
you should know that much
are the seats and *mudrās*,
and also the sizes of the deities,
in due proportion.'

This explains the size of the deities. ***The capacity of your* manas**: It means that you should draw or imagine all those deities that are drawn externally or imagined internally in the *manas* as large as you wish. ***The size of the deities, in due proportion***: As for the deities that you draw in the Mandala, those drawn in the matrix mandala should be drawn large since the area of the mandala site is also large, whereas the border areas become progressively smaller, so the deities there should also be small.

38. **'From whence the Buddhas arise,**
from there also arise the *mudrās*.
The trainees should be sealed
with the *mudrās* arising from the Dharma-[dhātu] [A]
Hence, in brief, it is said that
***mudrās* are the symbols of the continuum of reality.'**

(167b) This explains the source from which the *mudrās* arise. The Master should transform himself and the trainees into the bodies of deities with those *mudrās* which arise from the continuum of reality of the Buddhas and protect the trainees with them. I explained in detail earlier that you cannot be harmed by anything if you have been protected and sealed with the symbols (*cihna*) of the continuum of reality, with the words, 'Just as a person with the king's seal will not be hurt by anyone'.

39. **'There are three types of Initiation,**
therefore, listen with diligence!
There is the initiation by the *mudrās* [B]
without actions and activities.

A This couplet is based on C. T seems corrupt: *chos-las byung-ba'i slob-ma-rnams | chos-kyi phyag-rgyas gdab-pa bya | 'The trainees arising from the Dharma, should be sealed with the Dharma* Mudrā'.

B C: 若秘印方便 '*There is the secret* mudrā *method*'.

That initiation by the Protectors
is the most excellent and is the first.
The second is said to arise
from actions and activities.
The third is to be known as mental,
and is devoid of place and time.'

This section explains the three types of initiation. ***There is the initiation by the* mudrās *without actions and activities*** (*karma-kriyā-rahita*): This explains that the Master and trainees who have devoted interest in the Profound and Extensive should be initiated with the *mudrās* while in the Mandala Arisen from Great Compassion and the Mandala of the Revolving Wheel of Letters. They should be initiated with the *mudrās* of Samantabhadra and so on, and with the *mudrās* mentioned below, in the presence of either of those two Mandalas, without regard for the Initiation Mandala, the jars and so forth. '***Without actions and activities***' means without the rituals of the initiation jars, the mandala, conch, wheel and so forth.

The second is said to arise (samutthāna) ***from actions and activities***: This means that the initiation is done according to the rituals previously described, when the Initiation Mandala has been drawn in front of the Mandala Arisen from Great Compassion or the Mandala of the Revolving Wheel of Letters.

(168a) ***The third is to be known as mental and is devoid of time and place***: This is the mental initiation into the Secret Mandala, and is that dealt with below.

40. 'This initiation in which the guru
speaks of how it benefits [beings]
after they have pleased him
is praised as best by the Perfect Buddhas[A].'

This refers to the initiation with *mudrās* and spoken words of permission in the above two Mandalas. You should know that these are the words, 'From this day henceforth, you shall turn the Wheel of the Dharma' and so forth, spoken by the Master who has been pleased by the reverence and diligence of the trainees, following the initiation with *mudrās*.

The first initiation with *mudrās* and the second initiation [with rituals] should be done with regards to the Mandala Arisen from Great Compassion and the Mandala of the Revolving Wheel of Letters[16]. Since it is stated that the mental initiation is done for the Secret Mandala, you should know that it is not done for the above two. Furthermore, I have just explained the meaning of the words here, but I have defined and explained the initiations in my *Piṇḍārtha*[17].

41. 'The Buddhas, in brief, proclaim (173a)
that there are five who have *samaya*:
The first are those who only have the *samaya*

A C: 令尊歡喜故 如所說應作 現前佛灌頂 是則最殊勝 '*In order to please the guru, they should do as they have been instructed. The initiation [given] in the presence of the Buddhas is the very best of all*'. Contrary to Buddhaguhya, CC understands this section to concern the third type of initiation.

after having seen this Mandala,
but the *mudrās* should not be shown
nor should the mantras be given to them.'

The following sections explain the sequence of the *samayas.* Now with regards to entry into the mandala, generally speaking some of those trainees enter it because they want to have the *samaya,* some do so because they want to do the *sādhana* and others enter it because they want to become Masters. You should know that if a trainee were to enter only one of those three Mandalas and get the *samaya,* then that is done without reference to the remaining two, but [entry] through a desire to do the *sādhana* or become a Master is done with reference to all three Mandalas.

Those who first have the* samaya, *after having seen the Mandala*:** (168b) The meaning of 'samaya***' in the present case is 'not deviating from the [prescribed] method'. This means that if a trainee has seen any one of the three Mandalas, he is the first type of person who has *samaya.* So if he had previously cultivated *bodhicitta,* the *mudrās* and mantras would be given to him, but since he has not previously cultivated *bodhicitta,* it is not fitting to give the *mudrās* and mantras to him, hence it says, '***but the* mudrās *should not be shown, nor the mantras given to him***'.

42. **'Those who have received the *mudrās* and mantras**
due to the special nature of their *bodhicitta,*
and have seen the Mandala
are known as the second type of *samaya*-holder.'

A trainee who has thus entered the Mandala but has not been given the *mudrās* and mantras, should be made to cultivate *bodhicitta,* and when he has repeatedly cultivated it, the text indicates that he should be given the *mudrās* and mantras if he wishes, with the words, '***Those who have received the* mudrās *and mantras, due to the special nature*** (viśeṣa) ***of their* bodhicitta.**' ***[Those] who have seen the Mandala are known as the second type of* samaya-*holder*.** A trainee who has thus repeatedly cultivated *bodhicitta,* who has been introduced into the Mandala and who has been given the *mudrās* and mantras, should be known as the second type of person who has *samaya.*

43. **'Those who have seen the mandalas and *mudrās,***
and have also practised the actions and activities,
but have not yet received instructions from the Guru[A]:
they are also said to have *samaya.*'

This means that a trainee who has seen the mandalas, who has been made to study the Tantras, Kalpas and so on, but who has not yet been given the instructions (*āgama*) by the Master, is the third type of *samaya*-holder.

44. **'There is also the *mantrin***
who has been instructed according to the ritual

A C: 復次許傳教 '*and who have also received the instructions*'.

at the time of depicting the *mudrās* and mandalas,
but who does not have the Initiation
for that which arises from Secret Awareness[A].'

The fourth type of *samaya*-holder is one who has been initiated into both the Mandala Arisen from Great Compassion and the Mandala of the Revolving Wheel of Letters, or else into either one of them and who has been told to teach the drawing and description of the *mudrās* and mandalas to the others, according to the ritual, but who has not yet been initiated into the Secret Mandala.

45. 'The *mantrin* who is initiated by the ritual
within the Secret Mandala,
is called the fifth type of *samaya*-holder.
No others should be said to have *samaya*.'

(169a) The trainee who has been initiated into both the above two Mandalas and also into the Secret Mandala is called the fifth type of *samaya*-holder. *No others should be said to have samaya*: If anyone acts in any other way apart from those mentioned above, deviating from the prescribed ritual, he is not said to have *samaya*.

46. 'Any well-disciplined *mantrin* who cultivates
his mind for the sake of Enlightenment,
and who does not reify the three places,
is called a Bodhisattva[B].'

This [and the following two] sections are in answer to the questions about how a *mantrin* who exerts himself in the mantra practice is to become a Bodhisattva and All-knowing, and how he is to see truth (*satya*). If you continually cultivate *bodhicitta* and have dissolved the three bases – body, speech and mind, or the three abodes – the Desire Realm, the Form Realm and the Formless Realm, by entering *bodhicitta*, and treat them as being without any objective basis, you will be termed a Bodhisattva[18].

47. 'One who has attained practice without reifying,
yet having generated the energy of expedient means,
applies himself to the welfare of beings[C],
is known as the most excellent of Jinas.'

One who has attained the practice which is without cognitive objects (*anālambana*), and then arises from that and engages in benefitting beings with expedient means, while knowing phenomena to be like illusions and so forth, is called All-knowing. ***One who has attained practice without reifying***: One dissolves phenomena by the

---

A C: 未達心灌頂 秘密慧不生 '[*but*] *who has not yet reached the mental initiation and in whom the secret awareness has not arisen*'.

B C is somewhat different. It has 善住若觀意 眞言者覺心 不得於三處 說彼爲菩薩 '*When the* mantrin, *well-disciplined, cultivates his* manas, *he will realize* (√ *budh*) *mind, and not reify the three places. I call him a Bodhisattva*'.

C C: 方便利衆生 爲植衆善本 '*yet benefits beings with expedient means in order to plant a mass of wholesome roots*'.

entering *bodhicitta* during the phase of practice with devoted interest; then while abiding in emptiness, which is defined as the abiding *bodhicitta*, one realizes that all phenomena are without objective basis on the absolute level, and that phenomena are delusive or illusion-like on the relative level. Therefore one is said to have attained the practice without supports. ***The most excellent of Jinas*:** One who has thus realized that phenomena lack any objective basis both on the absolute and relative levels, has the air of being victorious over the Four Māras, even though he has not actually overcome them.

48. **'Whosoever's mind abides like Sumeru**
with regards the primordially tranquil phenomena,
which are without inherent reality:
that person sees the truth.'

This explains how truth is seen. If anyone realizes that all phenomena, which are primordially tranquil, are without inherent reality, with their mind becoming unshakable regarding that, like Mount Sumeru, they are said to have seen the truth. In brief, they have the entering *bodhicitta* to begin with. Seeing truth indicates the abiding *bodhicitta*, and being '***the most excellent of Jinas***' (169b) shows the arising *bodhicitta*. They should also be known as the virtues of abiding in the Level of Practice with Devoted Interest.

49. **' "This is true[A], that is real,**
and likewise not deceptive.
Just as the Buddhas beheld the truth,
like the Former Ones, I also see!"
What need is there for any attainment
other than the attainment of *bodhicitta*?'

This extols the special qualities of one who has attained *bodhicitta*. That which is attained by Bodhisattvas is true, real and not deceptive. Just as previous Buddhas did, he has also seen that it is real and not deceptive. It was explained above that having accomplished the attainment of *bodhicitta*, you '***should recite until the Bodhisattva Samantabhadra, Mañjuśrī, or Vajrapāṇi comes and caresses your head, or says "Excellent!". Then, if having prostrated to them you offer oblations, you will attain the* samādhi *of not forgetting* bodhicitta**' [VI.43]. To reach the occurrence of that is termed the '***attainment of* bodhicitta**'. (170a) If that has happened, that indeed is attainment, so what need is there for any other attainment? For the accomplishment of that *bodhicitta* is the cause of all others.

50. **'It is said that apart from that**
there are five types of attainment:
Those at entry into the practice,
also those during the ascent of the Levels,
the five mundane supernatural cognitions,
Buddhahood and those that remain.'

A C: 空 (*śūnya*) 'empty[ness]'.

This deals with the other five listed attainments apart from that accomplishment of *bodhicitta*, and they are those associated with entry into the practice and so forth. Of those, '***those at entry into the practice***' are the special categories of *samādhis* such as the attainment of light (*āloka-labdha*), the increase of light (*āloka-vṛddhi*)[19] and so forth, which are accomplished while rising up through the Level of Practice with Devoted Interest and entering the Level of Awareness. ***Also those during the ascent of the Levels***: Those attainments accomplished with the attainment of the Joyous Level and so forth. ***The five mundane supernatural cognitions***: The attainment of the five mundane supernatural cognitions. ***Buddhahood***: The attainment of becoming a *vidyādhara* with the appearance of a Buddha. ***And those that remain***: The attainment of becoming an ordinary *vidyādhara*, that is, the attainment associated with *dhāraṇīs*. The first three above should be known as the mental attainments.

51. 'While the stream-forming actions
remain unvitiated in one's stream,
and the effects have not yet fully matured,
that is the occasion for attainments[A].'

The following sections indicate the occasion when they will be accomplished. Also this occasion is of two types: with regards accomplishment in this lifetime and accomplishment in future lives. This section deals with accomplishment in this lifetime. [The attainments will occur] if the actions which form the stream remain unvitiated in one's mental stream, that is, if the stream previously accumulated by the six perceptual gateways remains unvitiated in the stream of this lifetime, and if one's psycho-physical constituents are preserved[20]. ***The effects have not yet fully matured***: If the results of the causes of life and merit, which were accumulated in the past, mature here in the present, your past karmic actions have not yet been exhausted, and so the causal basis for one's merits will be strengthened by the maturation of effects [such as] a long life. If (170b) you are thus protected by both life and merit when doing the *sādhana*, you will accomplish it at that time.

52. 'In brief, when action and birth
have been projected simultaneously[B],
then the *mantrin* will accomplish
the attainment which arises from *manas*.' (173b)

This means that if action and birth have not yet been exhausted when one has accomplished attainments and both karmic action and rebirth are projected[C]

A C: 修業無間息 乃至心續淨 未熟令成熟 爾時悉地成 '*When you cultivate the [ritual] actions continuously until the continuum of the mind is purified, that which has not yet matured will mature and then the attainments will be accomplished*'.

B C: 於彼一時頃 淨業心俱等 '*when he is endowed with pure action and mind at the very same time*'.

C T: *zad-par-gyur-na*, '*if they have been exhausted*'. This would seem to be an error. In commenting on this verse, the *Piṇḍārtha* uses *'phangs-pa* 'projected', which accords better with the meaning of the verse: if the karmic energy and potentiality for further births have not been exhausted, then after these have been projected into one's succeeding lifetime, attainments will be innately present.

simultaneously, then the results of the *sādhana* – birth in the Vajra Family, birth as a *vidyādhara* and so on – will be attained by that *mantrin* in his next lifetime, without his having to accomplish them again. ***Which arises from* manas**: Those attainments which are accomplished by the *manas* itself, without having to accomplish them through material substances, will be attained immediately upon rebirth.

53. 'When accomplished, you will travel in the sky,
just like a magician[A];
you will bewitch with a mantra net,
just like a great conjurer[B].'

The following sections give answers to the question about the results of *sādhana*. Here the attainment of travelling in the sky is explained. Just as a magician walks in the air and creates many kinds of illusions, that *mantrin* will travel in the air and manifest many different kinds of emanations (*nirmāṇa*) by the power of mantras, after having become a *vidyādhara* and so on.

54. 'Just as within a gandharvas' city
there are no bodies or communication,
likewise he who abides in that
is said to become invisible[C].'

This explains how the *mantrin* can become invisible after having become a *vidyādhara*, with the example of a gandharvas' city21. Just as bodies can dwell in the air in a gandharvas' city even though they are actually invisible, in the same way, when the *mantrin* has accomplished that attainment, (171a) he will become invisible in space and stay in the air, with neither his body being seen nor his speech heard.

55. 'Just as in a dream, in bed,
you may visit the Heaven of the Thirty Three,
[though] your body has not been abandoned,
and one does not go there with it.
In the same way, by that very yoga,
a *mantrin* who abides in the mantras
will attain a rainbow-like body
through his meritorious actions.'

A T reads '*ci-ltar sgyu-ma 'jigs-med bzhin*' in agreement with C: 如幻無畏者, '*Like one who has no fear of illusions*'. However, the line quoted in V reads '*ci-ltar sgyu-ma mkhas-pa bzhin*' (*like one who is skilled in illusions*) which accords better with Buddhaguhya's comments which refer to a '*sgyu-ma-mkhan*' or '*mig-'phrul-mkhan*'. This suggests that CT had '*māyābhaya*' (*without fear of illusions*) while V had '*māyākāra*' (*a magician*). V's reading makes better sense so I have adopted that.

B T reads '*mig-'phrul chen-po*' (a great conjurer) while C has 帝釋網 (*the net of Indra*). This suggests that the text originally had '*indrajx01la*' which can yield both interpretations.

C C: 如乾闥婆城 所有諸人民 身秘密如是 非身亦非識 '*Just as the inhabitants of a gandharvas' city are hidden, likewise he will be bodiless and undiscerned*'.

This explains with the example of dreams how the *mantrin* will travel in space and so on, without abandoning his present body, after having become a *vidyādhara*. Just as within the dreams of a sleeping person even the Heaven of the Thirty Three Gods is seen, likewise by virtue of his yoga, a *mantrin* may see himself travelling in the sky and so on, without abandoning his present body. This means that he will also be able to manifest himself in many different appearances, so he '***will attain a rainbow-like body***'.

56. **'Mantras, which arise from**
body, speech and mind,
are like a Wish-fulfilling Gem:
the things you wish for will arise [A]
without pause for reflection.'

This explains the mantra-attainment with the example of a Wish-fulfilling Gem. Just as a Wish-fulfilling Gem will spontaneously provide whatever things you wish for without having to reflect upon them, in the same way whatever results you desire of the mantras which have been accomplished will be spontaneously provided, without having to reflect upon them.

57. **'Just as the directions of space**
are unsullied by all conditioned objects,
likewise the *mantrin* regarding all imagined objects [B]**.'**

This explains that the *mantrin* who has accomplished the attainment of realization is unharmed by planets, stars, inauspicious omens and so on. For just as space is not sullied by conditioned (*saṃskṛta*) impurities and so on, (171a) likewise the *mantrin* who has become accomplished disregards the auspicious and the inauspicious and is not harmed by their omens.

58. **' "These are just ideas":**
thus he should consider them.
When he has considered [thus], the *mantrin*
will be joyful, in the company of perfect Buddhas.'

This indicates that the *mantrin* will gain the companionship of the Buddhas after he has accomplished the attainments. ***These are just ideas*** (*saṃjñā*): None of these conditions, phenomena and so forth really exist, but they are just ideas. By considering them in that way when cultivating *bodhicitta*, the *mantrin* will become joyful because he will accompany the perfect Buddhas and listen to the Dharma.

59. **'The Buddha, the Lord of Men,**
has described two kinds of Homa:
the internal and the external,
and the libations are also likewise.'

A C: 隨念雨衆物 '*a mass of things will rain down as you wish*'.

B C: 眞言者不染 一切分別行 '[*likewise*] *the* mantrin *will not be sullied by any conceptual activities*'.

The two questions concerning the homa ritual and fire have already been answered, and here the Bhagavat explains that the two types of homa are the external and internal fire. ***The libations are also likewise*:** This means that the libations (*tarpaṇa*) for the internal mental fire are the creation of the body-image of the deity from its own seed mantra, as previously described. The external fire should be should be satisfied (√ *tṛp*) with the propitiatory (*ārādhana*) offering materials.

60. 'When the individual natures of the deities
have been investigated[A], they will be understood.
I shall now speak of the scale
of the mantras of the mundane ones.
The very powerful ones, such as Maheśvara,
are the gods honoured by the world[B];
The very powerful mantras uttered by them,
together with their *mudrās* bestow
the ordinary results immediately:
That indicates their scale.
However, they have the qualities
of arising and perishing, and lack stability.'

The following sections describe the nature (*svabhāva*) and scale (*pramāṇa*) of the attainments of the deities. ***When the individual natures of the deities have been investigated, they will be understood*:** If you have understood the nature of the deities, the results of their attainments will also be known. Of these, the nature of the supramundane deities has previously been explained. (172a) Here the nature of the mundane deities is to be explained and then the scale of their results will also be known through their power (*prabhāva*). Therefore, the Bhagavat says, '***I shall speak of the scale of the mantras of the mundane ones***': The mantras and *mudrās* taught by those powerful gods such as Īśvara and so forth, bestow results in the present world and this is indicated as their scale. Their '***scale***' means their power. ***However they have the qualities of arising and perishing, and lack stability*:** This refers to their specific qualities (*viśeṣa*). Although the attainments of the mundane gods bestow results immediately in this lifetime, they have the qualities of arising and perishing, so they are impermanent.

61. 'The mantras of the supramundane ones
do not have a progenitor[C].
The scale of the mantras
of the Jinas who are free from faults
and have severed karmic action and rebirth,
and the rhinoceros-like Pratyekabuddhas,
likewise the victorious Śrāvakas,
and the Bodhisattvas, has already been described.'

A '*Have been investigated*' added from C.

B '*By the world*' added from C.

C C: 無作本不生 '*uncreated and primordially unborn*'.

This explains the b supramundane mantras. The mantras spoken by the Bodhisattvas, Śrāvakas, Pratyekauddhas and so on '***do not have a progenitor***'. ***Who have severed karmic action and rebirth***: Since the Jinas are free from the three faults, attachment, hatred and stupidity, they are without arising and perishing. The scale of their mantra attainments has already been described.

62. 'They utterly transcend the three times,
and yet have visible and invisible results
produced through inter-dependence, (174a)
arising from body, speech and mind.
The scale of the mundane results
is said to be one eon,
but the results of the mantras
of fully perfect Buddhas transcend eons.'

Therefore, the supramundane mantras do not only bestow results immediately, but they also bestow results both in the present visible world and in the future invisible world. The '***visible results***' are the attainments of men and gods. The '***invisible result***' is Nirvāṇa. (172b)

63. 'The *samādhis* of the Great Sage Buddhas
and their Children are pure,
without any perceptual forms.
The mundane ones have perceptual form.'

This section describes the *samādhis* of the *mantrins*. In general there are two types of *samādhi*: the absolute and the relative. Of those, the absolute *samādhis* are the letters beginning with *A* revealed by way of each of the letters. The relative *samādhis* are the qualities (*guṇa*) such as the Strengths and the Fearlessnesses [formed] from the syllables of the mantra garland. The letters of the *samādhis* which form those syllables have already been explained. Here the meaning (*artha*) of the *samādhis* is explained. ***The Great Sage*** (*mahāmuni*) ***Buddhas***: They are 'sages' because they are characterized by control over their body, speech and mind. This refers to the unlocalized Nirvāṇa, Perfect Buddhahood. ***Their Children*** are the Bodhisattvas and so on. Since the meaning of their *samādhis* is the primordial non-arising of all phenomena, they are '***pure and without perceptual forms***'. ***The mundane ones have perceptual forms***: After a Bodhisattva has arisen from *samādhi*, he engages in such actions with perceptual images as the adornment of the Buddha fields, he is incarnated, he becomes awakened and becomes enlightened. Then by the power of his previous aspirations, he produces the configurations of the Inexhaustible Body and so forth. That is the engagement in actions with perceptual forms, and '***the mundane ones have perceptual forms***' also refers to that. Secondly, since the Tīrthikas (173a) consider the *samādhis* of the mundane gods to be real, they are said to have perceptual forms.

64. 'The recompense here [in the present],
is the matured result of karmic action.
When you have accomplished the attainment,
then even karmic action will be averted.'

The results of karmic action which mature as [birth with] the body of a god [and so forth] will mature in the present five psycho-physical constituents which are the recompense for previous karmic action. When, however, you have accomplished the attainment of your own *samādhi* and so forth, that recompense for karmic action is overpowered by that attainment, and such results do not mature but are averted.

65. 'Because the mind lacks inherent reality,
it is devoid of causes and effects,
so you will be liberated from action and rebirth,
and become like space.'

This deals with the awakening with the ultimate attainment. The practitioner (*sādhaka*) realizes that his mind lacks inherent reality by cultivating the pure *bodhicitta*. Since the causes and results of phenomena are without any objective basis, he is also liberated from causal karmic action and resultant rebirth. When he has thus been freed from karmic action and rebirth, he is characterized by purity and is devoid of a perceiving subject and perceived objects, like space.

66. 'Lord of the Secret Ones, listen carefully and retain this carefully in your mind, for I shall explain the subject of the array in the forms of the symbols: the transformation of the deities into their specific abodes and the realization of the five *samādhis*[A], which was directly and completely understood by the previous Buddhas, for the benefit, welfare and happiness of those Bodhisattvas who engage in the Bodhisattva practice by way of the mantras, who have become capable of realizing the continuum of reality and who have vowed to liberate all realms of beings without remainder.'

The subject of the array in the forms (*rūpa*) ***of symbols***: In the Mandala Arising from Great Compassion and the Mandala of the Revolving Wheel of Letters, it (the array) was laid out in the form of bodies and syllables, but here it is laid out in the form of symbols (*mudrā*), since it is not really possible to set down the intrinsic nature of Mind. The '***subject***' (*paṭala*) refers to the Mandala which is arranged in the form of symbols. ***The transformation of the deities into their specific abodes***: The deities are transformed into those mandalas (173b) by the array in the forms of symbols. ***The realization of the five* samādhis**: Those same five mandalas of earth and so forth are transformed into the various specific Awarenesses. Through those five mandalas the special qualities (*viśeṣa*) of the *samādhis* of the five Awarenesses are realized. ***Directly and completely understood*** (*√ buddh*) ***by the previous Buddhas***: This shows the identity of action of all Buddhas. This should be construed as meaning, 'Listen carefully to what was also known and explained by previous Buddhas!'. ***For the benefit, welfare and happiness of those Bodhisattvas who engage in the Bodhisattva practice by way of the mantras***: This shows that the description of the Mandala is not given because Vajrapāṇi himself is unaware of it, but it is to be described for the sake of the benefit and happiness of those Bodhisattvas, who abide on the Level of Practice with Devoted

A C: 彼密印形相敷置聖天之位威驗現前三昧所趣如是五者 ... '*those secret* mudrās *and their features, the placing of the locations of the deities, the manifestation of their transformation and the* samādhis *which are to be realized: these five* [*were* ...].'

Interest and engage in the practice of a Bodhisattva by means of the secret mantras. ***For whom the realization of the continuum of reality has become accessible***: This describes the qualities of the insight of those who abide on the Level of Practice with Devoted Interest, and it means that their insight has become capable of perceiving the continuum of reality, which is like space. If the space-like continuum of reality has become accessible to them, what need is there to describe the mantra method to them? Although they have thus gained access to emptiness, they also act with expedient means to liberate beings, so the text says, '***who have vowed to liberate all realms of beings without remainder***'. Therefore listen to the Mandala which is described for the '***benefit, welfare and happiness***' of those who engage in Bodhisattva practice by means of the secret mantras who thus unite insight and expedient means. Here, '***benefit***' (*artha*) means for the benefit of the Bodhisattvas, for the bliss of Nirvāṇa or salvation (*niḥśreya*). '***Welfare***' (*hita*) means it is for their welfare in this and future lives. (174a) '***Happiness***' (*sukha*) means it is for their happiness in this life.

67. Then saying, 'Bhagavat, thus do I desire!', Vajrapāṇi listened to the Bhagavat, who said this to him, 'Lord of the Secret Ones, first is the topic of the layout of the Mandala of the fully perfect Buddha, which is the source of countless mundane and supra-mundane mandalas, the most secret of secrets, and which is called "That Arisen from the Matrix of Great Compassion", so listen to the ritual for drawing it!'

Lord of the Secret Ones, first is the topic of the layout of the Mandala of the fully perfect Buddha: This means that first the Bhagavat Vairocana should be established in the matrix mandala in the same way as in the previous Mandalas and this is connected with the words '***so listen to the ritual for drawing it***' which are mentioned below. ***Most secret of secrets***: It is secret because the intrinsic nature of his Mind cannot be drawn and perceived as a cognitive object. It is an even greater secret than that because it is not revealed to any person without the *samaya*. ***The source of countless mundane and supramundane mandalas***: The mundane mandalas are the representational mandalas, drawn with pigments. The supramundane mandalas are the intrinsically existent ones. Because the mundane mandalas emanate from it and because the intrinsically existent mandalas are known through seeing it, it is said to be their source. Moreover, this means that countless mandalas of mundane deities and supramundane deities arise from it.

68. 'It should be completely square,
one-gated, with a pavilion,
marked with a fine vajra, (174b)
and a hundred-pointed vajra in the centre[A].
Upon it, a lotus is drawn
full-blown, with seeds.
Upon that also there is a great lotus,
perfected with eight petals

A C: 羯磨金剛 '*karma-vajra*'. This is understood in the Sino-Japanese tradition to be a cross formed by a pair of three-pointed vajras.

adorned with *mudrās* and *anusvāras*,
and it has anthers, very fine.
On all the petals are arranged
the twelve component syllables.
In the midst of them, the Lord sits,
the Lord of Men, the Perfect Buddha.
He is completely encircled
by an entourage of eight mandalas.'

This section deals with the drawing of the matrix mandala in which the Bhagavat Vairocana resides. The rituals for measuring out the mandala, the sequence of the sections and the application of the pigments are as those mentioned in connection with the previous Mandalas. ***Completely square [border]***: (174b) This indicates that he is endowed with the Four Immeasurables. ***One-gated***: This indicates that many gates are gathered together in the one gate of the continuum of reality. ***With a pavilion*** (*vedikā*): The centre of the [area] which has been drawn in outline with pigment is filled in with yellow pigment. This means that it has a base upon which the Bhagavat sits. ***Marked with a vajra***: A five-pointed vajra should be drawn within it, on the western side. ***A hundred-pointed vajra in the centre***: This indicates that he has the hundred Awareness *Dhāraṇīs* of liberation during his causal phase. Also, with regards to these hundred Awareness which are the gates to liberation, it says in the chapter on the Revolving Wheel of Letters that there are twenty four letters from the *Ka* group down to *Ya, Ra, La* and *Va,* which make twenty five when headed by *A*. Likewise those with *A, Aṃ* and *Aḥ* also each make up twenty five letters. You should draw in it a hundred-pointed vajra which by its nature links one with the hundred Awarenesses through those hundred gates to liberation. *Śa, Ṣa, Sa* and *Ha* are included within the second area.

Upon it, a lotus should be drawn, full-blown, with seeds: Upon that vajra, you should draw a lotus with four petals and with its seeds. ***Upon that also there is a great lotus, perfected with eight petals, adorned with* mudrās *and* anusvāras, *and it has anthers, very fine***: You should additionally draw an eight-petalled great lotus on top of that. ***Adorned with* mudrās *and* anusvāras**: Since the '***anusvāra***' is the sign which indicates emptiness, this refers to the Twelve-membered *Vidyā* King[22] and it should be linked with the words, '***the twelve component syllables*** (pada) ***are arranged***'. The *mudrās* are the eight secret *mudrās* and this should be linked with the words, '***by the entourage of eight mandalas***'. (175a) You should know that since the upper lotus is distinguished by its size and by having eight petals, the one below it appears to be much smaller than it and has [only] four petals. Secondly, you should know that since it is the lotus of the causal phase, it is smaller. The great lotus with eight petals is the eight Awarenesses[23] in nature, as described before.

On all the petals are arranged the twelve component syllables: The eight paired essence and sub-essence letters of the Twelve-membered *Vidyā* King should be written upon the eight petals[24].

In the midst of them, the Lord sits, the Lord of Men, the Perfect Buddha. He is completely encircled by the entourage of eight mandalas: The Bhagavat sits in the matrix at the centre of the lotus, and the eight *mudrās* should also be drawn in that lotus matrix, surrounding the Bhagavat, with their own mandalas and seed syllables.

69. 'This Mandala arising from Great Compassion
should be known as the foremost.
From this the mandalas arise,
together with their rites, shapes,
attainments and layouts of the Valiant Ones,
each according to their texts'.

'***Foremost***' means the foremost of supports. The mandalas for the rites of Pacifying, Enriching and so forth should be laid out in their [respective] shapes, and you should know that the mandalas which are explained elsewhere in other parts of the text also arise from this Mandala. The abode of the Bhagavat Vairocana is an earth mandala.

70. 'Lord of the Secret Ones!
Furthermore, the mandala of the Tathāgatas
is like a pure[A] moon disc,
and resembles a conch in colour;
within it the triangle of all the Buddhas
rests upon a white lotus.
It is marked with an *anusvāra* sign,
and adorned with a vajra symbol[B].
Without doubt, there will emerge
two rays of light[C]
from that Lord of Mantras,
and then go to the ten directions.'

To the east of the Bhagavat you should draw the mandala of all the Tathāgatas who have gone before. (175b) ***Like a moon disc***: Means that the form of the base for the Bhagavat's lotus is like a moon disc. ***Resembles a conch in colour***: You should know that the water mandala is like a conch in colour. ***Within it the triangle of all the Buddhas rests upon a white lotus***: This means that upon the water mandala you should draw a triangular symbol on a white lotus. ***Marked with an* anusvāra *sign***: The letter *A* with an *anusvāra* should be placed there. ***Adorned with a vajra symbol***: A five-pointed vajra should be drawn there. ***There will emerge two rays of light***: Two rays of light should be drawn emerging from two corners of that triangular symbol. These should be known as the *saṃbhoga-kāya* and the *nirmāṇa-kāya*, which arise from the *dharmakāya*.

71. 'Lord of the Secret Ones!
Furthermore, Lokeśvara's mandala
should be drawn diligently by the noble one.
Its border is square all around,
and in the centre, a conch should be placed.
Upon that, a lotus is drawn

A '*pure*' added from C.
B C: 金剛印圍繞 '*encircled with vajra* mudrās'.
C C: 周匝放光明 '*rays of light are emitted from the edges of* [*this Mantra Lord*]'.

full-blown, with its seed-syllable.
Upon that, a great vajra[A]**,**
and on the vajra also a great lotus
marked with all the seed-syllables,
to which should be added his own seed-syllable[B]**.'**

This describes the mandala of Avalokiteśvara. ***Its border is square all around***: It is drawn as an earth mandala. ***In the centre a conch should be placed***: In its centre, a water mandala should be drawn. ***Upon that a lotus is drawn, full-blown, with its seed-syllable***: A white lotus with the seed-syllable *A* should be drawn upon that water mandala. ***Upon that, a great vajra***: A five-pointed vajra should be set upon the lotus. ***On the vajra, also a great lotus marked with all the seed-syllables, to which should be added his own seed-syllable***: Upon that vajra, an eight-petalled great lotus should be drawn, together with his own seed-syllable.

72. **'Also Tārā and Bhṛkuṭī,**
likewise Pāṇḍara-vāsinī,
the *Vidyā* Vasumati[C]**,**
and Mahā-sthāma-prāpta should be carefully made.
All the Noble Ones and their assistants
should be drawn within this mandala
as the *mudrā* symbols,
the attributes of their attainments.'

(176a) His entourage, Tārā and so forth, should be drawn in that mandala in the form of their symbols.

73. **'The activity**[25] **of Hayagrīva**
rests in a triangle as appropriate.
The mandala is marked[D] **with fine signs**
and it is like the colour of the rising sun. (175a)
It should be arranged by the wise one,
together with the *Vidyā* King.'

At the border of the western side of that mandala, the triangular mandala of Hayagrīva should be drawn. ***The mandala is marked with fine signs***: The mandala is adorned with triangular [marks]. ***It should be arranged by the wise one together with the Vidyā King***: That triangular mandala should be drawn with the *Vidyā* King, Hayagrīva. You should know that he is to be drawn in the form of his symbol.

74. **'Furthermore, Lord of the Secret Ones,**
I shall briefly describe your own mandala[E]**:**

A C: 上表金剛慧 '*on that, a vajra insight* [mudrā] *should be displayed*'.
B C: 善功以爲種 '*skilfully placing* [*him*] *there as his seed-syllable*'.
C T: *longs-spyod-ma.*
D '*Adorned*' added from V and C.
E C: 第二壇 '*the second mandala*'. Perhaps there has been some graphic confusion between '*tvayaṃ*' (your) and '*dvayaṃ*' (second).

It is completely square in shape,
marked with a vajra symbol;
all of it is in pleasing yellow.
In the middle a lotus is placed,
and in the centre a vase should be made,
with light like the moon.
On this, its sign should be marked,
and also adorned with an *anusvāra.*
Upon that also, the great wind[A],
the colour of summer rain clouds;
it should be made by the *mantrin*
as a moving banner,
and is adorned with an *anusvāra.*
Upon that also, a triangle,
with a fearsome appearance,
like the destroying fire,
and marked with a triangular design[B].
Its encircling aura of flames is most awesome,
like the colour of the rising sun.
Within that, a great lotus,
[red] like the fire at the end of time;
upon the lotus, there is a vajra,
with a radiating blazing aura;
it is marked with the excellent seed-syllable,
that has the sound "*Hūṃ*".
This mandala of yours, O Hero,
was spoken of by the Victorious Lords [in the past].'

This is the description of the mandala of Vajrapāṇi. Since Vajrapāṇi's intrinsic nature is the Accomplishment of Activities and he is all-doing (*sarva-karmika*), you should know that his mandala has four parts. ***It is completely square, marked with a vajra symbol, all of it is in a pleasing yellow***: First an earth mandala should be drawn as before. A lotus should be drawn in the middle of that earth mandala, then a water mandala upon that lotus. You should know the vase to be the water mandala. ***On this, its sign should be marked and also adorned with an* anusvāra**: That mandala should be marked with its sign, the seed-syllable *Va* with an *anusvāra.* (176b) Upon that water mandala, a wind mandala should be drawn, dark purple like summer rain clouds, with a banner which looks as though it is in motion[26]. ***Adorned with an* anusvāra**: You should know that its seed-syllable *Ha,* has an *anusvāra.* Upon that wind mandala, there is a fire mandala, triangular and fearsome, the colour of the fire of the destruction at the end of an eon. ***Marked with a triangular design***: It is also marked with the sign of that mandala, a triangle.

Within that, a great lotus: A second lotus, red in colour like the fire at the end of time, should be drawn in the middle of the fire mandala. Upon the lotus a maroon

A C: 大風印 '*the great wind* mudrā'.
B C: 三角以圍之 '*and encircled with triangles*'.

coloured vajra should be drawn. '*Blazing*' is the nature of the fire. '*Radiating*' is the wind portion. Since both the fire and wind are present, the vajra should be made red-maroon. ***It is marked with the excellent seed-syllable that has the sound "Hūṃ"***: This means that the letter *Hūṃ*, Vajrapāṇi's seed-syllable, should be placed upon it.

75. **'Māmakī and Vajra-śṛṅkhalā,**
likewise those arising from the Vajra Family[A],
Vajrāṅkuśī and Vajra-sūcī,
and the most powerful Mantra King[27]
should all be known
in this great mandala.
So that the actions may be accomplished,
their specific symbols and mandalas,
seed-syllables and colours,
should be done in sequence, as fitting.'

(177a) This explains that his entourage, Māmakī and so forth, should be drawn in [this] earth mandala. You should likewise know that their mandalas are in accordance with the specific colours of their individual symbols and seed-syllables, and they should be drawn according to the sequence previously explained.

76. **'Then there are also the chief**
great Vajradharas I have mentioned:
Vimala-ākāśa, Vajra-cakra,
Vajra-daṃṣṭra, Surata,
Vighuṣṭa, Mahā-bhaga,
the Vajradhara Vajra-nātha,
Śānti-vajra and Mahā-vajra,
Nīla-vajra, and the other Vajra[dharas]
Padma-vajra, Vimala-netra,
Suvajra, and Vajra,
Niḥprapañca-pratiṣṭha,
and Ākāśānantya-gati.' (175b)

In the area below Vajrapāṇi's mandala, you should draw the sixteen[B] Vajradharas who are listed, beginning with Vimalākāśa.

77. **'Their mandalas are said to be**
white, yellow, red and black.
Futhermore, the shape of their symbols
are three-pointed and single-pointed,
also neither of these two[C],

A C: 及金剛部主 '*and the Lord of the Vajra Family*'.

B Both commentaries have '*twelve*', but I have amended this to '*sixteen*' as that is the correct number.

C C: 二首皆五峰 '*All the double-headed ones have five points*'. This makes better sense than T, which I have had to retain for the sake of Buddhaguhya's comments (which in themselves are unclear).

and some are also like garlands.
They are distinguished by their various colours[A]**.**
All of them have their seed-syllables[B]**,**
and are very powerful.'

For their mandalas, you should also draw the four mandalas of earth and so forth. Their mandalas are described thus: '***Their mandalas are said to be white, yellow, red and black***'. These four types of mandalas should be repeated four[C] times, and linked with the sixteen Vajradharas in sequence. ***Furthermore, the shapes of their symbols are three-pointed, and single-pointed, also neither of these two, and some are also like garlands***: Their three-pointed vajra symbols are of two types – three points at [only] one end, and three points at both ends. The same applies to the single-pointed vajras. Therefore they hold both two-headed ones, and the one-headed ones which are vajra hammers (*thu lum*). ***Some are also like garlands***: These are vajra garland symbols. Those four should be multiplied by two to give a total of sixteen[28]. ***They are distinguished by their various colours***: The colours of those symbols should be the same as the colours of the corresponding Vajradharas. ***They are all completely victorious***[29], (177b) ***and are very powerful***: This praises those Vajradharas, saying that they are all victorious over those difficult to quell.

78. **'The mandala of the Lord Acala**
is said to be of wind and fire.
It should be drawn in the south-west,
below the area in front of me,
It has his seed-syllable as his sign
together with a sword symbol,
or it is permissible to make a noose.
[Thus] the wise one should depict him.'

This describes the mandala of the Lord Acala. ***It is said to be of wind and fire***: Draw a fire mandala upon a wind mandala, and then draw Acala's symbol on top of that, either a sword or a noose, together with his seed-syllable.

79. **'Trailokya-vijaya's is likewise,**
different in having his sign with a vajra
in the middle of a wind [disc][D]**,**
and he abides in the three bases.'

A T: '*The colours should be known by their special attributes* (viśeṣa)'. C makes better sense so I have adopted that.

B T: *rnam-par-rgyal*, C: 種子 '*seed-syllables*'. Confusion between *vijaya* 'victorious' and *bīja* 'seed-syllable'? On the basis of parallel passages above, the reading of C should be adopted, although T is quite possible.

C Both commentaries have '*three*' but this ought to be amended to '*four*', as there are sixteen Vajradharas.

D C: 降三世殊異 謂在風輪中 繞以金剛印 而住於三處 '*Trailokyavijaya's special feature is that he abides within a wind disc, surrounded with vajra* mudrās *and abiding in the three places*'.

Trailokyavijaya's is likewise*:** This means that you should draw a fire mandala upon a wind mandala as in the case of Acala. ***In the middle of a wind [disc] and so on: You should draw [another] wind mandala on top of the fire mandala and a Vajra *Mudrā* with his own sign should be drawn within it. ***He abides in the three bases*:** He abides in the three bases, the two wind mandalas and the one fire mandala.

80. **'Furthermore, Lord of the Secret Ones!**
You should arrange in a mandala
the form of the Mother of the Bodhisattvas.
First of all, the whole mandala therein[A]
is square, the colour of gold,
and is marked with vajra symbols.
This is an excellent mandala.
Then there is also the form of the goddess
[upon] a great lotus in the middle of it,
all yellow, with a flaming aura.'

This describes the mandala of Locanā, which is an earth mandala, as before. Also you should make the colour of that goddess yellow. She is seated upon a lotus.

81. **'The Uṣṇīṣa which is also placed there**
should reside in one third;
Omitting the second part,
Locanā should also be drawn there.
She abides in the midst of radiant light,
and should be accompanied by her seed-syllable.'

You should draw a lotus upon an earth mandala, and draw the threefold Uṣṇīṣa upon that lotus. ***Omitting the second part, Locanā should also be drawn there*:** You should omit the middle third below the Uṣṇīṣa symbol and draw the symbol of Locanā in the lower portion. ***Abiding in the midst of radiant light*:** That Uṣṇīṣa symbol should be located within blazing light. (178a) ***With her seed-syllable*:** It should be made with the letter of that Mother's seed-syllable.

82. **'As for the Wish-fulfilling Gem of all the Bodhisattvas,**
the Victorious One prescribes that
its mandala is of water, with crossed vajras[B]
It is utterly unsullied and most peaceful,
and causes all wishes to be fulfilled.'

A C: 先說漫荼羅 諸佛菩薩母 安置壇形像 '*I shall first explain the first mandala of the Mother of the Buddhas and Bodhisattvas who form should be placed in the mandala.* [*It is square* ...]'.

B T: *chu-yi yin-te thams-cad sgo*, while C has 圓白而四出, omitting '*of water*' in place of which it says 'completely white'. Moreover *thams-cad sgo* and ¥l ¥X are somewhat enigmatic. If we take into consideration CC's comments that a vajra-cross is to be placed within the water mandala, we can surmise that they are probably the equivalents for *viśva-mukha*, 'facing all directions'. To make the meaning clearer I have translated this as '*with crossed vajras*'.

This means that the Wish-fulfilling Gem, the symbol of all the Bodhisattvas, should be drawn upon a water mandala.

83. 'Then, Noble One, listen carefully
about the mandala of Śākyamuni!
It is the one called Mahendra
adorned with yellow colour,
and completely square on all sides.
In the centre is a vajra as before,
and upon it should be placed
a completely yellow lotus[A].
Upon that, a great begging bowl
which has vajra markings. (176a)
Or else the robes and staff
should be placed there in sequence.'

In the second area of the Mandala, you should draw Śākyamuni resting upon an earth mandala. The remainder is as before. You should place a yellow lotus upon an earth mandala, and upon that lotus you should place a begging bowl, or monks robes, or a mendicant's staff. That is also to be marked with blazing vajras.

84. 'You should also know the symbols
of the well-known five Uṣṇīṣas:
Sitāta-patrā's is a parasol,
For Jayā, the wise one should place
a sword as her symbol,
and it should emit rays of light.
Vijayā's is a wheel,
Vikiraṇa's is a hook,
and the Fortunate One says
Tejorāśi's is a fine *uṣṇīṣa*.
Mahodaya's is a vajra,
Abhyudgata's is a lotus
and Ananta-svāra-ghoṣa's is a conch.
Know them according to their different colours.'

This section describes the drawing of the symbols of the five Uṣṇīṣas, and their mandalas should match their individual colours. Both their colours and mandalas are as previously explained.

85. 'That of Ūrṇā is a Wish-fulfilling Gem.
Of Locanā's also, listen,
it is an *uṣṇīṣa*, completely yellow,
and marked with vajra symbols.'

A C adds: 周遍皆黄暈 '*the entire surroundings shine with yellow light*'.

The symbol of Ūrṇā should be drawn like a Wish-fulfilling Gem and her mandala should match her colour. The symbol of Buddha-locanā is drawn as a yellow *uṣṇiṣa* and marked with vajra signs. Because her colour is yellow, you should know that it should be drawn on an earth mandala.

86. **'That of Aparājitā**
is a hand holding a wondrous lotus.
That of Aparājita is a great mouth[30]
resting on a black lotus.'

(178b) The symbol of Aparājitā should be drawn as a raised lotus, with the hand drawn as a fist. The symbol of the *Vidyā* King called Aparājita should be drawn resting upon a black lotus.

87. **'Those who are said to dwell in the Pure Abode**
are those who have access
to the realization of purity.
Listen, Noble One, to the arrangement
of the symbols of their names:
A thinking-hand, an auspicious-hand,
a smiling-hand, and likewise also
a flower-hand, and a space-hand
should be drawn in detail as prescribed.'

This section describes the drawing of the symbols of the Pure Abode gods. ***Thinking-hand***: The palm of his hand rests upon his cheek. When drawing this symbol, the cheeks should not be drawn, but just the palms. ***Auspicious-hand***: A hand bestowing fearlessness should be drawn. ***Smiling-hand***: It should be drawn as though pulling back the mouth from the cheek. ***Flower-hand***: You should draw the ring finger and the thumb placed together. ***Space-hand***: It should be drawn as an upraised hand[31].

88. **'That of Pṛthivī is a vase,**
a water mandala marked with a vajra.
A beckoning hand is that of Agni,
and it should be drawn with the Ṛṣis[A]**:**
Kāśyapa and Gautama,
Mārkaṇḍeya, Gārgaṇa,
Vaśiṣṭha and Aṅgiras
are seated within Agni's abode.
They should be drawn diligently
according to sequence, with the Veda Hand.'

The symbol of Pṛthivī should be drawn as a jar filled with water, and adorned with vajras. The symbol of Agni should be drawn together with the Ṛṣis who are listed,

A C: 請召火天印 當以大仙手 '*The* mudrā *for inviting Agni should be* [*drawn*] *as a great* ṛṣi's *hand*'.

beginning with Kāśyapa. The '*Veda Hand*' is the symbol of the Ṛṣis – the thumb should be placed on the finger joints as with the Recitation Hand[32].

89. 'The club of Yama should be drawn
resting within a wind mandala.
That of the Lord of Death is a bell,
Kālarātrī's sign is a pennant,
Raudrī's is a trident,
Brahmī's is a lotus,
Kaumārī's is a spear,
Vaiṣṇavī's is a wheel,
and that of Camuṇḍā is a mallet[A].
Kauverī's is a human skull.
These should all be placed
within wind mandalas, (176b)
and are completely encircled
by crows, eagles, dogs and vultures[B].
Whoever wishes to accomplish the actions
should draw them as prescribed.'

The symbol of Yama, a staff, should be drawn resting upon a wind mandala. The mandala of Yama should be surrounded with the symbols of his entourage who are listed as the Lord of Death, Kālarātrī and so on, drawn in the wind mandalas and surrounded by crows, eagles and so on.

90. 'Draw a sword for Nirṛti,
and a wheel for Viṣṇu.
Skanda's[C] is a spear.
Those of Nanda and Upananda
are both clouds with lightning,
and both are water blue in colour.
To be placed in both gate areas
of Śākya-siṃha's mandala
are the trident of Śaṅkāra,
and the cobra of Umā.
A white vase with a lotus
is the symbol of Candra.
That of Āditya is a chariot,
resting upon an earth mandala[D].
Those of the great ladies Jayā and Vijayā

A Reading based on C which gives *mudgara* 'mallet' in transliteration, while T has *thod-pa* 'skull' which is probably wrong in view of the next line.

B C has *bhāsa* 'vulture' (*Gyps bengalensis*) in transliteration. However CC explains thus: '*A* bhāsa *resembles a kite, and has a small ochre-coloured or yellow crest. It is a type of sparrow-hawk. This bird is camouflaged*'. T has *wa* which normally translates Sanskrit words for 'fox', though the Mahā-vyutpatti also gives it for *kāka* 'crow'.

C C: '*Kumāra*' which is another name for Skanda.

D This line goes with the bow symbol of Jayā and Vijayā in C.

are endowed with a bow symbol.
The pennant symbol should be drawn
for the Maruts in the north-west.
That of Sarasvatī is a *vīṇā*;
Varuṇa is depicted holding a noose.
O Great One, you should know that
his mandala is of water.
They should be empowered with the seed-syllables,
and marked with their symbols.
The mandalas for their symbols
in the mandala of Śākya-siṃha
should be made as prescribed.
The symbols placed within them
should be accompanied by the seed-syllables.'

The symbols of those listed such as Viṣṇu and so forth should be known as stated. (179a) Also when the mandalas are not actually mentioned, you should match them up by their specific colours and shapes with the mandalas previously described.

91. **'Furthermore, listen carefully concerning**
the mandala of Vajra-varada[33]:
It is completely square on all sides
and marked with vajra symbols,
and within it should be made
the mandala arisen from fire.
The symbol placed within it
is an *utpala*, beautiful in form.
The mantra of the Wise One Mañjughoṣa
is surrounded by its light;
his bases are as prescribed,
and are sealed with their seed-syllables;
all the edges of the circumference
should be covered with *utpalas*.'

This describes the drawing of the mandala of the Noble Mañjuśrī in the third area of the mandala. There is an earth mandala, as before, and in the middle of that earth mandala you should draw a fire mandala. The symbol to be placed within that is an *utpala*.

The seed-syllable mantra of Mañjughoṣa himself should be placed upon that *utpala* and should be surrounded by light. ***His bases are as prescribed and should be sealed with their own seed-syllables***: Each of the seed-syllables, *A* and *Ra*, should be placed according to the prescribed rule upon an earth and a fire mandala. The edges of those mandalas should be surrounded with *utpalas*.

92. **'These Heroes are to be drawn within it,**
according to sequence:
The symbol of Jālinī-prabha is a hook,
for the youth Ratna-ketu, a jewel,

for the youth Vimala-prabha, a lotus bud; (177a)
As for those who are known as the Messengers
of the Wise One Mañjughoṣa,
their [symbols] should be known
by the fearless one, as appropriate.
You should know that a sword
is the symbol of Keśinī,
a trident is Upakeśinī's,
Citrā's is said to be a staff,
Vasumati's is a banner,
and that of Ākarṣaṇī is a hook.
They should all be marked
with the *utpala* emblems.
The symbols of the Servants
who are mentioned, are curved knives.'

The symbols of the Messengers, Keśinī and so forth should be drawn marked with *utpalas*. (179b) The symbols of Mañjuśrī's Servants previously described, should be drawn as the curved knives called '*khaḍgas*'.

93. 'Diligently in the south you should draw
the symbol of the energetic Sarva-nīvaraṇa-viṣkambhin,
which is a Wish-fulfilling Gem,
set within a fire mandala,
accompanied in sequence by his entourage.
You should know that these, in detail,
are the symbols of that entourage:
the symbol of Kautuhala
is a one-pointed vajra upon a jar,
Abhayaṃdada's is a hand bestowing fearlessness,
Apāya-jaha's is a hand which should be formed
as though drawing up from fire,
Paritrāṇāśaya-mati's is a hand placed over the breast,
Maitry-abhyudgata's is a hand holding a flower,
Karuṇā-mṛḍita-mati's is a hand placed on his heart,
with the middle finger hooked inwards.
Sarva-dāha-prasamita's is a hand granting favours,
with streams of water flowing from the tips.
Acintya-mati-datta's is a hand,
which hold a wish-fulfiling gem.
All of these rest upon lotuses,
which should be placed within their mandalas.'

The symbols of Sarva-nīvaraṇa-viṣkambhin with his entourage should be drawn as stated. ***A hand placed over his heart*:** Just a hand should be drawn, as though placed on his heart. ***All of these should rest upon lotuses which should be set within their mandalas*:** This means that all the symbols whose mandalas are not actually mentioned, following Jālinī-prabha, should be drawn upon lotuses within the above mandalas.

94. 'The symbol of Kṣiti-garbha in the north
abides within an earth mandala,
on which there is placed a seat as before;
on that there is a great lotus
which blazes radiantly with all colours.
Upon that there is a great pennant,
with a great jewel placed on its tip.
His is the most excellent of forms
described here in the shape of his symbol.
His entourage are without number,
the limitless qualities of the Lord.
Their symbols should also be
diligently generated and drawn. (177b)
The symbol of Ratnākara
is a three-pointed vajra
which rests upon a jewel.
Ratna-pāṇi's is a one-pointed vajra
which rests upon a jewel.
Dharaṇīṃdhara's is a two-headed vajra,
which rest upon a jewel.
Ratna-mudrā-hasta's is a five-pointed vajra
which rests upon a jewel.
Dṛḍhādhyāśaya's is a *viśva-vajra*
which rests upon a jewel.
All these symbols should be placed in mandalas.'

This describes the symbols of Kṣiti-garbha and his entourage. ***There is placed a seat as before***: Kṣiti-garbha's seat should be drawn within that earth mandala, as described previously in the Mandala Arisen from Great Compassion. Upon that seat you should draw an eight-petalled lotus. ***All colours***: The eight petals should be made in different colours – white, red, yellow, blue [and black], together with the other three which are mixtures, such as green. ***His is the most excellent of forms*** (180a) ***described here in the shape of his* mudrā**: The form of Kṣiti-garbha is described as the shape of his symbol.

His entourage are without number and so forth describes the drawing of the symbols of the chief members of the limitless and numberless entourage of Kṣiti-garbha. ***That of Dharaṇīṃdhara is a two-headed vajra which rests upon a jewel***: That vajra has two points, one pair up and one pair down. Since his vajra is thus distinguished, you should know that the previous two vajras have three points and one point in each direction. ***All these symbols should be placed in mandalas***: All those symbols should be placed upon earth mandalas.

95. 'The symbol of Ākāśa-garbha in the west
is a white lotus great throne,

in a pleasing water mandala[A].
Within it a sword-noose
with extremely sharp blades[B],
sealed with his seed-syllable,
should be placed there by the wise one.
To draw his entourage,
the shapes of their symbols are, in sequence:
A wheel sign within a wind mandala
is the symbol of Gaganāmala.
The symbol of Gagana-mati
is a conch within a mandala[C].
The symbol of Viśuddha-mati
is a white lotus within a wind mandala.
The symbol of Caritra-mati
is an *utpala* placed on a conch[D],
within a wind mandala.
The symbol of Sthira-buddhi also
is a vajra set upon a lotus[E].'

This section describes the drawing of the symbols of Ākāśa-garbha and his entourage.

For the colours and shapes of the deities in this Mandala who are not clearly mentioned here, you should refer to their colours and shapes as described in the previous two Mandalas. Likewise for the colours and so on not described in detail in the previous two Mandalas, you should know them from the mandalas of the individual deities as mentioned in this Mandala.

A C: 圓白悅意壇 '*a perfectly white pleasing mandala*'.

B C: 置大慧刀印 如是堅利刃 鋒銳猶氷霜 '[*Upon that*] *you should place a great insight sword* mudrā. *Its extremely sharp blade is as keen as hoar frost*'.

C C: 風漫荼羅 '*a wind mandala*'.

D C: 磗磲 '*giant clam*'. Note that CC specifically states that the shell in question is *not* a conch.

E C: 在風漫荼羅 '*within a wind mandala*'. C then follows with: 略說佛秘藏 諸尊密印竟 '*This completes a brief explanation of the secret* mudrās *of the deities in the Buddha's secret treasury*'.

XIV
ENTRY INTO THE SECRET MANDALA

1. Then the Bhagavat also spoke of the ritual for entering into the Secret Mandala:

> **'The *mantrin* who is fully trained,**
> **who is skilled in the Secret Mandala,**
> **should now burn up, according to [this] ritual,**
> **all the failings of the trainee.'**

(180b) This chapter explains the ritual for the introduction [of the trainees] into the Secret Mandala and their initiation. The stages in the entry into the Mandala which are the five explained for the previous Mandalas – staying by it [from the previous] evening, acceptance of the Discipline and so on, the protection, sprinkling with water, the generation of *bodhicitta* and so on – should also be done in this case. As for the distinctive elements, the trainee should be placed as before in the gateway of the Mandala. Then the Master should abide in his own *samādhi* and imagine a letter *Ra*[1] in the heart of the trainee, focussing his attention upon the true meaning of that letter, that all phenomena are free from dust. He then should reduce the body of that trainee to atoms and [know that] those atoms also lack any objective reality. By that, the body of the trainee is made empty on the absolute level. Having imagined thus, he should also imagine the body of the trainee being burnt up by the fire of the letter *Ra* and turning to ashes. Having dissolved the trainee into emptiness, he should again imagine a letter *A*[2] in that place and then imagine that *A* changing into the Body of the Bhagavat. This is the summary. The meaning of the sections will also be explained now.

The* mantrin *who is fully trained: The Master who has learnt the rituals of drawing both the Mandala Arisen from Great Compassion and the Mandala of the Revolving Wheel of Letters, of the initiations, the recitation, the *sādhana* and so forth. He is '***skilled***' because he is learned. In brief, the Master who has been initiated into the previous two Mandalas should carry out these actions. ***Should now burn up, according to this ritual, all the failings of the trainee***: This is the preliminary statement. '***All the failings***' refers to the accumulation of unwholesome tendencies in the [trainee's] mental stream (181a) which cause the growth of undesired recompense. Those failings of the trainee should be burnt up by the ritual which appears below[3].

2.

> **'So that it will not arise henceforth,**
> **his life should [also] be burnt up.**
> **But, when he has been burnt and become ash,**
> **he should be re-created.'**

This explains clearly how to burn up all the failings of the trainee mentioned above. '***His life***' refers to the five psycho-physical constituents of the trainee. ***So that it will not arise henceforth***: At the same time as the five psycho-physical constituents are thus being burnt up and dissolved into emptiness, not even the idea that the trainee's five psycho-physical constituents really exist should arise. ***But when he has been burnt and turned to ash***: When there is nothing remaining to be burnt up and the trainee's psycho-physical constituents have been utterly destroyed, he should be turned into emptiness. ***He should be re-created***: When he has been firmly established in emptiness, the trainee should then be united with the body-image of Vairocana, according to the words appearing below.

3. 'With a letter he should be burnt into the unchanging,
and with life[A] he should be re-created;
When all has been re-created by life, (178a)
he will be completely pure and unsullied.'

Though it has been stated in general that the life of the trainee should be burnt up at that time, you might wonder how or by what it is burnt up, so the text says '***With a letter*** (*akṣareṇa*), ***he should be burnt into the unchanging*** (*akṣara*)'. This means that the five psycho-physical constituents of the trainee should be consumed by the letter *Ra* as previously mentioned. '*Akṣara*' (letter) also means 'unchanging': that is, the five psycho-physical constituents should be made stable, not to arise again or change into anything other than emptiness. ***With life he should be re-created, and when all has been re-created by life***: This is linked with the previous words, '***he should be re-created***'. This means that after the trainee's life, his five psycho-physical constituents have become empty, he is transformed into the Body of Vairocana in the manner mentioned above, by the letter *A*, which is '***life***'. ***Completely pure***: He is white. ***Unsullied***: He is luminescent. In other words, he is transformed (181b) into the radiant white Body of the Buddha.

4. 'The twelve component syllables
should be arranged on their receptacle.'

The twelve component syllables should be arranged on his lotus seat[4].

5. 'This *samaya* of the Buddhas
and saviour Bodhisattvas is revered
by the Buddhas, Śrāvakas
and mundane gods.'[B]

It is fitting for Buddhas, Bodhisattvas, Śrāvakas, Pratyekabuddhas and the mundane [gods] to have trust in this *samaya*.

A C: 字 '*letter*'.

B This is quite different in C: 如是三味耶 一切諸如來 菩薩救世者 及佛聲聞衆 乃至諸世間 平等不違逆 '*With this* Samaya, *one becomes equal to and not parted from all the Tathāgatas, the saviour Bodhisattvas, Buddhas and Śrāvakas, and the mundane gods.*' CC comments thus: Samaya *means 'the same as'. That is you are equal to the Buddha and the Buddha is equal to you, without duality or separateness. Ultimately all are equal. The Master is equal to the Buddha and the Buddha is equal to the trainee. Not only is the trainee equal to all the Tathāgatas of the ten directions, but he is also equal to all the Bodhisattvas and all the Śrāvakas, Pratyekabuddhas and crowds of mundane deities. If he is equal to all beings in this way, he is the Body of Vairocana.*

6. 'Whosoever understands this *samaya*
dwelling within the Secret Mandala,
has entered all the tantras,
and is master of all the mandalas;
that mantra-holder will be like me:
no others are said to have *samaya*[A].'

Whoever is firm in this *samādhi* method within the Secret Mandala will be as one who has entered the mandalas of all Tantras, will have the *samaya* for them all and will be a master of drawing all mandalas. ***That mantra-holder will be like me***: It was stated in general above that he should be re-created and made radiant and white, and these words mean that he should be made into the very body-image of the Bhagavat Vairocana.

To have* samaya *refers to nothing else: If that *samādhi* is not done, and another is done in error, one cannot be said to have *samaya*. On this occasion '***samaya***' refers to the realization of the *samādhi* of emptiness. That *samādhi* which first burns is the entering *bodhicitta*. To abide unchanging in the intrinsic emptiness [of phenomena], after having been burnt up is the abiding *bodhicitta*. Then the re-creation and transformation into the Body of the Bhagavat is the arising *bodhicitta*.

A C: 我身等同彼 眞言者亦然 以不相異故 說名三味耶 '*Because my Body is the same as his, and likewise the* mantrin *himself is no different, I call this* "samaya" '.

XV
THE EIGHT SECRET *MUDRĀS*

1. Then the Bhagavat Vairocana gazed upon the circle of the entire assembly and spoke to the Bodhisattva Vajrapāṇi, 'There are eight secret *mudrās* which are most secret, which create the divine abode[A], which are marked with their own mantras, which have mandalas and which should be used for the yoga of one's tutelary deity.'

Now the eight secret *mudrās* should be described. These *mudrās* are used in order to make stable the *mantrin*'s transformation into the body-image of the deity. Also the transformation into the body-image of the deity is of two types: transformation into a Tathāgata's Body and (182a) transformation into a Bodhisattva's Body. At the time of transforming yourself into a Bhagavat's Body, the throne, the members, the light and so on should be formed according to the stages appearing below, with the following secret *mudrās*. Also when transforming yourself into the forms of Bodhisattvas and so forth, they will become stable if you do the transformation with these *mudrās*. If you transform yourself with these *mudrās* while changing yourself into the Body of a Tathāgata, you will become a Tathāgata in nature, because these *mudrās* are the *mudrās* of the Tathāgata.

The Body of the deity, which is to be perfected, is also of two types: the place which is to be perfected and the body which is to be perfected. The place is perfected with two *mudrās*, the *Mudrā* of the Indestructible Vajra and the *Mudrā* of the Lotus Bud. The remaining six bring about the perfection of the body. They are divided into three types: those which perfect the body, the speech and the mind. Those which bring about the perfection of the body are the *Mudrā* Producing All Limbs and the *Mudrā* Producing Brilliance. Those which bring about the perfection of mind are the *Dhāraṇī Mudrā* and the *Mudrā* of the Abiding of the Bhagavat's Dharma. The Adornment of the Array of Buddha Speech is the *Mudrā* which brings about the perfection of speech. The *Mudrā* of Upholding the Bhagavat's Yoga is that which brings about the perfection of the *samādhi* yoga.

As for the steps in which these are to be used, you should first transform the site where you are sitting into an earth mandala, a vajra seat, with the *Mudrā* of the Indestructible Vajra. Then having made the *Samaya Mudrā*, you should carry out in the specified sequence: the protection of yourself and the place, the requisite worship, the transformation into Vajrasattva and so forth. Then following the steps after that, you should transform yourself into the Body of the deity. First you should create the lotus seat with the Lotus Bud *Mudra*. (182b) Then you should transform yourself with stability into the Body of the deity with the *Mudrā* Producing All the Limbs. Then with the *Mudrā* Producing Brilliance, you should create the aura of light. Then with the *Dhāraṇī Mudrā*, the unforgetting recollection of the Dharma should be firmly established. Then your speech should be transformed with the *Mudrā* of the Adornment of the Array of the Buddha Speech. With the *Mudrā* of Abiding Dharma, the nature itself of Suchness is made to abide firmly. Finally, with the *Mudrā* of Upholding Yoga, the *samādhi* is made to abide firmly.

A C: 聖天之位威神所同 '*divine abodes whose majesty is equivalent to the deities*'.

This is the summarized meaning. Now the meaning of each section will be explained.

[Vairocana] spoke to the Bodhisattva Vajrapāṇi: The fact that the Bhagavat himself describes them without being asked by Vajrapāṇi, is in order to indicate the greatness of those *mudrās*. Although they are accessible to the Buddha Bhagavats, they are not accessible to others such as the Bodhisattvas, so even Vajrapāṇi cannot request for them to be explained.

Secret* mudrās**: Because they should not be shown to anybody who lacks the *samaya* and has not been initiated and so forth. ***Most secret: Because the vajra throne, the lotus, the aura of light and so forth are not shown in the form of the deity itself, but as hand *mudrās*. ***Which create the divine abode***: The divine abode is the vajra throne and the lotus, because the deities will abide there. This refers to the *Mudrās* of the Indestructible Vajra and the Lotus. Secondly, it also refers to all eight of the *mudrās* because if you transform yourself with those *mudrās*, your body will become a divine abode. ***Marked with their own mantras***: (183a) Those *mudrās* are marked by the signs of each of the mantras which appear below. This means that while making a *mudrā*, its mantra should also be imagined there. ***Which have mandalas***: Those *mudrās* also have their individual mandalas, such as the earth mandala and so forth as mentioned below. This means that each mandala should be imagined within the *mudrā* itself, and the vajra and lotus throne, and the aura of light should be imagined to be associated with the abode of each one.

Which should be done for the yoga of one's tutelary deity: You should use these *mudrās* when performing the rites of Pacifying, Enriching and the superior, medium accomplishments and so forth performing the yoga of the tutelary deity.

2. 'Bodhisattvas who engage in the Bodhisattva practice by means of mantras should know that they themselves may become stable in the body-image of that deity by this ritual and after knowing that, they will abide in the manner of the tutelary deity and then accomplish attainments.'

When the Bodhisattvas who engage in bodhisattva practice by means of mantras change themselves into the body-image of a deity by such rituals, they will become firmly established in the body-image of the deity if they create each element with these *mudrās* in the stated sequence. ***After knowing that, they will abide in the manner of the tutelary deity and then accomplish attainments***: It is not sufficient[A] just to transform yourself into the Body [of the deity] and firmly establish it, having created it with those *mudrās*. It should also be done when you are accomplishing the activities of the tutelary deity, such as the rites of Pacifying, Enriching and so on, and the superior and medium attainments. This qualifies the words '***There are eight secret*** mudrās' and so forth.

3. 'What are those eight *mudrās*? Place both hands together, leaving a hollow within and make both your little fingers and fore fingers like flaming shafts of light. This is the Mudrā of Producing the Brilliance of the Bhagavat. Its mandala is triangular, marked with a triangular pattern and has radiant light. Its mantra is *NSB RAṂ RAḤ SVĀHĀ*.'

A Amend '*cho-ga*' (B) to '*chog-pa*' (V).

You should know that the expression, '***from the previous*** **mudrā**' when making the *Mudrās* of the Indestructible Vajra, the Lotus Bud and the Array of the Buddha Speech, refers in all three cases to the *Mudrā* Producing Brilliance. With regards the three *Mudrās* beginning with the *Dhāraṇī Mudrā*, it should be understood to refer to the *Mudrā* Producing All the Members.

4. 'From the previous *mudrā*, crook both your fore fingers and hold them on top of your thumbs like pennants[A]. This is the *Mudrā* of the Bhagavat's Indestructible Vajra. Its mandala is like the letter *Va* and has a flaming vajra [in it]. (178b) **Its mantra is *NSB VAṂ VAḤ SVĀHĀ*.'**

5. 'From that same *mudrā*, stretch out both your middle fingers and ring fingers and leave the others as before. This is the *Mudrā* of the Lotus Bud[B]. The mandala is like a moon disc, with a lotus sign. Its mantra is *NSB SAṂ SAḤ SVĀHĀ*.'

6. From that same *mudrā*, both of your little fingers should be inserted below. This is the *Mudrā* of the Adornment of the Array of the Buddha's Voice[C]. The mandala is like a full moon and has a pennant, and is marked with two *anusvāras*. Its mantra is *NSB HAṂ HAḤ SVĀHĀ*.'

7. 'Likewise place both of your hands together leaving a hollow within. Separate both your thumbs and the remaining fingers just a little, making it like an *añjali*[D]. This is the *Mudrā* which Produces All the Bhagavat's Members. The mandala is a rounded pot[E]. Its mantra is *NSB AṂ AḤ SVĀHĀ*.'

8. 'From that same *mudrā*, crook both of your middle fingers and leave the others as they are. This is the *Mudrā* of the Bhagavat's *Dhāraṇī*. Its mandala is like a rainbow, with all the symbols. It is hung with a vajra-pennant. Its mantra is *NSB BUDDHA-DHĀRAṆI SMṚTI-BALA-DHĀNA-KARI DHARAYA SARVAṂ BHAGAVATY-ĀKĀRAVATI SAMAYE SVĀHĀ* (NSB. O Buddha *Dhāraṇī*! Supporter of the power of remembrance! Uphold everything! Noble One of fine appearance! O vow! *Svāhā*!).'

(183b) ***Dhāraṇī***: So that you will remember the things such as the vajra throne, the lotus and the aura of light as you have imagined them. To signify that it is endowed with all powers, it has the colours of all four mandalas, like a rainbow. ***With all the symbols***: It has the symbols of each individual mandala, a vajra, lotus and so forth. ***Hung with a vajra-pennant***: Because the shape of its mandala is like a rainbow, it is a wind mandala. To make the pennant – the symbol of the wind mandala – immovable, it is a pennant with a vajra.

A C: 如嚩字形 '*like the shape of the letter Va*'.
B C: 蓮華藏印 '*Lotus Matrix* Mudrā'.
C C: 如來萬德莊嚴印 '*the* Mudrā *of the Tathāgata's Adornments of a Myriad Virtues*'.
D C adds 未開敷華 '[*like*] *an unopened bud*'.
E C adds 滿月之形 '[*like*] *a full moon in shape*'.

9. 'From that same *mudrā*, both of your middle fingers should be removed and both of your little fingers hooked by your middle fingers and joined at the crown of your head. This is the *Mudrā* of the Bhagavat's Abiding Dharma. The mandala is that of space, with all colours and marked with two *anusvāras*. Its mantra is *NSB A VEDA-VIDE SVĀHĀ*. (NSB. *A*! *Knowing one*! *Svāhā*!).'

'***The two* anusvāras**' of the Abiding Dharma *Mudrā* are the symbols of emptiness and the emptiness of emptiness. Its mandala is ...[A]

10. 'From that same *mudrā*, both of your middle-fingers[B] should be interlaced together. This is the *Mudrā* of Upholding the Bhagavat's Yoga[C]. Its mandala is space, especially blue, with an *anusvāra* and has pride[D]. (179a) **Its mantra is *NSB MAHĀ-YOGA-YOGINI YOGEŚVARI KHĀÑJALIKE SVĀHĀ* (NSB. O Yogini of the Great Yoga! Mistress of Yoga! You who are like space in measure! *Svāhā*!).'**

The mandala of the Upholding Yoga *Mudrā* is that of space and should be made bluer than the colour of the sky. That signifies that it should be made greater (= bluer) than the wind mandala because it has all the powers of *samādhi*.

11. 'Lord of the Secret Ones! These are the secret *mudrās*. Since they are the great secret of the Tathāgatas, do not give them to anyone except those who are initiated, who are of good birth[E], who are energetic, firm in their resolutions, devoted to the guru, grateful, very pure and who have no regard for their own bodies or lives!'

They are secret *mudrās* because they should not be given to anyone else. They should not be given to anyone who does not have the *samaya* or such qualifications (*guṇa*) as the initiation and so forth, which are listed below, but they may be given to those who do have those qualifications. '***Initiated***' means initiated into the Secret Mandala. ***Good birth***: They can be given to *brahmins* and *kṣatriyas*, but they should not be given to those of the inferior castes such as fishermen and so on. Secondly, this means 'having a lineage', that is, relying upon and abiding with the deities of the Tathāgata family, the Lotus Family and so forth. Thirdly it refers to those who strive diligently in the practice of the mantras of the Tathāgata Family and so on. ***Energetic***: Diligent in the practice of the mantras. ***Firm in their resolutions***: (184a) They do not abandon whatever aim they wish for until it has been accomplished. ***Devoted to the guru***: Having trust in the guru. ***Grateful*** (*kṛta-jña*) Because they fully apply themselves in

---

A Textual corruption here in all editions of both V and B (conflation) which runs this section straight on to comments for the next section with a small portion lost.

B C: 以智慧三味手 '*both your hands*'.

C C: 世尊迅疾持印 '*the* Mudrā *of the Bhagavat's Swift Upholding*'. C probably read *yugapad* (迅疾) here in contrast to *yoga* (*rnal-'byor*) in T.

D I am not certain what is meant by this. T editions have *snyoms-pa* 'pride' or *snyams-pa* 'equal, proportionate'. C omits this.

E C: 其性調柔 '*who are well-controlled in nature*'.

earnest to whatever is taught by the guru, since they trust and revere the guru. ***Very pure***: Because when the body is cleansed, the mind will also be disciplined. ***Who have no regard for their own bodies or lives***: They do not spare even their own bodies and lives in such mantra practices as the rituals and *sādhana*. To such people these *mudrās* should be given.

XVI
ENTRY[1] TO UPHOLDING THE SECRET MANDALA

1. Then at that time, the Bhagavat Vairocana gazed upon all beings in the future and then entered a *samādhi* called 'Entry into All'[A]. As soon as the Bhagavat entered that *samādhi*, this Buddha field[B] was spread out flat like the palm of his hand: It was adorned with portals and arches built from the five kinds of precious gems, covered with hanging multi-coloured pennants, covered with jewelled awnings, with many jewel-bells, white whisks, silk ribbons and netting suspended [from it], and with jewelled pillars which were set up in the eight directions. Its eight directions were also adorned with lotus pools filled up with fragrant water having the eight qualities; [there were also] the cries of geese, ducks and swans and ever-blooming flowers and various trees. It was encircled with garlands and strings of the five precious gems and the ground was pleasant and soft to the touch, like velvet. There resounded various kinds of pleasant sounds of drums and musical instruments. It had mentally formed thrones, buildings and palaces [which were] built up by the merits of the many Bodhisattvas.

Now the chapter dealing with the depiction of the inner mental mandala will be explained. Concerning the mental mandala which is to be depicted, there are in general two types of mandalas: the intrinsically existent mandala and the representational mandala. Of those, the intrinsically existent mandala is extensive and inconceivable. You should know that it is the mental mandala which shows that in a condensed form. Even the representational mandala is difficult to complete as described, and it is the mandala described in the Continuation Tantra which reveals its condensed form. Therefore you will know by means of this mental mandala what the Secret Mandala – which is Mind in nature – is like, and you should view it as a gate of entry. To show the method of depicting that mental mandala, the text teaches that the Bhagavat entered into a *samādhi* and then this Buddha field was spread out flat like the palm of his hand, adorned with portals and arches built from the five kinds of precious gems. It shows that though all these lack objective reality, they emerged as imagined by the power of his Mind alone. Therefore, the yogin should resolve that all he generates by his *manas*, such as the mental mandala and so on, (184b) will be like that laid out by the Lord while his Mind was equipoised, and that when he has entered that *samādhi*, it will be as he has resolved.

The teachings concerning the method of depicting the mental mandala in that way begin with '***Then at that time, the Bhagavat Vairocana gazed upon all beings in the future and then entered a* samādhi**' and so forth. Since the Bhagavat's acts to benefit beings occur spontaneously by the power of his previous aspirations, it is not really necessary for him to enter a *samādhi*. Nevertheless, by entering into a *samādhi* to cause such phenomena to be manifested, beings to be guided such as the Bodhisattva Samantabhadra and so on will know for what reason the Bhagavat has entered a

A T: *thams-cad-kyi rjes-su-'jug*, C: 等至. On the basis of this, the underlying Sanskrit term was likely to have been *sam-ā-* √*pad*.
B C: 諸佛國土 '*these Buddha fields*'.

samādhi, and what he will manifest having entered it and so forth. Therefore the Bhagavat entered a *samādhi*.

Entry into All: When the Bhagavat entered into that *samādhi*, he directly realized the continuum of reality in all its entirety on the absolute level, and on the relative level he perceived that this Buddha field was laid spread out like the palm of his hand and so forth, which reveals the distinctive qualities of the abode. Because these absolute and relative realizations arose when the Bhagavat entered that *samādhi*, it is termed '***Entry into All***'.

He gazed upon all beings in the future: Although the completely pure Bodhisattvas such as Samantabhadra and Vajrapāṇi understood how these things actually are, the Bhagavat reveals that the many types of things arise by the power of mind alone, for the sake of future beings, without having any objective reality.

As soon as the Bhagavat entered that* samādhi**, (185a) ***this Buddha field was spread out flat like the palm of his hand: When you are to depict the mandala, you must level the heights and depressions of the ground and correct it. This shows the way it is. ***This Buddha field***: The great thousand three thousand realms of the *Sahā* universe. ***Was spread out flat like the palm of his hand***: That Buddha field was flat without mountains and valleys. These words show that when people in the future draw the mandala, they should correct the mandala site so that it is flat like the palm of one's hand.

The text indicates that after that Buddha field became flat, it was adorned with those ornaments. This shows the way in which the levelled site is to be adorned with such decorations as arches, portals, parasols, pennants and with patterned designs. ***Lotus pools filled up with fragrant water***: This shows that ponds and so on should be drawn in the mandala. ***The eight types of qualities*** are cooling, clear, sweet and so on[2].

It had mentally formed thrones, buildings and palaces built up by the merits of the many Bodhisattvas: In that Buddha field there were the individual thrones, houses and palaces of the Bodhisattvas, in measure with their individual merits produced by the Perfections. This also shows that you should place such deities as the Bodhisattvas with their respective abodes in the site of that mandala.

2. There also appeared a great king of lotuses, arisen from the Tathāgata's fervent application[A], marked with the sign of the realization of the continuum of reality. (179b) **In the middle of it there rested the Body of the Tathāgata, who cleaves to the continuum of reality[B] and who delights beings according to their wishes and interests. From all the members of the Tathāgata there emerged bodies with benign strength, adorning his Body with many kinds of colours and shapes, which arose from his fervent application to the Ten Strengths that were generated over many millions of eons by the merit of the Perfections of Generosity, Morality, Patience, Strenuousness, Meditative Concentration and Insight.**

(185b) The Tathāgata rests upon a lotus king in the centre of that Buddha field, and from the Body of the Tathāgata there emerged the Awareness Beings (*jñāna-sattva*)

A C reads '*arisen from the Tathāgata's fervent application*', with the last sentence of the previous section.

B C: 如來法界性身 '*the Body of the Tathāgata which is the continuum of reality in nature*'.

who only utter Dharma words. This also shows that the Bhagavat Vairocana, who rests in the centre of the mandala, should be surrounded by the deities formed from the Tathāgata's Body. ***Arisen from the Tathāgata's fervent application, marked with the sign of the realization of the continuum of reality***: These are the special attributes of that lotus king. ***The realization of the continuum of reality*** refers to the pure Awareness of Suchnes. ***Marked with its sign***: You should know that it is white, because that is the symbol of pure Awareness. In brief, this means that the pure Awareness of Suchness was transformed into the appearance of a great lotus king. The Body of the Tathāgata rests in its centre to show that the Body of the Bhagavat Vairocana arises from the Awareness of Suchness, which is an attribute of the continuum of reality. ***Who cleaves to the continuum of reality***: It is emptiness in nature. So although the intrinsic nature of the Bhagavat is [also] emptiness, he is not like one who has [entered] the Nirvāṇa without remainder, for he gives rise to all relative activities by the power of his previous aspirations, without pausing for reflection (*avikalpam*). In order to show this, the text says, '***who delights beings according to their wishes and interests***'.

[Bodies] with benign strength, which arose from his fervent application to the Ten Strengths: The power of those bodies which emerged from the Bhagavat's Body is completely benign. Furthermore, because during the causal phase of the Bhagavat himself, he had generated fervent application to the Ten Strengths which are an attribute of Perfect Buddhahood, (186a) the result arose from the Ten Strengths which had been perfected. ***Which adorned his Body with many kinds of colours and shapes***: This refers to the special attributes of the many bodies which emerged. It means that they had many different colours and forms. Also, in order to show that that multitude of bodies arose due to the mass of merit accumulated by the Bhagavat himself when he was engaged in Bodhisattva practice, through the Perfection of Generosity and so on over countless eons, the text says, '***over many hundreds of thousands of eons***'.

3. When they had emerged, speech was communicated[3] in all the world systems and this paean was uttered:

> **'Ah! The Insight and Expedient Means**
> **of all Buddhas are inconceivable!**
> **Having realized that [phenomena] are unlocalized,**
> **they then also teach localized phenomena[A].**
> **Whosoever knows that the intrinsic nature**
> **of phenomena cannot be perceived**
> **will accomplish the attainment which[B]**
> **all the Guides have accomplished.'**

When they had uttered this paean, they all re-entered the inconceivable *dharmakāya* of the Tathāgata.

A C: 無阿賴耶慧 含藏說諸法 '*the insight which is without substratum incorporates* [*the ability*] *to verbalize phenomena/teachings*'.

B C: 彼無得而得 '*will accomplished what they have not yet accomplished,* [*which all the Guides ...*]'.

When they had emerged, speech was communicated in all the world systems and this paean was uttered: Thus, the Dharma as realization which was revealed earlier by the Bhagavat as the actual appearance of the Buddha Field laid out flat like the palm of his hand and so forth, was also revealed as scriptural Dharma with the verses which appear above. And that was with the words, '***Ah! The Insight and Expedient Means of all Buddhas are inconceivable***' and so forth. ***Insight***: Its nature is to realize that all phenomena are without autonomous existence. ***Expedient means***: To teach the existence of various different kinds of phenomena for the benefit of beings, even though they have realized that all phenomena are empty. Both of these are wonderful and incomprehensible. In order to clarify those words, the text says, '***Having realized that phenomena are unlocalized*** (*anālaya*), ***they then also teach localized phenomena***'. (186b) This means that after they know by Insight that all phenomena are empty and devoid of polarization into a perceiving subject and perceived objects, '***then they also teach localized phenomena***'. They thus realize with Insight that all phenomena lack objective reality. Yet by their Expedient Means, they actually reveal phenomena (*dharma*) and so forth, which appear to have objective reality and be localized as perceiving subjects and perceived objects, in order help beings.

Whosoever knows that the intrinsic nature of phenomena cannot be perceived: Whosoever knows that the intrinsic nature of phenomena such as the psycho-physical constituents, the perceptual elements and sources is without any objective reality. ***Will accomplished the attainment which all Guides have accomplished***: Whosoever knows thus that all phenomena are without any objective reality will attain the resultant buddhahood achieved by the Buddha Bhagavat Guides. In brief, this shows that a person who realizes the emptiness of phenomena will become a Buddha.

When they had uttered this, they all re-entered the inconceivable continuum of reality of the Tathāgata: Thus they became invisible in the continuum of reality, which is emptiness in nature.

4. Then the Bhagavat spoke to the Bodhisattva Vajrapāṇi, 'Nobly-born One! Listen concerning the inner mandala! Lord of the Secret Ones, the physical site should be transformed by the transformational power of the mantra and *mudrā* which are the continuum of reality in nature, because it is intrinsically pure. Then transforming yourself into the Action Vajrasattva, you should imagine yourself free from dust and free from the thorn-like faults, that are [the beliefs in] a self, a being, a soul, a sustainer, a spirit, something derived from a spirit and an agent.'

First the Bhagavat revealed the intrinsically existent mandala in connection with the method of depicting the Secret Mandala, and now he will describe the method of depicting the Secret Mandala itself.

You should know that in this case the consecration (*adhivāsana*) of the trainees should be done that same evening, and the steps of that are as follows: First the Master should make ready those things that are mentioned in the text, such as the offering materials, and then gathering together the trainees, he should arrange them on the outside. Then the Master should enter into the mandala house and (187a) salute all the Buddhas and Bodhisattvas. Making the *Samaya Mudrā*, he should imagine in front of himself the intrinsically existent mandala in which there are either each individual seed-mantras or else the general essences, as taught for the

Mandala of Great Compassion. Then he should transform himself with the *Mudrā* and Mantra of the Continuum of Reality, then transform himself into Vajrasattva with the Turning the Dharma Wheel *Mudrā* and Mantra and protect himself with the Vajra Armour *Mudrā* and Mantra. Then having changed himself into the Action Vajrasattva, he should show the *Samaya Mudrā* to the deities and present them with the oblations (*argha*). Then empowering the offerings of flowers, perfume and so forth, with each of their mantras, he should offer these as well and he should also make mental offerings. When he has thus made the inner and the outer offerings, the Master should go outside and give flowers and perfume to the trainees. He should then protect them with the All-doing (*sarva-karmika*) Mantra, bind their forearms with the thread empowered by the All-doing Mantra and give them the tooth-wood. When that has been done, they should be made to confess their failings, offer their bodies and accept the Discipline. This is the consecration ritual (*adhivāsana-vidhi*).

Also, with regards the ritual for introducing them into the Mandala, if there is an assistant who is doing the *sādhana*, he should do it according to the sequence. If not, the Master himself should cause the trainees to make the *Samaya Mudrā*, transform them with the Mantra and *Mudrā* of the Continuum of Reality, transform them with the Dharma Wheel Mantra and *Mudrā* and cause them to generate *bodhicitta*, all in due sequence. Then the Master should enter again the place of worship and equipoise his mind. He should imagine a moon disc in his heart, upon which there is a letter *Ra*, white-coloured but slightly tinged with red. With the true meaning of the sound of that letter, which is the meditative observation that all phenomena are free from dust, he dissolves his own body by going through the process of viewing it as atoms and so forth. (187b) Those atoms also lack parts and so they are without any objective reality. Likewise he meditates that his consciousness and so forth also lack any objective reality. Imagining even the moon disc and the letter *Ra* to be empty, he should finally meditate that even the true meaning of the sound itself is without any objective reality, and he rests in emptiness as long as he wishes.

Following that, he should imagine first a wind mandala, then a water mandala and then a golden mandala. Upon that golden mandala, he also should imagine his own body, from the navel down, to be a square golden mandala. He should then imagine a lotus with a root, reaching up as far as his heart. In the middle of it there sits the Bhagavat Vairocana. On the eastern petal there is the Tathāgata Ratna-ketu, on the southern petal there is the Tathāgata Saṃkusumita-rāja, on the northern petal there is the Tathāgata Dundubhi-ghoṣa and on the western petal there is the Tathāgata Amitābha. On the south-eastern petal there is the Bodhisattva Samantabhadra, on the north-eastern petal there is the Bodhisattva Avalokiteśvara, on the south-western petal there is the Bodhisattva Mañjuśrī-kumāra-bhūta and on the north-western petal there is the Bodhisattva Maitreya.

In order that the casting of the flowers may be done easily, the Master should imagine all of the Bodies of the Bhagavat Vairocana and the Bodhisattvas and so forth coming up to his cranium. Then he should imagine that on all the stamens of the lotus there are the Mothers of the Bodhisattvas, and the Ten Levels, the Six Perfections and the *samādhis*, in the body-images of goddesses. At the stalk of the lotus, he should imagine the Bodhisattva Vajrapāṇi, and to its front, left and right, he should imagine in sequence the entourage of Avalokiteśvara, the Vajradhara *Vidyās*, (188a) the Wrathful Ones, the Gate Keepers and the Wrathful Messengers. In the outer area many gods and nāgas should be imagined. When all that has been made stable, he should correctly make mental offerings to them. Then when all this has been completed, the Master should signal with a snap of the fingers and cause the trainees to cast their flowers upon his head. He should give to the trainees whichever of the deities he has imagined upon whom those flowers fall. This is the summary and now the words of the text will be explained.

***The physical site should be transformed by the transformational power of the mantra and* mudrā *that are the continuum of reality in nature, because it is intrinsically pure*:** Having worshipped [the Buddhas] and so forth, in due sequence as previously indicated, he should transform his body with the *Mudrā* and Mantra of the Continuum of Reality, saying, 'Let it become empty!'. ***Then transforming yourself into the Action Vajrasattva*:** Following the previous sequence, he should transform himself with the Dharma Wheel *Mudrā* and Mantra and change into the Action Vajrasattva. Then he should make all the offerings, do the rituals for the disciples and so forth, in the sequence mentioned above. ***Free from dust*:** Then once again entering inside, the Master should imagine the letter *Ra* in his heart and he should follow the process of meditation that all phenomena are devoid of dust and so on, as described before. ***Free from the thorn-like faults, that are [the beliefs in] a self, a being, a soul, a sustainer, a spirit, something derived from a spirit and an agent*:** He should meditate that entities such as the self (*ātman*) and so on of the non-Buddhists (*tīrthika*) also lack any objective reality. Just as an external site is cleansed by the removal of such impediments and defects as stones, wood and so forth, so also is the inner site cleansed by this method.

5. 'Therein imagine a square mandala with four gates, the western one of which is always open. They are adorned with portals and a pavilion. In the centre there arises a great king of lotuses, mind-formed, eight-petalled with a stalk, (180a) and with extensive and beautiful stamens. And again within that there is the Tathāgata, who surpasses all mundane bodies, speech and minds, who completely transcends the mind levels, who has attained emptiness[A] and who bestows the special kinds of results one desires.'

(188b) He should thus have entered into the *samādhi* of emptiness and so forth, and then he should imagine the wind and water mandalas as described before. Upon them he should imagine an earth mandala, upon which his body up to the waist becomes a square mandala of gold. The pavilion (*vedikā*) should be made in the centre of the site and should also be imagined to be gold in colour. ***In the centre there arises a great king of lotuses, mind-formed, eight-petalled, with a stalk and extensive and beautiful stamens*:** The eight petals should be made in different colours, matching the body colours of the four Buddhas and four Bodhisattvas. Ratna-ketu is white, Saṃkusumita-rāja is yellow, Dundubhi-ghoṣa is maroon and Amitābha is red. Likewise, Samantabhadra is yellow, Avalokiteśvara is white, Mañjuśrī-kumāra-bhūta is yellow and Maitreya is red. Furthermore, you should know this is to linked with the

A Here T has *sems* 'mind' , but I have replaced that with 'emptiness', which seems to be more appropriate in view of Budhaguhya's comment. C omits this phrase altogether.

words, '***all [things] are also all the colours***' [XIII.37], that is, they are without limit. ***Within that there is the Tathāgata, who surpasses all mundane bodies, speech and minds***: The Body of the Bhagavat Vairocana, which is imagined in the middle of the lotus, is supremely excellent, surpassing all mundane ones. ***Who completely transcends all mind*** (citta) ***levels***: It is devoid of the phenomena of perceiving subject and perceived objects which are accessible to the mind. ***Who has attained*** (*anuprāpta*) ***emptiness***: The attribute of emptiness which is attained by immediate experience. (189a) These qualities show the perfection of self-benefit. ***Who bestows the special kinds of results one desires***: This shows the perfection of other-benefit. He bestows upon beings the results that are paradise, Nirvāṇa and so on.

6. 'In the east there is the Tathāgata Ratna-ketu, in the south there is the Tathāgata Saṃkusumita-rāja, in the north there is the Tathāgata Dundubhi-nirghoṣa and in the west there is the Tathāgata Amitābha[A]. In the south-eastern corner there is the Bodhisattva Samantabhadra, in the north-eastern corner there is the Bodhisattva Avalokiteśvara, in the south-western corner there is the Bodhisattva Mañjuśrī-kumāra-bhūta and in the north-western corner there is the Bodhisattva Maitreya. On all the stamens you should depict the Mother of all the Bodhisattvas, the Six Perfections and the *Samādhis*. Below, you should depict the crowds of *Vidyādharas* and Wrathful Ones. At the stalk is Vajrapāṇi. The remainder is a great ocean[B].'

The Buddhas and Bodhisattvas should be imagined upon the petals and stamens of the lotus following the sequence mentioned earlier. ***The remainder is a great ocean***: Below that mandala he should imagine a water mandala, a great ocean.

7. 'The *mantrin* should imagine
mind-generated lamps, flowers
incense, perfumes and food-stuffs,
for union with the embodied beings[C].'

The *mantrin* should imagine all those things, the flowers, perfumes and so forth. '***For union*** (*samaya*) ***with the embodied beings*** (*dehin*)' of this mandala. In order to cause beings to enter into union with the embodied deities, this mandala should be made by [those with] devoted interest in the Profound and the Extensive, as it is not possible to depict the representational mandala in detail.

8. 'Also the *mantrin* should diligently generate
and depict in this Mandala of the Great Self[D],

A C: 無量壽如來 '*the Tathāgata Amitāyus*'.

B C adds here: 一切地居天等其數無量而環繞之 '[*while*] *all the ground is inhabited by innumerable gods who surround it*'. T has transposed this material to Section 8.

C C: 一切皆以獻之 '*all of these should be used as offerings to it*'. This verse is also in prose in C. Despite Buddhaguhya's comments, C seems to have preserved the more appropriate reading. Note also that T has the same line in Section 12 below, so we perhaps have here a case of dittography or 'eye-skip'.

D C reads: 眞言者誠諦圖書漫荼羅 '*The* mantrin *should diligently depict the mandala*' and then follows on in the same verse with 自身爲大我囉字淨諸垢 '*then making his own body into the Great Self, he should purify all dust with the letter RA*'.

the countless gods and so forth
on all the ground below[A].'

Countless gods and *nāgas* should be drawn on all the peripheral ground below the central pavilion in this Mandala of the Great Self which is the Bhagavat.

9. 'Having cleansed his own body
by himself with a *Ra*,
the *mantrin* sits in the yoga-posture,
recollecting the Tathāgatas.'

After those yogins have done their own activities, the cleansing of themselves in emptiness with the letter *Ra* and so forth[B], in the manner mentioned above, they should do whatever rites they wish to do.

10. 'He should place an *A* with *anusvāra*
upon the heads of all the trainees.'

(189b) When the trainees enter the mandala, he should transform them into the continuum of reality and then to make them firm, he should imagine the essence of Perfect Buddhahood, *Aṃ*, upon their heads.

11. 'They should then be made to throw
flowers upon his fearless body[C].
Having ascertained which [deity it is]
that one should be revealed to them[D].'

After the trainees have cast their flowers upon his body, he should give the trainees whichever *vidyā* (deity) upon whom their flower falls. ***Having ascertained which [deity it is], that [one] should be revealed to them***: The manner of the mandala [deities] should be taught to them.

12. 'This is the foremost of mandalas,
for the sake of union with the embodied beings[E].'

A As mentioned above, C (and general sense) indicate that '*the countless gods ... below*' has been transposed from the end of Section 6.

B V: '*cultivating the letter* Raṃ *in their hearts*'.

C C: 智者傳妙花 令散於自身'*The wise one should give* [*them*] *flowers and have them thrown at his body*'.

D T adds here '*and furthermore the* vidyā *should be given to them*'. Buddhaguhya does not comment on this line and it is also omitted in C. Therefore I suspect that it is intrusive, possibly originally a marginal gloss.

E C: 此最上壇故 應與三味耶'*Since this is the foremost of mandalas, they should be given the* samaya'. Once again, T seems to have had '*dehin*' (*embodied being*) in its base text while C probably had '*deya*' (*should be given*).

***For the sake of union with the embodied beings*:** As explained earlier, it is so that they may be united (*samayin*) with this Mandala. ***This is the foremost of mandalas*:** It is the foremost one because it arises through the cultivation of the *samādhi* of emptiness, without conceiving external perceptual forms.

XVII
THE RITUAL OBSERVANCES FOR THE *VIDYĀS*

1. (180b) Then Vajrapāṇi asked the Bhagavat Vairocana about the ritual observances for the *vidyās* with these verses, for the sake of those Bodhisattvas who engage in the Bodhisattva practice by means of mantras:

'How is the ritual observance to be kept?
How does one dwell in the morality?
How does one practice without attachment
to anything in any situation?
After the elapse of how much time
will the observance be fully completed?
How should its power be recognized?
In which abodes should it be done?
Would the Guide also tell us the period
[of the time needed] until one speedily becomes
devoid of time, place, activity,
action, right and wrong?
I ask the All-knowing One,
the Lord of Men, Perfect Buddha,
about that taught by previous Buddhas
by which attainments will be accomplished,
for the benefit of future beings
to attract them to the Lord of Jinas!'

Now the chapter on the ritual observances for the *vidyā*-mantras will be explained. *Vidyā* refers to the Awareness of Suchness and also to the mantras and *mudrās* which emerge from it, because it is awareness (√ *vid*) of the truly real (*bhūta-artha*) as it actually is (*yathā-bhūa*). Its ritual observance[1] (*vrata*) is the style of behaviour which conforms to it, such as a style of behaviour resembling Śākyamuni, or a style of behaviour having the appearance of a monk – the shaved hair and beard, the wearing of monk's robes and so forth. Just as there are in this world the customs and practices of faith of mundane people towards the great gods, you should know that this ritual observance for *vidyā* has these four sections: practice in conformity with the body-image of one's tutelary deity, practice in conformity with the *samādhi* of the intrinsic emptiness [of phenomena], (190a) the practice in conformity with the realization that all phenomena are illusion-like in nature after having arisen from *samādhi*, and the recitation of the mantra. Now, some people keep this ritual observance [for a while] and do a hundred thousand [recitations] for the preliminary service as mentioned in the text and then they start on the *sādhana*. However, you should know that because it is desirable to be even more stable than that, one should abide in the earth mandala and so forth and keep this ritual observance for six months. Therefore this ritual observance should be viewed as the basis (*hetu*) for the ritual observance for abiding in the earth mandala and so forth, and you should consider that the ritual observance for abiding in the earth mandala and so forth arises from this. Therefore having first purified your mind completely with this ritual observance, you should subsequently start the next ritual observance.

Also, when keeping the subsequent ritual observances you should engage in i) the abiding in the body-image of the deity, ii) the abiding in the *samādhi* of emptiness, the conduct without attachment in the knowledge that all phenomena are illusion-like when you have arisen from the *samādhi* and the recitation of the mantras, in due sequence, and iii) next you should abide in the earth mandala and so forth, and make yourself into their nature and make the *mudrās* of earth and so on.

You should know that Vajrapāṇi's questions about the ritual observances for the *vidyās* are mainly (190b) with reference to the keeping of the ritual observances for the *vidyās* while abiding in the earth mandala and so on. The enquiry is made in verse so that the topics and the words do not become corrupted, because the topics are difficult and important.

For the sake of those Bodhisattvas who engage in the Bodhisattva practice by means of mantras: Vajrapāṇi does not ask about it because he himself does not understand the subject, but so that beings in the future who engage in the Bodhisattva practice by mantras might be helped.

Regarding the ritual observance for the *vidyās*, Vajrapāṇi says '***that taught by previous Buddhas***', so if it has already been taught by the past Buddhas, what need is there to ask about it now? Although Vajrapāṇi himself understands the topic since it was explained by earlier Buddhas, it is because future beings will have faith in it and be attracted to the Bhagavat if he teaches and explains it in the present.

2. **When he had asked that,**
the Bhagavat Vairocana then
out of pity for beings,
spoke these words:
'Excellent, O Great One,
Powerful Vajrapāṇi!
I shall teach the supreme ritual observance
which previous Buddhas spoke of!
Abide Buddha-like in the observance
which arises from the observance for the *vidyās*,
by which you will accomplish the attainments
that will aid the world!'

Which arises from the ritual observance for the* vidyās**: That [ritual observance] which arises from the four-membered ritual observance for the *vidyās*, which is characterized by a completely purified mind. This should be linked up with my words above, 'the practice while abiding in the earth mandala and so forth is to make one stable'. ***Abide Buddha-like in that observance: (191a) The Buddha Bhagavat, who is fully awakened, comprehends instantly that all phenomena are characterized by emptiness when he enters *samādhi* on the absolute level, and also acts without attachment by the knowledge that phenomena are like illusions when he acts on the relative level. Similarly, a person who abides in the ritual observance for the *vidyās* will also abide in the intrinsic emptiness of all phenomena while abiding in *samādhi*. When he has arisen from *samādhi*, he acts without attachment to anything while realizing that phenomena are like illusions. Therefore he resembles a Perfect Buddha.

3. **'After generating the true nature of self,**
if your *manas* ever freed from confusion
and always remains equipoised,
then the observance will have been kept.'

This section answers the question, '***How is the ritual observance to be practised?*'. *If your* **manas** *ever freed from confusion*: If just the body-image of the deity appears in your *manas* without any doubts and no other concepts appear in it apart from the perceptual image of the deity, through accomplishing the *samādhi* wherein the true nature of self (*ātma-tattva*) is changed into whatever is the body-image of your tutelary deity, '***then the ritual observance will have been kept***'. Hence it is said to be '***always remains equipoised***'. In brief, the mind should always be equipoised. This means that if the body-image of that deity has not been made to appear with stability in your *manas*, you will not enter into ritual observance for the *vidyās* merely by use of the mantras and *mudrās*, and thinking that you are as the deity. That is the practice of the body-image in conformity with the *vidyā* [deity].

4. **'One whose morality unites together**
into one characteristic
***bodhicitta*, phenomena,**
training, actions and results,
is said to be Buddha-like.
No other is said to have morality.'

This section is in reply to the question, '***How is one to dwell in morality*** (śīla)?' When one realizes that the entering *bodhicitta* associated with the introspection characterized by the refutation of phenomena, the perceptual images of psycho-physical constituents, the perceptual elements and sources, the training which consists of the ten wholesome actions, and conditioned (*saṃskṛta*) actions and results, all have an identical characteristic – emptiness, (191b) then that morality is an unsullied morality, devoid of actions and activities, and characterized by emptiness. Therefore the text says, '***[That person] is said to be Buddha-like***'. This means they are like the Buddha Bhagavat who realized the identical characteristic of phenomena that are all empty in nature. That is the practice of the *samādhi* of the emptiness [of phenomena] in conformity with the *vidyā* mantras. Furthermore, you should abide in the *samādhi* of emptiness in such a way that you do not have to think about it or dissolve each thing individually, when you have changed yourself into the body-image of the deity. Once you have changed yourself into the body-image of your tutelary deity, your mind will be completely purified.

5. **'If one who has mastery of all phenomena** (181a)
and gains realization for the sake of beings
treats gold and gravel similarly,
he will soon[A] act without attachment.'

A C: 常 '*always*'.

This section answers the question about how you are to practice without attachment in any situation. ***One who has mastery of all phenomena***: You realize that all phenomena are empty in nature and you do not come under the sway of the emotional afflictions such as attachment and so forth. If ***he gains realization for the sake of beings and treats gold and gravel similarly, he will soon act without attachment***: Even when you engage in Liberality and so forth for the benefit of beings on the relative level, after you have arisen from the *samādhi* of emptiness, you realize that conditioned phenomena are like illusions and feel no attachment for them. That is, if you do not have feelings of attachment to gold just as you do not have such feelings towards stones and gravel, you will be acting without attachment in any situation. Even when you practise on the relative level, that is practice in conformity with the *vidyā*-mantra.

6. **'When the amount of time has elapsed**
for a hundred thousand, or however many indicated,
with regards the quantity of mantras,
then the observance will be fully completed.'

This section answers the question about how much time will elapse before the ritual observance becomes fully completed. If you keep [the ritual observance] in the manner described above for whatever quantity of recitations, (192a) a hundred thousand and so forth, is mentioned in the text, then that ritual observance will be fully completed. Moreover, this refers to the ritual observance with four members which is characterized by completely purifying the mind, prior to the ritual observance for abiding in the earth mandala and so on.

7. **'Abiding in the earth mandala**
and meditating on earth[A]**,**
he should make the vajra *mudrā*,
and always drink milk for nourishment;
with breathing in and out well controlled,
that *mantrin* should recite for one month.'

This section answers the question about which abodes you should do it in. In order to explain that you should keep the ritual observance for the *vidyā*-mantra after abiding in the earth mandala and so forth, the text states, '***Abiding in the earth mandala and meditating on earth***' and so on. This indicates that you should abide for one month in the earth mandala, changing yourself into the body-image of your tutelary deity, meditating wholeheartedly (*prasaṅgena*) that just as it is the nature of the ground to be hard and firm, so also is your body, and doing the recitation. ***Abiding in the earth mandala, meditating on earth***: Having meditated on the true meaning of the sound of the letter *A*, the essence of earth, which shows that all phenomena are unborn from the very beginning, then you should imagine that that letter changes into the earth mandala, as before. Having changed yourself into the

A This line is based on C. The two Tibetan versions differ although V is closer to C: *dbang-chen-gyi ni dngos-po-yis* | *dbang-chen dkyil-'khor-la gnas-te* || (T + B); *dbang-chen-gyi ni lha lta-bur* | *dbang-chen-gyi dkyil-'khor-la 'dug-nas* || (V); 最初金輪觀 住大因陀羅 (C). I take *dbang-chen* and 大因陀羅 in their usual sense herein – 'earth'.

body of your tutelary deity upon it, you should make the vajra *mudrā* and meditate that you are hard and stable like the nature of earth. ***You should make the vajra* mudrā**: You should make the vajra *mudrā* because it accords with being hard and stable. ***Always drink milk for nourishment***: Your nourishment is also in accord with that, because if you drink milk, your body will grow up and become sturdy. For just as in the ordinary world the body is supported by the mind and food, (192b) here also it is in harmony with the earth *samādhi* if you meditate on stability with the mind and eat strengthening foods. ***With breathing in and out well controlled, the* mantrin *should recite for one month***: The *mantrin* should do the recitation for one month, having controlled inhalation and exhalation (*prāṇāyama*) as explained earlier.

8. 'Then in the second month,
conjoined with the water mandala,
he should make the lotus *mudrā*
and then drink water for nourishment.'

This explains the abiding in the water mandala. By meditating on the true meaning of the sound of the seed syllable of the water mandala, and meditating on the water mandala which arises from that seed syllable, you should follow the sequence below. You should meditate that your body is also blue, like water in nature, make the lotus *mudrā* and do the recitation for one month. You should make the lotus *mudrā* and drink water for nourishment in order to be in harmony with that [water *samādhi*].

9. 'Then in the third month,
he should meditate on the fire mandala,
and eat food not sought out,
as well as [making] the sword *mudrā*[A].
All failings arising through his body,
speech or mind, will be burnt up.'

This explains the abiding in the fire mandala. ***Eat food which is not sought out***: In order to act in accordance with fire. Just as fire consumes everything without considering whether it is wet or dry, good or bad, so you also should eat without considering or seeking out substances which are sweet and desirable. ***As well as [making] the sword* mudrā**: This also accords with fire. Just as fire consumes and cuts off everything, likewise a sword also cuts and annihilates all things. ***All failings arising through your body, speech or mind will be burnt up***: If the *mantrin* abides in a *samādhi* such as this, all the predispositions to negative actions done by body, speech or mind, (193a) which have been accumulated in the mind will depart from it.

10. 'In the fourth [month], conjoined
with the wind [mandala],
he should always eat wind for food.
Then making the wheel *mudrā*,
in equipoise, the mantra should be recited.'

A C: 大慧刀 '*a great insight sword*'.

This explains the abiding in the wind mandala during the fourth month. You should practise the *samādhi* of the wind mandala, which was explained earlier, and in particular you should mentally meditate that your body has the sensation of wind. ***You should always eat wind for food***: The food which you use should also be in harmony with it. If you imagine that the wind which courses internally descends the gullet and dissipates, then hunger and thirst will cease. That is 'eating wind'. ***Then making the wheel* mudrā**: Since a wheel is characterized by revolving and moving, it is made to be in harmony with the wind. ***In equipoise, the mantra should be recited***: You should do the recitation in accordance with the process described earlier, controlling the inhalation and the exhalation.

11. 'Then in the fifth month,
if the holy one rests immersed in yoga
with regards to both earth and water[A],
and then abandons profit and loss
and becomes completely without attachment,
he will become like a Perfect Buddha.'

You should engage in the ritual observance for the *vidyā* mantras abiding in both the earth and water mandalas. You should imagine the earth and water mandalas arising from their respective essences, as before. Imagining the lower part of the body to be earth in nature and the upper part of the body to be water in nature, you should drink both milk and water for nourishment and do the recitation for one month. ***And then abandons profit and loss***: You should neither be joyful when gaining something nor unhappy when losing something.

12. 'Conjoined with wind and fire,
free from all faults,
and abandoning gain and loss,
he should recite for another month.'

You should engage in the ritual observance for the *vidyā* mantras abiding in both the wind and fire mandalas. You should imagine the fire mandala arising from its seed-syllable *Raṃ*, above the wind mandala. (193b) You should imagine that your lower body is blazing fire in nature and that your upper body is wind in nature, as before. With regards your food, you should use both a little of the wind eating practice and a little of the fire food which has not been sought out. The recitation should be done for one month.

You should know that when practising the tutelary deity with regards to all of these, the colour of the body-image of the deity is similar to the colour of each mandala. It is should also be mentioned that you ought to control the inhalations and exhalations and do the recitations for each month according to the process which was described in the section dealing with the earth mandala.

A C: 金剛水輪觀 '*visualizing an earth (vajra) and water disc*'.

13. **'The gods Śakra, Brahmā and so on,**
***piśācas* and *mahoragas*[A],**
will salute him from afar
and will protect him.
They will all give ear to his orders
and do just as he has ordered.
Divine physicians, men and gods[B],
will come before him,
saying "What shall we do for you?"
When harmful obstructors and gremlins,
***rākṣasas* and the Mothers,**
see that mantra-holder,
they will salute him from afar[C].
Wherever the *mantrin* resides,
who abides in the *vidyā* observance,
that place will blaze fearfully,
like the fire of destruction.
He will attain all ranks of mastery,
like the Perfect Buddha;
he will subdue those difficult to train,
just as the mighty Vajrapāṇi;
he will help all beings, (181b)
like the compassionate Lokeśvara.'

This section answers the question about how its power is to be recognized. When the gods such as Śakra, Brahmā and so on, and the *piśācas* and *mahoragas* see the *mantrin* who has this type of ritual observance for *vidyā*, they will salute him from afar and protect that *mantrin*. Whatever that *mantrin* commands will be done [by them], and the divine physicians will sit before that *mantrin* and obey his orders, and medicines which have been sought but not found will be seen in his presence. Even such terrifying beings as the *rākṣasas* and the Seven Mothers will salute him from afar, and the abode of the *mantrin* itself will appear as though ablaze with fire. He will gain mastery over both the mundane and the supramundane just as the Buddha Bhagavat, he will chastise hostile beings just as Vajrapāṇi, and he will act most compassionately just as Avalokiteśvara.

14. **'When the six months have elapsed,**
he will accomplish the *siddhi* results he desires,
and he will always benefit
both himself and others.'

(194a) This section answers the question about the period of time needed until one becomes free from time, place, actions, activities, right and wrong. By the process of

A T adds '*and* rākṣasas', but delete on basis of C and general sense as *rākṣasas* are mentioned below.

B C adds 持明諸靈仙 'Vidyādharas *and Immortals* (*ṛṣi*?)'.

C C: 恭敬而遠之 '*they will treat him with respect and keep their distance*'.

meditating on the earth mandala and so on over six months, you will become unaffected by time and so forth, and accomplish the attainments which benefit both yourself and others. The length of time needed to attain that is six months.

XVIII
THE KNOWLEDGE OF THE MASTER'S TRUE NATURE

1. Then Vajrapāṇi also asked the Bhagavat about the essence of the mantras and mandalas:

'What is the essence of all mantras?
What should one understand to become a Master?'

This chapter explains the true nature of a Master. As for the true nature of a Master, if you know what the essence of the mantras and mandalas truly is you will be a Master, hence the essence, the source of mantras, will be described first, and then the true nature of a Master will be taught. Therefore Vajrapāṇi asked these questions. The first question, '***What is the essence of all mantras***', should be linked with the words '***I declare that A is the essence of all mantras***'. The second question, '***What should one understand to become a Master***', should be linked with the words, '***You should arrange the essence in your heart***' and so forth. It is not sufficient merely to arrange the letters, but if you know the true meaning of their sounds and so on, you will be called a '***Master***'.

2. When he had been asked thus,
the Bhagavat Vairocana
said to the Vajradhara:
'Excellent, excellent, O Great Being[A]!
I shall explain to you, my son,
the most secret of secret [Awarenesses],
the most exalted[B] mantra Awareness.
Listen with unwavering attention!'

(194b) ***The most secret of secret [Awarenesses]***: In addition to the method of practising the mantras being naturally secret, the essence of mantras – the letter *A* – is the gate from which arises the Awareness that realizes that everything is primordially unborn, and it is extremely profound. So it must not be taught to those who are unsuitable and do not have the *samaya*, therefore it is the ***most secret of secret [Awarenesses]***. ***The most exalted mantra Awareness***: Since it will be realized that all phenomena are empty through this essence gate, it [*A*] is called '***Awareness***'. The supreme result, the great realization, will arise from that Awareness, so it is called '***most exalted***' (*mahodaya* = great source). Although Awareness and the great result arise by way of the Perfections and so on, it is called '***most exalted mantra Awareness***' to distinguish it from them.

3. 'I declare that *A*
is the essence of all mantras,
and from it there arise
mantras without number;

A C adds 令彼心歡喜 復告如是言 '*and made his heart joyful; he then said to him* ...'.
B T: *cher-'byung* = *mahodaya*, 'most exalted', 'great source'; C: 大心 = *mahā-hṛdaya*, 'great essence'. Either version would be reasonable.

and it produces in entirety[A] the Awareness
which stills all conceptual proliferations.'

This section answers the question, '***What is the essence*** (*hṛd*) ***of all mantras***'. The '***essence***' is the source. Therefore it is a source both on the absolute level and on the relative level. For if all the letters beginning with *Ka* lacked an *A*, they could not be spoken, so you should know that all the letters beginning with *Ka* arise from *A*. Hence it is a source on the relative level. On the absolute level, the Awareness which is the realization that all phenomena are primordially unborn and unarisen, arises from that *A*. This is the source on the absolute level. '***Mantras*** (195a) ***arise without number***' from it. All mundane and supramundane mantras that might be spoken are composed of letters, and since those letters are formed with *A*, all those countless mantras arise from that *A*. This shows that on the relative level it is the source of them all.

It produces in entirety the Awareness which stills all conceptual proliferations: This shows that the Awareness which is free from the conceptual proliferations (*prapañca*) of the concepts of perceiving subject and perceived objects also arises from that *A*, by the realization that all phenomena are primordially unborn and unarisen, empty in intrinsic nature, through the *samādhi*-gate of *A*. This shows that it is a source on the absolute level.

4. **'Lord of the Secret Ones!**
Why is *A* the essence of all mantras?
The Perfect Buddhas, Lords of Men,
say that *A* is the vital-force[B].
Therefore this is everything,
and inheres in all members;
and the members also should be known
to be ever in all, as appropriate.
All are encompassed by the letters
and the letters also are pervaded by that.
The sounds formed from the letters
arise in each member[C].
Therefore this encompasses all things,
and the bodies arise from their diversity[D].'

A T: *mtha'-dag* = *sakala* 'entire'; C: 巧 = *kuśala* 'wholesome', 'skillful'.

B T: *'tsho-ba* = *jīva* 'vital-force'; C: 種子 = *bīja*.

C C: 支體由是生 '[*the sounds are formed from the letters*], *and the members arise from this*', V: '*The sounds arise from the letters, and they arise in all members*'.

D All versions differ for these two lines. T & B: *de-bas-na 'di kun thams-cad de | lus ni sna-tshogs-las byung-ba'o ||* '*Therefore this is all things, and the bodies arise from their diversity*'; V: *de-bas-na de kun thams-cad de | sna-tshogs-pa'i lus 'byung-ba'o ||* '*Therefore this is all things, and the diverse bodies arise* [*from it*]'; C: 故此遍一切 身生種種德 '*Therefore this encompasses all things, and bodies arise from* [*its*] *various virtues*]'. Naturally the comments in CC are entirely compatible with the reading in C, but I have adopted the version given by T and B as that fits Buddhaguhya's comments, while adopting '*encompasses*' from C.

This explains what was briefly taught in the above verses. Now, there are generally speaking five elements: *A*, *Aṃ*, *Aḥ*, *I* and *U*. They are the general nature (*prakṛti*) of all letters. The *anusvāra* of *Aṃ* is the intrinsic nature of *Ṅa*, *Ña*, *Ṇa*, *Na* and *Ma*. The *Ka* group is included within *Ṅa*, the *Ca* group in *Ña*, the *Ṭa* group in *Ṇa*, the *Ta* group in *Na*, and the *Pa* group in *Ma*. *Ya* is included within *A* and *I*. *Ra* and *La* are included in *Ṛ* and *Ṝ*, *Ḷ* and *Ḹ*. *Śa*, *Ṣa*, *Sa* and *Ha* are included within the *visarga* of the syllable *Aḥ*. You should know that all the members beginning with *Ka* arise from those vowels *A* and so forth.

A is the vital-force: That letter *A* is the vital-force of everything, both on the relative and the absolute levels. (195b) Relatively speaking it is called the vital-force, because as explained above the letters *Ka* and so on could not be pronounced if they lacked *A*. On the absolute level it is called the vital-force because [it produces] the Awareness that realizes that all phenomena are primordially unborn and unarisen. Not only does Vairocana thus teach that it is the vital-force, but this was also taught by earlier Buddhas. ***Therefore this is everything***: Since that *A* is thus the vital-force, all phenomena such as *Ka* and so on are this. How is that? The text says, '***It inheres in all members***'. This means that *A* inheres in the letters beginning with *Ka*. ***The members also should be known to be ever [present] in all, as appropriate***: You should know that the members (*aṅga*) beginning with *Ka* always inhere in all mantras as appropriate. ***All are encompassed by the letters***: This speaks of them (the letters) as being their receptacle, meaning that all the syllables of the mantras are encompassed by the letters beginning with *Ka*. ***The letters also are encompassed by that***: This means that the letters beginning with *Ka* are encompassed by that *A*. ***The sounds formed from the letters arise in each part***: This means that the partial aspects of the sounds such as '***All phenomena are devoid of purpose***' and so forth, arise from the sounds of the letters beginning with *Ka*. ***Therefore this encompasses all things and the bodies arise from their diversity***: Therefore that *A* is all phenomena such as *Ka* and so forth, and since those phenomena such as *Ka* and so forth are the seeds of all the deities, the body-images of the deities arise from the conjunction of those diverse letters as appropriate.

5. 'I shall teach where they are to be placed,
so listen carefully about the essence[A]!
You should place the essence in your heart,
and then arrange the members in your members.'

(196a) This explains the allocation of all those thirty two letters throughout the body of the Master. ***I shall teach where they are to be placed***: The allocation of that letter *A* in the heart has already been described. ***Listen carefully about the essence***: The word '***essence***'[1] does not refer only to *A* but you should also understand it to be what was explained earlier with the words '***The mind which is satisfied and fixed is what I describe as the heart. The mantras which are located there will bestow vast results***' [VI.103-104]. It is not sufficient just to allocate those letters, but they should be meditated upon until the true meaning of each individual sound satisfies and delights the mind. ***You should place the essence in your heart and then arrange the members in your members***: You

A C: 佛子一心聽 '*Son of the Buddha! Listen single-mindedly!*'

should place the letter *A* in your heart and arrange the letters *Ka* and so forth in your members following the sequence which is mentioned below with the words, '***Ka is placed in the throat***'.

6. **'Established in the yoga-posture**
and recollecting the Tathāgatas,
the wise one should make his own body (182a)
into the Body of the Perfect Buddha:
he should do all of this[A]**.'**

This means that a Master should change his own body into the Body of the Perfect Buddha and arrange all those letters therein. ***Established in the yoga-posture and recollecting the Tathāgatas***: He should think of the Tathāgatas and salute them, then having equipoised his body and mind, established in the yoga-posture, he should do the things mentioned.

7. **'When a person knows that vast Awareness**
according to the prescribed ritual,
then he will be called a Master
by all the powerful Buddhas.'

(196b) When he has arranged the letters thus and knows the true meaning of their sounds, the vast Awareness which realizes emptiness, having engaged in them according to the prescribed ritual, he will then be called a Master by the Perfect Buddhas.

8. **'He will be called a Tathāgata,**
or else a Perfect Buddha.
He will also be called
a Bodhisattva, Brahmā,
Viṣṇu and Maheśvara,
Candra, Āditya, Varuṇa,
Śakra, Prajāpati,
Kālarātrī and Yama,
Pṛthivī and Sarasvāti.'

This section deals with the praises of him. Buddhas and so forth are accomplished by two types of cause – merit and Awareness. The merits of Generosity and so on are the indirect cause and Awareness is the actual cause. Here this Awareness that he has actualized which realizes emptiness, the true meaning of the letters of the sounds of mantras, is the actual cause.

With regards to the praises, '***He will be called a Tathāgata***' and so forth, that Master is not really a Tathāgata because he abides on the Level of Practice with Devoted

---

A C: 一切如是作 即同於我體 安住瑜伽座 尋念諸如來 '*he should do all in this way and then he will become identical to me in substance. Establishing himself in the yoga-posture, he should recollect the Tathāgatas*'.

Interest. Since, however, he is creating the cause of becoming a Tathāgata and so on, you should know that the cause is named by the result. Just as it happens in the everyday world that one can say there will be a fine harvest if there is rain and good sprouts, even though the fruit is not formed.

The epithets are of four kinds: supramundane deities, mundane deities, supramundane humans and mundane humans. The supramundane deities are '***A Tathāgata or else a Perfect Buddha***'. The mundane deities are '***Brahmā, Viṣṇu and Maheśvara***' and so on. The mundane humans are '***brahmin and initiate and also a celibate***'. (197a) The supramundane humans are '***the noble monks who have exhausted all inflations***'.

9. **'Brahmin and initiate[2],**
and also a celibate[3],
a noble monk who has
exhausted his inflations[4],
a holder of all secrets,
all-knowing and all-seeing,
Lord Master of Dharma.'

A holder of all secrets: He holds all the secrets of body, speech and mind since he has changed his body into the body-image of a deity, filled his body with the letters that are speech in nature and has the Awareness which perceives the true meaning of the sounds of those letters. ***Lord Master of Dharma***: Because he has mastered both Dharma as realization and as scripture.

10. **'Whoever is firm in *bodhicitta*,**
and devoted to Awareness of the sounds,
without attachment to any dharma,
will be known in all [those] aspects,
Whoever has the Wheel of Letters
arranged throughout his body,
will be a mantrin, a mantra-holder,
a glorious mantra king, a Vajradhara.'

You do not become a Buddha or a Bodhisattva and so on just by having arranged the letters throughout your body, but if your *bodhicitta* is stable and you exert yourself in meditation on the Awareness of the true meaning of the sounds of those letters, you will become like those beings who have been mentioned. That is the *samadhi* of the Master and is the first one.

11. **'The letter *Hūṃ* between your eyebrows**
is the ground of He With Vajra[A];
The letter *Sa* in your chest[5]
is called the ground of Padmapāṇi;

A C begins these lines with: 所有諸字輪 若在於支分 '*If any of the letter discs are to be placed in the members, [then you should know ...]*'.

Mine is placed in the heart location:
it is Lord and Master of all,
and it pervades entirely
all the animate and inanimate.'

This is the second *samādhi* of the Master. They should be arranged upon [the mandalas of] the Three Families. ***The letter Hūṃ between your eyebrows***: As before, the Master should change himself into the Body of the Bhagavat Vairocana and he should imagine *Hūṃ*, the essence of Vajrapāṇi, upon its mandala between his eye-brows. ***The letter Sa in your chest is called the ground of Padmapāṇi***: This is the essence of Avalokiteśvara and should be imagined in the chest in conjunction with a moon disc. ***Mine is placed in the heart location***: He should imagine an *A*, the essence of the Bhagavat Vairocana himself, in his heart. ***It is Lord and Master of all and it pervades entirely all the animate and the inanimate***: (197b) This is praise of the qualities of that essence. '*Animate*' refers to such beings as the humans and so on. '***Inanimate***' refers to the earth, trees and so forth, and it pervades all of them.

12. **'*A* is the highest life-energy,**
_Va_ is called "speech"[A],
_Ra_ is called "fire",
Hūṃ is called "wrathful",
Kha should be known as space,
and the _anusvāra_ is the most empty.
One who knows this is called a Master,
for this is the supreme reality.'

This deals with the third *samādhi* of the Master. Since among the essences of the Great Hero the letter '***A is the highest life-energy***', you should imagine it as described before, in conjunction with the movement of the breath in your interior. ***Va is called "speech"***: Because *Va* is speech in nature, you should imagine it in your mouth. ***Ra is called "fire"***: You should imagine that letter *Ra* in conjunction with its mandala in the 'light-discs'[6]. ***Hūṃ is called "wrathful"***: You should imagine the letter *Hūṃ* with its mandala between your eye-brows. ***Kha should be known as space and the* anusvāra *is the most empty***: The letter *Kha* with an *anusvāra* should be imagined above your cranium. *Kha* shows that it is the attribute of all phenomena to be like space. The *anusvāra* is also empty in nature. ***One who knows this is called a Master, for this is the supreme reality***: Whosoever knows the true meaning of the sounds of the letters mentioned above and their arrangement is called a '***Master***'.

13. **'Therefore, if you exert yourself continually**
regarding this Awareness
of which the Perfect Buddhas have spoken,
you will attain the deathless state[B].'

A C: 水 = *paya*, 'water'; T: *tshig* = *pada* 'speech'. Buddhguhya's comments nonwithstanding, C probably preserves the original reading, given the context.

B C: 故應具方便 了知佛所說 常作精勤修 當得不死句 '*Therefore you should be endowed with expedient means and always exert yourself in the understanding taught by the Buddhas, and you will attain the deathless state.*'

This verse is in praise of them. Those essences have not only been explained by the Bhagavat Vairocana, but they were also mentioned by earlier Buddhas. Therefore, if you continually exert yourself in the meditation upon the Awareness which reveals the true meaning of their sounds in all aspects, (198a) you will attain the status of Buddhahood.

XIX
THE ALLOCATION OF LETTERS (182b)

'This is the way to allocate the letters,
which was taught by the Perfect Buddhas,
so listen carefully to it!
***Ka* is placed in the throat,**
***Kha* should be placed on the palate,**
***Ga* is in the neck,**
***Gha* is placed in the gullet;**
***Ca* should be placed in the tongue**
***Cha* is in the middle of the tongue,**
***Ja* is on the tip of the tongue,**
***Jha* is at the root of the tongue[A];**
***Ṭa* is known to be on the shins,**
***Ṭha* should be placed on the thighs,**
***Ḍa* is placed at the waist,**
***Ḍha* is placed on the buttocks;**
***Ta* is placed in the bladder,**
***Tha* is known to be the belly,**
***Da* is placed in the two armpits,**
***Dha* is placed on either side of the ribs;**
***Pa* is known to be the back,**
***Pha* is known to be the breast,**
***Ba* is placed on both shoulders,**
***Bha* is placed on both hands;**
***Ma* is placed in the *manas* location[B],**
***Ya* is called the penis,**
***Ra* is explained as the collar bones[C],**
***La* is known as the brow[D],**
***I* and *Ī* are the two eyes[E],**
***U* and *Ū* are called the lips,**
***E* and *Ai* are the two ears,**
***O* and *Au* are the two cheeks.**
***Aṃ* is the place[1] of the Perfect Buddha,**
and *Aḥ* is Nirvāṇa[2].
Know all this according to the ritual,
and make yourself enlightened

A C: 舌生處 '*place from where the tongue arises*'.

B *Ma* should be omitted as are all other nasals. T also follows this with '*Then it will be known how the body is*', which is apparently intrusive and is not found in C or CC.

C C: 眼 = **netra*, '*eyes*', T: *nam-mtshong* = *jatru*, '*collar-bones, scapula*'.

D T adds '*skyob-pa de-yi 'phral-ba yin*' here which makes little sense here and is not included in C or CC. It is probably an intrusion, perhaps originally a marginal gloss.

E C: 緣伊在二眥 'i *and* ī *are in the canthus* (*apāṅga*)'.

by the excellent ritual observance [A]!
If the All-knowing Treasure
always abides in your heart,
you will be called omniscient in the world,
like an All-knowing Hero [B].'

This chapter on the allocation of the letters indicates which of the letters *Ka* and so on, should be placed in which members of the body, which was mentioned in general above with the words, '***arrange the members in your members***' (XVIII.5). Those thirty-two letters which are to be arranged should be linked with the thirty-two marks of a Great Being. You should also know that the first *samādhi* of the Master should be employed at the time of the Mandala Arising From Great Compassion, the second one should be employed at the time of the Mandala of the Revolving Wheel of Letters and the third one should be employed at the time of the Secret Mandala.

A C: 知是一切法 行者成正覺 '*The practitioner who knows the entire method will become fully enlightened*'.

B C: 一切智資財 常在於其心 世號一切智 是謂薩婆若 '*The treasure of All-knowing will always be in his heart, and the world will call him omniscient: that is termed "All-knowing" (sarvajña)*'.

XX
THE BODHISATTVA'S TRAINING ACCOMPANIED BY EXPEDIENT MEANS

1. Then Vajrapāṇi, the Lord of the Secret Ones, asked the Bhagavat this, 'Bhagavat! Please explain how it is that the Bodhisattva Mahāsattvas are without uncertainty and confusion? How is that they are not harmed when they go around in *saṃsāra,* (183a) when they are in possession of that basis of training of the Bodhisattva Mahāsattvas which is upheld by expedient means and insight?'

This chapter explains the path of the ten wholesome actions of a Bodhisattva's training, which is accompanied by expedient means. Regarding this, the extraordinary training of the Bodhisattvas who engage in the Bodhisattva practice by means of mantras, which is characterized by *samaya,* has already been explained. Here you should know that it is the general training, accompanied by expedient means of both the Bodhisattvas who engage in the Perfections and those who engage in Mantras, which is to be explained.

Bodhisattva: (198b) '*Bodhi*' (Enlightenment) is defined as Suchness and the person (*sattva*) who has the intention which seeks to directly experience that is called a 'bodhisattva'. '***Mahāsattva***' refers to the person who knows that all phenomena are like illusions and realizes that although no phenomena really exist at all[A], nevertheless on the relative level, they do bring about effects by means of the certainty of the cause-result relationship, in the manner of illusions, and who then continues in the training accompanied by expedient means in order to completely liberate beings. On this occasion, the text especially mentions the Bodhisattva Mahāsattvas with reference to the explanation of that sort of training. ***The basis of training*** (śikṣā-pada): This refers to that which is defined as the adoption of the method of the ten wholesome actions and the abstinence from the ten unwholesome actions, which is dealt with below. ***Which is upheld by expedient means and insight:*** '***Insight***' (*prajñā*) is defined as the realization that all phenomena are primordially unborn. '***Expedient means***' (*upāya*) is to engage in this type of training, and in Generosity and so forth with purity of the three elements (*tri-maṇḍala-pariśuddhi*) on the illusion-like relative level, by way of expedient means, although it is understood that all phenomena are primordially unborn and unarisen, and are without any objective reality. ***Upheld by insight and expedient means:*** Like the Śrāvakas, they do not lack the expedient means to abstain from the ten unwholesome actions, but when they perceive the great benefit with their insight, they will also countenance the actions which lead to the miserable states, without guile. They give themselves to beings and engage in the things which should not be done. Hence, their training is said to be upheld by expedient means and insight. ***Please explain how it is that the Bodhisattva Mahasattvas are without uncertainty and confusion and are not harmed when they go around in*** **saṃsāra**: (199a) Vajrapāṇi is asking the Bhagavat to explain how it is that those Bodhisattvas who are free from any doubt that [this] instruction was proclaimed by the Bhagavat, or confusion through not

A V: '*the individual also lacks any substantial existence...*'

knowing whether it is or is not [thus], do not fall into the miserable states and do not become emotionally afflicted even though they go around in *saṃsāra* by having that training.

2. When he had asked this, the Bhagavat Vairocana gazed upon all the continuums of reality with his Tathāgata Eyes and then he said this to Vajrapāṇi, the Lord of the Secret Ones, 'Lord of the Secret Ones! If Bodhisattva Mahāsattvas abide in the skill which I shall teach concerning the method of engaging in the practice of a Bodhisattva, they will gain understanding of the Mahāyāna, so listen carefully to it!'

'***Tathāgata Eyes***' refer to the Buddha Awareness. '***The continuums of reality***' refers to the realms of beings. With that Buddha Awareness, he perceives in all realms of beings who among these beings are suffering and who are happy. Or else he perceives what kinds of happiness or suffering will arise among these beings, based on their engaging in such and such wholesome or unwholesome actions. ***If they abide in the skill which I shall teach concerning the method of engaging in the practice of a Bodhisattva***: In this case ***the practice of a Bodhisattva*** refers to the training accompanied by expedient means. '***Method***' refers to what leads them to it, because by this training they will attain whatever aim they desire. ***Skill***: Because they train in the kind of method described above which is upheld by insight and expedient means, unlike that of the Śrāvakas. ***They will gain understanding of the Mahāyāna***: When one is established in that training upheld by insight and expedient means, with skill in the method of practice of Bodhisattvas, one is said to have undertaken the training. (199b) So the Bhagavat tells him to hear how the Bodhisattva Mahāsattvas, who have undertaken the training, will enter into the Mahāyāna.

3. 'Lord of the Secret Ones, a Bodhisattva should turn away from the taking of life, the taking of what is not given and sexual misconduct. He should turn away from lying, abuse, slander and idle talk. He should turn away from covetousness, malice and perverse opinions. Lord of the Secret Ones! This is the Bodhisattva's training which is equivalent to the practice of Buddhas and Bodhisattvas if you engage in it.'

This lists the ten unwholesome actions from which one should abstain and they will be explained below. ***This is the Bodhisattva's training which is equivalent to the practice of Buddhas and Bodhisattvas if you engage in it***: If you have trained in that training mentioned above, you will have trained in the practice of Buddhas and Bodhisattvas, so you will attain the status of Buddhas and Bodhisattvas. Therefore, by training yourself thus, your training may be said to be identical to the training in which the Buddhas and Bodhisattvas engaged.

4. Then Vajrapāṇi, the Lord of Secret Ones, asked the Bhagavat, 'The Bhagavat has explained this path of ten wholesome actions in the Śrāvaka Way and since the mundane non-Buddhists accept and dwell in the path of ten wholesome actions, so what is special about this, what makes it different?'

Vajrapāṇi asks in what way is this training special when it is spoken about among Bodhisattvas, Śrāvakas and mundane people. '***The mundane non-Buddhists***' refers to those ascetics who undertake this teaching concerning the points of training (*śikṣā-vastu*), which are not followed by the common mass of mundane people. ***What is special about this?***: Vajrapāṇi asks about the distinctive qualities of the nature of that training. ***What makes it different?***: This is an enquiry about its causal basis and should be linked up with what will explained below.

5. When he had asked this, the Bhagavat said to Vajrapāṇi, the Lord of the Secret Ones, 'Excellent, Lord of the Secret Ones, it is excellent that you ask the Tathāgata about this matter. Therefore, Lord of the Secret Ones, listen well, for I shall teach the Dharma discourse which reveals the single method which has distinct methods. (183b) **The training which I have taught to the Śrāvakas lacks expedient means and insight and only brings about the fulfilment of the literal sense and the realization of partial knowledge. Therefore their training and this path of ten wholesome actions are not similar. The mundane [non-Buddhists] undertake them while attached and in dependence upon the objective reality of a self (*ātma-bhāva*). In order that the Bodhisattvas who fare on the Mahāyāna may enter into sameness, they should undertake the benefitting of both themselves and others, upheld by expedient means and insight, without regard for anything else. Therefore, Lord of the Secret Ones, the Bodhisattva Mahāsattvas should strive to perceive all phenomena[A], upheld by expedient means and insight.'**

The distinct methods: (200a) The differentiation of the methods of the Bodhisattvas, Śrāvakas and mundane people by means of the specific qualities taught below. ***The one method***: Because it shows the similarity in nature of the ten wholesome actions.

The training which I have taught to the Śrāvakas and so forth: Although the Noble Śrāvakas accomplish it according to the instructions (*āgama*) taught by the Teacher, they do not adhere to or deviate from the scriptures and reason (*yukti*) and act as appropriate with insight as Bodhisattvas do. Lacking insight and expedient means, they remain in the partial knowledge which is [only] the realization that the person lacks any autonomous existence, so their training is not similar.

The mundane [non-Buddhists] undertake them while attached to and dependent upon the objective reality of a self (*ātma-bhava*): Mundane people say that all arising, perishing, happiness, suffering and the points of training are experienced by an entity (*bhāva*) called the 'self' (*ātman*) and they undertake the training dependent upon another so-called 'self'. Since their training relies upon the entity which they think is the 'self', it is not similar.

In order that the Bodhisattvas, who fare on the Mahāyāna, may enter into sameness: They will enter into the sameness of all phenomena on the absolute level, as they are empty in nature and they will enter into the sameness of all phenomena on the relative level, as they are illusion-like in nature. ***Without regard for anything else***: It is not like the dependent undertaking of the mundane people who imagine a 'self' to exist. ***Upheld by expedient means and insight***: As explained earlier. ***Who undertake the***

A C: 一切法平等 '*the sameness of all phenomena*'.

benefitting of both themselves and others: (200b) They themselves undertake that sort of training which is upheld by expedient means and insight, and also others are caused to undertake it, being drawn to it by the Four Methods of Attracting. To this you should add the words, 'Therefore the trainings of mundane people, Śrāvakas and Bodhisattvas are dissimilar'.

Therefore the Bodhisattva Mahāsattvas should strive to perceive [the sameness] all phenomena, upheld by expedient means and insight: With these words, the Bhagavat summarizes what he has explained above. It means that they should apply themselves to all phenomena with the method that has been described, which has expedient means and insight, unlike the training of the Śrāvakas and mundane people which lacks them.

6. Then the Bhagavat gazed upon the realms of beings with eyes of great loving-kindness and great compassion and then said to the Bodhisattva Vajrapāṇi, 'Regarding that, the Bodhisattva should deliberately turn away from severing life, he should cast away weapons and feelings of hatred. He should guard the life of another as though it were his own. On the other hand, such [actions] may be done to save an individual from the effects of his evil actions, but even these should be done without feelings of hatred and with a compassionate mind.'

The Bhagavat is about to speak in order to explain each point of the Bodhisattva's training which has been listed by name only. '***Loving-kindness***' is defined as establishing beings in happiness and '***compassion***' is defined as removing them from suffering. Those two, loving-kindness and compassion, are the eyes of the Bhagavat, because with friendliness he perceives who in the realms of beings ought to be made happy and with compassion, who ought to be removed from suffering.

Elsewhere Vajrapāṇi is referred to as the Lord of the Secret Ones, but here he is called a Bodhisattva, because this training is for Bodhisattvas in general.

(201a) The taking of life, which is defined by five types and is well known from the Vinaya and other texts, should be abandoned. That is, you should '***cast away weapons and feelings of hatred***'. The Bodhisattva ***should guard the life of another as though it were his own***: Since the possession of weapons and the making of enemies, with feelings of hatred, is a subsidiary element to the taking of life, these also should be abandoned in order to fulfil even the subsidiary elements of the abandonment of the taking of life.

7. 'He should turn away from taking what is not given. If he does not even have feelings of attachment to the possessions of others, how much less inclined is he to take the possessions of others which are not given! Or, on the other hand, if he sees some beings who are greedy and avaricious and who do not give [to others] or act meritoriously, he may do such actions exceptionally in order to remove avarice from such persons, and he should give away [those things] as gifts for their sakes, without attachment to them. (184a) He should frequently speak in praise of generosity[A]. If a Bodhisattva

A C: 獲妙色等 '[*by which*] *one will acquire a beautiful appearance and so on*'.

is attached to something, then you should know, Lord of the Secret Ones, that Bodhisattva has impaired the elements of Enlightenment and has irreparably fallen away from the Dharma Vinaya[A].'

Likewise the remainder, such as the taking of what is not given, are just as described in the text.

8. 'He should turn away from sexual misconduct. If even thoughts of attachment to the wives of others, those who are betrothed, those who are protected by their families or else by religious vocation do not arise in him, how much less is he inclined to use the improper parts or join both organs together! Or, on the other hand, he may do such acts to safeguard beings.'

9. 'He should turn away from lying. He should not wilfully utter lies, by which the Buddha's Enlightenment is slandered, even to save his life. Lord of the Secret Ones, to slander the Buddha's Enlightenment is the greatest of lies for a Bodhisattva dwelling in the Mahāyāna[B]. Lord of the Secret Ones, you should understand in this way that you should not forsake truthful speech.'

10. 'Lord of the Secret Ones! Furthermore, he should turn away from abuse. He should speak to beings with tender, gentle and gratifying words. Why is that? Because, Lord of the Secret Ones, the words of a Bodhisattva, who gives priority to the benefitting of others, should be gentle. But on other occasions, exceptionally, a Bodhisattva may speak harshly in various situations to those beings in whom there are the causes of the miserable states of existence.'

11. 'Lord of the Secret Ones! Furthermore he should turn away from slander. He should act so as not to bring about discord or harm and the like, anywhere. Bodhisattvas do not cause dissension among beings. (184b) **But on other occasions, exceptionally, if he sees beings who have become bogged down in various heretical positions (*dṛṣṭi-sthāna*), he will cause division by means of that, so that those beings may be established in this single method of the All-knowing One.'**

12. 'Lord of the Secret Ones! Furthermore, a Bodhisattva should turn away from idle talk. He should use words which are appropriate to the time and place, conform to the topic, which are pleasing to beings and which purify aural activity. Why is that? Because a Bodhisattva has a diverse vocabulary. But on other occasions, a Bodhisattva may even speak valueless, trivial words because he wishes to establish beings in the Buddha Dharma, by first

---

A C: 無爲 '*the unconditioned* [*Dharma Vinaya*]'.

B C: 設爲活命因緣不應妄語即爲欺誑諸佛菩提. 秘密主, 是名菩薩住於最上大乘. 若妄語者越失佛菩提法. '*Even to save his life,* [*the Bodhisattva*] *should not lie, for this falsifies the Enlightenment of the Buddhas. Lord of the Secret Ones, this is termed the Bodhisattva's abiding in the highest vehicle. A liar will lose the Buddha's Enlightenment Dharma.*'

telling legends and delighting people. In that way, a Bodhisattva will not be obstructed, even when he moves around in *saṃsāra*.'

13. 'Furthermore, Lord of the Secret Ones, a Bodhisattva should turn away from covetousness. He should not even give rise to thoughts of attachment to the possessions and wealth of others. Why is that? Because a Bodhisattva does not have a clinging attitude. If a Bodhisattva gives rise to grasping, he will partially degenerate from the gate to All-knowing[A]. Lord of the Secret Ones, a Bodhisattva should make himself joyful and consider as follows: "It is excellent that whatever I must do will become the wealth of others!", and repeatedly become joyful at the fruitfulness (*avipranaśa*) of the possessions of those beings[B].'

14. 'Furthermore, Lord of the Secret Ones, he should turn away from malice. He should be very tolerant, friendly and even-minded, without hatred. (185a) **He should treat his enemies as he would his beloved. Why is that? Because a Bodhisattva does not have an evil mind (*dauṣṭhūlya-manas*), but the thoughts of a Bodhisattva are naturally pure. Therefore, Lord of the Secret Ones, the Bodhisattva should be free from malice.'**

15. 'Furthermore, Lord of the Secret Ones, a Bodhisattva should be without perverse opinions. He should fix his thoughts upon the Buddha, Dharma and Saṅgha, with true views, views fearful of the next life, without wavering, without deceit, without artifice and with directness. Why is that? Because, Lord of the Secret Ones, perverse opinions are the greatest of faults (*avadya*) for a Bodhisattva and will sever all his wholesome roots. They are the grandmother[C] of all unwholesome roots. Therefore, Lord of the Secret Ones, you should not give rise to perverse opinions even in jest!'

Although permission has been given for Bodhisattvas to do occasionally the things which ought not to be done, the Chapter on the Bodhisattva's Morality[1] says that that only refers to the lay Bodhisattvas and not to those who have become monks (*pravrājita*), because that would contradict the Vinaya.

16. Then Vajrapāṇi, the Lord of the Secret Ones, said to the Bhagavat, 'Bhagavat! Please explain in detail how it is that the restraint of this path of ten wholesome actions is not ruined in a Bodhisattva, how it is not cut off from the root? How does he not fall even though he is surrounded by the ruler of the country, a house[D], a wife, sons and daughters, relatives and kinsmen and also experiences both divine and human comforts?'

A C: 若菩薩心有染思彼於一切智門無力而墮一邊 '*If a Bodhisattva's mind has attachment, he will become incapable of that gate to All-knowing and will fall into a limited* [*state*].'

B C: 勿令彼諸衆生損失資財故 '[*and repeatedly become joyful*], *for he should not cause beings to lose their possessions*'.

C C: 母 '*mother*'.

D Added from C.

Then Vajrapāṇi asks these questions about their distinctive qualities, regarding the destruction or otherwise of the root (*mūla*) of the topics (*vastu*) of the ten wholesome actions which were explained above. Now, the restraints (*saṃvara*) for monks are explained in the chapters of the *Pratimokṣa* so it will not be dealt with here. In this case, since it deals with the lay Bodhisattvas, there are two types of [restraint]: the acceptance of the restraint of the Five Precepts and the maintenance of the vow without having accepted the discipline. Of those questions, that about '***the ruin of the restraint of this path of the ten wholesome actions***' asks the Bhagavat to explain how the path of the ten wholesome actions of a Bodhisattva who has accepted the discipline of the Five Precepts will be destroyed. That about '***the complete severance from the root***' asks him to explain how the maintenance of the vow by oneself without having accepted the Five Precepts will be destroyed.

The question about '***how he does not fall even though surrounded by the rulers of the country*** (*rājyaiśvarya*), ***a wife***' and so on (201b) is to clarify the causal characteristics (*nimitta*) and asks the Bhagavat about the distinctive qualities (*viśeṣa*) of lay Bodhisattvas. Although lay bodhisattvas are surrounded by their family and entourage, engage in and control divine and human pleasures (*bhoga*), how is it that they do not come under the sway of those things, and with skilful expedient means, they do not degenerate from the discipline of the ten wholesome actions? These questions should be linked up with the Bhagavat's replies given below.

17. When he had asked this, the Bhagavat said to him, 'Excellent, Lord of the Secret Ones, excellent! I shall explain to you the skill in determining the Vinaya of the Bodhisattvas[A], so listen well and bear it in mind! Lord of the Secret Ones, there are two types of Bodhisattva: (185b) **householders and monks. Of those, the householder Bodhisattvas live in houses and uphold the five bases of training, and they control the kingdom[B] by various kinds of methods and expedient means. Lord of the Secret Ones, the Bodhisattva who wishes to attain All-knowing [Awareness] by mastery of time and place upheld by expedient means, will display different kinds of arts (*śilpa-sthāna*) such as singing, music and magic, and gather together beings by the Four Methods of Attracting, with these various methods and means, so that they may wish for the supreme perfect Enlightenment. The householder Bodhisattvas should accept the five bases of training: To reject the severance of life, the taking of what is not given, sexual misconduct, lying and perverse opinions.'**

Furthermore, the lay Bodhisattvas are specified and described with, '***they control the kingdom by various kinds of methods and expedient means***' and so forth. Monks strive and exert themselves during this lifetime, but the lay Bodhisattvas are not limited by time and space. They contemplate and exert themselves not only in this lifetime, but also in many different lifetimes, and they strive to be born in various places such as Buddha fields and so on, by way of their many different kinds of expedient means. Hence the text says, '***upheld by expedient means***'. Even the music and so on, and the

A Reading adopted from C. T: '*lapses in the Vinaya of Bodhisattvas*'.
B C: 勢位自在 '[*they*] *exercise full authority*'.

many crafts which they display are in order to attract beings to them by means of the Four Methods of Attracting, used in accordance with the individual types of being and to raise them up to the supreme and perfect Enlightenment. This section concludes with an enumeration of the items of the Five Precepts of a Bodhisattva.

18. 'Then faithfully engaging in that training as has been taught, they should train in the wake of former Tathāgatas. Abiding in the agglomeration of the supreme unconditioned morality which is praised by the Tathāgata, they should engage in the conditioned morality which is upheld by expedient means and insight and not infringe the four root failings, even for the sake of their lives. What are those four? They are the abandonment[A] of the holy Dharma, the abandonment of *bodhicitta*, avarice[B] and causing harm to beings. Why is that? Because these are lacking in expedient means and insight, are emotionally afflicted by nature and are irreparable.'

(212a) If the lay Bodhisattva faithfully trains in this five-fold training which has been mentioned, he will have trained in a training similar to that of the earlier Tathāgatas, which was praised by the supreme Tathāgatas. Why is that? Because even the earlier Tathāgatas dwelt in the agglomeration of the unconditioned morality (*śīla-skandha*), and having trained in the conditioned morality which is upheld by expedient means and insight, they attained the supreme [Enlightenment]. Therefore if you train thus you train in their wake. ***Abiding in the agglomeration of the supreme unconditioned morality***: Abiding in the realization that all phenomena, which are primordially unborn and unarisen, are empty in nature. ***The conditioned morality***: That which was enumerated as turning away from the taking of life and so on.

Thus a trainee should not infringe these four root infractions[2] which are listed above, even for the sake of his life. These four were also explained earlier in the section on *Samaya* [II.93]. ***Why is that? Because they are irreparable.*** If any of these four have occurred you should not even be called a Bodhisattva, and it is not possible to repair. These four things lack expedient means and insight and are emotionally afflicted by nature. They '***lack expedient means and insight***' because those four destroy them.

19. 'All the Buddhas of the past
likewise those of the future,
and such Lords in the present,
with expedient means and insight train in that,
and by that they all attain
the unconditioned supreme Enlightenment[C].
Though ways of training have been taught
with the awareness lacking expedient means[D],

A C: 謗諸法 '*defamation of the Teachings*'.
B C: 慳悋 '*meanness*'.
C C: 得無漏悉地 '*They gain the unsullied attainment*'.
D C: 離於方便智 '*lacking in expedient means and awareness*'.

the Great Hero expounded them
in order to help the Śrāvakas to it.[A]'

(202b) Therefore, if these four have occurred and you are without expedient means and insight, you will not attain the supreme unconditioned Enlightenment, so it is irreparable. If it is irreparable because of the lack of expedient means and insight, how does one explain the training of the Śrāvakas which lacks expedient means and insight? To explain the training of the Śrāvakas in the Awareness which lacks expedient means, the Bhagavat says that although he has taught such a training to the Śrāvakas, which lacks expedient means and insight, it was not taught as the definitive (*nitārtha*) one, but in order to guide them in accordance with their capacity.

A C: 誘進諸聲聞 '*to guide the Śrāvakas*'.

XXI
THE ARISING OF THE HUNDRED LETTERS (186A)

1. Then the Bhagavat Vairocana gazed upon the entire assembly. Desiring that the teaching might be fruitfully accomplished, he spoke gently to the most powerful one, Vajrapāṇi, in order to proclaim the Lord of all Mantras, the King of Mantras, the Protector of all Mantras, the Great Majesty, that he might be caused to dwell in the Three *Samayas* and perfect the Three Paths[A]:

'Listen, O Hero, with unwavering mind
to the Mantra Protector of Mantras!'

Following the transformation herein of these configurations of the Vajra Adornments of the Inexhaustible Body and so forth of the Bhagavat Vairocana, first the four-membered inner and outer recitation was taught in the case of the mantra recitation. Next, the four-membered inner recitation was taught in the case of the four essences (*A*, *Ā*, *Aṃ*, *Aḥ*) of the Tathāgata. Then the three-membered inner recitation was taught in the case of the essence of the Great Hero (*A*, *Va*, *Ra*, *Ha*, *Kha*). It was also said that one should do the [preliminary] service (*seva*) with a fixed number of recitations and duration. Now in this Chapter on the Hundred Letters, the one-membered recitation and the signs of the recitation without [preliminary] service of a fixed number and duration, from the *sādhana* of the Perfect Buddha's Body until completion, is explained.

(203a) Therefore you should know that these recitations may be explained in a sequence going from coarse to subtle. First, the four-membered inner and outer recitation is coarse because you focus your attention on both the inner and the outer bases. Next, the four-membered inner recitation is subtler than that because you do not focus your attention on the Body of the Buddha externally, but you imagine the Tathāgata's Body within your heart and do the recitation. Then in the case of the Great Hero, you should abandon even the imagining of the Tathāgata's Body in your heart, but imagining any one of the mandalas of earth and so on, you should do the recitation, doing it with three members, and so it is still subtler than the previous one.

In this section on the Hundred Lettered [Mantra], you should abide in the *samādhi* of emptiness yourself, focussing your attention on just the sound of the essence [*Aṃ*], and then do the recitation with just one member. Therefore you should know that it is subtler than all those above.

Now, although all the hundred letters are the Perfect Buddha, they are also transformations of the letter *Aṃ*. You should know that the explanation of the Hundred Lettered [Mantra] is made up of five chapters: the Arising of the Hundred Lettered [Mantra] (XXI), the Manifestation of the Acquisition of the Result of the Sound (XXII), the Accomplishment of the Arrangement of the Hundred Lettered [Mantra] (XXIII), Self Accomplishment (XXIV) and the Teaching of the Nature of Enlightenment (XXVI).

A C: 三法 '*the three phenomena*'. CC states that these are the basic principle, the practice and the result of the mantra training.

Of those, first the Chapter on the Arising of the Hundred Lettered [Mantra] will be explained. Now, you should know that the hundred letters are included within that one *Aṃ*, in the following way – *Ṅa*, *Ña*, *Ṇa*, *Na* and *Ma* are the *anusvāra* in nature; the *Ka* group is included in *Ṅa*, (203b) the *Ca* group in *Ña*, the *Ṭa* group in *Ṇa*, the *Ta* group in *Na* and the *Pa* group in *Ma*. Then relating these twenty five letters to what was explained in the *Vijñāna* Chapter [XVIII.4], *A* is also included in *Aṃ*, *Ṛ* and *Ṝ*, *Ḷ* and *Ḹ* are included within *Ra* and *La*. *Ya* is included in *I* [and *Ī*], and *Va* is included in *U* and *Ū*. In that way *Ya*, *Ra*, *La* and *Va* are also included within it. Since they are each conjoined with an *Aṃ*[1] and so on, when you link those twenty five letters with the four – Enlightenment, Practice, Perfect Buddhahood and Nirvāṇa – they make one hundred, and thus they are all included within the one letter *Aṃ*.

Aṃ is defined as the emptiness of the knower and the known, for the *anusvāra* is the sign (*lakṣaṇa*) of emptiness, and the four part letter *A* is included within it, therefore that *Aṃ* itself which is the Bhagavat Perfect Buddha in nature, is the Hundred Lettered [Mantra].

Since *Ṅa*, *Ña*, *Ṇa*, *Na*, *Ma*, *Śa*, *Ṣa*, *Sa*, *Ha*, *A*, *Aṃ* and *Aḥ* govern all *samādhis*, they are not counted here as letters.

He gazed at the entire assembly: As previously explained. ***Desiring that the teaching should be fruitfully accomplished***: The word '***teaching***' means the teaching to train those beings who are to be guided, so it can refer to all of the Sutra Collection and so forth, but here it refers to the mantra teachings. Furthermore, concerning what was previously explained above about the necessity to do the *sādhana* after having done the preliminary service of recitation of a fixed number and duration, it is said, '***The number of mantras, three hundred thousand, that I have generally prescribed, is the number of recitations stipulated for the pure* mantrins, *beings who are free from failings; in no other way should it be done.***' [IX.5] (204a) Hence it is possible that beings with impure mental streams may not accomplish it, even though they have done the preliminary service of the requisite number and duration, so the previous service and so forth will not be fruitful. Since it says here that you should recite until the signs of the transformation of the basis (*āśraya-paravṛtta*) occur, that very occurrence itself of the signs is the accomplishment, and as it is impossible for you not to be accomplished after the signs appear, it is said to be fruitful.

The epithets '***The Lord of all Mantras, the Great King, the Great Majesty, the Protector of all Mantras***' also qualify that *Aṃ* which is Perfect Buddhahood in nature. Moreover, its intrinsic nature should be understood to have three aspects. These three aspects are its attribute of being [Dharma as] realization, which is both absolute and relative, and its attribute of being scriptural [Dharma]. Of those, realization which is on the absolute level in nature, is the letter *Aṃ* and the similar letters of mantras. Regarding that, it says, '***the Lord*** (*Īśvara*) ***of All Mantras***'. '***All mantras***' refers to the partial aspects of the Awareness of Liberation, such as 'All phenomena are devoid of tranquility' and so forth. These are the *samādhis* of Mañjuśrī-kumāra-bhūta and so forth in nature, and their appearance in those Bodies on the relative level, and the letters *A* and so on in the scriptural Dharma. The '***Lord***' of them is the Hundred Lettered [Mantra] of the Bhagavat Perfect Buddha. Even the partial aspects are included within it, for on the relative level it is the ordinary forms of the mantras which emerge from the Body of the Bhagavat; also it is the scriptural Dharma which is produced from all the letters beginning with *A* and so forth. Because all mantras are connected with it on the absolute and relative levels and are formed by its power, that *Aṃ* is called the '***Lord of Mantras***'. (204b) It is the '***Great King***' because it is superior to all ordinary mantras in its qualities, both on the absolute and the relative levels. '***Great Majesty***' (*tejas*) indicates the perfection of its power and this means that it has great power. ***The Protector*** (*nātha*) ***of all Mantras***: This means that it is a refuge (*śaraṇa*), because all mantras arise from it and are included in it, as explained above.

He spoke of that essence to Vajrapāṇi in a gentle voice. And what was Vajrapāṇi to become? He was to be '***caused to dwell in the Three* Samayas**' and completely perfect the Three Paths: The '***Three* Samayas**' refer to the Vajra Adornments of the Inexhaustible Body, Speech and Mind of the Bhagavat. During the initiation associated with Great Awareness, Bodhisattvas such as Vajrapāṇi who have completely perfected the Ten Levels, behold and enter those Vajra Adornments of the Inexhaustible Body and so on. By its transformational power [in the form of] rays of light emitted from the Body of the Bhagavat, so he is said to '***be caused to dwell in the Three* Samayas**'. ***Completely perfect the Three Paths***: They are '***Paths***' because they lead to the attainment of the Three *Samayas* and they were to be perfected by Vajrapāṇi.

2. Then he entered into the *samādhi* called 'The Supreme Awareness'[A] and then uttered this Mantra which produces various kinds of Awarenesses and emits a hundred rays of light: *NAMAḤ SAMANTA-BUDDHĀNĀM AṂ*.

Then he entered a *samādhi* called '***The Supreme Awareness***', after which he proclaimed the letter whose intrinsic nature is the Supreme Awareness of Perfect Enlightenment (*saṃbuddha*), which is the understanding that all phenomena are primordially unborn and unarisen, so that *samādhi* is also named 'The Supreme Awareness'. Therefore, '***which produces various kinds of Awarenesses***' refers to the different aspects of that letter. '***Various Awarenesses***' refers to the understanding of the various types of Dharma as realization and as scripture, on the absolute level and the relative level, and refers to the arising of such Awarenesses from this letter *Aṃ*. (205a) ***Which emits a hundred rays of light***: Because on the absolute level, the mantras which are partial aspects of Awareness emerge from the Awareness of Suchness, which is like an ocean, and on the relative level it completely pervades the Three Realms with the many mantra Bodies which emerge from the Tathāgata's Body. It is also because the hundred letters arise as the scriptural Dharma from the letter *Aṃ* and encompass all mantras in the manner described above.

3. 'Vajrapāṇi!
This is the Protector of all mantras,
the Great Majesty of all mantras[B];
this is itself the Perfect Buddha,
the Lord of all Dharma, the Sage,
the Destroyer of the dark gloom of ignorance,
which shines like the rising sun.'

A Probably Skt. *jñānodaya*, understood by C to mean 智生三昧 '*The Source of Awareness*'.
B C: 成就大威德 '*which accomplishes the great majesty*'.

This is the Protector of all mantras and so on: As explained above. ***This is itself the Perfect Buddha***: This letter *Aṃ* is the Nirvāṇa With Remainder (*sopadhiśeṣa-nirvāṇa*) in nature. ***The Lord of all Dharma***: Because it is the knowledge of all Dharma as realization and as scripture. ***The Sage***: That is the attribute of one who has control of body, speech and mind, and this refers to Śākyamuni himself. ***The destroyer of the dark gloom of ignorance, which shines like the rising sun***: It removes the obscurations regarding both Dharma as realization and as scripture. In the same way as you do not know of what substance objects are that lie in darkness, but can see this clearly when the sun rises, in the same way when the gloom of ignorance has been cleared away by that All-knowing Awareness, you can know clearly [the nature of] phenomena on the absolute and the relative levels. This indicates its perfection of abandonment, and the previous words indicates its perfection of Awareness.

4. 'Having thus transformed itself
into the Great Sage himself
it manifested emanations in order to aid beings.
As many minds of beings as there are,
then that many supreme states
of emanations were created[A].'

Having thus transformed itself into the Great Sage himself: That same Perfect Enlightenment whose intrinsic nature is the Awareness of emptiness, [was] transformed into the Body of Śākyamuni. What did it do when it had thus been transformed? ***Manifested emanations in order to aid beings***: Having transformed into the Body of Śākyamuni, various kinds of emanations for the sake of beings were manifested. (205b) How many of such emanations were manifested? *b*: It created emanations in just as many bodies as there are varieties of minds, and in just as many as there are desires. That shows the arising from emptiness. Therefore the implication of this is that when you have first rested in the *samādhi* of emptiness on the absolute level, you should subsequently do the practices of changing yourself into an embodiment of Perfect Enlightenment and so forth on the relative level.

5. 'Therefore those who desire to attain
the Perfect Buddhahood
should always persevere in all ways
with a pure inner self[B].'

This is the concluding summary. It means that because the intrinsic nature of Perfect Enlightenment is thus, anybody who desires to become an embodiment of Perfect Enlightenment should strive to cultivate the Body of the Perfect Buddha, which is the Hundred Lettered [Mantra] in nature. ***In all ways*** (*sarvathā*): By means of all modes of body, speech and mind. ***Always***: At all times. ***With a pure inner self***: This mainly refers to the mind, for it is not sufficient just to change your body into the Body of the Bhagavat, but you should also zealously apply yourself to the internal pure mental *samādhi*.

A C: 悉能爲施作 '*they all are capable of functioning in order to bestow* [*that supreme state*]'.
B C: 淨身離諸垢 '*a pure body free from taints* (mala)'.

XXII
THE ACQUISITION OF THE RESULT

1. Then the Bhagavat Vairocana also said to Vajrapāṇi, the Lord of the Secret Ones, 'Lord of the Secret Ones! At the moment the Bhagavat Buddhas attain the Level associated with the Initiation into Direct Knowledge[A] and the Great Awareness, those Bhagavat Buddhas behold themselves abiding on the Path of the Three *Samayas*[B].'

(206a) Of the three natures of the Hundred Lettered [Mantra], you should view its nature which is realization – the Awareness of Suchness on the absolute level and the Body of the Bhagavat on the relative level – as the meaning (*artha*) of the letter *Aṃ*, and letter *Aṃ* [itself] should be viewed as being word (*pada*) in nature. Of those, this letter *Aṃ*, which is Perfect Buddhahood in nature, is the gate which radiates forth and gathers together the various kinds of Adornments of the Bhagavat's Speech. Although it is thus divided into three aspects through the distinction of meaning and word, there is no difference in its being the gate which performs the Buddha activities – the functions of Speech activity are also performed by the Body and Mind, and the functions of Body activity are also performed by the Speech and Mind, and the functions of Mind activity are also performed by the Body and Speech. Therefore, in this case the Inexhaustible Speech of the Buddha is revealed by the acquisition (*yoga*) of the result of the Hundred Lettered [Mantra], and through it the result of the letter, which is Perfect Buddhahood, liberates matured beings and matures those who are not matured.

While the Bodhisattvas who had perfected the Ten Levels, such as Samantabhadra, sat there delighted by the various types of magical displays of their individual power and cognitive range, and by the power which adorned the Buddha field in various manners, an array of light rays which emerged from the *ūrṇā* of the Bhagavat's *abhisaṃbodhi-kāya* struck the tops of those Bodhisattvas. By the transformational power of these rays of light, those Bodhisattvas attained the Level associated with the initiation into the direct knowledge of the Great Awareness (206b). Then at that moment the Vajra Adornments of the Inexhaustible Body, Speech and Mind of the Bhagavat, which are the Three *Samayas* in nature, were realized and witnessed by those Bodhisattvas.

Buddha Bhagavats*:** Those Bodhisattvas who have completely perfected their passage through the Ten Levels and have gained possession of the Ten Masteries, and who have realized that phenomena are like illusions in all perceptual images, are called Buddhas. ***Great Awareness refers to the Awareness of Suchness, and in order to cause those Bodhisattvas to know directly that Awareness, they were initiated with rays of light, hence the text says '***Initiation into direct knowledge***[1] (*abhijñā*) ***of the Great Awareness***'. Or else [a second interpretation] could be 'Great Awareness *and* Direct Knowledge', so in that case the Great Awareness is the realization of the emptiness of all phenomena as before, on the absolute level. '***Direct knowledge***', that is, Awareness on the relative level, is the Six Supernatural Cognitions. The initiation for the

A T omits '*Direct Knowledge*'.
B C: 三三昧耶句 '*the three* samaya *states*'.

attainment of that absolute and relative Awareness by those Bodhisattvas is called 'Initiation into Great Awareness and Direct Knowledge'. Those who have that Initiation '***attain the Level associated with the Initiation***', which refers to the distinctive qualities of their minds.

[At the moment] those Buddha Bhagavats refers to those same Bodhisattvas. ***The Three Samayas***: This refers to the encompassing of the entirety of the Three Realms by the Vajra Adornments of the Inexhaustible Body, Speech and Mind of the Bhagavat. On this occasion, the word '*samaya*' denotes 'universal realization' or 'attainment'. The Adornments of his Inexhaustible Body and so forth arose throughout the Three Realms so that they might be seen at that moment by the Bodhisattvas and realized by their Awareness. '***Path***' refers to that which leads to the realization of those *Samayas*. (207a) The Bhagavat's cognitive range (*gocara*), which is those Three *Samayas* in nature, also became the cognitive range of those Bodhisattvas and was seen and realized by them, and this fact was beheld by the Bodhisattvas themselves.

2. 'Lord of the Secret Ones! At that moment also, the Bhagavat who is associated with the Initiation into the Direct Knowledge of Great Awareness (186b) **reveals Buddha activities, in the form of *dhāraṇīs*. At that very same moment, those Bhagavat Buddhas become witnesses to the revelation of the Path of the Three *Samayas*[A] to all beings with Buddha activities.'**

At the moment when the Bodhisattvas who reside on the Tenth Level comprehend those Three *Samayas* which are Buddha activity, that Bhagavat Perfect Buddha who is the Hundred Lettered [Mantra] in nature, the gate which unites together the various kinds of Buddha Speech, changes into the form of the *dhāraṇīs* and reveals Buddha activities to those Bodhisattvas who are known as Buddhas. The word '***Bhagavat***' refers to the Perfect Buddha himself. ***Who is associated with the Initiation into Direct Knowledge of the Great Awareness***: This indicates the special qualities of that same Perfect Buddha. '***Great Awareness***' is as before. '***Direct Knowledge***' means the direct realization (*abhisamaya*) of that Great Awareness. He is associated with the Initiation for the direct realization of the Great Awareness. ***In the form of* dhāraṇīs**: These are the *dhāraṇīs* of meaning (*artha*) and word (*pada*) – the mastery of entry into non-conceptualization, and the [word] *dhāraṇīs*. That same Bhagavat Perfect Buddha, who is associated with the Initiation into the direct knowledge of the Great Awareness changes into *dhāraṇīs* and then reveals to those Bodhisattvas various kinds of expedient means that mature and liberate beings, which are the Buddha activities. Hence the text says he '***displays Buddha activities***'.

At that very same moment, those Buddha Bhagavats become witnesses to (*pratyupasthita √ bhū*) ***the revelation of the Path of the Three Samayas to all beings by Buddha activities***: (207b) Thus that Bhagavat Perfect Buddha displays the Buddha activities to those Bodhisattvas who are called Buddhas and they see and realize the nature of the Three *Samayas* in that way. They also comprehend the revelation of the Path of those Three *Samayas* by that manner of Buddha activity. '***The Buddha Bhagavats***' refers to those Bodhisattvas as mentioned earlier. ***To all beings***: To both pure and impure beings in whatever way suitable. ***By Buddha activities***: as before. ***The Path of the Three***

A C: 三三昧耶句 '*the three* samaya *states*'.

Samayas: The Path by which the Vajra Adornments of the Bhagavat's Inexhaustible Body and so forth may be attained. ***They become witnesses to the revelation***: Because those Bodhisattvas comprehend the manner in which the Vajra Adornments of the Bhagavat's Inexhaustible Body and so forth, which are the Three *Samayas* in nature, are attained by beings through the revelation of that Path, which causes the attainment of the Three *Samayas*, to beings who are suitable.

3. 'Lord of the Secret Ones, behold the vast emanations of the Mandala of my Speech Configuration which pervade limitless world systems, which are gates of purity, gates which satisfy all beings according to their wishes and make known the continuum of reality to each of them individually. They are at present engaged in the performance of Buddha activities as Śākyamunis in unlimited world-systems that are more extensive than the realm of space. Yet, Lord of the Secret Ones, concerning that, beings do not know that this is the arising of the Mandala of the Bhagavat's Speech Configuration, that they are Buddha Bodies arisen from the Essence[A] [*Aṃ*] of the arrayed of Adornments of the Speech of the Buddha, which produces them to satisfy beings according to their wishes.'

This explains that the Tathāgata emanates Bodies of Śākyamuni from his Speech configuration, the various kinds of Buddha Voice Adornments, which perform the Buddha activities for those mature and immature beings who are suitable, throughout all the world systems. ***Speech Configuration***: It is called a 'configuration' (*chakra* = wheel) because the Buddha Speech of the Tathāgata which arises in various kinds of forms, enters the [consciousness] streams of beings. ***The vast emanations of the Mandala***: (208a) They are *vast* because the emanations of Śākyamuni Bodies from that Speech configuration reveal Buddha activities throughout all world systems, which are as extensive as the entire realm of space. '***Which pervade limitless world systems***' connects with '***and make known the continuum of reality to each of them individually***'. Those *nirmāṇa-kāyas* reveal the words and meanings of the continuum of reality to all beings throughout all world systems. They are also '***gates of purity***'. The '***gates of purity***' are the methods for entering into the pure continuum of reality. ***Gates which satisfy all beings according to their wishes and make known the continuum of reality to each of them individually***: This kind of revelation of all phenomena is in accordance with the faith of individual beings, and so a Buddha teaches the Dharma to those who are to be trained by a Buddha. In the same way, the Dharma is taught by Śrāvakas, Pratyekabuddhas, Śakras, Brahmās and so forth, in accordance with the individual faith of beings, and all that is also the expedient means to cause them to enter into the continuum of reality. ***As Śākyamunis in unlimited world systems that are more extensive than the realm of space***: Moreover, the revelation of the Dharma in that way is not just by one or two Śākyamuni Bodies, but throughout unlimited world-systems that are more extensive than the realm of space, Śākyamuni Bodies teach the continuum of reality in such a way that beings are satisfied according to their wishes. Therefore they are said to be '***engaged at present in the performance of Buddha activities***', meaning that those Śākyamuni Bodies are engaged in Buddha activities to mature the immature and to liberate the matured among beings who are suitable, throughout that quantity

A C: 胎藏 'matrix' (*garbha*).

of world systems. Those Śākyamuni Bodies which perform Buddha activities (208b) arose from the essence [= *Aṃ*] of the arrayed Adornments of the Buddha Speech. Yet people do not know that those Bodies are forms of the Buddha emanated from the Speech configuration of the Bhagavat, but claim that he [Śākyamuni] became such through the body of Śuddhodana, the King of the Śākya clan.

4. 'And yet those Bodhisattvas who strive that they may be perfectly enlightened with regards to the continuum of reality and who have arisen from the Practice of the Bodhisattva Samanta-bhadra, in ocean-like infinite world-system gates, because they are upheld by me in this universe of world systems adorned with a lotus-base matrix, with its oceans of species – they purify the Buddha field by way of various kinds of pure aspirations. They directly accomplish the core of Enlightenment, perfectly realize Enlightenment, turn the Wheel of the Dharma and manifest Buddha activities. (187a) **Since they additionally desire the rank of utterly pure Buddhahood, they attain[A] an infinitude of bodies because of the infinitude of their minds, an infinitude of Awareness because of the infinitude of bodies, an infinitude of beings because of the infinitude of Awareness and an infinitude of the space realm because of the infinitude of beings.'**

Even though Śākyamunis are manifested with Bodies emanated thus from the Speech configuration which perform Buddha activities throughout all the world-systems, people are unaware that those emanations arose from that Speech configuration. But the Bodhisattvas who strive that they might perfectly understand the continuum of reality, who arise by the Practice of the Bodhisattva Samanta-bhadra and who appear in infinite world-systems, adorn the ocean of creatures of the world-systems, this universe of world-systems adorned with a lotus-base matrix, this Buddha field, since they are upheld by the Bhagavat Vairocana and attain direct and perfect awakening in the core of Enlightenment and so forth. This is not done, however, by the personal power of those Bodhisattvas alone, but that adorning of the Buddha field and so forth is done through the power of the Bhagavat Vairocana. And although such things are indeed done by those very Śākyamuni Bodies, those completely pure Bodhisattvas who are to be guided, see those Śākyamuni Bodies as *saṃbhoga-kāyas*. Therefore this last instance should be understood as indicating that the *saṃbhoga-kāyas* operate for the benefit of those Bodhisattvas. (209a) This is the summarized meaning and now the meaning of the text will be explained.

'***And yet***' means that although ordinary people do not know that the Śākyamuni Bodies which manifest Buddha activities are emanations of the Tathāgata, nevertheless those Śākyamunis perform the things which were mentioned above. ***Ocean-like infinite world-system gates***: This refers to the source of those Bodhisattvas who have been described above. They are said to be '***ocean-like***' because those infinite world systems are difficult to know and estimate, being like oceans. They are '***gates***' because those Bodhisattvas arise from these world-systems. ***Who strive that they may perfectly understand the continuum of reality, arisen from the Practice of the Bodhisattva Samantabhadra***: This qualifies those Bodhisattvas who adorn the Buddha fields and so on. The '***continuum of reality***' refers to the Awareness of Suchness. They '***strive that they may perfectly understand it***' means that they strive in order to perfectly understand

A C: 知 '*know* [*there is*]'.

that continuum of reality, which is the Awareness of Suchness. ***Arisen from the Practice of the Bodhisattva Samanta-bhadra***: They are born from the Bodhisattva Samanta-bhadra's Resolution. ***In this universe of world-systems which is adorned with a lotus-base matrix***[2]: This denotes the *Sahā* Universe. ***Lotus-base***: That universe of world-systems is adorned with a lotus. ***Matrix***: The place of origin. ***Adorned***: Since that universe of world-systems which is adorned with a lotus arises because of those beings who have engaged in merit, (209b) the result of such merit is to be born in such a universe, and this means that it is also the ornament of those beings. ***[With its] oceans of creatures***: That Buddha field is also one that has streams of consciousness equivalent to an ocean in quantity. ***[Because] upheld by me***: By the power of the *saṃbhoga-kāya* and this is to be connected with the words '***they purify the Buddha field***'. ***They purify the Buddha field by way of various kinds of pure aspirations***: Those Bodhisattvas purify the Buddha field by way of their various kinds of pure aspirations, and since they also apply themselves to that by the power of the Bhagavat, this is to be linked with the words '***because they are upheld by me***'. ***They directly accomplish the core of Enlightenment***: The '***core of Enlightenment***' (*bodhimaṇḍa*) refers to the place of Perfect Enlightenment in the Akaniṣṭha realm and to the places of awakening to the Great Enlightenment in the abode of men. These are completely perfected by those Bodhisattvas. ***Perfectly realize Enlightenment***: They directly realize that Enlightenment which is cleansed of the obscurations of emotional afflictions and wrong understanding, which is space-like in character. ***Turn the Wheel of the Dharma***: The turning of the Wheel of the Dharma which is well-known from the scriptures. ***Manifesting Buddha activities***: They manifest Buddha activities which are defined as the maturing and liberating of beings. ***Since they additionally desire the state of utterly pure Buddhahood***: When they have thus performed the purification of the Buddha field and so forth, they rise up to Perfect Buddhahood. At the moment when they directly realize and so actualize the Awareness of Suchness, which is defined as the realization of the emptiness of all phenomena, (210a) they attain such qualities mentioned below as the infinitude of minds and so on.

Of those, regarding the '***infinitude of minds***', their minds, being free from all perceptual images such as concepts (*vikalpa*) and so forth, realize the emptiness of all phenomena and become like space in nature. Since space which has the attribute of emptiness, is unsullied by anything and there is nowhere it does not pervade, it has no limit that can be grasped. Likewise, since a mind which is emptiness in nature also encompasses everything, that mind is infinite. ***The infinitude of bodies***: Since they have attained that infinitude of mind their bodies are also as all-pervasive as their minds, therefore their bodies are infinite. ***The infinitude of Awareness***: When their bodies have thus become infinite, then all those bodies, however many there are, will be accompanied by transformed Awareness. Because as much Awareness will arise as there are bodies, their Awareness is also infinite. ***The infinitude of beings***: Both their bodies and their Awareness arise in the same quantity as there are beings and as they are infinite so also are beings. ***The infinitude of space***: The realms of beings are as numerous as the extent of the realm of space, and when they realize the infinitude of the realms of beings, they will also attain the realization of the infinitude of the realm of space.

5. 'Thus, Lord of the Secret Ones, by the infinitude of their minds[A], they will attain the four infinitudes. When they have attained them, they will become completely perfect Buddhas and have the strength of the Ten Strengths, conquer the Four Māras and utter the roar of bulls[B] and lions.'

***Thus by the infinitude of their minds, they will attain the four infinitudes*:** When they have attained the realization that their minds, which are empty in nature, are like space in character, (210b) they do so also with regards to bodies, Awareness, beings and the realm of space. ***When they have attained them, they will become completely perfect Buddhas*:** When they have thus actualized the Awareness of Suchness, they will immediately attain Perfect Buddhahood, which is the Nirvāṇa with remaining psycho-physical constituents in nature. ***They will have the strength of the Ten Strengths and conquer the Four Māras*:** These are the distinctive qualities of a Perfect Buddha, which are well known from the scriptures. ***They will utter the roar of bulls and lions*:** Just as the roar of a lion surpasses that of all animals, likewise the Bhagavat Perfect Buddha surpasses all non-Buddhists who posit [the existence of] permanence, bliss and so forth, by uttering the sound of the Teaching that all conditioned things are impermanent, suffering and so on.

6. 'Having trained in this hundred-gated Essence,
proclaimed by the Perfect Buddhas,
all these supreme states
will be realized by those Heroes.'

After all the qualities mentioned above have been attained by those Bodhisattva Heroes, they will awaken to that supreme state of Perfect Enlightenment (*saṃbuddha*). Also that awakening to the supreme state is attained through the recitation and meditation of that Hundred Lettered Essence [*Aṃ*] of the Buddha. Also the revelation of the distinctive qualities of the three aspects of the acquisition of the result of the Hundred Lettered Essence should be known as a cumulative process. After those Bodhisattvas who are called 'Buddhas', of the Eleventh Level have resided on that Eleventh Level, they are urged on by the Bhagavat's rays of light and enter into the path of the Three *Samayas*. They then rise above that Eleventh Level and reside on the Level of those having the Initiation into the Direct Knowledge of the Great Awareness. (211a) Then, when they have changed into the body-image of the Perfect Buddha and manifest Buddha activities in general with the Śākyamunis which are a Tathāgata's *nirmāṇa-kāyas*, those Bodhisattvas should be known to abide on the All-good (*samanta-bhadra*) Level. When they arise from the practice of the Bodhisattva Samanta-bhadra, they aid [beings] with *saṃbhoga-kāyas* and purify the Buddha fields. Hence, you should know that they abide on a Level which is like a bridge leading to entry on the Perfect Buddha Level after having risen beyond the All-good Level until they attain the Perfect Buddha Level.

A T has *sems-can* which should be corrected to *sems*.
B C: 無所畏 '*fearless*', instead of '*bulls*'.

XXIII
THE ACCOMPLISHMENT OF THE ARRANGEMENT OF THE HUNDRED LETTERS

1. Then Vajrapāṇi, the Lord of the Secret Ones, said this to the Bhagavat:
'Bhagavat! This Lord of Mantras,
which generates [all] mantras,
proclaimed by the Buddha[A]
is a great wonder!
By whom, how and where should
the abode of the Great Sage be known?
Tell me how and by what
mantras arise from that!
Lord, most excellent of speakers,
please explain all this to me!'

In general there are two kinds of beings to be guided: the completely pure for whom realization is the main thing, and the impure who remain with the scriptural Dharma. The chapter dealing with the acquisition of the results of the Hundred Lettered [Essence] was taught for the benefit of those to be guided who are completely pure. This chapter was taught for the benefit of those beings who are not completely pure. Therefore Vajrapāṇi questioned the Bhagavat so that the practitioner (*sādhaka*) might imagine in his heart the causal and resultant qualities of the Bhagavat transformed into the form of *Aṃ*, the essence of the Perfect Buddha, defined as the Hundred Lettered Essence, with the process appearing below, and accomplish the Body of the Perfect Buddha.

Bhagavat! This Lord of Mantras which produces all mantras, proclaimed by the Buddha, is a great wonder!: The nature of the Hundred Lettered Essence explained earlier is a great wonder because of its qualities and great power. (211b) '***Lord of Mantras***' and '***produces all mantras***' qualify of that essence, and were explained earlier. ***By whom, how and where should the abode of the Great Sage be known?***: This concerns this Chapter, called the 'Accomplishment of the Arrangement of the Hundred Letters'. '***By whom?***' means by what kind of practitioner should it be known. This should be linked with the description of the practitioner's attributes mentioned below with the words '***Whoever has been initiated into the Mahāyāna Mandala Arising from Great Compassion***' and so on. '***How?***' means in what way should that essence be understood and this should be linked with the words, '***It is golden in colour, shining brightly***' and so on. '***Where?***' means in what place should that essence be arranged and this should be linked with the words, '***The place in which the Guide resides is the heart***' and so on.

Tell me how and by what mantras arise from that!: This question concerns the contents of the Chapter on Self Accomplishment [XXIV] and it means, 'For what reason and how do ordinary mantras arise when they arise from that essence?' This

---

A This is based on C: 佛說眞言救世者 能生一切諸眞言 '*The Lord of Mantras proclaimed by the Buddha can generate all mantras*'. T: *sngags-rnams-kyis ni sngags 'byung-ba'i* | *sngags-kyi mgon-po 'di bshad-pa* | '*The Lord of Mantras, which generates mantras, proclaimed by the mantras*'.

should be linked with the words, '***Rays of light emitted from its Body, always shine forth everywhere***' and so on, which will be dealt with in the Chapter on Self Accomplishment.

2. **When he had been asked that,**
the Bhagavat, Master of the Dharma, Great Sage,
the All-knowing Vairocana,
then spoke these words in a gentle voice,
that penetrated all world systems[A]**:**

(212a) When Vajrapāṇi asked those questions, the Bhagavat Vairocana replied as follows. ***Master of the Dharma***: This qualifies the Bhagavat. He is master of both Dharma as realization and as scripture, and has power over body, speech and mind. He spoke these words which penetrated all of the infinite world systems.

3. **'Most seng, excellent, excellent!**
I shall explain to you entirely
the uttermost secret, the great wonder
the supreme nown tocret of the Buddhas,
which is unk powerful Vajrapāṇi,
Great Bei all logicians[B]**.'**

The uttermost secret: It is most subtle, mind-arisen in character. ***The great wonder***: It is a great wonder because the letters imagined with the mind change into the Body of the Perfect Buddha and so forth. ***The supreme secret of the Buddhas***: Because the logicians (*tārkikas*) cannot comprehend the nature of that essence on the absolute and the relative levels, even though they investigate it by way of inference (*anumāṇa*) and so on, so it is '***unknown to all logicians***'.

4. **'Those who have been initiated into**
the Mahāyāna Mandala Arising from Great Compassion,
who are honest and pliant[C]**,**
and who always have great compassion,
who never view Enlightenment
as having an objective basis, (187b)
they will know the Great Self in their hearts[D]**.'**

This section gives the answer to the question, '***By whom should it be known?***'. The general sense is that the practitioner who has been initiated into that Mahāyāna Mandala Arising from Great Compassion and who then has tranquillity (*śamatha*) and

---

A C: 爾時薄伽梵 法自在牟尼 圓滿普周遍 悉遍諸世界 一切智慧者 大日尊告言 '*Then the Bhagavat, Master of the Dharma, the Sage, who is completely perfect, who is all-pervasive, who encompasses all world systems, who is All-knowing, the Lord Vairocana, spoke these words.*'

B C: 外道 '*the heterodox non-Buddhists*' (*tīrthika*).

C C: 調柔具善行 '*who are self-controlled and behave well*'.

D This line could also be interpreted as '*They know their hearts to be the Great Self*'.

insight (*vipaśyanā*) will know this essence. Now, the meaning of the individual phrases. ***Whoever has been initiated into the Mahāyāna Mandala Arising from Great Compassion***: This essence will be known by the practitioner who has been initiated into that Mandala. '***Yāna***' is a term for 'going' (*gati*), so you go to the intrinsically existent Mandala which is defined as the Inexhaustible Body and so forth, or else you go by this representational mandala, and this term refers to the Mandala Arising from Great Compassion. Although the word '***mahā***' (great) has a broad usage, (212b) in this case '***mahā*** ' is not used for both the Body and the Speech Mandalas since they are relative in nature, but that Mind Mandala is termed '***mahā*** ' because it is on the absolute level by nature. In brief, this refers to the Initiation into the Secret Mandala. Because when you have been initiated into the Secret Mandala, you will hold the Five *Samayas* and the three part initiation in the manner explained earlier, and you will have thus become a practitioner who has completed that training in the three part Mandala, according to the sequence.

Who are honest and pliant: It is not enough for that practitioner merely to have been initiated into the Secret Mandala, but in this instance the practitioner should possess the accomplishments which arise from recitation, such as those mentioned above. '***Honest***' means that his mind is free from unsteadiness and deceit. '***Pliant***' is to be without arrogance and aggression. Whoever is honest and pliant is in harmony with *samādhi*, so this indicates that he has tranquillity.

Who always have great compassion and who never views Enlightenment as having an objective basis: Even though he has tranquility on its own, if he lacks insight he will view it as having an objective basis. Whoever causes all beings to be freed from suffering by his compassion and does not view that *bodhicitta*, which is Suchness in nature, as an objective phenomenon (*bhāva*), is said to have the insight which realizes emptiness. This essence, the Great Self, will be known by those who thus have tranquillity and insight.

5. **'The place in which the Guide**
resides is the heart,
where there is a mind-made lotus,
beautiful with eight petals,
in a disc like a full moon,
which resembles an unsullied mirror;
there resides the Lord of Mantras,
most powerful, which is ever present[A].'

This section answers the question '***Where is the abode of the Great Sage?***'. The practitioner should first imagine clearly all the Buddhas and Bodhisattvas and salute them. (213a) Then he should confess his failings in their presence and so forth, and make the *Samaya Mudrā* and so on according to the sequence. Then in his own heart, he should imagine a white lotus with eight petals, with a moon[B] disc. Upon this moon disc which shines like a mirror, he should then imagine the Bhagavat, the Hundred Lettered *Aṃ*. Moreover, it should be seen there calmly just as a reflection is within a mirror. This is the summarized description of its abode.

A C omits this line.
B B: *rlung* 'wind'.

Now, the meaning of the individual phrases. ***The place in which the Guide resides is the heart***: The practitioner's heart should be made into the abode of that Guide. ***A mind-made lotus, beautiful with eight petals***: Furthermore, regarding that abode of the Guide, the heart, he should imagine a mind-made lotus which is very radiant and white in his heart, and above it, he should also imagine a moon disc with that Guide in its centre. ***Which resembles an unsullied mirror***: Although the moon is white, it is obscured by impure darkness, so it should be imagined to be more radiant than that. Hence this indicates that the essence should be imagined in [that disc] which is like a mirror, extremely pure and with a clear image. ***There resides the most powerful one, ever present***: That essence should always be located in that mirror. The epithet, '***ever present***', refers to both its nature on the absolute level and also to the nature of his Body on the relative level. The Awareness of Suchness, its nature on the absolute level, is said to be ever present by way of its unchanging consummacy. On the relative level as his Body, that Adornment of the Inexhaustible Body of the Bhagavat is ever present by way of its authentic consummacy for the sake of beings and by virtue of his previous [resolutions], (213b) until the end of *saṃsāra*. Furthermore, this means that as long as the practitioner abides in *samādhi*, that essence is also present unwaveringly.

6. **'It is golden in colour, shining brightly,**
free from faults, dwelling in *samādhi*,
difficult to behold, like the sun.
All of this person is entirely[A]
pervaded and transformed by it,
both internally and externally.'

This section answers the question, '***How should it be known?***'. ***Golden in colour, shining brightly***: The colour of the essence is like gold, emitting rays of light. ***Free from faults***: This praises the nature of the result. It is free from obscuring thoughts such as the emotional afflictions and wrong understanding. ***Dwelling in* samādhi**: It is not possible to separate the letter from the *samādhi*, therefore this indicates that the essence is present in one who sits in the *samādhi* for its accomplishment. ***Difficult to behold, like the sun***: This indicates that it should be imagined with majestic radiance. Just as you cannot focus on the sun surrounded by rays of light and cannot bear to gaze at it, in the same way you should imagine that this essence is also surrounded by the rays of light it emits and is difficult to look at. In brief, the practitioner should imagine that essence, whose colour is like gold in the middle of that mirror disc in his heart, and he should imagine his body totally changing into the Body of a Buddha. When he has thus changed, he should also imagine the essence located in the moon disc in his heart as before. Therefore the text says, '***All of this person is entirely pervaded and transformed by it, both internally and externally***'. (214a) ***All of this person***: All of the five psycho-physical constituents of that practitioner will be completely pervaded and transformed by this essence. The external transformation is his external body changing into the Body of the Perfect Buddha. The internal transformation is the location of the moon disc in his heart. Also, '***all of this person***' can be interpreted as

---

A C: 諸衆生亦然 '*the beings are also thus*'.

referring to such mantra deities as the Noble Mañjuśrī and Avalokiteśvara. They are entirely pervaded by this method because both the external form which is changed into their body-images, and the internal letters *A* and so forth, which are to be imagined in the moon disc, arise through the transformational power of this essence. When you have thus cultivated the changing of your own body into that of the Perfect Buddha and have imagined the moon disc in your heart with that essence, you will become a *vidyādhara*, endowed with the Body of a Perfect Buddha. This should be linked with the words appearing below, '***Likewise when those with pure selves just see or converse with him***' and so forth.

7. 'Know the mirror to be your *manas*!
The eye of insight is also thus[A].'

Having said that you should also know the moon disc in the heart to be the mirror, [the Bhagavat] indicates the technique for changing that letter which is imagined there into the Body of the Perfect Buddha. ***Know the mirror to be your* manas!**: That mirror which you imagine in your heart is no other than the stuff of your *manas*, for the mind (*citta*) endowed with perceptual images is called '*manas*', and you should know that that *manas* takes on the image of the mirror disc. ***The eye of insight is also thus***: The mental function (*citta*) which arises in the instant after the *manas* has been transformed into the mirror disc, whose disposition is to discriminate and define clearly, is called 'insight' (*prajñā*). Since that insight reflects upon the essence, (214b) it is also called '*manas*'.

8. 'When the *mantrin* has perceived
the mirror with the eye of insight,
he will see himself serene
in the nature of a Perfect Buddha.
Then from his body, the body image,
and from his *manas*, the mind-made,
which are pure and beautiful,
will arise by his own actions.'

When you one-pointedly reflect upon the moon disc with the essence, with the insight [arising] in the following instant, then rays of light will be emitted and gather together from that essence. Following this, your own body will be seen to change into the nature of the Perfect Buddha's Body as explained above. Therefore the text says, '***Then from his body, the body image*** (*rūpa*)'. This means that you should make your own body into the body-image of the Body of the Bhagavat. That is the technique for imagining your external body as that of the Buddha. ***Then from his* manas, *the mind-made***: This means that you should imagine the mirror disc with the essence arising from your *manas*. In other words, when changing your external body into that of the Buddha, you should also imagine the moon disc internally with the essence. ***Which are pure and beautiful will arise by his own actions***: When you have thus cultivated both the external and the internal [aspects], your external body will become the beautiful

---

A C: 以如是慧眼 了知意明鏡 '*You should know* [*that*] *the* manas *is that shining mirror*'.

and pure Body of the Perfect Buddha, and your internal *manas* will also become a radiant and pure moon disc with the essence. Such purity arises from the actions you have done of imagining your own body as that of a Buddha and the essence internally. Also, in this instance '***pure***' does not refer to the 'purity' which defines Awareness and so on, but to 'purity' due to the radiance of those internal and external forms. '***His own actions***' does not refer here to the wholesome actions and so on, of your previous lifetimes, but to the actions of the practice which generates the internal and external forms in this way.

9. **'Then its rays of light,**
by which the *mantrin*
effects all Buddha activities,
will be emitted and illuminate [all places][A].
Likewise, if [beings] see or converse
with he whose self is pure,
any needs they wish for
will completely be accomplished.'

(215a) When the practitioner has changed himself into the Body of the Perfect Buddha, he will be able to do all the Buddha activities by the power of the rays of light which are emitted from it. Moreover, when the rays of light are emitted from that essence, the vowels *A* and so forth will arise from its *A* and the consonants *Ka* and so on will arise from its *anusvāra*. These are also the essences of the mantra deities of Mañjuśrī and so forth. They all '***arise from the mind-formed***' in sequence as mentioned in the Chapter on Self Accomplishment [XXIV.1] below. This praises the person who has changed himself into the Body of the Perfect Buddha. ***He whose self is pure***: He is a *vidyādhara* who has the Body of the Perfect Buddha and he fulfils whatever needs are wished for by those beings he sees. Likewise, whoever speaks with that *vidyādhara* will also have their aims accomplished. In the same way, if that *vidyādhara* just thinks, 'May that being be thus!', all will be done. You should also know that any beings who are able to see that *vidyādhara* and so on, accumulate merit and enjoy good fortune. Although those beings will be benefitted by him, he is not accessible to the sight of ordinary people.

10. 'Lord of the Secret Ones! Furthermore, Bodhisattvas who engage in the Bodhisattva practice by way of mantras, should generate that body-image in their bodies thus: There is nobody who surpasses a completely perfect Buddha. The Tathāgatas have perfectly understood that one's eyes, ears, nose, tongue, body, mind and so forth are an assemblage (*saṃghāta*) of the four elements and lack inherent reality[B], that they are perceived just by name, that they are similar to space and cannot be perceived as objects, and that they arise from causes and karmic action[C], like reflections. (188a) **Also, they are mutually connected in unbroken dependent arising, for that which**

A C: 如電焰 '*like flashes of lightning*'.
B C: 自性空 '*are empty of inherent existence*' or '*empty by nature*'.
C C omits '*and that they arise … karmic action*'.

has been produced in dependence upon something arises in a similar way to a reflection. Therefore, because of this mutual interdependent arising, the deity is oneself and oneself is the deity. In that way the body-image should be generated as the Body of the deity, with [one's own] body[A].

'Lord of the Secret Ones, behold! Realization arises in dependence upon the Dharma and the Dharma arises in dependence upon realization, yet because they both lack self-existence, they are not established as mutual agents and products.'

(215b) Because it is possible for one to become arrogant about that Buddha Body, this shows that the reasons for its coming about are gathered together and accumulated by conditions on the relative level, through the certainty of the cause-result relationship. Bodhisattvas ***should generate that body-image in their bodies thus***: They should generate the Body of the Perfect Buddha in their own bodies in the manner mentioned above. ***There is nobody who surpasses a completely perfect Buddha***: This praises the Body of the Perfect Buddha, and it means that since no other person's body is superior to that of the Perfect Buddha, you should generate the Body of the Perfect Buddha in your own body. ***The eyes, ears, nose*** and so: Although the Body of the Perfect Buddha which you have generated is devoid of any physical reality (*rūpa-bhāva*) on the absolute level, it is not devoid of the intrinsic nature (*dharmatā*) of the certainty of the cause-result relationship on the relative level. For example, although such phenomena as the eye, ear and so on which are an assemblage of the four elements (*mahā-bhūta*) in nature are understood by the Buddha Bhagavats to be emptiness, not being anything on the absolute level, however it is said, 'Nevertheless they appear to arise from the assemblage of causes and conditions and would not be [so] without causes and conditions'.

They also lack inherent reality: This either means that those phenomena, such as the eyes, ears and so on, which are compounds of the four elements are primordially unborn and unarisen, or else that if you dissolve them by the 'atomic direction' method[1] and so on, you cannot establish that they have self-existence. ***They are perceived just by name***: They only have nominal existence (*saṃjñā-kṛta*), because they lack objective reality. If they lack objective reality, how is it that even those named things exist? The text says that '***they are similar to space***', for although space also lacks objective reality, it is named 'space', likewise, although those [phenomena] also lack objective reality, (216a) they are given such names as 'eyes' and 'ears'. They ***cannot be grasped as objects*** (*agrāhya*): They cannot be perceived [as objects] because they lack self-existence, and those statements indicate that those phenomena such as the eyes and so on are empty in nature, like space. ***They arise from causes and karmic action***: This shows their emotionally afflicted aspect. '***Causes***' are the emotional afflictions such as ignorance and so on. '***Karmic action***' is the present behaviour of body, speech and mind, which is wholesome and unwholesome. So although they lack any objective reality on the absolute level, they appear to arise from causes and karmic action on the relative level. ***[They are] like reflections***: Though they appear on the relative level, they only appear [thus] through your not having considered them as reflections, but

A C: 身所生身尊形像生 '*The body produced by the body arises as the body-image of the deity.*'

if you examine those reflections with reason and scripture, they cannot withstand that examination and their existence cannot be established. ***The Tathāgatas have directly and completely understood [this]***: Earlier Tathāgatas comprehended those phenomena in that manner.

Also they are mutually connected in unbroken interdependent arising, and that which has been produced in dependence upon something, arises in a similar way to a reflection: If they are thus like reflections, will they not be discontinuous in the same way as a reflection is in the absence of an object? They are not discontinuous like reflections, for even though there is no emotionally afflicted element in the previous instant, the karmic action and rebirth generated by the emotionally afflicted will cause the occurrence of the result. So they are not like reflections which do not appear if an object is lacking, but they arise continuously in mutual interdependence. But ***they arise in a similar way to reflections***: Those phenomena which arise from conditions cannot withstand examination, and on the absolute level they do not exist, like reflections for example.

Therefore because of that mutual interdependent arising, the deity is oneself and oneself is the deity: (216b) Thus, although phenomena do not exist on the absolute level, they do arise interdependently on the relative level; so the deity is generated in dependence upon yourself, and you are generated in dependence upon the deity, therefore this is called 'self-generation'. ***The deity is oneself***: Because the *Aṃ*, which is the Hundred Lettered Essence in nature, located in your heart arises through having been imagined by you. ***Oneself is the deity***: Because you generate yourself as the Body of the Perfect Buddha by that essence. ***In that way the body-image should be generated as the Body of the deity in one's own body***: Because they arise in that manner through the mutual assemblage of causes and conditions, you should generate your own body-image as the Body of the Perfect Buddha.

Lord of the Secret Ones, behold! Realization arises in dependence upon the Dharma and the Dharma arises in dependence upon realization: Those words '***the deity is oneself and oneself is the deity***' can be expressed in other ways. '***The Dharma***' is the letter *Aṃ*. '***Realization***' is to become the Body of the Perfect Buddha in dependence upon that letter, and having become it, the heart letter should once again be imagined, the one arising in dependence upon the other. Consider them to be thus! ***Yet because they both lack self-existence, they are not established as mutual agents and products***: Because both the letter and the body-image lack self-existence, the letter does not cause the generation of the body-image and the body-image does not cause the generation of the letter.

11. 'Lord of the Secret Ones! How is the mind-made body-image to be generated in your *manas*? It is thus, Lord of the Secret Ones: when you have thought of white, yellow or red, your *manas* will also be perceived with that perceptual image[A], therefore you should also accomplish your aims[B] in just such a way. So, Lord of the Secret Ones, if you imagine a mandala in your *manas* and place it in one who has an illness, that person will at that instant be cured of illness, without a doubt.'

A T should read *rnam-pa* not *rnam-par-shes-pa* (*vijñāna*).

B C: 如是身轉 '*in that manner you should transform the body*'.

This explains the causal characteristics of the way in which the letter arises, in order to make firm that mantra letter you have generated, which rests on the moon disc in your *manas*. (217a) ***When you have thought of white, yellow or red, your* manas *will also be perceived in that perceptual image.*** When you have imagined the water, earth or fire mandalas, your *manas* also takes on that perceptual image. ***Therefore you will also accomplish your aims in just such a way.*** The functions of the earth mandala and so on will be carried out [only] by that *manas* which has taken on the perceptual image of the earth mandala and so forth. Therefore the Bhagavat says '***So if you imagine a mandala in your* manas *and place it in one who has an illness, that person will at that instant be cured of illness without a doubt***'. When someone is afflicted by a fever, you should imagine the water mandala in an upturned jar upon the patient's cranium, as described earlier, and you should imagine that the patient is gradually being filled with white nectar water which flows out from it, from his head down to his feet, both inside and out. At the same time as the water is acting thus, you should imagine all the fever being expelled outside. If you do that two or three times, there is no doubt that the patient will be cured of the illness. Likewise you should use the earth mandala as well. If you imagine the fire mandala as described earlier for a person afflicted with a cold and shivering illness and then imagine that the patient is placed upon it, with the fire moving upwards from below and pervading his entire body, both inside and out, he will be freed from the cold disease (*pratiśita*).

12. 'There is no mandala without the *manas*, nor is there a *manas* without the mandala[A]. Why is that? Because its attributes are identical to the mandala. So, Lord of the Secret Ones, if an illusory man made by a magician were to manifest another man[2], do you think, Lord of the Secret Ones, that there would be any distinction between them?'

When the Bhagavat said that, Vajrapāṇi said to him, 'There would be no difference between them. Why should there be, Bhagavat? Because both of those men arose from the unreal, and illusion lacks self-existence[B].'

'Lord of the Secret Ones! Thus it is because both the phenomenon which arises from the *manas* and the *manas* itself are conceptual creations, therefore they lack self-existence[C].'

(217b) It is not the case that those earth mandalas and so on exist as phenomena elsewhere and their perceptual images are imagined by the *manas*. But because the *manas* itself takes on the perceptual images of those mandalas, both the *manas* and those mandalas are of a single nature and are inseparable. Though neither of them exists on the absolute level, they are merely conceived on the relative level by the mind (*citta*) which has perceptual images. Therefore, in order to prove this with an example, the Bhagavat says '***If an illusory man made by a magician***' and so on, speaking

A C: 非漫荼羅異意非意異漫荼羅 '*the mandala is not other that the* manas, *and the* manas *is not other than the mandala*'.

B C: 非實生故是二男子本性空故等同於幻 '*because they have not actually been born, those two men are identical as illusions since they are inherently empty*'.

C C: 意生衆事及意所生如是俱空無二無別 '*In this way, both the* manas *which generates things and that which is generated by the* manas *are empty. They are not dual, not separate.*'

of an illusion's emanation. In brief, although the moon disc and the essence which are generated in the *manas* lack self-existence and do not exist on the absolute level, however because they carry out their functions on the relative level due to the certainty of causes and conditions, you should exert yourself in imagining the moon disc with the essence in your *manas.*

XXIV
SELF ACCOMPLISHMENT (188B)

1. Then the Bhagavat also said to Vajrapāṇi, the Lord of the Secret Ones, 'Lord of the Secret Ones! Listen to the indivisibility of the Body of the Mantra Lord and the bodies [of the deities]!

'They arise from the mind-formed,
when the *manas* is utterly purified,
rays of light emitted from the Body
of the Lord who dwells there
always shine forth everywhere
from the members of the member[A].'

Now in order to show that the Bodies and the letters of the mantras of Mañjuśrī, Avalokiteśvara and so on, arise from the Hundred Lettered [Essence] which is the Perfect Buddha in nature, the Bhagavat also said to Vajrapāṇi, '***Lord of the Secret Ones! Listen to the indivisibility of the Body of the Mantra Lord and the bodies [of the deities]***' and so forth. He tells Vajrapaṇi to listen to him speak about the indivisibility of the Body of the Perfect Buddha and the bodies of the other mantra deities which arise from it. ***Arising from the mind-formed***: Both those bodies and that *Aṃ*, the gate which encompasses the Inexhaustible Speech of the Bhagavat, which is imagined in your heart resting on a moon disc, are '***the mind-formed***'. (218a) Because the Body of the Perfect Buddha, or else the Bodies of the other mantra deities arise from that, the text says '***arising from the mind-formed***'. ***When the* manas *is utterly purified***: It is not sufficient just to imagine the Body for it to arise, but it arises from that *manas* which is utterly purified through the practice of tranquillity and introspection. ***The rays of light emitted from the Body of the Lord who dwells there***: The essences of the mantra deities are emitted from that essence which rests located in that utterly purified mind. '***The rays of light emitted from the Body***' are the letters *Ka* and so forth which arise from that essence.. They ***always shine forth everywhere from the members of the member***. The '***member***' (*aṅga*) refers to the *A* itself and the '***members of the member***' are the *anusvāra*, the vowels *I*, *U* and so on, and the mantras formed from them, so it says '***always from the members of the member***'. In brief, when you are changing yourself into the Body of Mañjuśrī or Avalokiteśvara, the remainder is as with the previous sequence. You imagine that the letter *Maṃ* and so forth as appropriate arises from the *anusvāra* of that *Aṃ* and changes into the Body of Mañjuśrī, through the radiation and contraction of its light rays. You should also imagine it in the same abode of the *Aṃ* and change into the Body as before.

2. **'The stupid are completely ignorant**
because they do not know these methods.
Just as the varieties of bodies

A C: 意從意生令善淨除普皆有光彼處流出相應而起遍諸支分 '*The* manas *arises from the* manas *and when it has been completely purified, rays of light will flow out everywhere from that place, and accordingly arise throughout the members.*'

are more numerous than can be expressed[A],
likewise it is said that the varieties
of the Mantra Lord are countless.
Just as the glorious Wish-fulfilling Gem
brings about all aims[B],
likewise the Body of the Lamp of the World
also brings about all aims.'[C]

***The stupid are completely ignorant because they do not know these methods*:** Out of ignorance of this method which is dealt with below, they do not believe it or know how it is that those many Bodies of the mantras arise from that single Body of the Perfect Buddha. ***Just as the varieties of bodies are more numerous than can be expressed, likewise it is said that the varieties of the Mantra Lord are countless*:** (218b) Just as the many types of Bodies of Buddhas and Bodhisattvas arise in many forms from the letters which are utterances in nature, likewise countless types of mantra deities arise from the Perfect Buddha Mantra Lord.

If that nature of the Perfect Buddha has utterly transcended judgemental thought (*vikalpa*), how does he generate these multitudes of Bodies? ***Just as the glorious Wish-fulfilling Gem brings about all aims, likewise the Body of the Lamp of the World also brings about all aims*:** Just as the Wish-fulfilling Gem brings the hopes and aims of everybody to fulfilment, spontaneously without thought (*avikalpaṃ*), likewise that Lord of Mantras, Lamp of the World, produces the multitudes of forms of Bodies and carries out all aims by the power of his previous resolutions, spontaneously without thought.

3. 'Lord of the Secret Ones! How does the continuum of reality bring about all needs spontaneously without thought? Lord of the Secret Ones! It is thus: for example, the realm of space is not a being, not a life force, not a spirit, not a creator, not an experiencer, not a perceivable object, not a perceiver and is devoid of thought and judgemental concepts[D], yet it is incontrovertible that the infinite realms of beings do everything such as coming, going and so forth within it.

'Likewise this unlocalized All-knowing[E]
which does not conceptualize,
definitely accomplishes everything,
both internally and externally for beings[F].'

This section illustrates that by the example of space.

A C: 乃至身所生分無量種故 '[*nor even the varieties of bodies, for there are innumerable types...*'

B C adds: 隨諸樂欲 '*according to the aspirations* [*of beings*]'.

C All of the above two sections are prose in C.

D C: 分別及無分別 '*of both conceptualizing and non-conceptualizing*'.

E C: 如是無分別一切智智等同虛空 '*Thus non-conceptualizing All-knowing Awareness is equal to space ...*'

F This verse is prose in C.

4. Then he [the Bhagavat] spoke the words which purify infinite realms of beings: the words which accomplish *samādhi*, the words which are inconceivable, the words which are the gate to the development [of others][A]:

[The text] has described the yoga practice in which you imagine that Hundred Lettered *Aṃ* transforming into the Bhagavat Perfect Buddha and the Bodies of the mantra deities, and then arrange them in the *manas* moon disc. Here it explains that the mind should be completely purified so that the mind-qualities conforming to the Perfect Buddha may be generated, after you have transformed your own body into the Body of the Perfect Buddha in that way.

The phrase, '***the words which purify infinite realms of beings***', refers to the phrases '***words which accomplish* samādhi**' and so on, which are mentioned next, (219a) because those words purify beings by means of removing the obscurations of emotional afflictions from them and cause the distinctive types of Awarenesses to arise.

Also, regarding the mind of the practitioner which is to be completely purified, there are the entering, abiding and arising minds. Of those, the entering mind is indicated with, '***the words which accomplish* samādhi**', and this is linked with the verse beginning, '***When from the beginning there has not been the slightest bit of arising***'. The abiding mind is indicated with, '***words which are inconceivable***', and this is linked with the verse beginning, '***When so-called phenomena are intrinsically unobtainable***'. The arising mind is indicated with, '***words which are the gates to the development [of others]***', and this is linked with the verse beginning, '***Then the compassion which accords with all worlds will be born***'.

The words which accomplish* samādhi**: Because those words teach the arising of the *samādhi* which realizes that all phenomena are unborn and unarisen from the very beginning. *b*: Because those words teach that mind, which is like space, which does not objectify any phenomenon. ***The words which are the gate to the development of others: Because those words teach that you should arise from that *samādhi* and then benefit beings by virtue of compassion.

5. 'If from the beginning there has not been
the slightest bit of arising or perishing[B],
then how will the Awareness of emptiness,
arise in that yogin?'

Because phenomena such as the psycho-physical constituents, the perceptual elements and sources are unborn and unarisen from the very beginning, there is also no perishing. If there are no phenomena externally perceived, then the consciousness which apprehends them is also unborn, because there is no place for it to arise. In that way both the perceiving and the perceived parts do not exist and are lacking, so even the yogin's Awareness of emptiness will also be unborn.

A Added from C.
B C: 若本無所有 隨順世間生 Cf. 7b '*If entities arise in conformity with the world, though they are primordially non-existent*'.

6. 'When so-called phenomena
are intrinsically unobtainable,
then the mind, which is like space,
Enlightenment, will be generated[A].'

(219b) When you have dissolved both the internal consciousness and the external phenomena into non-existence by means of the process described above, the mind which abides in the realization that there is no objective basis for all these phenomena will become like space, free from all judgemental thought. Because the Awareness of Suchness which is a definition of Enlightenment arises from that non-conceptualizing mind, it is said '***Enlightenment will be generated***'.

7. 'Then the compassion which accords (189a)
with all worlds will also arise;
Abiding in a state of "name-only"[B],
one is given the name "Buddha" here.'

After you have arisen from that *samādhi*, the mind associated with generosity, practice, the transformation into the Body of the deity and so forth, which benefits beings by virtue of compassion, will arise.

To summarize these points briefly, the intention is that first you should dissolve phenomena into their intrinsic nature of emptiness with the entering mind that is accompanied by deliberation (*vitarka*). Then having remained for as long as you wish in the non-conceptualizing mind, which realizes emptiness, you should appear with the body-image of a deity by virtue of compassion and carry out the deeds benefitting beings, such as generosity and so on.

Abiding in a state of "name-only": Even such activities do not exist on the absolute level, but you should abide in the realization that they are just names. If everything is thus nothing but names, what need was there previously to exert yourself greatly in the transformation into the Body of the Perfect Buddha? The text says '***One is given the name "Buddha" here***'. This means that even the Perfect Buddha does not really exist here, but is nothing more than a name.

8. 'Then both emptiness and non-emptiness
are really just figures of speech.
Therein the numerical divisions
of one, two, three and so on, also arise[C].'

Then both emptiness and non-emptiness are really just figures of speech: At that time even such statements as 'Space and so forth is emptiness' and 'Phenomena such as jars and

---

A C: 若自性如是 覺名不可得 當等空心生 所謂菩提心 '*As* [*their*] *intrinsic nature is thus,* [*the yogin*] *will realize that names are unattainable, then the space-like mind,* bodhicitta, *will arise.*'

B C: 唯想行 '*a state of thought-only*'. For both T and C, the underlying term was likely to have been '*saṃjñā-mātra*' which permit both interpretations.

C C: 當知想造立 觀此爲空空 如下數法轉 增一而分異 '*You should also know that* [*even emptiness*] *is a mental construct, and if you perceive that you will treat emptiness as empty. Thus numerical differentiation* [*arises*] *with the development of subsequent numbers*'.

so forth are not empty on the relative level' are just figures of speech. (220a) ***Therein the numerical divisions of one, two, three and so on, also arise***: From that single letter *A*, there are also formed the many divisions of letters such as *I* and so on, by way of figurative speech.

9. 'Thus, O Hero, through the transformation
of that emptiness by the Self-arisen One,
***A* and so forth expand according to sequence.'**

Thus the intrinsic nature of emptiness expands into the many different types of letters, such as *A*, *I* and so on, that is, they arise from the essence which rests in the *manas*. The '***Self-arisen One***' (*svayaṃbhu*) refers to the intrinsic nature of the Bhagavat Perfect Buddha, because he is not generated by anyone.

10. ***A SA VA***

KA KHA GA GHA	***CA CHA JA JHA***
ṬA ṬHA ḌA ḌHA	***TA THA DA DHA***
PA PHA BA BHA	***YA RA LA VA***
ŚA ṢA SA HA	***ṄA ÑA ṆA NA***

'Lord of the Secret Ones! Behold the accomplishment of the *samādhi* method, the billowing forth of emptiness which is transformed by the symbol *A*. Lord of the Secret Ones, *A* itself abides as the inherent nature of the array of various different forms[A]. It also reveals by its own nature that all phenomena are unborn. To some it reveals with the form of *Va*, the meaning "inexpressible". To some it reveals that all phenomena are devoid of purpose, with the form of *Ka*. To some it reveals that all phenomena are like space, with the form of *Kha*. To some it reveals that all phenomena are without movement, with the form of *Ga*. To some it reveals that all phenomena lack cohesion, with the form of *Gha*. To some it reveals that all phenomena lack perishing, with the form of *Ca*. To some it reveals that all phenomena are like autumn clouds, with the form of *Cha*. To some it reveals that all phenomena lack birth, with the form of *Ja*. To some it reveals that all phenomena are devoid of impurities, with the form of *Jha*. To some it reveals that all phenomena are devoid of pride, with the form of *Ṭa*. To some it reveals that all phenomena are devoid of creation, with the form of *Ṭha*. To some it reveals that all phenomena are devoid of disorder, with the form of *Ḍa*. To some it reveals that all phenomena are devoid of deception, with the form of *Ḍha*. To some it reveals that all phenomena are devoid of Suchness, with the form of *Ta*. To some it reveals that all phenomena are devoid of location, with the form of *Tha*. To some it reveals that all phenomena are devoid of giving, with the form of *Da*. To some it reveals in the form of *Dha* (189b) that all realms are without objective basis among phenomena. To some it reveals in the form of *Pa* that the Absolute has no objective basis in any dharma. To some it reveals that all phenomena are

A C: 住於種種莊嚴布列圖位 '*abides as the various adornments which are arranged in the depiction*'.

insubstantial like bubbles, with the form of *Pha.* To some it reveals that existence has no objective basis in any dharma, with the form of *Bha.* [To some it reveals that death has no objective basis in any dharma, with the letter *Ma*][A]. To some it reveals that no ways have an objective basis in any dharma, with the form of *Ya.* To some it reveals that all phenomena are devoid of pollution, with the form of *Ra.* To some it reveals that no attributes have an objective basis in any dharma, with the form of *La.* To some it reveals that all phenomena are devoid of peace, with the form of *Śa.* To some it reveals that all phenomena are dull by nature, with the form of *Ṣa.* To some it reveals that no truths have an objective basis in any dharma, with the form of *Sa.* To some it reveals that all phenomena are devoid of causes, with the form of *Ha.*'

11. 'Lord of the Secret Ones, in that way you should know that through each of the gates which bring about *samādhi*, there are thirty two gates which bring about *samādhi.* Lord of the Secret Ones, you should see that the Thirty Marks of a Great Being also arise from there. *Ṅa, Ña, Ṇa, Na* and *Ma*[B] cause mastery over all *samādhis*, and you should see that the [eighty] subsidiary marks of the completely perfect Buddha are also brought about [through them].'

12. 'Lord of the Secret Ones, (190a) therefore a Bodhisattva who engages in the Bodhisattva practice by means of mantras should know the *samaya* of the hundred letters which arise from the total of the ten minds multiplied ten times, which is the conclusion of the Buddha's task, is thus revealed.

'All these are perfected and expanded
by the Perfect Buddhas;
since I also have them all,
I am a supreme victor Buddha!'[C]

A C omits this.
B '*and Ma*' added from C.
C C omits all of this section, which therefore could be a later addition to the text.

XXV
THE RITUAL OF THE MANTRA OF THE HUNDRED LETTERS

1. 'Furthermore, Lord of the Secret Ones, all these are syllables that accomplish the *samādhi* method and if transformed by this emptiness, you will become just like the Perfect Buddha, who has mastery over all phenomena.'

2. 'Therefore, the letter is the deity[A];
***A*, the supreme state**
surrounded by the letters,
illumines everywhere.'

3. 'That deity is without attributes,
free from ground and attribute;
yet from the deity without attributes
these attributes emerge.'

4. 'All the Protectors have taught that
from the sound, the letters arise,
and from the letters, the mantras arise,
and from the mantras, the results arise.'

5. 'You should know sound to be empty,
just as [space] does not think of
all the kinds of beings,
therefore all of it is empty.'

6. 'There is also sound which is not empty,
and its applications are manifested.
One who comprehends that sound [will attain]
the bases of the deities and the *samādhi*;
since the yoga of laying out the letters
is manifested by the letters,
it becomes the basis for the conventional designations
that are the multitudes of mantras.'

There seems to be no commentary on Chapter 25[B].

A C reads this line in prose at the end of the last section, and then continues in verse: '*Lord of the Secret Ones! You should know that* ...'

B This comment was inserted by gZhon-nu dPal, the reviser of this commentary.

XXVI
THE NATURE OF ENLIGHTENMENT

1. **'Just as space is always**
unlocated in any direction,
likewise the Lord of Mantras
is not located in any phenomenon[A].'

Now the intrinsic nature of the Tathāgata's Perfect Enlightenment: just as space is not fixed in the directions north, south, east and west, that Lord of Mantras which by nature abides on the absolute level, is not fixed by way of an objectifier and objectified in such phenomena as colour-form and so forth.

2. **'Just as all things are located** (190b)
in space, always visible,
yet it does not function as their support,
likewise is the Mantra Lord[B].'

Just as material things appear to be located in space, though space does not support them, likewise though the Tathāgata produces the many different forms of the Vajra Adornments of his Inexhaustible Body and so forth (220b) at the moment of his Perfect Enlightenment by virtue of it, the intrinsic nature of that Enlightenment does not abide in the Vajra Adornments of his Inexhaustible Body and so forth by way of objectification.

3. **'Just as space is said to be[C]**
separated from the three times and so on,
likewise the Mantra Lord also appears
although devoid of the three times.'

Just as space transcends the three times because it does not change from its single nature, likewise the Mantra Lord which is Suchness in nature, is unchangingly consummate and yet although not located in the three times, the qualities of the Strengths, the Fearlessnesses and so on are made visible.

4. **'It abides merely as verbal expression,**
and is devoid of agent and so forth:
the wise ones refer to space
only by conventional usage.'

A C: 譬如十方虛空相 常遍一切無所依 如是眞言救世者 於一切法無所依 '*For example, just as it is the characteristic of space in the ten directions to pervade everywhere though it is itself without support, similarly the Lord of Mantras itself is without support* [*though it pervades*] *all phenomena*'. ('*phenomena*' here refers to the mantras, adornments etc.)

B C adds: 非彼諸法所依處 '*likewise the Mantra Lord is not the support of those phenomena*'.

C C: 世間成立虛空量 '[*Just as*] *that which is designated* (vyavahāra) *as space on a mundane level*'.

This indicates that the Adornments of the Inexhaustible Speech of the Tathāgata, which have been transformed into letters, do not have any objective reality on the absolute level.

5. **'Just as space does not exist**
in the slightest way, apart from its name;
likewise the Mantra Lord
merely appears as verbal expression[A].'

Just as space only exists in a nominal sense, yet is itself intrinsically non-existent and lacks objective reality. It is nothing more than the utterance 'space', for there is no phenomenon called 'space' over and above the name. Likewise while that Essence, the Mantra Lord, merely appears [to exist] on the relative level, it does not exist as a phenomenon.

6. **'It is not fire, water, or wind,**
nor earth, nor the sun;
it is not the moon, nor any of the planets,
it is not day nor night,
it is not death nor old-age[B],
it is not an instant nor an hour,
nor is it a year and so forth.
It is not destruction nor growth,
it does not even have a number of eons,
and does not have the results
that arise from the wholesome and unwholesome[C].'

The intrinsic nature of the Enlightenment of the Tathāgata is not the nature of such things as are listed, like the four elements or the sun and moon which are derived from the four elements, (221a) or time like day and night.

7. **'Those who desire the state of All-knowing**
should always exert themselves
in that which is entirely
free from various kinds of concepts[D].'

Whoever wishes to attain the state of All-knowing should strive towards that intrinsic nature of Enlightenment, which is devoid of these things listed.

A C: 名字無所依 亦復如虛空 眞言自在然 現見離言說 '*Just as words are without support, likewise is space. The Mantra Lord is also thus: though it manifests, it is unconnected with verbal expression*'.

B C: 非生非老病 非死非損傷 '*it is not birth, nor old-age and sickness, its is not death nor decay*'.

C C: 非淨染受生 或果亦不生 '*it does not* [*lead*] *to birth in the pure nor the impure, nor even do results arise*'.

D C: 若無如是等 種種世分別 '*Given that such various mundane concepts do not exist,* [*those who desire the state of All-knowing should always exert themselves in that*]'.

XXVII
THE PRACTICE OF THE THREE *SAMAYAS*

1. Then Vajrapāṇi, the Lord of the Secret Ones, asked the Bhagavat this, 'Bhagavat! What phenomena are designated by that expression "the Three *Samayas*"?'

Now the Three *Samayas* will be explained. They have two aspects: the causal Three *Samayas* and the resultant Three *Samayas*. Of those, the causal Three *Samayas* are the entering mind, the abiding mind and the arising mind. The resultant Three *Samayas* is the threefold Inexhaustible Body and so forth of the Bhagavat. Now, the word '*samaya*' also means 'conduct' (*ācāra*), meaning that you conduct yourself with these entering, abiding and arising minds. It also means 'what one attains' (*āpti*) or 'what one realizes', and since the Vajra Adornments of the Inexhaustible Body and so forth are to be attained or realized, '*samaya*' also refers to them. In this chapter the causal *Samayas* will be explained.

2. When he had asked the Bhagavat that, the Bhagavat Vajrapāṇi replied to Vajrapāṇi, 'Lord of the Secret Ones, what you have asked me is excellent, excellent! I shall explain it to you, so listen carefully and bear this in mind!'

3. Vajrapāṇi, the Lord of the Secret Ones, said 'Bhagavat, let it be so!' and then he listened to the Bhagavat, (191a) **who said the following, 'That arising in an unimpeded manner with regards to a threefold set of phenomena is the Three *Samayas*. What is this set of phenomena? The first mind is to know phenomena. It is the generation of [*bodhi*]-*citta* whose inherent nature is meditative observation, which is [endowed with] the insight that arises in the wake of that, and which is also free from the infinite web of ideas through having completely known reality as it is by that [insight]. The second is non-conceptualization, Enlightenment in character[A] and is the state of Perfect Buddhahood.**

'Lord of the Secret Ones, though one has seen reality as it is, one should gaze upon the infinite realms of beings, without objectifying them, and being impelled by compassion, one should generate *bodhicitta*, thinking, "I shall cause beings to be established in that Enlightenment which is free from all conceptual proliferation and is without attributes". That is the third *samaya*.'[B]

A I have relocated this phrase to here from the previous sentence on the basis of C.

B This section presents considerable difficulties in interpretation as the various Tibetan and Chinese versions with their commentaries differ radically in their understanding of it, for reasons I have discussed in the Introduction. C reads: 有三種法相續除障相應生名三三昧耶.云何彼法相續生所謂初心不觀自性從此發慧如實智生離無盡分別網是名第二心菩提無分別正等覺句秘密主彼如實見已觀察無盡衆生界悲自在轉無緣觀菩提心生所謂離一切戲論安置衆生皆令住於無相菩提是名三三昧耶句 '*The continuous and unimpeded arising in union* (yukti) *of any three kinds of phenomena is called the Three Samayas. What is that continuous arising of phenomena? It is the first mind which has not meditated upon the intrinsic nature* [*of phenomena*]. *The insight which arises after that produces the awareness of the true nature of things, devoid of the inexhaustible net of concepts. This is called the second mind. That which*

The threefold set of phenomena: (221b) Because the three minds – entering, abiding and arising – are different, there is the threefold set of phenomena. Through having engaged in those three minds, the Vajra Adornments of the Inexhaustible Body, Speech and Mind, which are the Three *Samayas* in character, arise without hindrance.

What is that set of phenomena? That is, what are the specific qualities of those three minds? The Bhagavat poses this question [rhetorically] so that he may explain them.

Of those, the entering mind is, '***The first mind is ... the generation of* bodhicitta *whose inherent nature is meditative observation*** and so on. ***Whose inherent nature is meditative observation***: Such phenomena as the psycho-physical constituents, the perceptual elements and sources and so forth have been dissolved[A] by insight. The ***insight which arises in the wake of that***: The insight which knows that phenomena are without autonomous existence, in the wake of meditatively observing them. ***Having also completely known reality as it is by that***: By that insight, the authentic (*aviparyāsa*) knowledge of phenomena is generated. Therefore, you should add that it is '*b*', because ideas that the attributes of phenomena such as the psycho-physical constituents and so forth really exist and arise are an obstacle to liberation, and so those ideas are said to be a '***web***'. The mind which is free from the web of thoughts is the mind which realizes emptiness, which is Enlightenment in character[1]. This should be linked with the words '***the first mind***' above and this is the entering mind.

The second is non-conceptualization and is the state of Perfect Buddhahood: This is the abiding mind. That same insight whose attribute is the Enlightenment devoid of all the web of thought, abides in [a state of] non-conceptualization, having realized that all phenomena are empty in nature. That is termed '***the state of Perfect Buddhahood***' (*saṃbuddha*).

The third is the arising mind. ***Though one has seen reality as it is***: Even having correctly realized Suchness through the entering and abiding minds, (222a) one does not remain in that [state of] non-conceptualization but acts for the benefit of beings. Therefore the text says, '***one should gaze upon the infinite realms of beings***'. Furthermore, though there is an objective basis to that gazing over realms of beings, one does not gaze upon them for profit or respect, so it says one should gaze upon them, '***without objectifying them, being impelled by compassion***'. What is that *bodhicitta* which one should generate? "***I shall cause beings to be established in that Enlightenment which is devoid of all conceptual proliferation*** (*niḥprapañca*) ***and is without attributes***". In brief, this means that though resting in non-conceptualizing Suchness, nevertheless *bodhicitta* then arises in him with the thought, 'May all beings be established in that Enlightenment I have realized, which is free of concepts, free of all verbalization and is without characteristics', by the power of his previous resolutions, being impelled by

---

is enlightenment in nature (lakṣaṇa) *without judgmental concepts is the state of Perfect Enlightenment. Lord of the Secret Ones! When one has seen the true nature of things, one gazes upon the infinite realms of beings, and impelled by mastery of compassion, one gazes upon them without reifying them, generating* bodhicitta *with the thought, "I shall cause all beings to dwell in the Enlightenment which is without attributes, establishing them in that which is free from all conceptual proliferations* (prapañca)*!" These are called the states of the Three Samayas.*' It should also be noted that the word '*samaya*' in this context is understood by CC to mean 'equality, sameness'.

A T: *ma-bshig-pa* amended to *bshig-pa* here and below.

compassion without any objectifying. ***These are the Three* Samayas**: The entering, abiding and arising minds, as mentioned earlier.

4. 'Furthermore, Lord of the Secret Ones,
What are the Three *Samayas*?
The first mind is the Buddha,
the second mind is the Dharma,
and the mind which arises together with that
is said to be the Saṅgha[A].
O Hero, those Three *Samayas*
are taught to you by the Guiding Ones.'

This section explains the synonyms (*paryāya*) for the entering mind and so on. ***The first mind is the Buddha***: Because the first entering mind is the realization that the psycho-physical constituents and so forth lack autonomous existence, it is called 'Buddha' as the term 'Buddha' is a synonym for 'realization'. ***The second mind is the Dharma***: This is the abiding mind which is termed 'Dharma' because it upholds (√ *dhṛ*) the attribute of being Suchness in nature. ***The mind which arises together with that is said to be the Saṅgha***: (222b) By virtue of compassion, it transforms into the Bodies of the deities who are defined as the Saṅgha of the non-regressive Bodhisattvas, at the very moment of realizing that all phenomena are empty.

O Hero, those Three Samayas are taught to you by the Guiding Ones: These Three *Samayas* which have been explained are not only explained to Vajrapāṇi by the Bhagavat, but they were also explained by earlier Buddha Bhagavats. This indicates the unity of activity of the Buddhas.

5. 'When one abides in these Three *Samayas*,
then, by way of various modes[B],
O Hero, for the sake of benefitting beings,
one will engage in the practice of Enlightenment.'

Having abided in these Three *Samayas*, the Bodhisattvas who engage in the practice of Enlightenment, act for the sake of beings by way of various kinds of modes (*naya*), such as the many modes of the ordinary (*laukika*) people and the modes of the supramundane, such as Śrāvakas, Pratyekabuddhas and so forth.

6. 'Lord of the Secret Ones, when those who have mastery of the three modes of embodiment have become Perfect Buddhas[C], they then first transform themselves into a single *nirmāṇa-kāya* in order to establish the

A C: 彼心相續生　所謂和合僧 '*The continuous arising of that mind is termed the communion of the Saṅgha*'.

B C: 諸導門上首 '*beginning with the gates of guidance*'. C often translates *-ādi* 'and so forth' with 上首 'beginning with', 'headed by'.

C C reads part of this as verse with the previous section: 當得成菩提　三身自在轉。秘密主三藐三佛陀 ... '*Then* [*you*] *will achieve Enlightenment and be able to transform freely the Three Bodies. Lord of the Secret Ones,* [*in order to establish the teachings,*] *the Perfect Buddha* [*is transformed into one Body*]'.

teachings[A]. Furthermore, Lord of the Secret Ones, they display that single Body in three aspects, that is, as the Buddha, the Dharma and the Saṅgha. Furthermore, Lord of the Secret Ones, they teach by establishing the Three Ways. When they have carried out extensive Buddha activities, they then reveal their *Parinirvāṇa*, (191b) and completely mature beings.'

This shows the resultant Three *Samayas*. When they have become perfectly enlightened, they manifest themselves as the son of the King Śuddhodana with a *nirmāṇa-kāya* and teach until their Nirvāṇa. ***Who have mastery of the three modes of embodiment*** (*tri-kāya*): At the very moment of becoming perfectly Enlightened in the Akaniṣṭha Heaven, [the being who] realizes the emptiness of all phenomena, which is Suchness in nature, has mastery of the *dharmakāya*. Because he then appears as a *saṃbhoga-kāya*, he has mastery of the *saṃbhoga-kāya*. Because he then appears as a *nirmāṇa-kāya* in the world, he has mastery of the *nirmāṇa-kāya*.

They ***first transform themselves into a single* nirmāṇa-kāya**: this is linked with the words, '***in order to establish the teachings***'. (223a) Having first become perfectly Enlightened in the Akaniṣṭha Heaven, they transform into *nirmāṇa-kāyas* and reveal the teachings by manifesting themselves as the son of the King Śuddhodana and engaging in the youthful pleasures, the going forth, the ascetic practices, the approaching of the core of Enlightenment and so forth.

'***Buddha***' refers to that same *nirmāṇa-kāya*. '***Dharma***' is the teaching of the twelve branches of discourses, by way of his Inexhaustible Speech. '***Saṅgha***' is the Saṅgha of the eight types of noble individual. After that single *nirmāṇa-kāya* has been manifested as these, they reveal the teachings of the Perfect Buddha.

Furthermore they teach by establishing the Three Ways: That *nirmāṇa-kāya* expounds the Śrāvaka Way to the Śrāvakas, beings who are interested in the realization that the individual has no autonomous existence. They expound the Pratyekabuddha Way to those beings who are interested in being liberated by dissolving phenomena by means of their interdependent arising and seeing their impermanence. They expound the Mahāyāna to those who are interested in the realization that both the individual and phenomena are without autonomous existence.

When they have carried out extensive Buddha activities, they then reveal their* Parinirvāṇa *and completely mature beings: They reveal their *Parinirvāṇa* in order to mature the beings who strive for liberation from *saṃsāra* through making them see the impermanence [of the *nirmāṇa-kāya* Buddha]. When that Nirvāṇa has been seen by beings, they will think 'If even the Buddha Bhagavat, the Lord of Men and Gods, who has accumulated a mass of merit and awareness, (223b) is impermanent, how much more so others!'; then exerting themselves in the Noble Path they will be matured.

These are the Three *Samayas* taught for the sake of both the Bodhisattvas who engage in the Perfections and those who engage in the Mantras. The causal Three *Samayas* are those from the Level of Practice with Devoted Interest up to the Samantabhadra Level, because during that period one has the entering mind and so on. The resultant Three *Samayas* are as before.

A C adds 所謂初變化身 '*which is called the first* nirmāṇa-kāya'.

7. 'Lord of the Secret Ones! Behold, whosoever engages in the Bodhisattva practice by way of mantras, who has complete knowledge of the Three *Samayas* and who accomplishes the mantra rituals, will be free from the hindrances arising from concepts, except those [people] who are faithless, lazy, gossipers, who have no trust in the mantras and who accumulate many possessions. One should also neither drink alcohol nor sleep in beds.'

In order to praise those the Bodhisattvas engaged in the mantras, who abide on the Level of Practice with Devoted Interest, who know these Three *Samayas* and who abide in them, the Bhagavat says, '***Lord of the Secret Ones! Behold, whosoever engages in the Bodhisattva practice***' and so forth. Generally there are three types of hindrances: those arising from judgemental concepts (*vikalpa*), those arising from karmic action and those arising from carelessness (*pramāda*) not yet abandoned. The hindrances arising from karmic action are frequent illnesses and so forth. The hindrances arising from carelessness not yet abandoned are poisons, weapons and entering precipitous places. The hindrances arising from judgemental concepts are those formed by previous concepts. These Bodhisattvas will be free from those hindrances. ***Except those who are faithless***, *lazy* and so forth: Those who do not wish to carry out the *sādhana* even though they have these Three *Samayas*, and those who are listed such as the lazy and so on, are not included among those free from hindrances because that very lack of desire to do the *sādhana* and the laziness and so on are hindrances for them. ***One should also neither drink alcohol nor sleep in beds***: The consumption of intoxicants is the root of all incapacity so it should be abandoned[2].

XXVIII
THE TATHĀGATA

1. **'What is a Tathāgata?**
What is a Supreme Jina?
What is a Bodhisattva?
What is a Buddha?
I ask the Great Sage
to clear away my confusion!
After their confusion and doubts
have been cleared away,
the renowned Bodhisattvas
will engage in the Mahāyāna,
the supreme king of practice!'

(224a) Now regarding the questions put by Vajrapāṇi to the Bhagavat with the verses beginning, '*What is a Tathāgata?*', the Bhagavat earlier said, '*This is the mantra of a Tathāgata, this is the mantra of a Bodhisattva*' when he was speaking about the mantras of Buddhas and Bodhisattvas. Now Vajrapāṇi asks for his uncertainty to be cleared away since he does not know what attributes or distinguishing qualities Tathāgatas and Bodhisattvas have, and what they are. Furthermore Vajrapāṇi did not ask these questions because he himself really does not know this, but in order to clear away the uncertainties that future beings may have. His four questions are answered in separate sections with the verses, '*Enlightenment is like space in character*' and so forth. Vajrapāṇi requests the Bhagavat to clear away uncertainties so that the renowned Bodhisattvas might engage in the Mahāyāna mantra practice, when they have abandoned their doubt and uncertainty. *The supreme king of practice*: This refers to the mantra practice itself.

2. Then the Bhagavat Vairocana gazed upon the entire assembly and said to Vajrapāṇi, the Lord of the Secret Ones,
'Vajrapāṇi, your question is excellent!
Therefore listen, for I shall explain
the Mahāyāna method to you[A].'

3. **'Enlightenment is space[-like] in nature,**
devoid of all judgemental concepts:
whoever desires to realize that[B]
is called a Bodhisattva.'

This section replies to the question, '*What is a Bodhisattva?*'. Enlightenment is the Awareness of Suchness, the realization of the emptiness of all phenomena, (224b) which like space is devoid of all judgemental concepts such as those concerning a perceiving subject and perceived objects, and is without the obscurations of emotional afflictions and wrong understanding. One who desires to realize such an

A This is prose in C.
B C: 彼菩提 '*that Enlightenment*'.

Enlightenment is called a 'Bodhisattva'. Furthermore, it refers to the Bodhisattvas from those abiding on the First Level up to the Ninth Level.

4. **'One who has accomplished the Ten Levels,**
and has attained the Ten Masteries,
who comprehends that phenomena
are empty and illusion-like,
and who knows the fortunes of all people[A]**,**
is called a Buddha.'

This section replies to the question '***What is a Buddha?***'. The Bodhisattva who has completely perfected those Levels and who has gained control of the Ten Masteries as mentioned, who realizes that such phenomena as the psycho-physical constituents and so forth are illusion-like and knows the absolute and relative attributes of the [existential] streams of people in the world – emptiness and illusoriness – at the time of abiding in and arising from *samādhi*, is called a 'Buddha'. Even though the ordinary Bodhisattvas realize the emptiness and the illusoriness of phenomena, and also know the [existential] streams of people in the world, they have not yet abandoned all the inimical elements. So when they arise from the equipoise (*samāpatti*) which realizes the emptiness and illusoriness of phenomena, they become obscured by those inimical elements. Therefore, since the text specifically mentions those who have become completely awakened through the Ten Levels and Ten Masteries, the title 'Buddha' refers to those who have abandoned the antidotes to the perverse and who directly experience [reality] authentically.

5. **'One with the Ten Strengths**
who has fully realized
that phenomena are space-like in nature,
non-dual, with a single attribute,
is said to be a Perfect Buddha.'

This section replies to the question '***What is a Supreme Jina?***'. The Bodhisattvas of the Tenth Level called 'Buddhas' are (225a) those who have realized that all phenomena are empty and have realized the individual attributes. The 'Perfect Buddhas' (*saṃbuddha*) are those who have additionally realized that even the individual attributes are empty, and who having become perfected with the Ten Strengths, fully realize that all phenomena are like space in nature, non-dual with a single attribute, in this manner: the emptiness of colour-form is the emptiness of feeling, and the emptiness of colour-form and the emptiness of feeling are non-dual and cannot be divided into two and so forth. Moreover, this refers to the Bodhisattvas who abide on the Samantabhadra Level, the Nirvāṇa With Remainder. ***The Supreme Jina***: Because he is victorious over the Four Māras.

6. **'Because he has eliminated "idea-only",**
one whose Awareness is self-knowing,

A C: 知此一切同 解諸世間趣 '*who knows that all these things are the same, and who comprehends the various mundane modes of existence*'.

the intrinsic nature of which is inexpressible,
is termed a Tathāgata[A].' (192a)

This section is in reply to the question, '***What is a Tathāgata?***'. One who has abandoned even the idea of the single attribute of the emptiness of all phenomena at the time of becoming a Perfect Buddha, whose self-aware intrinsic nature is inexplicable, (225a) and who has entered the Nirvāṇa Without Remainder, is called a 'Tathāgata'.

A C: 唯慧害無明　自性離言說　自證之智慧　故說名如來 '*One who has eliminated ignorance with insight alone, who has the self-knowing Awareness whose intrinsic nature is inexpressible*'. The first portion of this verse seems to have been mistranslated: the 唯慧 '*insight alone*' is probably based on a misreading of '*saṃjñā-mātra*' (idea-only) as '*prajñā-mātra*'.

XXIX
THE *HOMA* RITUALS

Now the explanation of the lineage of Agni will be given. (225b) You should know that when the Bhagavat was formerly engaged in the Bodhisattva practice, the Bhagavat himself taught the virtuous instructions that appear in the Tīrthika scriptures, such as, 'You should not kill creatures apart from doing so as offerings (*bali*) to the gods'. The explanations about Agni in the Vedas of the Brahmins were also taught in order to reduce the amount of slaughter of creatures among the *tīrthikas* and so forth, who being disposed to perversity, engage in such evil deeds. How is that known to be so? Because as it says in the *Noble Mañjuśrī Tantra*, 'Even that with a small amount of truth was taught by me.'

1. 'Furthermore, Vajrapāṇi, at one time I was a Bodhisattva, and when I was engaged in the practice of a Bodhisattva and resided in the Brahmā Heaven, Brahmā questioned me, saying, "O Great Brahmā, I should like to know what types of fire there are!" '

When the Bhagavat engaged in the Bodhisattva practice, he took on the form of Brahmā and dwelt in the Brahmā Heaven (*brahmā-loka*). He was questioned thus by the Brahmā King who is master over the three thousand great thousand world systems.

2. **'And in reply, I said to him:**
"Abhimānin Agni was self-arisen[A]**;**
next born from him were the Brahmā sons.
The mundane fire Pāvaka
was the first Brahmā son.
His son was Brahmodana,
and his son was Bharata[B]
His sons were Vaiśvānara,
Havana and Havya-vāhana.
Parśva-saṃbhida was the son
of Atharvan, famed in the ocean
[Thus were the fire deities
born from each other in succession][C]**." '**

Abhimānin Agni was self-arisen (*svayaṃbhu*): When all the worlds arose spontaneously at the time of the first eon, not created by anyone and moving through space, consuming blissful food, Agni also arose spontaneously in the Brahmā World. Since he was proud, thinking, 'I am self-arisen, not created by anyone', he is termed '***Abhimānin, the self-arisen one***', and in that way Agni[1] first arose.

Next were the Brahmā sons born from him. The mundane fire Pāvaka was the first Brahmā son: After the self-arisen Agni, the Fire which is the chief of the mundane ones called

A C: 所謂大梵天　名我慢自然 '*Thus, Mahā-Brahmā is called Abhimānin, the self-arisen*'.
B 畢怛囉 '*Pitara*' (father).
C Inserted from C.

Pāvaka, which burns, arose from Brahmā, and he was also the first of the Brahmā sons. ***His son was Brahmodana***: He was the son of the mundane Fire called Pāvaka. ***His son was Bharata***: The son of that Brahmodana (226a) was Bharata. ***His sons were Vaiśvānara, Havya and Havya-vāhana***: Those Fires were the sons of Bharata. ***Parśva-saṃbhida***: He was the son of the Fire called Atharvan. He is also well-known as living in the ocean called Puṣkara.

3. **'The fire called Māruta**
is prescribed for the ritual of conception.
The fire to wash one's wife
is the Pavamāna fire.
Maṅgala is for the ceremonial hair-parting[A].
Pragalbha is for the birth rites,
The fire for naming is Pārthiva.
Likewise for ritual feeding, Śuci.
Ṣaḍbhi is for the hair-shaving.
For receiving vows, Samudbhava.
Sūrya is for the presentation of a cow,
Yojaka is for marriage.
Agni is for setting-up a new house[B].
For the making of oblations, that same Fire.
The fire called Pāvaka is used
to offer to the various gods.
For the House-holder[C], the Brahmā Fire.
Likewise for the *dakṣiṇa* offering[2], Śānta.
Likewise for binding the sheep,
the fire called Avahanika.
For transgressions, Viveci.
For sacrificing cooked foods, Sahasa.
For the Twilight Ritual, Haviṣya.
Likewise for the Soma-saṃsthā, Nidhi.
Mṛḍa[D] is for the full-ladle offerings.
For Pacifying, Dāruṇa is used.
Yama is the funerary fire.
Likewise for Enriching, Balada[E].
The Wrathful Fire is well-known
for all acts of destroying.

A C reverses the purpose of these last two.

B C omits this line. I suspect there may be some kind of textual corruption here. For the next line C reads: 造作衆事業 跛那易迦火 '*Upanāyika* (*that appropriate for offerings*) *is the fire for performing various tasks*'.

C C: 造房 '*House-building*'.

D C: 阿密栗多火 '*Amṛta Fire*'.

E This text used for C probably had an omission at this point, as both '*Yama*' and '*Balada*' are omitted. It says '*Kṛtānta* (= funerary fire!) *is the fire for Enriching*', thus conflating two lines. T also shows signs of corruption as it says '*Kṛtānta is the fire for Yama*'. My translation is based on V.

The fire called Kāmada[A]
is prescribed for Mastery.
Dūta fire is for burning forests.
The stomach[B] **fire is Jaṭhara.** (192b)
Bhakṣa is that for flesh-eating[C]**.**
Vaḍavā-mukha is in the ocean.
Yugānta is famed as the fire
which destroys at the end of time[D]**.**
These Fires which have been explained
to you in brief, Noble One,
are called the Sons of Brahmā,
by those engaged in the Veda *śruti*.
These forty four were taught
by me at that time[3]**.'**

Maruta (Wind): The fire used for the *homa* at the time of causing conception, according to the Brahmanical ritual is Maruta. ***Pāvamāna*** (Purifying): When [the woman] has conceived and become pregnant, the fire for the *homa* at the time of washing her hair is Pāvamāna. ***Maṅgala*** (Auspicious): The fire to be used in the *homa* when the child is being delivered is Maṅgala[4]. ***Pragalbhi*** (Resolute, confident): The fire to be used in the *homa* when the child has been delivered is called Pragalbhi. ***Pārthiva*** (Sovereign, princely): The fire to be used in the *homa* when the name of the child is given is Pārthiva. ***Śuci*** (Pure): The fire to be used for the *homa* at the time of the ritual [first] feeding of the child is Śuci. ***Ṣaḍbhi*** (?): The fire to be used for the *homa* when putting the child's hair into a top-knot is called Śadbhi. ***Samudbhava*** (Source): The fire to be used for the *homa* when the child is made to accept the vows, from the age of eight until he takes a bride, is called Samudbhava. ***Sūrya*** (Sun): The fire to be used for the *homa* when taking a bride is called Sūrya[5]. ***Yojaka*** (Joiner): The fire to encircle the couple (226b) at the time of marriage is called Yojaka. ***Agni*** (Fire): The fire to be used for the *homa* when setting up a new household is Agni[6]. ***The Same Fire***: The fire used in the *homa* for the ritual called *Upanāyika* is that same fire. ***Pāvaka*** (Purifier): The fire used in the *homa* for the various gods of the planets and constellations is called Pāvaka. ***Brahmā Fire***: The fire used in the *homa* for the ritual of the Householder is called the Brahmā Fire. *Śānti* (Peaceful): The fire used in the *homa* for presenting offerings is **Śānti**. Secondly the word '*dakṣiṇa*' (offerings) can also mean 'the southern direction', so it means that both the Brahmā Fire and Śānti Fire should be placed in the southern quarter and tended there. ***Avahanika*** (Slayer): The fire used in the *homa* for killing a cow and offering it to the deity is called Avahanika. ***Viveci*** (Separater): If any transgressions have been committed through intoxication, then the fire for the *homa* to purify one of that intoxication

---

A C: 迦摩奴 *Kāmada.*

B C: 所食令消化 '*which digests what has been eaten*'.

C The 'flesh-eating' (**kravyāda*) refers to the cremation of a corpse as mentioned by Buddhaguhya below, which C alludes to: 若授諸火時 '*when consigning to fire*' although CC is silent at this point.

D I have based this rendering on C and V. T understands the line as follows: '*Destroyer* (*saṃvartaka*) *is famed as the fire at the end of time*'.

after one has repented is Viveci[7]. ***Sahasa*** (Powerful): The fire used in the *homa* for the ritual of sacrificing cooked food is called Sahasa. ***Haviṣya*** (Fit for Offering): The fire used in the *homa* for the ritual called '*Sandhya*' should be Haviṣya[8]. ***Nidhi*** (Treasury): The fire used in the house for the ritual called '*Soma-saṃsthā*' is called Nidhi[9]. ***Mṛḍa*** (Mild): The fire used for the three measures of burnt offerings with the full ladle of materials (*dravya*) prior to the [main] homa is called Mṛḍa. ***Dāruṇa*** (Harsh?): The fire for the Pacifying *homa* is called Dāruṇa. ***Kṛtānta*** (Termination): (227a) The fire used for the *homa* when a person has died is called *Kṛtānta*[10]. ***Balada*** (Strength-giver): The fire used in the Enriching *homa* is Balada. ***Wrathful***: The fire used for the Destroying *homa* is the Wrathful One. ***Kāmada*** (Giving desire): The fire used for the Mastery *homa* is Kāmada. ***Dūta*** (Messenger): The fire used for burning forests is called Dhūta. ***Jaṭhara*** (Stomach): the fire which digests food and so on which is in the stomach is called Jaṭhara. ***Bhakṣa*** (Eater): The fire for cremation is called Bhakṣa. ***Vaḍāva-mukha*** (Mare-mouthed): The fire which abides in the ocean. ***Yugānta*** (Eon-destruction): The fire at the destruction of the world.

From '***Proud Agni was self-arisen***' to '***famed in the ocean***' teaches the lineage of the Fires. From '***The fire called Māruta***' to '***is prescribed for mastery***' teaches the nature of the fires through their action. From '***Dhūta fire is for burning forests***' to '***as the fire at the end of time***' (227b) teaches the nature of fires through their characters (*śīla*). All these fires are well-known from the mundane scriptures of people such as the Brahmins and they carry out mundane functions.

4. 'Lord of the Secret Ones!
Now, whoever [tries to] perform *homa*
without knowing the nature of the fires[A],
is unable to perform *homa*, or the preparatory rites[B],
nor will he have any results from the rites.'

If you do not know the nature of the fires, you will not be successful in performing the *homa* because of errors in the ritual. [***Nor***] ***the preparatory rites***: Even the preparatory rites (*sukṛta, saṃskṛta*) for the *homa*, such as spreading the *kuśa* grass will not be successfully done. Because of that, the *homa* ritual being performed will not be fruitful.

5. 'Having become perfectly
awakened to Enlightenment,
I have taught twelve kinds of Fire.
What are those twelve?
The first is the Fire of Awareness
who is called Mahendra,
with a golden complexion,
with a blazing aura, in *samādhi*,
who bestows fine features,
enrichment and strength,

A C: 我於往昔時　不知諸火性　作諸護摩事　彼非護摩行　非能成業果 '*In past times, I did not know the nature of the various fires, so when I performed* homa *rites they were not the [true]* homa *practice and they were not able to accomplish any results*'.
B C omits '*or the preparatory rites*'.

and is the perfecter of Awareness.
The second is called Sustainer,
like the colour of the autumn moon,
noble, wearing white robes,
he holds a rosary and a water pitcher[A].
The third is called Wind,
his complexion is black and rough[B].
The fourth is called the Red One (*rohita*),
and is like the red at dawn[C].
The fifth is called the Gentle One (*mṛḍa*),
he is hairy, tawny in colour[D],
he is long-necked and very brilliant;
he brings benefit to all.
The sixth is called Wrathful,
with crooked eyes, the colour of smoke,
his hair up-ended and emitting a great sound,
he is four-fanged and most powerful.
The seventh is called Belly (*jaṭhara*),
and is piercing[E], with all colours.
The eighth is called Destruction (*kṣaya*)
and seems like a mass of lightning shafts.
The ninth is called Mind-born (*manoja*),
he has various forms and is very powerful.
The tenth is called World-supporter.
Apart from that, there is Kravyāda,
red-black and marked with an *Oṃ*[F].

A C: 吉祥圓輪中 珠鬘鮮白衣 '[*Seated*] *within a noble disc,* [*holding*] *a rosary and* [*wearing*] *clean white robes*'.

B C: 黑色風燥形 '*black with a wind-parched appearance*'. CC says that it is as though he were smeared with ashes.

C Both V and C have '*dawn*', but T and B have '*evening*'.

D C: 多髭淺黃色 '*he has prolific moustaches and is pale-yellow in colour*'.

E C: 迅疾 '*rapid*', '*swift*'.

F The text of C reads as follows: 第十羯囉微 赤黑唵字印 '*The tenth fire is Kravyāda, red-black and marked with an Oṃ*'. There then follows a note which says that the name of the eleventh fire was missing from the Sanskrit text, and then it continues with details of the twelfth fire, which correspond to those in T. On the other hand, T reads '*bcu-pa 'jig-rten-pa yin | sha-za'i me ni de-las gzhan*' (*The tenth is called World-supporter. Apart from that there is Kravyāda*). Therefore, it is actually the tenth fire (*World-supporter*) which was missing in the base text for C. Moreover, the text of T is also unsatisfactory, as it looks as though at least one line is missing: that describing the Kravyāda Fire '*red-black and marked with an Oṃ*' found in C. It is also possible that the description of the tenth fire is missing from T since the majority of the fires have two lines each for their names and descriptions. It is interesting to note that the missing portion here is approximately the same amount of text which seems to be missing in C above in Section 3 dealing with Yama and Balada. Due to their close proximity, this suggests that the recto and verso of the folio were damaged in the same place. This hypothesis is corroborated by the fact that the locations of these two missing segments occur at almost exactly the same place on two successive folios (192a7–192b7).

The twelfth is called Deluding (*mohana*),
who is the deluder of all beings.'

While the Bhagavat was engaged in the Bodhisattva pratice, he taught the Fires mentioned above, which appear in the Vedas of the Brahmins and after he became enlightened he also taught twelve Fires so that the supramundane *homa* could be performed.

The Awareness Fire: These are the attributes of the fire for the Enriching *homa*. It is so-called because it is the fire of the Awareness Being (*jñāna-sattva*). ***Sustainer***: These are the attributes of the fire for the Pacifying *homa*. The third fire called '***Wind***' is summoned when lighting the hearth. The fourth (228a) fire, the '***Red One***' (*rohita*) is used for the Subduing *homa*. The '***Gentle One***' (*mṛḍa*) is the fire used for the full ladles of offerings in the *homa*. ***Wrathful*** (*krodha*): These are the attributes of the fire used in the Destruction *homa*. ***The seventh is called Belly*** and so forth: These briefly mention the attributes of the remaining five fires.

6. **'Lord of the Secret Ones!**
Thus the forms of Agni are transformed;
and both one's own colour
and the materials should be made the same.
This is the external *homa*,
and you should burn offerings
according to the attainments you desire.'

Immediately after having described the fires, the Bhagavat explains the *homas*. ***Thus the forms of Agni are transformed*** and so forth: The colours of both the person who performs the ritual with the fire of Pacifying or Enriching and the materials should be changed [as appropriate]. ***This is the external homa***: That which has the three elements – oneself, the fire and the materials – is called the 'external *homa*'.

7. **'Lord of the Secret Ones!**
As for the internal one,
That which has one tripartite nature
by means of uniting the three places,
is called the internal *homa*.' (193a)

With regards the internal *homa*, it is one in its intrinsic nature of emptiness. You might ask how many places are gathered together into one, so the text says that it '***has one tripartite nature by means of uniting the three places***'. This means that those three places – oneself, the fire and the materials – which are united together, should be made one in their intrinsic nature of emptiness. This is also commented on below.

8. **'Lord of the Secret Ones!**
That with great loving-kindness
and great compassion is the Pacifying.

That endowed with joy is Enriching.
The Wrathful Fire is for the fierce practices,
and these should be done forcefully[A].
The Wind Fire should be placed in the centre.'

For performing the Pacifying *homa* (228b) you should mainly generate loving-kindness and compassion. For the Enriching *homa* it should mainly be joy. Regarding the Destroying *homa*, you should not perform it with anger although it should be done fiercely. ***The Wind Fire should be placed in the centre*:** When you first light the fire in the hearth, you should summon the Wind Fire and light the fire with a fan.

9. **'Lord of the Secret Ones!**
Thus you should perform *homa*
in those places which have been prescribed,
which are fitting [for the action],
and with what is appropriate.'

You should perform the Pacifying *homa* and so forth in whichever of those places[11] that have been prescribed for Pacifying and so forth is appropriate.

10. **Then Vajrapāṇi asked the Bhagavat this[B]:**
'Bhagavat, please tell me
how should the hearth be made[C]?
How should the sprinkling be done?
How should the *kuśa* grass be spread?
How should [the deity] be imagined[D]?'

Vajrapāṇi asks the Bhagavat about the teaching which was given in brief above, concerning how the hearth should be made, how the water is to be sprinkled in order to cleanse the fire, how the grass is to be strewn and how Agni is to be placed in the hearth.

A The Tibetan text for these lines seems to include additional material (underlined), perhaps previous marginal glosses, which is also ignored by Buddhaguhya. T reads in full as follows: '*The Wrathful Fire is for the fierce practices. Having made the Wrathful One forcefully, insert the name [of the one to be destroyed] between* pha *and* ta [= phat], *and also place their image within the Wrathful Mandala*. [*The deed*] *should be done wrathfully*'. *The Wind Fire should be placed in the centre*.' C simply has: 忿怒從胎藏而造衆事業 '[*Generating*] *wrath from the matrix, you should perform the multitude of actions*'. This portion of C is likely to be based on a misreading of '*garbha*' 胎藏 (*matrix*) for '*galbha*' (*forceful, bold*). However, CC provides a rational explanation for this apparent mistranslation, which can be reconciled with Buddhaguhya's comments, saying that '*garbha*' in this case refers to the Matrix of Compassion, that is, the wrath used in the fierce practices arises from compassion, not hatred as with mundane wrath. I have included '*The Wind Fire should be placed in the centre*' for the sake of Buddhaguya's comments, although I consider this line to be intrusive.

B C has the following section in prose first and then follows with the same in verse as T. This is probably dittography as CC does not comment on this.

C C: 云何火爐三摩地 '*What is the* samādhi *for the fire hearth*?'.

D C: 云何具衆物 '*What materials are to be used?*'.

11. And when he had asked this, the Bhagavat Vairocana then said this in reply to Vajrapāṇi, the Lord of the Secret Ones:

'Lord of the Secret Ones!
Now the pit for the hearth
should measure one cubit entirely[A],
and the rim should be made four inches [in size],
and it should be marked with a vajra sign[B].'

This section is in reply to the question, '***How is the hearth to be made?***'. The diameter of the fire-pit should be one cubit and the rim should be made four inches in breadth and height. A vajra sign should be marked on the bottom.

12. 'Fresh *kuśa* grass should be spread
going around to the right of the hearth pit:
the tips should be placed over the roots,
and the roots should also be placed over the tips[C].'

This section is in reply to the question, '***How should the* kuśa *grass be spread?***' and is easy to understand.

13. 'You should then sprinkle with water
to the right, as you laid the grass around[D].'

(229a) This section is in reply to the question, '***How should the sprinkling be done?***'. The sprinkling of the water (*prokṣaṇa*) to purify the fire should also be done going around to the right, in the same manner as the *kuśa* grass was put down around it.

14. 'Perfume, flowers and incense,
should *be given to the Mṛḍa Fire.*
***The mantrin* should carefully place**
the *Mṛḍa* Fire in his own form,
with one flower, in that hearth;
then the purificatory sprinkling should be done[E].
The wise one should present him
[three] ladles full with his mantra.'

A C adds 四方相均等 '*the four sides equal to each other*'.

B C: 周匝金剛印 '*and the circumference [marked] with vajra signs*'.

C C: 不以末加本 應以本加末 '*The tips should* not *be placed over the roots, but the roots should be placed over the tips.*' According to CC this refers to the method of placing the kindling criss-cross over the hearth-pit, resting on its rim.

D C: 次持吉祥草 依法而右灑 '*Then taking some kuśa grass, sprinkle water to the right, according to the rule.*'

E C: 以塗香華燈 次獻於火天 行人以一華 供養没栗荼 安置於座位 復當用灌灑 '*Then offerings should be made to Agni with perfumes, flowers, and lamps. The yogin should offer a single flower to Mṛḍa. When* [*the deity*] *is installed in his seat, the sprinkling should be done again.*'

This section is in reply to the question, '***How should [the deity] be imagined?***'. This means that first you should place one flower in the hearth and summon the *Mṛḍa* (gentle) Fire and then make offerings to it with perfume and flowers. Then it should be sprinkled with water, presented with three ladles full of offerings (*pūrṇa-huti*), while reciting the mantra of that Fire.

15. 'Then either the Pacifying *homa*,
or the Enriching *homa*, should be performed.
This mundane *homa* ritual
is called the external one.'

Following the process described above, you should carry out the hearth ritual, make offerings to the *Mṛḍa* Fire and establish that Fire in its own place. Then having invited either the Pacifying or the Enriching Fire, you should perform the Pacifying or the Enriching *homa*, or whichever one you wish. Because these are focussed on external things like the hearth, the fire and so forth, they are called the mundane *homas*.

16. 'Moreover, the internal *homa*
counter-acts karmic action and rebirth.
It should be known by the *manas*,
devoid of form, sound and so forth.
The eyes, ears, nose, tongue and body
are all generated by the *manas*,
and depend upon the mind king.
These things generated by thought: (193b)
***bodhicitta*, the objects, the eyes and so on,**
and also the Wind Fire should be
counteracted by the non-arising insight[12]**,**
and burnt in the mental fire[A]**.**
This is called the inner *homa*,
which I have taught to you, Noble One.'

A There are major differences between T and C in this section, and, furthermore, the explanations given by Buddhaguhya and Śubhakarasiṃha are at considerable variance. Generally speaking, the text preserved by C seems superior. C has translated the entire passage in verse, whereas T (although this is not evident from my rendering) gives up any attempt to translate the section as verse after the first four lines, and instead lapses into prose, and also completely omits some of the lines found in C. This may be due to recensional variations as many other differences between T and C can be noted elsewhere in this chapter. C reads: 復次内護摩 滅除於業生 了知自末那 遠離色聲等 眼耳鼻舌身 及與語意業 皆悉從心起 依止於心王 眼等分別生 及色等境界 智慧未生障 風燥火能滅 燒除妄分別 成淨菩提心 此名内護摩 爲諸菩薩說 '*Next there is the internal homa, which counteracts karma and rebirth. It should be known by your* manas, *devoid of form, sound, and so forth. The eyes, ears, nose, tongue and body, and also the action of speech and thought, all arise from your mind, and depend upon the mind-king* (= manas). *The eyes and so forth, born of discrimination, and the perceptual spheres of form and so forth, which obstruct the undeveloped insight, should be destroyed by the Wind Fire. When you burn away delusive discrimination your* bodhicitta *will become pure.*'

This explains the internal *homa*. You should dissolve your five psycho-physical constituents into emptiness. Also the material objects, such as the external hearth and so forth, and likewise the perceptual awarenesses of the six senses which arise should also each be dissolved. Then preventing them from arising again, you should abide in the non-conceptualizing *samādhi*, [in which] even that *bodhicitta* which thus destroys and suspends them is counteracted by non-arising insight. That is the internal *homa*. ***The Wind Fire also should be counteracted by non-arising insight and should be burnt in the mental fire*.** The Wind Fire is counteracted (229b) by controlling the breath (*prāṇāyama*). It should be burnt up in the motionless mind.

XXX
THE TRANSMISSION[1]

1. Then the Bhagavat spoke to the entire assembly saying, 'You should practise by adhering assiduously to this Dharma discourse. Apart from my Children[A], do not give it to any others[B]!

'I shall explain their attributes,
so listen to them, all of you!
Those born from the Sun lineage
who are honourable, with discerning minds,
who are grateful and desire the Dharma,
and who also know and exert themselves in it,
whose complexions are pure,
and have very fine features,
whose noses are high and sharp-pointed,
and whose heads and foreheads are very broad[C]:
These are all my children,
and they will ponder on the meaning of the teachings.
To them you should always give this in earnest.'

This Dharma discourse is not to be given without due consideration to beings who are not suitable receptacles[2]. Therefore, the Bhagavat says, '***Do not give it to any others [whose capacity you do not know] apart from my Children!***'. Although you may give it to his Children who have the attributes described above without any need for ascertaining their capacity, this profound Dharma discourse should only be given to others when you have ascertained and know if they have intelligence or not, whether or not their faculties are diffused into objects of attachment and so on, and if they are suitable receptacles without such faults. Because it is said, 'It is a mistake for a Bodhisattva to teach the profound and extensive Dharma to those who are devoted to the inferior.'

2. Then they all became most joyful,
and said 'We shall do as the Tathāgata bids!'.
Then, at that moment, they all
made prostrations to the Tathāgata,
and also made offerings to him.
Then sitting with joined palms in his presence,
they uttered these verses:

A C: 具標相者 '[*apart from*] *those who have the signs*'.

B C adds: 若不知根性 '*if you do not know their quality*'.

C C gives a slightly different version for this list of attributes: 若於吉祥執宿時生志求勝事有微細慧當念恩德生渴仰心聞法歡喜而住其相青白或白色廣首長頸額廣平正其鼻修直面X圓滿端嚴相稱 '*Those whose birth was astrologically auspicious, who desire superior things, who have discerning intelligence, who always recollect their good fortune, who have an ardent attitude, who hear the Dharma with joy and abide in it, whose complexions are bluish white, who have broad heads and long necks, whose brows are broad and level, whose noses are straight, whose faces are well-balanced, and who are virtuous and moderate.*'

'We request the Lord
to teach the words of empowerment
for this teaching, so that
the Dharma method[A] may remain
for a long time in the world!'

Then the Bhagavat spoke the words which empower this Dharma discourse: *NAMAḤ SAMANTA-BUDDHĀNĀṂ SARVATHĀ ŚIṂ ŚIṂ TRAṂ TRAṂ GUṂ GUṂ DHARAṂ DHARAṂ STHĀPAYA STHĀPAYA BUDDHA-SATYA-VĀG DHARMA-SATYA-VĀK SAṄGHA-SATYA-VĀG HŪṂ HŪṂ VEDA-VIDE SVĀHĀ* (Salutations to all Buddhas, in all places! *Śiṃ Śiṃ*! *Traṃ traṃ*! *Guṃ guṃ*! *Dharaṃ dharaṃ*! Maintain, maintain! True speech of the Buddha! True speech of the Dharma! True speech of the Saṅgha! *Hūṃ hūṃ*! Knowing One! *Svāhā*!). When the Bhagavat had said this, those Vajradharas and the Bodhisattvas headed by Samanta-bhadra were enraptured and praised what the Bhagavat had said. (194a)

Then that entourage headed by Vajrapāṇi asked the Bhagavat to empower this *Vairocana-abhisaṃbodhi-vikurvita-adhiṣṭhāna-dharma-paryāya* with the mantra of empowerment, so that it might remain uncorrupted in the world and last a long time, because if this Dharma discourse is empowered by this mantra it will be protected.

A C: 法眼道 '*the path of the Dharma eye*'.

Part III

THE MAHĀ-VAIROCANA-UTTARA-TANTRA

I
THE RITUAL FOR THE PACIFYING *HOMA*

1. Then Vajrapāṇi, the Lord of the Secret Ones, said, 'I shall explain how to bind those [who endanger] this teaching for the benefit and comfort of those who devote themselves to the *sādhana* in this manner, so listen attentively!'

2. 'The *mantrin* should raise his left foot,
then firmly set down his right foot;
his eyes looking towards his waist,
he should raise up both his arms,
the right one stretched out,
held like a serpent,
making it into a wheel.
By using the Wheel *Mudrā*,
they will be quelled in all directions.'

3. 'Seeing the most powerful *mudrā*,
myself, the Vajradhara,
or else any mundane being,
will all be frightened [by it].'

4. 'Placing both his feet together,
he should let out a thunderous "*Hūṃ*",
raging, clench his teeth on his lower lip,
with fury, he should hold his head up.'

5. 'The sinful will be cowed,
if he puts his heels together
and quells them with the spear *mudrā*:
they will turn to dust that instant.'

6. 'Having swiftly stepped back one pace
raising up a leg and bending his body,
he will completely vanquish
the gods, *asuras* and *yakṣas*
who dwell here upon the earth.'

7. 'Then the *mantrin* who dwells here
will annihilate demons for ever.
Bending their left legs,
and joining their hands like lotuses,
they will devoutly circle above the *mantrin*.'

8. 'If he strides in the manner of a lion,
and wrathfully quells demons,

then even if they were impelled by Buddhas,
those demons will be turned to dust,
or perish, without a doubt.'

9. 'If the wise one were to summarize
the various attainments
mentioned in all the Tantras (194b),
they would all be included in four groups:
the first rite is Pacifying,
likewise there is Enriching,
Subduing and Ferocious rites.'[1]

10. 'Of those, Pacifying is for the attainment of liberation and so forth, and calming the harm of spirits and so on. Those skilled in the mantras say that anything to do with the obtainment of wealth, such as possession of the wish-fulfilling gem and sword *vidyās*, or the kingdom of a Universal Monarch (*cakravartin*), is connected with Enriching. The *vidyādharas* say that Subduing is for the control and attraction to one of men or women, boys and girls, kings, ministers and so on, or those such as gods, *nāgas* and *yakṣas*. The *vidyādharas* say that the Ferocious rite is for binding, causing harm, cutting-off limbs, confining, causing hatred, killing and parching – in brief, it is for anything that causes harm to the bodies of beings.'

11. 'By the propitiating *homa* rites
the mantras will speedily grant attainments.
All the gods will empower you,
and grant you favours.'

12. 'They will safeguard you from all things like
the harm of insufficient or incomplete rituals,
excess or omission of letters and vowels,
and possession by oppressors or demons.'

13. 'There will be no attainments
from rites without *homa*.
Therefore you should definitely
undertake the *homa* rites.
You should engage in the various *homas*
according to the distinctions
of the Pacifying, the Enriching,
the Subduing and the Ferocious.'

14. 'Of those, first of all the *homa* for the Pacifying rites is to be defined. You should go to the north of the town, some two miles distant and carefully search out a site. Wherever there is white coloured earth, such as on the banks of the Ganges, on the shores of a lotus lake, beside a river or on a beach, is suitable. There you should transform yourself into Vajrasattva and

do the anointing and purification of the ground and so forth. (195a) Then on the fifth day of the new moon or at the full moon, you should begin the Mandala in the following way. *Uttara-bhādra-pada*, *Pūrva-phalgunī*, *Aśleṣā* and *Maghā* are the constellations[2] for Pacifying. As for the planets, you should begin it under the influence of the Moon and Venus.'

15. 'Then changing yourself into the Body of Avalokiteśvara, you should place the Bhagavat Vairocana as his sword symbol or as his letter *A*, upon a lotus. To the north, you should place the triangular symbol of all the Buddhas or the letter *AṂ*, upon a lotus. To the west of the Buddhas, you should place Ākāśa-garbha as his sword symbol or as his letter *I*. Mañjuśrī is to the west of Ākāśa-garbha. He should also be set upon a lotus as his *utpala* symbol or his letter *MAṂ*. To his west you should place the symbol or letter *GAṂ* of Gagana-locanā. To the east of the Buddhas, you should place Śākyamuni as his bowl symbol or his letter *BHAḤ*. In front of him you should place the Wish-fulfilling Gem symbol or the letter *BHRUṂ* of Ūrṇā. You should also draw that with the Wish-fulfilling Gem symbol or the letter of all the Bodhisattvas. The letter is *KA*. Then on the right side of Mahā-vairocana, you should place Avalokiteśvara as his lotus symbol or his letter *SA*. On the left side of Avalokiteśvara, you should place Mahā-sthāma-prāpta as his lotus symbol or his letter *MA*. In front of Mahā-sthāma-prāpta, you should place Bhṛkuṭī as her water-jar symbol or her letter *BHṚ*. On the right side of Padma-dhara you should place the goddess Tārā as her *utpala* symbol or as her letter *TAṂ*. In front of her you should place Pāṇḍara-vāsinī as her lotus symbol or as her letter *PAṂ*. On the left side of the Bhagavat you should place the vajra symbol of the letter *VAṂ* of Vajradhara. (195b) On his right side you should place Māmakī as her vajra symbol or as her letter *MĀ*. In front of her you should place the *Vidyā* Queen Sumbhā as her vajra symbol or her letter *SAṂ*. On the left side of Vajradhara you should place Amṛta-kuṇḍali as his vajra symbol or as his letter *MṚ*. In front of him you should place the vajra symbol or the letter *HŪṂ* of all the Vajradharas. Below the Bhagavat you should place Acala as his sword symbol or as his letter *HĀṂ*. Below the Bhagavat to the south-west you should place Trailokya-vijaya as his vajra-mace symbol or as his letter *HĀ*. In front of the two gates you should place the names of the two Nāga kings, Nanda and Upananda. Within the portals you should place the four Guardians. In the east you should place a sword or the letter *CA*. In the north you should place a sword or the letter *BA*. In the west you should place a mace or the letter *SA*. In the south you should place a mace or the letter *KṢA*. Then the five [gods] of the Pure Abode should be drawn in the small abode bands within the outer lines: in the first band you should put *SAṂ SAṂ SVĀHĀ*, in the second band *MANO-MAYA*[3], in the third band *DHARMA-SAṂBHAVA*, [just] to put *SAṂ SAṂ SVĀHĀ* in the small abode bands. You in the fourth *VIBHAVA* and in the fifth band *KATHANA*. Or else, it is also permissible should place the symbol or letter of whichever family your tutelary deity belongs to in the abode of its Family Lord. You should then draw lotuses filling the whole of the interior of the outer lines.'

16. 'Then the fire-pit should be made within the courtyard in the area of the right gate of the Mandala.

'It should be made completely circular,
measuring one cubit in size,
and twelve inches in depth.
The rim around it
should be made four inches in size.
In the centre of the bottom (196a)
you should make a wheel,
one inch in height.'

17. 'Then sitting down, you should make the *Samaya Mudrā* and recite the *samaya* Mantra. Transform yourself into Avalokiteśvara with the letter *SA* and his Lotus *Mudrā*. Then set the letter *A* in its own mandala and imagine it changing into the exact form of the Body of Mahā-Vairocana. Or he can be manifested with his symbol. Then making the Sword *Mudrā*, you should transform yourself into the Body of Mahā-Vairocana from the letter *A*. Imagine that all the letters in the Mandala change into the body-images of their respective deities, or they can be manifested as their respective symbols. Then recite the mantra of the Noble Acala. Make the Action Vajra [*Mudrā*] and then offer perfumes, flowers and so forth to all the deities who reside in their respective mandalas. You should actualize a *samādhi*, thinking, "They are also devoid of dust", with the letter *RA* and then consecrate the perfumes, flowers and so forth with their respective mantras. You should also consecrate the perfumes and so on with their respective essences and offer them. You should also exhort each of them, saying, "Please accept this perfume and think of me!". You should do likewise for all of them.'

18. 'The mantra of the Noble Acala: *NAMAḤ SAMANTA-BUDDHĀNĀM TRAṬ AMOGHA-CAṆḌA MAHĀ-ROṢAṆA SPHOṬAYA HŪṂ TRAṬ HĀṂ MAṂ*. The mantra for the perfume: *NSB VIŚUDDHA-GANDHODBHAVAYA SVĀHĀ*. The mantra for the flowers: *NSB MAHĀ-MAITRY-ABHYUDGATE SVĀHĀ*. The mantra for the incense: *NSB DHARMA-DHĀTV-ANUGATE SVĀHĀ*. The mantra for the lamps: *NSB TATHĀGATĀRCI-SPHURAṆA-AVABHĀSANA-GAGANODĀRYA SVĀHĀ*. The mantra for the food offerings: *NSB TRYADHVIKĀNĀM ARARA-KARARA BALI DE BALIṂ DADĀMI SVĀHĀ BALIṂ-DADE MAHĀ-BALIṂ SVĀHĀ*. (196b) **The mantra for the oblations: *NSB GAGANA-SAMĀSAMA SVĀHĀ*. These should done both at the beginning and the end. For rituals where you recite the essence mantras, you should recite: *OṂ BHAGAVĀN VAIROCANA IDAṂ GANDHI PRĪTI GṚHYA IDAṂ ME KĀRYA KURU SVĀHĀ*, doing likewise for them all.'**

19. 'For the Pacifying ritual, you should offer white sandalwood mixed with camphor. If you do not have these, offer one *uśīra*[4]. Likewise you should offer sweet-smelling and auspicious white flowers such as white lotuses, roses, jasmine and *yūthika*[5]. The perfumes for the Pacifying rituals are

camphor, sandalwood or else pine. For the food-offerings you should offer such white foodstuffs as yoghurt, cooked rice and so forth. The oil for the lamps should be poured in to white containers and offered. You should offer oblations of water poured into conches and such-like white receptacles, mixed with sandalwood, camphor and white flowers.'

20. 'Having thus made the offerings of such things as described, you should then withdraw and transform yourself into Avalokiteśvara and then make the cast-offerings (*bali*) for the [ten] directions outside.

'With parched grain and with oil,
with water and with boiled rice,
with flowers and with beans,
with *kṛśara*[6] and with oil-pressings,
the Master should take in his hand
such cast-offerings as these and joyfully
cast them in each of the directions.
He should also offer incense and oblations.'

21. 'First he should offer them to Rahu
and his entourage in the north-east.
Then the wise one should offer them
to Indra himself in the east.
Then, without fear, the *mantrin*
should offer them to the south-east.
Then, without fear, the *mantrin*
should offer them to the south.
Then the wise *mantrin* should offer them
to Nirṛti with his entourage in the south-west.
Reciting the mantras, the fearless-one should offer
to the Nāgas in the west. (197a)
Having offered them to those Lords,
he should go to the north-west,
and offer them to Vāyu with his entourage,
calling out their names,
and then offer the cast-offerings with mantras.
Having gone around to the north,
with a lucid mind,
desiring to accomplish his attainment,
he should give cast-offerings to the *yakṣas*.
The wise one should cast the offerings
for the *rākṣasas* and the *piśācas*,
and the flesh-eating ghosts,
and other types of beings.
He should bring to mind
the various beings upon the earth
who dwell in trees and bushes,
and present them with such cast-offerings.'

23. 'These are the mantras for the cast-offerings for the [ten] directions – For the north-east: *RUDRĀYA SVĀHĀ.* For the east: *ŚAKRĀYA SVĀHĀ.* For the south-east: *AGNAYE SVĀHĀ.* For the south: *VE VI SVĀHĀ.* For the south-west: *RĀKṢASĀDHIPATAYE SVĀHĀ.* For the west: *MEGHĀŚANĪYE SVĀHĀ.* For the north-west: *VĀYAVE SVĀHĀ.* For the north: *YAKṢA-VIDYĀDHARI SVĀHĀ.* For the *rākṣasas*: *KRAṄKERI SVĀHĀ.* For the *piśācas*: *MICI MICI SVĀHĀ.* For the hungry ghosts: *GU I GU I.*'

24. 'When you have thus made the cast-offerings everywhere, you should wash and rinse your hands. Then going inside, you should make obeisances to all the Buddhas. Then you should cleanse all the materials to be burnt, however much there are, with the Mantra of the Noble Acala, and place them on your right. On your left you should place two oblation vessels filled with a mixture of perfume and water, and *kuśa* grass. One should be consecrated with the Mantra of the Noble Acala and the other with the Mantra of Mañjuśrī. You should spread *kuśa* grass all around the hearth to encircle it. You should also spread *kuśa* around the place where you are to sit. Place a long and a short spoon made of *udumbara* or *aśvattha* wood (197b) in front of yourself, with the liquid butter.'

25. 'Then you should sprinkle the hearth with sandalwood and also strew it with some sweet smelling white flowers. Taking fire from the house of a brahmin, purify it with the Mantra of the Wrathful King and light *plakṣa* or *udumbara* kindling with it, using a fan. You should sit there facing the north, rub both your hands with perfume and make the *Samaya Mudrā* and so forth. Then you should transform yourself into the exact form of the Body of Mahā-vairocana residing upon a water mandala, using his Mantra and *Mudrā.* You should imagine a water mandala on the bottom of the hearth and then imagine the letter [*RA*] you have placed within the fire as before change into the body-image of Agni. He is the colour of a conch, jasmine or the moon. He has his hair bound up upon his head and is three-eyed. He has four hands in which he holds a rosary, a water-jar and a club. With the other, he makes the *Mudrā* of Bestowing Fearlessness. He is dressed in white robes, wears a white cord crossed over his chest and has a triangular design upon his heart, marked with the letter *RA.* He emits white tongues of fire and is Awareness in nature. You should sprinkle Agni in a circular manner, with water consecrated with the Mantra of the Noble Acala which you have previously prepared. You should also recite the Mantra of Vajra-varada (Mañjuśrī) three times: *NSB MAṂ SVĀHĀ.*'

26. 'Then, offer perfumes, flowers and so forth to Agni with his own mantra. Next offer three measures of a mixture of sugar, ghee and honey. Taking hold of the long spoon, offer three full measures of butter. Then dipping both ends of *aśvattha* or *udumbara* sticks (*samit*) into butter, burn seven pieces. Then also offer three full measures of butter and sprinkle the fire as before. *NSB OṂ VARADĀGNAYE ŚĀNTIṂ KURU SVĀHĀ.* (198a) In the same way burn offerings for each one of the deities and sprinkle the fire. This is the mantra for Pacifying: *NSB HŪṂ A MAHĀ ŚĀNTI-GATA ŚĀNTI-KARA PRAŚAMA-DHARMA-NIRJĀTA | ABHĀVA-SVABHĀVA-DHARMA SAMANTA-PRĀPTA AMOGHASYA SVASTI ŚĀNTIṂ VAṂ KURU SVĀHĀ*.'

27. 'Then imagine all the Buddhas and meditate that because your inner self is pure, it is *bodhicitta* just as it is. Placing your *vidyā* upon a moon disc, make the *mudrā* of your tutelary deity and visualize the body-image of your deity. Again, as before, offer three full measures of butter and sprinkle in a circular manner. You should burn offerings of the materials which are mentioned in your tantra for as long as you do not become tired. If you do become tired, gaze upon the Body of the Perfect Buddha, or meditate on *bodhicitta*.'

28. 'Then offer oblations and making obeisances to the deities, ask them to depart. Having asked the deities to depart, cover the mass of symbols with a new cloth and next imagine them again as the deities residing upon their respective mandalas, as before. You should follow that sequence for the ritual until the Pacification has taken place.'

29. 'When a *mantrin* who knows the ritual
has pacified without laziness
according to this ritual,
he will attain pacification.
If done for a fortnight, without a doubt,
a whole realm will be pacified.
For a king, twelve days,
and ten days for a region.'

30. 'You should engage in the ritual thus,
by performing the ritual of Pacification:
Wearing white clothes, clean and calm,
cleaving to *bodhicitta*,
you should sleep on a bed of *kuśa*.
Then drinking ghee or milk,
you should set your mind on the *homa*.
You should engage in the Pacification ritual,
performing the *homa* at the three times and reciting.
The face-cooling is with Vajra-varada, (198b)
the sprinkling with the Lord Acala.
Here, just in brief, is the *homa* ritual.'

II
THE RITUAL FOR THE ENRICHING *HOMA*

1. 'Moreover the Fortunate one,
foremost of those wise in the mantras,
out of kindness for beings,
also explained the great Enriching *Homa*,
desiring to benefit them.'

2. 'Listen with concentration!
In order to do the ritual for enrichment
in all matters, the hero should seek
a site located in the eastern area
of a town or countryside,
doing as before.'

3. 'The wise one should draw the Mandala
for the accomplishment of Enriching
on a mountain peak, in a cow-pen,
or by a stūpa containing relics.'

4. 'When the wise one has dug the soil
carefully according to the ritual,
he should place gem-stones
mixed with herbs in the centre.
He should also fill up the site
with yellow soil.
Having carefully made it level,
he should draw the Mandala upon it.'

5. 'Now, first of all the *mantrin* who is skilled in the rite should transform himself into Vajra-varada (Mañjuśrī), who resides in his own mandala, with his mantra and *mudrā*. Next he should set off the boundary and take possession of the site with the Noble Acala. The third, fifth or seventh day of the new moon, or at the full moon are all suitable. The auspicious planets are Mercury or Jupiter, and the constellations are *Abhijit*, *Dhaniṣṭā*, *Jyeṣṭhā* or *Rohiṇī*[1]. The *mantrin* should transform himself into Mahā-Vairocana and taking a yellow cord he should mark out the Mandala according to the previous measurements. Then circumambulating the mandala, he should enter within. (199a) Next he should recite the *Prajñā-pāramitā* and make obeisances.'

6. 'Having transformed himself into Vairocana, he should take up yellow pigment and
'Set the letter *KA* there,
which is then Kanaka-muni,
with golden shining light,

who resides in *samādhi*,
and has overcome harm-doing.'

7. 'Then having drawn the Mandala with its archway, the gateway should always be opened out towards the west. The exterior should be enclosed with three squares and the deities should be arranged therein as before. Its specific details are as follows: Samantabhadra should be placed as his banner symbol with his letter *SA*, in the place of the Noble Ākāśa-garbha. The Noble Jambhala should be placed as his citron[2] fruit symbol and his letter *JAṂ*, which has the attribute of nectar, in the place of Ūrṇā. Yaśovatī should be placed as her *priyaṅgu*[3] symbol with her letter *YA*, in the place of the Noble Bhṛkuṭī. The Noble Gaurī should be placed as her lotus symbol with her letter *ŚRĪ*, in the place of the Noble Pāṇḍara-vāsinī. Subāhu should be placed as his vajra symbol with his letter *HŪṂ*, in the place of the Noble Sumbhā. Vajra-sena should be placed as his vajra symbol with his letter *SA*, in the place of Amṛta-kuṇḍali. Śakra and the Four World Guardians should be arranged in the places of the Gods of the Pure Abode. Then vajras should be drawn all around, between the two outer lines and in the corners.'

8. 'Next the hearth should be made within the courtyard on the right side of the Mandala:

'It should be made square with a rim,
two cubits measure in width.
It should be encircled with vajras.
Make it just one cubit in depth,
the rim raised a little-finger's height.
Smear it with a plaster of yellow clay, (199b)
and mark it with a six inch lotus symbol,
four inches in height.

'At the three watches of the day, smear it with cow's dung which has not fallen to the ground.'

9. 'Then as before, imagine accurately the features and signs of the chief deity of the Mandala and so forth, and worship them with perfumes, flowers and so on. Regarding that, the distinctive features are these: when you ask the Bhagavat Vairocana to take up his abode and worship him with the offerings of perfumes, flowers and so forth, you should do that having transformed yourself into Vajra-varada.'

10. 'Now the distinctive features of the flowers and so forth should be described:

'The most excellent perfume for Enriching
is saffron mixed with camphor.
If you cannot obtain that, you should mix
anything which is sweet-smelling and yellow.
You should get *campaka* flowers,
yūthika and yellow jasmine,
or any other fragrant yellow ones

and offer those.
The incense the wise one should offer
to accomplish the rite of Enriching
is saffron mixed with *agaru*[4],
and those mixed with sugar.
The most excellent incense
is *gugguli*[5] and sandalwood mixed with butter.
The wise *mantrin* should also offer incense
of *sāla*[6] resin mixed with saffron.
The wise one should also offer lamps
with wicks made of yellow cotton
in fine gold receptacles,
or else yellow dishes are permissible.
He should make the oil fragrant
with grains of incense,
or else he should offer pure lamps
using oil from sesame seeds.
He should offer yellow rice-gruel,
with *kṛśara* and fine butter,
and also yellow broths,
and similar fruit-cakes.
The oblations for Enriching
should be with perfumed water,
mixed with yellow flowers,
and likewise rice and *dūrvā*[7] grass,
put into yellow containers.' (200a)

11. 'Having thus prepared the offerings as they should be, he should next transform himself into Vajra-varada, and going to the exterior, he should make the cast-offerings for the [ten] directions. Then having rinsed his hands, he should enter within.'

12. 'He should make obeisances to all the Buddhas and place the materials to be burnt which have been sprinkled, in front of the hearth as before. He should sit in the lotus position on *kuśa* grass that has been spread upon the ground and next he should imagine himself to be the Body of Mahā-vairocana. He should anoint the interior of the house with yellow incense and also scatter yellow flowers, and spread *kuśa* grass there. Then taking fire either from the house of a *kṣatriya* or from a king's palace, he should purify it by sprinkling. *Plakṣa*[8] or *udumbara*[9] wood should be lit. Next he should imagine an earth mandala at the bottom of the hearth and also the letter *YA* with an *anusvāra* resting upon a lotus: *YAṂ*. He should imagine Agni appear from that letter *YAṂ* within the hearth. He resembles gold in colour and has his hair bound up upon his head. He is three-eyed and has four hands in which he holds a rosary, a water-jar and makes the *Mudrā* of Bestowing Fearlessness. He is dressed in yellow robes, wears crossed yellow cords over his chest and has a triangular design made with the impressions of three

finger-tips, marked with the letter *RA*, which is golden coloured. He emits blazing tongues of fire and has great power. Thus imagining Agni arisen from the shining light of the king of mantras, the *mantrin* should then cleanse him with sprinkled water, wash his face and offer him the oblation. Perfume, flowers and so forth should also be offered with his specific mantra. *NSB OṂ AGNAYE SVĀHĀ.* Next, three measures of yoghurt mixed with honey and butter, or with black sesame, should be offered to the fire. (200b) Then seven full measures of butter should be offered with the long and short spoons, which are to be made of *bilva*[10] wood. Next he should burn three offerings of firewood cut from the heart-wood of *plakṣa* or *udumbara*, the full thickness of the wood and a cubit in length, which has been dipped in butter, and also three full measures of butter.'

13. 'Then, imagining the body-images of the deities as before, he should burn three measures of offerings to them, with their essences. Next, thinking of all the Buddhas and meditating on *bodhicitta*, he should imagine the body-image of his tutelary deity and burn three measures of offerings as before and burn the materials described in his *sādhana* for the attainment. He should first recite with *OṂ*, followed by the words, 'glory', 'noble', 'possessions', or 'wholesome treasure', to which *SVĀHĀ* should be added. Or else, he should burn measures of offerings, mentioning whatever material he wishes to transform with *SVĀHĀ*. When he has made the burnt offerings in that manner, he should follow the sequence of *bodhicitta* and so forth as before.'

14. 'Now, the practitioner who engages in the ritual
should dress himself in yellow robes,
and hold a clean yellow towel.
His mind firm and extensive,
silently and free from avarice,
he should always delight in *bodhicitta*.
When he first does the ritual at the three times,
he should drink rice gruel or milk,
and then undertake the rite of Enriching.
Whatever enrichment he wishes for
will swiftly be attained.
Swords, wheels, vajras,
realgar, antimony, bezoar,
wish-fulfilling gems, vases, clothes,
showers of wealth, shoes,
parasols, carriages, horses,
likewise many-storied buildings, (201a)
lotuses, tridents,
rosaries, maces, water-pots,
vīṇās, javelins or arrows,
begging bowls and staves,
or whatever item he wishes
will be transmuted in this Mandala.'

III
THE RITUAL FOR THE SUBDUING *HOMA*

1. 'Furthermore, this *homa* which
accomplishes the rite of mastery,
was taught with a kind heart
by the Illuminator of the world.
I shall explain all about it
so listen if you desire union.'

2. 'First a site should be sought out,
which is in the south-east
of a town or else a wood:
an uninhabited house,
a solitary tree or a cemetery,
or else a shrine to Śiva,
a shrine to the Mothers or a cave.
There the *mantrin* should draw the Mandala
and undertake the rite of subduing
on the ninth day of the new moon.
The wise one should draw the Mandala
at the time of the Sun or Mars,
with the constellations *Puṣyā*,
Kṛttikā, *Maghā* or *Viśakhā*[1].'

3. 'Regarding that, the *mantrin* should first transform himself into Vajrapāṇi and carry out the purification and taking possession of the site which has red-coloured earth. Next he should transform himself into Mahā-vairocana and take up a cord reddened with safflower dye, which has been empowered with the Mantra of the Noble Acala, and mark out the Mandala. It should be triangular, with a gate facing towards the east. It should also be carefully constructed with portals, archways and a border.'

4. 'Then taking up fine red pigment,
he should place there the blazing letter, (201b)
the letter *RA* which has an *anusvāra*,
resembling the rising sun.
It is the most excellent conqueror
of those who are very hard to guide.
Having brought to mind all the Buddhas,
he should fully draw the Mandala,
the triangle of which may be five cubits,
or else seven or nine in size.
In accordance with the mantra attainment
it should be divided into three parts.
The deities should be arranged as before,
The wise one should act as the Lord of the Family,

and the other deities should be arranged
by the wise one as appropriate.'

5. 'He should place both Keśinī and Upakeśinī as their mace and noose symbols in the place of Ākāśa-garbha. Vajrāṅkuśī should be placed as her arrow symbol in the place of Sumbhā. Mūrdhaṭaka should also be placed as his arrow symbol. On the outside, the four assistants should be drawn as noose symbols. Then he should carry out all the rituals as before. He should offer red perfumes, flowers and so forth.'

6. 'The hearth should be made in the same place as before. It should be twenty inches in length with a two inch high rim around it and one little-finger in depth. In the centre he should paint an eight inch vajra in red. That hearth should also be made triangular in shape.'

7. 'Next he should transform himself into Vajrapāṇi and make the cast-offerings outside. Then taking fire from the house of a washerman, he should purify it by sprinkling as before. He should light the fire with *khadira*, *aśoka* or *karavīra* wood[2]. Likewise he should transform himself into Vairocana and imagine a fire mandala on the bottom of the hearth, in which he places a *RA* letter. He should imagine that *RA* letter which radiates out a blazing garland of fire changing into the body-image of Agni. (202a) He is the colour of the rising sun, difficult to restrain, with three eyes and has his tawny hair bound up upon his head. He has four hands which hold a mace, a noose, a rosary and a water-jar. He is dressed in red robes and wears red cords crossed over his chest and he is marked with the letter *RAṂ*. He radiates red light from blazing tongues of fire. Having imagined Agni in this manner, the *mantrin* should purify him with sprinkled water and offer him the oblation. While reciting his mantra, the *mantrin* should give him perfumes, flowers and so forth.'

8. 'Then he should burn seven measures of *karavīra* firewood which has been smeared with mustard oil and red sandalwood. Next he should burn seven measures of offerings to the deities who have been arranged in the Mandala and, as before, he should imagine the body-image of his tutelary deity and place it there. Likewise, he should burn measures of offerings and the materials which are prescribed in the rules for the ritual. Likewise at the end, he should do the meditation on *bodhicitta* and other rituals. For this ritual, all the utensils for the Mandala should be red. The hearth should also be anointed with red sandalwood and strewn with pieces of red flowers at the three watches of the day.'

9. 'The noble one should wear red robes,
adorned with red perfume and garlands,
with red cords crossed over his chest.
He should know the special features of *bodhicitta*.
Moreover, he should eat fruit as food.

He should always recite and burn the offerings
with joy, smiling and silent,
uniting his mind with the mind [of the other].
One who imagines the body-image of the deity
will be able to undertake with the fire,
all the attainments without exception
of the rite of Subduing.
Whoever has undertaken the rite,
in this manner, knowing the ritual,
will gain control after one month
of his beloved or her daughter,
If he does the *homa* for two months,
the *mantrin* will quickly draw to himself
***yakṣiṇīs* and likewise**
girls of the subterranean realm (202b)
with the male and female assistants.
This praises in brief here
the *homa* for Subduing.'

IV
THE RITUAL FOR THE *HOMA* OF THE FIERCE ACTIONS

1. 'I shall now explain completely
the ritual for the Fierce Actions.
Whether *yakṣas*, *mahoragas* or fierce ghosts,
asuras, *gandharvas*, *kinnaras*,
wrathful beings who delight in harming,
likewise obstructors and gremlins,
ghosts, witches, *rākṣasas*,
ḍākiṇīs and goblins,
or wrathful, arrogant humans
who are powerful and do cruel deeds:
in order to control these, the *mantrin*
should engage in the Ferocious Rite.
But the Ferocious Ritual should not be used
against those whose faults are small.'

2. 'To the south of the town
the ascetic should seek out a site
with black soil, in a lonely cemetery,
a hermitage or a tranquil old grove.
On the eighth day of the new moon
or else on the fourteenth day,
with the planets Saturn or Mars,
under the constellations *Hasta*,
Citrā, *Aśvinī*, *Uttara-phalguṇī*,
and likewise *Punar-vasu* and *Svāti*[1].
such are the Ferocious constellations.'

3. 'At the time of any one of these,
the *mantrin* furious like Yama
should draw the fearful Mandala
which severs the life of opponents.
The *mantrin* should transform himself
into Vajrasattva with his *mudrā*.
He who is without fear regarding mantras
should prepare the site as before.'

4. 'Then having taken possession of it
with most powerful Acala,
he should make himself into Vairocana
with his letter and *mudrā*.'

5. 'Taking a blue cord spun by a young girl, (203a)
he should mark out the Mandala.
He should make it triangular

and circular on the outside.
The wise one should fix the size
according to the rite,
either four cubits, five or eight,
likewise twelve or sixteen.'

6. 'Then with black pigment
or else cemetery ashes,
the wise one should place there a *Hā*,
[which changes into Trailokya-vijaya]
radiant with a garland of tongues of fire,
fearful like the fire at the end of time,
the colour of monsoon clouds,
his fangs are bared in his mouth,
he is crowned with a vajra in his hand.
He threatens all the armies of demons
and all wrathful ones.'

7. 'Having placed such a letter there
he who is wise in painting,
the wise one should draw the Mandala.
It should be decorated with many pennants,
with archways and portals,
and pierced with a great gate.
The placement of the Lord of the deities
should be fixed as before.
Having opened the gate to the north,
he should make the remaining gates.'

8. 'Next he should place Yama as his spear symbol in the place of the Noble Ākāśa-garbha. The Wrathful Noble Aparājita should be placed as his axe symbol in the place of Ūrṇā. Amogha-paśa, Ekajaṭā and Haya-grīva should be placed as their noose, axe and vajra-mace in sequence in the place of Mahā-sthāma-prāpta, Bhṛkuṭī and the Noble Tārā. The Wrathful Candra-tilaka should be placed as his vajra symbol in the place of Sumbhā. Durdharṣa and Abhimukha should be placed as mace symbols before the gate. Yama and Kālarātrī should be placed together in the place of the gods of the Pure Abode. Nirṛti should also be placed as his sword symbol.'

9. 'The hearth should face the gate within the courtyard. (203b) All around the outside of the Mandala, pennants should be drawn. The hearth for the fire should be made like that for Subduing. Its special features are that it should have a circular rim around the outside and be decorated with many pennants. He should imagine the deities of the Mandala in their respective body-images as before and perform the acts of offering. Then having made offerings as should be done, the *mantrin* should transform himself into Vajrapāṇi and make the cast-offerings for the [ten] directions outside as

before. In regard to the specific types of incense and so forth, he should offer black perfume or red sandalwood mixed with juniper charcoal, blue *aparājita*[2] flowers or else other blue flowers. For incense, *sāla* resin mixed with molasses should be offered. For the lamps, pungent mustard oil in black receptacles with black wicks should be used. The foodstuffs to be offered should be *kṛśara*, or else salty and bitter black foods and broths. Beans, *kṛśara*, cooked or raw meat and fish should be given as the cast-offerings for the [ten] directions.'

10. 'Having made the cast-offerings according the specified ritual, the *mantrin* should obtain fire from the house of an outcast or a cemetery, he should light the fire with wood from a cemetery, *bhallātaka* or *vibhītaka* wood[3].'

11. 'Transforming himself into Mahā-vairocana, he should imagine a wind mandala at the bottom of the hearth and place the letter *HŪṂ* there. That letter *HŪṂ* should be imagined changing into the body-image of Agni. He is a smoky, three-eyed and four-faced Acala, black in colour, who is extremely terrible. He is difficult to look at and has his tawny hair bound up on his head. His radiance is smoky like blue rain clouds. He wears blue robes and wears blue cords crossed over his chest. Four fangs are bared in each of his mouths and his face is extremely wrathful. In his hands he holds a sword, a noose, a mace and a water-pot. (204a) He is marked with the letter *RA*. His brows are creased in anger. He is surrounded with blazing fire which is sooty and harsh, that emits *Hūṃ* sounds, with garlands of radiant rays of light which are copper coloured. Having imagined that Agni who is like the fire which appears at the end of time, the *mantrin* should offer him perfumes and so forth with his mantra. *OṂ AGNAYE JĀTI TRAṬ HŪṂ PHAṬ*.'

12. 'Next he should burn three measures of *kṛśara* mixed with pungent mustard oil and seven measures of poison, blood and black mustard. Also he should offer *bhallātaka* or *vibhītaka* firewood with sharp points, smeared with pungent mustard oil and black mustard. Then imagining the Lord of the Mandala and the other deities as before, he should burn measures of those materials as offerings for them, with their specific mantras.'

13. 'Next he should imagine and establish his tutelary deity as before and offer as much as he wishes of the materials described in his own ritual text, holding them with his thumb and fore finger, in a wrathful manner, and reciting the mantras accompanied with *PHAṬ*.'

14. 'Then he should perform the purification with meditation on *bodhicitta* and so forth.'

15. 'Any *mantrin* who performs
this kind of fierce rite

should do it here in this manner,
burning such things as *kuśa* grass
for thirty three sessions.
The noble one should wear blue robes,
adorned with blue perfumes and garlands,
and wear blue cords crossed over his chest.
He should always cleave to *bodhicitta.*
For food, he should eat salt, pepper,
black mustard and *kṛśara* foodstuffs.
He should be skilled in arranging the deities,
pure and endowed with the highest morality,
energetic and heroic,
wrathful like the destroyer of the world.
Facing the south silently,
he should sit with his face turned upwards,
and continually undertake the *homa* and recitation.
He who is skilled in guarding and protecting,
who does the *homa* at night,
should engage in the Fierce Practice.' (204b)

V
THE ARRANGEMENT OF THE MEDITATIONAL LETTERS AND INITIATION

1. Then the Bhagavat Vairocana expounded the Dharma concerning the inherent nature of the continuum of reality which is emptiness, the non-dual sphere of experience, the essence of interdependent arising, the causal basis of the attainment of non-conceptualizing Awareness by those who engage in the Bodhisattva practice, which is free from all proliferations, which is radiant and pure, which is accomplished by the *manas*, which is perfect and causes perfection.

2. Then at that moment, the Bodhisattva Mahāsattva, the most compassionate Avalokiteśvara entered into the *samādhi* of All-knowing Awareness and said to Vajrapāṇi, the Lord of the Secret Ones, 'Lord of the Secret Ones! How are those who have undertaken to establish themselves in the Mantra Method to attain the experiential sphere of All-knowing Awareness, which is in harmony with emptiness, which bestows the attainments of all mantras, which is unlocalized, which is without substantial existence, which is devoid of both a ground for attributes and the attributes themselves, which causes the attainment of the Mahāyāna and which bestows immortality?'

3. When he had asked that, Vajrapāṇi, the Lord of the Secret Ones, who reveals the secrets of all the Tathāgatas, looked at the face of the Bhagavat Vairocana and asked him this, 'Bhagavat! As the most compassionate Bodhisattva Avalokiteśvara, who looks upon the lives of all beings, has questioned me in this way, I ask the Bhagavat to expound the Dharma concerning that experiential sphere which benefits all beings, which causes the attainment of the Mahāyāna, which is non-dual and without attributes, which bestows the attainments of the all mantra methods, (205a) whose inherent nature is the quintessence of interdependent arising, which is in harmony with the continuum of reality, which causes all the realms of the worlds of the ten directions to arise and which is the experiential sphere of emptiness!'

4. When he had asked this, the Bhagavat Vairocana, Tathāgata Arhat Samyaksaṃbuddha, who has completely perfected the Three Ways, who thinks of all beings to liberate them from the ocean of all concepts, [taught] the inconceivable essence[1] of all the Bodhisattvas. This essence bestows the attainments of all mantras, causes obstacle-makers to be fearful, exorcises all ghosts, is without form, sound, odour, taste, touch, location, *manas*, consciousness and letters, is inexpressible, without proliferations and is unique. Vairocana spoke this to Vajrapāṇi, the Lord of the Secret Ones:

5. 'The Great Sage says that the Tathāgata
has taught the causes
of causally produced phenomena,

and likewise their cessation[2].
Because the relative does not exist,
and the consummate is also different,
duality does not exist:
that is the nature of the eight consciousnesses.'

6. Then after those multitudes in the assembly directly comprehended those two verses in accordance with their meaning, by various diverse ideas and understanding, through the power of the miraculous creations formed by each one of the letters, those Bodhisattvas cried out, 'Excellent! Excellent!' to the Bhagavat.

'Those who abide in the Mantra Method,
who meditate on this reality
which is praised by the Perfect Buddhas,
will become Buddhas themselves.'

7. Then at that moment, the Bodhisattva Mahāsattva Avalokiteśvara, empowered by the Bhagavat Vairocana, asked the Bhagavat the following: (205b)

'If the *mantrin* accomplishes attainments
by the unadulterated mind itself
which has transcended concepts,
how much more so conditioned phenomena!
When one has tamed the horse-like mind
by means of equipoise,
and has made both compassion
and loving-kindness steady,
one will swiftly accomplish firm attainments.
Most excellent *A* is the seed-syllable
of the eternal non-arising of phenomena;
the holy Jinas have said
that *A* is emptiness.
It is all the letters of the alphabet
and likewise the two extensions[3],
therefore you should imagine
the changeless that is endowed with letters.
From it appear *I*, *U*, *Ṛ* and *Ḷ*
and the augmented vowels[4].
Most excellent *A* is the best manifestation,
through it liberation will be attained.
The five groups of sounds:
the *Ka* group, the *Ca* group,
likewise the excellent *Ṭa* group,
the *Ta* group and the *Ba* group,
the five with a nasal sound,
and *Ya*, *Ra*, *La*, *Va* and *Śa*,
are all perfected by the supreme lord *A*.

Most excellent of those vast meanings,
it carries out many kinds of aims.
Enlightenment is attained with *A*,
likewise *I* is also a magnetizer,
slaying is accomplished with *U*,
***Ṛ* is for rites of subduing,**
***O* is the conqueror of *rākṣasas*,**
***E* is said to be for binding,**
and *AI* is the essence of the *nāgas*:
all of them are excellent and holy.
If you meditate and recite
all the augmented letters,
together with the *anusvāra* and *visarga*,
ever conjoined with the continuum of reality,
you will accomplish attainments.'

8. Then the Bhagavat Vairocana said to the Bodhisattva Mahāsattva Avalokiteśvara:
'Excellent! Excellent! O Great Being
who has realized the Tenth Level!
You have explained in totality the true nature
of inexhaustible reality of the Sugatas.
You have understood the profound secret
of which Vajrapāṇi spoke!
It is excellent you know that!'

9. Then Vajrapāṇi, the Lord of the Secret Ones, asked the Bhagavat this:
'O Hero, most excellent Wheel-turning King (206a)
who is the continuum of reality in nature,
* * * * * * * * * * * * * * * * * * [A]
Having imagined yourself thus
with the *mudrā* of the World Hero
and the unborn letter,
well controlled by *bodhicitta*,
all activities will be accomplished
by non-dual union with emptiness.
If you imagine the Lord of the pure continuum of reality
accompanied with his seed letter,
and then recite in pellucid equipoise,
you will accomplish the attainments.
The *mantrin* who bathes, confesses his sins,
who is devoted to solitude,
and imagines the *mudrā* and garland of letters
will accomplish steadfast attainments.

A There seems to be a hiatus at this point in all editions. Vajrapāṇi's question to the Buddha is missing. What follows is clearly the Buddha's reply to Vajrapāṇi.

If accomplished with these mantras
that are conjoined with the continuum of reality,
there will be nothing unaccomplished
in the human and non-human realms.'

10. 'Lord of the Secret Ones! Therefore, one who performs the recitation should establish the revolving wheel [of letters] in its own Mandala, on the occasion of that initiation ritual.'

VI
THE RITUAL FOR RECITATION

1. Then Vajrapāṇi asked the Bhagavat this: 'Bhagavat! Please explain the actual nature of the inconceivable continuum of reality which transcends the levels of mind, which you have perfectly realized, to Bodhisattvas according to their wishes and inclinations, with various expedient means. Please explain this, Sugata!'

2. 'First of all, you should confess each of your sins with this ritual: "May all the Buddhas and Bodhisattvas think of me! I, [name], confess in the presence of all the Buddhas and Bodhisattvas all those sins, those unwholesome deeds which I have done, caused to be done, or have consented to be done in this and earlier lives, while wandering in *saṃsāra*, from now until I reside in the core of Enlightenment!" This should be recited a second and a third time.' (206b)

3. 'Then you should take refuge in the Three Jewels, in the presence of all the Buddhas and Bodhisattvas: "May all the Buddhas and Bodhisattvas think of me! I, [name], take refuge in the Buddha Bhagavat, I take refuge in the self-aware supreme and tranquil *dharmakāya* of the Tathāgata and I take refuge in the Saṅgha of the irreversible Noble Great Bodhisattvas of the four quarters, from now until I reside in the core of Enlightenment!" This should be recited a second and a third time.'

4. 'Then you should offer yourself: "May all the Buddhas and Bodhisattvas think of me! I, [name], offer everything I have to all the Buddhas and Bodhisattvas, so I ask them all to accept me out of pity for me, from now until I reside in the core of Enlightenment!" This should be recited a second and a third time.'

5. 'Then you should make the *Samaya Mudrā* and recite its Mantra: *NSB ASAME TRISAME SAMAYE SVĀHĀ*. Next, you should transform yourself into the continuum of reality: *NSB DHARMADHĀTU-SVABHĀVĀTMAKO 'HAṂ*. Next, transform yourself into Vajrasattva: *NSB VAJRĀTMAKO 'HAṂ*.'

6. 'Then you should generate the aspiration to Enlightenment: "May all the Buddhas and Bodhisattvas think of me! Just as the Buddhas and Bodhisattvas direct their thoughts to Enlightenment [knowing that] their minds are primordially unborn and empty in nature, because they are devoid of all entities, free from the psycho-physical constituents, the perceptual elements and sources, perceived objects and perceiving subject, without autonomous existence and are [characterized by] sameness, in the same way I, [name], also direct my thoughts from now until I reside in the core of Enlightenment!" (207a) This should be recited a second and a third time.'

7. 'Then making the *Mudrā* of Fulfilment on the crown of your head, you should imagine such offerings as perfumes, flowers and so forth, in all the assemblies of Tathāgatas, and recite this *Vidyā* Queen three times: *NSB ABHISMARAYE SPHARAṆA HI MĀṂ GAGANA KHAṂ* | *DHARMADHĀTV-ĀKĀŚA-SAMATĀYA* | *SARVA-TATHĀGATA-PARIŚODHANA-MAṆḌALE MAMA PRANIDHI PUṆYA-JÑĀNA-BALENA* | *SARVA-TATHĀGATA-ADHIṢṬHĀNA-BALENA DHARMA-DHĀTV-ADHIṢṬHĀNA-BALENA CA SVĀHĀ.* The *Mudrā* of Fulfilment is the one which is like an open lotus upon the crown of one's head. That is the definition of the *Mudrā* of Fulfilment.'

VII
THE GREAT MANDALA FROM WHICH THE *TATHĀGATAS* ARISE

1. Then, having revealed the play of the inconceivable continuum of reality, the Bhagavat Vairocana desired to reveal the inconceivable sphere of experience (*gocara*) as well. From the *uṣṇīṣa* on his head, he emitted a web of light rays called the Dharma Treasury, with which he illumined the darkness of an infinite number of minds in the realms of beings. Then that great arrayed web of light rays encircled all the Tathāgatas who were abiding in the palace of the continuum of reality, the transformation and vast play of the Tathāgata, which was as extensive as the realm of space, and then illumined all the circles of the assemblies of all beings and brought about the complete protection of all realms of beings without remainder. It both satisfied those beings born in the hell, animal and ghosts states of existence, and it also transformed the worlds of gods and humans to include them within the matrix of the Tathāgata, the *Ghana-vyūha* [realm]. Then it also transformed the inconceivable continuum of reality with the outflow of the transformational power of the Tathāgata's merit. Since the Bhagavat had not completed the task of the continuum of reality, he entered the *samādhi* of the great King of Mandalas, the matrix which protects infinite realms of beings, (207b) called the "Treasury from which Emerges the Matrix of Great Compassion".

2. When he had entered it, he said to the Vajradharas such as Vajrapāṇi who were equal in number to all the atoms in the Buddha fields of the ten directions, 'Nobly-born Ones! There is a mandala called the "Source of All Tathāgatas", the regal matrix which protects infinite realms of beings, by which Bodhisattvas will attain the Tathāgata Level and actualize the inconceivable continuum of reality, with little difficulty, if they rely upon it.'

3. When he had spoken thus, all the Vajradharas such as Vajrapāṇi who were equal in number to all the atoms in the Buddha fields of the ten directions spoke with one voice, 'Bhagavat! Now is the time! Sugata! Now is the moment! Bhagavat! It is excellent, so out of pity for us, we ask the Bhagavat to explain the great Mandala which is the transformed array.

'Dharma Master, Dharma Lord,
you who are unending,
you who are the Teacher endowed
with great Awareness,
you who are the sole Lord of the Levels,
you who have successfully
accomplished the accumulations,
you who have put down the burden
and reached the end of existence,
Great Lord of Physicians,

Knower of reality,
You who are unobstructed
and uninterrupted,
You who have realized
Suchness and the limits of being,
without proliferations,
You who are refuge, support, ground,
Nirvāṇa and tranquility,
you who bring about liberation,
you who are free from illness,
you who are free from imperfections,
you who are beyond all verbalization,
you who destroy all phenomena!'
When all those Vajradharas
had thus praised him with those titles
with constantly joyful minds,
they asked him to guide them.

4. **The All-knowing One who is free from malady**
understood what they had requested and said, (208a)
'I shall explain the Mandala which arises
from the matrix of great compassion!'

5. Then Vajrapāṇi, the Lord of the Secret Ones, bowed down at the feet of the Bhagavat and then asked him this, 'Bhagavat! What is the name of this Mandala?' When he had asked this, the Bhagavat said to Vajrapāṇi, the Lord of the Secret Ones, 'Vajrapāṇi! The name of this Mandala is "That Which Reveals The Arising Of Buddhas In World Systems Where There Are No Buddhas".'

6. Then Vajrapāṇi, the Lord of the Secret Ones, asked the Bhagavat this, 'Has not the Bhagavat said that the Tathāgata Arhat Samyak-saṃbuddhas are like space? Bhagavat, if the Tathāgatas neither arise nor perish, why is it that the Bhagavat speaks of Buddhas arising in world systems where there are no Buddhas?' The Bhagavat replied, 'Vajrapāṇi! When Buddhas who have been emanated enter complete Nirvāṇa, then the Bodhisattvas who engage in the Bodhisattva practice by way of mantras in those world systems cause beings to be fully matured through the transformation of the array of the Great Mandala.'

7. When he had said this, Vajrapāṇi then said to the Bhagavat, 'Bhagavat! This is wonderful! It should be known that those great Bodhisattvas undertake a task of great difficulty, who completely perfect beings of diverse beliefs who have attachment, hatred, stupidity, dissimulation, deceit or doubts, according to their individual inclinations.'

8. The Bhagavat replied, 'Vajrapāṇi! You should know that because those Nobly-born Ones do not venerate just one Buddha, those Nobly-born Ones

generate the roots of wholesomeness in the presence of many Buddhas. They also arise from three gates to the beholding of reality (*dharmāloka-mukha*). What are those three? They are the gate to beholding it by way of great compassion, the gate to beholding it by way of the profound Dharma and by way of making offerings to and revering the Tathāgatas. You should know that those Nobly-born Ones are endowed with these three gates to the beholding of reality.'

9. Then the Bhagavat gazed upon the Bodhisattvas who were residing in the great palace of the continuum of reality, with his eyes of Great Compassion and Kindness, and said to Vajrapāṇi, the Lord of the Secret Ones, 'Vajrapāṇi! Listen to the attributes of the Vajra Master! With regards those, first the Master should have generated the aspiration to Enlightenment, he should engage in the Bodhisattva training, be controlled by the Bodhisattva discipline, be compassionate, have great faith, abide in the profound Dharma, be skilled in the Perfection of Insight method, be adept in the arts, sagacious and careful.'

10. 'Whoever has trained in the mantra practices,
the *mudrās* and the mandala actions,
and has received the authority from a guru
to carry out the task of drawing mandalas,
who is free from doubts
about the Buddha, Dharma and Saṅgha,
and who strives to protect
unlimited realms of beings:
that wise one is fit to draw
the Mandala of the Buddhas.'

11. 'The resolute one who has
fully perfected all attributes,
and who is intelligent and heroic,
is able to pacify obstacles,
whether his own or of the trainees.
Any *mantrin* who has realized
the meaning of ultimate truth,
whose faith is extensive,
who is skilled in crafts, without pride,
whose actions are exalted,
who also has faith in the exalted,
who is joyful after hearing
the vowed aspirations of Buddhas
and the protector Bodhisattvas,
who is always satisfied,
who undertakes the mantra practice,
and exerts himself in recitation,
whose thoughts are without insincerity,

**who has no regard for worldly things,
and who cleaves to the mantras:
if he has those qualities
he is esteemed as a Master by the Teacher.'**

**12. 'Moreover, anyone who dwells
detached from all phenomena
is also said by all the Buddhas
to teach the Arising of the Buddhas.'**

**13. 'Also, the *mantrin* who abides in
the Three *Samayas* praised
by all the Perfect Buddhas,
or in the abandonment of all faults,
is fit to draw the Mandala
even though he lacks some attributes.'**

**14. 'Anyone who has seen the rituals for the task
is suitable to make all mundane
and supra-mundane mandalas,
if they have all of such qualities.'**

15. 'If he is treated as a Master by others and if he knows that the trainees are well-motivated and have trust in him,

**'Then, knowing this, that Master
should carefully seek out a site:
lakes and delightful groves
that are adorned with ponds,
woods with fruits and flowers,
likewise such places where
there are bushes and large trees,
with geese, cranes, peacocks,
herons, parrots and mynahs;
he should diligently use those places.'**

**16. 'The *mantrin* should draw
the wealth-increasing Mandala
amongst mountains with fruits and flowers,
or by pure and pleasing ponds,
streams with clean water,
or places where rivers bend to the right.'**

**17. 'The wise one should draw the Mandala
for use in the rite of Pacifying
in places which are very smooth,
where there are monasteries and houses,
temples and shrines,
or by a solitary tree or at a crossroad.'**

18. 'The Mandala for the wrathful rites
should be drawn in empty houses
or cemeteries, places which are rough,
foul and harsh, where fierce deeds are done,
likewise in unpleasant and fearful
caverns in the mountains.'

19. 'Peform the wrathful rites wrathfully,
the pacifying rites peacefully,
and the enriching rites luxuriously.'

20. 'Or, wherever one feels is definitely pleasing,
in that place one should apply oneself
to the task of drawing the relevant Mandala.'

21. 'Any person with a pure mind
who has abandoned doubts and so forth,
will thenceforth accomplish
all rites, without any fears.
The abandonment of concepts
is non-conceptualizing Enlightenment:
that will be attained by one
who has abandoned concepts,
but not by anyone else.'

22. 'Hence the wise one should abandon
confusion in all respects,
and wisely draw the Mandala
out of a desire to aid all worlds.
Neither time nor space exist,
nor creator and created,
with regards to all phenomena:
there is only [non-dual] reality.
The stupid who are veiled by ignorance
are intoxicated by causes and conditions,
so they do not realize that phenomena are empty,
but are always in the control of demons.'

23. 'Thus the Teacher who is endowed with Awareness
and whose realization is free from proliferations
taught the immeasurable Dharma
which is devoid of all concepts.'

24. Then the Bhagavat Vairocana entered into the *samādhi* called the "King of the Array of the Adornments of all Buddhas". When he had entered into that *samādhi*, rays of light called the "Adornment of all Buddha Fields" emerged from between his eyebrows. When they had emerged, everywhere

became illuminated. When they had illumined this Buddha Field, this universe of world-systems adorned with a lotus-base matrix formed from the maturation of the Tathāgata's [wholesome roots], adorned with divine portals, whose perceptual images and qualities could not be comprehended in even a hundred billion eons, became spread out like the palm of a hand. Having created this inconceivable array of the Tathāgata, those rays of light then became invisible in the crown of Vajrapāṇi's head.

25. No sooner had those rays of light (210a) become invisible, than Vajrapāṇi, the Lord of the Secret Ones, bowed down at the Bhagavat's feet and then asked him the following, 'Bhagavat! Please explain the transformation of the array of the Great Mandala!'. When he had asked this, the Bhagavat replied to the Bodhisattva Mahāsattva Vajrapāṇi, 'Vajrapāṇi! Listen to the transformation of the array of the Great Mandala!'. When he had said this, Vajrapāṇi listened to the Bhagavat.

26. 'Vajrapāṇi! The Mandala should be made in such suitable places as those mentioned, of any size from one cubit up to a *yojana*[1] but it should not be made more than a *yojana* in size.

27. 'There the site should be level and smooth,
well anointed with perfumes,
or else the *mantrin* should daub
it carefully with clean clay.'

28. 'Then empowering eight-inch pegs (*kīla*) one hundred and eight times with the All-purpose Mantra, the entire Mandala will be empowered so that it cannot be damaged by anything when he has inserted them squarely in the four corners. *NSV HAṂ KOṬAYA SAME MAHĀ-CAṆḌALI HŪṂ PHAṬ*.'

29. 'Then he should next gather together the articles needed for the Mandala and prepare them. Having protected them with either the All-purpose Mantra or the Mantra of the Noble Acala, he should have them placed to the north of the Mandala, or else he should empower them and place them there himself.'

30. 'Following that the trainees should be accepted. They should have great faith, be very pure, exert themselves in the Dharma, be of noble lineage and be highly motivated. He may accept one, two, three or as many as he wishes. He should tie three knots in cords spun by a young girl or any other cord, or even *kuśa* grass is acceptable, with the All-purpose Mantra, or the Mantra of the Noble Acala or the Unbearable One[2].

'Then consecrating them with the mantra
a hundred times or even more,
he should tie them onto their left arms (210b)
so that the trainees' actions may be successful.'

31. 'He should make tooth-sticks of *udumbara*,
that have been smeared with the scent of flowers,
that are very fine and have been protected.
They should be eight inches long,
one-pointed and of pleasing appearance.
Then the wise one should give them out;
facing the north or the east,
they should bite on the tooth-sticks
and then they should cast them down,
without looking and without deliberation.
According to where they fall,
so their actions will be successful.'

32. 'They should be made to hear
such sutras as the *Prajñā-pāramitā*.
To encourage the trainees
he should give them edifying teachings.'

33. 'If they see either dreams
that are auspicious or inauspicious,
they should relate these to the guru
so that their fortunes may be divined.
If they dream of stūpas, groves,
monasteries, books or gods,
wish-fulfilling gems, precious clothes,
or else of getting flowers and fruit,
or of obtaining in their dreams
various kinds of materials to be transmuted,
such as swords, wheels or *vīṇās*,
then such attainments as they desire will arise.
Whoever sees the sun, moon, fire
or sharp weapons, or else ocean-crossing,
elephants and horses,
will obtain the attainments without difficulty.
Such dreams as these are good
and so indicate certain success.
The opposite dreams are inauspicious:
if they see fearful things they will not succeed.
Asses, camels, dogs
owls, tigers, rats or crows,
people with oil smeared on their bodies,
rough and ugly naked people;
such inauspicious dreams as these
should be rejected by the wise one.'

34. 'Or else knowing that phenomena
are like dreams and gandharvas' cities,

the wise one should explain
that dreams lack any substantiality.'

35. Then Vajrapāṇi questioned the Bhagavat as follows, 'Bhagavat! Due to what cause and conditions are Bodhisattvas who engage in the Bodhisattva practice by way of mantras, unwavering with regard to such phenomena as these from the very first?' The Bhagavat replied, 'It is because those nobly-born ones are endowed with great compassion and view all phenomena (211a) as being complete liberation (*parinirvāṇa*). They know that both the attributes ordinary people perversely [believe in] and the absence of attributes are as one, so they are certain and unwavering as regards all those things.'

36. Then having transformed the vast and inconceivable continuum of reality, the Bhagavat said to Vajrapāṇi, the Lord of the Secret Ones, 'Vajrapāṇi! Listen for I shall tell you about the transformation of the array of the Great Mandala! Regarding that, the Master should first make himself clean and go to the south-west. Having made the divisions of Mandala on the ground, he should make obeisances to all the Buddhas and Bodhisattvas. Recollecting the pure continuum of reality, he should gaze upon the transformation of the infinite vast expanse of the array. Having gazed upon it, he should transform himself into Vajrasattva.

37. 'The wise one should measure out
the abodes of the deities with certainty,
using either a five coloured cord
or else he may do it mentally.
He should draw it with a pure mind,
so that it is completely square,
with four gates and archways,
together with extensive portals.
The *mantrin* should draw the mandala
with five types of powdered jewels
or else powdered rice,
or even with incense or ash.
It should have gates on the four sides,
and the west gate should be opened.
Then he should recollect the *Vidyā* Queen,
the great protectress Unbearable One,
or else the Noble Acala.
Having recollected the Perfect Buddha,
he should go to the south-western region,
and then having stretched out the cord,
he should go around it and return.
Then the perspicacious one
should go to the west,
and there he should face east

and stretch out the cord eastwards.
He who knows the technique for the cord
should always do thus at the beginning.'

38. 'Then sitting in the middle,
he should recollect the Tathāgatas:
the Lord Apāya-jaha,
Amitābha, the best of beings,
likewise Sarva-nīvaraṇa-viṣkambhin,
the Sage Saṃkusuma-rāja,
the Jina Vairocana (211b),
the Great Sage who has overcome Māra,
likewise he who is called Akṣobhya,
and the Buddha Dundubhi-svara-nirghoṣa.
With fervent feelings, the ascetic
should measure out three areas there.'

39. 'When he who is skilled in the rite
has carefully measured out the site thus,
he should read the *Prajñā-Pāramitā Sūtra*,
the Mother of the Buddhas and the wise Bodhisattvas,
or else other profound sutras
which define the Levels.'

40. 'Then having read, the perspicacious one
should circumambulate with incense.
Next he should make obeisances to the Buddhas
and to the Children of the Supreme Jinas,
and then the wise one should draw
the body-images of the Buddhas or their symbols.
Or else he should draw them all
in any other suitable way.'

41. Then the Bhagavat Vairocana said to Vajrapāṇi, the Lord of the Secret Ones, 'Lord of the Secret Ones! There are practices for the accomplishment of the inconceivable continuum of reality state, which when possessed by Bodhisattvas who engage in the Bodhisattva practice by way of mantras, will enable them to liberate with little difficulty the limitless realms of beings from the ocean of existence that is *saṃsāra*.' When he had said this, Vajrapāṇi asked the Bhagavat this, 'Bhagavat! Please explain that basis for accomplishment which, when possessed by the Bodhisattvas who engage in the Bodhisattva practice by way of mantras, will perfect all rituals and also delight the Tathāgatas!'

42. When he had asked this, the Bhagavat Vairocana transformed the vast continuum of reality state into the basis for accomplishment and then he explained the excellent practice.

43. 'Lord of the Secret Ones! For that, the Master should draw the Revolving Wheel Mandala about one *yojana* in size, with a residence made from fine "serpent's venom" sandalwood, (212a) **hung with large and small bells and jewelled awnings. It should be perfumed with various incenses of fine *agaru*, adorned above with nets of large and small bells made of many kinds of jewels linked with cords of fine gold, and resound with various melodious sounds of drums. The arches in the four directions should have garlands of pearls attached to them. It should be filled with cloth dyed in various colours, constructed with various structures and ornaments, and also illumined with many jewelled lamps.'**

44. 'Then while seated in the midst of the assembled Tathāgatas, he should transform himself into the pure continuum of reality itself or visualize its perceptual image. Making the Dharma Source *Mudrā* or the *Samaya Mudrā*, he should make those [trainees] who have entered the intrinsic nature of emptiness accept the Discipline of the Buddhas and Bodhisattvas, and the aspiration to Enlightenment. Then in order to purify the eye of supreme Awareness, he should teach them the *samayas*. These are the symbols of the inner Mandala for that: He should draw the triangular symbol of all the Buddhas in the east resting upon a lotus. This is its mantra: *NAMAḤ SARVA-BUDDHA-BODHISATTVĀNĀṂ A SARVA-TRAṆAKA SVĀHĀ.* To the right of the Bhagavat he should draw the banner of the wish-fulfilling gem of all the Bodhisattvas. Its mantra is *NAMAḤ SARVA-BUDDHA-BODHISATTVĀNĀṂ SAMANTA AMṚTE JVĀLA SVĀHĀ.* Below that he should draw the sword of Samantabhadra inserted into its mandala abode. Its mantra is *NAMAḤ SARVA-BUDDHA-BODHISATTVĀNĀṂ VAJRA RĀJA MĀLA SVĀHĀ.* To the left of the symbol of all the Buddhas, he should draw the Dharma Wheel symbol. Below that he should draw the symbols of Śākyamuni, a begging-bowl and monk's robes. On the right hand side of the Bhagavat he should draw the symbol of Gagana-locanā, (212b) **like an *uṣṇīṣa* resting on a lotus. Below her he should draw the symbol of Vajra-varada, a vajra placed upon an *utpala.* To the north of Samantabhadra he should place the symbol of Maitreya, a water-jar. To the west of the Bhagavat he should draw the symbol of Acala, infinite and with a vast radiance. To the south of the Bodhisattvas he should draw the symbol of all the Vajradharas.'**

45. 'Then omitting the courtyard in the outer area of the Mandala which has been divided into three parts, he should draw the symbol of all the messengers in the east. In the south-east corner he should draw the symbol of all the female messengers. The symbol of the messengers is a hook. The symbol of their entourage is a noose. On the southern and northern sides he should draw the symbols of the male and female servants. The symbol of the male servants is a sword, whilst curved knives and vajra spikes are the symbols of the female servants.

46. 'Then the *Prajñā Pāramitā Sūtra* should be read. When it has been read, he should arise and circumambulate the Mandala. Having done that he

should also make obeisances to the Bhagavat Buddhas. Then he should make the trainees circumambulate the Mandala. These trainees should have generated the wish for Enlightenment, have faith, be very clean, be firm in their vows, uphold the discipline, desire to protect all beings and be very compassionate. They should be blindfolded and not empty-handed, with their minds focussed one-pointedly upon the Mandala. Standing in the gateway of the second section of the Mandala, they should make the *Mudrā* of Fulfilment, the Dharma Source *Mudrā* or the *Samaya Mudrā*, recite the *Samaya* Mantra and be received into the Mandala. Then they should be made to cast their flowers. Wherever their flower falls, that is their deity. Those who are thus firm in the *samaya* should generate the idea that the Master is their teacher. The Master should also regard them as his children.'

47. 'Then taking into consideration the superior, middling and inferior mental streams of the trainees, he should bestow upon them the ritual for the yoga of entry into the practice of mantras. When he has done so, they will see the *samayas* in this array of the Great Mandala. Whether they have entered into the mundane or supramundane mandalas, they will enter into union (*samaya*). Those who have thus been transformed in the Great Mandala, who are devoid of sins, who are born of the Tathāgata lineage and who are motivated to protect limitless realms of beings, should be made to recollect the ritual for the yoga of entry into the practice of mantras.'

48. Then the Bhagavat Vairocana gazed upon the Bodhisattva Mahāsattvas who were arrayed in the abode of the continuum of reality with his eyes of great kindness and compassion. Smiling a little, he emitted the laugh called the 'Vow to Liberate Beings from all the Oceans of Samsaric Existence', desiring to reveal the utterly pure, supreme continuum of reality by means of entry into the Tathāgata's detailed knowledge[3]. Then rays of light called the 'Arising of the Realm of All Tathāgatas Everywhere' emerged from the orb of his great *uṣṇīṣa*. When those rays of light had emerged, they caused all the Bodhisattvas arrayed in the entourage of all the Tathāgatas to appear in the expanse of the world systems in the ten directions which exceeds the realm of space. They manifested the realm of entry into the inconceivable continuum of reality, they were seen in the mental activities of all beings, they made the pure and infinite continuum of reality perceptible, (213a) they revealed the sameness of phenomena which are equal to space, and they disported by way of the play of the continuum of reality[4]. Then they adorned the wind mandala[5] formed and created through the inconceivable maturation of the wholesome roots of the Tathāgata and through the intentions of the Tathāgata, with the array of the Buddha Fields of the ten directions. Having arranged the transformation of the Mandala of the Great Array in the region of space, they came to rest there.

49. No sooner had those great rays of light come to rest, than the following thought arose in the mind of Vajrapāṇi, the Lord of the Secret Ones, 'It is truly miraculous how these rays of light arisen from the Bhagavat, which

reveal formations never seen before, cover the region of space with various kinds of structures and reveal the great play of the Tathāgata, and then become invisible in the Tathāgata's face. Because of this, I am sure that today the Bhagavat desires to teach the Dharma-discourse of the play of all the Tathāgatas, the pure principle of entry into sameness by means of the pure accomplishment of the great detailed knowledge, so I shall ask the Bhagavat about it.'

Then Vajrapāṇi bowed down at the Bhagavat's feet and asked the Bhagavat this, 'Bhagavat! I have served you from the time when you first generated the wish for supreme and perfect Enlightenment up until the time when you actually became perfectly enlightened. (214a) While I did so, I never saw such a great miracle on those occasions when you previously had a great wish [to do something], while now thousands of rays of light, equal in number to all the atoms of the ten Buddha Fields, arise from the orb of your *uṣṇīṣa* and illumine all world systems which exceed the realm of space. So regarding this, I thought, "Today we shall obtain the pure principle which accomplishes the means of entry into the great detailed knowledge, the Dharma-discourse which is the emanation of the Perfect Enlightenment of all Tathāgatas, that the Bhagavat desires to teach to us!". Bhagavat! As that will be excellent, I ask you to teach us the pure principle which accomplishes the means of entry into the great detailed knowledge, the Dharma-discourse which is the emanation of the Perfect Enlightenment of all Tathāgatas, out of pity for us. It will also be made visible for creatures living in future times.'

50. When he had asked this, the Bhagavat replied to Vajrapāṇi, 'Excellent! Lord of the Secret Ones, excellent! It is excellent that you have asked about this matter. Lord of the Secret Ones! Therefore listen carefully and retain this in your mind, for I shall teach to you the Dharma-discourse which is the emanation of the Perfect Enlightenment of all Tathāgatas, the pure principle of entry into sameness by the pure means which brings about entry into the great detailed knowledge.'

51. 'Bhagavat! (214b) Let it be so!', said Vajrapāṇi and listened to the Bhagavat. The Bhagavat then said to him, 'Lord of the Secret Ones! The principle of emptiness is the principle of Perfect Enlightenment. The principle that there are no attributes is the principle of Perfect Enlightenment. The principle of the Tathāgata is the principle of Perfect Enlightenment. Thus these principles of Perfect Enlightenment should be cultivated by Bodhisattvas. Lord of the Secret Ones! This is the Dharma-discourse, the principle of entry into sameness by the pure means which brings about entry into the detailed knowledge of all Tathāgatas.'

52. Then the Bhagavat Vairocana transformed the vast and extensive infinitude of the continuum of reality and entered into the *samādhi* called the 'Maturation of the King of Unsullied Space, which is as Vast and Extensive as Space Itself'. No sooner had the Bhagavat entered this *samādhi* than from

his *uṣṇīṣa* there emerged rays of light called the 'Illumination of the Realm of all the Tathāgatas, the Revelation of the Inconceivably Extensive Realm'. When they had emerged, they appeared just like all the Tathāgatas and encircled the Bhagavat Vairocana many hundreds of thousands of times. They lit up the world systems in the ten directions with their great light and rested in the sky above. Then, having spread out the Great Mandala of the Secret Matrix, they illumined all world systems (215a) that are more extensive than the realm of space with the light of the three great *samayas*, and then transformed the realms of beings so that the sprouts of the three *samayas* might arise. Then those rays of light gathered together from the sky and flowed down onto the crown of Vajrapāṇi's head.

53. No sooner had those rays of light flowed down onto the crown of Vajrapāṇi's head than Vajrapāṇi, the Lord of the Secret Ones, attained the great *samādhi* called the 'Arising of the Realm of the Tathāgatas' at that instant. By attaining it, he became capable of abiding without duality on the Level of Tathāgatas. Then Vajrapāṇi, the Lord of the Secret Ones, was soothed by the delight of Tathāgata Awareness and with eyes unwavering he gazed at the Bhagavat Vairocana for a while. Smiling a little, he mentally asked the Bhagavat,

> 'What is a Tathāgata?
> What are the holy Jinas?
> What is a Bodhisattva?
> Why is one called a Buddha?
> Lord! I beg the Great Sage
> to clear away my confusion!
> When the famed Bodhisattvas
> have abandoned doubt and confusion,
> these Children of the Jinas will engage in
> the Mahāyāna, the King of Practices.'

54. When he had asked this, the Bhagavat replied to Vajrapāṇi, the Lord of the Secret Ones, 'Lord of the Secret Ones! It is excellent that you have thought of asking about this matter! Rare are beings who do not become terrified, very terrified, after having heard about this kind of principle which accomplishes the Dharma method. Lord of the Secret Ones! You should know that those Nobly-born Ones do not serve just one Buddha, but they cultivate wholesome roots under many thousands of Buddhas. (215b) Lord of the Secret Ones! Therefore Bodhisattvas who engage in the Bodhisattva practice by way of mantras should first of all realize an understanding of the Mahāyāna. Why is that? Lord of the Secret Ones, the Bodhisattvas who realize an understanding of the Mahāyāna will succeed in the Bodhisattva practice by way of mantras with only a little hardship. In this way, the Bodhisattva who engages in the Bodhisattva practice by way of mantras fully purifies the great direct knowledge (*mahā-abhijñā*).'

55. Then the Bhagavat Vairocana said to the Bodhisattva Vajrapāṇi, 'Lord of the Secret Ones! Listen carefully and retain this in your mind for I shall

explain this to you!'. When he had said this, Vajrapāṇi listened to the Bhagavat. Then the Bhagavat said this,

'One who is perfectly aware that
phenomena are like space in character,
and are non-dual with a single attribute,
with the Ten Strengths[6],
is called a [Perfect] Buddha.
One whose very nature is imperceptible
because he has abandoned even "ideas-only",
but knows intrinsically by Awareness,
is said to be a Tathāgata.
Enlightenment is space[-like] in nature,
devoid of all judgmental concepts:
whoever desires to realize that
is called a Bodhisattva.
One who has perfected the Ten Levels,
and has realized the Masteries,
who fully comprehends that phenomena
are empty and illusion-like,
and knows the mind-streams of all the world,
that one is called a Buddha.'

56. 'Lord of the Secret Ones! Thus, these are the mind states to be established by a Bodhisattva. (216a) Lord of the Secret Ones, by that discourse also you should know that there is no establishing or accomplishing of their minds by Bodhisattvas.'

57. Then Vajrapāṇi, the Lord of the Secret Ones, asked the Bhagavat this, 'Bhagavat! It is a great wonder that the Bhagavat Tathāgata Arhat Samyaksaṃbuddha teaches the Dharma-discourse for the direct understanding of the Mahāyāna to the Bodhisattva Mahāsattvas. Sugata! It is a great wonder! Bhagavat, I cannot say that those Nobly-born Ones are afraid of the miserable states of existence, nor that they fear the acts of demons, nor that they fear the eight obstacles[7], while they wander in the *saṃsāra* of the five states of existence. What is the reason for this? The Bodhisattvas who abide in a direct understanding of the Mahāyāna, do not abandon the supramundane path while living together with mundane people, but display all mundane activities out of expediency in order to mature beings fully. They do not fall from the direct understanding of the Mahāyāna.'

58. Then Vajrapāṇi, the Lord of the Secret Ones, entreated the Bhagavat, 'Bhagavat! Please explain the Mandala of the Great Secret Matrix, for that will bring about benefit and happiness for many people.' When he had asked this, the Bhagavat said this to Vajrapāṇi, the Lord of the Secret Ones, 'Lord of the Secret Ones! Listen carefully and retain this in your mind, for I shall explain the Mandala of the Secret Matrix to you! (216b) Regarding that, first of all the Master should be wise in distinguishing the Three *Samayas* and should himself dwell in the Three *Samayas*. Lord of the Secret Ones! What

are those Three *Samayas*? They are the set of three phenomena. That is, comprehension in an unobscured manner while connected with the three times through that set of phenomena is called the Three *Samayas*. Lord of the Secret Ones! What is that set of phenomena? The mind is this set of phenomena. Lord of the Secret Ones, he who fully knows that all concepts of mind do not exist sees the Perfect Buddha. The facet which is the self-awareness that realizes the continuum of reality here is the attribute of a Tathāgata. That which evolves a body, speech and mind is the attribute of emanation. Lord of the Secret Ones! These are the Three *Samayas*. If they cannot be comprehended even by Śrāvakas and Pratyekabuddhas, how less so by others such as the Tīrthikas!'

59. Then the Bhagavat spoke these verses,

'Foolish people blinded by ignorance
who do not know this method
seek Buddhahood elsewhere,
but do not realize it exists here.
Buddhahood will not be attained
even in any other world system.
The mind itself is Perfect Buddhahood,
no other Buddhahood than that is taught.
Therefore, the yogin
should always abandon doubt
and examine the three aspects of mind,
and then he will know the three *samayas*.'

60. Then when the Bhagavat had spoken these verses, he also said to Vajrapāṇi, the Lord of the Secret Ones, 'Vajrapāṇi! Now the Master, who is skilled in making known the three *samayas* (217a), should convince himself that he is the continuum of reality and purify the site by means of the technique which makes use of that. By having thus purified the site and cleaving to it as though it were the realm of space, he should consider that he is the continuum of reality, the realm of unobscured Awareness, and transform himself into Vairocana.'

61. 'Having transformed himself thus, he should transform his body into the Mandala and the Mandala into his body, by means of the technique of [establishing] their non-duality due to the purity of the continuum of reality. He should divide [the site] by means of the ritual given earlier, using pigments of five colours, mentally created, or else with others. Lord of the Secret Ones! Then he should perform the ritual of entry into the *samaya* of the Secret Matrix, in order to protect suffering beings.'

62. Then the Bhagavat Vairocana carried out an empowerment of the Dharma, by which empowerment (*adhiṣṭhāna*) the Bodhisattvas who engage in the Bodhisattva practice by way of mantras will be able to attain the Tathāgata Awareness in this one present lifetime.

Then the Bhagavat gazed upon the realms of beings with his eyes of great kindness and compassion, and said to Vajrapāṇi, 'Lord of the Secret Ones! Listen to what I shall say concerning the principles of the transformation of the continuum of reality, for even the All-knowing Awareness of Tathāgatas which is difficult to attain will be established in the minds of other beings who have not acted meritoriously, by these principles which brings about the transformation.'

63. When the Bhagavat had said this, (217b) Vajrapāṇi joined his hands together and asked the Bhagavat this, 'Bhagavat! It is a great wonder that the Buddha Bhagavats, the bull-like ones who are endowed with the Ten Strengths, who have the Four Fearlessnesses and who utter the roar of lions, possess [All-knowing] Awareness. Bhagavat! Those nobly-born sons or daughters who are wise in nature [do not] endure the unendurable sufferings of beings in the hells over a number of eons in excess of the infinity of space, for the sake of this All-knowing Awareness. Bhagavat! Hence the wise nobly-born one who seeks to learn this should learn it from the Tathāgatas. So, Bhagavat, because this is excellent, please explain these principles of transformation of the continuum of reality, out of pity for us.'

64. When he had asked this, the Bhagavat replied to Vajrapāṇi as follows, 'Lord of the Secret Ones! Because they are similar to space in character, all phenomena have a single attribute. Because the continuum of reality is without objective basis, all phenomena are transformations of emptiness in character. Lord of the Secret Ones, these are the principles of the transformation of the continuum of reality which I cultivated and practised many times formerly while I was engaged in the practice of a Bodhisattva up until I sat in the core of Enlightenment. Lord of the Secret Ones! Therefore, that is the supreme and perfect Enlightenment of Tathāgatas. Nobly-born One, even while seated in the core of Enlightenment, I attained the Perfection of Insight gate, the abandonment of all concepts, through pondering on these.

65. 'I also attained the Dhāraṇī Gate called the "Infinite Sounding Forth of Melodious Sounds" (218a) and the *Vidyā* Queen called the "Melody which Defeats the Four Māras", which transcends all mundane states of existence, which is unlocalized, which encompasses space, in which there are no attributes, no creatures and no experiencer or agent. Lord of the Secret Ones! What are those *Vidyā* Queens which cause that which is infinite and extensive to be revealed? *NAMAS TRY-ADHVIKĀNĀṂ BUDDHA-GATE PRATIṢṬHITEBHYO* | *APRATIHATA-ŚĀSANEBHYAḤ MAHĀ-KṚPEBHYAḤ GAGANA AMALA-RŪPA-DHĀRAṆĪ* | *TATHĀGATA-RŪPA-BHAVENA* | *PARA-RŪPA-DHARE MAHĀ-KṚPE VIMALE* | *SARVA-GATE VIŚODHANI.* This is the peerless vajra verse. *A MAHĀ-VISMAYE HŪṂ KHAṂ.* Vajrapāṇi, this is the *Vidyā* Queen called "Unsullied like Space", the Mother of all the Buddhas and Bodhisattvas, which is empowered by the transformational power of all the Tathāgatas. Nobly-born One! I cannot perceive any Buddha Fields

where Tathāgatas do not expound and utter this *Vidyā* Queen. Lord of the Secret Ones! You should know that Bodhisattvas who engage in the Bodhisattva practice by way of mantras, who desire to enter into the Mandala, *Mudrās* and *samayas* of the Secret Matrix declare with this formula as follows, "I shall engage in this Queen of Bodhisattva practice by way of mantras!".'

66. Then Vajrapāṇi, the Lord of the Secret Ones, asked the Bhagavat the following, 'Bhagavat! How are Bodhisattvas who engage in the Bodhisattva practice by way of mantras to be shown the nature of Mantras, (218b) what is to be done for them to gain mastery of all Dharmas?'

67. When he had asked that, the Bhagavat replied to Vajrapāṇi, 'Lord of the Secret Ones! Regarding this, a Bodhisattva who engages in the Bodhisattva practice by way of mantras should receive the initiation from a Master. He should consider thus, "This Master is my teacher and he will arouse the supreme and perfect Enlightenment in me!". He should then join his hands together and approaching the Master, entreat him. The Master also should make himself very compassionate, knowing that he is a suppliant, and say the following, "Nobly-born one, I shall reveal that supreme Eye of the Tathāgata to you!".'

68. 'Then searching out a pleasing site, he should clean the ground according to the ritual described earlier and draw a square, one-gated mandala, in which he has carefully fixed the distinct abodes of the deities, set out the various different places for the offerings and placed in its centre a transmuted jar filled with water fragrant with incense.

'Those trainees, who visualize themselves in the body-image of their own deities seated upon a lotus, their *manas* become *bodhicitta*, who wish to protect a limitless number of creatures and who desire to join the lineage of the Tathāgata, should be consecrated upon their heads with water from that jar by the Master. He should also say to them, "Nobly-born one! You have been born into the lineage of the Tathāgata! The Eye of the Tathāgata has been opened!".'

69. 'Lord of the Secret Ones! You should know that the divine body-image to be utilized by those Bodhisattvas who engage in the Bodhisattva practice by way of mantras can be any one of the Bodies of the Tathāgata, or else one of the diverse forms of all the limitless Beings[8], and (219a) it should be created through transforming oneself with the [appropriate] mantra and *mudrā*. Lord of the Secret Ones! What is that transformation with the mantra and *mudrā*? Lord of the Secret Ones, the seat created by the Master with the Lotus *Mudrā* at the time of the initiation, which is inconceivably hard and stable, and as indestructible as a vajra, should be made of gold, copper or clay, or else it should be drawn and set there. In order to cause the person who sits upon it to gain control of all phenomena, he should consecrate him by pouring fragrantly perfumed water from a jar over his head. [The trainee]

should say[9] what the Master himself says and do similar actions with the *mudrās*. With the Conch *Mudrā* and Mantra, the Master should empower him to turn the Wheel of the Tathāgata's Speech. With the Sword *Mudrā* and Mantra, he should empower him to overcome all beliefs in the reality of the person. With the Vajra *Mudrā* and Mantra, he should empower him to destroy the citadel of ignorance. With the *Uṣṇīṣa Mudrā* and Mantra, he should empower him to be invisible like an *uṣṇīṣa*. With the *Ūrṇā Mudrā* and Mantra, he should empower him so that he possesses an *ūrṇā*. With the *Mudrā* and Mantra that Produce All Members, he should empower all his members.'

70. 'Lord of the Secret Ones! Of these, the Lotus *Mudrā* is produced as follows: join both your hands together and bending them back at the joints, make the tips of all your fingers equally outspread. This *Mudrā* is the Vajra Seat of all the Tathāgatas, (219b) which is most powerful and firm. Its Mantra is the gate to all great wonders. *NSB GAGANĀMALA-PRABHĀ-VAJRODYOTANA MAHĀ-KṚPĀTMAKA*. These are the peerless vajra words: *ATI VISMAYA MAHĀ-KṚPA-ĀTMA JAḤ HŪṂ*.'

71. 'Linking together both your hands back to back, with your fingers interlaced so that they are mutually linked, and turning your left thumb backwards, join it with your right thumb at the nails.

'This *Mudrā* is a great *mudrā*,
renowned as the Dharma Wheel.
The Saviour Protectors of the world
all turn this holy Wheel.'

NSB TATHĀGATA AMṚTE VIJAYA-VARṆA SARVA-JAYA-GĀTHA-DHARATHA-KĀRI MAHĀ-KṚPE HŪṂ HAṂ TRAHI MAHĀDBHŪTE HŪṂ.

72. 'From the *Mudrā* of Fulfilment, insert both your thumbs into the palms of your hands, encircle them at their bases with both your forefingers and leave the others standing upright.

'This *Mudrā* with which
the Saviour Protectors of the world
always benefit beings speedily,
is renowned as the Dharma Conch.'

NSB TYADTVA BHAGAVATI PRATIṢṬHITE | ANANTA-SĀRA-VINIRGHOṢAṂ SARVA-TATHĀGATA VĀK PRASĀRA VISMAYAKA DHARA MAHĀ-DHARA-MAṢAKA SARVA-SATTVA ŚĀNTA ŚANĀRĀ MAHĀ MAHĀ HŪṂ.

73. 'From that same *Mudrā* of Fulfilment, crook both your forefingers and hold them on top of the nails of both your thumbs, in the manner of a sword.

'This most powerful *mudrā*
is famed as the Sword *Mudrā*,
and it severs the innate beliefs
in the reality of the person of all beings.'

NSB A MAHĀ-KHAḌGA-PRAJÑĀTE JITA SATKĀYA-DṚṢTI-CCHEDANA-KĀRA TATHĀGATA-ADHIMUKTI-NIRJĀTA VIDHUTA SAṂKALPA MAHĀ MAHĀ HŪṂ JaḤ.

74. 'From that same *Mudrā*, stretch both your forefingers outwards and hold them at the third joint of the middle fingers, separated by a space the size of a grain of barley, and make them like a vajra. Your thumbs, ring fingers and little fingers (220a) should be inserted inside.

'This renowned *mudrā* of the Buddhas,
Lords of the World,
is famed as the Vajra *Mudrā*
which shatters the citadel of ignorance.'

This is its Mantra: *NSB MAHĀ-VISMAYA-TEJODBHAVA MAHĀ-CAṆḌA-DURDĀNTARA BHAÑJA HĀ.*'

75. 'From that same Vajra *Mudrā*, place both your forefingers on the sides of both middle fingers, like an *uṣṇīṣa*.

'This is the *Uṣṇīṣa Mudrā*
of the Lord Protectors of the world.
For whoever makes this *Mudrā*
it will become an *uṣṇīṣa* for him.'

This is its Mantra: *NSB SARVATRA APRATIHATA BHAVATI DHARMA-JVĀLINĀṂ*[10] *SARVA-TATHĀGATA-GAṆODDHARYA-VAŚĀYA MAHĀ-BUDDHA-SARVA-TATHĀGATA ADHIṢṬHĀNA* | *ADHIṢṬHITE SPHURA MAHĀ-MAHOṢṆĪṢA SVĀHĀ.*

76. 'Make the right hand into a fist and place it between your eye-brows.

'This *Mudrā* is ever famed as the *Ūrṇā*
of the most excellent Jinas.'

This is its Mantra: *NSB A ŚIKHENA DUVAM PRABHA SARVA-SATTVA-KLEŚA ŚĀNTĀVAPRAŚĀMANAGARA MAHĀTI-DHARA SARVA-TATHĀGATA-ALAṂKĀRA MAHĀ-PURUṢA-RŪPA-DHARA KOṬI-GATA SVĀHĀ.*

77. 'Lord of the Secret Ones! It is these Mantras and *Mudrās* which involve Bodhisattvas who engage in the Bodhisattva practice by way of mantras, in the activities of the Buddha. Therefore, Lord of the Secret Ones, Bodhisattvas who engage in the Bodhisattva practice by way of mantras, who have been empowered by these Mantras and *Mudrās*, manifest bodies appropriate to those to be trained in realms of beings, using a variety of different body forms, just like a Wish-fulfilling Gem.'

78. Then the Bhagavat Vairocana also said to Vajrapāṇi, the Lord of the Secret Ones, 'Lord of the Secret Ones! (220b) There is a discipline by which Bodhisattvas who engage in the Bodhisattva practice by way of mantras, control their bodies, speech and mind, if they are endowed with such a discipline (*saṃvara*) regarding the Mandala of the Secret Matrix. Lord of the Secret Ones, what is that discipline? To make secure is the discipline, for the body, speech and mind which are restrained, fully

restrained, will be cleansed of internal and external suffering, and that is the discipline.'

79. When he had said this, Vajrapāṇi asked the Bhagavat, 'Bhagavat! How should the Bodhisattva who engages in the Bodhisattva practice by way of mantras, be made to receive the discipline?' When he had asked this, the Bhagavat replied to Vajrapāṇi thus, 'Vajrapāṇi! For this, the Master should read the Perfection of Insight in the presence of the deities and sit facing the Mandala. He should call the trainee and exhort him thus: "Child! Receive the discipline for entry into the great *samaya* which abides unobstructed in the three times!". The trainee should join his palms and bend his knee and entreat the Master as follows, "I, [name], entreat the Master to give me the discipline for entry in the great *samaya*, from today until I am seated in the core of Enlightenment. I accept upon my head the teacher's command!". Then the Master should also say this, "Remember, nobly-born one, you should offer yourself with fervent determination to the Buddhas and Bodhisattvas, (221a) until you are seated in the supreme and perfect core of Enlightenment!".'

80. 'Lord of the Secret Ones, this is the discipline called "Entry into the Great *Samaya*". The Bodhisattvas who engage in the Bodhisattva practice by way of mantras, who abide in this discipline firmly uphold the morality and dwell in the supreme morality of the Tathāgatas.

81. 'Lord of the Secret Ones! Listen also concerning the *bodhicitta* by which one is established in the Awareness of the Tathāgatas.'

82. Then Vajrapāṇi said to the Bhagavat, 'Bhagavat! Please tell us about that kind of *bodhicitta*, out of pity for us.' When he had asked this, the Bhagavat said to Vajrapāṇi, 'Lord of the Secret Ones! Enlightenment has the nature of space. Space is without form and cannot be seen. The attributes of Enlightenment are also the attributes of mind. Therefore, Lord of the Secret Ones, the Mind, space and Enlightenment are without duality. Regarding this, supreme and perfect Enlightenment is that realization of the sameness of phenomena, the direct understanding of the continuum of reality. Lord of the Secret Ones, that mind which arises by means of aspiration to that and by means of relying upon that is called *bodhicitta*.

83. 'Moreover, Lord of the Secret Ones, (221b) Enlightenment will be realized by Bodhisattvas by five principles of abiding. What are those five? Bodhisattvas will realize that it is devoid of all phenomena. Some will realize that they are without psycho-physical constituents, perceptual elements and sources, a perceiving subject and perceived objects, empty and like illusions. Others will realize this by relying upon phenomena. Or else, Lord of the Secret Ones, Bodhisattvas who engage in the Bodhisattva practice by way of mantras will realize the primordially unborn nature and emptiness of their own minds, by the sameness of phenomena which are

without autonomous existence, without psycho-physical constituents, perceptual elements and sources, a perceiving subject and perceived objects. Lord of the Secret Ones, regarding that "absence of phenomena" therein, the Tathāgata has taught that the mundane path should be completely abandoned for no self, being, soul or spirit exists in them, but they are just psycho-physical constituents, perceptual elements and sources. Regarding the abandonment of psycho-physical constituents, perceptual elements and sources, a perceiving subject and perceived objects, the realization of the Mahāyāna by the Bodhisattvas is established by way of their fully understanding[11] the realization of the Śrāvaka Path. By the sameness and lack of autonomous existence of phenomena, Bodhisattvas who engage in the Bodhisattva practice by way of mantras see that their own minds are primordially unborn and realize the emptiness in nature, insubstantiality and lack of attributes [of their minds]. Therefore, Lord of the Secret Ones, a Bodhisattva should generate a mind which is unlocalized, unobscured and devoid of all proliferations.'

84. 'Lord of the Secret Ones, you should also know by this discourse (222a) that there is nothing more conducive to the [attainment of] supreme and perfect Enlightenment for the Bodhisattvas who fully abide in the Mahāyāna than the gate of liberation which accomplishes the mantra practice method. Why is that? For while Bodhisattvas who have striven over many eons and have also undertaken difficult renunciations will become perfectly awakened to Enlightenment, the Bodhisattvas who engage in the Bodhisattva practice by way of mantras will become fully awakened to the supreme and perfect Enlightenment in this very lifetime. What is the reason for that? Lord of the Secret Ones, that which is called "life" is only applied as an idea to arising by the Tathāgata. Because that idea also perishes for Bodhisattvas prior to their attaining the *samādhi* wherein they directly experience the nature of phenomena.'

85. Then the Bhagavat also said to Vajrapāṇi, the Lord of the Secret Ones, 'Lord of the Secret Ones! Bodhisattvas who desire to enter this *samaya* of the Mandala and the *mudrās* of the Secret Matrix should separate themselves by a long distance from five factors. What are those five? Avarice, harming beings, doubt, laziness, and disbelief in the mantras and so forth. Lord of the Secret Ones, Bodhisattvas who desire to enter into the supramundane path in this very lifetime should separate themselves by a long distance from these five factors. Lord of the Secret Ones, I cannot say that the Bodhisattva who dwells in these factors has perfected even the slightest of the Bodhisattva practice. Lord of the Secret Ones, why is that so? Because these factors (222b) are a great hindrance to Enlightenment for Bodhisattvas.'

86. Then Vajrapāṇi, the Lord of the Secret Ones, asked the Bhagavat this, 'Bhagavat! How much will the merit of a nobly-born son or daughter who abides in the *samaya* of this Secret Matrix increase?' When he had asked this,

the Bhagavat replied to the Bodhisattva Vajrapāṇi, 'Lord of the Secret Ones! Can you comprehend the limits of the realm of space?'

'Bhagavat! Since the realm of space is immeasurable, it is not possible to grasp its extent.'

'Even if you were able to comprehend the limits of the realm of space, you would not be able to comprehend the amount of merit generated by a nobly-born son or daughter who has seen the *samaya* in the Mandala of the Secret Matrix. Why is that? Because they see the arising of Buddhas in this Mandala. Lord of the Secret Ones, the word "mandala" means the best (*la*) of essences (*maṇḍa*), the ultimate point of all essences. There is no mandala of the Tathāgatas above that. It is the matrix, the support and the refuge of all wholesome roots. Therefore, Lord of the Secret Ones, though all worlds were completely filled with burning coals, a nobly-born son or daughter who desires to enter into the Mandala, the *mudrās* and *samaya* should wade through them on foot and go to wherever they will gain entry into that Mandala, the *mudrās* and *samaya*.

87. 'Those nobly-born sons and daughters should come to regard (223a) those Bodhisattvas who engage in the Bodhisattva practice by way of mantras as spiritual friends, as parents and as teachers. Why is that? For if they do not become resentful when they offer their flesh and blood to those Bodhisattvas, how much more so will they be able to offer other things.'

88. 'Lord of the Secret Ones, how are those Bodhisattvas repaid who engage in the Bodhisattva practice by way of mantras, in reliance upon which the life-stream of hell beings is severed and the burden of life in the animal state and the world of Yama[12] becomes nothing? You should know that those Bodhisattvas dwell in equality with the unequalled, they are empowered by the transformational power of all the Tathāgatas and are endowed with a sphere of experience which is unsupported like space.'

89. 'Lord of the Secret Ones, I urge you, you should know this: in future times, foolish people who rely upon objective supports, who are attached to the belief in the reality of the person, whose spirits are perverted, and who have not investigated the basis of their minds, will be lost in confusion. There will be those who say that this is not the Buddha's word, that it was composed by poets. Lord of the Secret Ones, you should know that those foolish people will enter two states of existence. What are those two? The hells and the animal realm. It cannot be said that they have even the slightest basis for wholesome roots. Why is that? Because they have entered into that which severs the roots, (223b) they cause themselves to be cut off from the Buddha's Enlightenment, they are overcome by Māra, stupid in nature. There will be those who have not cultivated the Mahāyāna, but who think that the Śrāvaka Way is best. They will censure those nobly-born sons and daughters who exert themselves in this Dharma-discourse, saying "Where is the Buddha's Enlightenment in immorality and engaging in sinful deeds?". Because they utter these insults, those foolish people will fall into the two

miserable states of existence. Yet all of these things were taught by the All-knowing Bhagavat so that this engagement in the practice of mantras might benefit beings. Because feelings of aversion arise in them towards those things, they will have suffering as their lot. Why is that? You should know that a person who holds the secret of the Tathāgata is worthy of salutation by all the world and the gods.'

90. Then the Bhagavat Vairocana said to Vajrapāṇi and the Vajradharas who were as numerous as all the atoms in the ten Buddha Fields, 'Extend your hands to protect, safeguard and shelter those nobly-born ones! You should continuously protect and safeguard those nobly-born ones! Turn all harm away from them!'

When he had said that, Vajrapāṇi and all those Vajradharas who were as numerous as all the atoms in the ten Buddha Fields, cried out with one voice, 'Bhagavat! We shall do everything as the Tathāgata Dharma Lord has commanded! We shall protect those nobly-born ones until they are seated in the core of Enlightenment!' (224a) The Bhagavat said, 'That is excellent, Nobly-born Ones, that is excellent! You should do whatever is necessary so that the Teacher's teachings will not perish.'

91. Then Vajrapāṇi, the Lord of the Secret Ones, said to all those Vajradharas, 'Friends! That accomplishment of many hundreds of thousands of ascetic deeds by the Tathāgata Arhat Samyak-saṃbuddhas is this supreme and perfect Enlightenment. Therefore, all of you should rouse yourselves and protect them! Why is that? For it will be said that we are obedient to the Tathāgata's commands, that we protect the Tathāgata's teachings, that we are equal to the unequalled, that we possess the Ten Strengths. Therefore, we should always strive to protect, safeguard and shelter this Dharma-discourse. We should also strive to protect, safeguard and shelter those nobly-born ones.'

When he had said this, all those Vajradharas cried out with one voice, 'We shall certainly do whatever is necessary so that the Teacher's teachings will abide for a long time and not perish!'

92. Then the Bhagavat Vairocana gazed upon creatures living in the future and motivated by great compassion, he spoke the words of this mantra so that this Dharma-discourse might abide for a long time: *NAMAS TRY-ADHVIKĀNĀṂ SARVA-TATHĀGATĀNĀṂ SARVA-TATHĀGATA-SAMATĀ-GATIṂ-GATE | EKA-DHARMA-SAMAVASARAṆE | VICITRA-RŪPA-DHĀRIṆI* (224b) *SARVA-SATTVA-ABHIPRĀYA PARIPŪRAṆE | SARVA-VIDHI SATTVA-GATI MANASE | TRAHI MAṂ SARVA-DHARMA-SAMA-MAHĀ-MAHE VAIROCANA GARBHA SAṂBUDDHA SARVA-TATHĀGATA ADHIṢṬHITE TRAHITE BHAGAVATE HŪṂ.*

93. Then Vajrapāṇi who was authorized by all the Tathāgatas and empowered by the Bhagavat Vairocana, generated great compassion and spoke the continuation of this very Tantra, 'First the Master should purify himself and

transforming himself into Vairocana by his *Mudrā* and Mantra, with his *manas* having become the continuum of reality, he should draw the Mandala.

'The *mantrin* should take white powder
always according to the previous rules
for the secret mantra rituals,
and then with a mind imbued with compassion,
he should apply the first colour,
ever recollecting Acala.
Then taking the second colour, red,
he should apply that.
The third colour, yellow, also
should be carefully applied.
Then that like emerald should be applied,
followed by that like sapphire.'

94. 'Such colours as these
are those of the Mandala itself.
The colours of the deities are likewise,
Pacifying, Enriching and Destroying
are said to be those of their mantras[13]:
this is the secret teaching.'

95. 'All the mandalas[14] of the Tathāgata
are renowned as *mahendra*,
Padmapāṇi's is of water,
and Vajrapāṇi's is of wind.
The mandalas of such servants as the messengers,
of those associated with the name "wrathful",
and of those who act without obstruction,
should all be of fire and wind.'

96. 'Moreover, all of these beings
endowed with all capabilities
should be propitiated with the nectar of emptiness.
With unsullied eyes of compassion,
garbed in the armour of kindness,
with unsullied joy and skill,
they strive to save beings (225a)
drowning in the oceans of *saṃsāra*.
Neither dwelling in *saṃsāra*,
nor dwelling in Nirvāṇa,
they rest in the limitless,
and act for the benefit of beings.'

97. Then Vajrapāṇi, the Lord of the Secret Ones, looked at all the entourages in the assembly and spoke these words,

'Friends! You should all listen
to this definition of the places
where obstructors appear,
described by the Bhagavat Teacher
who is All-knowing and free of sins.
There are many kinds of obstructors,
gods, *asuras*, *yakṣas* and humans.
Regarding those, there are two types,
those of the external and internal realms.
You should know that the internal ones
are those illnesses arising
from hot and cold *vāta*[15]
that are of a chronic nature,
such as tuberculosis, asthma,
fevers and vomiting,
anaemia and loss of appetite.
The great external obstructors
are human and also non-human.
These thorns to Awareness
appear in order to upset the world
by various kinds of deeds.
Those who cause confusion in hermitages
will be repelled by seeing
the ritual of the actions.
Obstructors that come when they are hot
should be pacified by being cooled.
The wise one should cure
each of those by their antidotes.
Or else the *mantrin* should
exclude all those obstructors
by demarcation [of the site].
It is said that Awareness is best
for pacifying all obstructors.'[16]

Translated and checked by the Indian Pandita Śīlendra-bodhi and the Zhu Chen Translator, Ban-de dPal-brTsegs.

Part IV

THE PIṆḌĀRTHA

Buddhaguhya's Condensed Commentary on The Vairocana-Abhisaṃbodhi Tantra

INTRODUCTION

Because he is Enlightenment, which causes
those who do not know that his Body and Speech
are just the embodiments of his Mind
to seek the Body and Speech which arise from
the Sugata who calms the life-streams of the world,
I prostrate to that Vairocana
who should be served by Vajradharas
and children of the Jina,
together with his Body and Speech.
Having done that, I shall explain in brief
the summarized meaning of the *Vairocana Tantra.*

After the Buddha Bhagavat had realized the perfection of the benefitting of self and others, he revealed that same perfection of the benefitting of self and others by way of the scriptures which (2b) teach the Mantra practice and those which teach the Perfection practice, in order to guide to reality those who are to be trained. Hence, this Tantra is intended to encompass the Bhagavat Vairocana's perfection of the benefitting of self and others by two approaches: the condensed and the extensive. The condensed approach aims to encompass all the topics which are taught by this Tantra through just its title: *Vairocana-abhisaṃbodhi-vikurvati-adhiṣṭhāna.* The extensive approach aims to encompass Vairocana's perfection of self-benefitting, characterized by the threefold perfection of the cause, the nature and result [of Enlightenment] by way of analysis, and his perfection of the benefitting others, characterized by such skilful means (*upāya*) as the *mudrās,* mandalas and mantras, by way of revelation and analysis, through the whole of this *Vairocana Tantra.*

[First, regarding the perfection of self-benefitting][1], the perfection of the cause [by which one attains the state of Vairocana] is described herein by teaching the stages of the path by which [the state of] the Bhagavat Vairocana is accomplished. [Secondly,] the perfection of the nature [of Vairocana] is described by teaching the attributes of Full Enlightenment (*abhisaṃbodhi*). The perfection of the result [which is Vairocana] is described by way of showing the attributes of the manifestations (*vikurtvita*) of the Inexhaustible Array of his Body and so forth.

[Secondly,] the perfection of the benefitting of others is described by way of the arrangement of the *mudrās,* mantras and mandalas which are transformations of that same Inexhaustible Body and so forth, together with the expedient means. [That which is thus arranged for the benefit of others has two aspects: the practice of the Master (3a) and of the practitioners. What are those practices? The practice by means of the rituals for the mandala of the Master, and preliminary practice by the practitioners by means of mantra recitation and so forth.] Moreover, you should understand that what is arranged for the benefit of others, by way of the transformation of these manifestations into the *mudrās,* mantras and so, on has twenty one topics:

1 The description of the mandala Master's attributes.
2 The analysis of the trainees' attributes.
3 The three items of the teachings about the attributes of the mandala site, the attributes of purifying it, the attributes of taking hold of it.

4 The description of the ritual for the preparation of the trainees.
5 The three items of the specifications for the marking-out of the mandala, the attributes of its sections, and of its gateways.
6 The description of the transformation of the Inexhaustible Array of the Bhagavat's Body by the arrayed bodies of the mandala deities in the Mandala Arising from Great Compassion.
7 The description of the arrangement of the mandala deities by the letters of their seed-syllables, which are transformations of the Inexhaustible Array of the Bhagavat's Speech, in the Mandala of the Revolving Wheel of Letters.
8 The explanation of the special features of the arrangement of the deities in the Secret Mandala, by the different types of *mudrās* which reside in earth, water, fire and wind mandalas, which are transformations of the Inexhaustible Array of the Bhagavat Vairocana's Mind.
9 The explanation of the different types of pigments to be used.
10 The explanation of the practice for the transformation of the mandala deities after having drawn the mandalas.
11 The explanation of the branches of worship, in order to make internal and external offerings to them.
12 The description of the ritual for the acceptance of the trainees.
13 The explanation of the ritual making the *samaya* known to them. (3b)
14 The explanation of the ritual to initiate them.
15 The description of the ritual to cause them to uphold the *vidyās*.
16 The explanation in detail of the different types of *vidyās*, mantras and *mudrās*.
17 The explanation of the categories of the branches of *sadhana*.
18 The explanation concerning the branches of *sādhana* such as the mandalas for the accomplishment of the *vidyās*, mantras and so forth.
19 The description of the signs of internal and external attainments.
20 The explanation of the ritual to be done with fire.
21 The explanation concerning the different branches of accomplishment.

Therefore, [this Tantra] reveals the attributes of these topics by way of the sequential, reverse and the detailed explanations, hence I shall appropriately summarize and delineate the topics encompassed by these [items] in order that intelligent people might bring them to mind. In brief, each separate word of the title '*Vairocana-abhisaṃbodhi-vikuvita-adhiṣṭhāna*' reveals how the meaning of the entire Tantra has been encompassed [in it].

THE TWO TYPES OF TRAINEES

There are two types of people to be trained. There are those who have savoured the good fortune of men and gods characterized by that beatitude which is preceded by the completion of the accumulation of merit and awareness through the repeated cultivation of the Perfection of Generosity and so forth as taught in the Mahāyāna sutras, who then aspire to reach the state of Vairocana in stages. Then there are others who accumulate the accumulation of merit and awareness by way of propitiating the *vidyās* and mantras, and who experience the good fortune of men and gods which is the result of that, and who then aspire to reach the state of

Vairocana. Thus, to help in a real way those who are orientated towards in the Perfections, (4a) the sutras which are mainly concerned with the practice of the Perfections such as the *Daśabhūmi*, the *Ratnamegha*, the *Akṣayamati* and so forth were taught, as well as the sutras which are mainly concerned with the profound and the extensive such as the *Samādhirāja*, the *Gaṇḍavyūha* and the *Prajñā-pāramitā Sūtras*. In order to help some of those who are orientated towards Mantra Practice, there are the *Tattva-saṃgraha*, the *Śrī-paramādya* and so forth of the Yoga [Tantra] approach, which are mainly concerned with the cultivation of the yoga for the accomplishment of [Four *Mudrās*] beginning with the *Mahāmudrā*, and which teach the different types of practices concerning the body appropriate to [that of] one's tutelary deity which is to be propitiated, and the special types of the branches of worship. Then, apart from these, there are the Tantras for other trainees, related to the Kriyā approach, such as the *Trisamaya-rāja*, the *Trikāya-uṣṇiṣa*, the *Vajrapāṇy-abhiṣeka* and so on, which teach the different types of external activities [such as cultivating ritual purity] by way of faith, which are mainly concerned with the cultivation of means and insight, and which cause the perfection of the benefit of self and others. [Like the Yoga Tantras], the *Vairocana-abhisaṃbodhi-vikurvita-adhiṣṭhāna Tantra* fully teaches the application to *sādhana* preceded by the cultivation of expedient means and insight, which is renowned as the method associated with the absolute level. However, because it also teaches the inferior *sādhana* of engaging in external purity and so forth, which forms a basis for the cultivation of yoga on the absolute level, in order to attract those trainees who are orientated towards the Kriyā Tantra type of approach, it can also be called a Kriyā Tantra. (4b)

THE THREE TYPES OF MANTRA TRAINEES

There are three types of trainees who are orientated towards the Mantra Method: those who comprehend solely by the title of a text (*udghaṭita-jña*), those who comprehend by analysis into topics (*vipañcita-jña*), and those who rely on the words of the text. Of those, the people who have acute intelligence and much understanding of the Mahāyāna Dharma and so forth comprehend solely by means of the title of a text, because they are able to understand all the techniques by the topics the title implies, even with the phrases and words abbreviated. Those who have middling intelligence and middling understanding of the Mahāyāna Dharma comprehend by way of analysis into topics, because they are able to grasp the meaning of the words and phrases when they have been analyzed into topics. Those with ordinary intelligence and ordinary understanding of the Dharma rely on the words because they are only able to grasp the meaning by having each word explained.

Now, with regards to trainees who understand solely by the mention of a title, they only need to be told the names of sutras, tantras, *samādhis*, gates of liberation or Bodhisattvas and so forth, which accord with their contents, for they are able to understand in detail the contents implied by the titles, even though these [contents] are abbreviated. In order to help those who comprehend by analysis, the contents of a text is indicated just by division into topics. In order to help those who rely on the words of a text, the sub-divided segments of the text of the tantras and so forth have to be extensively expanded by verbal conventions and then explained.

ELUCIDATION OF THE TITLE

Therefore, in this instance, the title '*Vairocana-abhisaṃbodhi-vikurvita-adhiṣṭhāna*', which accords with the contents [of the Tantra], was revealed by the Bhagavat for the benefit of those who understand by the mention of the title alone. (5a) Because they have extremely sharp intelligence and much understanding of the Mahāyāna Dharma, such people as these comprehend the contents in the following way, even though they just hear the name of this Tantra. The Bhagavat *Vairocana* has attained the optimum accumulation of merit and awareness. *Full Enlightenment* (*abhisaṃbodhi*): He has directly understood that all phenomena lack inherent reality. In the first instant [of Enlightenment], he attained, by his own Awareness, that Enlightenment which is devoid of both the obscurations of afflicting emotions and of wrong understanding that are the intrinsic nature of the various modes of existence, which is cleansed of all the foundations of habitual dispositions for proliferations like the sky, and which is extremely radiant and self-aware in nature. At that very moment, the Array of his Body, Speech and Mind, which are naturally obtained, were manifested – that is, the Array of his Body which resembles both pure and impure beings, the Array of Buddha Speech which is skilled in all the languages of beings, and the Mandala of Awareness which has access to truth on both the absolute and relative levels. This is the '*manifestation*' (*vikurvita*) of Vairocana's Full Enlightenment. As the *Tathāgatotpatti-nirdeśa* [II.322] mentions in detail: '*Nobly born son! After the Tathāgata has become fully enlightened he enters a* samādhi *called " The Utter Buddha Awakening", and no sooner does he enter it than as many Bodies appear everywhere as there are beings, and as much Speech as there are Bodies, and as many Minds as there are Bodies and Speech appear everywhere. O Son of the Jina! In that way you should understand that the Bodies, Speech and Minds of Tathāgatas are vast and measureless,* (5b) *since the realms of beings are also without measure.*' Furthermore this same point is also taught by the passage in this Tantra which states at length that those Bodhisattvas Mahāsattvas such as Samantabhadra then '*saw the [unmoving] Body of Vairocana seated in the most excellent core of Enlightenment*' [10.8], and you should refer to the Tantra concerning this.

'*Manifestation*' (*vikurvita*) refers to the display with playful ease (*vikrīḍita*), and this '*manifestation of the array of Body and so forth*' can be explained as another way of saying that they caused all beings to be completely joyful. Therefore, [the title] speaks of the '*transformation*' (*adhiṣṭhāna*) of the manifestation of the Full and Perfect Enlightenment of Vairocana. This signifies that [Vairocana] reveals that manifestation of the attributes of this inexhaustible array in the form of the bodies, speech and minds of all beings as appropriate, by way of the *mudrās*, mandalas and mantras, and empowers and transforms them in order to cause beings to be completely joyful according to their fortune as long as *saṃsāra* lasts. That which relates all of that is this '*Tantra*'.

Those people to be guided who understand just by mention of the title are able to understand in summary the entire meaning of the Tantra by just ascertaining the meaning of this name. It is given this name '*Vairocana-abhisaṃbodhi-vikurvati-adhiṣṭhāna*', which accords with its contents, in order to aid those who understand just by mention of the title. (6a) Moreover, not only does this name which accords with its contents aid those who understand just by mention of the title, but also it shows the causal relationship (*saṃbandha*), the subject matter (*abhidheya*) and the purpose (*prayojana*) of this Tantra. Thus, you should understand by this title that the Array of Vairocana's Body and so forth are the cause of this Tantra and this Tantra is their result, because it indicates the manifestation of the Inexhaustible Body, Speech and Mind of Vairocana by way of the *mudrās*, mandalas and so forth. You should understand the subject matter is that same revelation of the Array of Inexhaustible Body and so forth by the *mudrās*, mandalas and so on. Its purpose is to reveal them by the *mudrās*, mandalas and so on. You should understand the purpose of that revelation as '*the attainment of salvation and beatitude*'.

Because the trainees who only understand by elaboration are unable to understand in detail the contents taught by the words [of the title] and their associated significance, the Bhagavat expounded this Tantra with the words '*the transformation of the Tathāgatas*' and so forth to aid them. (6b) Thus, you should understand that it is necessary to relate to them the cause of Vairocana and what his essential nature is like, the cause of his Full Enlightenment and what its essential nature is like, when its manifestation arises and what its essential nature is like, and how that manifestation is revealed by way of the *mudrās*, mandalas and so on, and so all these things are taught in this Tantra in order to aid them. Therefore, I shall bring together the words of the Tantra which teach the meanings variously encompassed by those themes.

A. THEORETICAL BASIS

I. THE CAUSE OF VAIROCANA

Now, the cause leading to the attainment of the state (*pada*) of Vairocana is thus: [It has two causes, the proximate and the distant, by way of the direct (*pratyakṣa*) and the indirect (*saṃbandha*) causes. The indirect cause is also twofold.] It is commenced by the mundane path and accomplished by the supramundane path.

1. The Mundane Path

This process of commencement by the mundane path is fully indicated in this Tantra [by way of view and practice], thus when beings in *saṃsāra* who are solely enmeshed by a particular belief in a self through attachment to the self and what belongs to the self, are tormented by the three kinds of suffering, the idea of the Dharma causes them to generate the eight minds such as the mind concerned with fasting and so forth, as it says in this Tantra, '*Lord of the Secret Ones! Furthermore, it sometimes happens that someone among the animal-like foolish people has a virtuous idea, namely, they think: "I shall undertake a fast"*', (7a) down to '*the Jinas have explained this as the eighth mind, which is like the digestion of the fruit*'.

Therefore, those who have undertaken the teachings which posit Viṣṇu, Mahādeva, Brahmā and so on as the teachers of the mundane path, come to understand the meaning of their scriptures, through the gradual cultivation of generosity and morality, upheld by the belief in a self and so forth. After they have formed the idea of 'isolation' (*kaivalya*) through the path which has been taught by those scriptures, they call the solitary entity of the *ātman* freed from the innate and adventitious fetters of karma and emotional afflictions, 'isolation'. Therefore, they imagine that all these unreal cities (= the mundane world) do not exist in this liberation which is characterized as 'aloneness', for only that solitary self remains, which is minute, invisible, one ten thousandth the size of a hair tip.

Therefore, the Bhagavat teaches that this also is an extreme which ought to be abandoned and is not the true path (7b) because they merely realize the nothingness of phenomena by belief in a self (*ātma-graha*). That is dealt with by these words, '*Lord of the Secret Ones! There are others who understand the different type of self and adhere to one of these types as they have been propounded. They arrive at the idea of "isolation" and claim that this is real, thinking that mere emptiness is an actual entity*' down to '*Whoever does not know emptiness does not know Nirvāṇa*'. [1.20]

2. The Supramundane Path

Therefore, this section next teaches about virtuous spiritual friends. Having ascertained by reason and scripture with the insight which arises from hearing and pondering that the mundane path is not one which brings about liberation, they rely on virtuous spiritual friends who teach the supramundane path and thereafter they exert themselves zealously in order to be liberated by the supramundane path which they have learnt from them. This signifies that, in this case, even that path is a liberating path which has the attribute of causing the attainment of the state of Mahā-vairocana.

Entry into that path is taught here in two categories, with reference to people with dull faculties and people with sharp faculties: i) by way of the realization of the lack of autonomous existence in the individual, and ii) the realization of the lack of autonomous existence both in the individual and in phenomena, Those with dull faculties first abandon the mundane path, the path of 'isolation', and then enter the path which leads to the realization that the individual lacks autonomous existence. They reject the hundred and sixty mundane minds, which are characterized by attachment and so forth, mentioned below, and realize the absence of autonomous existence in the individual, (8a) as mentioned in detail with '*there is the mind of attachment, the mind of non-attachment, the mind of hatred, the mind of friendliness, the mind of stupidity*' [1.21] and so forth. Having transcended the hundred and sixty mundane minds after three eons, the supramundane mind arises, which is mentioned thus:

> '*This is just the psycho-physical constituents,*
> *and there has never existed a self.*
> *Through the faculties, perceptual sources and elements,*
> *the mundane world is understood to be valueless.*' [1.23]

From the start, the yogins with sharp faculties clear away the concepts of autonomous existence and so forth, the psycho-physical constituents, the perceptual sources, the perceptual elements, the perceiving subject and perceived objects, and transcending the hundred and sixty mundane minds, they enter into the lack of autonomous existence both in the individual and in phenomena, which is mentioned [1.25] thus: '*Lord of the Secret Ones! Moreover, there are those who fare in the Mahāyāna and have no regard for the other Ways, and who give rise to the thought that phenomena lack autonomous existence. Why is that? Because when they break down the basis of the psycho-physical constituents by practising those previous practices, they fully comprehend the intrinsic nature of phenomena and give rise to the idea that they are like magical illusions, mirages, shadows, echoes, a wheel of fire or a* gandharvas' *city. Lord of the Secret Ones! Therefore, since they have come to be dominated by these ideas, even the notion of the lack of autonomous existence of phenomena must be abandoned.*'

Therefore, regarding those with dull and sharp faculties, although both cultivate the path of no autonomous existence in the individual, (8b) those with sharp faculties cultivate the path of the realization that both the individual and phenomena lack autonomous existence, while yogins with dull faculties, who have abandoned as a preliminary the hundred and sixty mundane minds beginning with attachment, attain in sequence the eight results such as the Stream-entry fruit and so on. They subsequently comprehend that those psycho-physical constituents and so on are like illusions, mirages and so forth in nature, and are unassociated with all ideas concerning [the reality of] psycho-physical constituents, perceptual elements and perceptual sources, so they realize that they are merely characterized by tranquillity and nothingness, as the text says [1.24] in detail: '*Lord of the Secret Ones! There also arises in those who abide in this supramundane mind, the idea that the psycho-physical constituents really exist. Then, they give rise to the mind which is devoid of attachment to the psycho-physical constituents, and because they dissolve them by considering them to be like froth, bubbles, a plantain tree, a mirage or a phantom, they become free from that notion. Thus, whoever has abandoned the psycho-physical constituents, the perceptual elements, the perceptual sources, the perceiving subject and perceived objects, will directly realize the continuum of tranquility, the intrinsic nature of reality. Lord of the Secret Ones! This supramundane mind which is free from the net of emotional afflictions and karmic actions associated with the sequence of eight complete and incomplete minds, will be transcended by yogins with the elapse of one eon.*'

3. The Hundred and Sixty Minds

Now, some of those minds beginning with attachment are defined by way of definitions which summarize the view-point taught in scriptures (*āgama*). Such words in the Tantra as '*what is the mind of attachment? It is that which has recourse to religion with desire*' [1.22] should be explained by summarization and analysis. The sense of the word '*attachment*' is any desire or longing (*abhi-ni-√ veś*) for any visual, auditory, gustatory or tactile object as appropriate, (9a) operating in the Realm of Desire, and likewise any desire or longing for and enjoyment of activities, the absence of inflations, meditative absorptions, *samādhis*, equipoises (*samāpatti*), liberations (*vimokṣa*) and so forth in the Realms with and without Form. Any being whose mind is accompanied by that mental factor, characterized by attachment to something, is said to be endowed with desire. So what does that [mind] do in order to attain such objects as mentioned which are not possessed, and to augment and increase what is possessed? It says it has '*recourse to religion*'. As for the word '*religion*' (*dharma*), it is 'religion' because it upholds (√ *dhṛ*) one from falling into the lower levels of the hells, the pretas and animals. In brief, it has the characteristics of the cultivation of generosity, the discipline of morality and the meditative absorptions and so forth. Hence, the implication is that if a person is attached to a certain object because of a desire to acquire or to augment that specific object, they undertake such religious practices (*dharma*) as generosity just for the sake of acquisition, but do not undertake the meditative absorptions, *samādhis* and *samāpattis* free of inflations, which form the path of salvation from the prison of *saṃsāra*, without savouring them. In that way, even this mind should be abandoned by one who desires liberation, by way of cultivation of either the path of [the realization] that there is no autonomous existence in the individual, or the path of [the realization] that there is no autonomous existence both in the individual and in phenomena. This should be understood as the summarized explanation of the words of the Tantra from here to the end of the description of the hundred and sixty minds.

The transcendence and the classification of the other subsequent minds such as hatred and so forth (9b) which are mentioned below, should generally be inferred by this method. I shall mention here those which are exceptional. The meaning of '*it is to have recourse to the religion with aversion*' is that it engages in religious practices which are defined as recitation, burnt offerings, generosity, morality and so on, with the wish to kill an enemy. *To have recourse to religion without reflection*: This is to undertake religious practices defined as generosity, morality and so on, without reflecting that such are its visible and invisible results, like a herd of cows. In that way, because it is easy to understand the words '*it is to have recourse to religion endowed with friendliness*' down to '*the ocean-like mind*' at the end, they should be understood without my analyzing them. As for the meaning of '*what is the mind of kinship? It is that which accompanies, with a like nature, any mind which has arisen*', a mind, which has arisen associated solely with a motivation factor (*saṃskāra*) of attachment and so forth with regards some object, will perish whether it ceases instantaneously together with that same mental factor or else endures and then ceases, but since the continuity of the mind, associated with the motivational factors of attachment and so forth, will acquire another continuation of the object of that stream, there will be no exertion in the religious practices of generosity, morality and so forth.

In order to show how these sixty minds, from the mind which arises with attachment and so on down to the end, become one hundred and sixty, the text says: '*By doubling* [*the five basic emotional afflictions*] *five consecutive times, one arrives at the one hundred and sixty mundane minds, and after the elapse of three eons.*' [1.23] Therefore, regarding the implied meaning, (10a) [first] the multiplication by two of one, two, three, four and five [means that by doubling in sequence one, two, three, four and five], one arrives at two, four, six, eight and ten. Hence the products are to be multiplied. Of the products of the multiplication by two of one, two, three, four and five, six, eight and ten should be retained, but it is not necessary to retain two and four since they are already included among the multiplicands. What should one do with these products? In brief, their purpose is to make one hundred and sixty, since it is possible to get sixty with the numbers between two and ten. By doing that, one will arrive at one hundred and sixty by counting the minds of attachment and so forth once, twice and so on. Here, '*multiplied by two*' seems to mean that one should multiply by two each one of the five minds of attachment and so forth, which are [the multiplicands] one, two, three and so on, because it is not the case that the others [six, eight and ten] are to be multiplied by two. Therefore, the intention is this: when each of the minds with attachment and so forth perceive their own objects continuously, then there are sixty of these minds which perceive the objects of attachment and so forth of the Three Realms. When that same object-stream of any one of the minds of attachment and so on, is perceived in conjunction with any other second mind such as hatred as appropriate, then these sixty minds form [a further] thirty linked (*prabandha*) minds. As it says in detail in the Abhidharma, '[*The mind*] *which is associated with the fetter of attachment, is also associated with the fetter of anger*' and so forth. (10b) Likewise, when anyone perceives that same object-stream of three of the minds of attachment and so forth, in conjunction with any three minds out of attachment, hatred and stupidity, then these sixty minds associated with attachment and so forth form twenty linked minds. When one perceives that same object-stream of any four of the minds of attachment and so forth, in conjunction with any four minds out of these sixty minds of attachment and so forth, then these sixty minds associated with attachment and so forth form fifteen linked minds. When one perceives that same object-stream of the Three Realms, which forms an objective support for four minds such as attachment and so forth as appropriate, in conjunction with any five minds out these sixty minds, then these sixty minds form twelve linked minds. Now, one should carry out the multiplication by two of each one of these with one and so on of these one, two, three, four and five minds. Now, when one perceives objects in the Three realms, as appropriate, with each of the minds of attachment and so forth, they will not total [one hundred and sixty] since it has been explained above that there are sixty of these minds. When one perceives that same object of the minds of attachment and so forth with two minds, then one will still not arrive at the total, since they will [only] make thirty if one does the calculation by doubling them as above. (11a) Hence though the multiplication by two of one has been calculated above, the subsequent ones have not been added up. Likewise, the multiplication by two of two makes four linked minds, and though it has been calculated in the enumeration above for the number four, it has not been added on, but if one doubles three which was previously multiplied one gets six. Hence, the intention is this: when one perceives just one object stream with six minds, then you should know that these sixty minds form ten linked minds. Likewise if one doubles the number four which was previously explained, it forms eight. Thus, when eight of these sixty minds of attachment and so forth are associated, they form seven linked minds. Because the linked minds with four elements which form just one unit have already been calculated above as the number four linked minds, they will not be enumerated here. Likewise, if one doubles the number five explained above, these minds of attachment and so forth make ten. Hence you should know these minds of attachment and so forth which are divided into ten linked minds, form six. In that way, the minds which are explained above are sixty. Multiplied by two, they are thirty. Likewise trebled, they are twenty. Quadrupled, they are fifteen. Multiplied by five, they are twelve. Also three doubled is six. Four doubled is seven. Five doubled is six. Therefore you should know that the sixty minds of attachment and so forth form one hundred and sixty in this way. (11b) Since they are inimical to those yogins who apply themselves to realize that there is no autonomous existence in the individual or who apply themselves to realize that there is no autonomous existence in both the individual and the phenomena, they should be abandoned by the realization of the path of no autonomous existence in the individual, and by the realization of the path of no autonomous existence both in the individual and the phenomena, which is mentioned in detail in the Tantra thus, *'after the elapse of three eons these are transcended and the supramundane mind arises. That is to say,*

> *This is just the psycho-physical constituents,*
> *and there has never existed a self.*
> *Through the faculties, perceptual sources and elements,*
> *the mundane world is understood to be valueless.'* [1.23]

That completes this digression linked to the 160 minds.

4. The Level of Practice with Devoted Interest

I shall now return to the main [topic]. After those yogins with acute faculties and those with dull faculties have entered in stages the path of no autonomous existence in the individual and phenomena in the manner explained above, and have comprehended that all phenomena appear like illusions and confuse the mind, they both exert themselves zealously in order to realize the Level of Practice with Devoted Interest (*adhimukti-caryā-bhūmi*). This is the sequence: they repeatedly cultivate that experience of such paths which involve the understanding that the individual and the phenomena lack of autonomous existence, by the cultivation which actualizes the entering (*praveśa*), abiding (*prasthāna*) and arising (*utthāna*) minds, and they assist beings with the Four Methods of Attracting which is a preliminary to the engagement in the Perfections of Generosity and so forth which are to be accomplished, so even though they have not attained [the minds] which cause them to enter the Ten Levels and the qualities (*guṇa*) of the body, speech and mind which result naturally from them, (12a) by the power of their insight which understands by hearing and pondering, they are firmly convinced that what is taught by the words of the Dharma which refer to those things is just so. That is *devoted interest.*

That preliminary devoted interest in the Bodhisattva practice, whose nature is the accomplishment of the benefit of self and others as appropriate is practice with devoted interest. It is practice with devoted interest in the sense of 'basis'. The Bhagavat teaches that the Level of Practice with Devoted Interest will be transcended in one eon, with these words:

> *'The Level of Practice with Devoted Interest*
> *is the cultivation of the Three Minds.*
> *Through the practice of the Perfections*
> *and the Four Methods of Attracting,*
> *the Level of Devoted Interest is unequalled,*
> *immeasurable and inconceivable.*
> *The emergence of immeasurable Awareness*
> *will come about by the ten minds.*
> *Everything that I have spoken a little about*
> *will be attained through this [Level].*
> *Therefore the All-knowing One*
> *calls this "devoted interest".*
> *The intelligent person will perfect*
> *this Level with the elapse of one eon.'* [1.27]

5. The Three Minds

Moreover, an elucidation of the meditative cultivation of the three minds which is termed the Level of Practice with Devoted Interest and these ten minds of the Level of Devoted Interest in the Dharma which perfects the Ten Awareness Levels is given by this passage in the Secret Chapter which is part of the *Uttara-tantra* of this *Vairocana Tantra* thus: '*Lord of the Secret Ones! What is complete knowledge of the three minds of practice with devoted interest? Lord of the Secret Ones! The first instant of mind which is characterized by the understanding through conceptual thought that the mind is without arising and perishing is the first realization* [the entering mind]. *The second* [the abiding mind] *is non-conceptualizing and transcends the entire web of concepts.* (12b) *Having gained the realization which is without obscurations, one can generate the compassion which would establish all beings on the true path. This is the third* [arising] *mind. Lord of the Secret Ones! When the three minds have been accomplished, the Levels, the Perfections and the Methods of Attracting will be accomplished.*

'*Lord of the Secret Ones! As for the practices for the accomplishment of the Levels and Perfections, Bodhisattvas who engage in the Bodhisattva practice by way of mantras and who are endowed with expedient means, insight and awareness, cause beings to accept* [*the Dharma*] *by the Four Methods of Attracting. This giving of the gift the Dharma in a joyful spirit is application to a branch of the Levels and Perfections. Lord of the Secret Ones! Moreover, he Bodhisattva who abides in the pure unconditioned morality will give that Dharma, he will establish beings in the morality they wish for and will also abide there himself. This should be viewed as application to a branch of the Levels and Perfections. Lord of the Secret Ones! At the time when the mind of a Bodhisattva is radiant and pervades all phenomena in the ten directions, he himself will attain the acceptance of the non-arising of phenomena and he will cause others to be established therein. This should be viewed as application to a branch of the Levels and Perfections. Lord of the Secret Ones! Moreover, one who has the light of Awareness, exerts himself with skilfulness to a greater and higher realization with that mind and also causes others to be established there. Lord of the Secret Ones, you should view this as his application to the accomplishment of the branches of the Levels and Perfections.*

'*Lord of the Secret Ones! When the Bodhisattva who engages in the Bodhisattva practice by way of mantras* (13a) *meditates on that mind, with a spirit of awareness, without regard for any of the meditative absorptions and also causes others to accept that, then you should view this as his application to the accomplishment of the Levels and Perfections. Lord of the Secret Ones! Moreover, when he himself abides there endowed with that mind, with a spirit of awareness, without regard for the mundane and supramundane meditative absorptions and immeasurable states of the Śrāvakas, and also establishes others therein, then you should view this as his accomplishment of the Levels and Perfections. Lord of the Secret Ones! Moreover, the Bodhisattva who engages in the Bodhisattva practice by way of mantras and who aspires in that way for meditative absorption with that mind, will himself abide in the practice of mundane and supramundane Insight* (prajñā) *with a spirit of awareness and also establish others therein. Lord of the Secret Ones, you should view this as his accomplishment of the Levels and Perfections.*

'*Lord of the Secret Ones! Moreover, the Bodhisattva who has been well-assisted by a spiritual friend and who is skilled in attracting beings with expedient means, will generate and uphold the first mind* (bodhicitta), *having aspired to all the Dharma of the Buddha, and attract beings with those Four Methods of Attracting. This is the Perfection of Expedient Means, and it should be viewed as the accomplishment of the application of the Level which Goes Far. Lord of the Secret Ones! Moreover, he whose spirit of awareness is unmoving and not agitated, will indeed not be overcome by any assailant or the Māra family of gods. This should be viewed as the application of the Unshakable Level and of the Perfection* [*of Devoted Interest*]. (13b) *Lord of the Secret Ones! Moreover, the Bodhisattva who has been well-assisted by a spiritual friend, for whom all phenomena have become identical as illusions, and who is endowed with the Perfection of Great Compassion, will pervade all the Buddha fields of the ten directions with the Perfection of Great Compassion and completely satisfy beings equally with his body, speech and mind, and then with prickling hair and much joy, he will see the Tathāgatas who abide in the ten directions. Endowed with the Great Compassion which is devoted to beings, he causes it to pervade all beings by his firm adherence to space, to beings, to awareness and to consciousness, and when he has developed the Strengths of trust, exertion and insight, he will see Buddhas and Bodhisattvas both in dreams and in actuality, and will also acquire the* samādhi *of not forgetting* bodhicitta. *You should know that this is the Bodhisattva who has entered the mandala of the* samādhi *of devoted interest.* You should understand this according to the Secret Chapter taught in detail in the *Uttara-tantra.* That concludes this digression.

6. The Bodhisattva

I shall now return to the main [topic]. At the conclusion of this explanation, which states that the Level of Practice with Devoted Interest will be transcended in one eon, the Bhagavat also teaches that those who are going to enter the Awareness Level, the Joyous One, which is characterized as the first generation of *bodhicitta,* who have the qualities (*guṇas*) which are the bridge (from) the Level of Practice with Devoted Interest, will pass beyond that Level when they have repeatedly cultivated it for a quarter of an eon, and enter into the Awareness Levels, saying

> '*Moreover he will transcend devoted interest* (14a)
> *after just a quarter* [*of an eon*]'. [1.27]

Following that, the Bhagavat teaches that while they are directly experiencing that path which involves the understanding that the individual and phenomena lack autonomous existence, by way of the entering, abiding and arising minds, they are entirely absorbed in the accomplishment of merit and wisdom through countless eons, because they repeatedly cultivate the Perfections of Generosity and so forth. Consequently, they will attain the mind which counteracts dualistic concepts regarding the illusory, mirage-like nature of the psycho-physical constituents and so forth, which is the characteristic of the First Level, by way of perceiving the suchness of all phenomena: '*Lord of the Secret Ones! Moreover, there are Bodhisattvas who engage in the practice of Bodhisattvas by means of the secret mantra path, who have accumulated an immeasurable mass of merits and awareness in countless hundreds of thousands of millions of eons*' down to '*furthermore, there arises the mind whose essential nature is emptiness, without substance, which is without attributes, without perceptual forms, which transcends all proliferations, which is limitless like space, which is the ground of all phenomena, which is separate from the conditioned and the unconditioned realms, which is free from actions and activities, separate from eye, ear, nose, tongue and body, and is without any self-existent nature whatsoever. Lord of the Secret Ones! This is spoken of by the Jinas as the first* [*level*] *of* bodhicitta'. [1.26] (14b)

Hence, the Bhagavat teaches that the name '*Bodhisattva*' is given to those endowed with the qualities which bring about entry into the Bodhisattva's Ten Awareness Levels, who have undertaken to cultivate them sequentially and accomplish them sequentially during the Bodhisattva's Ten Levels, through the process just explained. It is also said that:

> '*Enlightenment is space*[*-like*] *in nature,*
> *devoid of all judgemental concepts:*
> *whoever desires to realize that*
> *is called a Bodhisattva*'. [28.3]

'*Whoever desires to realize that*' is their specific characteristic, and it implies that they have undertaken it in order to realize, in stages, the *bodhicitta* which is focussed upon suchness.

7. The Buddha

Following that, the Bhagavat teaches that you will be termed a '*Buddha*' when you arrive at the accomplishment of the Ten Bodhisattva Levels and the Ten Masteries, realize that even illusion-like phenomena are empty and also undertake the relative path. You will also know all the types of karmic actions of beings which draw them to the fortunate and unfortunate realms and the predictability of their specific causes and effects through (15a) having actualized the Awareness [which perceives] such objects (*viṣaya*), for then:

> '*One who has accomplished the Ten Levels,*
> *and has attained the Ten Masteries,*
> *who comprehends that phenomena*
> *are empty and illusion-like,*
> *and who knows the fortunes of all people,*
> *is called a Buddha*'. [28.4]

One who has realized that all phenomena lack even existence as illusions is termed a '*Buddha*'.

8. The Perfect Buddha

Now, the Bhagavat teaches that you will become perfectly enlightened (*saṃbuddha*) when you truly comprehend that, on the absolute level, all phenomena which you hitherto not understood are characterized by emptiness, are non-dual like space and have a single attribute, while you will also attain the Ten Strengths by Awareness on the relative level:

> '*One with the Ten Strengths*
> *who has fully realized*

that phenomena are space-like in nature,
non-dual, with a single attribute,
is said to be a Perfect Buddha'. [28.5]

One is also termed a Perfect Buddha (*saṃbuddha*) because one has realized that the suchness of all phenomena is identical, hence it also says in the *Prajñā-pāramitā*: '*The characteristic of the realization that all phenomena are identical in being nothingness is thus: the purity of colour-form is the purity of feeling, and the purity of feeling is the purity of colour-form. Thus this purity of colour-form and the purity of feeling is non-dual, indivisible, not separate and not distinct.*'

9. The Great Hero

This occasion, when the Awareness of Perfect Enlightenment is realized, is also mentioned in the text, in the teaching on the *Samādhi* of the Great Hero. It says that when the Bhagavat was still a Bodhisattva, he assumed birth in the Realm of Desire, went forth, engaged in asceticism and so forth in order to mature beings by his projected creations. He sat in the core of Enlightenment, was victorious over the Four Māras through the prior realization of the five-membered *Samādhi* of the Great Hero, and then he attained [Perfect Enlightenment]. What it says in the section where the *Samādhi* of the Great Hero is taught is this:

Then the Bhagavat said to the Bodhisattva Vajrapāṇi:
'Because I sat in the core of Enlightenment
and overcame the Four Māras,
I am called the Great Hero:
This was joyfully proclaimed
with voices free from all fear
by the crowds of gods such as Brahmā.
Thereafter, I who am mighty,
have been renowned as the Great Hero.
I directly realized that there is no arising,
and abandoned the perceptual range of words;
I became free from all faults,
and separated from causes and conditions.
There arose in me, as it really is,
the Awareness which is empty, like space,
the utterly pure reality,
which is devoid of all darkness.
To abide in the mode of "idea alone":
this is the attribute of Perfect Enlightenment.
Hence I revealed this reality
in the form of letters,
by the power of transformation,
to illumine the world,
and out of pity for beings
I teach everything to them'. [2.73]

Now the letters which characterize the Great Hero Essence which is the basis for this *Samādhi* of the Great Hero are *A Khaṃ Vī Ra Hūṃ*, and you should understand that the basis of five-membered *Samādhi* of the Perfect Enlightenment of Great Hero is formed with these five seed-syllable letters. Furthermore, the power and accomplishment of this essence are taught in detail later in the chapter on the Great Hero. (16b)

Likewise, in order to aid beings here who have devoted interest in the mantra practice, this same Bhagavat went to the Ghanavyūha Buddha Field and entered the core of Enlightenment located there, prior to displaying Perfect Enlightenment. Then, being encouraged by all the Buddhas in the manner of the *Tattvasaṃgraha Tantra*, he transformed himself into the Body of a Buddha by the five part application to Perfect Enlightenment (*abhisaṃbodhi*) and went to the top of Mount Sumeru. Then, he helped the gods who are active in the Realms of Desire and Form and restrained hostile beings by generating the Vajradhātu Mandala and so forth. Having also come to Jambudvīpa, he entered the core of Enlightenment and explained the Mantra Method. By this process, he displayed Enlightenment in the manner of the Yoga style of tantras, in order to aid those humans and gods who have interest in [the Mantra Method]. This theme is taught in detail in the *Tattvasaṃgraha Tantra.*

Therefore, by showing the power of the realization of Perfect Enlightenment (*abhisaṃbodhi*) in various ways, the Bhagavat's intention is that you should comprehend the manner in which he became fully and perfectly enlightened in order to attract trainees variously by way of the Mantra Tantras and the Perfection Sutras. Thus this [process], beginning with the eight mundane minds, which were explained previously, up to the Great Hero Level which is the occasion of Perfect Enlightenment, is the cause of becoming the Bhagavat Vairocana, the nature of which is the accumulation of merit and awareness.

II. THE ESSENTIAL NATURE OF VAIROCANA

1. The Attainment of the Four Modes of Embodiment

The essential nature of the Bhagavat Vairocana is defined as the four modes of embodiment (*kāya*). Thus, dividing the *nirmāṇa-kāya* into two, four modes of embodiment are taught in this Tantra. These are the *dharmakāya*, the *abhisaṃbodhi-kāya*, the *saṃbhoga-kāya* and the *nirmāṇa-kāya.*

This is the process of realizing (*abhisamaya*) these embodiments on the absolute level: As previously described, a person becomes disillusioned with *saṃsāra* and enters the mundane path which has the characteristics of fasting, religious observances and certainty. By reliance upon reason and spiritual friends, they gradually accumulate the mass of merit and awareness which precedes the realization of the tenth Bodhisattva Level. Having realized [everything] up to this state of Perfect Enlightenment, they then transcend the Three Realms. They are born equal in fortune with those who reside in the Ghanavyūha Buddha Field and see with the Eye of Awareness that the realms of beings are tormented by the burning fire of the three kinds of suffering. Generating the resolute mind of a extremely compassionate mother, they think: 'This realm of beings is clearly unable to separate itself from the three kinds of suffering without the full perfection of the Vajra Array of the Inexhaustible Body and so forth, but because that full perfection of the Inexhaustible Body and so forth will not come about without the attainment of Enlightenment, I shall sit in the core of Enlightenment and actualize the Light of Awareness (*jñāna-āloka*) which is free from the hostile hordes of concepts and without any foundation for the predispositions that result in conceptual proliferations, which is the supreme truly perfect Enlightenment in nature. Then having actualized that, through the force of my previous aspirations, these Vajra Arrays of Body, Speech and Mind will arise, whose sole end is to satisfy beings according to their lot.' Having resolved thus, they transform themselves solely for the accomplishment of that intention and attain the four modes of embodiment.

2. The *Dharmakāya*

The *dharmakāya* is the state of unlocalized Nirvāṇa which is endowed with an accumulation of Awareness from which all supports for conceptualization have been cleared away, which is radiantly luminous because it has been freed from all perceptual images, and which continues in an unbroken stream of moments as long as there is *saṃsāra* since it is bounded by self-awareness (*svasaṃvedana*) alone. The attributes of that *dharmakāya* are mentioned in the text thus:

> '*Because he has eliminated "idea-only",*
> *one whose Awareness is self-knowing,*
> *the intrinsic nature of which is inexpressible,*
> *is termed a Tathāgata*'. [28.6]

Therefore, the ascertainment by reason and scripture that even the essential nature of this *dharmakāya*, which characterizes the Tathāgata, has neither been born nor will be born, is undertaken through the preparatory path in which attachment to phenomena is completely abandoned. If you have ascertained thus by reason that all phenomena, which you imagined to be pure and impure in nature, have intrinsically neither been born nor will be born on the absolute level, you will not believe that [the *dharmakāya*] has any substantial existence, as it has been said:

> *No essential nature can be discerned*
> *through any intellectual examination,*
> *hence it has been taught that they are unborn*
> *and without essential nature.*

Furthermore, the ascertainment by reason that all phenomena are unborn is developed in detail and explained in many Mādhyamika treatises by the Master Nāgārjuna and others, so I shall not endeavour to do so here. Therefore, as even this pure *dharmakāya* which characterizes the state of a Tathāgata arises by interdependence (*pratītya-samutpāda*), you should not think that it has any substantial existence (*dravya-sat*) on the absolute level, for as the *Sarva-buddha-viṣaya-*[*avatāra-*]*-jñāna-āloka-vyūha Sūtra* says: '*Mañjuśrī! This "unbornness" is a epithet* (adhivacana) *for the Tathāgata*'. And also from the same:

'The unborn is always the Tathāgata,
all phenomena are like the Tathāgata;
by apprehending perceptual forms, those with foolish minds
become involved in non-existent phenomena in the world.
Since the Tathāgata is wholesome, he is free from inflations
but takes on physical appearances here;
though they have no reality and are not the Tathāgata,
these physical manifestations appear in all the worlds.'

This same method should be applied to abandon completely through reasoning any belief in the substantial existence of all entities such as the *saṃbhoga-kāya* and so forth.

3. The *Abhisaṃbodhi-kāya*

Therefore, the aspect of the peerless Mahā-vairocana which initially appears by virtue of this *dharmakāya*, at such times as when he is revealing himself to the Great Bodhisattvas with pure [mental] streams, by means of manifesting the *saṃbhoga-kāya* and the *nirmāṇa-kāya* which have the characteristics appearing below, is the *abhisaṃbodhi-kāya* of this Bhagavat. Because the core of Enlightenment is always manifested thus to those who are to trained, it is called the *abhisaṃbodhi-kāya*. As for its characteristics, text says that '*the Great Bodhisattvas such as Samantabhadra then saw the Bhagavat who had entered the most excellent core of Enlightenment*' [10.8].

4. The *Saṃbhoga-kāya*

Likewise, when he had just attained the *dharmakāya*, any [embodiment] from among his manifestations in the three levels of existence by the naturally acquired Array of his Inexhaustible Body, Speech and Mind which satisfy beings according to their interest, which solely teaches the profound and extensive Dharma whose substance is scripture and realization to just the pure Bodhisattvas, and which is perceived by those Bodhisattvas in indefinite places and times, whether at the core of Enlightenment or elsewhere, while he appears in a peerless Body, is shown here to be the essential nature of the *saṃbhoga-kāya* of the Bhagavat Vairocana. That *saṃbhoga-kāya* of the Bhagavat Vairocana is also shown by these words of the Tantra thus: '*Thus, teachers were seen resembling the bodies of the Vajradharas, the Bodhisattvas Samantabhadra, Padmapāṇi and so on, who taught the Dharma with the pure words of the Mantra Method in the ten directions. They taught it in order to perfect completely those beings who have nurtured lives of action, from the first generation of* bodhicitta *up to those who dwell in each of the Ten Levels, and to bring about the acquirement of the sprout of existence in those who have suppressed lives of action*'. [1.3]

5. The *Nirmāṇa-kāya*

Those embodiments which appear as gods, humans and non-humans, and which are manifested to undertake the teaching of the Dharma to gods, humans and non-humans according to their lot, causing the foolish ordinary people to accept the mundane or supramundane paths as appropriate, should be known here as the *nirmāṇa-kāya.* Regarding their characteristics, the text says: '*Bhagavat! How do the Tathāgata Arhat Samyak-saṃbuddhas, having achieved the All-knowing Awareness themselves, reveal that All-knowing Awareness to beings and teach* [*it to them*] *with various methods, intentions and expedient means. For they teach the Dharma to some beings with the Śrāvaka-yāna method, to some with the Pratyekabuddha-yāna method, to some with the Mahāyāna method, to some with the method of the Five Supernatural Cognitions, to some with activities in the shape of gods, to some in human shape, or in the shape of* mahoragas, nāgas, yakṣas, gandharvas, asuras, garuḍas *and* kinnaras*? How is it that each of those beings to be guided see them in the shape of a Buddha, or in the shape of a Śrāvaka, or in the shape of a Pratyekabuddha, or in the shape of a Bodhisattva, or in the shape of Maheśvara, or in the shape of Brahmā, or in the shape of Nārāyaṇa, or in the shape of Vaiśravaṇa, or in the shape of* mahoragas, kinnaras *and so on? How is it that they use the modes of speech appropriate to each being and are seen behaving in various ways, and yet the All-knowing Awareness has the sole taste of the Tathāgata's liberation?*' [1.4]

Likewise, this is the description of the emanation of the Array of the Buddha Speech: '*Lord of the Secret Ones, behold the vast emanations of the Mandala of my Speech Configuration which pervade limitless world systems, which are gates of purity, gates which satisfy all beings according to their wishes and make known the continuum of reality to each of them individually. They are at present engaged in the performance of Buddha activities as Śākyamunis in unlimited world-systems that are more extensive than the realm of space. Yet, Lord of the Secret Ones, concerning that, beings do not know that this is the arising of the Mandala of the Bhagavat's Speech Configuration, that they are Buddha Bodies arisen from the Essence* [*Am*] *of the arrayed of Adornments of the Speech of the Buddha, which produces them to satisfy beings according to their wishes*'. [22.3]

6. The Arrangement of the Four Modes of Embodiment in the Mandalas

The transformation of these four modes of embodiment is revealed visibly in the arrangement of the Mandala Arising from Great Compassion by the perceptual forms of the body-forms, *mudrās, vidyās* and mantras of the Buddhas and Bodhisattvas. Thus the transformation of the *dharmakāya* of all the Tathāgatas is revealed in the arrangement of the triangular symbol. The Bhagavat Vairocana, as the embodiment of the core of Enlightenment, should be placed in the centre of the core mandala, with a *samādhi mudrā.* Likewise, in the same core area you should view those with the divine characteristics of deities encompassed by the Three Families, such as Lokeśvara, Vajradhara and so forth, as the body-forms of the transformation of the *saṃbhoga-kāya.* Likewise the *nirmāṇa-kāyas* reside all together with the others in the second area – appearing as the *nirmāṇa-kāya* of the Bhagavat Śākyamuni and the body-forms of the mundane deities such as Indra, Yama, Varuṇa, Vāyu, Agni, Brahmā, Viṣṇu, Śiva and so forth who fully satisfy the beings who have faith in them. Thus, you should consider the *dharmakāya,* the *abhisaṃbodhi-kāya,* the *saṃbhoga-kāya* and the *nirmāṇa-kāya* of the Bhagavat Vairocana to be encompassed by the arrayed deities of the first and second areas of the Mandala Arising from Great Compassion. In the third area, there are arranged the Perfection Beings, the great Bodhisattva Lords of the Ten Levels, such as the Bhagavats Mañjughoṣa, Sarva-nīvaraṇa-niṣkambhi, Kṣitigarbha and so forth with their entourages, who draw near out of a desire to see the Bhagavat Vairocana's *abhisaṃbodhi-kāya* and so on. In that way you should understand that this [Mandala] shows the essential nature of the Bhagavat Vairocana since it reveals the attributes of the four modes of embodiment.

7. The Multiplicity of Tathāgatas

Now this should be considered: It has been explained that even though the Tathāgata primarily abides in the *dharmakāya* since the continuity of a Buddha is uninterrupted, he appears in the *abhisaṃbodhi-kāya* each time he is to guide a certain great Bodhisattva. Hence, if a multitude of embodiments of the Tathāgata are [said to be] generated and appear in that way, is it actually possible for a great number of embodiments of the Tathāgata with the attributes of Full Enlightenment to appear at a single time? If that is the case, then what problem would there be were it so? The Mahāyāna asserts that the Buddhas who manifest as the *saṃbhoga-kāya* and *nirmāṇa-kāyas* do gather together at a single time, as is mentioned in the *Buddha-saṃgīti Sūtra* and so on. Also, such Mantra Sutras such as the *Tattva-saṃgraha* and so forth, mention that these manifestations as the *abhisaṃbodhi-kāya* also occur in the presence of people to be trained thus. What is wrong with this? Elsewhere it has been said that,

> '*All the Buddhas are equal*
> *due to their accumulations,*
> dharmakāyas *and engagement*
> *in the benefitting of creatures*',

so even though the *abhisaṃbodhi-kāya* manifestation of all Buddhas is identical, they benefit the entire mass of people to be trained, hence there is nothing wrong with this. On the other hand, would it not be valueless for additional Tathāgatas to arise, since the benefitting of all beings can come about through a just single manifestation of the Tathāgata's Body? There is no problem with this, for, on the absolute level, [a Buddha's attainment of] Perfect Enlightenment characterized by the abandonment of his own obscurations of emotional afflictions and wrong understanding is sequentially revealed for the sake of people to be trained, who rely upon and enter the true path which arises as the union of expedient means and insight, in order to calm the burning fire of the three kinds of suffering of *saṃsāra* which is present in their streams [of existence]. Therefore, one engages in the benefitting of beings initially as an element (*aṅga*) leading to the attainment of Enlightenment, while subsequently one spontaneously engages in the benefitting of beings by the Inexhaustible Array of the *abhisaṃbodhi-kāya* and so forth. You should not think that this benefitting of all beings is just done by a single Tathāgata and hence there is nothing for you to do. It is indeed fitting because it is quite consistent. This concludes the explanation of the attributes of the four modes of embodiment which are the essential nature of the Bhagavat Vairocana.

III. THE CAUSES OF ENLIGHTENMENT

Hence, the cause of obtaining these four modes of embodiment is twofold, due to the distinctions of the direct (*pratyakṣa*) cause and the indirect (*saṃbandha*) cause. Of these, the attributes of the indirect cause have already been explained, beginning with the mind of mundane generosity up to the state of the Great Hero which is perfect Enlightenment.

The direct cause is Enlightenment and All-knowingness. Now, the attributes of Enlightenment and All-knowingness are mentioned in the *Buddha-bhūmi Sūtra* thus: '*Enlightenment is the Awareness of Sameness, and All-knowingness is the Investigating Awareness and so forth*'. Thus, by engaging in the practice of a Bodhisattva, the Bhagavat repeatedly cultivated over a long period of time [the view] that the many different kinds of creatures are like an illusion, and that in truth all phenomena are nothingness. (21a) Consequently, there are just these two categories: i) the Awareness of Sameness and ii) Investigating Awareness and so on, as the result of those two causes. At the time of Perfect [Enlightenment], the fourfold[2] [division] into the Awareness of Sameness, the Investigating Awareness and so forth is absent in the first moment, and they are merely termed Enlightenment and All-knowingness, arising through the perception of the Suchness of all phenomena. After that, they are called '*dharmakāya*'. Hence, the *Vairocana Tantra* explains in the [Chapter on] the Mandala Arising from Great Compassion that there is a five-pointed vajra of Awareness in the centre of a triangular symbol which is the transformation of the *dharmakāya*. Therefore, this fivefold Awareness[3], which is Enlightenment and All-knowingness in nature, is said to have a single essential nature on the absolute level. This is either because it perceives Suchness or else because it is logically impossible [for it to be otherwise], as it is unborn and unarising from the very beginning, for it is said that both Enlightenment and All-knowingness are non-dual and cannot be divided into two. In order that these two might be realized, three causes are described in the text: i) Great compassion, ii) *Bodhicitta* which has the attributes of the First Level, and iii) the continuous cultivation of the Perfections of Generosity and so forth. Thus, the text says that '*All-knowing Awareness has* bodhicitta *as its cause, compassion as its root and is upheld by the expedient means of the Perfections*'. Therefore, three causes which bring about the realization of Enlightenment and All-knowingness are described: the initiating cause (*praveśa-hetu*) for realization, the immediate cause (*upādāna-hetu*) for realization and the co-operating cause (*sahakāri-hetu*) for realization. Of those, great compassion is the initiating cause of one who aims for the supreme truly perfect Enlightenment. Its attribute is the desire that all beings might be freed from suffering. The immediate cause is the *bodhicitta* which has the attributes of the First Level. Having purified it on higher and higher Levels, by means of antidotes to the inimical, it becomes of the same nature as All-knowingness which has the attributes of supreme truly perfect Enlightenment. The co-operating cause is said to be the accomplishment of the Six Perfections.

IV. THE ESSENTIAL NATURE OF PERFECT ENLIGHTENMENT

When one directly understands one's own mind and all phenomena, the Awareness arising at the first moment which has the attribute of realizing that they are unborn and unarising is called 'Enlightenment'. The means to realize that is taught with the words '*What is Enlightenment? It is to know your mind as it really is*' [1.7]. Now there are two types of [dualistic] concepts (*kalpa*) regarding phenomena: i) the concept which posits the existence of perceived objects and a perceiving subject in the psycho-physical constituents, perceptual elements and perceptual sources, through the interdependent arising of external things (*bāhya-artha*) and a mind unconnected with such appearances (*ābhasa*), and ii) apart from that, the concept which posits the existence of a perceiving subject and perceived objects due to the appearance of blue and so forth without there being external things. Therefore, these two are incompatible with the attainment of the Bhagavat Vairocana's four modes of embodiment, because they are the very causes of the obscurations of emotional afflictions and wrong understanding, so they should be abandoned. Moreover, the path to their abandonment is supreme truly perfect Enlightenment, and so to teach initially in brief that [Enlightenment] forms the antidote to the mind which has the attributes of a perceiving subject and perceived objects, it says '*Enlightenment is to know your mind as it really is*'. Now, since '*Enlightenment*' (*bodhi*) is given as 'understanding' in lists of verbal roots (*dhātu*), the word '*Enlightenment*' indicates 'knowing' in a general sense. Therefore, Enlightenment is defined as knowing your mind as it really is. Here 'your mind' connotes the mind which appears as a perceiving subject and perceived objects, and which is the faculties, the intellect and so forth in nature. *To know it as it really is*: The Enlightenment which fully knows things as they really are is the understanding that all images are without reality, through investigating the essential nature of that mind which has the aspects of a perceiving subject and perceived objects, by reasoning and scripture which show that they are without inherent reality. The word '*really*' is used in the sense of veridical (*aviparyāsa*). As it says in the text, '*even though one searches, one will not find it in any percepts, colours, shapes, sense objects, form, feeling, ideation, motivation, or consciousness, nor in any I and mine, nor in any perceiving subject nor in perceived objects, nor in the pure or the impure, nor in the perceptual elements, nor in the perceptual sources, nor in any other perceptual data*' [1.12].

This Enlightenment, which is characterized by the full knowledge of one's mind as it really is, is also differentiated from that of the Śrāvakas and the Pratyekabuddhas by the term '*supreme and fully perfect Enlightenment*'. Hence, this implies that the Enlightenment of the Śrāvakas and the Pratyekabuddhas is not the antidote to the obscurations of the emotional afflictions and wrong understanding, due to the presence (*ābhasa*) of the psycho-physical constituents and so forth. Because of that, the *Vairocana Tantra* says '*therein neither exists nor can be perceived any phenomenon whatsoever*' [1.7], which shows that this Enlightenment is the antidote to emotional afflictions and wrong understanding in all aspects since, it is devoid of such appearances as the psycho-physical constituents and so forth. The same point is also shown by '*in that supreme and fully perfect Enlightenment there neither exists nor can be perceived any phenomenon whatsoever which forms perceived objects or a perceiving subject*' [1.7]. Therefore, this implies that [Enlightenment] is radiant through being intrinsically unassociated with all perceptual images, so there neither exists nor can be perceived [within it] the slightest phenomenon with the aspects of a perceiving subject and perceived objects. Because of that, it says '*Enlightenment has the attribute of space*' [28.3].

As an simile for Enlightenment, space shows that it is radiantly luminous because it is intrinsically unassociated with all perceptual images, but that does not cause you understand that it is an unborn entity in nature. Because of that, it says '*therein there is neither that which becomes enlightened nor that to which one is enlightened*' [1.7].

(23a) Hence, this implies that there is only Enlightenment whose essential nature is intrinsic luminosity and Awareness of Sameness, which is formed from the full knowledge of one's mind as it really is, and yet is devoid of the dualistic concepts that there is one who is enlightened and that to which one is enlightened.

Moreover, should you wonder why it is not possible for the dualistic concepts of one who is enlightened and that to which one is enlightened to exist in that Enlightenment, it says '*because Enlightenment is without attributes*' [1.7]. Hence, this implies that if we say that an 'attribute' (*lakṣaṇa*) is any mental concept (*vikalpa*) of blue and so forth, by which one knows, defines and understands an object to have the qualities of blue and so forth, then that Enlightenment is without them because it lacks perceptual images and does not conceptualize, hence it is said to be without attributes. Having stated that Enlightenment is in that way the antidote to the mind which has the perceptual images of a perceiving subject and perceived objects, it then says, '*Lord of the Secret Ones! All phenomena are also without attributes*' [1.7], in order to show that it is also the antidote to the psycho-physical constituents, perceptual elements and perceptual sources. '*All phenomena*' are the psycho-physical constituents, perceptual elements and perceptual sources. Their attributes are given in the *Abhidharma-*[*kośa*] (1.14) thus: '*The attribute of colour-form is that which can be beheld, the attribute of feeling is experience, the attribute of ideation is the apprehension of perceptual forms in nature*', and so forth. (23b) When you investigate these attributes with the arguments which show phenomena are without autonomous existence, [you will find that] they do not exist, so it is said that all phenomena are also without attributes. Although this negation (*pratiṣedha*) of attributes merely shows that the psycho-physical constituents and so forth are without inherent reality on the relative level, that attribute of all phenomena being empty, which is their essential nature on the absolute level, has not been negated, so this is shown with the example of space: '[*all phenomena are also without attributes*], *just as space is*'. Then whatever has the attribute of being like space, empty in nature, is said to have the attribute of space. In this case, the example of space is intended as an explanation to show that the relative nature of the psycho-physical constituents and so forth is without inherent reality. Thus, to say that Enlightenment is the realization that one's mind and all phenomena are without inherent reality describes the attribute of Enlightenment.

This mind which is intrinsically radiant and whose nature is understanding is also called Enlightenment at the first moment of arising on the Tathāgata Level. You should understand that it is given the names 'unlocalized Nirvāṇa' and '*dharmakāya* of the Tathāgata' thereafter. By virtue of this *dharmakāya*, various different embodiments appear which teach in whatever state, occasion and language is appropriate to those to be trained. Therefore, it is taught that the four part embodiment which has the attributes explained here also has Enlightenment as cause.

It is not possible to conceive any substantiality in this intrinsically radiant Awareness whose nature is Perfect Enlightenment and unlocalized Nirvāṇa, either in itself or in anything else apart from that. This is because it is intrinsically extremely radiant, because it causes familiarity (*parijaya*) with the emptiness which is characterized by the sameness of self and other, and because the light of non-conceptualizing Awareness perpetually forms a vast realm.

So that the concepts which trainees have regarding existence and non-existence might be negated, the Bhagavats say that the apprehension of substantial existence should be negated, through the reasoning based on the scriptures which teach the Mahāyāna, mentioned both here and elsewhere, to show that both pure and impure things which arise interdependently are in general primordially unborn and unarising, thus:

> '*No essential nature can be discerned*
> *through any intellectual examination,*
> *hence it has been taught that they are unborn*
> *and without essential nature.*'

Consequently it says in the *Sarva-buddha-viṣaya-jñāna-āloka Sūtra*:

> '*The unborn is always the Tathāgata,*
> *all phenomena are like the Tathāgata;*
> *by apprehending perceptual forms, those with foolish minds*
> *become involved in non-existent phenomena in the world.*'

This point is also made in the *300 Prajñā Pāramitā Sūtra*:

> '*They who see me as colour-form,*
> *and who follow me by my voice,*
> *are devoted to perverse efforts:*
> *those people do not see me!*'

As for how one is to see the Bhagavat on the absolute level, likewise it also says therein:

> '*The Buddha should be seen as reality,*
> *the Guides are the* dharmakāya*;*
> *yet the reality cannot be discerned,*
> *nor can one be conscious of it.*'

Though the Bhagavat cannot be seen as a Tathāgata on the relative level, and his essential nature of emptiness does not have any objective reality, it is said that:

> '*The Tathāgata takes on a form*
> *which is wholesome and free from inflations;*
> *though this is not really so, not the Tathāgata,*
> *his form appears in all worlds.*'4 (24b)

Also in the *Great Prajñā-pāramitā Sūtra*, Subhūti looked upon those to be guided and explained to them the [false] belief (*graha*) in pure and impure phenomena as real phenomena thus: *'Even the Enlightenment of a Buddha is like an illusion, like a dream!' The gods said, 'Subhūti! Is even Nirvāṇa like an illusion, like a dream?' Subhūti answered, 'Even Nirvāṇa is like an illusion, like a dream. Were there any phenomenon more distinguished than Nirvāṇa, I would say that it too is like an illusion, like a dream!'*[5]

Therefore you should understand the Bhagavats, who soothe beings with the rain of great compassion and who are the Guides leading us to the city of Nirvāṇa, are aware that the obscurations of emotional afflictions and wrong understanding, which are preceded by the beliefs in a self and what belongs to the self, evolve through the concepts which treat impure and pure (relative and absolute) phenemona as though they have substantial reality, so they help those people who are to be guided and teach that all phenomena are primordially unborn and unarising, in order that attachment to them may be abandoned. Yet, though they may teach for a hundred eons that relative phenomena are primordially unborn and unarising, they do not appear to sever conventional usage (*vyavahāra*). Thus in the *Samādhi-rāja Sūtra* also it says:

> '*That which is conceived is merely imagined,*
> *no end to it can be perceived in* saṃsāra'.[6]

Moreover, some people treat scriptures which express the true nature (*tattva*) of relative and absolute phenomena as implicit meaning (*neyārtha*) even though they are actually explicit in meaning (*nītārtha*), (25a) and thus those who explain the words [of sutras] may even be led to treat what has rational meaning as irrational by the acuity of their intellects, so what hope is there for people like us who are involved with the confusion of attachment? Therefore, if the wise ones think 'I shall ascend the to the peak of the mountain of true views, and having shot the thieves which are the untrue concepts (*asat-vikalpa*) with the arrows of recitation and meditation, I shall devote myself to the perfection of perfect Enlightenment', we can say that they have approached the Dharma sensibly. I [Buddhaguhya] also genuflect to the Holy Ones, joining my hands at my head, and then pray always thus:

> Holy Sugatas, let me do all the tutelary deity yoga,
> the recitations and the mantras which you have taught,
> and then let me be accomplished!
> May the Jinas gaze upon me,
> and then let me know them!

Regarding this, the 'union of the relative and the absolute natures of one's tutelary deity' is the characteristic of union (*yoga*) with one's tutelary deity. This is also the sequence mentioned in related tantras. In this Tantra it says: '*Having convinced yourself that whatever phenomena are seen and heard have the characteristic of being unborn in their absolute nature, by logically [establishing] that they are primordially unborn and unarising, you should next examine what exists on the relative level which one imagines to be the psycho-physical constituents, perceptual elements and perceptual sources through its parts, by the reasoning which considers their unity and multiplicity. Having actualized the mind which is isolated from what appears as them, you should engage in the accomplishment of the tutelary deity yoga on the absolute level and the relative level.*'

Now, the nature of the deity on the absolute level is the continuum of reality, and union with it, through the conviction that the suchness of the tutelary deity and yourself is characterized by indivisibility, is the tutelary deity yoga on the absolute level. (25b) The sequence of union with the relative tutelary deity is also taught here, with two parts. One of these is to accomplish the appearance of yourself as your tutelary deity, by transforming the image of your mind isolated from all appearances into the image of the moon disc and so forth. The other is to arise from the mind isolated from appearances and be convinced that you have the body-image of the deity, through believing in your inherent unity in sameness, preceded by the belief that yourself and the tutelary deity are identical in being like illusions. You should have the pride that the image of one's matured (*vipāka*) body-form is indeed the tutelary deity. These are the two types of yoga for the relative tutelary deity. You should know that this is taught in the chapter on the 'True Nature of the Deity' and so forth in this Tantra. That concludes this digression.

V. THE MANIFESTATION OF ENLIGHTENMENT

1. When Enlightenment arises

Now the portion of the text dealing with the analysis of the direct and perfect Enlightenment of Mahā-vairocana should be dealt with. You should know that it is the manifestation (*vikrīḍita*) of Enlightenment which pervades all the vast realms of the world with the appearance of Vairocana's extensive Body, Speech and Mind, in the semblance of all beings and non-beings as appropriate to the lot of those beings, at the very moment of his realization of that Perfect Enlightenment, by the force of his previous aspirations. The characteristics of that were mentioned earlier in the *Vairocana Tantra*: '*Then those Bodhisattvas headed by Samantabhadra,* (26a) *and those Vajradharas headed by Vajrapāṇi, being empowered by the Bhagavat, entered into the display of the treasury of the manifestations of the sameness of his Inexhaustible Body*' [1.3].

The moment of Vairocana's Perfect Enlightenment is also spoken of elsewhere, thus it is also taught in the *Tathagatotpatti-nirdeśa Sūtra*. I shall repeat in this section what I previously quoted because it is relevant here: '*Nobly born son! After the Tathāgata has become fully enlightened, he enters a* samādhi *called "The Utter Buddha Awakening", and no sooner does he enter it than as many Bodies appear everywhere as there are beings, and as much Speech as there are Bodies, and as many Minds as there are Bodies and Speech appear everywhere. O Son of the Jina! In that way you should understand that the Bodies, Speech and Minds of Tathāgatas are vast and measureless, since the societies of beings are also without measure*' [II.322].

2. The Nature of Enlightenment

These Arrays of the Inexhaustible Body and so forth which were revealed also benefit pure beings such as the Bodhisattva Samantabhadra, since the Bhagavat revealed them as perfect means (*upāya*) in order that they might understand his intrinsic nature (*svarūpa*). Those who are impure such as sages, humans, gods, *asuras, gandharvas* and so forth do not have the capability of seeing the nature of the three Arrays of Vairocana's Inexhaustible [Body and so forth] as they are in themselves, therefore they are transformed into the perceptual forms of the mantras, *mudrās* and mandalas of the Array of Vairocana's Body and so forth, and taught in this Tantra in order to help those beings. Thus, since [such beings] are made to delight in the intrinsic nature of the mandalas, *mudrās* and mantras of the Array of his Body (26b) and so forth by those [perceptual forms], they will also be delighted merely by these instructions of the Bhagavat and will rely on the results which are beatitude and salvation.

The perceptual form [of this manifestation] also has three aspects, based on the categories of its cause, intrinsic nature and result. Of those, its cause is twofold by the distinct categories of the two types of cause: the direct and the indirect causes. The indirect cause should be known through the four categories of *samādhis*: those of the mundane beings, of the Bodhisattvas, of the Buddhas and of Perfect Buddhas. The direct cause is Perfect Enlightenment (*saṃbuddha*) and the *dharmakāya*. The essential nature of this manifestation is the attributes (*lakṣaṇa*) explained earlier. Its result is activities (*prayoga*) using various kinds of expedient means, for the guidance of all beings.

3. How Enlightenment is revealed

Therefore, according to this Tantra, the transformation of this manifestation (*vikrīḍita*) of Perfect Enlightenment (*saṃbuddha*) is threefold in nature. You may deduce from it, as appropriate, those transformations when it teaches about them in the perceptual forms of the mandalas, *mudrās*, mantras and *samādhis*. Of those, the transformation of the Array of his Body is actually shown in the *Vairocana Tantra* by way of the Mandala Arising from Great Compassion. It describes the arrangement of the body-images of the deities, in the [ritual] procedure for the Mandala. Thus it says:

> '*In the centre of the matrix, he should draw*
> *the most excellent Lord of the Jinas,*
> *golden in colour, blazing in light,*
> *with his topknot and crown.*' [2.23]

and

> '*To the north of the Lord,*
> *there is the heroic Avalokiteśvara.*
> *He should be drawn*
> *seated upon a white lotus,*
> *and he is white himself*
> *like a conch, jasmine, or the moon.*
> *His face is smiling and*
> *on his head there is Amitābha.*' [2.26]

and

> '*To the south of the Lord Vairocana,*
> *Vajradhara should be drawn;*
> *he fulfils all wishes,*
> *and in colour he is like a* priyaṅgu *flower,*
> *greenish-yellow, or like an emerald.*
> *This Lord has a crown and is adorned*
> *with all the ornaments of a Great Being;* (27a)

he holds a vast vajra which penetrates all places,
and he is encircled with rays of light.' [2.34]

and so forth at length. This should be understood as the transformation of the Mandala which has the Matrix of Great Compassion.

The transformation of the Array of Inexhaustible Speech is actually shown here as the Mandala of the Revolving Wheel of Letters. Thus, it is explained that the deities should be arranged there as their *mudrās* or seed-syllables. As is mentioned among the teachings on the Mandala of the Revolving Wheel of Letters, the Lord of the Mandala, the Bhagavat Vairocana, should be arranged in either his body-form, *mudrā* or seed-syllable, and then it says that the others apart from him should be arranged as either their *mudrās* or their seed-syllable, thus '*In the east, the letter A with an* anusvāra, *the essence of the* dharmakāya *of all the Buddhas: AṂ* [10.19], and *In the south-east, he should draw the symbol of all the Bodhisattvas, the Cintāmaṇi, or its syllable KA*' [10.19]. In the same way, apart from these, the majority are indicated just as seed-syllables in this description of the Mandala.

Likewise the Secret Mandala epitomizes and reveals the Array of the Inexhaustible Mind, hence the *Vairocana Tantra* states that the deities should be arranged in the Secret Mandala as their distinct symbols which correspond with the content (*artha*) of their liberation such as a lotus or vajra, and as the specific manifestations of their minds, which are the structures of the fire, wind, earth and water mandalas, that are spoken of thus:

'*Lord of the Secret Ones!*
Furthermore, the mandala of the Tathāgatas
is like a pure moon disc,
and resembles a conch in colour;
within it the triangle of all the Buddhas
rests upon a white lotus.
It is marked with an anusvāra *sign,*
and adorned with a vajra symbol.
Without doubt, there will emerge
two rays of light (27b)
from that Lord of Mantras,
and then go to the ten directions.' [13.70]

and

'*Furthermore, Lokeśvara's mandala*
should be drawn diligently by the noble one.
Its border is square all around,
and in the centre, a conch should be placed.
Upon that, a lotus is drawn
full-blown, with its seed-syllable.
Upon that, a great vajra,
and on the vajra also a great lotus
marked with all the seed-syllables,
to which should be added his own seed-syllable.' [13.71]

This should be understood in detail from the instructions on the Secret Mandala.

Although it is explained that these three Mandalas by their number encompass the three secrets of the Body and so on, yet there is no Speech without the Body, and also there is generally no Mind without Body, so you should understand that the three aspects – Body, Speech and Mind – are manifested in each of the Mandalas. Thus, because the Mandalas are generally tripartite, the arrangement of the body-forms, seed-syllables and symbols which are the transformations of the Body, Speech and Mind also appear in each one.

Likewise, you should refer to the Secret Chapter in the supplement to this Tantra regarding other mandalas which are characterized by having fewer sections than this, and understand that this is also the intention in their case.

Moreover, the Array of [Vairocana's] Body and so forth are taught here as the internalized or externalized body-forms of the Buddhas and Bodhisattvas, and form objects of meditation (*dhyeya*) to teach the four-membered recitation to the practitioner. This is mentioned in the text thus:

> '*Letter should be joined to letter,*
> *likewise ground becomes ground.*
> *You should recite 100,000 times*
> *mentally, with restraint.*
> *The [first] letter is* bodhicitta,
> *the second is said to be sound.*
> *[One] ground is your tutelary deity,*
> *which should be created in your body.*
> *The second ground should be known as*
> *the perfect Buddha, the most excellent of men.*
> *The* mantrin *should imagine him*
> *located in a pure moon disc.*
> *He should carefully arrange*
> *the letters within that in sequence.*
> *If attended by the drawn-in syllables,*
> *life and exertion will be purified.*' [5.2 - 5]

Likewise, you should also understand the [Array of the Inexhaustible Body] by way of the transformation into the perceptual images of the representational body-images. Also the Array of the Inexhaustible Speech is revealed here by way of the transformation into the seed-syllables of the *vidyās* and mantras. Thus the mantras are *NSB A Vī Ra Hūṃ Khaṃ* and so forth, and *NSB asame trisame samaye svāhā* and so forth. The seed-syllables of the *vidyās* are *A Ā Āṃ Aḥ* and so forth. Likewise, you should also view the Array of the Inexhaustible Mind as being revealed through the manual *mudrās* or the drawn symbols which you are to arrange.

In that way, the *Vairocana Tantra* states that *you should see such things through their revelation* with regards to the cause, the essential nature, and the perceptual forms of the result of this Array of the Body and so forth.

This condensed form into which the manifestation of Perfect Enlightenment (*saṃbuddha*) is transformed, is revealed in this [*Vairocana Tantra*] as the Mantra [Method] which involves the practices of the Body, Speech and Mind, so that [their] purpose may be naturally achieved through the propitiation of the essences of the mandalas, the *vidyās*, the mantras, the *mudrās* and the seed-syllables, into which the manifestations (*vikrīḍita*) were transformed. Those practices form two categories. The first of them teaches in detail the ritual of the Mandala. (28b) The others apart from that are defined by the teachings about the *vidyās* and mantras, and should be known appropriately in accordance with the Tantra.

B. THE PRACTICAL APPLICATION

I. THE RITUALS FOR THE MANDALA AND INITIATION

Now, regarding what is specified for the ritual of the Mandala, that is taught herein with fourteen parts. These are:

1 The teaching about the Master's attributes.
2 The teaching about selecting the mandala site.
3 The teaching about the attributes of its purification and the ritual for its transformation.
4 The teaching about the attributes of the trainees.
5 The teaching about the ritual to prepare the trainees.
6 The description of the ritual to mark-out the mandala.
7 The division of the sections of the mandala and so forth.
8 The attributes of the colours for the mandala.
9 The teaching about the ritual to apply them.
10 The technique of drawing down the mandala deities.
11 The teaching about the branches of the ritual of worshipping them.
12 The teaching about the ritual to accept the trainees.
13 The description of the ritual to initiate them.
14 Teaching about the ritual to be done with fire.

1. The Attributes of the Master

Of those, the attributes of the Master are of three types: those present in the Master himself, those related to his performance (*abhisaṃskāra*) as a Master and those which have been accomplished. Of those, the attributes present in the Master himself are '*to be compassionate, be skilled in the arts, be ever wise in the methods of the Perfection of Insight, know the differences between the Three Ways, be skilled in the true nature of mantras, know the inclinations of beings, have trust in the Buddhas and Bodhisattvas*' [2.3] and so forth.

The attributes related to his performance as a Master are [indicated] by way of those who are profound and who are not profound:

> '*There are two types of Masters*
> *who comprehend the mantras and* mudrās;
> *you should know their attributes through*
> *the categories of profound and not-profound.*
> [*The first*] *should know the Profound and Extensive,*

and does not have recourse to beings, (29a)
he is a beloved child of the Buddhas,
and he has abandoned the present world.
The second type is intoxicated
by the present world and relies on supports.
He is given permission and empowerment
by the Best of Men, the Buddhas,
in order to draw all mundane mandalas.' [13.14]

The second type is this Master who performs [the rituals] with objective supports.

The *Vairocana Tantra* indicates the attributes of those who have accomplished the Master initiation (*upāya*) in two categories: those who are initiated as Masters who can draw the Mandala with the Matrix of Great Compassion and the Mandala of the Revolving Wheel of Letters and those who are initiated to draw the Secret Mandala:

'*The first are those who only have the* samaya
after having seen this Mandala,
but the mudrās *should not be shown*
nor should the mantras be given to them.
Those who have received the mudrās and mantras
due to the special nature of their bodhicitta,
and have seen the Mandala
are known as the second type of samaya-*holder.*
Those who have seen the mandalas and mudrās,
and have also practised the actions and activities,
but have not yet received instructions from the Guru:
they are also said to have samaya.
There is also the mantrin
who has been instructed according to the ritual
at the time of depicting the mudrās *and mandalas,*
but who does not have the Initiation
for that which arises from Secret Awareness.
The mantrin *who is initiated by the ritual*
within the Secret Mandala,
is called the fifth type of samaya-*holder.*
No others should be said to have samaya.' [13.41 – 45]

Therefore those who have got the Master initiation for the three mandalas by this process, should do the service with the twelve-branched *Vidyā* King[A] when drawing the mandala, as the text says (29b):

'*Listen attentively to what should be done*
beforehand for the Mandala!

A All versions have '*Vidyā* Queen', presumably in error.

The most powerful Vidyā *King*
formed from the syllables of its twelve components
should be recited in due sequence,
abiding in your own samādhi.
Then knowing the appropriate method,
you should perform each action as wished.' [13.13]

Therefore, it is taught that both the trainee who has repeatedly cultivated *bodhicitta* and who has become a mandala Master, and also one who relies on objective supports since they have not yet repeatedly cultivated *bodhicitta*, should do the service of the twelve branched *Vidyā* King beforehand on the occasion of drawing the mandala. The significance of '*abiding in one's own* samādhi' is that the Master should abide in his own *samādhi* and recite this *Vidyā* King. The *Vidyā* King formed from twelve component syllables is *NSB asamāpta dharmadhātu-gatiṃ gatānāṃ sarvathā aṃ khaṃ aṃ aḥ saṃ saḥ haṃ haḥ raṃ raḥ vaṃ vaḥ svāhā hūṃ raṃ raḥ hra haḥ svāhā raṃ raḥ svāhā.* This is also the description of the attributes of the Master's *samādhi.* He should transform himself into the Body of Vairocana with *A* and arrange the entire wheel of letters in his body. That arrangement of the letters in sequence in his body that is indicated by *Ka is placed in the throat* and so forth. That is the first *samādhi* of the Master. Likewise, to have made himself into the Body of Vairocana in the same way and to arrange the three seed-syllables of the three Lords of the Families is the second *samādhi* of the Master. Or else, to transform himself into the Body of Śākyamuni by having arranged the five letters of the Great Hero is the third *samādhi* of the Master. In answer to 'What should one understand to become a Master?', the text says:

'*I declare that* A (30a)
is the essence of all mantras,
and from it there arise
mantras without number;
and it produces in entirety the Awareness
which stills all conceptual proliferations.' [18.3]

and

'*The Perfect Buddhas, Lords of Men,*
say that A *is the vital-force.*
Therefore this is everything,
and inheres in all members;
and the members also should be known
to be ever in all, as appropriate.
All are encompassed by the letters
and the letters also are pervaded by that.
The sounds formed from the letters
arise in each member.
Therefore this encompasses all things,
and the bodies arise from their diversity

I shall teach where they are to be placed,
so listen carefully about the essence!
You should place the essence in your heart,
and then arrange the members in your members.
Established in the yoga-posture
and recollecting the Tathāgatas,
the wise one should make his own body
into the Body of the Perfect Buddha:
he should do all of this.
When a person knows that vast Awareness
according to the prescribed ritual,
then he will be called a Master
by all the powerful Buddhas.
He will be called a Tathāgata,
or else a Perfect Buddha.
He will also be called
a Bodhisattva, Brahmā,
Viṣṇu and Maheśvara.' [18.4 – 8]

and so forth. The benefits should be understood in detail from the Tantra.

Regarding the arrangement of the Wheel of Letters in his body by the Master who has cultivated *bodhicitta* well, in order to show that the benefits are great because that is the method of entry into the absolute level, the text says:

'*Whoever is firm in* bodhicitta,
and devoted to Awareness of the sounds,
without attachment to any dharma,
will be known in all [those] aspects,
Whoever has the Wheel of Letters
arranged throughout his body,
will be a mantrin, *a mantra-holder,*
a glorious mantra king, a Vajradhara.' [18.10]

This is the extensive process for the Master's *samādhi* in which (30b) the wheel of letters is to be arranged. This ritual of the Master's yoga is that of the extra-ordinary Master who is devoted to the profound and the extensive, who relies upon *bodhicitta,* and who is skilled in the true nature of the sounds.

Now I shall describe the two ordinary Master's yogas, based on the process for the brief and the medium ritual for the second type of Master. In order to teach the brief one, by which the Master himself focuses upon the true nature of the sounds, after having arranged the three seed-syllables of the three Lords of the Families in his matured (*vipāka*) body[7], the text says:

'*The letter* Hūṃ *between your eyebrows*
is the ground of He With Vajra;
The letter Sa *in your chest*
is called the ground of Padmapāṇi;

Mine is placed in the heart location:
it is Lord and Master of all,
and it pervades entirely
all the animate and inanimate.' [18.11]

Likewise, regarding the medium ritual for the Master's yoga, he should arrange these five letters in his body matured beforehand, on the occasion of drawing the Secret Mandala. In order to teach that, it says:

'A *is the highest life-energy,*
Va *is called "speech",*
Ra *is called "fire",*
Hūṃ *is called "wrathful",*
Kha *should be known as space,*
and the anusvāra *is the most empty.*
One who knows this is called a Master,
for this is the supreme reality.' [18.12]

You should know that these five letters should be arranged in the pelvis, the navel, the breast, the eyebrows and the cranium, according to the sequence in the section on the arrangement of the Essence of the Great Hero. Therefore the *Vairocana Tantra* prescribes that you should abide in any one of those *samādhis* in that way and recite the *Vidyā* King with twelve component syllables.

2. The Mandala Site

Now, the site of the mandala is of two types: inner and outer. (31a) In order to teach the attributes of the outer site, the text says:

'*Pure and pleasing places with water,*
having fruit and flowers' [2.5]

and so forth, and these should be known in detail from the Tantra.

3. The Purification of the Mandala Site

Moreover, the text prescribes the purification on the relative level thus: '*he should clear away stones, broken pottery, pebbles, hair*' and so forth. It specifies that the Earth Goddess should be first informed of the purification, with these words:

'*O Goddess! You are a witness*
to the Levels and Perfections,
the special methods of practice
of all the Protector Buddhas' [2.7],

and so forth.

The absolute site is the mind itself of the Master who engages in the profound. To purify that you should repeatedly cultivate *bodhicitta*. In order to teach both of these it says:

> '*First you should know the site*
> *which is specified as the mind,*
> *and it should be purified as taught before:*
> *by that you should completely purify it*' [13.16],

and so on in detail down to

> '*appearing as perfect Enlightenment,*
> *so it is said to be stable*' [13.16],

and the *Vairocana Tantra* states that the purification [of the mental site] is by application to repeated cultivation of *bodhicitta*. Therefore, the import of this is that the faults of the site will be purified by just the abandonment of all false concepts (*vikalpa*), by way of repeated cultivation of *bodhicitta*, even without the purification of the outer site. Therefore it says:

> '*Any* mantrin *who [tries] to carry out*
> *the purification of the site,*
> *abiding in conceptual thought,*
> *while lacking in* bodhicitta,
> *will not be able to purify it.*
> *Hence you should abandon thoughts*
> *and then purify the whole of the site.*
> *Of those mandala rituals*
> *I have taught in detail,*
> *these which I prescribe as preliminary*
> *are not understood by the stupid.*
> *Concepts are the cause of suffering,*
> *and as long as they are not abandoned*
> *you will not be enlightened in this world,*
> *nor will you be called All-knowing.*' [13.18]

This meaning of the purification of the mental site is taught in detail in the *Vajra-samaya-abhyudaya Tantra*[8].

4. Taking Possession of the Site

Then you should take possession of the site because you will commence to draw the Mandala from the third day. Regarding the attributes of that, the text says:

> '*The first transformation of the site*
> *is said to be done by the Perfect Buddhas,*
> *and the second by virtue of your mind;*
> *here it should be done in no other way.*' [13.22]

There, '*by virtue of your mind*' means by the power of the Master's mind who resolves in this manner: 'I shall depict the Mandala on this site!'.

The possession of the site by the perfect Buddhas is described in ten parts:

1 Smearing it with cow's urine and dung which has not fallen to the ground on the occasion of taking possession.
2 The pacification of obstacles by subduing them with mantras.
3 Making the mandala of the deities with perfume.
4 Causing the perfect Buddhas to draw near to the Mandala site as appropriate.
5 Worshipping them with fragrances, flowers and so forth.
6 Placing one's hand on the site with the intention of taking possession of it, reciting the mantra of either Trailokya-vijaya or Acala.
7 Inviting the deities of the Mandala, the Buddhas and the Bodhisattvas.
8 Pleasing the Earth Goddess with mantras.
9 Sleeping on the site itself of the Mandala and investigating the auspicious dreams.

These ten parts are taught for the taking possession of the site. This is dealt with in detail from '*Having firmly trodden down the site at one of the suitable places that have been mentioned, the Master should smear it with clean cow's urine mixed with cow's dung that has not fallen to the ground*' [2.10] down to (32a)

> '*Then having arisen, the* mantrin
> *with a compassionate heart,*
> *should place himself on the west side,*
> *and with a pure inner nature,*
> *he should think of* bodhicitta,
> *and like that he should go to sleep.*
> *Then the* mantrin *will see a dream,*
> *either of renowned Bodhisattvas,*
> *or of Buddhas and the Blessed Ones,*
> *who exhort him to undertake*
> *the task of drawing the Mandala,*
> *in order to benefit beings;*
> *or else they say to him:*
> *"O Great Being! It is excellent!*
> *You should quickly draw the Mandala!"*
> *or anything else suitable to encourage him.*' [2.11]

5. The Attributes of the Trainees

Having taking possession of the site in that way, the Mandala should be drawn the next day and the trainees should be thoroughly investigated and accepted. Of those, the attributes of the trainees are of three types: the special attributes, the ordinary attributes and the classificatory attributes. In order to teach the special attributes, it says:

> '*faithful trainees of noble families,*
> *they should have trust in the Three Jewels,*
> *and have profound understanding*' [2.12],

and so forth. However, because it is not possible for them to have many of these attributes, the specific number is shown thus:

> '*They are suitable whether they have ten*
> *or eight, or seven, or five,*
> *or one, two, four or more* [*of these*]' [2.12].

Therefore, concerning them, it says '*whosoever has repeatedly practised the accomplishment of the limitless gates of the method of the Mahāyāna mantra practice previously is a Vajrasattva, and it is for his sake that this number* [*of qualifications*] *has been made*' [2.13].

So that even those who do not have those qualities may be accepted into the Mandala, the ordinary attributes are mentioned. Therefore, it says '*Furthermore, the Master who has great compassion should just vow to liberate all realms of beings without remainder and he should accept beings without limits, in order that that may become the cause of* bodhicitta' [2.14].

With reference to the classificatory attributes of trainees, it says: (32b)

> '*There are four types of trainees*
> *to be known through the categories*
> *of their readiness or otherwise:*
> *those to be accomplished on a single occasion,*
> *those to be accomplished on two,*
> *and those who are neither of those,*
> *but he who has all attributes perfected*
> *is the trainee dearest to the Jinas*' [13.15].

'*Those to be accomplished on a single occasion*' are those trainees who have seen the Mandala, who have repeatedly cultivated *bodhicitta* and made it become pellucid, who have received the *mudrās* and mantras from the Master, who know the rituals that should be done to practise the mantras through having heard the Tantra, and who are skilled in the rituals for the actions of Pacifying and so forth and the actions for the most excellent attainments. This means that those who have such qualities should be accomplished and perfected after having been initiated in the Initiation Mandala just at the end, so that they can accomplish the Master initiation, at the [same] time as being introduced into the Mandala. Those who have received the mantras should accomplish the recitation since they have been given the mantras, hence it says '*those to be accomplished on a single occasion*'.

Those to be accomplished on two: They have not repeatedly cultivated *bodhicitta* and should be made to cultivate *bodhicitta* after having been introduced into the Mandala, and they should also engage in the recitation after being given the *mudrās* and mantras. Therefore, since they are to be accomplished on the second occasion, they are '*those to be accomplished on two*'. Moreover, after they have been made to hear the Tantra and have become skilled in the actions which are to be done, they may initiated as Masters. That is, they should be accomplished by way of completing the Master initiation, hence this also is the meaning of being accomplished on the second occasion. This signifies that the occasion when they are introduced into the Mandala for the first time is one [occasion], and since the occasion when they are initiated as Masters is different to that, they will be accomplished on the second occasion. Because one whose *bodhicitta* has not been repeatedly cultivated and become pellucid is not worthy of the *mudrās* and mantras when entering the Mandala first, nor capable of cultivating *bodhicitta* afterwards, and because in the same way they are incapable of retaining the Tantras and so forth which they hear, they are said to be those who are neither of those.

He who has all attributes perfected is the trainee dearest to the Jinas: Whoever has been initiated into all three Mandalas – that with the Matrix of Great Compassion, the Revolving Wheel of Letters and the Secret One – is perfected in all the attributes of a Master, so of him it is said *he who has all attributes*. Thus, you should also understand that one who already has got that Master initiation may be included among the trainees in order to augment his merits, in order to pacify obstacles, in order to exhaust failings and to let him see the mandala well-drawn by another Master, as the *Subāhu-paripṛcchā Tantra* mentions in detail:

> '*As often as you see the meritorious mandala*
> *where the congregation of* Vidyās *reside,*
> *your body will be empowered by them.*
> *All obstructing demons will be terrorized*
> *if they see your vast vajra-like body*[A] '. [Tsha 180b]

You should understand this sequence according to the section teaching the attributes of the five kinds of *samaya*-holders. As it says in this Tantra:

> '*The first are those who only have the* samaya
> *after having seen this Mandala,*
> *but the mudrās should not be shown*
> *nor should the mantras be given to them.*
> *Those who have received the* mudrās *and mantras*
> *due to the special nature of their* bodhicitta,
> *and have seen the Mandala*
> *are known as the second type of* samaya-*holder.*
> *Those who have seen the mandalas and* mudrās,
> *and have also practised the actions and activities,*
> *but have not yet received instructions from the Guru:*
> *they are also said to have* samaya.
> *There is also the* mantrin

A There is some difference between Buddhaguhya's quote and the canonical version. Buddhaguhya: *ji lta ji ltar rig sngags tshogs kyis ni | bsten-pa'i dkyil-'khor bsod-nams can mthong-ba | de-lta de-ltar rdo-rje rigs bsten-pas | lus la 'dir ni byin-rlabs kun-du-'jug | rdo-rje'i lus ni rgya-che mthong-gyur na | bgegs rnams mtha' dag 'jig par rab tu 'gyur ||* Q: 180b8: *ci-ltar ci-ltar dkyil-'khor mthong-ba dang | de-ltar de-ltar rdo-rje rigs bsten dang | rig-pa'i tshogs la bsten-pa'i bsod-nams kyis | de-yi lus la ma-lus byin-brlabs 'jug | mi-tshugs rdo-rje'i bdag nyid de mthong dang | sa-phyogs rdo-rje'i me 'bar de shes nas | lha klu lha-min gnod-sbyin grub-pa'i rnams | bzlas-brjod byed-pas skrag nas 'byer-bar-'gyur ||*

who has been instructed according to the ritual
at the time of depicting the mudrās *and mandalas,*
but who does not have the Initiation
for that which arises from Secret Awareness.
The mantrin *who is initiated by the ritual*
within the Secret Mandala,
is called the fifth type of samaya-*holder.*
No others should be said to have samaya.' [13.42 – 46]

The meaning of this has just been explained, so I shall not explain the parts.

6. The Preparation of the Trainees

The preparation of the trainees has nine parts: (34a)

1. Taking refuge in the Three Jewels.
2. The confession of failings.
3. Making them accept the Discipline of Awareness which is Unobscured in the Three Times.
4. Causing them to wait in readiness and the offering of flowers, incense and so forth.
5. The divination of omens by the bitten tooth-wood.
6. The ceremony of protection and binding with thread over which the mantra of the Noble Acala and so forth has been recited.
7. The ceremony to make the trainees who abide in readiness joyful.
8. Distinguishing the good and bad dreams seen by the trainees when asleep.
9. Generating enthusiasm in them by explaining the Dharma to them.

Concerning these nine rituals which are necessary when they are being made ready, the text teaches: '*he should make the trainees take refuge in the Three Jewels, he should also explain to them the evils which should not be committed*' [2.15] down to '*because Bodhisattvas do not uphold the training without completely giving their bodies, speech and minds*'. [2.16]

7. The Marking-out and Division of the Mandala

Now there are the six acts for the ritual of marking-out the Mandala:

1. The actualization of the deity yoga mentioned for the marking-out of Mandala in connection with the Master and the cord he holds.
2. The teaching about the size of the Mandala.
3. The teaching which defines the marking-out of the Mandala.
4. Its division into sections.
5. The description of the arrangement of the places of the Mandala deities.
6. The setting off of the gates, arches and portals.

When marking-out the Mandala endowed with the Matrix of Great Compassion, the *Vairocana Tantra* just indicates that the Master should do the yoga of Vairocana, which is taught in detail in the section dealing with the marking-out of the Mandala endowed with the Matrix of Great Compassion thus: '*Taking a thread of five different colours, he should transform himself into the Bhagavat Vairocana*'. [2.19] (34b)

For the marking-out of the Mandala of the Revolving Wheel of Letters, he should mark it out with the conviction that he is the Body of Vajrasattva, which is stated thus: '*He should transform himself into the primordially tranquil, the form of the non-dual yoga, the form of the Tathāgata, the form of the essential nature of nothingness*'. [10.15]

For the marking-out of the Secret Mandala, he should transform himself with the Body of the Perfect Buddha which is endowed with the four mandalas of earth and so forth, and do the marking-out and drawing of it, which is stated thus in the text:

> '*First the* mantrin *should arrange*
> *those mandalas in his own body:*
> *from his feet up to his navel*
> *he should imagine that of earth;*
> *from above that to his heart*
> *he should resolutely imagine that of water;*
> *above that of water is that of fire,*
> *and above that of fire is that of wind.*
> *When he has imagined them* [*thus*],
> *the wise one should establish*
> *the representation upon the ground*'. [13.7]

When the trainees are accepted, you should understand that the Master should generate the extensive, the medium or else the brief Master's *samādhi*, by way of the yoga for the arrangement of the letters described earlier. The various kinds of the Master's *samādhi* at the time of marking-out the Mandala have already been described.

Now, the ritual of the measurement of the Mandala should be examined. The number of the cubits and spans of the seats, the pattern of the enclosure, the body-forms of the deities and *mudrās* are not definitely indicated for any of the three Mandalas in this Tantra, for it teaches them without specifying the size in cubits and so forth. While the mandala portion appears definitely as seven or eight cubits and so on for other great mandalas in order to define the pattern of the enclosure, and while in the tantras, where a great mandala is laid out, the body-forms of the deities and the *mudrās* which are to be depicted are specified and given in cubits and spans, (35a) in this *Vairocana Tantra* the measurements of the pattern of the enclosure of the perfect Buddhas, body-forms of the deities and *mudrās* which are to be drawn are not defined in that way for the Mandala endowed with the Matrix of Great Compassion and so forth. Therefore, one can just say that this measurement in cubits and so forth is indefinite with regards these three Mandalas. As it says in the section teaching the Mandala Arising from Great Compassion, in explaining the attributes of the lotus which is Vairocana's seat:

> '*As for its size, it is taught that*
> *it should be sixteen inches or more*' [2.22].

This signifies that although the size of Vairocana's lotus seat should be sixteen inches (*aṅguli*) or more, such as seventeen or eighteen inches, it should not be made less than sixteen inches in size, such as fourteen or fifteen inches. Thus, you should view this as prescribing that in all three Mandalas, Vairocana's lotus seat should not be made less than sixteen inches in size, but that [the size of] the lotus seats for the remainder of the different deities of the Mandalas are not defined. In that way, regarding all three Mandalas the text teaches in general that the size of the body-forms of the deities, the seats and *mudrās* are indefinite, thus:

> '*As much as the capacity of* manas,
> *you should know that much*
> *are the seats and mudrās,*
> *and also the sizes of the deities,*
> *in due proportion*' [13.38].

In this manner you should understand that whatever measurement is generated for Vairocana's lotus seat according to the capacity of one's *manas*, the body-forms of the deities and the *mudrās* in the enclosure of the Mandala which are not defined should be generated in correlation with the lotus seat of Vairocana. Let it just be said that this Mandala with the Matrix of Great Compassion and so on encompasses the arrangement of the Inexhaustible Body and so forth. (35b)

Now, regarding the marking-out of the Mandala, it is taught that there are two types of five-coloured cords: the cord for marking-out the intrinsically existing Mandala in the air, and the cord for marking-out the transformation Mandala, which is its representation, upon the ground, which is stated thus:

> '*The cords are said to have four parts,*
> *that is, white, yellow, red and black.*
> *The fifth is described as being like space.*
> *Having held* [*one cord*] *in the air,*
> *the mandala should be fixed there.*
> *With a second cord, the mandala*
> *should be laid out upon the ground*' [13.24 – 25].

There '*having held* [*the cord*] *in the air*' signifies that having twisted a cord of five colours for the Mandala Arising from Great Compassion and so on, he should mark-out the Mandala in the air with the ritual of the Brahmā cord. *With a second cord*: The five-coloured cord, the cord used for marking-out the Mandala in the air, should not be used to mark-out the Mandala on the ground. The reason for this is that it would be discourteous to use a cord previously used for the other Mandala. Though the attributes of the wet-line are not indicated, you should understand that it should be just white, in order to avoid confusion of the colours.

Now, this is the explanation of the ritual for marking-out the Mandala Arising from Great Compassion and so forth. Here also there are two types of line. One is the line for dividing the Mandala in the air, and with reference to that it says: (36a)

> '*To mark out a line to the east,*
> *the cord should be held in the air,*
> *level with his navel.*

Then going to the south,
it should be marked out to the north' [2.19].

The meaning of this is that the Master should place the two ends of the first line of the mandala level with his navel, then holding it level with his navel, he should quickly imagine the features of the Array of the Inexhaustible Body and so forth, the intrinsically existent Mandala of the Bhagavat Vairocana. Next, in order to make that visible, he should mark-out the transformed mandala, which is its representational form, with the other five-coloured cord on the ground. Moreover, the ritual of the Brahmā cord is taught in order to first ascertain the centre of the site of the Mandala, thus:

'*Then taking up a second cord*
and recollecting the Tathāgatas there,
he should face east and mark the line.
Then going to the south,
he should mark the line to the north' [2.19].

The text teaches that, following this, the lines of the whole Mandala should be marked out:

'*Then the wise one turns around,*
and standing in the south-west,
he should mark a line northwards.
Then he should turn around to the right,
and having do so, he should stand there,
and mark a line to the south. (36b)
Then leaving that place,
he should go and stand in the south-east,
then the mantrin *who abides in the mantra ritual*
should mark a line eastwards.
Then likewise going to the north-east,
he should face westwards,
he should mark a line northwards
to the north-western quarter.
In that way the mantrin
should make a complete square' [2.19].

8. The Division of the Mandala into Sections

Now, it teaches that the interior of the squared Mandala abode should be partitioned into three areas through division:

'*Then having gone into the interior,*
he should divide it into three'. [2.20]

The process for dividing the Mandala site into three parts is as follows: The interior of the Mandala site which has been completely squared should divided up with eight lines from both directions, to make a grid of eighty-one squares (*koṣṭha*). Those squares should also be divided into three parts, with twenty-seven squares in each portion. The first [outer] section of the Mandala is made by the first band of squares around the four sides. If you count that first chain of squares around the four sides, there are thirty-two squares. Because of that, there are five squares extra here. I explained above that there are twenty-seven squares in each part, therefore it is obvious that one should join these five squares to the inner sections, for without them the squares of the inner sections will not come to twenty seven. Therefore, these five squares should be subtracted from the squares of the first section of the site and added to the area of the inner second section. The procedure for that is as follows: First of all, four of those squares should be divided into eight parts, those four squares then forming thirty-two parts. Therefore, you should subtract one part from the band of thirty two squares of the first section and add it to the area of the inner second section. In that way, four squares will be subtracted from the band of squares of the first section. If you divide the fifth square into four parts and then divide each part eight times, they make thirty-two. Therefore, in this case also you should subtract a single part from the band of thirty squares around the four sides of the first section and add it to the area of the inner second section, in the previous manner. In that manner, these five squares will be subtracted from the band of squares of the first section and added to the squares of the second inner section. In that way, the squares of the first section total twenty-seven. Although the five squares which are thus subtracted from the first section and are added to the area of squares in the second section, make the second area equivalent to the area of the twenty-seven squares, if, however, you use the previous method of division for the squares, it is not possible to make this second inner section. Therefore, in order to divide the second inner section, you should combine all those squares which were subtracted from the area of the squares of the first section with the squares of the second inner section, and make as one the inner part from the outside, all together, and then dividing it with six lines, you should mark out forty-nine squares. Therefore, the band of squares in the first section and the four sides adjacent to them form twenty four squares and the second section should be fixed with these. Of the group of twenty-five squares which remain in the interior, twenty-four should be made as the third inner section. Here also, half of that area of twenty-five squares should be established as the central section and the other half should form sixteen squares. For the size of each one of those parts, you should reduce each part from the band of sixteen squares around the four sides which are connected with the central section, and increase the area of the second section on all four sides. In that way the second and the third sections will each be made with the area of half twenty-five squares. Therefore, you should understand that the three sections should be marked-out with their individual areas equivalent to twenty-seven squares, by the dimensions of their length and breadth. Following that, each section on four sides should be marked out with the dimensions of their length and breadth and one third part of each section should be made into a courtyard. The remaining two parts of each section left over should be fixed as the abode of their specific deities. It is thus indeed explained in this *Vairocana Tantra* that the parts of the three sections of the Mandala Arising from Great Compassion and so forth should each be fixed the same size in length and breadth. According to the summary in the *Guhya Tantra* concerning all the things not explained for the mandala ritual, it says that the first section should be made larger, where the Bhagavat Vajradhara says regarding the summary (*saṃgrāhya*) of the mandala: *It can have two, three, or four sections, or even many sections. That which is the outer section should be larger and fixed with one gate.* Why is that? If, according to the method explained above, you only subtract one square from the outer section and do not add it to the area of the second inner section, then this first section will be larger than the second inner section by one square. Thus this is what is clarified by these words:

> *'Then having gone into the interior,*
> *he should divide it into three.*
> *Having divided into three parts* (38b)
> *the whole of the site,*
> *then each one of those parts also*
> *should be divided into three parts'*. [2.20]

You should understand that this is the general marking-out and division of the Mandala Arising from Great Compassion and so forth.

Regarding those, I explained above that you should understand that the Mandala Arising from Great Compassion is the transformation of the emanated treasury of the Array of the Inexhaustible Body, the Mandala of the Revolving Wheel of Letters is the transformation of the emanated treasury of the Array of the Inexhaustible Speech, and the Secret Mandala is the transformation of the emanated treasury of the Array of the Inexhaustible Mind. You should know that the *mudrā* which is drawn as a triangle in the three Mandalas [symbolizes] all the Tathāgatas who have entered into the *dharmakāya*, for its core is marked with a five-pointed vajra of Awareness. It indicates the three Liberations – nothingness, absence of perceptual forms (*nimitta*) and the absence of aspiration – which are transformed into the three sides of the triangle. In the case of the Mandala Arising from Great Compassion, the transformed Body attained at the moment of Mahā-vairocana's realization of direct and perfect Enlightenment, resides in the inner mandala together with the special features (*viśeṣa*) of his Body which appear as the Three Families, characterized as Lokeśvara, Vajradhara and so forth, who are the *saṃbhoga-kāya* in nature. The passage quoted above shows that Lokeśvara, Vajradhara and so on who reside in the core mandala are the *saṃbhoga-kāya* in nature, thus: (39a) *Thus, teachers were seen resembling the bodies of the Vajradharas, the Bodhisattvas Samantabhadra, Padmapāṇi and so on, who taught the Dharma with the pure words of the Mantra Method in the ten directions. They taught it in order to perfect completely those beings who have nurtured lives of action, from the first generation of bodhicitta up to those who dwell in each of the Ten Levels, and to bring about the acquirement of the sprout of existence in those who have suppressed lives of action.* [1.3]

The *nirmāṇa-kāya* of the Bhagavat Vairocana himself, the pure *nirmāṇa-kāya* of Śākyamuni, resides together with the impure deities in the second section. In the third section there resides the emanated treasury of the Inexhaustible Array of the Sameness of the Body and so forth of the Bhagavat Vairocana himself, attained on the occasion of Perfect Enlightenment, and likewise the Great Bodhisattvas who appear in a variety of Bodies, such as the Bhagavat Mañjuśrī who have come to see and hear the many methods of benefitting beings.

In the same way, the sections of the deities to be arranged in both the Mandala of the Revolving Wheel of Letters and the Secret Mandala are similar to these. However, it is taught in the *Vairocana Tantra* that the Mandala of the Revolving Wheel of Letters is the transformation of the Treasury of the Inexhaustible Array of Speech. Thus it is taught in the *Vairocana Tantra* that those same deities of the Mandala are to be arranged as the letters of their seed syllables which are the transformations of [Vairocana's] Speech which reveal the *samādhis*. When it says in the text that the deities of the mandala should be arranged as seed-syllables or as symbols, (39b) the implication there is thus: those symbols such as vajras and so forth are the perceptual forms of the Awarenesses of the mandala deities. By virtue of their Awarenesses, they appear to those to trained as the Body, Speech and Minds of the deities. Therefore, because those Awarenesses actually appear in that way, the Body and Speech are what the Awarenesses are. As the perceptual form of Speech is also indicated by those perceptual forms of Awareness, there is no [logical] flaw. Likewise, you should understand that the mandala deities should be arranged in the Secret Mandala as their specific symbols such as swords, lotuses and vajras into which the Treasury of the Inexhaustible Array of the Mind is transformed, located in mandalas of fire, wind, earth and water.

Regarding these three Mandalas, it is only taught that there are gates in each section and that the *mudrā* within the gate of the inner mandala should be made the size of the Vairocana's lotus. You should understand that the gates of the second and third sections should be made slightly larger in stages in accordance with that, which is stated thus:

> '*The first gate is the same* [*size*]
> *as the matrix mandala,*
> *and the wise one should know that*
> *the others should be gradually larger*'. [2.70]

Also regarding the outer mandala, you should draw archways in the four directions or make them from wood and so on. Likewise you should draw the portals associated with the archways in the outer mandala, which are mentioned thus:

> '*In the four directions, the wise one*
> *should make portals in each portion,*
> *with care and restraint,*
> *as the places of the Lords of the deities*', [2.21]

and in order to indicate the dimensions of these three parts it says:

> '*Also the size of the archways* (40a)
> *should be the same as the central mandala,*
> *and the portals are also the same;*
> *the lotus is said to be sixteen inches*'. [2.70]

The meaning of this is that the archways and the portals should be made the size of the width of one strip of the central section. Likewise, '*the lotus is said to be sixteen inches*' describes the width of Vairocana's lotus as sixteen inches, and the intention is that the size of the portals in the four directions is anything above the sixteen inches of the lotus. The meaning of '*you should make the portals of the chief deities in each direction*' is that you should make the seats of the deities in their portals, yet you should make only one portal in one side. You should arrange the *mudrās* of all the Tathāgatas, Lokeśvara and Vajradhara according to their direction within the portals of the lotus seat of Vairocana in the central mandala. In the second section, you should make the portals which connect with the courtyard of the central mandala. In the eastern direction, there you should arrange the Jina Śākyamuni, and likewise in the northern direction you should place the King of the Gods (Indra). In the southern direction you should place Yama. Likewise in the portals of the eastern direction and so forth, which connect with the second section, you should place the Lords of the third mandala such as the Bhagavat Mañjuśrī who in nature are the leaders of the deities in the four directions.

9. The Attributes and Application of the Colours

Now, after the marking-out of the Mandala, the colours of the Mandala should be applied. (40b) This has five parts:

1 The instruction about the *samādhi* with which the Master transforms the colours
2 The ritual of the transformation of the colours.
3 The *samādhi* of applying the colours.
4 The instruction about the sequence of the process for the coloured bands of the mandala.
5 The method of applying the colours.

Of those, regarding the *samādhi* for transforming the colours, you should transform yourself into the Body of the Bhagavat Vairocana, mentioned with the words: '*Then transforming himself into the Bhagavat Vairocana with his* mudrā, *he should imagine* [*the pigments*] *to be the vast continuum of reality*'. [10.17]

As for the transformation of the colours, for the colour white, one should arrange *Ra* and transform it into the nature of the continuum of reality. For the colour red, one should arrange *Aṃ* and imagine it is the nature of the perfect Buddha Durdharṣa. For the colour yellow, one should arrange *Ka* and imagine it is the nature of Kanakamuni. For the colour green, one should arrange *Va* and imagine it is the nature of Mahā-bodhimaṇḍa-muni. For the colour black, one should arrange *Ha* and imagine it is the nature of the wrathful Trailokyavijaya. This is dealt with thus: '*He should first take up the white pigment, which should be transformed thus:*

> *This is the pure continuum of reality*
> *which purifies the realms of beings.*
> *This itself is the Tathāgata,*
> *devoid of all faults*',

down to

> '*he threatens in every way*
> *all the hostile demon armies*'. [10.17]

Arising from that *samādhi* for applying the colours, it says that '*he should circumambulate the Mandala and enter within. With the power of great kindness and compassion, he should focus his attention upon the trainee practitioners* (sādhaka) *and transform himself into the Action Vajra-sattva with* Va, *together with Varada-vajra, and then he should draw the Mandala which Arises from Great Compassion*'. [10.19]

Regarding the sequence for the bands of colours white and so forth, it says:

> '*First white should be applied,*
> *and then red and then yellow.*
> *Next green should be applied.*
> *All the inner parts are black.*
> *Thus the colour method is explained*'. [2.69]

With reference to the method for applying the bands of the colours white and so on, it says:

> '*Colour should be applied from inside,*
> *and not from the outside*'. [2.69]

10. Offerings

Having drawn the Mandala, offerings should be made. This has four parts:

1 The offering *samādhi* which is to be actualized.
2 The protection of the Mandala.
3 Imagining that the Mandala deities are present.
4 The accomplishment of the four types of offerings.

Of those, with reference to the offering *samādhi*, the text says:

> *Then the* mantrin *who cleaves to the continuum of reality*
> *should be seated and then*
> *abide facing towards the east,*
> *his thoughts imbued with* bodhicitta,
> *that is the continuum of reality in nature,*
> *then making the vajra* mudrā,
> *he should become the Action Vajra*[*sattva*]
> *and diligently make offerings.* [10.19]

The protection of the Mandala should be done with the *Sīma-bandha Mudrā* and so forth which are described in the Chapter on *Mudrās.*

As for the imagining that the deities are present, according to all Tantras there are two types, those deities who have been invited to the Mandala and those who have not been invited, depending on whether you are inclined to believe that they have arisen from the continuum of reality [or not]. According to all the Tantras of both the Yoga School, such as the *Tattva-saṃgraha,* and the Kriyā [School], the deities are thought to be present everywhere, [though] generally they are only seen by those who have first invited them. (41b) Thus, those Tantras teach that the Bhagavat dwells in undefined times and places in the presence of people to be guided. Thus, in the *Tattva-saṃgraha* it is mentioned that having become directly and perfectly enlightened in the Ghanavyūha Buddha Field, the Bhagavat went to the top of Mount Sumeru and taught the Dharma which comprises the scriptures and realization. Then, he also went to others places such as Jambudvīpa and did acts of benefitting. It is clear that such things as these are taught in the Yoga Tantras. Even in the Kriyā Tantras, the *Vidyā* and Mantra deities are said to have undefined abodes, since the appropriateness of the preliminary ritual of invitation, in order to make offerings to the deities, is mentioned in those Tantras and should be done just to perceive them. This *Vairocana Tantra* explains that one should imagine the deities to be truly present just by making the *Samaya Mudrā* and imagining them, without having invited the deities for the mandala rituals and for the rites of recitation and so forth. So it mentions herein that the Bhagavat who resides in a non-conceptualizing *samādhi*, in the core of Enlightenment, and who perpetually encompasses the Three Realms with the Inexhaustible Body and so forth, attained at the time of Enlightenment, acts for the benefit of beings according to their circumstances with manifestations in perceptual forms which are the mundane and supramundane *vidyā* mantras and so forth in nature, without coming from anywhere nor going anywhere. Thus it states in detail herein: '*The Bhagavat was in the regally jewelled great residence, which is most splendidly adorned with royal gems, a domed pinnacle with neither boundary nor centre*' [1.1] (42a) and so forth down to '*Also there were the great Bodhisattvas assembled around, headed by Samantabhadra, Maitreya, Mañjuśrī and Sarva-nīvaraṇa-viṣkambin. The Sun of the Tathāgata, that transcends the three times, was transformed and manifested thus* [*as Vairocana*] *and revealed the teachings of the Dharma Gate known as The Ground of the Sameness of Body, Speech and Mind . Then those Bodhisattvas headed by Samantabhadra and those Vajradharas headed by Vajrapāṇi, being empowered by the Bhagavat, entered into the display of the treasury of the manifestations of the sameness of his Inexhaustible Body and likewise they entered into the display of the treasury of the array of the sameness of his Inexhaustible Speech and Mind, and yet they could not discern any engagement [in activities] or disengagement on the part of the Body, Speech and Mind of the Bhagavat Vairocana. All the activities of his Body, all the activities of his Speech and all the activities of his Mind were seen by all of them to reveal the Dharma with the words of the Mantra Method continually throughout all realms of beings. Thus, teachers were seen resembling the bodies of the Vajradharas, the Bodhisattvas Samantabhadra, Padmapāṇi and so on, who taught the Dharma with the pure words of the Mantra Method in the ten directions. They taught it in order to perfect completely those beings who have nurtured lives of action, from the first generation of* bodhicitta *up to those who dwell in each of the Ten Levels, and to bring about the acquirement of the sprout of existence in those who have suppressed lives of action*' [1.2-3]. (42b)

Here, '*those who have suppressed lives of action*' signifies the Śrāvakas and Pratyekabuddhas who abide in the realm of the Nirvāṇa with remainder. '*To bring about the acquirement of the sprout of existence*' signifies that they teach the Dharma so that those who are born in the pure Buddha Fields might attain such Buddha qualities as the Levels, the Perfections and so forth. Thus by having generated the strength of the *kṛtsnas, anutpādas, nirodha-jñāna* and *samāpattis*, they experience the bliss of *samādhi* for some time. They are encouraged by the Buddha Bhagavats, and acquire from them, in the pure Buddha fields, the method which completely perfects the Levels, Perfections and so forth. Then they devote themselves to the accomplishments, and they go on until they arrive at the city of unlocalized Nirvāṇa through the attainment of the state of truly perfect Buddhahood. Thus, this matter is taught in detail in the Secret Chapter included in the *Uttara-tantra* of this very *Vairocana Tantra*.

Having described in detail the Bodhisattvas who engage in the practice of Bodhisattvas, knowing the path of the mantra gate, and the Śrāvakas and Pratyekabuddhas, who are aware of the path and abide on the level with objective supports but whose minds have not yet attained access to the mind itself, the *Vairocana Tantra* says that those who are obscured by the obscurations of emotional afflictions and wrong understanding focus on themselves[A] and suppress the emotional afflictions. Because they have not [achieved] the cessation of causes and results, the absence of the two extremes (43a) and the suspension of mind, yogins who arise from the *samādhi* of the unpurified Awareness-eye of the Śrāvakas have [merely] suppressed colour-form, appearances and the conditions arising from them, which cause them to get reborn through latent dispositions and emotionally afflicted behaviour in the Three Realms. Having abandoned their psycho-physical constituents by virtue of their previous aspirations, they get to be born in a pure Buddha field. But they strive to obtain All-knowing [Awareness] by suppressing the Levels and Perfections from the first generation of *bodhicitta* onwards. They are impelled by the force of the *kṛtsnas*, *anutpādas*, *nirodhas* and *samāpattis* and dwell intoxicated in the heart of the lotus for sixty thousand years. Following that, they will be purified in the supreme and full Enlightenment, according to their aspirations. You should understand this in detail according to the Secret Chapter.

Therefore, if the Bhagavat Vairocana's Body and so forth are present everywhere in the form of mundane and supramundane mantras and *vidyās*, then what need is there to invite him and ask him to come? The purpose of this is summarized by the Bhagavat and shown by this passage from this Tantra: '*Lord of the Secret Ones! Furthermore, the Tathāgata who is in tune with all and who pleases all beings in accordance with their wishes, appears before the Bodhisattvas who engage in all actions and mantra practice, like a reflection.* (43b) *A Tathāgata does not conceptualize and is inaccessible to the* manas, *and transcends time, place, actions, activities, right and wrong,*

> '*Yet he grants the rank of All-knowing,*
> *that arises from mantra practice;*
> *hence All-knowing, attainment,*
> *and the best state will be accomplished*' [6.96 – 98].

Does not the *Vairocana Tantra* say that you should draw the Bodhisattvas such as Samantabhadra who have been born from the Perfections in the third section? If it is necessary to invite them in order to imagine that they are definitely present, because they are not the emanations of the Inexhaustible Body and so forth of the Bhagavat Vairocana which perpetually pervade the Three Realms, then why is the process for their invitation not related? There is no logical defect in this, for those Bodhisattvas are always devoted to observing with the Eye of Awareness the nature of

---

A CD: '*focus on the sameness of the path themselves*'.

the Bhagavat Vairocana's Array of his Inexhaustible Body and so forth and how these are applied to benefitting beings. Therefore, they are witnesses to the appearance of the Bhagavat in any place through the Mandala with the Matrix of Great Compassion and so forth for the benefit of beings, so they also reside there by virtue of the *samaya*. Or on the other hand, they also have attained the illusion-like *samādhi*, so though they reside in a single place, they appear thus for the benefit of beings by virtue of their aspirations. Due to this also, there is no logical flaw. Moreover, the presence of the *Vidyā* and Mantra [deities] of the mandala without (44a) the invitation is not only described in this *Vairocana Tantra* alone, but if many rituals appear in all of those Yoga and Kriyā Tantras, which teach the rite for the mandala without invitation, concerning the protection of oneself and one's abode with the site-*mudrā*, the offering of flowers and so forth which are mantrified, and the threatening of obstacles, without having invited the *Vidyā* and Mantra deities, any such *Karma-mudrās* and Mantra [deities] will be present without having been invited. Therefore, since the invitation is not specifically mentioned in those Tantras, there is no logical flaw. This *Vairocana Tantra* teaches that you should imagine the *Vidyā* and Mantra [deities] to be present in all respects without having invited them.

For this, two parts are taught: i) first the visualization (*nirdhyai*) of [the deities] in the sky region, and ii) the drawing of the mandala on the ground. In order to imagine that they are present in both of these two types of mandalas, you should make the *Mudrā* of the Three *Samayas*. Then reciting the Mantra of the Three *Samayas*, you should first imagine the all-pervading inherently existent Mandala which arises from the continuum of reality in the sky region, and then having mentally accomplished the attributes of the Mandala Arising from Great Compassion on the ground, you should make offerings. This is what is spoken of thus:

> '*He should become the Action Vajra[sattva]*
> *and diligently make offerings.*
> *Then in an all-encompassing spirit,*
> *he should show the* mudrā *called*
> *The Samaya of All the Saviour Buddhas,*
> *and recite the mantra three times*' [10.19].

This concludes the explanation that it is acceptable to imagine (44b) by such a process that the deities are present in the Mandala without having invited them.

11. The Ritual for Making Offerings

Now I shall relate the offering ritual. It is taught in this Mandala that there are two types of offerings based on the distinctions of the external and the internal offerings. Of those, the external offerings are sevenfold as follows: flowers, perfume, incense, food, lamps, clothing and jars. This is spoken of in detail with:

> '*Then the* mantrin *should earnestly make offerings*
> *to the deities, with pleasing yellow,*
> *white and red flowers*',

down to

> '*Cotton scarves should be offered,*
> *one to each of the main deities,*
> *and one per group for the ordinary Great Beings*' [2.88].

The method for this is as follows: it is taught that the deities whom you have imagined to be present in the sky mandala, by the manner described in the above ritual of marking-out the mandala, do not depend upon the perceptual forms of the external application of the colours and so forth, so they are said to be '*supramundane*'. Those deities who are depicted in the mandala placed on the ground by the ritual explained previously are dependent upon the actions of applying the external colours and so forth, so they are said to be '*mundane*'. In this way, when you hereafter do the recitation, homa and offerings, in dependence upon the branches (*aṅga*) of the external recitation, homa and offerings, then they are generally called 'mundane' by this Tantra. When one accomplishes those recitations and so forth just by conceiving them mentally, without dependence upon external perceptual forms, then the *Vairocana Tantra* generally calls them '*supramundane*'. (45a) Therefore, you should know that these definitions should be applied according the circumstances when the text speaks of '*supramundane deities*', for in some cases it is only the category of mundane deities which is indicated. You should also understand that, according to the circumstances, some are supramundane.

Now for the technique of presenting flowers to the category of deities imagined in the sky mandala who are called 'supramundane', it says:

> '*The thumb and ring finger joined together*
> *is called the Auspicious* [Mudrā].
> *The flowers should be taken with that*
> *and presented from the area of your heart*' [13.31].

To show the method for presenting flowers to those depicted in the mandala on the ground, called 'mundane', it says:

> '*For the mundane deities, know that*
> *it should be done from your navel*' [13.31].

The *Vairocana Tantra* describes the features of the technique for presenting the incense to the supramundane deities thus:

> '*The incense should be held up in the air*
> *with the Vajra Fist or the Lotus Garland* [Mudrā],
> *and then presented to the mundane Protectors*' [13.32].

Likewise, concerning the ritual to present it to those depicted in the mandala on the ground, it says:

> '*Do it in due order*
> *for the other mundane deities*' [13.32].

In that way, this shows the process for making the external offerings such as flowers to the deities of the Mandala Arising from Great Compassion who are imagined in the sky mandala or who are depicted in the ground mandala, by the manner previously explained.

Now there are said to be three types of internal offerings: joining the palms in salutation, the cultivation of kindness (45b) and compassion, and likewise the mental offerings. With addition of the external offerings previously explained, there are four types altogether. Therefore the *Vairocana Tantra* says:

> '*There are four types of worship*
> *which should be presented to all Saviours:*
> *salutations with joined palms,*
> *likewise kindness and compassion,*
> *mundane flowers and incense,*
> *and flowers produced with the fingers.*
> *Making the* Mudrā *which Produces All the Members*
> *and then cultivating* bodhicitta,
> *they should be made diligently*
> *for each one of the Protectors and their Children.*
> *These are the faultless flowers,*
> *sweet-smelling and splendid,*
> *the trees of the continuum of reality which arise*
> *to be offered to the Jinas;*
> *they are created by mantras,*
> *changed by virtue of* samādhi;
> *excellent vast multitudes of clouds*
> *arisen from the continuum of reality,*
> *always pour [flowers] like rain*
> *in the presence of the Buddhas.*
> *For the other ordinary deities*
> *these are the specified flowers,*
> *they should be offered as appropriate,*
> *with their specific mantras and* mudrās' [13.29 – 30].

The '*mundane flowers and incense*' here were dealt with in the teachings on the external offerings, and because they depend upon the branches of the external offerings of flowers and so forth, they are said to be '*mundane*'. Flowers produced with the fingers and so forth indicate the technique for the mental offerings. Here also the words,

> '*excellent vast multitudes of clouds*
> *arisen from the continuum of reality,*
> *always pour [flowers] like rain*
> *in the presence of the Buddhas*', [13.30]

actually indicate the technique for offerings which are to be offered mentally in the intrinsically existent mandala. Therefore it says:

'*For the other ordinary deities*
these are the specified flowers' [13.31],

and the word '*ordinary*' includes those supramundane deities who are depicted in the ground mandala, but the word '*ordinary*' does not include the mundane deities such as Viṣṇu and Brahmā since you might otherwise omit the external offerings of such things as flowers to the supramundane deities who are depicted in the ground mandala. In this Mandala, the mundane deities, who are known as Viṣṇu and Brahmā and so on, are not depicted. Herein you should view any categories of mundane deities in the central mandala as embodiments of the Bhagavat Vairocana's *nirmāṇa-kāya*, as is mentioned in detail at the end of the chapter on the *mudrās* of the mundane and the supramundane deities: 'Mudrās *such as these which emerge through the fervent inclination of the Tathāgatas are extensive* Mudrās *that become the symbols of the Bodhisattvas*' [11.100].

The procedure for the presentation of the four types of offerings is as follows: Having first visualized yourself as the Action Vajrasattva, you should mantrify with Acala's Essence Mantra the branches of the external offerings such as perfume and flowers which have been purified by the letter of the continuum of reality. Then you should mantrify the perfume, flowers and so forth with the mantras of the offerings. Next, you should protect the mandala drawn upon the ground. Then making the *Samaya Mudrā*, you should recite the *Samaya* Mantra and imagine the intrinsically existent mandala in the region of the sky. You should imagine how the mandala which is its representation is to be depicted upon the ground, as though it were alive. (46b) Having made each one of the *mudrās* of the deities depicted there, you should recite their mantras and speedily contemplate them. Then you should make the four types of offerings. The sequence for this is as follows: first plant both your knees on the ground, join your palms together and make obeisances. This is the first offering, the offering of salutations. Then in the manner previously explained, you should make offerings with such perfumes and flowers as are mentioned. This is the second offering, that characterized by external offerings. Then making the *Mudrā* of Producing All Branches which is described in the chapter on the Eight Secret *Mudrās*, you should think 'Let fine incomparable branches of offerings issuing from the Samantabhadra practice arise for all the Tathāgatas who abide in the vast world systems!'. Then having actualized *bodhicitta*, you should arise and recite three times the Gagana-gañja *Vidyā*. This is the third offering, that characterized by mental offerings. Then you should do the two parts of the accomplishment offering (*pratipatti-pūja*) which is characterized as the repeated cultivation of kindness and compassion. This is the technique for it: you should wish 'May the sufferings of the miserable states be soothed in all beings by the wholesome roots of whatever wholesome deeds I have done! May mundane and supramundane perfections arise!' This is the fourth offering and is said to be the accomplishment offering characterized by the repeated cultivation of kindness and compassion towards all beings.

12. The Ritual for the Acceptance of Trainees into the Mandala

Now I shall explain the ritual for the acceptance of the trainees. (47a) I explained above that there are three types of attributes of trainees: the special attributes, the ordinary attributes and the classificatory attributes. Whether those trainees have previously accepted the *vidyās* or not, they should be introduced into the Mandala. Among them, those who have not accepted the *vidyās* because they have not previously seen the Mandala but have just accepted the *Samaya* before and so enter the Mandala are one type. Others strive to attain the superior, medium and lower attainments, and having been introduced into the Mandala they are made to cultivate that *bodhicitta* which they have not yet cultivated, and exert themselves in the preliminary accomplishment of the *vidyās*. Others who have accepted the *vidyās* and mantras, whether they have already cultivated *bodhicitta* or not, have become quite certain about the *vidyā* and mantra rituals (*kalpa*) by the insight arisen from hearing and pondering. Having been introduced into the Mandala Arising from Great Compassion or the Mandala of the Wheel of Revolving Letters, they then strive to attain the Master initiation which follows on from that. Likewise, there are others who aim to obtain the initiation into the Secret Mandala although they have already received the Master initiation by the process described earlier, and having entered the Secret Mandala accept the initiation which follows on from that. Others have the *samaya* from the first, and whether they have accepted the *vidyās* or not, and similarly whether they have obtained the Master initiation or not, behold any Mandala just in order to increase their own merit. Others delight in seeing the Mandala because they either strive to calm the mischiefs of obstacles (47b) or they desire wealth. Therefore, only these have the *samaya* due to the fact that they have seen the Mandala as appropriate from the start. All others do not have the *samaya* because they have not seen even one Mandala.

Therefore, I shall explain something of the general ritual for those trainees to enter the three Mandalas. Regarding that, first of all, the Master should transform himself by the process described earlier in the Action Vajrasattva and produce the offerings which were described. Then he should transform himself into the Body of Vairocana with any one of the Master yogas described earlier. Calling the trainees, he should seat them outside the door of the Mandala and sprinkle them with water over which the [mantra] of Trailokya-vijaya has been recited and then the Master himself should make the *mudrā* of the Three *Samayas* and mantrify the cotton scarves with the mantra of the Three *Samayas* three times. Then he should blindfold the trainees with those cotton scarves and set them within the portal of the gate of the third [section of the] mandala. Having placed them there, they should take refuge in the Three Jewels and receive *bodhicitta*. Making the *Mudrā* of the Continuum of Reality and reciting the mantra [for them], the trainee should be transformed into nothingness, the nature of the continuum of reality. Following that, the trainee should make the Dharmacakra *Mudrā* and then, reciting its mantra, he should imagine himself to be the Body of Vajrasattva. Then the Master should place a flower in the [trainee's] hand with that trainee making the Three *Samaya Mudrā*, and the mantra of the Three *Samayas* should be recited three times. Following that (48a) the letter of the continuum of reality should be imagined upon that [trainee's] head. Then [the Master] should cause the [trainee] to make a declaration of sincerity (*satyādhiṣṭhāna*) and make him cast into the Mandala the flower resting in his hand-*mudrā*. Wherever that flower falls, the trainee should be given that mantra [deity]. Trainees who have already seen other Mandalas previously, who have the *samaya* and have accepted a mantra, should remove their blindfolds and then they should present the flower inserted into their hand-*mudrā* either to the Lord of the Mandala or to the *Vidyā* [deity] they have received in another mandala previously if it is present. The reason is that those who have previously seen the mandala, received a mantra [deity] and who have the *samaya* may want cast their flowers with the prior declaration of sincerity but without being blindfolded. A practitioner (*sādhaka*) may not be suitable to accomplish a multitude of *Vidyās* due to the multiplicity of *Vidyā* aspects, so if their flowers fall upon another *Vidyā* unconnected with the *Vidyā* they have previously received, they will be in the situation of having to recite two *Vidyās*. On the other hand, if they recite either one of the *Vidyās* and reject the other *Vidyā*, misfortune will arise. It has been said,

> '*Wherever the flower falls*
> *that is to be accomplished,*
> *if you recite any other* vidyā
> *you will be destroyed* '[9].

Also, regarding this ritual for the trainees who are to be accepted into the three Mandalas, it is as this passage in this Tantra indicates:

> '*The trainees are led before the Mandala,*
> *and are sprinkled with water by the* mantrin.
> *He should give them perfumes and flowers,*
> *and when they have called upon the Tathāgatas,*
> *they should be made to accept* bodhicitta.
> *Because of this, they will all be born*
> *into the wholesome Family of the Jinas.*
> *He makes for them the* Mudrā
> *which arises from the continuum of reality,*
> *and the Dharma Wheel* Mudrā *also,*
> *then they are transformed into Vajrasattvas.*
> *He should then firmly make*
> *the* samaya *of all the Buddhas,*
> *at the same time reciting aloud three times*
> *over the scarves, in accordance with the mantra ritual.*
> *Then with a compassionate mind,*
> *he should blindfold them.*
> *Having recited the* samaya *three times,*
> *he should place upon their heads*
> *the letter* Ra *with an* anusvāra.
> *It shines like the risen moon,*
> *white in colour and radiates*
> *a flaming garland.*
> *In the presence of all the Protectors,*
> *he then makes them throw their flower,*
> *and wherever their flower falls,*
> *that deity should be given to them.*
> *The trainees should be held*

in front of the outer mandala gate,
in between the two gates,
in the central area of the portal.
With them abiding there, all the rituals
should be done well, following the sequence' [2.89].

This is general ritual for entry into the three Mandalas. Since another ritual is specially taught for entry into the Secret Mandala, that should also be mentioned. First of all, a trainee who has had the initiation into the Mandala Arising from Great Compassion and the Wheel of Revolving Letters Mandalas should be introduced into the Secret Mandala by just the ritual explained earlier. Having been established there, a *Raṃ* located in a fire mandala encircled by a flaming garland should be imagined in [the trainee's] heart and the whole of his body should be imagined to be reduced to ashes by its fire. In the midst of the ashes, the Master should conceive the letter *Aṃ*, (49a) white like a *kunda* flower or the moon. Having transformed [the trainee's] body into the Body of the Bhagavat Vairocana by that, the twelve component letter *vidyā* should be imagined upon his lotus seat. The trainee should be exhorted thus 'You also should meditate thus!', as it is said in the text, '*Then the Bhagavat also spoke of the ritual for entering into the Secret Mandala:*

'*The* mantrin *who is fully trained,*
who is skilled in the Secret Mandala,
should now burn up, according to [this] ritual,
all the failings of the trainee.
So that it will not arise henceforth,
his life should [also] be burnt up.
But, when he has been burnt and become ash,
he should be re-created.
With a letter he should be burnt into the unchanging,
and with life he should be re-created;
When all has been re-created by life,
he will be completely pure and unsullied.
The twelve component syllables
should be arranged on their receptacle.
This samaya *of the Buddhas*
and saviour Bodhisattvas is revered
by the Buddhas, Śrāvakas
and mundane gods.
Whosoever understands this samaya
dwelling within the Secret Mandala,
has entered all the tantras,
and is master of all the mandalas;
that mantra-holder will be like me:
no others are said to have samaya' [14.1 – 6].

As for the meaning of this, '*The* mantrin *who is fully trained, who is skilled in the Secret Mandala*' signifies that he has trained zealously with the insight arisen from hearing, pondering and cultivating, as far as he is able, in the rituals for drawing the Mandala

Arising from Great Compassion and so forth, and the rituals for the branches of the accomplishment of all the *vidyās* and mantras. (49b) [*He*] *should now burn up, according to* [*this*] *ritual all the failings of the trainee.* Here the word '*failings*' signifies the dispositions towards undesirable actions which lead to misfortune. '*Burn up*' is the cleansing of the [existential] stream of the trainee. The significance of that is that the letter of the continuum of reality should be arranged in the heart of the trainee and he should be conceived to be the continuum of reality in nature by way of thinking of its meaning. The trainee himself should also be convinced that he is thus. Therefore because of that conviction about the continuum of reality, it is contrary to the dispositions towards undesirable actions, so it explains '*all the failings should be burnt up according to the ritual*'.

His life should [*also*] *be burnt up*: '*Life*' refers to his own body. Hence the significance is the conviction that he is the continuum of reality is not only counteracts the dispositions towards failings, but also it is also counteracts appearance in his own body. *So that it will not arise henceforth*: This shows the utter conviction of both the Master and the trainee about the continuum of reality. *When he has been burnt and become ash*: This indicates that not only should the trainee be transformed into the continuum of reality through considering the meaning of that letter of the continuum of reality which is arranged in his heart, but that he should imagine that the trainee has been reduced to ashes by way of the letter *Raṃ* encircled by a garland of fire, which has been arranged in his heart. *He should be re-created*: This signifies that he should be made to appear in his own body. Since the words '*his life also should be burnt up*' do not mentioned with what is to be burnt up, the text says '*with a letter he should be burnt into the unchanging*'. (50a) Here the words *with a letter* should be understood to mean with the *Raṃ* which is located in its mandala. *He should be burnt into unchanging*: Because it is inherently unchanging it is 'the unchanging'. '*Should be burnt*' is explained as 'thoroughly burnt'. Although it says '*he should also be recreated*', how he is to be recreated has not yet been described, therefore it says '*and with life he should be recreated*'. The word '*life*' here refers to the letter *A*, which is the life of all letters, as it is said, '*the Perfect Buddhas, Lords of Men, say that A is life*'. Therefore, it signifies that he should be transformed into the Body of Vairocana by *A*. Because of that, it says '*when all has been re-created by life, he will be completely pure and unsullied*'. He should be transformed sitting upon a lotus seat. One should imagine the twelve-syllabled *Vidyā* King on the petals of that lotus, hence it says '*the twelve component syllables should be arranged on their receptacle*'. '*Receptacle*' here means 'support'.

Hence, that transmutation of the trainee into the Body of Vairocana by this process is *samaya* in the sense of 'union' or in the sense of 'realization'. Furthermore, that *samaya* which makes you believe that you are in the form of the Body of the Bhagavat Vairocana is revered and desired by all, and is a synonym for 'not to be transgressed'. Therefore it says:

> '*This* samaya *of the Buddhas*
> *and saviour Bodhisattvas is revered*
> *by the Buddhas, Śrāvakas*
> *and mundane gods*' (50b) [14.5].

In order to show that this *samaya*, which is the Body of Vairocana in character, is the *samaya* of transformation just within the Secret Mandala but not in the others, it says:

> '*Whosoever understands this* samaya
> *dwelling within the Secret Mandala*' [14.6].

In order to show the benefits of this *samaya* made within the Secret Mandala, the text says:

> '[*He*] *has entered all the tantras,*
> *and is master of all the mandalas*' 14.6].

There the words '*entered into all the tantras*' signifies that they become possessed of the *samayas* for the mandalas in all tantras. '*Master of all the mandalas*' means that they become Masters for the mandalas of all tantras. The words explained above '*when all has been re-created by life, he will be completely pure and unsullied*' did not show clearly that the trainee should be transformed into the Body of Vairocana, so it says,

> '*that mantra-holder will be like me:*
> *no others are said to have* samaya' 14.6].

The meaning of this is that that trainee should visualize himself as the Body of the Bhagavat Vairocana.

13. The Rituals for Initiation

Now, the process for the initiation should be summarized. The meaning of the word '*initiation*' (*abhiṣeka*) is this: Initiation is that wetting or lustration in the presence of the deities of the Mandala who have been depicted. Regarding that, these three topics should be mentioned: to what kind of trainee should that initiation be given, how should it be done and why should it be done. (51a) In that connection, this Tantra speaks of the characteristics of two trainees who ought to be initiated. That is, the trainee who has seen the *samaya* mandala, who has profound insight due to have repeatedly cultivated *bodhicitta*, who comprehends the true nature of the meaning of the *vidyās*, mantras, tantras and rituals (*kalpa*) as they really are, by the extremely certain insight arising from hearing and pondering, whose interest has been made very stable by the spirit arising from convinced devotion to the profound method of the Mahāyāna, is the first type who should be initiated. The second type who has seen the *samaya* mandala and likewise, who has made his mental stream quite unsullied by having heard, pondered on and cultivated the *vidyās*, mantras, tantras and rituals, but who has not cultivated the *bodhicitta*, is attached to external activities because of his reliance on objective supports. Furthermore, the characteristics of these two should be understood in this Tantra through what I taught earlier about the categories of Masters. There I explained that the first type is the trainee who has convinced interest in profound insight who is to be initiated as a Master in order to draw the mundane and supramundane mandalas. The other is the one who is to initiated as a Master for the mundane mandalas. As the *Vairocana Tantra* says:

> '*There are two types of Masters*
> *who comprehend the mantras and* mudrās;
> *you should know their attributes through*
> *the categories of profound and not-profound.*
> [*The first*] *should know the Profound and Extensive,*
> *and does not have recourse to beings,*
> *he is a beloved child of the Buddhas,*
> *and he has abandoned the present world.*
> *The second type is intoxicated*
> *by the present world and relies on supports.* (51b)
> *He is given permission and empowerment*
> *by the Best of Men, the Buddhas,*
> *in order to draw all mundane mandalas*' [13.14].

Regarding the words '*in order to draw all mundane mandalas*' here, I explained above that 'mundane' just refers to those supramundane mandalas which are connected with such activities as the application of the colours and so forth. Is it not stated that,

> '*the first are those who only have the* samaya
> *after having seen this Mandala,*
> *but the* mudrās *should not be shown*
> *nor should the mantras be given to them*' [13.42],

or how does one who relies on objective supports and has not repeatedly cultivated *bodhicitta* arrive at the state of initiation to be a Master? And how should that trainee who has thus been given neither the *mudrās* nor mantras and who is involved in that with objective supports be given the initiation to be a Master? There is no logical flaw here, for it should be explained that such words refer to the practitioner. The mantras should not be given to any trainee who desires to accomplish attainments by mantras without their having repeatedly cultivated *bodhicitta.* It signifies that those who desire to benefit beings by being a mandala Master or those who desire to accomplish merit by the recitation of the mantras and so forth, should be given the mantras even though they have not repeatedly cultivated *bodhicitta.* Therefore, both the trainees with the qualities mentioned who rely on objective supports and those who do not, should be given the Master initiation. (52a) Also I explained above that there are two types of mandalas according to the distinctions of mundane and supramundane, thus when one accomplishes the Mandala Arising from Great Compassion and so on which are connected with the external activities of drawing with colours and so forth, then it is called 'mundane'. Hence, in this Tantra the recitation with the external branches in order to propitiate the mantras and the other accomplishments such as the *homas* and offerings are described, but it explains that the *homas* and so forth which have those characteristics are 'mundane'. The idea is that this is because they are associated with the external perceptual forms such as flowers and so forth. You should understand that when the Master mentally accomplishes either the Mandala Arising from Great Compassion and so forth or any other mandala which is described as mental in character, for the sake of only the trainees who are in tune with the profound and extensive mind, and engages in the activities of giving the trainees the *samaya* and so forth, this Tantra describes that as 'supramundane' due to that mandala not being associated with such external activities as the application of colours and so forth. In that way, you can infer that those who have repeatedly cultivated *bodhicitta* and who have convinced interest in the profound and extensive may be initiated to draw both the mundane and supramundane mandalas unconditionally, and that the trainees who rely upon objective supports are only given permission to draw the mundane mandalas. It is also taught that there are three types of initiation with regards the Mandala Arising from Great Compassion and so forth. Regarding this method, it is obvious that the intention of the Bhagavat's [words] is that a trainee will come to have the fully perfected attributes of a Master having received the three part initiation in stages.

Regarding this, the process for accepting the initiations into the three Mandalas should be mentioned. First of all, the trainee should be initiated by just the transformation into the Body of Vajrasattva as when he enters into the root mandala, in the Initiation Mandala which accords with the core of Enlightenment that has been drawn in front of the drawn Mandala Arising from Great Compassion, in order to that he may acquire everything from the Master himself. Then, the *samaya* should be declared. You should understand that this is the Initiation associated with core of Enlightenment, so that the trainee may acquire the *abhisaṃbodhi-kāya* of the Bhagavat Vairocana, and it is the first one. The attributes of this initiation are mentioned where the Mandala Arising from Great Compassion is taught: '*Lord of the Secret Ones! The* mantrin *should draw a second mandala, square with one gate, in front of the main mandala, two cubits apart. In the four corners he should allocate four Vajradharas. Which are the four? Niḥprapañca-pratiṣṭha, Vimala-ākāśa, Vimala-netra and Vicitra-vastra. In the centre a great lotus with eight petals and stamens should be placed. On four of the petals he should draw the four associated Bodhisattvas who are endowed with power from their previous aspirations: Dhāraṇīśvara-rāja, Smṛtiprajanyin, Hitādhyāśayin and Kāruṇya. On the other four petals, he should draw their four attendants:* (53a) *He Who Acts According to Different Attitudes, He Who Fulfils What is Desired, He Who is Unattached and He Who is Liberated. In the centre he places the form of the inconceivable continuum of reality. Then having empowered four precious jars filled with jewels and medicines, with [the mantras of] Samantabhadra, Maitreya, Sarva-nīvaraṇa-viṣkambhin and Sarvāpāyajaha, he should consecrate the trainees on their heads.*

'*The* mantrin *should place him*
in that holy lotus,
and then he should make offerings
with incense and flowers,
lamps and food offerings should also be given.
He should propitiate the deities
with parasols, banners, pennants,
pleasing drum beats,
auspicious and extensive melodious words.
In the presence of the Protectors,
he prepares the trainee and consecrates him.
With fine incense and flowers,
he should also make offerings to him.
Then taking a golden stylet,

and sitting in front of him,
he should recite these words
to stir the heart of the trainee:
"Just as the great physicians of the past
cleared away the world's blindness,
so the Jinas also remove
your blinding film of ignorance."
Then taking up a mirror,
he should explain the attributes of phenomena:
"Phenomena are like reflections:
pellucid, pure and without turbidity,
they cannot be perceived or expressed.
Arising from causes and action,
they are without inherent reality or duration.
When you have thus understood these phenomena,
act for the unequalled benefit of beings,
and you will be born as a son of the Buddha!"
Then he should place a Dharma-wheel
between his legs and also give him
a very fine conch in his right hand: (53b)
"This day forth you will turn
the Wheel of the Protectors in the world
and blow the supreme Dharma-conch
throughout all places.
Do not have any doubt about this,
but with a fearless attitude
expound to all the world
the excellent method of mantra practice.
One who has acted thus is praised
as an assistant of the Buddhas.
Also all the Vajradharas
will protect you in all things!"' [2.92].

There the '*four precious jars*' signifies ones made from precious materials whose colours appear as white, yellow, red and green, or ones made from clay similar to them. *Then having empowered four precious jars filled with jewels and medicines, with Samantabhadra, Maitreya, Sarva-nīvaraṇa-viṣkambhin and Sarvāpāyajaha*: This signifies the initiation with the four jars by the blessed Bodhisattvas whose names correspond with their purpose. Thus, they should be initiated with the jar empowered by the Bodhisattva Sarvāpāyajaha in order to exhaust all the actions leading to misfortune. Likewise, they should be initiated with the jar of Sarva-nīvaraṇa-viṣkambhin in order to suppress all emotional afflictions. Therefore these two initiations are sow the seeds of the antidotes which overcome karmic action and all emotional afflictions, in order to avert all the faults of *saṃsāra*. The initiation with the jar empowered by Samantabhadra is to sow the seed of the state in which the accumulations of merit and awareness are completely perfected. The initiation with the jar empowered by Maitreya is to sow the seed for the attainment of the Regent Level. (54a) Therefore you should view these two as sowing the seeds for the cause of attaining the Bhagavat Vairocana's rank (*pada*). Hence you should understand that the Master should give the initiation with these jars in this sequence, and that the initiation should be given with the jars, uttering words with that kind of meaning to make them joyful beforehand.

The trainees who have thus been initiated should be introduced into the root mandala. Those who have acted in accordance with the above in the presence of the mandala deities, and have then been initiated in order to hear the mantras and to draw the mandalas should be made to accept the *samaya* whose nature is the training of body, speech and mind, the undertaking of the wholesome and the turning away from the unwholesome. That training is called '*samaya*' in this Tantra because by it the attainments and so forth will be fully acquired. That is also called '*samaya*' in the sense of 'what ought not be transgressed'. Regarding the ritual for the acceptance of the *samaya*, the *Vairocana Tantra* says:

> '*Then taking those trainees*
> *the* mantrin *should instil*
> *a compassionate frame of mind in them,*
> *and teach the* samaya *commitments to them:*
> *"From this day forward, you should never abandon*
> *the holy Dharma and* bodhicitta, (138b)
> *even for the sake of your life.*
> *You should not be parsimonious,*
> *nor do what harms beings.*
> *All the Buddhas prescribe*
> *these* samaya *commitments*
> *to you, well-disciplined one.*
> *You should guard them*
> *just as you guard your life!"*' [2.93].

Regarding the Master's injunctions about the *samayas* and the precepts to be adopted by the trainees, the *Vairocana Tantra* says:

> '*With faith and devotion, the trainees*
> *should bow at the guru's feet,* (54b)
> *and then with very certain minds*
> *they should accept all of that*' [2.93].

Following that, in order to initiate the trainee who has received the initiation into the Mandala Arising from Great Compassion, in the presence of the Mandala of the Revolving Wheel of Letters which has been drawn, he should be made to sit in a drawn mandala with a lotus and the continuum of reality letter depicted as a seed syllable. The trainee should be transformed into the *saṃbhoga-kāya* of the Bhagavat Vairocana with the *Mudrā* Producing All Limbs, the Body in which the letters have been arranged beforehand in the sequence which appears below, and he should be initiated with the four jars that have been mantrified by the four great Bodhisattvas as before. Then, in the sequence that appears below, he should be convinced that he is the Body of Vairocana by way of the arrangement of the letters *A* and so forth. This is as mentioned thus: '*Lord of the Secret Ones! For that, the Master should transform himself into the body-image of the Tathāgata with his mantra or* mudrā. *He should then call the trainees and establish them in the Great King of Lotuses whose substance is the continuum of reality. He should make the* Mudrā *which Produces All the Members, and he should then sprinkle then sprinkle water on their heads from four jewelled jars empowered by the four great Bodhisattvas.*

> '*The wise one should place on their heads*
> *an* A *with an* anusvāra,
> *and then he should place* A *in their hearts,*
> *and place* Ra *on their breasts.*
> *Or else he should place* A *in all places,*
> *golden coloured with radiant light,*
> *with topknot and crown,*
> *seated upon a white lotus throne,*
> *the excellent Jina who resides in* samādhi' [10.19]. (55a)

The significance of initiation in the continuum of reality lotus is thus: the continuum of reality is the nothingness of all phenomena. The seed-syllable which expresses that is said to be *Raṃ* in this Tantra. The lotus marked with it is said to be the continuum of reality in nature. The initiation should be given to the trainee who sits there, for just as the continuum of reality is free from all faults, likewise the trainee who has been initiated here will have the two seed-syllables for the attainment of the *saṃbhoga-kāya* and the *nirmāṇa-kāya,* and attain those two modes of embodiment in sequence. Then, though he teaches the Dharma which is devoted to the benefit of beings, he will not be defiled by any faults just as the continuum of reality [is not]. In the same way, he should be led, with the ritual explained earlier, into the Secret Mandala which has been drawn. Having been set within it, he should be initiated with the *Dharmakāya* Initiation [using] the instructions about the cultivation of *samādhi,* '*he should be burnt up into the unchanging with a letter*' and so forth. This should be seen as the initiation for the attainment of the Bhagavat Vairocana's *dharmakāya,* and is the third. Though it is not mentioned in the Secret Mandala [Chapter] that the initiation mandala should be drawn as described and moreover the ritual for the initiation into the Secret Mandala is not fully taught, however in the section where the advantages of entry into the Secret Mandala are taught, the text says:

> '*Whosoever understands this* samaya
> *dwelling within the Secret Mandala,*
> *has entered all the tantras,*
> *and is master of all the mandalas*' [14.6].

'*All the mandalas*' here includes both the mundane and the supramundane ones. (55b) To be '*master*' of them is to be able to draw them and impart the instructions for them and so forth. It also says that will be attained as a result by those who have had the Master initiations. It may be inferred that the imagining of the trainee as the *dharmakāya* by the process of burning up the [trainee's] body by the Master with the letter, characterized by the instructions for the cultivation of *samādhi*, '*burnt up into the unchanging by a letter*' and so forth, when he has been placed within the Secret Mandala, is the initiation into the Secret Mandala. You should also refer to the Chapter on the Entry into the Secret Mandala for the characteristics of this initiation into the Secret Mandala. This concludes the explanation of the ritual for the initiation of the trainee into the three Mandalas.

In that way, two external initiations have been explained for the Mandala Arising from Great Compassion and the Mandala of the Revolving Wheel of Letters. [But the *Vairocana Tantra*] describes a second [type of] initiation by the mind for the trainee who engages in the profound and extensive regardless of whether or not one possesses the equipment for those two [external] initiations. For the ritual of the mental initiation, having set the [Mandala] Arising from Great Compassion in front of the Mandala of Revolving Wheel of Letters, [the Master] should mentally visualize the ritual of initiation into the two Mandalas as appropriate, saying 'I have initiated you as far as possible in the ritual, but now enter into the Mantra Method!'. Therefore, there are three with this mental initiation, the initiation by the *Mudrā* Which Produces All Limbs with the ritual which appears below, and the external initiations explained above. (56a) The attributes of these three initiations are also explained in the Tantra:

> '*There are three types of Initiation,*
> *therefore, listen with diligence!*
> *There is the initiation by the* mudrās
> *without actions and activities.*
> *That initiation by the Protectors*
> *is the most excellent and is the first.*
> *The second is said to arise*
> *from actions and activities.*
> *The third is to be known as mental,*
> *and is devoid of place and time.*
> *This initiation in which the guru*
> *speaks of how it benefits [beings]*
> *after they have pleased him*
> *is praised as best by the Perfect Buddhas*' [13.39 – 40].

There, the trainee '*who is initiated by the* mudrās' means the trainee who deserves to be given initiation should be led into the Mandala Arising from Great Compassion or the Mandala of the Wheel of Revolving Letters which have been drawn, and being placed in front of the Mandala, he should be initiated with *Mudrā* Producing All the Members. In particular, when being initiated in front of the drawn Mandala Arising from Great Compassion, the trainee should be transformed into the Body of Vajrasattva for any one of the three types of initiation as appropriate. When being initiated into the Mandala of the Revolving Wheel of Letters, the trainee should be initiated after having visualized himself as the Body of the Bhagavat Vairocana. For the initiation into the Secret Mandala, he should be led into that Mandala after having visualized himself as the Body of Vajrasattva, and then initiated with the *Dharmakāya* Initiation which has the attributes explained in the *Vairocana Tantra*. It was explained earlier that you should understand that the initiation of the trainee into the Mandala Arising from Great Compassion causes him to attain the embodiment of the core of Enlightenment (*bodhimaṇḍa-kāya*), the initiation into the Revolving Wheel of Letters (56b) next causes him to attain the *saṃbhoga-kāya* and the *nirmāṇa-kāya*, and the initiation into the Secret Mandala causes him to attain this *dharmakāya*.

Now, regarding the explanation here of the attributes of entry into the embodiment of the core of Enlightenment and so forth, the *Vairocana Tantra* says:

> ' "*I shall expound the Dharma which is unequalled,*
> *primordially tranquil and supreme*
> *to the first in the world*
> *by whom I am called the Protector of the World.*" '

'*Then, when the Bhagavat had spoken these verses, he performed an empowerment, such that when the Bodhisattvas and Vajradharas were empowered by it, they saw the Bhagavat who had entered the most excellent core of Enlightenment, which is devoid of proliferations like space, in non-dual union with practice and is like the fruition of karmic action*' [10.7 – 8].

There the verse '*I shall expound the Dharma which is unequalled*' means 'I shall teach the Dharma to the world by the *saṃbhoga-kāya* and *nirmāṇa-kāya*'. There, the first arisen in the world are the '*first in the world*', that is, Viṣṇu, Mahādeva, Brahmā and so forth of the Tīrthikas, because they arise in the first evolving eon (*vivarta-kalpa*). Amongst those first-worlders, he is the '*Protector of the World*' (*lokanātha*). In way is he the Protector of the World? The words '*I shall expound*' signify 'the reason why', meaning because he teaches the supreme Dharma which is primordially tranquil, and without equal. Therefore, the implication of this is that since they teach paths which are sullied and have objective supports, those [first-worlders] are not truly world protectors. (57a)

'*They saw the Bhagavat who had entered the most excellent core of Enlightenment*' shows the entry of the Vajradharas and the Great Bodhisattvas into the *abhisaṃbodhi-kāya*, for their initial entry into the Bhagavat Vairocana's *saṃbhoga-kāya* and *nirmāṇa-kāya* is shown by this passage: '*Then those Bodhisattvas, Samantabhadra and so on, and those Vajradharas such as Vajrapāṇi and so on, through empowerment by the Bhagavat, entered into the display of the treasury of the manifestations of the sameness of his Inexhaustible Body, and likewise they entered the display of the treasury of the array of the sameness of his Inexhaustible Speech and Mind*' [1.3]. Therefore, you should understand that by seeing the Inexhaustible Body and so forth of the Bhagavat Vairocana, they come to know the Bhagavat Vairocana's *abhisaṃbodhi-kāya* endowed with perfectly special qualities through]the Inexhaustible Body and so forth] which form the way of seeing it. However, according to some, the meaning of the verse,

> '*I shall expound the Dharma which is unequalled,*
> *primordially tranquil and supreme*
> *to the first in the world*
> *by whom I am called the Protector of the World*'

can be considered differently, by relating it to the *dharmakāya*. That is, the embodiment of the Bhagavat Perfect Buddhas has three [modes] due to the distinctions of the *dharmakāya*, the *sambhoga-kāya* and the *nirmāṇa-kāya*. Since the *dharmakāyas* of all Buddhas have the same nature and are unchangingly consummate, (57b) they are perpetually prior (*ādi*) to all creatures who arise and perish without beginning. Therefore, having placed that *dharmakāya* in his heart, the Bhagavat says '*I shall expound the Dharma which is unequalled*', and so forth. Hence the implied meaning is 'I am prior to the mundane beings who are subject to birth and death, because of the essential nature of the *dharmakāya*'. You should understand that this viewpoint does not elucidate the meaning of *first* in accordance with the verse. Moreover, these people think that '*I shall expound the Dharma*' means that it is because the Bhagavat accomplishes Adornment of the Array of Buddha Speech, which delights all beings, by virtue of the *dharmakāya*.

Moreover the entry into the *dharmakāya* is shown in the chapter which teaches the Secret Mandala in the section which explains the *Vidyā* King which is formed from twelve component letters, thus: '*Then Vajrapāṇi entered into the Level of the Bhagavat Vairocana's Body, Speech and Mind and perceived the sameness of all phenomena, and thinking of future beings, he uttered this* Vidyā *King which severs all doubts*' [13.8], and so forth down to

'*Then the glorious Vajrapāṇi*
became most joyful in thought,
and being empowered by the perfect Buddhas
he spoke the following verses:
These phenomena are without attributes,
without inherent reality, unlocalized,
liberated from karmic action and rebirth,
and are said to resemble ideas.
After being encouraged by the expedient means
of the Protectors, Masters of Compassion,
I have understood this nature of phenomena!' [13.10].

This concludes the explanation of the three part ritual of initiation into the Mandalas as Master. (58a) This is the summarized significance of the ritual dealing with the actions concerning the three types of Mandalas.

14. The *Homa* Rituals

The ritual to be done with fire [are not explained here since this commentary is for those of medium ability][A].

II. THE PRACTICES TO PROPITIATE THE MANTRAS

Now I shall summarize the description given in the Tantra of what should be done by the practitioners in order to propitiate the *vidyās* and the mantras, together with the results. Regarding that, the practice of the practitioner is of three types: i) the

A There seems to be a small hiatus in the commentary at this point, with none of the editions mentioning the *homa* rituals. I have supplied the bridging comment.

preliminary practice for the mantra which is to be propitiated, ii) the application practice characterized by the ritual of prior service in order to propitiate the mantra, and likewise, iii) the accomplishment of the mantra, by which the result of the mantra will come about. As for the results, the results of the mantra is, in essence, characterized by the attainments.

1. The preliminary practices

Of those, the preliminary practice for the mantra which is to be propitiated is of two types due to the distinctions of inner and outer.

A. The outer preliminary practices

The outer [preliminary practices] are characterized by entry into the mandala and initiation which have been explained. Apart from these, the remainder have the nature of the *samaya* commitments of those who propitiate the *vidyās* and mantras. These are spoken of thus:

> *'From this day forward,*
> *you should never abandon*
> *the holy Dharma and* bodhicitta,
> *Repeatedly recollecting*
> *a kind and compassionate attitude,*
> *you should not be parsimonious,*
> *nor do what harms beings.*
> *You should not treat the guru with disrespect:*
> *He is like all the Buddhas*[A]' [2.93].

Indeed, these are the ordinary duties for the preliminary practice of those who propitiate the mantras in general. (58b) As for the others apart from that, they are the practices of those following the Bodhisattva Way and those who strive in the mantra practice, which are explained here generally. Moreover, in Chapter XX on maintaining the training whose nature is the path of the ten wholesome actions upheld by expedient means, the text says: '*Bhagavat! Please explain how it is that the Bodhisattva Mahāsattvas are without uncertainty and confusion? How is that they are not harmed when they go around in* saṃsāra, *when they are in possession of that basis of training of the Bodhisattva Mahāsattvas which is upheld by expedient means and insight?*' down to '*a Bodhisattva should turn away from the taking of life, the taking of what is not given and sexual misconduct. He should turn away from lying, abuse, slander and idle talk. He should turn away from covetousness, malice and perverse opinions*' [20.1 – 3].

The transgression or otherwise of this [training] which is upheld by expedient means and insight should be ascertained according to this Tantra. This preliminary practice by the practitioner is also said to be the outer one because the practitioner undertakes it in an unequipoised state.

A This differs somewhat to MVT and includes several extra lines.

B. The inner preliminary practice

The inner one is the preliminary practice of the practitioner in accordance to his equipoise. You should know that two types are also indicated herein in accordance to the equipoise of the mental stream with perceptual forms and without perceptual forms. These are taught in accordance to the practitioners' power of repeated cultivation. (59a)

i. The preliminary practice without perceptual forms

Of those, the preliminary practice of the practitioner without perceptual forms is characterized by the repeated cultivation of *bodhicitta*, regarding which the text says:

> '*The first are those who only have the* samaya
> *after having seen this Mandala,*
> *but the* mudrās *should not be shown*
> *nor should the mantras be given to them.*
> *Those who have received the* mudrās *and mantras*
> *due to the special nature of their* bodhicitta,
> *and have seen the Mandala*
> *are known as the second type of* samaya-*holder*' [13.42].

Indeed the preliminary practice for all mantra *sādhanas* is characterized by the repeated cultivation of *bodhicitta*. Likewise, in particular, in the section on the accomplishment of the Essences of the Tathāgata, it is explained that the preliminary practice is characterized by the repeated cultivation of *bodhicitta*, in reference to which it says '*you should stay in a grove, a monastery, a cave, or wherever there is mental solitude, cultivating* bodhicitta *until signs appear*' [6.22]. Here the *sign* is when the mind is able to rest stably for as long as one wishes in the *samādhi* of the realization that all phenomena are without inherent existence, which is explained herein thus: the trainee should carefully purify himself by *bodhicitta*, and

> '*When a trainee is not swayed at all*
> *by any objects of perception,*
> *he will then be without impurities,*
> *like space and become utterly pure*' [13.21].

Likewise, it is said elsewhere (= *Subāhu-paripṛcchā Tantra*) that the mind which has reached equipoise is the one capable of recitation since it is able to rest stably for as long as wished upon a single object through the repeated cultivation of the *samādhi* which focuses upon [an object] with perceptual forms and without perceptual forms. It mentions that characteristic of the complete purification of the mind, thus:

> '*Looking at the tip of one's nose*
> *and abandoning conceptualization:* (59b)
> *when the mind is unmovable*
> *even though engaged in activity,*
> *then you should know the mind*
> *is said to have become*
> *established on the object*'.[10]

In order to teach that the mind which rests stably on one object is capable of meditatively cultivating the recitation deity, through the emergence of certain physical and mental qualities, it also says:

> '*The most excellent human joy*
> *will arise in the practitioner who has meditative absorption,*
> *by that joy his body will become pellucid,*
> *and through his body being pellucid,*
> *he will be granted bliss.*
> *If he is joyous and blissful*
> *then without any doubts,*
> *he will be one-pointedly concentrated*
> *on the recitations*'.[11]

Similarly, it explains there the advantages of doing the recitation with a stable mind, thus:

> '*By recitation all the failings done*
> *throughout one's lifetimes*
> *will be destroyed entirely,*
> *If evil failings are utterly destroyed,*
> *pleasing attainments will be accomplished*'.[12]

Similarly, it teaches there the instructions for the practice of the recitation when the mind has not been made stable, thus:

> '*The mind which delights in laziness*
> *and is associated with suffering,*
> *should be carefully turned away from*
> *whatever acts as a cause for that,*
> *and applied to the worthy mantra letters*'.[13]

In connection with this sign of the equipoised mind, the complete purification of one's mind should also be understood by way of the [practice] with perceptual forms and [the practice] without perceptual forms, which are dealt with below.

Likewise, the preliminary practice is also explained as being characterized by repeated practice of the yoga without perceptual forms, by way of the repeated practice of *samādhi* without perceptual forms thus: '*A Bodhisattva who engages in the Bodhisattva practice by means of mantras, who desires to accomplish the* samādhi *without perceptual forms should think as follows: "From whence do perceptual forms arise? Is it from my body, or from my mind, or from my* manas*?" With regards to these, he should ascertain that the body is produced from [previous] karmic actions and by nature lacks creative power [of its own], like grass, trees and pebbles, and is insensate and resembles external things (*ākāra*), as though it were a statue. Though some person gets angry with such a statue, or destroys, burns or cuts it with fire, poison, swords, water or vajras, it is not the least bit discomforted. Even if one makes offerings to that statue of various different kinds of divine and human articles, such as food, drink, baths, incense, garlands, clothing, sandalwood or camphor and so forth, it will not* *become joyful. Why is that? For whoever makes offerings or does harm to that figure, which lacks any inherent reality, due to perverse delusive ideas generated by his arrogance, is a fool in nature. Lord of the Secret Ones! In that way you should meditate on the lack of self-existence in the body, by the recollection which attends to the body. Moreover, Lord of the Secret Ones, the mind should be considered to be without inherent reality, devoid of all perceptual forms and lacking in self-existence. Lord of the Secret Ones, the three times cannot be found in the mind. You should consider that that which is devoid of the three times is also inherently devoid of perceptual forms. Furthermore, Lord of the Secret Ones, foolish ordinary people imagine that the* manas *has perceptual forms. But this is just a designation* (adhivacana) *for what is falsely imagined. They do not know that that which is not real is unarisen. Lord Of the Secret Ones! If a Bodhisattva who engages in the Bodhisattva practice by means of mantras, has thought in that way, he will attain the* samādhi *without perceptual form. Lord of the Secret Ones, when he abides in the* samādhi *without perceptual forms, the mantra deities uttered by the Tathāgatas will draw near and come into his presence'* [8.1–6].

Here the word '*mind*' includes the six perceptions of the eye and so forth which focus on colour-form and so forth. If you investigate those objects of the mind such as colour-form and so forth, either by the reasoning of one and many parts or the fact they are primordially unarisen and unarising, you will find that what is without inherent reality cannot be perceived by the mind defined here as visual perception and so forth. Hence, objects such as colour-form do not exist, so the visual perception and so forth which perceive them are also unarisen. Whatever has not arisen cannot be established in the past, present or future. Therefore, the three times do not exist in the mind. In that way, you should ascertain the non-existence of the mind, whose nature is the psycho-physical constituent of visual perception and so forth, which perceives the nature of the four psycho-physical constituents of colour-form and so forth.

Now, regarding the instructions to ascertain whether the mind, which is the perceiving subject and perceived objects in nature, is also primordially unborn and unarisen, it says that '*foolish ordinary people imagine that the* manas *has perceptual forms. But this is just a designation* (adhivacana) *for what is falsely imagined. They do not know that that which is not real is unarisen*'. Here the word '*manas*' signifies the perception (*vijñāna*) with the aspects (*ākāra*) of a perceiving subject and perceived objects, (61a) as it says herein:

> '*White, yellow, or red,*
> *are imagined by the* manas,
> *for whatever is distinguished there,*
> *that is a function of mind.*
> *The mind which is satisfied and fixed*
> *is what I describe as the heart.*
> *Abiding in that yoga, you should imagine*
> *the Perfect Buddha, the best of humans*'[A] [6.102 – 103].

Here, '*white*' is the moon disc, '*yellow*' is the earth mandala, '*red*' is the fire mandala, and they are described as appropriate in this Tantra as the actual seats of the yogins

A This is significantly different to *Vairocana Tantra* VI.102/3 who engage in the cultivation of the *samādhi* of the Perfect Buddha and so forth. Since what appears in that *manas* as white, yellow or red, is untenable according to the reasoning previously mentioned, yogins also comprehend that even the *manas* which has those perceptual images does not exist. Because of that, it is said, '*this is just a designation for what is falsely imagined. That which is not real is unarisen*'. This is mentioned elsewhere thus:

> '*Representations of reified objects and beings*
> *appear to the consciousness;*
> *yet they lack reality though they arise,*
> *because the one does not exist, nor does the other*'.[14]

In that way, the yogin who wishes to accomplish the *samādhi* without perceptual forms does not meditate on his body, but first of all understands that colour-form itself is not a causal basis for the concepts (*vikalpa*) of blue and so forth, since it is intrinsically insensate. Following that, having understood that the psycho-physical component of external colour-form and so forth does not exist, in the manner explained earlier, he should then consider that the mind which perceives them is also unborn. Because of that, the yogin (61b) will also understand that the *manas* which appears as objects and beings does not exist either, because of the fact that it is linked to objects, like consciousness in the case of illusions, mirages or dreams. He should [just] act in the state of *samādhi* without perceptual forms by way of hearing, pondering, and cultivating.

The advantages of this are described thus:

> '*When he experiences the* samādhi
> *without attributes, as it really is,*
> *then the* mantrin *will accomplish*
> *the attainment arising from the* manas' [6.41].

Likewise, in the section where the advantages of the yoga without perceptual forms are taught, it is said that attainments with perceptual form will also arise from that without perceptual form, thus:

> '*The Jinas say that attainments with forms*
> *come from that with perceptual forms;*
> *but you will also accomplish those with forms*
> *by abiding in that without perceptual forms.*
> *Hence, you should, in all cases,*
> *rely on that without perceptual forms*' [7.4].

ii. The preliminary practice with perceptual forms

The practitioner's preliminary practice with perceptual forms is said to be 'inner'. Moreover, in the explanation about the attributes of cultivating the four branches which are the transformation of oneself into the deity and so forth, in the section on the four branches of the general recitation of all mantras, the text says of the first:

> '[*One*] *ground is your tutelary deity,*
> *which should be created in your body*' [5.3],

and so forth in detail.

Likewise, it is additionally explained by way of cultivating the transformation of oneself into the Body of the Perfect Buddha in the section on the *sādhana* for the Essences of the Tathāgata, where it is prescribed thus: '*then starting with any one of those essences, you should accomplish the ground until it becomes definite*' [6.23] and so forth. (62a)

Likewise, the characteristics of the purification of mind is additionally explained by way of the cultivation of yoga with and without perceptual forms for all the preliminary practices of the practitioner in general, in the following manner: By the light of *Ra* arranged in both of your eyes, you should visualize the *abhisaṃbodhi-kāya* of the Bhagavat Vairocana which has been accomplished by the essence *A*, seated upon a lotus in the moon disc in your heart. In your cranium there is also the essence *Aṃ*, which indicates the *dharmakāya* that characterizes the state of a Tathāgata. Resting in the vajra mandala which abides in the *Dharmodaya Mudrā* of all the Tathāgatas described in the Mandala Arising from Great Compassion, you should cultivate [that essence] until you see the *abhisaṃbodhi-kāya* of the Bhagavat Vairocana seated on a lotus in a moon disc like a reflection, by the light of the *Ra* which is arranged in your eyes. Then, sending your mind upwards on the path of the light rays of the moon, you should make that essence *Aṃ* which is arranged in your cranium appear vividly, white like the moon and very minute. You should cultivate it for as long that takes. Then, having arranged *Laṃ*, white like the moon, in the place where *Ra* was arranged in both your eyes, you should then consider that all phenomena are devoid of attributes (*lakṣaṇa*) and cultivate the emptiness of your entire body and all of the Three Worlds, by fervent recourse to the *dharmakāya*, as long as you wish. The concluding process for that (*upasaṃhāra*) should be done by seeing your body as whatever has been arranged in association with the Tathāgata and so forth, (62b) while the concluding process for the appearance of the Tathāgata and so forth should be done by seeing just your own body. Therefore, you should consider this as the inner preliminary practice of the practitioner by way of attention to the two *samādhis* – those with and without perceptual forms in sequence. As it says in detail:

> '*White, yellow, or red,*
> *are imagined by the* manas;
> *for whatever is distinguished there,*
> *that is a function of mind.*
> *The mind which is satisfied and fixed*
> *is what I describe as the heart.*
> *The mantras which are located there*
> *will bestow vast results.*
> *Imagine a lotus there,*
> *with eight petals and stamens.*
> *The* A *that is located there,*
> *with a beautiful radiant aura,*

as though pulsating everywhere.
[*It is*] *the Lord who has various forms,*
like the flashing of a thousand lightning bolts,
manifesting his appearance everywhere,
like a mirror in a cave,
present before all [*beings*]
like the images of the moon in water.
The mantrin *who abides in the mantra place*
should know his manas *to be thus*
Then the mantrin *should imagine*
within the expanse of his cranium
an A, *marked with an* anusvāra,
stainless, pure and beautiful,
like crystal, the moon, or snow;
it is the tranquil dharmakāya
and the ground of all.
Through it the mantra attainment
will be accomplished in various forms
When you see that abode of the Tathāgata,
you will attain paradise and beatitude.
Having placed a Ra *in your eyes,*
which shines like a lamp,
bend your neck a little
and press your tongue on your palate,
then gazing within your heart,
equipoised, look at your manas.
It is unsullied and extremely pure,
always present like a mirror.
That is the true nature of manas
spoken of by the Buddhas of the past.
The consciousnesses will become radiant
when one is on the path illumined by manas.
Then the mantrin *will see*
the Lord of humans, the perfect Buddha.
The mantrin *who sees him will always*
accomplish the supreme attainment.
Then having previously transformed it,
the letter you should imagine
is a La *with an* anusvāra.
It should be imagined in your eye sockets;
If you see this as the emptiness of everything,
you will attain the imperishable state
If you desire to attain the splendid Awareness
or else the Five Supernatural Cognitions,
or the attainments of the vidyādharas,
or to be long-lived and youthful,
you will not attain them

as long as you do not engage in this,
This Awareness arising from the mantra
is the most excellent true Awareness' [6.102 – 107].

Therefore, this is the explanation of the nature of yoga with and without perceptual forms, characterized by the [preliminary] practice of the practitioner for the mantra-practitioners who should train in the expedient means and insight which accomplishes all mantras.

Likewise, in particular, the Bhagavat says that the *sādhana* practice of those who accomplish the Great Hero Essence is preceded by the cultivation of *bodhicitta,* characterized by the accomplishment of the so-called 'true nature of self', which is the state of the Perfect Buddha residing in an earth mandala, thus:

'*He who knows the ritual should first*
in sequence carry out the true nature of self.
The mantrin *sits as before,*
and having recollected the Tathāgatas,
he should make himself into an A
augmented with an anusvāra.
All is quite yellow and beautiful,
square and marked with vajras.
The mantrin *should imagine*
the Lord of all perfect Buddhas dwelling there.
This is called the true nature of self
by all the Buddhas.
When the mantrin *has become free of doubts*
concerning the true nature of self,
then he will indeed be a benefactor
of all those in the world.
He will be endowed with various wonders
and will live like a magician.
When the mantrin *is equipoised*
he will eliminate all karmic actions
accumulated by ignorance from beginningless time
in the confines of samsaric existence.
If the mantrin *visualizes his mind*
as the supreme bodhicitta,
he will always be unsullied by the results
arising from wholesome and unwholesome actions,
like a lotus is unaffected by the water,
and then how much more so
if he transforms himself
into the most excellent Jina!' [6.47 – 50].

This is the explanation of the inner preliminary practice with perceptual form to bring about the accomplishment of the mantras.

2. The Application Practice (Prior Service)

The yogin, characterized as one who has thus thoroughly done either the inner or the outer preliminary practice as appropriate, should undertake the practice of application to the mantra which is to be propitiated, which is defined as the prior service recitation. That is also of two types because of the distinctions of the application to recitation with and without perceptual forms.

A. The application practice of recitation with perceptual forms

Of those, regarding the application practice involving recitation with perceptual forms, I only explained the characteristics of the four-membered external recitation in general for all accomplishing of the mantras. (64a) So, regarding the ritual for that, the text says:

> '*Letter should be joined to letter,*
> *likewise ground becomes ground.*
> *You should recite 100,000 times*
> *mentally, with restraint.*
> *The [first] letter is* bodhicitta,
> *the second is said to be sound.*
> *[One] ground is your tutelary deity,*
> *which should be created in your body.*
> *The second ground should be known as*
> *the perfect Buddha, the most excellent of men.*
> *The* mantrin *should imagine him*
> *located in a pure moon disc.*
> *He should carefully arrange*
> *the letters within that in sequence*' [5.2 – 4].

The application involving the four-membered inner recitation of those who do the recitation with the four essences of the Tathāgata is also described. These are manifested from the continuum of the Tathāgata, thus 'A *is of Enlightenment,* Ā *is practice,* Aṃ *is the state of Perfect Enlightenment, and* Aḥ *is Nirvāṇa*'. Therefore, these four essences encompass the aspects of the Awarenesses of Enlightenment, Practice, Perfect Enlightenment and Nirvāṇa of the Bhagavat Vairocana. Of those, Enlightenment is the realization that one's mind is unborn in all aspects and that Awareness is unborn. That aspect which is the realization of Enlightenment is symbolized by the essence *A*. Likewise, at the moment when he became directly and perfectly awakened to Enlightenment, he pervaded the Three Realms with the Inexhaustible Arrays of Body, Speech and Mind – the *saṃbhoga-kaya* and *nirmāṇa-kaya* – which he automatically attained (64b) and which undertake the benefitting of beings according to their lot, and he acted for the benefit and liberation of beings. That which has those characteristics is called the Bhagavat's Practice, and is symbolized by the lengthened *A* essence. When that Awareness which is characterized as Enlightenment does not get involved in the objective aspect of cognition (*jñeya*) through the absence of referential objects (*alambāna*), just as fire goes out after the fuel has been consumed, then that essence of Enlightenment with the *anusvāra* which expresses the nothingness of the objective aspect of cognition is said to be Perfect Enlightenment, because of the realization that mind and its objects are unborn. Also, that aspect of the realization of his Awareness is symbolized by that *Aṃ*. Consequently, both the Awareness and the objective aspect of cognition of the Bhagavat Vairocana are nothingness, and even their substance lacks inherent reality. The state in which that is realized is the state of the realization of infinite nothingness (*ananta-śunyatā*), which is like Nirvāṇa. That is symbolized by the essence *Aḥ* with a *visarga*, which expresses the nothingness of nothingness. These four essences are the application [practice] of the inner four-membered recitation. Thus you should imagine yourself as the Body of the Perfect Buddha Śākyamuni with any one of the four essences *A* and so forth, and then imagine a moon disc in the heart of the Perfect Buddha who have been indivisibly united with you by that essence. (65a) Then, imagining another Perfect Buddha Body, the Bhagavat Vairocana, seated upon a lotus throne there, you should imagine that same essence located in the moon disc in his heart and recite it. In order to teach that the text says: '*Then starting with any one of those essences, you should accomplish the ground until it becomes definite. Placing the essence in* [*your*] *heart, you should accomplish your mind, until it appears to be very pure, unsullied, stable without wavering, free from conceptualization, like a mirror, and very subtle. You should do it with continual application to the practice until you see your body as the body of the deity. The second ground is the perfect Buddha who sits upon a great royal lotus within that same mirror disc, abiding in* samādhi, [*as though*] *within a cave. He has a top-knot and a crown, and is surrounded by infinite rays of light. He is devoid of all thoughts and concepts and is peaceful from the very beginning, like space. Imagining that the sound abides in him, you should recite in equipoise*' [6.23].

B. The practice of recitation without perceptual forms

Likewise, the Tantra explains the *samādhi* without perceptual form which is the ritual of recitation of all the *vidyās* and mantras, as appropriate, by way of the application [practice] involving the *dharmakāya* as your tutelary deity. The text teaches that the deity's Body is of two types based on the division into an impure and a pure Body according to that with and that without perceptual form respectively. The pure one is defined as the *dharmakāya*, which is the *samādhi* without perceptual form in essence and non-conceptualizing awareness in nature. (65b) The impure is defined as the body-form which has been [mentally] created (*parikalpita*) in essence, which is the Body of a Perfect Buddhas in character, whether *saṃbhoga-kāya* or *nirmāṇa-kāya*, and which is formed of colour and shape with regards to its appearance to people to be guided. The colour-form bodies of the other types of deities, apart from the pure and impure ones, may appear in accordance with whatever causes of merit they possess, yet they are also impure by being [mentally] created in essence. Also, this Tantra establishes that whatever they have realized concerning the attributes of repeated cultivation of their minds by their gates of liberation is also their *dharmakāya*[15]. As it is said elsewhere regarding the general definition of mantras, '*mantras are* bodhicitta'.

The characteristics of these two modes of embodiment are indicated herein, thus: '*The natural form of the deity is of two types, the completely pure and the impure. Of these, the completely pure is realization in nature, which is devoid of all perceptual forms. The impure is the body-image with perceptual forms,* [*with*] *colour and shape. By these two natural states of the deity, two types of aims may be accomplished: attainments with perceptual forms will arise through that with perceptual forms and those without perceptual forms will arise through that without perceptual forms.*

> '*The Jinas say that attainments with attributes*
> *come from that with attributes;*
> *but you will also accomplish those with attributes*
> *by abiding in that without attributes.*
> *Hence, you should, in all cases,*
> *rely on that without attributes*' [7.3 – 4].

That method for undertaking the Body of the deity without perceptual form is the same as was described earlier in the Chapter on the *Samādhi* Without Perceptual Forms. The accomplishment of the four-membered recitation, beginning with one's tutelary deity, by the mentally created Body characterized by its appearance in the form of colour and shape, was explained earlier. This is process of application for the accomplishment of recitation by way of repeatedly cultivating the *samādhi* without perceptual form, which is the one's tutelary deity with the attributes of the *dharmakāya*: First you should actualize all the four branches of recitation for a while as before, and then analyze the manifestation of the created (*parikalpita*) colour, shape and so on, of your tutelary deity who is identical to yourself, breaking them down into atoms. Or it is also acceptable to do this by way of the reasoning that it is unborn and unarising from the very beginning, or similarly by way of the technique of drawing-in the vital-energy (*prāṇa*) through the yoga of turning your mind inside, or by way of not focussing on its appearance [as colour and shape]. In accordance with that realization, you should then actualize the mind which is just self-aware, free from the body-image of your tutelary deity and without appearance [as subject and object], and mentally recite your *vidyā* mantra as appropriate. In order to teach this, the text says:

> '*The supramundane is that done mentally,*
> *ceasing to do the drawing-in and so on.*
> *You should make yourself one with the deity,*
> *perceiving both to be identical,*
> *it should be inseparable from the nature of your* manas.
> *In no other way should it be done*' [10].

This concludes the explanation of the application practice for practitioners to propitiate the mantra at the time of doing the prior service.

3. Accomplishment Practice

Now I shall deal with the practice of yoga for accomplishing the attainments of mantras for which the prior service has been done, (66b) and this is also of two types due to the distinctions of external and internal.

A. External accomplishment practice

Of those, the external one is this mandala of the accomplishment of all mantra attainments, and the text speaks of the attributes of the mandala of the mantra accomplishment thus:

> '*Draw an excellent vajra mandala,*
> *which is completely square,*
> *one-gated, with a perimeter,*
> *completely coloured in gold.*
> *The vajras should be joined to each other,*
> *in the manner of a vajra mesh*' [6.31].

Having dealt in detail with the attributes of the mandala, it then says:

> '*Then having safeguarded the place, stay there.*
> *Having obtained cleansed material,*
> *with a pure inner self,*
> *you should recite the whole night long.*
> *Then, at midnight or else at sunrise,*
> *the material will be transmuted*
> *as though brilliant with a flaming aura*' [6.35 – 36].

Therefore, this actually describes the mandala for the external accomplishment, in order to accomplish external attainments with such attributes as the sword and so forth.

B. Internal accomplishment practice

You should understand that the attributes of those internal attainments are actually taught in the Chapters on the Great Hero and the Hundred Letters. Likewise, the attainment of mastery of the *samādhi* without perceptual forms in order to bring about the internal attainments is additionally spoken of in the text thus:

> '*When he experiences the* samādhi
> *without attributes, as it really is,*
> *then the* mantrin *will accomplish* (67a)
> *the attainment arising from the* manas' [6.41].

What is stated here about the attainments arising from the *manas* is mentioned where all the attainments are categorized, thus:

> '*What need is there for any attainment*
> *other than the attainment of* bodhicitta*?*
> *It is said that apart from that*
> *there are five types of attainment:*
> *Those at entry into the practice,*

also those during the ascent of the Levels,
the five mundane supernatural cognitions,
Buddhahood and those that remain' [13.49 – 50].

Therefore, this explanation of the characteristics of entry into the mandala for internal and external preliminary practice, the repeated cultivation of *bodhicitta*, the purification of the mind and so forth, leads on to entry into the application practice characterized by the four-membered recitation and so forth.

Now, these are the characteristic of the four-membered recitation and so forth for application [practice], thus: first of all, you should recite for a while until the prior service recitation of the mantra is completed as described, by way of the recitation application with and without objective supports, in any sequence. Moreover, the [prior] service recitation of the mantra is said in this Tantra to be fixed in three modes: fixed in number and time, and in the arising of signs. It says that a service of a hundred thousand recitations in number is to be done for the repeated cultivation of *bodhicitta*, done while in the nature of the relatively real or else absolutely real deity, (67b) at the start of the time when you do the prior service for all mantras in general and for any one of the four essences of the Tathāgata particular, and that the preliminary recitation should be fixed for two months [duration]. Regarding the prior service for the Great Hero letters, it just says that the practitioner should recite with the yoga base while in a state characterized by the true nature of the self, but the number for each is not specified. Regarding that, the Bhagavat explains a little the attributes of the fixed recitation of general service for all the mantras with this passage thus, from

'*Letter should be joined to letter,*
likewise ground becomes ground.
You should recite 100,000 times
mentally, with restraint',

down to

'*Then, well restrained, the* mantrin
should recite for one month.
The preliminary practice of the mantras
is entry from one ground to the other.
This is called preliminary practice
by all the renowned Buddhas.
After that he should offer
just a few flowers, perfume and so on.
So that he may become a Buddha
he should also dedicate [*to others*] *his* bodhicitta.
Thus, without fear, the mantrin
should recite for a second month.
Then at the time of the full moon
that person should start the accomplishment' [5.2 – 10].

Likewise, the prior service of those four essences of the Tathāgata in particular is specified by this passage in detail thus, from '*Then starting with any one of those essences, you should accomplish the ground until it becomes definite*' down to

> '*Imagining that the sound abides in him,*
> *you should recite in equipoise.*
> *It is taught that the preliminary service*
> *should be done a hundred thousand times.*
> *Then in the second month,*
> *you should offer flowers, perfume and so on,*
> *acting helpfully towards beings*
> *in many different ways,*
> *regardless of profit and loss,*
> *you should recite for another month.*
> *"By the power of my merits*
> *may all beings be happy!*
> *May they be free from all ills!*
> *May they also perfect all wishes*
> *praised by the Tathāgatas!"*' [6.23 – 25],

which indicates in detail the yoga praised for benefitting beings. This summarizes in general what arises from application to the recitation of the fixed prior service for the four essences of Tathāgatas. You should get the details from the Tantra.

i. The attainments arising from A

Likewise, after you have done the four-membered internal yoga, the maintenance of life-energy and the removal of poison, which arise from the essence *A* in particular by the practice of imagining without even recitation, are mentioned: '*When he has united* A *with his breath and cultivated this at the three* [*specified*] *times* [*of the day*], *desiring that his life-energy be maintained, he will live for a long time. If he places the* anusvāra *on top of it, he will draw out all abiding and moving poisons*' [6.43].

This practice for controlling [someone] with the essence *A* by way of visualization is also mentioned: '*Then if he wishes to control a lover, he should make himself into an* A *and likewise the person to be controlled into a* Va. *He should place a lotus in himself and in the other he should place a conch, with each looking at the other, then at that instant he will gain control.* [6.44]. (68b)

This means that for the practice for control you should visualize yourself as Vairocana with a red-coloured Body and imagine a red-coloured lotus upon your tongue, and also visualize the person to be controlled as a red-coloured Vajrasattva with the letter *Va*, imagining a red-coloured conch upon his tongue also. You should then place that person facing you.

Therefore, the fixed recitation for the prior service of the four essences of the Tathāgata and the fixed application to activities involving the repeated cultivation of imagining are described in that way.

Also, this text teaches the prior service of those who accomplish the Great Hero essence letters, which has a fixed number of recitations preceded by the accomplishment of the object of union[16] (*yoga-sthāna*), for the sake of the attainments which arise through the recitation. You should know that the text also shows the application involving recitation with those same essences in order for the actions which arise from imagining to be accomplished, and the practices of the attainments which arise from the visualization of them. Regarding the attributes of the object of union, it says

> '*You should know that the excellent* A
> *has a* mahendra *mandala;*
> *both inside and outside*
> *it is a vajra mandala.*
> *Imagine all of them abiding thus.*
> *This is explained as the yoga-posture*' [6.56].

The Bhagavat Mahendra Body is mentioned here thus:

> '*A perfect Buddha dwelling in* samādhi,
> *shining, golden in colour,*
> *with top-knot and crown,*
> *is called the* mahendra *ground.* [6.61]

In that way the object of union is to be accomplished. (69a) Having arranged any one of those Great Hero essence letters in that object of union, you should engage in the three kinds of yoga as appropriate in order that the perfection of one's own or other's benefit might be accomplished. These are the application to what is to be accomplished through the imagination process, the practice of attainments which are accomplished by the month-long prior service recitation, and the practice of accomplishing the attainments which arise from repeated cultivation by the visualization of those letters.

First of all, the text teaches the action of attracting all beings and the action of expelling poisons and fevers, by way of the imagination practice in which you imagine the A essence with the attributes of the Perfect Buddha, as described earlier, as the object of union, the *mahendra* (earth) mandala, thus:

> '*You should know that the excellent* A
> *has a* mahendra *mandala;*
> *both inside and outside*
> *it is a vajra mandala.*
> *Imagine all of them abiding thus.*
> *This is explained as the yoga-posture.*
> A *is the supreme life-energy,*
> *and is called the most excellent magnet.*
> *When you surmount it with an* anusvāra,
> *it will become the attracter of all beings*' [6.56 – 58].

Likewise, by way of having done the accomplishment (*sādhana*) of the prior service recitation at the three times for a month, by the repeated cultivation of the essence *A* which is located therein, the actions of enrichment, and the attainments of the lotus, vajra and so forth should be accomplished, which spoken of thus:

'*When the* mantrin *has recited at the three times,*
for one month, while making the vajra-like mudrā,
the fortress of ignorance will be destroyed,
and he will become firm,
unshakable even by gods and asuras.
In order to obtain possessions
or for some degree of enriching action,
all these should always be done
by the mantrin *in the centre of the mandala*' [6.59 – 60],

and

'*You should meditate and transmute*
in the mahendra *mandala* [*such things as*]
a vajra, a lotus, a sword,
or else a goose, pure gold or earth
or else a wish-fulfilling gem, as appropriate' [6.62].

'*Meditate in a* mahendra [*mandala*]' signifies 'abiding in the *mahendra* ground'. Its attributes are as mentioned above:

'*A perfect Buddha dwelling in* samādhi,
shining, golden in colour,
with top-knot and crown,
is called the mahendra *ground*' [6.61].

Therefore, this should be viewed as the attainment through having recited the essence *A* for a month with the ritual explained earlier.

In order to show that all beings, such as armies, will indeed be suppressed by the yogin who has imagined himself abiding in the *mahendra* ground, it says:

'*Now I shall also explain subduing,*
so you should listen one-pointedly!
In brief, the mantrin *should imagine*
an eight-peaked Sumeru, on top of which
he should place a lotus,
and subsequently a vajra;
on top of that the chief holy letter.
If the yogin presses that on the head,
he will remain motionless' [6.63].

This means that you should imagine Mount Sumeru upon the one who is to be subdued, and a lotus resting upon an earth mandala, and an eight pointed vajra on that. Then you should imagine the Bhagavat the colour of the earth, absorbed in *samādhi*, until he comes to appear clearly.

Likewise, so that the yogins who have the *mahendra* ground may cure the illnesses of themselves and others, (70a) they should drink medicine suitable as an antidote to the sickness, over which they have recited a hundred times, as it says:

> '*If it is recited one hundred times*
> *over medicine to be drunk by someone,*
> *his illnesses which arise from*
> *previous actions will be cured*' [6.64].

This concludes the explanation of the actions and attainments of the essence *A*.

ii. The attainments arising from Va

The actions of *Va* should also be mentioned. Regarding these, one should imagine a white lotus resting on a vajra mandala in the middle of the navel of the object of union, as described earlier, which has become indivisible from yourself. Also imagining a water mandala there, you should imagine a *Va*, like the moon in colour and like a jar in shape, and then you should see nine streams of nectar flowing from it. You should imagine the jar-like *Va* to be encircled by them, spreading outwards from the surface of the jar. Also imagining it surrounded by a mass of hoar-frost, you should recite the essence *Va* as before. Then the attainments of clarified butter, milk and so forth will be accomplished, as it says:

> '*Then furthermore, listen carefully*
> *about the excellent* Va,
> *which is* [*white*] *like snow, milk or a conch,*
> *and arises in the middle of the navel.*
> *It rests in the middle*
> *of a fine white lotus.*
> *The excellent Lord is tranquil,*
> *like the light of the autumn moon.*
> *That mandala is said to be*
> *wonderful by the perfect Buddhas.*
> *It should be imagined completely white,*
> *and also encircled with nine swirls.*
> *That which calms all torments*
> *rests within dew-drops.*
> *If the* mantrin *imagines it in his mind,*
> *with streams of water flowing all round*
> *like milk, strings of pearls,*
> *crystal or moonlight,*
> *then he will be freed from all torments.*
> *These things should be transmuted*
> *in this mandala, while equipoised:*
> *such materials as clarified butter,*
> *milk, strings of pearls,*
> *likewise lotus-root, crystal,*
> *yoghurt, or even water, as are appropriate,*
> *should be transmuted for the accomplishment*
> *of various attainments*' [6.65 – 67].

In order to show the results of these attainments, it says:

> '*Your life will be long,*
> *your appearance will be very wonderful,*
> *you will be free from all illnesses,*
> *you will have excellent good fortune,*
> *your intelligence will be sharp and retentive,*
> *your vision will be free from impediments:*
> *with these transmuted materials,*
> *all these things will quickly come about.*
> *This noble mandala is called the "pacifier"*' [6.67].

If you locate that *Va* in such a mandala, with an *anusvāra*, and imagine it in the direction of the navel of the one to be accomplished, they will be cleansed of fevers, poison and so forth, as it says that:

> '*If done with an* anusvāra,
> *it will be the most excellent purifier*' [6.68].

Here you should also imagine streams of water flowing from this *Va* with *anusvāra*, which is white like clouds. This concludes the explanation of the actions and attainments of *Va*.

iii. The attainments arising from Ra

Likewise, the text teaches the attainments and actions [arising from] a hundred thousand recitations of the letter *Ra* resting in its own mandala, arranged in the region of the chest of the object of union which has become indivisible from yourself, as explained earlier, preceded by imagining the true nature (*tattva*) of its sound. It says that,

> Ra, *most excellent truth,*
> *is called the best of the luminous ones.*
> *By it, whatever arises from actions,*
> *even from the five heinous deeds,*
> *will all be destroyed,*
> *if the yogin imagines it, while equipoised.*
> *He should place it in his heart,*
> *where it abides in the form of a triangle,*
> *pleasing and completely red,*
> *and marked with a triangular sign,*
> *tranquil yet encircled with a flaming aura.*
> *Placed therein, the yogin*
> *should imagine* Ra *with an* anusvāra.
> *Fearlessly he should transmute*
> *these things as appropriate with it:*
> *If the sun and all the planets,*
> *and likewise fire,*
> *all things to be controlled,*
> *and furthermore making angry,*

parching, killing,
and also confining and harming,
are done in conjunction with fire here,
they will all be carried out' [6.69 – 73].

iv. The attainments arising from Ha

Likewise, you should imagine the letter *Hūṃ* resting on a wind mandala between the eye-brows of the object of union, which has become indivisible with yourself. You should do the recitation preceded by [imagining] the true nature of its sound, successively for a month at the three times, and then one will accomplish the attainments of sky-walking and so forth, which is mentioned thus:

'Ha, *the most excellent truth*
arising from the wind' [6.74].

This teaches the attributes of the causal basis of the wind *samādhi.*

'*Causes, karmic actions, results,*
by which seeds are produced,
all these will be destroyed
if you unite this with an anusvāra' [6.75].

This shows that the expression of the true nature of its sound is associated with the attribute of entry into the absolute *samādhi.*

'*To describe its appearance also,*
it is black in colour, with great light
and is encircled with a fierce flaming aura' [6.76].

This explains that its appearance is of the nature of the wind, and is black.

'*The wise one should imagine it* (71b)
on the disc located between his eyebrows' [6.76].

This states that this [letter] located on the wind mandala should be placed between the eyebrows. In order to teach the attributes of the wind mandala, it says:

'*Indigo, like a crescent moon* [*in shape*],
it ripples like the emblem on a flag,
the supreme letter which is unchanging
should be imagined located there by the mantrin' [6.76].

In order to teach the attainments which originate through having visualized and recited it in that way for a month, it says that:

'*Whosoever just sees them*
in the middle of that mandala

will then transmute the objects
which benefit beings.
Travelling in the sky,
also the magical powers,
the divine sight and hearing,
will likewise be attained by the mantrin.
The equipoised mantrin *will carry out*
all [these] things if he abides in the mandala,
both the general and the specific things
that have been spoken of, such as invisibility' [6.77].

This is the causal basis for the attainments characterized by the gaining of the happy (*niḥśreya*) state since it is also the causal basis for the conquest of the four Māras, by way of imagining the true nature of its sound defined here as the lack of objective reality to causes. In order to teach that, it says that:

'*By this [letter], the renowned Bodhisattvas*
will be victorious over demons,
[dwelling] in this Enlightenment Essence,
through the absence of any objective basis to all causes' [6.78].

v. The attainments arising from Khaṃ

Now, the text shows that the recitation of *Khaṃ* for a month is the causal basis for accomplishment of the attainments of the sword, wheel and so forth. For this, you should become indivisible with the object of union, and then make the Sword *Mudrā* and be convinced of the emptiness of all things that are imagined. It says that,

'*Since there are no causes,*
there are also no results,
and even actions do not exist. (72a)
As those three phenomena do not exist,
the Awareness of emptiness will be attained.
The perfect Buddha, of great power,
has fully described its appearance:
With an anusvāra, Khaṃ *is called*
the most excellent of space' [6.79 – 80].

You should understand that this shows that *Khaṃ* expresses the *samādhi* of the emptiness of all phenomena, and also that the *samādhi* of emptiness is transformed into the form of *Khaṃ*.

'*He who has the Sword* Mudrā,
will definitely transmute
that which is to be transmuted. [6.81]

You should understand that this refers to the ritual of the prior service for one month.

C. Generalities concerning the attainments

In order to show the attainments of the prior service for one month, it says that,

> *If you have such articles as*
> *swords, nooses, wheels,*
> *iron arrows, and hammers*
> *you will accomplish the best state*' [6.81].

This explains that these are the attainments of the five essence letters of the Great Hero, by way of imagining and also reciting each of the letters, preceded by the firm conviction [that you are indivisible with] the object of union as described.

Now, by intensively applying yourself to the meditation which removes instability in the yoga while in a state of equipoise, the object of union, indivisible from yourself, will appear just as you imagine it. In order to indicate the attainments such as salvation and magical powers which then come about through cultivating meditation with these letters which have been taught, the text says: '*Lord of the Secret Ones! When the Bodhisattva who engages in the practice of a Bodhisattva by means of mantras has transformed himself into the nature of* A, *and without perceiving any thing related to the external or the internal,* (72b) [*views*] *both gravel, stones and gold in the same way, and abandons sinful actions and such faults as attachment, hatred and so forth,*

> '*Then he will become pure*
> *like the perfect Buddha Sage,*
> *he will be capable of all deeds*
> *and will be free from all faults*' [6.82].

Here the significance of '*without perceiving any thing related to the external or the internal* ' is that having repeatedly cultivated the object of union as described, so that its bare perceptual image appears in his *manas* for as long as he is in a state of equipoise, the yogin disregards both emotionally afflicted and unafflicted appearances, whether related to his own personal colour-form or that of external entities.

While the yogin is equipoised in that way, he will attain the *manas* in which the object of union appears to exist in him. Because of that, according to special circumstances, there are other [attainments]which arise through cultivating the path and through repeated recitation, using these letters, *A* and so forth, which are transformations of the *samādhi* of the Great Hero. Regarding that, the text explains:

> '*Then furthermore, he who is devoted*
> *to the mantra yoga and knows the ritual*
> *should carry out the actions of* Va,
> *desiring to aid all beings.*
> *Perceiving the sufferings of the world*
> *with a compassionate mind,*
> *his body will be completely filled*
> *by that Lord, with a white stream of water,*
> *like snow or cow's milk.*
> *Then when he has become certain about it,*

an extremely pure flow of water (73a)
will come forth from all the follicles
on all parts of his body,
and all these realms without exception
will be completely filled with that water.
Whosoever drinks that water
or else even touches it with their hands
will all definitely become Enlightened,
of this there is no doubt!' [6.83].

This signifies that you should actualize the whole of the yoga for the water mandala as explained earlier, and completely fill the whole of your body with the streams emerging from it. Then the streams of water will pour forth from your pores and purify completely everything up to the peak of existence.

Likewise, to teach the actions of *Ra* also, it says:

'[*Or else,*] *equipoised, he should imagine*
Ra *in all parts of his body,*
surrounded with a peaceful lustrous aura,
which flows out to all places.
Then if the yogin releases outwards
the all-illuminating radiance,
the mantrin *will do as he wishes*
by manifestations with Ra' [6.84].

This means that you should imagine the letter *Ra* located in the fire mandala in any part of your body united with the object of union, and fill the interior of your body with its peaceful flames and then they should flow out and appear externally.

The various other actions of these Great Hero essences, which arise from their recitation and visualization, should be understood with reference to the Chapter on the Great Hero. You should understand that these attainments and actions come about by their appearance in the yogin's own mind faculty and the transformational power of the Tathāgatas. With reference to the occurrence of the afore-mentioned actions and attainments by virtue of their appearance in one's own mind, (73b) it says: '*Lord of the Secret Ones! Such levels of attainments arise from one's* manas. *Lord of the Secret Ones, you should see that the various different formations* [*arise*] *from immaterial entities by just having imagined them, and the results of the seed-syllables of all actions arise by just having uttered them*' [6.94 – 95].

From immaterial entities: From the mind and mental factors. *The various different formations*: The attributes (*lakṣāṇa*) which appear as the earth and water mandalas and so forth. *The results of the seed-syllables of all actions arise by just having uttered them*: Herein, '*the results of the seed-syllables*' means the essences of the Great Hero should be imagined as the specific mandalas which are the results of the seed-syllables. *By just having uttered them*: This signifies that you should know those essences through engaging in their recitation. Likewise, you should understand that the yogin also accomplishes these actions and attainments by the Tathāgata's transformational power. Thus, by the power of his previous aspirations, the Tathāgata spontaneously and continuously manifests *vidyās*, mantras, deities and so forth, to those who engage in mantra practice and have undertaken the actions of attainments, and they are at hand to fully satisfy beings according to their lot. Hence, you should understand the attainments and actions are accomplished by virtue of his transformational power and benefaction (*varada*), as it says: '*Lord of the Secret Ones! Furthermore, the Tathāgata who is in tune with all and who pleases all beings in accordance with their wishes,* (74a) *appears before the Bodhisattvas who engage in all actions and mantra practice, like a reflection. A Tathāgata does not conceptualize and is inaccessible to the manas, and transcends time, place, actions, activities, right and wrong,*

> '*Yet he grants the rank of All-knowing,*
> *that arises from mantra practice;*
> *hence All-knowing, attainment,*
> *and the best state will be accomplished*' [6.96 – 98].

Furthermore, regarding the application to the *vidyā* and mantra practice, from where [the Bhagavat] prescribes the number of months and amount [of recititation] regarding the application to the ritual of prior service, such as the four-membered external recitation and so forth, down to the specification of the individual number of months and the amount for the prior service of the four essences of the Tathāgata regarding the four-membered internal recitation, and likewise the specification of the months and so forth for the object of union in connection with the prior service of the letters of the Great Hero essences, with the specified preliminary *sādhana* – all of these were revealed with reference to the purification of the practitioner's [mental] stream, and the Bhagavat says in this Tantra that:

> '*The number of mantras, three hundred thousand,*
> *which I have generally prescribed,*
> *is the number of recitations stipulated*
> *for the pure* mantrins,
> *embodied beings free from failings.*
> *In no other way should it be done*' [9].

Here, the practitioner is shown to be pure due to three factors: i) he is without the dispositions which generate those wholesome and unwholesome actions in present and future lives which contradict the mantra attainments, (74b) and likewise ii) he has already present in his [mental] stream the seeds of wholesome actions, arisen from past or current lifetimes, which accord with the mantra attainments, and iii) he has the qualities of having trained in the practitioner's entry practices such as the cultivation of *bodhicitta*, which are internal and external in nature as have previously been explained.

This Tantra makes clear that such attainments that are desired will arise through three causes even with regards to the practitioner who is not endowed with the above three factors. They are: i) the arising of signs which accord with the desired attainments [from] an unlimited time of recitation, meditative concentration and so forth, likewise ii) the experience of the fruition of the dispositions towards wholesome and unwholesome actions which contradict whatever attainments one desires, and iii) and the attainment of the *samādhi* without perceptual forms by the repeated cultivation of the suchness (*tathatā*) of all phenomena, with respect to the fact that all phenomena are unborn and unarising from the very beginning.

It is explained that such mentally produced attainments as the supernatural cognitions and so forth actually arise by way of the *samādhi* without perceptual forms, when it is said that:

> '*Then the* mantrin *will accomplish*
> *the attainment arising from the* manas' [6.41].

It is also taught that attainments with perceptual forms [will arise] by way of the cultivation of the *samādhi* without perceptual form, with the words '*attainments with perceptual forms also will arise through that without perceptual forms*'. (75a)

Likewise, the text teaches the specific time when attainments are obtained arising from such wholesome actions as propitiating the mantras, meditation, homa and so forth. Thus, the result of a wholesome action such as propitiating the mantras may for one person be manifested in another existence, while for another it will come to fruition in this present life by virtue of their aspiration and application. To show that, it says that:

> '*While the stream-forming actions*
> *remain unvitiated in one's stream,*
> *and the effects have not yet fully matured,*
> *that is the occasion for attainments*' [13.52].

Here '*in one's stream*' signifies 'in the mind-stream of a person who accomplishes wholesome actions by propitiating the mantras'. '*Stream-forming*' is the stream which functions as the causal basis for special attainments such as becoming a *vidyādhara* and so forth. It says '*while the actions remain unvitiated*', [meaning] in any such being for such a time. '*While*' is the time. '*Actions*' indicates that action of propitiating the mantras. *Unvitiated*: If a previous act of propitiating the mantras has not been exhausted by the result having been granted in a succession of lifetimes. In order to show that it is [unvitiated] if the result of that action has not been experienced, the text says '*and the effects have not yet matured*'. To show that this is the occasion for the [accomplishment] of attainments, it says, '*that is the occasion for attainments*'. Hence, you should know this signifies that if the effects of that action of propitiating the mantras has not been experienced in a succession of lifetimes, then the occasion for its result to be granted is when there is an accumulation [of merit]. (75b) You should understand whatever result is experienced in either the present life or in other lifetimes is just the result of that.

In order to show the occasion when the results of actions actualized in the present world are granted, it says that:

> '*In brief, when action and birth*
> *have been projected simultaneously,*
> *then the* mantrin *will accomplish*
> *the attainment which arises from* manas' [13.53].

This signifies that when the results of actions characterized as mantra attainments emerge from the [mind]-stream of the practitioner during any lifetime from a [previous] lifetime when wholesome actions were accumulated by propitiating the mantras, then action and birth will be have been projected simultaneously.

This is the explanation of the practice of yoga in order that the practitioners may propitiate the mantras when they are doing the prior service.

Now, the practice of yoga to accomplish the mantra attainments when the prior service has been finished should be mentioned. That is also of two types based on the distinctions of external and internal.

Of those, the external refers to those mandalas which accomplish all the attainments of all the mantras. Regarding the attributes of the mandala for the accomplishment of the mantras, it says that:

> '*Draw an excellent vajra mandala,*
> *which is completely square,*
> *one-gated, with a perimeter,*
> *completely coloured in gold.*
> *The vajras should be joined to each other,*
> *in the manner of a vajra mesh*' [6.31],

and so on down to

> '*Having obtained cleansed material,*
> *with a pure inner self,*
> *you should recite the whole night long.* (76a)
> *Then, at midnight or else at sunrise,*
> *the material will be transmuted*
> *as though brilliant with a flaming aura*' [6.35 – 36].

Therefore, this external accomplishment mandala is explained solely to accomplish external attainments characterized as the sword and so forth.

The internal mandalas are characterized as fire, wind, earth and water. Having repeatedly cultivated them, the internal attainments such as the supernatural cognitions and so forth, which depend only on the power of the mind, will be accomplished. You should understand that the attributes of these internal attainments are actually taught in the chapters herein on the Great Hero and the Hundred Letters. Likewise, the mastery of the *samādhi* without perceptual forms which is the means for the internal attainments is also taught by such [passages] as:

> '*When he experiences the* samādhi
> *without attributes, as it really is,*
> *then the* mantrin *will accomplish*
> *the attainment arising from the* manas' [6.41].

The teaching of the categories of attainments is also mentioned herein thus:

'*What need is there for any attainment*
other than the attainment of bodhicitta*?*
It is said that apart from that
there are five types of attainment:
Those at entry into the practice,
also those during the ascent of the Levels,
the five mundane supernatural cognitions,
Buddhahood and those that remain' [13.50].

CONCLUSION

In the above manner, I have summarized the essential meaning (*piṇḍārtha*) of the matters revealed by just the name '*Mahā-vairocana-abhisaṃbodhi-vikurvita-adhiṣṭhāna-tantra*' under four headings: i) the description of the cause and nature of the Bhagavat Vairocana, (76b) ii) the elaboration the topics herein which fully describe the manifestation (*vikurvita*) of Enlightenment and its transformational creations, iii) the revelation of the transformation (*adhiṣṭhāna*) of the manifestations into the perceptual forms of the mantras, *vidyās*, *mudrās* and so forth, the methods of propitiating them, and the entry practice, and likewise iv) the practices for the application (*yoga*), the process of accomplishment (*sādhana*) and the attainments (*siddhi*). You should know that having condensed the words of this Tantra, I have briefly shown the summarized topics so that they may be understood by those trainees who comprehend the meaning when it is thus analyzed in detail. You should understand that since those who rely on the words of the text, will only understand the meaning by way of hearing and pondering on the entire text of the *Vairocana Tantra*, this summary of the essential meaning is not to be regarded as a means for them to understand it.

This completes the *Mahā-vairocana-abhisaṃbodhi-tantra Piṇḍārtha* written by the Master Buddhaguhya. Translated and redacted by the Indian Pandita Silendrabodhi and the Chief Translator dPal brTsegs Rakṣita. This contains two thousand three hundred *ślokas*.

NOTES

T: Tibetan version of MVT (Q 126)
C: Chinese version of MVT (Taishō 848)
V: Unrevised edition of Buddhaguhya's Commentary (Q 3487)
B: Revised edition of Buddhaguhya's Commentary (Q 3490)
CC: Śubhakara-siṃha's Commentary (Manji-zoku Ed. 36-3-5)

PART I INTRODUCTION

1 Although the *Mahā-vairocana-abhisaṃbodhi* is called a *sūtra* in its title, Buddhaguhya and later writers refer to it as the *Mahā-vairocana-abhisaṃbodhi-tantra.* I have adopted this title throughout to bring it in line with Buddhaguhya's comments, but it should be understood that this change would probably have been made some time after 714 CE when Śubhakara-siṃha arrived in China, as he does not seem to know or use the term '*tantra*' at all. Hereafter I shall abbreviate the title of our text to MVT.

2 *Guhya-samāja*, Chapter 18, vv 34-35. *Prabandham tantram ākhyātaṃ tat prabhandaṃ tridhā bhavet | ādhāraḥ prakṛtiś caiva asaṃhārya-prabhedataḥ || prakṛtiś cākritiś hetur asaṃhārya-phalam tathā | ādhāras tad upāyaś ca tribhis tantrārtha-saṃgrahaḥ ||*

3 This list was inspired in part by that given in *Hindu Tantrism* (Brill, 1979)by Teun Goudrian *et al.*

4 Taishō vol 75 p. 431a.

5 See however, the recent translation of this work by Rolf Giebel (1995), who gives convincing identifications for a large number of these eighteen tantras.

6 As with several other early figures in the history of tantric Buddhism, Dharmagupta is said to have lived for a prodigious length of time – over 800 years according to some sources. However, we know that he was still alive around 715 CE from Śubhakara-siṃha's biography.

7 There are however a few fragments in Sanskrit surviving as quotations in various other texts. These are noted where they occur in the translation.

8 The Tibetan translation of the MVT is immediately followed by a Continuation Tantra, which is not found in the Chinese version. Though my conclusions are highly speculative, this Continuation Tantra contains information which may be interpreted to give us some idea when it was composed. To begin with, it would seem that the Continuation Tantra was intended originally as a short manual containing the main rituals and doctrines of the MVT in summary, perhaps for the convenience of the Master. Although it has now achieved canonical status, it was probably intended to be somewhat more ephemeral. Now, in each of the chapters dealing with the rites of Pacifying, Enriching and so forth, a selection of planets and constellations (*nakṣatras*) are given. The rite is likely to be most effective if performed when one of those planets is in conjunction with the prescribed constellations. The list for the rite of Destroying is the most interesting, for instead of the random pattern of constellations we find given for the other rites, we see that there is a consecutive block of four – *Uttarā-phalgunī, Hasta, Citrā* and *Svāti* – which covers a 53° sweep of the sky. I suspect that the reason for this is linked to Saturn, which together with Mars is indicated for the rite of Destroying. Saturn, as no doubt the reader will be aware, is a slow moving planet, for it takes almost twenty nine years to complete one revolution around the sun. If the constellations prescribed for Destroying were as random and spaced out as for the other rites, there would often have been gaps of several years before Saturn was conjoined with an appropriate constellation, leaving Mars as the sole planet in use for this rite and thereby limiting the occasions when one could perform it. Indeed, it is even possible that Mars was inserted here

later, as it is also listed for the Rite of Subduing, and thus is the only planet to be listed twice. Whoever compiled the Continuation Tantra seems to have included this block of four constellations to avoid that kind of situation, as Saturn would have taken about five years to pass through them all. Naturally this presupposes regular updating of the text, which was probably not done. Anyway, *if* we accept that such was the reason for this block of four constellations, then we have an important means of generating possible dates for the composition of this text. By calculating back, we find that Saturn entered the first of those constellations in the following years: 682, 711, 740 and so on every 29 years either way. Of these dates, 682 CE may be too early, bearing in mind that Śubhakara-siṃha seems to have had no knowledge of it. On the other hand, though not impossible, 740 seems just a bit too late, so we may tentatively suggest that the Continuation Tantra was composed around 711. Though fairly speculative, such a date would fit in with the general chronological sequence of the tantras.

Another clue may also be contained in the Continuation Tantra. unlike the MVT itself, the phrase *gsang-ba'i snying-po* is used a number of times. It is not clear whether this is being used solely as an epithet or not, but it takes on a new light when we reconstruct the most likely Sanskrit form of this phrase: *guhya-garbha,* that is, 'secret matrix'. Does this have any connection with the *Guhya-garbha Tantra,* which I believe has its roots in the early eighth century?

9 The Bhauma-kāras migrated from Assam and had occupied the Utkala region by the beginning of the eighth century CE, eventually extending their kingdom over a wide area of present-day Orissa and beyond. The Bhauma dynasty in Orissa normally is considered to begin with Śivakara I, who began his reign in 736. Buddhism flourished in Orissa at this time under the patronage of at least the first three kings of the Bhauma dynasty who were keen and devout patrons of Buddhism. The ninth century saw a vigorous re-establishment of Śaivism under the later monarchs, at the expense of Buddhism.

10 Now, at this point in Śubhakara-siṃha's biography we are given an interesting piece of information regarding the rulers of Udyāna by the use of Turkic titles for members of the royal family. Namely, that Udyāna was at that time under Turkic rule, having been annexed shortly before by the qaghans of Kapiśa (the area around present-day Begram, 70 miles north of Kabul) and ruled by them for most of the eighth century. Unfortunately, the significance of this fact seems to have generally escaped the attention of many Buddhist scholars who depend on Indo-Tibetan materials alone. The political situation in this area during the 8th century is confirmed by a number of entries in the *Tang Shu* and several other reliable records in Chinese such as the accounts of Hye-cho and Wu-kong who visited the area around 726 CE and 750 CE respectively. It should however be noted that although these kings were of Turkic origins, the several Chinese travellers passing through this region stress that these kings were all devout Buddhists.

But this has serious implications for the location of Oḍḍiyāna (Uḍḍiyāna) and by extension the identity or even the historicity of King Indrabhūti who figures so largely in the early history of Anuttara-yoga tantras such as the *Guhya-samāja.* Although it is customary for most scholars nowadays to locate Oḍḍiyāna in the Swat Valley in the northern region of present-day Pakistan, surprisingly there does not seem much concrete evidence to identify Oḍḍiyāna with the country called Udyāna that was undoubtedly located in that region. It may therefore be more fruitful to re-examine the case for locating Oḍḍiyāna elsewhere. Recently Lokesh Chandra has argued quite convincingly that Oḍḍiyāna was in fact Kāñcī in southern India, adducing a startling piece of new information to support his claim. He shows that '*oḍḍiyāna*' is in fact a Tamil word meaning a gold or silver girdle worn by women as an ornament, and also a belt worn by yogins to support themselves during meditation. The connection with Kāñcī can be made because the Sanskrit word *kāñcī* also has exactly this meaning, and is in fact translated into Tamil by the word '*oḍḍiyāna*'. Surely this is more than just a coincidence! Moreover, in Tibetan *O-rgyan* or *U-rgyan* is commonly used to indicate Oḍḍiyāna. It seems that the *O* or *U* is phonetic, while *rgyan* should be understood as the

Tibetan semanteme meaning 'ornament'. A number of notable tantric personages are also associated with the Kāñcī area which gives further weight to this theory. For example, Nāgārjuna was born in Kāñcī, Tilopa resided in the cemetery at Kāñcī where he was visited by Nāropa, Vajrabodhi lived in Kāñcī and probably received teachings on the *Sarva-tathāgata-tattva-saṃgraha* there from Nāgabodhi, and there is even a King Indrabhūti of Kāñcī mentioned in the 'Biographies of the Eighty Four Siddhas'. All this evidence suggests that at least we seriously consider the likelihood that Oḍḍiyāna was Kāñcī. But whatever the truth may be it is also clear that Oḍḍiyāna eventually took on mythic characteristics reminiscent of legendary Shambhala in the minds of Tibetans.

As for the Indrabhūti problem, we are faced with a morass of conflicting and confusing information. Unfortunately much of what is available from native Tibetan sources is probably pious fiction. For example, mention is sometimes made of a King Dza who is equated with King Indrabhūti, but as Samten Karmay has recently shown from a Tun Huang document, this King Dza is in fact the Tibetan King, Khri-srong lde-bstan. A King Indrabhūti of Oḍḍiyāna is often linked with origins of the *Guhya-samāja Tantra.* But, if it had not even been composed by the beginning of the 8th century for reasons I have suggested above, this King Indrabhūti must have reigned some time during the first half of that century. This leads us to several possible conclusions. Although Oḍḍiyāna is popularly identified with the Swat valley area (*Udyāna*), no king of that name is known to have ruled there around that time, because as we have seen all the rulers there were Turks whose names are known from the *Tang Shu.* (The king mentioned in the *Tang Shu* earlier in 642 CE has been erroneously identified as Indrabhūti by some, but this king's name should actually be restored to some like Dharmendrahasa.) Therefore if King Indrabhūti of Oḍḍiyāna was a historical figure, his kingdom must be located elsewhere, and as we have seen this could be Kāñcī in South India. An alternative and radical view has been suggested by Dr H. Hadano, namely that there was no King Indrabhūti connected with the *Guhya-samāja Tantra* at all. He bases his arguments on a detailed analysis of all known lineages for the *Guhya-samāja Tantra* preserved in Tibetan sources, which indicates that the association of King Indrabhūti with that Tantra is spurious, and he maintains that a conflation of several disparate traditions has occurred. It should be noted that there were possibly several other Indrabhūtis, such as the King Indrabhūti of Zahor (which is thought to have been somewhere in Bengal) associated with the Yoga Tantras. I am presently preparing a paper for publication dealing in detail with various aspects of the above problems.

11 I have not included a translation of this appendix due to lack of space, but it may be viewed as a kind of alternative Continuation Tantra. It exists in three versions – an earlier translation made by Vajrabodhi, that by Śubhakara-siṃha, and a Tibetan translation (Q 3488) which is attributed to a dPal-bzang rabs-dga', included in the Tenjur. The Sanskrit title given with the Tibetan translation is *Mahā-vairocana-abhisaṃbodhi-tantra-saṃbaddha-pūja-vidhi* – 'The Ritual of Worship Linked with the Mahā-vairocana-abhisaṃbodhi Tantra'. Several accounts of its origin are given by the Sino-Japanese tradition. One is that Śubhakara-siṃha obtained it on his way to China, while he was in Gandhara or Udyāna. There he began teaching the MVT itself to the qaghan and his court, but as this was too lengthy and too profound, the qaghan asked Śubhakara-siṃha for an abbreviated version giving instructions for the ritual of worship. Śubhakara-siṃha was given two copies of this Ritual of Worship by Mañjuśrī who appeared to him in front of the stūpa erected by King Kaniṣka. One of these copies was given to the king, and the other was brought by Śubhakara-siṃha to China and translated there. However, even when we divest it of its miraculous elements, this account is dubious because there is also another translation of the text made by Vajrabodhi at a slightly earlier date. Vajrabodhi in his turn is said to have obtained it in Southern India, where it had been taken from the Iron Stūpa before by Nāgārjuna.

12 Details of Prajñā's life have been preserved for us in the Chinese Song Biographies. He was born in the Udyāna area and became monk at seven years of age. After studying the Four *Āgamas* and the Abhidharma, he later he went with his teacher to Kashmir and received full

ordination at the age of twenty (c. 755 CE). There he studied the Sarvāstivādin Abhidharma, the *Abhidharma-kośa* and the *Vibhāṣa*. When he was twenty three (758 CE), he went to Nālandā and studied Yogācāra, Prajñā-paramitā-sūtras and the five sciences (grammar, medicine, logic and so forth) under Jñānapāla, Vīramitra and Jñānamitra. Hearing that the *Vidyā-dhara Piṭaka* was flourishing in Southern India at that time, he went there and sought out what he had not yet obtained. He visited a Master (*ācārya*) called Dharmayaśa (or Dharmakīrti?) living in Uḍra at that time. Going there, he served this master and received secret yoga (*guhya-yoga*) from him as well as entering the mandalas. He received the 'threefold secret' (*tri-guhya*) protection of body, the 'fivefold *mudrās*' and so forth. However he thought that the time had come for him to go to China to spread the Dharma there, so he decided to go there. After several shipwrecks, he finally arrived at Kan-shu in 781, and at last reached Chang-an in 786. Kūkai met Prajñā c.805, during his stay in Chang-an. He wrote that he learnt from Prajñā and Muniśrī that Nāgabodhi was still alive in Southern India. We may also note further hints from Prajñā's biography that the famed centre of tantric activities, Oḍḍiyāna, is not to be located in Udyāna. As a native of that area, Prajñā would surely have known if tantric teachings were available there, but instead we see that it was necessary for him to go to Southern India to receive tantric initiations.

13 Works attributed to Buddhaguhya are as follows:

A. Kriyā Tantra Commentaries
Dhyānottara-ṭīkā (Q3495)
Subāhu-paripṛcchāa-piṇḍārtha (Q3496)
Vajra-vidāraṇa-ṭīkā (Q3504)
Vajra-vidāraṇa-sādhana (Q3751)
Vajra-vidāraṇa-bali-vidhi-krama (Q3752)
Vajra-vidāraṇa-snāha-vidhi (Q3755)

B. Commentaries on MVT
MVT Piṇḍārtha (Q3486)
MVT Vṛtti (Q3487 & Revision Q3490)

C. Yoga Tantra Commentaries
Sarva-durgati-pariśodhana-vārttika (Q3451)
Sarva-durgati-pariśodhana-maṇḍala-vidhi-krama (Q3461)
Tantrārthāvatāra (Q3324)

D. Guhyagarbha Commentaries etc.
Abhiṣekārtha-nirbheda (Q4722)
Vajrasattva-māyājāla-prabha-krama (Q4731)
Mārga-vyūha (Q4736)
Citta-bindūpadeśa (Q4738)
Śrī-guhyagarbha nāma cakṣuṣ-ṭīkā (Q4756)
Krodha-māyābhiṣeka-maṇḍala-vajra-karmāvali (Q4761)
Māyābhiṣekasyaka-mūla-vṛtti (Q4762)

E. Miscellaneous
Yoga-kalpa-vighna-nibarhaṇa (Q3283 & Q5449)
Śrī-vajrapāṇi-sādhana (Q3687)
Karmopāya (Q3754)
Dharma-maṇḍala-sūtra (Q4528)
Maṇḍala-kriyā-vidhi (Q4581 & Q5439)
Bhoṭa-svāmi-daśa-guru-lekha (Q5693)

14 For example, his *Yoga-bhāvanā-mārga* and his commentary on the *Catur-devī-paripṛcchā Tantra*.

15 No other information about this Śrī-gupta (*dPal-sbas*) seems to be available. Two suggestions may be made regarding his identity. First, one wonders whether he is the same person as the

Dharmagupta who taught Śubhakara-siṃha? We know that Dharmagupta was alive at least until 714 CE when Śubhakara-siṃha left Nālandā, so it would just be possible for him to have taught Jñānagarbha during that latter's early youth, if we assume that Jñānagarbha was born in 700 CE or just before then. Though entirely speculative, this is an intriguing possibility! On the other hand, it is possible that this is none other than an alternative form of Buddhaguhya's name, for there is actually some uncertainty about the correct Sanskrit form of Buddhaguhya's own name. In Tibetan this is usually given as *Sangs-rgyas gsang-ba* which would normally be equivalent to *Buddhaguhya*. But in several colophons to his works in the Tenjur, both Buddhaguhya and Buddhagupta are given in transcription. Also the Den-kar-ma, the oldest catalogue of Tibetan translations compiled in the early ninth century CE, gives the name as *Buddhagupta* in transcription. Given the age of the *Den-kar-ma*, it may not be unreasonable to think that Buddhagupta is the correct form. In that case, could not Jñānagarbha's teacher called Śrī-gupta be the same person? That there was some link between Buddhaguhya and Jñānagarbha may be surmised from the fact that he was a member of the party which went to invite Buddhaguhya to Tibet. There is also the problem of the identity of the *Sangs-rgyas sbas* known from rNying-ma sources to have also been active during the second half of the 8th century, for this name may also be reconstructed as Buddhagupta!

16 B.K. Matilal, *Ignorance or Misconception?* in *Buddhist Studies in Honour of Walpola Rahula* (Gordon Fraser 1980). See also J. Gonda's excellent monograph, *Some notes on the Study of Ancient Indian Religious Terminology*.

17 I should hasten to add that a knowledge of recent philosophical trends is indeed of great use in furthering our understanding of Buddhism, but the use of terminology derived from existentialism or phenomenology in *translations* seems to be quite misleading for the general reader. It is also interesting to read E. Conze's views on this matter in his review of Alex Wayman's *Analysis of the Śrāvakabhūmi Manuscript* reprinted in *Further Buddhist Sudies* (Bruno Cassirer 1975).

18 I also occasionally had recourse to the revised version (義釋) of this commentary in 14 *juan*, Manji-zoku Vol 36, 254 – 463.

19 It is surprising that a fully collated Tibetan edition has not yet been produced in Japan, as far as I know, given the particular propensities for such work among Japanese scholars. If it remains undone in a few years time, I may take on the task myself. I am currently producing a textual edition of the *Susiddhi-kāra-tantra* using eleven Kanjur editions so far!

20 See Chapter XIII.10.

21 Though Sanskrit is a highly inflected language, it often makes use of various kinds of compounds (*samāsa*), so a text may contain quite long strings of words without any inflections to indicate their precise grammatical relationship. Part of the task of any commentator worth his salt is to resolve these compounds into their component parts, indicating the implied case inflections. But the situation in Tibetan is different, for it does not naturally use the complex compounds found in Sanskrit. So when translating such a compound, a translator normally has to resolve it into its component words anyway and use the Tibetan case particles to indicate their relationship. Hence even if Buddhaguhya gives an analysis of a compound occurring in the MVT to aid the understanding of the reader, this often becomes redundant in Tibetan, which has already had to analyze the compound in question for the purposes of translation! Likewise such analysis is unnecessary for the same reasons in an English translation.

22 I might also stress here the that teachings of the MVT are addressed as equally to women as to men, for as the attentive reader will note, Vairocana or Vajrapāṇi always speak of 'noble sons *and* noble daughters'. Wherever possible I have tried to phrase my translation so statements are applicable to both women and men. For example, where the text uses a third person singular pronoun which in English we would tend to (although unfairly) translate as 'he', I have sometimes converted this either to the second person pronoun 'you' or the third person plural 'they' and slightly recast the translation accordingly. So apart from specifically

male or female figures as in the case of the named Bodhisattvas like Vajrapāṇi or Tārā, it is important to remember that a Bodhisattva, a *mantrin*, a Master or a trainee is just as likely to be a woman as a man, even if I have referred to these as 'he' on occasion. Moreover, as the text says, in Enlightenment there is no male or female!

23 Any particular sutra or theory was deemed to be 'Buddhist' if it taught the three signs of existence-impermanence, suffering and the absence of a self. Later it was held that 'anything which is well-spoken (= true) is the Buddha's word', which naturally allowed the acceptance of a very wide range of views.

24 Similar references may be found in *Samyutta* V. 92, *Aṅguttara* I. 257 and III. 16.

25 Apart from these two usages of *citta*, the term is also used occasionally in a neutral sense for the total perceptual and ideational system.

26 Moreover, it should be noted that all the motivating factors (*saṃskāras*), which include the wholesome elements as well as the unwholesome emotional afflictions (*kleśa*), are available for use in this process as they also form part of the *manas*.

27 This is commonly misunderstood to mean that the Yogācārins totally denied the existence of an external basis for perception. See T. Kochumutton, *A Buddhist Doctrine of Experience* and A. Wayman, *Yogacara and the Buddhist Logicians*, for a rebuttal of this misunderstanding.

28 In this context it is interesting to note that one of the special functions of *manas* is to produce 'free' images such as the *manomaya-kāya* (the *manas*-created body) (D I 77).

29 *Himma* is defined by Corbin in *Creative Imagination in the Sufism of Ibn Arabi* as the act of meditating, conceiving, imagining, projecting, ardently desiring i.e. of having something present in the soul or heart, intention, thought, desire and so forth. This corresponds very well with the functional meaning of *manas* in the MVT.

30 In the MVT, the mind (*citta*) is symbolized by a white moon disc, a mirror. Just as a mirror has two sides, one black and non-reflective and the other clear and reflective, so also the mind can be thought of as having two sides, as described here. One aspect of the mind reflects reality and the other aspect (= *manas*) conceals it.

31 This is also reminiscent of the wonderful phrase used in some recent theories to decribe the primordial cause of the cosmic big-bang – 'fluctuations in the quantum vacuum'.

32 It should be noted that in some ways the above techniques parallel those taught for *Mahāmudrā*.

33 The word *guhā* 'secret' here also means 'cave'.

PART II THE MAHĀ-VAIROCANA ABHISAṂBODHI TANTRA WITH BUDDHAGUHYA'S COMMENTARY

Chapter I

1 It appears that this standard opening to sutras was omitted in the Sanskrit text, as will be seen from Buddhaguhya's comments below. This is corroborated by the remarks in CC where it states that the Sanskrit text lacks the five words '*Evaṃ mayā śrutaṃ ekasmin samaye*'. Yi-xing reports that, according to Śubhakara-siṃha, this is because the present version of the MVT is a summarized compilation in some 3,000 *ślokas* of the unwieldy large version in 100,000 *ślokas*. However, they have been added to both T and C, by the translators in the case of C and possibly likewise for T.

2 There is some controversy as to how the standard opening words of a sutra, *Evaṃ mayā śrutaṃ ekasmin samaye* [*Bhagavan … viharati sma*], are to be interpreted. They may be read either as 'Thus I have heard at one time (or: on one occasion), [the Bhagavat was residing at …]', or else as 'Thus I have heard. On one occasion, [the Bhagavat was residing at …]'. It would seem that both these interpretations were current among Buddhists in India, and from his comments it is clear that Buddhaguhya favoured the latter one.

3 The original Sanskrit term used here must have been '*adhiṣṭhāna*' as T has '*byin-gyis rlob-pa*' and C has 加持, both standard equivalents for that term, and hence both the Chinese and

Tibetan translators seem to have understood it in its specialized sense of 'transformational power'. However, Buddhaguhya glosses '*adhiṣṭhāna*' as *lhag-par-gnas-pa*' suggesting **adhivāsa*. In other words, Buddhaguhya understands the term not in its specialized sense but merely as 'abode' or 'residence'. This is one example of the cases where Buddhaguhya's comments are somewhat at odds with the sense of the text as we have it in its translated form. However, either could be correct since it is not possible to determine which understanding was actually that intended by the compiler of the text.

4 *Piṇḍārtha* 20a-20b.

5 Buddhaguhya's explanation of '*dhara*' is based upon the various meanings of the verb √*dhṛ*.

6 The name '*Vairocana*' also means 'sun', 'illuminating'. In the Sino-Japanese exegesis of the MVT, Mahā-vairocana as the *Dharmakāya*, is distinguished from 'Vairocana', the *Saṃbhoga-kāya*.

7 *Pada*. This may be translated variously as 'word' or 'syllable' in English. A word in Sanskrit is considered as the minimal meaning-bearing unit, and so even what we might consider as a syllable can also be classed as a word. However, grammarians like Bhartṛhari taught that the only true unit of meaning is the complete sentence, and not what we would call words. I have translated *pada* by 'word' or 'syllable' as seems appropriate, although a certain amount of ambiguity is never absent.

8 *Akṣara*. Translation of this term is problematic, as it covers a range of meanings. As will be mentioned elsewhere by Buddhaguhya, one of these meanings is *a-kṣara* 'unchanging', which is used as a synonym for *bodhicitta*, Enlightenment and so forth. The other meaning, which concerns us here, oscillates between 'letter' and 'phoneme'. Although a distinction exists, unfortunately neither Sanskrit nor Tibetan clearly indicates which sense is implied. Generally speaking, when *akṣara* is used in the sense of 'phoneme', it indicates (in the MVT) a higher level of reality, the 'unspoken sound', or the manifestation of Buddha Speech on the *saṃbhoga-kāya* level, thus linking it with the meaning 'unchanging', whereas when used in the sense of 'letter' it usually refers to the low level written equivalent. I was tempted to translate *akṣara* by 'phoneme' when it seems that the sound aspect is primarily meant, and by 'letter' when the written grapheme seems appropriate, but as there are many cases where either connotation would be appropriate, I concluded that it would be best to leave *akṣara* as 'letter' in all cases. However, the reader should bear this ambiguity in mind when 'letter' occurs, and realize that two levels of meaning are usually involved. Also, even when the graphic aspect seems to be foremost, as for example when one imagines various seed-syllables in *samādhi*, the phonemic aspect is not absent. In other words, when doing such practices, one should hear the sound as well visualize the shape of the letter, or better still, one visualizes the sound as shape and colour.

9 The entering (*praveśa*), abiding (*prasthāna*) and arising (*utthāna*) minds. For details, see under the comments for Chapter I Section 25.

10 Sanskrit for the above passage has been preserved in the *Nāma-mantrārthāvalokinī*, a commentary on the *Nāma-saṃgīti*: *Bhagavantas tathāgatā arhantaḥ samyaksaṃbuddhās sarvajñajñāmam prāpya tat sarvajñajñānaṃ sarvasattvebhyo vibhajya nānānayair nānābhiprāyair nānopāyair dharmaṃ deśayanti* || *keṣāñcic chrāvakānanayam* | *keṣāñcit pratyekabuddhayānanayam* | *keṣāñcid mahāyānanayam* | *keṣāñcit pañcābhijñajñānanayam* | *keṣāñcid devopapattaye* | *keṣāñcid manuṣyopapattaye* | *yāvat mahoraga-yakṣa-rākṣasāsura-gandharva-garūḍa-kinnarādy-upattaye dharmaṃ deśayanti sma* || *tatra kecit sattvā buddhavaineyikā buddha-rūpena paśyanti* | *kecic chrāvaka-rūpena* | *kecit pratyekabuddha-rūpena* | *kecid bodhisattva-rūpena* | *kecid maheśvara-rūpena* | *kecis brāhmaṇa-rūpena* | *kecid nārāyaṇa-rūpena paśanti* | *kecid vaiśravaṇa-rūpena yāvat mahoraga-manuṣyāmanuṣya-rūpena paśyanti* || *svaka svakair vacanodāharana-nayair vividheryāpatha-vyavastitam* | *tac ca sarvajñajñānam ekarasam yad uta tathāgata-vinirmukta-rasam* ||

11 This line is quoted by Kamalaśīla in his *Bhāvanā-krama*, which is available in Sanskrit: *Tad etat sarva-jña-jñānaṃ karuṇā-mūlaṃ bodhicitta-hetukam upāya-paryavasānam.*

12 This is the same process as is described in Vasubandhu's *Triṃśika* (26–28): '*As long as consciousness does not abide in the state of representation-only, the tendency towards the twofold grasping*

will not cease to operate. Though one may think "This is representation-only", one is still regarding it as something placed before one. One is therefore still not abiding in the state of representation-only. However, when consciousness no longer perceives objects (ālaṃbana), *one is then abiding in the state of representation-only, because where there is nothing to be perceived* [*as an object*] *there is also nothing perceiving it.*'

13 *Piṇḍārtha* (23a): '*An attribute* (lakṣaṇa) *is that mental concept* (vikalpa) *by which one knows, defines, and understands an object which has the perceptual forms* (nimitta) *of blue and so forth*'.

14 *Puruṣa*, the Saṃkhyā 'soul' as opposed to *prakṛti*, the world-ground.

15 The *Piṇḍārtha* (21a-21b) says there are three causes which bring about the realization of Enlightenment and All-knowing Awareness: the initiating cause (*prasthāna-hetu*), the immediate (*upadāna-hetu*), and the cooperating cause (*sahakāri-hetu*).

16 One could also translate this in the wider sense of abstinence. What is probably implied here is observance of the *poṣadha*, a kind of Buddhist 'sabbath-day'. Lay people would undertake to observe a number of precepts for the duration of the day – the most common being abstinence from harm-doing, stealing, sexual misconduct, lying, the consumption of intoxicants, dancing and singing, sleeping on a high bed, and the untimely consumption of meals.

17 Due to an ambiguity in the original Sanskrit text, this can be read with or without the negative. Buddhaguhya gives an explanation for both possibilities in his comments. C reads it without the negative.

18 I have translated *dharma* here by 'religion' because the text is decribing all the various motives and attitudes mundane people have when they are involved in religious conduct. See Buddhaguhya's discussion of this in the *Piṇḍārtha* 9a. Further on in the *Piṇḍārtha*, Buddhaguhya also says '*dharma which is defined as recitation, burnt offerings, generosity, morality and so forth*' (9b).

19 The *Piṇḍārtha* (9b) says that this is when one engages in religious practices with the intention of killing an enemy and so forth.

20 What exactly is involved here is problematic. Although the Tantra has just listed the details for sixty types of mind in Section 21 and 22, it also refers to one hundred and sixty minds in Sections 16 and 23. Are the calculations referring to a way of deriving one hundred and sixty minds from sixty? According to Buddhaguhya's lengthy explanation in his *Piṇḍārtha* 9b – 11b, this is the case. However, there he uses a complicated system of *division* rather than the multiplication the text clearly prescribes. The solution given by CC is rather more elegant, but introduces another factor into the equation: the five basic emotional afflictions (*kleśa*), while apparently disregarding the sixty minds just given. CC states that 5 X 2 = 10, 10 X 2 = 20, 20 X 2 = 40, 40 X 2 = 80, and 80 X 2 = 160. Could it be that the "original" long version of the Tantra or its source had a full list of one hundred and sixty minds which have been truncated to the sixty we now have?

21 These are the eight minds associated with the four Hīnayāna levels of *Śrotāpana* (Stream-enterer), *Sakṛdāgamin* (Once-returner), *Anāgamin* (Non-returner) and Arhat. Each level has two phases: one incomplete and one complete. See Commentary below for details.

22 This analogy is succinctly explained in Vasubandhu's *Trisvabhāva-nirdeśa* (27-30): '*Just as a magical creation may appear as an elephant by the power of a spell, though there is actually no elephant there at all but only the image* (ākāra) *of one. The elephant stands for the imagined* (kalpita) *mode of being, and its image for the relative mode* (paratantra), *and the non-existence there of the elephant is the consummate mode of being* (pariniṣpanna). *Likewise, the imagination of the unreal appears in the nature of duality from the basic mind. There is no duality at all, but only an image there. The basic mind is like the spell, and suchness is like the piece of wood. Conceptualization* (vikalpa) *is like the image of the elephant, and duality is like the elephant.*'

23 *Karma-kriyā-rahita*. Generally speaking all actions and activities carried out by body, speech, or mind, but often implying the actions of the ritual meditation (*sādhana*) and the various other activities done in the course of mantra practice.

24 A good summary of this argument is given by Vasubandhu in his *Viṃśatika* (11-15): It should be remembered here that an atom is defined by the Buddhists as the smallest indivisible unit of matter: '*The object is not a single atom nor discrete atoms, nor is it a comglomerate of them, because the atom cannot be proven [to exist]. One atom joined to six others must have six parts. If the six occupy the same place, then the mass would only be one atom. If there is no conjunction of atoms, how can there be one for a conglomerate of them? One cannot prove their conjunction because they have no parts. It is illogical to claim oneness for that which has different directions. [But if it has no parts] how can there be shadow and concealment? For they cannot refer to a mass [of atoms] unless that is something other [than the atoms]. If it were a single unit, there would be no gradual movement, no simultaneous perception and non-perception, no co-existence of the multitude of separate things, and no invisibility of minute things.*'

Chapter II

1 This indicates their *saṃbhoga-kāyas.*

2 This indicates their *nirmāṇa-kāyas.*

3 *Tri-maṇḍala-viśuddhi*: the purity of the giver, the gift and the recipient, and similarly for other actions.

4 That is, not by telepathy.

5 The Sanskrit text for these words of the Master have survived in a Javanese ritual text, the *Sang hyang Kamahāyānikan*, with some small differences to T and C, thus:

ehi vatsa mahāyānaṃ mantra-cārya-nayam vidhim ।
deśayiṣyāmi te samyak bhājanas tvaṃ mahā-naye ।।
atītā ye hi saṃbuddhāḥ tathā caivāpy anāgatāḥ ।
pratyutpannāś ca ye nathāḥ tiṣṭhanti ca jagad-dhitāḥ ।।
taiś ca sarvair imaṃ vajraṃ jñātvā mantra-vidhiṃ param ।
prāpta sarva-jñatā vīraiḥ bodhi-mūle hy alakṣaṇa ।।
mantra-prayogam atulaṃ yena bhagnaṃ mahā-balam ।
māra-śainyaṃ mahā-ghoraṃ Śākya-siṃhena tāyinā ।।
tasmān matim imāṃ varya kuru sarva-jñatāptaye ।

6 These verses have been preserved in the Chinese Commentary, transcribed into Chinese characters. They may be read as follows:

tvaṃ devi sākṣībhūtāsi sarva-buddhānāṃ tāyinām ।
caryā-naya-viśeṣeṣu bhūmi-pāramitāsu ca ।।
māra-śainyaṃ yathā bhagnaṃ Śākya-siṃhena tāyinā ।
tathāhaṃ māra-jayaṃ kṛtvā maṇḍalāṃl likhāmy aham ।।

7 In Ch. XIII.15.

8 The Sanskrit name of the Mandala, '*Mahā-karuṇā-garbhodbhava*' can be interpreted in two ways: 'Arising from the Matrix of Great Compassion' and 'Matrix-source of Great Compassion'.

9 That is, diamond-like.

10 These verses are also preserved in transcription in the Chinese Commentary and may be read as follows:

adya yuṣmābhir atulā lābhā labdhvā mahātmabhiḥ ।
yena sarve jinā yūyaṃ saputrair iha śāsane ।।
sarvaiḥ parigṛhītāḥ stha jāyamānā mahodaye ।
tena yūyaṃ mahāyāne śvo jāta hi bhaviṣyatha ।।

11 These words are also quoted in the *Sang hyang Kamahāyānikan*:

eṣa mārga-varaḥ śrīmān mahāyāna-mahodayaḥ ।
yena yūyaṃ gamiṣyanto bhaviṣyatha tathāgatāḥ ।।
svayam-bhuvo mahā-bhāgāḥ sarva-lokasya cetiyāḥ ।
asti-nāsti-vyatikrāntam ākāśam iva nirmalam ।।
gambhīram sarva-tarkebhir apy atarkyam anāvilam ।
sarva-prapañca-rahitaṃ prapañcebhiḥ prapañcitam ।।

karma-kriyā-virahitaṃ satya-dvayam anāśrayam I
idaṃ yāna-varam śreṣṭhaṃ labhiṣyatha naye sthitāḥ I I

12 The *Pratimokṣa* forms part of the Vinaya, and lists a set of rules primarily for the conduct of the monastic Saṅgha, although Mahāyāna Pratimokṣa texts are also relevant for lay people. Through the observance of these rules, one counteracts unwholesome actions which bind one to *saṃsāra*, hence the literal meaning of the Pratimokṣa C 'liberation'. Several versions originating with different Schools have survived, in which the number of rules vary. One of the most popular Mahāyāna *Pratimokṣa* texts was the *Upāli-paripṛcchā Sūtra*, which specifically deals with the conduct of Bodhisattvas. Taking refuge would have involved accepting the discipline of such a text.

13 *Danta-kāṣṭha*. This is the ancient Indian version of a tooth-brush made of bamboo, and was one of the eighteen articles a monk was allowed. Its use and benefits are described in various Vinaya texts, for example in the *Mūla-sarvāstivāda Vinaya Saṃgraha* (T 1458) we read: 'There are five benefits to be gained from using a tooth-stick in the morning: you will remove bile, you will be able to stimulate the appetite, your mouth will be cleansed, you will enjoy your food and drink and your eyes will become clear. There are three types of tooth-stick: a long one of twelve inches, a short one of eight inches, and a medium one in between. When you are going to use it, you should first clean your hands with bean-powder (used as a kind of soap), and then wash the tooth-stick. After that you can use it. When you have finished you should rinse the end and throw it away. If you live in a place where water is scarce, rub it with sand and then throw it away ...'. The same text also states that if you do not have a tooth-stick, you should use bean-powder or dried cow-dung! It seems from the explanation given that it was used before eating. One gargled and washed out one's mouth with water after meals. It was also the custom in India to send tooth-sticks decorated with flowers to monks the day before when inviting them to a meal. In the case of the tantric initiation, they are given to the trainees for them to bite upon. This symbolizes the cleansing of faults. Following that, their suitability for initiation is divined from the way in which the cast-down sticks have fallen, as is described by Buddhaguhya.

14 *Yakṣinī* are a type of female nature divinities, particularly associated with trees, and usually worshipped as local divinities by village communities. They are frequently depicted in Indian art as beautiful, sinuous young women. They were thought to possess the secrets of various magical powers, and the rites referred to here were presumably performed to gain such powers from them.

15 The five precious things: Gold, silver, pearl, coral, and turquoise. The five grains: Rice, wheat, beans, husked and unhusked barley. There are several lists in existence for the five medicines. In the *Sāmānya-vidhāna-guhya Tantra* they are *siṅgri*, *vyāghra*, *karṇika*, *saha*, and *sahadeva*. In the *Susiddhi-kāra Tantra* they are *kaṇṭakārī*, *bṛhatī*, *saha*, *sahadeva*, and *giri-karṇika*. Ānandagarbha in his commentary on the *Māyājāla Tantra* gives *saha*, *danta-utpala*, *kaṇṭakārī*, *śata-aparājita*, and *bṛhatī*. Beyer (*The Cult of Tara*) gives *stag tser* (*vyāghra-kantaka*?), *kaṇṭakāra*, *aparājita*, *utpala* and *indrapāṇi*, which he identifies as *Potentilla discolor*, *Sambucus racemosa*, *Clitoria ternata*, *Nymphaea caerulea*, and *Belamcanda chinensis*. Additionally, the five perfumes (white and red sandalwood, saffron, camphor and musk), and the five essences (sesame, butter, molasses, honey and salt)are also put into the jar.

16 See *Piṇḍārtha* (29b) for details of the first Master's *samādhi*.

17 See *Piṇḍārtha* (29b) for details of the second Master's *samādhi*.

18 See *Piṇḍārtha* (29b) for details of the third Master's *samādhi*.

19 The wet-cord, which should be white, is not actually wet, but it is rubbed with chalk and snapped down on the surface of the ground, in the same way as carpenters used to mark out timber.

20 See *Piṇḍārtha* (36b B 38a) for a very detailed explanation of this process.

21 Skt: *aṅguli*.

22 I must confess to being puzzled by this comment. Buddhaguhya's arithmetic seems a little strange but this is what he says. One wonders whether somebody has clumsily altered the

number of consciousnesses (*vijñāna*) from four to five, which is the usual number of sensory consciousnesses. Normally, Yogācāra theory posits a set of eight consciousnesses: the *ālaya-vijñāna*, the *manas*, the *mano-vijñāna* and the five sensory consciousnesses. These are transformed at Enlightenment into the Mirror-like Awareness, the Investigating Awareness, the Awareness of Sameness, and the Awareness which Accomplishes Activities respectively. Loosely speaking, one can also refer to the eight consciousnesses as *jñānas* C 'uncapitalized' awareness. This is probably the most reasonable interpretation of Buddhaguhya's comments.

23 These are elephants, lions, fire, snakes, robbers, captivity by kings, the sea and flesh-eating demons. Tārā's efficacy in protecting one from the harmful effects of these fearful things was a popular theme of Indian religious verse. See, for example, the Praises by Candragomin in M. Willson's *In Praise of Tara*, pp.226-37.

24 Several identifications exist for this plant, including millet. But in this instance it is most likely to be *Aglaia odorata*, a graceful tree with small fragrant yellow flowers.

25 I have not been able to find a better term for her function than 'summoner', used in the Chaucerian sense of one who summons wrong-doers to answer for their deeds before a court.

26 A *tilaka* mark is like that which many present-day Indian women put between their eyebrows.

27 The image of the flowers of the *Udumbara* tree (*Ficus glomerata*) is used throughout Buddhist literature as a simile for the rarity of certain events, like the appearance of a Buddha or a Universal Monarch in the world. The *Udumbara* is said to flower only once every three thousand years or else only when a Buddha is born in the world. Actually, the *Udumbara* flowers rather more often than that, but it is a species with small flowers concealed within the fruit.

28 Sanskrit verses similar to this portion have survived in the *Kriyā-saṃgraha* as noted by Wayman:

sarvajñānāṃ kadā loke saṃbhavo jayate na vā ।
udumbarasyaiva kusumaḥ kadācit karhicid bhavet ।।
tato 'pi durlabhotpādo mantra-caryānayasya hi ।
[*yena sattvārtham atulaṃ kartuśakto hy anivṛtaḥ* ।।]
aneka-kalpa-koṭibhir yat kṛtaṃ pāpakaṃ puraṭi ।
tat-sarvaṃ hi kṣayaṃ yāti dṛṣṭvā maṇḍalam īdṛśaṃ ।।
kim utānantayaśasāṃ mantra-caryā-naye sthitāḥ ।
yad apy anuttarapāde japan vai mantrān tāyināṃ ।।
ucchannā durgati teṣāṃ sarva-duḥkhasya saṃbhavāḥ ।
yeṣāṃ vai caryā-vare 'smin matir anyaṃ na niścalā ।।

29 The *Piṇḍārtha* indicates that this method of applying colours refers to enclosing walls (*prakāra*) of the Mandala.

30 The original text probably had the word *rāga* or *raṅga*. Among their various meanings, they mean both 'colour' and 'attachment'.

31 Green symbolizes the capacity to perform various different actions because it is not a primary colour but can be produced by the mixture of several other colours, thus combining the functions those colours symbolize.

32 Although the standard technical definition of *samādhi* is the one-pointedness of mind upon something (*citta-ekagrāhatā*), other alternative definitions are known. Here the MVT defines *samādhi* as 'the complete satisfaction of mind' (*cittasya samādhāna*), as one of the meanings of the verbal root *sam-ā* √*dha* from which the word '*samādhi*' is derived is 'composure' or 'peace of mind'. It is noteworthy that apart from this, the verb also conveys the ideas of creation, manifestation and so forth. This explains why the Tathāgata always enters into a *samādhi* before revealing various miraculous displays or uttering *vidyā*-mantras. Likewise, when the Master or practitioner is to engage in any of the practices to imagine, transform or empower the mandalas, mantras, *mudrās* and so forth, it is necessary for him to enter that creative state of mind.

33 The distribution of these plants and trees in India gives a useful clue to the area in which the MVT was compiled.

Keśara (*Mesua ferrea*): East Himalayas, hills of East Bengal.

Punnāga (*Terminalia arjuna*): The Deccan, North-west Himalayas and other places throughout India.

Campaka (*Michelia champaca*): East Nepal and warm-wet areas of the Himalayas.

Aśoka (*Saraca indica*): East Himalayas, Central India.

Tilaka (*Clerodendrum philomoides*): Lower Himalayan region, Bihar, Orissa.

Patalā (*Streospermum suaveolens*): Warm-wet areas of the Himalayas.

Śala (*Shorea robusta*): Warm areas of the Himalayas, Assam and the hills of West Bengal.

Tagara (*Tabernaemontana coronaria*): Throughout India, but especially North-west Himalayas.

Spṛkkā (*Trigonella corniculata*): Bengal and Kashmir.

Kuṣṭha (*Costus specious*): Central and Eastern Himalayas.

Agaru (*Aquileria agallocha*): East Himalayas, Assam and Bhutan.

Śrīvāsa (*Pinus longifolia*): Himalayas, Bhutan and the Indus area.

It will be seen that virtually all of these plants and trees are to be found in the East Himalayan region. This points to a north-east Indian origin for the MVT. There are many other Buddhist texts, especially tantric ones, which include the names of plants, trees and herbs. A detailed study of these would provide much useful data to pin-point the likely areas or origin of such texts. I am currently working on an edition and translation of the *Susiddhi-kāra Tantra* which contains a vast compendium of such information.

34 That is, in the east.

35 *Kuśa* grass (*Desmostachya bipinnata*) which has been considered sacred in India from ancient times is used in many religious practices, both Buddhist and non-Buddhist. Concerning this grass, CC says, '*In India, mantra reciters often use* kuśa *grass to make mats for themselves. This has many benefits. Because that is what a Tathāgata sits on when he becomes enlightened, everybody considers it to be auspicious* (kuśala). *If the* mantrin *uses this kind of mat, obstacles will not arise nor will he be assailed by poisonous insects.* Kuśa *grass has a fragrant odour. It also has very sharp tips, so if they brush against one's body, they will leave stab wounds. If the* mantrin *sprawls or sleeps on this grass when he feels like a rest, it will prick him so he will be unable to indulge in his laziness!*'

36 With slight differences, the Sanskrit for the verses spoken by the Master in this portion survives in CC and also the *Sang Hyang Kamahāyānikan*:

ajñāna-paṭalaṃ vatsa punitaṃ jinanes tava |
śalākair vaidya-rājendraiḥ yathā lokasya taimiram ||
pratibimba-samā dharma acchāḥ śuddhā anāvilaḥ |
agrāhyā abhilāpyaś ca hetu-karma-samudbhavāḥ ||
evaṃ jñātvā imān dharmān niḥsvabhāvān anāvilān |
kuru sattvārtham atulaṃ jāto 'sy urasi tāyinām ||
adya-prabhṛti lokasya cakraṃ vartaya tāyinām |
sarvatra pūrya vimalaṃ dharma-śaṅkham anuttaram ||
na te 'tra vimatiḥ kāryā nirviśaṅkena cetasā |
prakāśaya mahā-tulaṃ mantrācārya-nayam param ||
evaṃ kṛta-jño buddhānām upakārīti gīyate |
te ca vajra-dharāḥ sarve rakṣanti tava sarvaśaḥ ||

37 This has also survived in Chinese transcription and may be read as follows:

adya-prabhṛti te vatsa api jīvita-kāraṇāt |
aparityajeḥ sad-dharmaṃ bodhicittaṃ varta-pāraṃ ||
mātsaryaṃ sarva-dharmeṣu sattvānām ahitaṃ caritaṃ |
ete samayāḥ saṃbuddhair ākhyātāḥ satva su-vrata ||
yathā sva-jīvitaṃ rakṣyaṃ tathā rakṣyā ime tvayā |
praṇipata gurūṃ śiṣyaś caraṇayor bhakti-vatsalaḥ ||
abhyupeya sattā-sarvaṃ niścittenātra ātmanā |

38 This may refer to kings who acted as regents, or to dual reigns which were not uncommon in India, where a father and son ruled together, with the son taking over completely upon the death of his father.

39 *Mukhato jāta.* This means 'born in the presence of'.

40 Hereafter, throughout the translation, I abbreviate all occurrences of '*namaḥ samanta-vajrānām*' to NSV.

41 Hereafter, throughout the translation, I abbreviate all occurrences of '*namaḥ samanta-buddhānām*' to NSB.

Chapter III

1 *vināyaka.*

2 Lit. 'Wind Direction'.

3 The text has *mahendra* throughout for 'earth'. I have usually put 'earth' in the translation for clarity's sake.

4 Green is viewed here as a secondary colour, produced by mixing white, red, yellow, blue and black. Hence deities who are green are thought to be appropriate for all of the activities associated with those primary colours.

Chapter V

1 As already mentioned in Note I . 6, the Sanskrit word '*akṣara*' means both 'imperishable, immutable' and 'phomene, letter'.

2 Although not very clear from the text, the process being described here is the visualization of a garland of mantras flowing with the breath, going out from one's heart into that of the Tathāgata, and then once again being drawn into oneself from the Tathāgata's heart.

3 *Prāṇa.* This should be understood as 'life-energy' rather than just the ordinary gross breath, which is its external manifestation.

4 *Āyama.*

5 Also described in VI . 24 – 26.

6 Also described in VI . 30 – 33.

7 Also described at length in VI . 35 – 37.

Chapter VI

1 Chapter IV.15.

2 These and the following verses are reproduced by CC in transliteration:
gaganāmala-niḥsvabhāvaka viśva-jñāna-vicitra-dāyakā ||
śūnyatā svabhāvataḥ sadā pratyayādhina-gambhira-durdṛśā |
santataṃ tu viśeṣa-gaminā phalam agraṃ dadati vicintitaṃ ||

3 *yathā sarva-gatīnām ālayo gagano bhonti asaṅga-gocaraḥ* |
tathā eṣa viśuddhi-dharmatā tri-bhāvāśeṣa-viśuddha saṃbhāvā ||

4 *caratetra yāgra-jo vibhuḥ bhavati sarva-jinaika-gocaraḥ* ||

5 *na paraṃ padam asti durlabhaṃ* |
sakalāloka-karaṃ yathā jinaṃ | *kathitā su-viśuddhi-dharmatā* ||

6 *carātra vikalpa-varjita vipula* | *dharma-gambhiram avyayaṃ* ||

7 That is, those gods who control the emanations of others.

8 *Lāsya* (T: *rol-mo*) is dance with musical accompaniment.

9 *Grāha.* The symptoms of this would be generally considered today as a form of schizophrenia.

10 Likewise, the water mandala has a lotus, the fire mandala a triangle, and the wind mandala a pennant.

11 *Ākarṣaka*.
12 The five *anantārya* (immediates), evil deeds which are so grave that the perpetrator experiences their effects immediately in the present lifetime. They are matricide, patricide, killing of an Arhat, causing a schism in the Saṅgha, and intentionally injuring a Buddha.
13 CC indicates that this means controlling eclipses of the sun and so on.
14 Lit. 'wind-arising', which can be interpreted in either of the ways given in the Commentary.

Chapter VII

1 The six modes of the deity (*devatā*) are attribute (*lakṣaṇa*), form (*rūpa*), *mudrā*, letter (*akṣara*), sound (*śabda*) and emptiness (*śūnya*). These will be explained by Buddhaguhya below.
2 The fourth member of recitation.
3 The third member of recitation.
4 The first member of recitation.
5 The second member of recitation.
6 The Sanskrit text for the following passage has been preserved in the *Pradīpoddyotana*, a commentary on the *Guhya-samāja Tantra* attributed to Candrakīrti: *Devatā-rūpam api Guhyakādhipate dvividhaṃ pariśuddham aśuddham ceti. Tatra pariśuddham adhigata-rūpaṃ sarva-nimittāpagataṃ. Apariśuddhaṃ nimittam rūpaṃ varṇa-saṃsthānañ ca. Tatra dvividhena devatā-rūpeṇa dvividha-kārya-niṣpattir bhavati. Sa-nimittena sa-nimitta-siddhir upajāyate. Animittenānimitta-siddhis.*
7 This is the well-known expression which appears in many other sutras: *Utpāda vā tathāgatānām anutpāda vā tathāgatānāṃ sthitaivaiṣa dharmānām dharmatā.*
8 This verse has also survived in the *Pradīpoddyotana*:
Iṣṭā jina-varaiḥ siddhiṃ sa-nimitte sa-nimittam
animitte sthitvā vai sa-nimittaṃ prasādayate
tasmāt sarva-prakāreṇa nir-nimittam niṣevyata.

Chapter VIII

1 C treats these as two items only: body and mind.
2 It seems that the Commentary is slightly confused here as it has the word (*mano-vijñāna*). In view of the *Piṇḍārtha* (60b) which says that the word 'mind' here refers to the six consciousnesses, visual and so forth, which focus on colour-form and so on, I think this should be deleted and the comments amended accordingly. In fact *mano-vijñāna* should refer to *manas*, as can be seen from the next note.
3 The *Piṇḍārtha* (60b) says that *manas* is the consciousness (*vijñāna*) with the perceptual images associated with a perceiving subject and perceived objects.
4 That is, one cannot find a past, present or future phase in the mind. C reverses this and says that one cannot find the mind in the three times.

Chapter IX

1 There is a disparity between the line of T which reads '*Alone with one or one with one*' and C, which only has 一一諸眞言 '*[You should recite] each one of the mantras*'. One wonders whether the Sanskrit original only had *ekaikaṃ*, and Buddhaguhya in his comments is indicating that this can be explained in two senses. In that case T has translated *ekaikaṃ* twice to accommodate these two possible meanings.
2 Further comments relevant to this Chapter may be found in Chapter XXI.

Chapter X

1 This refers to the three *samādhis* that the Master must use prior to drawing the three mandalas described in this Tantra. For the drawing of the Mandala Arising from the Matrix of Great Compassion, he should transform himself into the Body of Vairocana using the essence *A*, and then arrange all the letters throughout his body as described in Chapter XVIII.5 and XIX, '*Ka is placed in the throat*' and so forth. For the Mandala of the Revolving Wheel of Letters he should transform himself with seed syllables of the Three Families, *A, Sa* and *Va*, mentioned in Chapter XVIII.11. For the Secret Mandala, he should transform himself with the five essences of the Great Hero, *A, Va, Ra, Hūṃ* and *Kha*, described in Chapter XVIII.12.

2 *Daśa-bodhisattva-vaśita.* These are mastery and freedom with regards life, mind, possessions, actions, birth, fervent conviction, the Dharma, aspirations, magical powers and Awareness.

3 An epithet for Mañjuśrī.

4 It is hard to make sense of Buddhaguhya's comments unless we assume that he read a negative in his text. On this line, CC says: '*He salutes him out of great gratitude as the one who anciently generated* bodhicitta, *accomplished the result, and revealed it to beings, for although all beings have this* bodhicitta, *they are not aware of it themselves*'.

5 There are five types of result in Buddhism. Two of those are mentioned here – *vipāka-phala* and *niṣyaṇḍa-phala.* The result which is recompense, maturation (*vipāka*), is the gradual ripening of wholesome or unwholesome phenomena and actions. Rebirth in the various levels of existence as a god, human, animal and so forth is attributed to this. When the force of the original cause has been exhausted, the result itself also ceases to operate. The result which is the natural outflow (*niṣyaṇḍa*) of the cause corresponds to the nature of its cause in activity and experience. Thus a person who habitually engages in wholesome activities will naturally be drawn to doing and experiencing the wholesome in the future, and vice versa for one who engages in the unwholesome. Thereby they will generate in turn further causes for such effects, setting up a kind of chain-reaction. Cf. *Abhidharma-kośa* II.56 – 58 for details of all these results.

6 That is, Mañjuśrī. The meaning of this is not clear. CC seems to imply that the Master should also transform himself into Mañjuśrī with his seed-syllable, *Maṃ.*

7 According to C, his seed-syllable is *Va.*

8 According to C, his seed-syllable is *Bhaḥ.*

9 According to the *Piṇḍārtha* (44a), this is how the Master is to imagine that the Awareness Beings (*jñāna-sattva*) are present in the mandala he has drawn. In many rituals and *sādhanas* this is done by some form of invitation, concluded by the mantra '*Jaḥ Hūṃ Vaṃ Hoḥ*', but Buddhaguhya says that the Tantra indicates that it is acceptable to imagine the deities to be present without any invitation.

10 Into the Body of Vajrasattva (*Pind.* 47b).

11 In other words, he gives them each a flower which they will cast upon the Mandala.

12 According to the *Piṇḍārtha,* this is the Initiation Mandala, in which the continuum of reality is represented either by its seed syllable (*Raṃ*) or as a lotus. After having been brought before that Mandala, the trainee should be transformed into the *saṃbhoga-kāya* of Vairocana with the *Mudrā* which Produces all the Members, and then sprinkled with water from the four jars.

13 This is the fifth of the *mudrās* described in the Chapter on the Eight Secret *Mudrās.*

14 No commentary from Section 19 to the end of this chapter. Buddhaguhya says that he has already dealt with the contents elsewhere.

Chapter XI

1 *Satkāya-dṛṣṭi.* This is glossed as *ātmātmīya-grāha,* 'attachment to the self and what belongs to the self' in *Abhidharma Kośa* V.15. Also in the *Laṅkāvatāra Sūtra* 117.17 it is said to be of two types: that which is innate (*sahaja*) and that which is deludedly imagined (*parikalptita*).

Chapter XII

1 Readers should bear in mind that Sankrit phonemes and letters are all syllabic in nature. When written, all letters are considered to have an inherent 'a' if no other vowel is indicated. Other vowels, (except initial vowels which have their own letters) are indicated by one of a special set of vowel signs placed above at the side or below the basic 'simple' letter which in itself is unaltered.

2 That is, without lengthening, *anusvāra* nasalization, or *visarga* aspiration as is the case with the subsequent sets of letters.

3 CC: '*A dancer in the ordinary world will display various kinds of physical movements, such as bending, stretching, bowing down and looking up, and perform songs with various kinds of subtle techniques, in the midst of an audience according to their wishes. She will cause some to feel joyful, and others to feel sad or fearful. She will bring about a variety of different benefits for beings with the skills arising from the one body and voice, because her knowledge is adapted to the hearts of beings. Likewise, a Bodhisattva also manifests many different modes of behaviour, all of which are actually mudrās, and delivers many different kinds of teachings, all of which are mantras, and so brings about great benefit for beings without any selectivity. It is therefore called the Dance of the Bodhisattva's Practice.*'

4 Based on T *rnam-par-mdzes-pa* and C 照, one could reconstruct *vi-√raj* as the underlying Sanskrit word for 'illumine'. This would have a semantic echo in *Vairocana* which also means 'illuminating', and 'the sun'

Chapter XIII

1 V adds: '*Its essence Va should be known as before*'.

2 This explanation does not accord well with what Buddhaguhya has just said about the emergence of the Array of the Sameness of the Tathāgatas from the continuum of reality, which he defined as Suchness!

3 The Mahāsaṅghikas and their derivative branch, the Lokottara-vādins, are said to have held the view that the Buddha, following his Enlightenment, spoke only one single word which was heard and understood by all beings as the Dharma suitable to their specific aptitude. This theory is particularly relevant to the ideas of the MVT, according to which this single word would have been *Aṃ*.

4 CC says that these Buddhas emerged from the pores of the Tathāgata Bodies, and then in turn further Buddhas emerged from their pores, and so on in succession.

5 That is, peaceful, angry, joyful and so on.

6 *Sāmānya-vidhi-guhya-tantra.*

7 Chapter II.11.

8 The root mantra (*mūla*) is *ASAMĀPTA-DHARMADHĀTU-GATIṂ-GATĀNĀṂ SARVATHĀ*, the essences (*hṛdaya*) are *AṂ KHAṂ AṂ AḤ SAṂ SAḤ HAṂ HAḤ RAṂ RAḤ VAṂ VAḤ SVĀHĀ*, and the subsidiary essences (*upahṛdaya*) are *HŪṂ RAṂ RAḤ HRA HAḤ SVĀHĀ RAṂ RAḤ SVĀHĀ*.

9 There are two phases to the mind orientated towards Enlightenment (*bodhicitta*). Aspiration (*praṇidhāna*) *bodhicitta* is the wish or resolution to become enlightened, and is like a person's wish to undertake a journey. Application (*prasthāna*) *bodhicitta* is characterized by having begun to engage in such practices as the Six Perfections, which is like a person who has actually set out on the journey. However, it would be possible, as Buddhaguhya describes, for a person to have begun to cultivate the application *bodhicitta* without having formally made the aspiration.

10 The *Piṇḍārtha* (32a) says that this is the Master's resolution: 'I shall depict the Mandala on this site!'.

11 This is dealt with in detail in Chapter II.11 -12.

12 This is for the marking-out of the intrinsically existing mandala in the air.

13 This is a play on the Skt. word *rakta* which means 'red' and 'passion, attachment'.
14 This *Mudrā* is described in Chapter XV.7.
15 See *Piṇḍārtha* 46a for further details about these types of offerings.
16 In other words either one of these two types of Initiation can be used for the first two Mandalas, depending upon the trainee's ability.
17 See *Piṇḍārtha* 56a for details.
18 As is often the case, CC also gives an alternative explanation for this verse. It says that '*Well-disciplined*' (*su-vrātya*) can refer either to Vajrapāṇi, reading it as '*O Well-disciplined One!*', or else to the person who engages in the practice associated with Vajrapāṇi. '*Cultivates his manas*' indicates the visualization of the deity in his *manas* with the clarity of an image in a mirror. '*Realize*' (√ *budh*) refers to the realization of the true nature of one's mind and its perceptual sphere. The '*three places*' are one's mind internally, its perceptual objects externally, and the perceptual connection between the two. The *mantrin* should understand that these three are primordially pure, unborn, without independent existence, and have the single attribute of sameness.
19 There are four stages of *samādhi* associated with the Level of Practice with Devoted Interest: The attainment of light, the increase of light, partial understanding of the true nature of things, and the immediate proximity to full understanding.
20 Buddhaguhya gives a slightly different explanation in his *Piṇḍārtha.* He says '*in one's stream*' signifies 'in the mental stream of the person who accomplishes wholesome actions by propitiating the mantras'. The '*stream-forming actions*' are the actions of propitiating the mantras which form the mental stream that becomes the causal basis for such special attainments as becoming a *vidyādhara* and so forth. '*Remain unvitiated*' is when the actions of propitiating the mantras have not been exhausted through their results having been received already.
21 The mythical idea of a *gandharvas'* city (*gandharva-nagara*) is inspired by mirages or other natural phenomena in the sky.
22 T inconsistently refers to this as both *Vidyā* King and *Vidyā* Queen. As 'King' would seem to be the intended reading, I have amended 'Queen' to 'King' wherever it occurs, such as here.
23 In other words the four *vijñānas* and the four *jñānas* into which they are transmuted.
24 I assume that this refers to *Saṃ* and *Saḥ*, *Haṃ* and *Haḥ*, *Raṃ* and *Raḥ*, and *Vaṃ* and *Vaḥ*. In connection with the arrangement of the letters of this *Vidyā*, the CC says elsewhere that the letters should be arranged through one's body thus: *Aṃ* on the crown of one's head, *Khaṃ* in the right ear, *Aṃ* in the left ear, *Aḥ* on one's brow, *Saṃ* and *Saḥ* on the right and left shoulders, *Haṃ* in the heart, *Haḥ* on one's back, *Raṃ* in one's belly, *Raḥ* in the small of one's back, *Vaṃ* in one's left and right thighs, and *Vaḥ* in one's feet.
25 That is, the symbol of Hayagrīva's activity. However, unfortunately neither the text nor the commentaries make it clear what exactly this is. However there is some indication from Japanese sources that this might be a white lotus.
26 In other words, with the letter *Ha* (ཧ) which resembles a banner. In many countries in the East, flags and banners were hung downwards from a T-shaped pole. Hence the shape of the letter *Ha* was seen to resemble a flag fluttering in the wind.
27 Candra-tilaka.
28 The comments for this section are puzzling. From the C and CC it is clear that there are four types of vajras: one, three and five-pointed ones, and vajra-garlands. Each one of these vajras should be repeated four times in a different colour to account for the sixteen Vajradharas. However, it is difficult to make sense of B. The comments on the different types of vajras are unclear, and B reads '*These six should be multiplied by two to give a total of twelve*', which is cannot be reconciled with the four types of vajras and the sixteen Vajradharas. I suspect that some kind of textual corruption had occurred in the Sanskrit original by Buddhaguhya's time, evidence for which can also be seen in the subsequent lines of this section. I have tentatively amended the numbers given in the translation.

29 I have given the alternative reading to '*All of them have their seed-syllables*' here for the sake of Buddhaguhya's comments, which do give the impression that he had *vijaya* 'completely victorious' in his Sanskrit text, though I consider C to have preserved the original sense.
30 *Mahā-mukha.* This also means 'crocodile'.
31 The five gods of the Pure Abodes named in II.47 are Īśvara, Saṃkusumita, Prabhamāla, Manobhava and Vighuṣṭa, but there is no indication which of them corresponds to which symbol.
32 Various simple *mudrās* are used by Brahmins when reciting the Vedas.
33 An epithet for Mañjuśrī or Mañjughoṣa.

Chapter XIV

1 The *Piṇḍārtha* has *Raṃ* here.
2 The *Piṇḍārtha* has *Aṃ* here.
3 The *Piṇḍārtha* (49b) indicates '*that the letter* [Raṃ] *of the continuum of reality should be arranged in the heart of the trainee, and* [*the Master*] *should think of him as the continuum of reality in nature by means of considering the meaning of the letter. The trainee himself should also be convinced that he is thus.*'
4 The *Piṇḍārtha* says that the twelve-syllabled mantra should be arranged on the petals of the lotus-seat upon which the letter *A* rests. CC understands the '*receptacle*' to refer to the trainee's transformed body in which the twelve letters are to be arranged.

Chapter XVI

1 CC states that the word 'entry' (Skt. *praveśa*) used in the title of this chapter has a different sense to that in the title of Chapter XIV. It says that this 'entry' implies 'comprehension, familiarity', as in the case of a person who has already entered a house and understands each part of it in detail, who has freedom of movement and knows everything that is contained in the house, in contrast to a person who enters it for the first time.
2 The full list is: coolness, sweetness, lightness, softness, clearness, freedom from impurities, soothing to the stomach when drunk, clearing and soothing the throat.
3 T implies that they spoke, but according to C the sounds came from the Tathāgata himself.

Chapter XVII

1 CC says that *śīla* refers to long term disciplinary observances, while *vrata* refers to a short term ritual observance.

Chapter XVIII

1 *Hṛdaya* means 'essence' and 'heart'.
2 *Snātaka* 'bather', an initiated householder.
3 *Brahmacārin.*
4 *Āśrava.* I have used 'inflation' following R. Johansson, *Dynamic Pyschology of Early Buddhism,* to which the reader should refer for a useful discussion of this term (pp 177-183). The literal meaning of this term is 'influx', but it implies an unrealistic psychological superstructure in an individual formed by i) cupidity (*kāma*), ii) becoming (*bhāva*), iii) false opinions (*dṛṣṭi*) and iv) ignorance (*avidyā*).
5 CC says that this should be four inches above the heart.
6 The '*light-discs*' are the eyes

Chapter XIX

1 CC states that this is the top of the cranium.
2 CC states that this has no location, but pervades all members

Chapter XX

1 Probably Chapter 10 in the *Bodhisattva-bhūmi*, which deals with all aspects of the Bodhisattva's Morality in great analytical detail.
2 These are equivalent to the *pārājayikas*, the four grave offences which merit expulsion from the Saṅgha: the taking of life, stealing, unchastity and falsely claiming to have attained superhuman qualities.

Chapter XXI

1 That is, with an *anusvāra*.

Chapter XXII

1 Apart from the technical meaning, 'supernatural cognition', *abhijñā* is also 'recognition'.
2 *Kusuma-tala-garbha-alaṃkāra-lokadhātu*. This is the name normally given to a particular Buddha realm. There are several theories regarding its nature. The best known version is that to be found in Book Five of the *Avataṃsaka Sūtra*, devoted to a description of this realm. Here, this realm is said to be manifested by virtue of the Bhagavat Vairocana's previous aspirations and practices. Beneath this realm there is a wind mandala, upon which there lies an ocean of fragrant water. A vast lotus grows in the midst of this ocean, and this world-system is located in the heart of this lotus. Furthermore, there are countless other subsidiary world-systems to be found around this central world-system arranged in twenty tiers. All of these worlds seem to form a great jewelled web, and the Bhagavat Vairocana also manifests himself within this universe, causing beings to attain Enlightenment. However, there does seem to be a certain imprecision regarding the nature and relationship of the various Buddha realms in Buddhist literature. So in the MVT, this term seems to imply the entire group of ten pure Buddha fields, with *Ghaṇa-vyūha* at its centre, and can be seen as equivalent to the Great Akaniṣṭha Realm. On the other hand, it is interesting that Buddhaguhya identifies this with the *Sahā* universe of world-systems, which is the universe we ourselves inhabit. For if he also accepts the view that this *Kusuma-tala-garbha-alaṃkāra* universe is manifested by the Bhagavat Vairocana, then our own universe, to which it is equivalent, is also manifested by him.

Chapter XXIII

1 Vasubandhu's *Viṃśatika* vv11–15 gives a full description of this form of analysis.
2 The same example is found in Nāgārjuna's *Madhyamaka-kārikā (17.31-32):*

yathā mirmitikaṃ śāstā nirmimīta ṛddhi sampadā |
nirmito nirmimītānyaṃ sa ca mirmitakaḥ punah ||
tathā nirmitakārah kartā yat karma tat kṛtaṃ |
tad yathā nirmitenānyo nirmitas tathā ||

'Just as a teacher, through magical power, were to create a figure, and this created figure were to create another, that in turn would be a creation. In the same way, an agent is like a created form and his action is like his creation. It is like the created form created by another who is created.' See also *Sāmaññaphala-sutta* (D1.76-77) and also *Majjhima-nikāya* 1.295.

Chapter XXVII

1 I have left this comment in place here although it should properly go with the next mind. On several occasions elsewhere Buddhaguhya has defined the abiding mind as that which abides in emptiness [XIII.48, XIV.6].

2 CC says that there are two causal factors that give rise to the above impediments – drinking alcohol and sleeping on beds. The drinking of alcohol causes all kinds of unwholesomeness to arise, and the sleeping in comfortable beds give rise various kinds of desires and careless thoughts. The yogin should spread kuśa grass and use that instead.

Chapter XXIX

1 In other words, Agni is viewed here as Mahā-Brahmā.

2 The *dakṣiṇa* offering is a present given as renumeration to Brahmins for the performance of a ritual and so forth.

3 Actually, only forty fires are mentioned.

4 CC reverses the above two functions. It also notes that this ritual washing and parting of the woman's hair is done when she is six months pregnant.

5 CC says that when a child has completed the period of his education, he should give the gift of a cow and its calf to his teacher, who then speaks to him of his duty to marry.

6 As mentioned earlier, C omits this fire altogether.

7 CC speaks of all transgressions in one's conduct, especially those occurring in connection with caste, that is, in cases of ritual impurity.

8 This is the ritual at the two twilight periods of sunrise and sunset.

9 CC understands this ritual to concern the rising of the moon. But the normal sense of *Soma-saṃsthā* is the ritual concerning Soma. However, it should be noted that the word *soma* means 'moon' as well as the ritual intoxicating substance.

10 As mention above, V reverses the words *Yama* 'the God of Death' and *Kṛtānta.*

11 This refers to the shape of hearths to be used: round for Pacifying, square for Enriching, and triangular for Destroying.

12 T's rendering of '*counter-acted by the non-arising insight*' reflects a quite different understanding of the Sanskrit, which probably had something like *ajāta-prajñā-niṣedha.* As it stands, this is a compound in which the three elements do not show any obvert grammatical relationship and which may be interpreted in several ways as we can see. Furthermore T and C understand *ajāta-prajñā* differently. Following Buddhaguhya, T interprets it as *phro-ba med-pa'i shes-rab,* in the sense of the insight which is free from the arising of perceptual activity. On the other hand, Śubhakarasiṃha in CC has understood this as the unborn, undeveloped insight. But once again, there is no way of deciding definitely which would have been the intention of the MVT itself. Since Śubhakarasiṃha was probably active during the period when the MVT first came to light or soon after, it is not unreasonable to suppose that his comments reported in CC do reflect views closer to those of the MVT itself.

Chapter XXX

1 This chapter runs on from the previous one in T without any break.

2 As Buddhaguhya has not commented on the requisite attributes, some of the comments in CC regarding these may be of interest: *Who desire superior things* (*ābhimānika*): They only desire the practice associated with the Tathāgatas, and when they generate *bodhicitta,* all that they do is for that and nothing else. *Who always recollect their good fortune* (*kṛta-jña*): From the time they first hear the meaning of a single phrase from their teachers until they attain Buddhahood, they do not forget their debt to them. Regarding the physical attributes, the general message of the comments in CC is that these should be balanced, free from extremes of size and shape.

The matter of the colour of their complexions is open to several possible interpretations. While C has 青白 '*bluish white*', T has *sngo bsangs*, which in Tibetan basically means 'dark-blue, indigo'. However, *sngo bsangs* may be used to render two Sanskrit words: *avadāta* and *śyāma*. Both of these cover a range of meanings which would include most skin colours C *avadāta* means 'spotless', 'pure', 'white' and 'yellow', while *śyāma* means any dark colour, such as black, dark-blue, brown or green! In view of C, *avadāta* may well be the underlying Sanskrit word, which we could then understand in the first two of its meanings, to avoid any repugnant implications of racial criteria in the selection of people who are suitable to receive these teachings. In any case, it would have been quite difficult for Masters to require the listed physical attributes from prospective trainees with any degree of strictness as the popularity of the MVT spread throughout India to China, Japan, Tibet and elsewhere. If this list is read in conjunction with the desirable attributes given in II.4 and II.12, it will be seen that it is the spiritual qualities of prospective trainees which are of greatest importance. Spiritual acumen is not dependent upon one's colour or sex.

PART III THE MAHĀ-VAIROCANA-UTTARA-TANTRA

Chapter I

1 As mentioned in the Introduction, there is no commentary available for this section of the text. Only Q includes sections 1 – 8, the other editions I utilized begin from Section 9.

2 Ancient Indian astronomy and astrology used a set of twenty eight (or twenty seven) constellations (*nakṣatras*) for the compilation of calendars, divination and so forth. They were in general use for this purpose from early Vedic times until 3rd – 4th century CE when a different system based on Greek astronomy gradually gained popularity, using the constellations associated with the twelve zodiac signs. *Uttara-bhādra-pada* is to be identified with α Andromedae, *Pūrva-phalguṇī* with δ Leonis, *Āśleṣā* with α Hydrae and *Maghā* with α Leonis (Regulus).

3 The mantra in Chapter 4 has *mano-rama*.

4 *Andropogon squarrosus*. A kind of grass found in the Himalayan foothills, the roots of which are used to prepare a fragrant incense and medicine.

5 White lotus (*Nelumbo nucifera*), roses (*rosa glandulifera*), jasmine (*jasminum sambac*), and *yūthikā* (*jasminum auriculatum*). Some editions have *pūtika* for this last flower, which is identified with *Caesalpina fonducella* or *Rasella rubra*.

6 *Kṛśara* is a kind of porridge usually made of rice, beans and sesame.

Chapter II

1 The constellations for Enriching are as follows, identified by their chief stars: *Abhijit* is Vega, *Dhaniṣṭā* is α Delphini, *Jyeṣthā* is Antares and *Rohiṇī* is Aldebaran.

2 *Bīja-pūra* (*citrus medica*). The word '*jambha*' included in Jambhala's name also means 'citron'.

3 The *priyaṅgu* is likely to be *Aglaia Odorata*, although it is also identified with *Setaria italica* or else *Cyperus rotundus*, a fragrant grass particularly found in sandy costal areas of India.

4 *Agaru*, the black incense made from the sap of *Aquileria agallocha*, a tall tree growing especially around the East Himalayas, Assam and Bhutan.

5 *Guggulu* is made from the yellow-coloured sap of *Boswellia thurifera*, found in wooded valleys of the Himalayas.

6 The *sāla* (*Shorea robusta*) is a tall thin tree with small pale yellow flowers, found in warm areas of the Himalayas, Assam and the hills of West Bengal. It is a sacred tree for Buddhists, as a Buddha of the past, Viśvabhū, became fully enlightened seated under it, and also the Buddha Śākyamuni passed into Parinirvāṇa lying between two *sāla* trees at Kushinagara.

7 *Dūrvā* (*Cynadon dactylon*) is a kind of grass growing up to 40 cms in length with narrow pointed leaves growing at intervals along the stem. It is found throughout India, Burma, Sri

Lanka and up to 5000' in the Himalayas, and was a sacred grass of comparable importance to *kuśa* grass.

8 *Ficus lacor.*

9 *Ficus glomerata.*

10 *Aegle marmelos.* It was traditionally thought that the use of a vessel made from its wood would lead to the acquisition of wealth.

Chapter III

1 *Puṣyā* is δ Cancri, *Kṛttikā* is the Pleiades, *Maghā* is Regulus and *Viśakhā* is β Libra.

2 *Khadira* is *Acacia catechu,* which is found in the Himalayas, Sikkim and the Punjab, up to 4000' – 5000'. *Aśoka* is *Saraca indica* or *Jonesia asoca,* found in the valleys of the East Himalayas up to 2000' and in Central India. *Karavīra* is *Nerium indicum,* a kind of oleander, found in Nepal up to 6500'.

Chapter IV

1 Identified by their chief stars, these constellations are as follows: *Hasta* is Arcturus, *Citrā* is δ Corvi, *Aśvinī* is Spica, *Uttara-phalguṇī* is β Arietis, *Punar-vasu* is β Leonis and *Svāti* is β Gemini.

2 *Clitoria ternata.*

3 *Bhallātaka* is *Semecarpus anacordium* and *vibhītaka* is *Terminalia belerica,* a tall tree which grows throughout India except in the west. Its fruit are used medicinally, and also for the manufacture of black dye and ink.

Chapter V

1 This is probably the letter *A.*

2 This section is made up of the well known verse, '*ye dharma hetu-prabhavā hetuṃ teṣāṃ tathāgato hy avadat | teṣāṃ ca yo nirodha evaṃ vādī mahā-śramaṇaḥ*' and a second stanza which also has the air of being a quotation, but I have been unable to trace its provenance. As it mentions the eight consciousnesses, and the relative and consummate natures, it is most likely to be from a Yogacāra text. My translation is tentative and may need correction.

3 I am not certain what is intended by the Tibetan *'dren-pa gnyis.* In view of the context, it may possibly refer to the two symbols, the *visarga* and the *anusvāra.*

4 The augmented vowels are probably *E, AI, O* and *AU.*

Chapter VII

1 This is an Indian unit of length, which varies between six to twelve miles according to different authorities. One finds such large sizes prescribed for mandalas from time to time, but it is difficult to know how seriously one should believe this. Quite apart from anything else, the trainees would have considerable problems throwing their flowers upon the deities of the mandala, unless catapults were allowed!

2 This refers to the mantra and *mudrā* given in Chapter XI.24.

3 *Pratisaṃvid.* This is of four types: detailed knowledge of the Dharma, of the value and meaning of that which the Dharma deals with, of etymology and language and of rhetorical aptitude.

4 I have adopted the reading given by N and S for part of this passage (*nam-mkha' dang mnyam-par-gyur-pa'i chos mnyam-pa-nyid rnam-par-bstan-pa | chos-kyi-dbyings-kyis rnam-par-rol-pa'i sgo-nas rnam-par-rol-nas* ...) as it seems to be better than that given in Q and is closer in meaning to parallel passages elsewhere.

5 Buddha fields or other kinds of world-systems are usually thought of as resting upon vast discs (*maṇḍala*) of wind and of water in space.

6 The text has 'ground' (*gzhi*), but I have amended this to 'Strength' (*stobs*) on the basis of the parallel passage in Chapter 28.

7 The eight obstacles (*aṣṭa-akṣaṇa*) are to be born in the hells, to be born as an animal, as a hungry ghost, as a long-lived god, to be born in barbarian regions, to be born with a perverse mentality, to be born stupid and to be born when there is no Buddha to teach the Dharma.

8 That is, the Bodhisattvas and so forth.

9 Q here reads *mos-par-bya-ba* 'should believe', but this has been emended to *smos-par-bya-ba* on the basis of other editions.

10 Q: *hvalinan*, N: *hāvalaṃnīṃ*, S: *hāvaliṃnāṃ*. I suspect this should be amended to *jvālināṃ*.

11 The text has *yongs-su-shes-pa*, 'full understanding/ knowledge', but in view of the context, one wonders whether this is a mistake for *yongs-su-spangs-pa*, 'complete abandonment'.

12 That is, the realm of the hungry ghosts. Yama, the Lord of Death, was regarded as the ruler of that realm.

13 Should this be amended to '*mandalas*'?

14 Text has '*mantras*' (*sngags*), but in the context this probably ought to be amended to 'mandalas'.

15 Classical Indian medical theory traces diseases to the imbalance of the three 'humours': wind (*vāta*), phlegm (*kapha*) and bile (*pitta*) or combinations thereof. Heat increases *vāta*, whereas cold causes an insufficiency.

16 In his *Piṇḍārtha*, Buddhaguhya quotes a long passage which he says is from the Secret Chapter of the *Uttara-tantra*, an alternative title for Chapter VII, although it is not to be found in the present Tibetan version. It may be surmised that our version of the *Uttara-tantra* preserved in Tibetan represents a somewhat earlier stage of development than that of the text used by Buddhaguhya. It is therefore not certain where this passage would have occurred, so I have appended it here 'Lord of the Secret Ones! What is complete knowledge of the three minds of practice with devoted interest? Lord of the Secret Ones! Because it realizes the first instant of mind that which is characterized by the understanding that the mind is without arising and perishing is the first realization. The second is non-conceptualization which transcends the entire web of concepts. Having realized without obscurations, the compassion which would establish all beings on the true path is generated. This is its third mind. Lord of the Secret Ones! By the accomplishment of the three minds, the Levels, the Perfections and the Methods of Attracting will be accomplished. 'Lord of the Secret Ones! The practices for the accomplishment of the Levels and Perfections are those when the Bodhisattvas who engage in the Bodhisattva practice by way of mantra and who are endowed with expedient means, insight and awareness, cause beings to accept [the Dharma] by the Four Methods of Attracting. This giving of the gift the Dharma in a joyful spirit is application to a branch of the Levels and Perfections. Lord of the Secret Ones! Moreover the Bodhisattva who abides in the pure unconditioned morality will give that Dharma, he will establish beings in the morality they wish for and will also abide there himself. This should be viewed as application to a branch of the Levels and Perfections. Lord of the Secret Ones! At the time when the mind of a Bodhisattva is radiant and pervades all dharmas in the ten directions, he himself will attain the acceptance of the non-arising of dharmas and he will cause others to be established therein. This should be viewed as application to a branch of the Levels and Perfections. Lord of the Secret Ones! Moreover, one who has the light of Awareness exerts himself with skill to a greater and higher realization with that mind and also causes others to be established there. Lord of the Secret Ones, you should view this as the application to the accomplishment of the branches of the Levels and Perfections. Lord of the Secret Ones! When the Bodhisattva who engages in the bodhisattva practice by way of mantras meditates on that mind, with a spirit of awareness, without regard for any of the meditative absorptions and also causes others to accept that,

you should then view this as his application to the accomplishment of the Levels and Perfections. Lord of the Secret Ones! Moreover when he himself abides there endowed with that mind, with a spirit of awareness, without regard for the mundane and supramundane meditative absorptions and immeasurable states of the Śrāvakas and also establishes others therein, then you should view this as his accomplishment of the Levels and Perfections. Lord of the Secret Ones! Moreover the Bodhisattva who engages in the bodhisattva practice by way of mantras, who aspires in that way for meditative absorption with that mind, will himself abide in the practice of mundane and supramundane Insight (*prajñā*) with a spirit of awareness and also establish others therein. Lord of the Secret Ones, you should view this as his accomplishment of the Levels and Perfections. 'Lord of the Secret Ones! Moreover the Bodhisattva who has been well-assisted by a spiritual friend and who is skilled in attracting beings with expedient means will generate and uphold the first mind (*bodhicitta*), having aspired to all the Dharma of the Buddha, and attract beings with those Four Methods of Attracting. This is the Perfection of Expedient Means and should be viewed as the accomplishment of the application of the Level which Goes Far. Lord of the Secret Ones! Moreover he whose spirit of awareness is unmoving and not agitated will indeed not be overcome by any assailant or the Māra family of gods. This should be viewed as the application of the Unshakable Level and of the Perfection [of Devoted Interest]. Lord of the Secret Ones! Moreover, the Bodhisattva who has been well-assisted by a spiritual friend, for whom all dharmas have become identical as illusions, and who is endowed with the Perfection of Great Compassion, will pervade all the Buddha-fields of the ten directions with the Perfection of Great Compassion and completely satisfy beings equally with his body, speech and mind, and then with prickling hair and much joy, he will see the Tathāgatas who abide in the ten directions. Endowed with the Great Compassion which is devoted to beings, he causes it to pervade all beings by his firm adherence to space, to beings, to awareness and to consciousness, and when he has developed the Strengths (*bala*) of trust, exertion and insight, he will see Buddhas and Bodhisattvas both in dreams and in actuality and will also acquire the *samādhi* of not forgetting *bodhicitta*. You should know that this is the Bodhisattva who has entered the mandala of the *samādhi* of devoted interest.'

PART IV THE PIṆḌĀRTHA

1 The Qian-long Edition alone of the *Piṇḍārtha* contains a number of interlinear comments in small print, possibly from the hand of dPal-brtsegs. I have included some of these in smaller type enclosed in square brackets as they are interest, but unfortunately many are illegible in the copy available to me and I have had to omit them.

2 *Vajracchedika* 26.

3 *Aṣṭasāhasrikā* ii.40.

4 *Samādhi-rāja* 37.32.

5 This refers to one's body visualized as the tutelary deity.

6 T: *rdo-rje dam-tshig mngon-par-'byung-ba'i rgyud*. This Tantra is also mentioned in the Chinese Commentary with some verses quoted from it. The Chinese gives *Vajrābhyudaya* in transcription. No Tantra of this name is known to have survived.

7 This is not found in the MVT.

8 Q 428, p188a: *sna-rtser blta-zhing rnam-par-rtog-pa spong | nam-zhig bskyod kyang rnam-par mi-g.yo-ba | de-tshe dmigs-la gnas-pa thob-pa-ste | sems ni las-su-rung-bar-'gyur-bar nges |*

9 Q 428, p188a: *rtse-gcig sems dang ldan-pa'i mi-la ni | yid-las-byung-ba'i dga'-ba rab-tu-skyed | dga'-bas lus ni shin-tu-sbyangs-pa 'thob | lus skyangs-pas ni bde-ba'i skal-ldan 'gyur | lus bde rtse-gcig sems dang ting-'dzin-gyis | de tshe bzlas-brjod thogs-pa med-par-'gyur ||*

10 Q 428, p188a-b: *tshe-rabs gzhan-du gang dang gang byas-pa'i | sdig-pa ma-lus bzlas-brjod byas-pas 'byed | bzlas-pas sdig-pa ma-lus byang-gyur-nas | dang-ba'i yid-kyis dngos-grub thob-par-'gyur ||*

11 Q428, p188a: *le-lo 'dod-chags mi-dgar ldan-pa'i sems | gang-dag gang-du g.yo-zhing rgyu-ba-dag | de dang de-nas myur-du bzlog-nas ni | gsang-sngags yi-ge mchog-la legs-par sbyar ||*

12 I have not found the source of this quotation, although it has the hallmarks of a Yogācāra viewpoint.
13 This probably refers to Chapter 4.1.
14 Throughout the *Piṇḍārtha*, the Tibetan text has '*rnal-'byor-gyi gnas*' (**yoga-sthāna*) which I have translated as 'the object of union', whereas the translation of the MVT, as well as V and B, has '*rnal-'byor-gyi stan*' (**yoga-āsana*), translated there as 'yoga-posture'. Whatever the reason for this apparent disparity, the two terms are referring to the same thing.

GLOSSARY

[It should be noted that many of the definitions and explanations given here are specific to the MVT and its Commentary and so may not be appropriate in other circumstances.]

Abhidharma One of the three main traditional corpuses of Buddhist literature, which deals with establishment and analysis of the true nature of phenomena. Apparently all the early schools of Buddhism possessed their own versions of the Abhidharma which had achieved canonical status, the best known of which is that preserved in Pāli. In the Mahāyāna, many works written by known historical figures such as Vasubandhu and Asaṅga were accepted as parts of the Mahāyāna Abhidharma.

Abhisaṃbodhi-kāya A Buddha's mode of being or embodiment which perpetually dwells in the *Bodhimaṇḍa* (q.v.) from the time of Perfect Enlightenment.

Absolute Level (*paramārtha*) The true nature of things, which is emptiness (*śūnyatā*) or suchness.

Ācārya The accomplished master who has received all appropriate initiations and authorizations to practice and teach the Mantra Method.

Accumulations of Merit and Awareness Through the practice of the first five of the Perfections, merit is accumulated which enables one to overcome the obscurations caused by the emotional afflictions. Awareness is accumulated by engaging in the Perfection of Insight and enables one to overcome the obscurations caused by wrong views about reality.

Akaniṣṭha **[Heaven]** The highest of the eighteen heavens in the Realm of Form, at the very limit of forming-bearing existence. At times, *Akaniṣṭha* is also used in the sense of the entire universe in its pure aspect, comprising all the Buddha fields of the ten directions.

All-knowing Awareness (*sarvajña-jñāna*) This is said to comprise the Mirror-like Awareness, Investigating Awareness and the Awareness of Accomplishing Activities, which arise in the instant after Enlightenment is attained. Buddhaguhya states that "there are two types of All-knowing Awareness, the relative and the absolute. The relative type is to know in all forms the Ten Strengths, the Four Fearlessnesses and the Eighteen Uncommon Qualities of a Buddha and so forth. The absolute type is to know emptiness".

Anusvāra The nasalization of vowels in Sanskrit, which is indicated in script by a small circle over the letter. It also symbolizes emptiness or nothingness, probably because the mathematical concept of zero and the use of a small circle or dot to denote it was first devised in India.

Aspiration and application minds There are two phases to the mind directed towards Enlightenment (*bodhicitta*). Aspiration (*praṇidhi / praṇidhāna*) *bodhicitta* is the wish or resolution to become enlightened, and is like a person's wish to undertake a journey. Application (*prasthāna*) *bodhicitta* is characterized by having begun to engage in such practices as the Six Perfections, which is like having actually set out on the journey.

Asura One of the classes of beings in *saṃsāra*, these powerful beings rank just below the gods against whom they are constantly engaged in jealous conflict. Various malevolent demon-like beings such as the *piśācas*, *rākṣasas* and *yakṣas* (q.v.) are generally included in this category.

Attribute (*lakṣaṇa*) The defining qualities or functions of any phenomena (*dharma*). Buddhaguhya defines the term in his *Piṇḍārtha* as "that mental concept (*vikalpa*) by which one knows, defines and understands an object which has the perceptual forms (*nimitta*) of blue and so forth".

Authentically consummate in character (*aviparyāsa-pariniṣpanna-lakṣaṇa*) A Yogācāra term for the true nature (*dharmatā*) of things on the absolute level. It implies the absence of the dualistic split in a perceiving subject and perceived objects, and so is equivalent to emptiness (*śūnyatā*) in meaning.

Autonomous existence (*ātman*) The unchanging independent essence thought to underlie the various attributes and qualities a thing possesses. When used in reference to the person, *ātman* is often equivalent to "self". Buddhism asserts that all phenomena lack this essence.
Awareness beings (*jñāna-sattvas*) Not explicitly used in the MVT as a part of the pair *jñana-sattva* and *samaya-sattva*, but refers to the beings that are embodiments of Buddha qualities, especially the Awarenesses, who may appear in the forms of Buddhas, Bodhisattvas or even mundane gods in order to teach beings the Dharma.
Awareness of Accomplishing Activities q.v. Five Awarenesses.
Awareness of Sameness q.v. Five Awarenesses.
Awareness of Suchness q.v. Five Awarenesses.
Bhagavat One of the commonest titles for a Buddha; "Blessed One" or "Lord".
Bodhicitta "There are two aspects to *bodhicitta*: the mind (*citta*) directed towards Enlightenment (*bodhi*), and the mind whose intrinsic nature is Enlightenment." These correspond to its absolute and relative aspects. The relative aspect also has two parts: the *bodhicitta* of aspiration and of application (q.v.). In the MVT it is symbolized by a moon-disc or mirror.
Bodhimaṇḍa-kāya Used interchangeably with *abhisaṃbodhi-kāya* (q.v.), it is the mode of being which is the embodiment of All-knowing Awareness, taken on by Buddhas at the time of their Enlightenment.
Bodhisattva "*Bodhi* (Enlightenment) is defined as suchness (*tathatā*), and the person who has the intention which seeks to directly experience that is called a "*bodhisattva*".
Bodhisattva Samantabhadra's Resolution (Practice) The ten resolutions and practices of the Bodhisattva Samantabhadra described in detail in Ch 56 of the *Gaṇḍavyūha Sūtra*: homage, praise and offerings to all Buddhas, the confession and repentance of all one's wrongdoing, joy at the attainments of others, the request to the Buddha to teach the Dharma and to remain in the world, application to the Buddha's Teachings at all times, the benefitting of all beings in ways suitable to their needs, and the transference of one's merit to all beings.
Buddha Fields (*buddha-kṣetra*) Realms of enormous size composed of millions of world systems throughout the ten directions of the universe in which a Buddha resides and reveals the Dharma for the benefit of the countless beings living there. The Buddha Field *par excellence* in the MVT is that of Mahā-vairocana, which is implicitly the entire universe.
Cakras The structured configurations ("wheels") in various perceptual forms of the qualities of Vairocana's Body, Speech and Mind which are spontaneously manifested throughout the universe upon his attainment of Perfect Enlightenment for the purpose of liberating beings. These *cakras* which are equivalent to the intrinsically existent mandalas of Body, Speech and Mind are also transformed into mandalas, mantras and mudras for the sake of ordinary beings.
Cognitive object (*ālambana*) Anything functioning as the objective support or basis of perception, here particularly during meditation.
Concepts / Conceptualization q.v. *vikalpa*.
Continuum of reality (*dharmadhātu*) i. The universal "matrix" which is space-like or emptiness (*śūnyatā*) in nature, from which all phenomena arise. It also forms the objective content of the Four Awarenesses (*jñāna*). Buddhaguhya states that there are two aspects to the continuum of reality: the Profound and the Extensive. The Profound is the *Bodhimaṇḍa* (q.v.), and the Extensive is the *Cakras* of the Vajra Adornments of Vairocana's Inexhaustible Body and so forth. ii. The universe itself with all its world systems and societies of beings.
Core of Enlightenment (*bodhimaṇḍa*) This literally means the "essence of Enlightenment", and traditionally refers to the place where a Buddha becomes perfectly enlightened, thus it is "the place of Perfect Enlightenment in the Akaniṣṭha realm, and the places of awakening to the Great Enlightenment in the abode of men". The term also implies the beholding of reality or Enlightenment itself. Buddhaguhya also states that there are two aspects to the continuum of reality (*dharmadhātu*): the Profound and the Extensive. The Profound is the *Bodhimaṇḍa*, and this is the causal basis for the Extensive, the Cakras of the Vajra Adornments of Vairocana's Inexhaustible Body and so forth.

Cultivation (*bhāvanā*) i. The cultivation of *bodhicitta* and so forth, by means of the practices implied by the Six Perfections. ii. The meditative observation of such things as the dharmas. iii. Meditation on the meaning of mantric letters and so forth.

Deity (*devatā*) The Buddhas and Bodhisattvas who are transformations and emanations of the qualities and facets of Mahā-vairocana's Enlightenment and All-knowing Awareness. These deities can have various forms – mantras, *mudrās* or body-images. See Chapter VII for details.

Destroying (*abhicāra*) The most extreme of the four rites that a *mantrin* may undertake to facilitate practice of the Dharma by himself and others.

Dhāraṇī "support", this basically implies the means by which something, especially the Dharma, is retained. Although originally many *dhāraṇīs* were mnenomic strings of syllables, the term *dhāraṇī* is generally used in the MVT in sense of *mantra*, the only apparent difference being that *dhāraṇī* are usually fairly lengthy!

Dharma A headache for any translator! *Dharma* is a multivalent word for which up to ten meanings are traditionally listed. I have retained the word "*dharma*" for the following: i. Dharma in the sense of realization, that is, the content of a Buddha's Enlightenment (*adhigama-dharma*); ii. Scriptural Dharma (*āgama-dharma*), the discourses which reveal this realization.

Dharmakāya q.v. *tri-kāya.*

Dispositions (*vāsanā*) The latent energy resulting from one's actions, "imprinted" into one's substratum consciousness (*ālaya-vijñāna*), which then predisposes one to particular patterns of behaviour in the future.

Eighteen Uncommon Qualities of a Buddha (*aveṇika-buddha-dharma*) Several variant lists are found in the Sutras. One which is fairly common is: A Tathāgata does not make mistakes; he does not shout and so on; he is not forgetful; his mind is ever composed; he treats all beings equally; he is not indifferent to beings; he does not lose his interest, his strenuousness, recollection, *samādhi*, insight and liberation; all his physical, vocal and mental actions are preceded and accompanied by awareness; his insight and awareness is unattached and unimpeded regarding all things in the past, present and future.

Emotional afflictions (*kleśa*) The mental factors (*dharmas*) which destabilize and afflict a person, and prevent the attainment of Enlightenment. The basic emotional afflictions are attachment, aversion, unknowing, pride, doubt and false opinions. From these there arise a multitude of subsidiary afflictions.

Emptiness (*śūnyatā*) Equivalent in meaning to suchness and the continuum of reality (*dharmadhātu*), it is the direct realization of the non-existence of a perceiving subject and perceived objects, the natural state of mind. Moreover the MVT tells us that "emptiness is neither an actual entity nor is it not an actual entity. It does not exist or not exist, and nor does it exist and not exist". *Great Emptiness* is the abandonment of even the idea of emptiness.

Enriching (*pauṣṭika*) The second of the four rites a *mantrin* can undertake to facilitate the practice of the Dharma by himself and others.

Equipoise (*samāpatti*) The state where the body and mind abide in a state of tranquil composure. Often *samāpatti* is equivalent to *samādhi* (q.v.).

Essence (*hṛdaya*) The condensed energy pattern in the form of a seed-syllable from which a deity, divine attribute or abode is generated, especially in the process of creative imagination.

Evil states of being (*durgati*) The three lower modes of existence – the hells, the hungry ghosts and the animals. On a popular level, rebirth into these states is taken literally, but a more sophisticated view implies that these states are concerned with experiential modes, that is to say, how the person experiences the world and himself or herself. So a person may be "in hell", though in the eyes of other people he may still retain a human form. The same may be said for the higher modes of existence.

Expedient means (*upāya*) The practical functioning of compassion by which Buddhas or Bodhisattvas mature and liberate beings on the illusion-like relative level, according to their needs.

Five Awarenesses (*jñāna*) The five facets of Perfect Enlightenment. They are i) the Awareness of Suchness (*tathatā-jñāna*) (also called the Continuum of Reality Awareness) which is the bare non-conceptualizing awareness of emptiness (*śūnyatā*) or suchness and is the basic ground unifying the other four; ii) the Mirror-like Awareness (*ādarśa-jñāna*) which is devoid of all dualistic thought and ever united with its "content" as a mirror is with reflections; iii) the Awareness of Sameness (*samatā-jñāna*) which perceives the identity of all phenomena (*dharma*); iv) the Investigating Awareness (*pratyavekṣaṇa-jñana*) which perceives the general and specific qualities of all phenomena; and v) the Awareness of Accomplishing Activities (*kṛty-anuṣṭhāna-jñāna*) which spontaneously carries out all that has to be done for the welfare of beings, manifesting itself in all directions.

Five Supernatural Cognitions (*abhijñā*) Supernormal hearing, supernormal sight, the knowledge of the thoughts of others, the recollection of past lives and the knowledge of supernatural powers.

Four Bases of Supernatural Power (*ṛddhi-pāda*) Intense aspiration, intense strenuousness, intense imagination, and intense concentration.

Four Divine States (*brahma-vihāra*) Kindness, compassion, joy and equanimity.

Four elements The four forces which produce materiality – solidity, fluidity, heat, and movement, commonly referred to as earth, water, fire and wind. They are both manifestations and symbols of the qualities of Vairocana's Mind, the *dharmakāya*.

Four Fearlessnesses (*vaiśāradya*) A Buddha has unshakable confidence in all dealings with other beings. This arises from his All-knowing Awareness, his having eliminated all inflations (*āśravas*), his confidence that he teaches the Path to salvation, and his confidence that he teaches the Path to the elimination of suffering.

Four Methods of Attracting Beings (*saṃgraha-vastu*) The methods used by Bodhisattvas to draw beings to the Dharma by means of generosity, kind words, beneficial acts, and appropriate help.

Four Noble Truths (*ārya-satya*) The four fundamental teachings of Buddhism – Samsaric existence is suffering, emotional afflictions are the cause of suffering, there is a state (*nirvāṇa*) in which all suffering is extinguished, and there is Path which leads to this.

Four Recollections (*smṛty-upasthāna*) The mindfulness that the body is impure, that feeling is suffering, that the mind is impermanence, and that dharmas lack any autonomous existence. Particular types of meditation are prescribed for each of these, and these may be found in such works as the *Smṛty-upasthāna Sūtra* or Buddhaghosa's *Path of Purity.*

Gandharva A class of heavenly beings, famed particularly for their musical skills. Their name (*fragrance-eater*) derives from the belief that they feed themselves only on fragrances.

Garuḍa A mythical class of large bird-like beings who are always in a state of enmity with the nāga-serpents who they eat.

Go-rocana A yellow substance produced from solidified bile of cows, used medicinally for its laxative, antiseptic, antispasmodic and cooling properties.

Habitual tendencies q.v. dispositions.

Homa The ancient Vedic fire ritual in which offerings are burnt, adopted and adapted by Buddhists for the elimination of internal and external obstacles.

Hungry Ghosts (*preta*) One of the miserable modes of existence in Saṃsāra. There are various kinds of *pretas*, but they are all subject to suffering in the form of insatiable and unsatisfiable appetites in recompense for greed and avarice in previous lives.

Immediate Path (*anantarya-mārga*): According Buddhaguhya this is the interim period from the Tenth Level up to the attainment of Perfect Enlightenment.

Inclination (*adhimokṣa*) This implies open-mindedness and trusting willingness to become involved in something, especially the Dharma.

Insight (*prajñā*) Buddhaguhya defines its nature as the realization that "all dharmas are without autonomous existence" or that "all dharmas are primordially unborn" and as "the total understanding of the intrinsic nature of all dharmas".

Interdependent origination (*pratītya-samutpāda*) The process by which all phenomena and events arise each in dependence upon the other. Although used as a general term for the nature of causality in Buddhism, it often refers to the twelve links in the process which gives rise to suffering. Insight into the workings of this process enables one to reverse the process and bring suffering and rebirth to an end.

Investigating Awareness q.v. Five Awarenesses
Jina A title for Buddhas meaning "Victorious One".
Judgmental thought q.v. *vikalpa*
Kalpa A measurement of time. Several accounts exist of the precise number of years involved, and there are also small, medium, great and "uncountable" *kalpas*. The most common values given for an "uncountable" (*asamkhyeya*) *kalpa* are 10^{51}, 10^{59} or 10^{63} years. A Bodhisattva is said to become a Buddha after three of these "uncountable" *kalpas*.
Kinnara A class of heavenly beings, similar to centaurs. They act as musicians in Śakra's heaven.
Kriyā Tantra The first of the four classes of tantras, which mainly teaches external, object-based practices and rituals.
Levels (*bhūmi*) The successive stages in the career of a Bodhisattva, of which there are ten. These are dealt with in I.27.
Liberations (*vimukti*) In the MVT these refer to the modes of approaching reality, the Three Gates of Liberation: Emptiness, the absence of perceptual forms and the absence of purpose. A fourth item is sometimes included: luminosity by nature.
Life-energy (*prāṇa*) The pulsating energy of life which appears on the physical level as breath, while in its purest form it is the energy of Perfect Enlightenment manifesting as the unborn sound of *A* which is emptiness (*śūnyatā*) in nature and penetrates the entire universe.
Logicians (*tārkika*) Philosophers who engage in sophistic discussions without recourse to practice, whose views have little relevance to the real nature of things.
Lotus Family (*padma-kula*) One of the Three Buddha Families taught in the MVT. It is headed by Amitābha, and includes such Bodhisattvas as Avalokiteśvara and Tārā, and protectors like Hayagrīva.
Mahāsattva A title given to advanced Bodhisattvas. "The person who knows that all dharmas are like illusions, and realizes that although no phenomena really exist at all, nevertheless on the relative level, they do bring about effects on that level by means of the certainty of the cause-result relationship, in the manner of illusions, and who then trains in the training accompanied by expedient means in order to completely liberate beings".
Mahoragas A class of demons, lit. "great serpent".
Manas An aspect of the mind which synthesizes perceptual forms derived from the six modes of perceptual awareness (sight, hearing, taste, smell, touch and mental awareness) into images, hence Buddhaguhya regularly defines the *manas* as "the mind (*citta*) associated with perceptual images". In many ways one may think of *manas* as the faculty of creative imagination, and hence it plays a central role in the creation of the alternative world view of mandalas and deities taught in the MVT.
Mandala Multi-dimensional configurations of the manifested qualities of Vairocana's Body, Speech and Mind. Buddhaguhya states that there are two kinds of mandala: the intrinsically existent mandala (*svabhāva-maṇḍala*) and the representational mandala which is the mandala as painted.
Mantra Manifestations of the Speech aspect of Perfect Enlightenment, in the form of various deities and also as the sounds and letters which reveal the qualities embodied by them. Through using mantras in creative imagination and meditation, one is able to tap the power of the various qualities they represent. See 2.80 – 86, 6.12 – 17 for further details.
Mantra Method (*mantra-naya*) The form of practice leading a Bodhisattva to Enlightenment by the use of mantras, mudras and mandalas, in contrast to the Perfection Method (q.v.).
Mantrin One who practises the Mantra Method.
Māra The Buddhist embodiment of evil and death, symbolizing all that may tempt, deceive and destroy in the spiritual life.
Mind (*citta*) The cognitive ground underlying the dynamic system of psychological operations. In its natural state, the mind is intrinsically luminous, free from all attachments and conceptualizing, and is emptiness (*śūnyatā*). In this sense "mind" is equivalent to *bodhicitta* (q.v.). When the natural state of mind is obscured by the false split into a perceiving subject and perceived objects, our everyday "minds" arise which are fragmentations of the natural state.

Mirror-like Awareness q.v. Five Awarenesses.

Mothers (The Seven) Wrathful goddesses who bring sickness and catastrophe to wrongdoers. See 6.15 Commentary, 11.96 and 13.90.

Mount Sumeru The Buddhist *axis mundi*, the mountain at the centre of the world upon which the two lowest heavens of the Realm of Desire are located. Around it the four continents of traditional Buddhist cosmology are arranged. Some scholars believe that the idea of Mount Sumeru was partly inspired by the Mesopotamian ziggurats.

Mudrā Any symbol used to represent physically the qualities of Buddhas and Bodhisattvas, either in the form of such things as swords, lotuses and so forth or as hand gestures. Ultimately the practitioner is to view all appearances as *mudrās*.

Mundane people (*laukikas*) Those following non-Buddhist religions, which in the Buddhist view do not directly lead to liberation from *saṃsāra*. However, these religions are not without value as the MVT sees them as indirect causes of Enlightenment, for they are manifestations of Mahāvairocana's Compassion suited to the capabilities of their adherents, which prevent them from falling into the miserable states of existence and facilitate their eventual entry into the supramundane Buddhist path.

Mundane i) Whatever does not lead directly to liberation from *saṃsāra*. ii) In the case of the mandalas and so forth, it refers to that which has perceptual form.

Nāga A class of serpent-like beings, who live in the underworld and water. They are frequently considered to be benevolent and act as guardians of hidden Mahāyāna texts. Nāgārjuna is said to have been given many scriptures by them, such as the *Prajña-pāramitā Sūtras*.

Nirmāṇa-kāya q.v. *tri-kāya*.

Nirvāṇa The state of peace in which one is released from the suffering of *saṃsāra*. When used in contrast to *Nirvāṇa without localization* (q.v.), it usually indicates an inferior quiescent state attained by Śrāvakas and Pratyekabuddhas.

***Nirvāṇa* with remainder** (*sopadhiśeṣa-nirvāṇa*) The situation when one has severed all emotional afflictions and ended rebirth, yet remains alive with a residual physical body due to previous karma, as in the case of Sākyamuni after his Enlightenment at Bodhgaya until his physical death many years later.

***Nirvāṇa* without localization** (*apratiṣṭha-nirvāṇa*) Perfect *Nirvāṇa*, when a Buddha does not dwell in Saṃsāra because of his great Insight and Awareness, and does not dwell in ordinary *Nirvāṇa* because of his great compassion.

***Nirvāṇa* without remainder** (*nirupadhiśeṣa-nirvāṇa*) Not only have the emotional afflictions been severed and rebirth ended, but the residual physical body is also finally cast off, as in the case of Śākyamuni at his death in Kusinagara.

Obscurations (*āvaraṇa*) The emotional afflictions (*kleśa*) and the wrong understanding of reality which block the realization of Enlightenment.

Pacifying (*śāntika*) The first of the four rites a *mantrin* can undertake to facilitate the practice of the Dharma by himself and others.

Perceiving subject and perceived objects (*grāhya-grāhaka*) When the natural state of mind is lost due to a mistaken understanding of reality (*avidyā*), a dualistic split (*vikalpa*) occurs which fabricates and superimposes upon reality the false idea of a conscious self which perceives and objects which are perceived by it. This state of affairs is *saṃsāra*.

Perceptual elements (*dhātu*) The group of six faculties, their six corresponding objects, and the six perceptual awarenesses: eye, colour-form, sight awareness; ear, sound, aural awareness; nose, fragrance, olfactory awareness; tongue, flavour, gustatory awareness; body, touch, tactile awareness; and mind, phenomena (*dharma*), mental awareness. This group, which comprises the elements present when perception occurs, is used in the Buddhist analysis of perceptual situations to show that all the elements involved in perception are impermanent, unsatisfactory and without autonomous existence.

Perceptual forms (*nimitta*) The basic data of perception such as colours, shapes, sounds and so forth.

Perceptual images (*ākāra*) The images constructed by the *manas* from the input of perceptual forms by which a structured view of the world is created. These images range from those of everyday things to those of the deities and the mandalas in which they dwell. Experientially all of these have the same validity as they are all constructed by the *manas*, although the images of the "divine" are preferable as they enable one to create an alternative liberating view of the world nearer the true state of things.

Perceptual sources (*āyatana*) The group of six faculties and their six corresponding objects – eye, colour-form; ear, sound; nose, fragrance; tongue, flavour; body, touch; and mind, dharmas. This group, which constitutes the elements required for perception to arise, is used in the Buddhist analysis of perceptual situations to show that all the elements involved in perception are impermanent, unsatisfactory and without autonomous existence.

Perfect Buddha (*saṃbuddha*) One who is perfectly Enlightened, referring especially Śākyamuni in the MVT.

Perfect Enlightenment (*saṃbodhi, abhisaṃbodhi*) The Enlightenment associated with a Tathāgata. It is the complete awareness of the emptiness of all dharmas on the absolute and the relative levels, and arises when the last traces of the habitual tendencies of the obscurations of emotional afflictions and wrong understanding have been abandoned without remainder.

Perfection Method (*pāramitā-naya*) The form of practice leading a Bodhisattva to Enlightenment by engagement in the Six Perfections, in contrast to the Mantra Method (q.v.).

Perfections (*pāramitā*) Generally speaking, there are six of these to be practised by a Bodhisattva during his progress to Enlightenment: Generosity, Morality, Patience, Strenuousness, Meditative Concentration, and Insight. Details are given by Buddhaguhya in his comments to I.27. Some texts also speak of a further four Perfections, bringing the number to ten.

Piśāca A class of flesh-eating demons, similar to the *rākṣasas* and *yakṣas* (q.v.).

Practitioner (*sādhaka*) One who engages in *sādhana*.

Pratyekabuddha "Solitary Buddha", the second of the three categories of saintly persons in Buddhism. They achieve an inferior type of Nirvāṇa, without reliance upon a teacher, through an understanding of interdependent arising. However, after they have gained this understanding, they do not communicate the Dharma verbally.

Proliferation (*prapañca*) This refers to the selective concepts (*vikalpa*), which involve the false division into perceiving subject and perceived objects.

Psycho-physical constituents (*skandha*) The group of five elements into which the individual (and environment) is analyzed: colour-form, feeling, ideation, motivations and perceptual awareness. By this analysis one should realize that the individual lacks permanence and autonomous existence (*ātman*), and hence is generally a source of suffering.

Pure Abodes The five highest heavens in the Realm of Form, culminating in Akaniṣṭha (q.v.).

Rākṣasa A class of evil flesh-eating demons who also cause sickness and misfortune.

Reality (*dharmatā*) Intrinsic nature or reality of phenomena when freed from a perceiving subject and perceived objects. Equivalent in meaning to suchness (*tathatā*) and emptiness (*śūnyatā*).

Realm of Desire (*kāma-dhātu*) The lowest of the Three Realms, which forms a large of Saṃsāra as it contains the first five of the six modes of existence: the Hells, Hungry Ghosts, Animals, Humans and *Asuras*, together with the lower Gods who form part of the sixth.

Realm of Form (*rūpa-dhātu*) The second of the Three Realms in Buddhist cosmology and meditation theory. It comprises seventeen heavens where the faculties of smell and taste, sexual organs, physical suffering and certain unwholesome mental factors are absent. The highest of these heavens is *Akaniṣṭha* (q.v.). These states can also be reached through meditation (*dhyāna*), hence their association with the Four *Dhyānas*.

Realm of Formlessness (*arūpya-dhātu*) The third and most subtle of the Three Realms, in which no spatiality or perceptual forms exist at all. It comprises four levels of progressive subtlety, and the beings "dwelling" there remain in a perpetual state of equanimity.

Relative [Level] (*saṃvṛti*) The conventional view of things, which has the effect of concealing their true nature, derived from dualistic concepts (*vikalpa*).

Ṛṣi A Vedic sage or seer.

Sādhana The meditative processes for accomplishment of *siddhis.*

Samādhi One-pointed concentration or composure of mind. It also implies a state of pure creativity due to the attainment of emptiness (*śūnyatā*) which is the source of unbounded possibilities, through the elimination of the subject / object split.

Samaya A multivalent term used with great frequency in tantric texts. Its main uses in the MVT are: i) the conduct required of a tantric practitioner, often as a set of pledges, ii) realization (*abhisamaya*) of Buddhahood, iii) union with the Body, Speech and Mind of Vairocana, and iv) the means expressed by way of symbols which guarantee the attainment of this union.

Saṃbhoga-kāya q.v. *tri-kāya.*

Saṃsāra The general term for the cyclic state in which we find ourselves that is caused by the obscuration of mind's intrinsic purity. It is characterized by impermanence, lack of autonomous existence and suffering, and is often spoken of in contrast to *Nirvāṇa* which has the opposite qualities.

Saṅgha Traditionally, the community of Buddhist monks and nuns. In Mahāyāna, it also includes all Bodhisattvas.

Selective concepts q.v. *vikalpa.*

Self (*ātman*) q.v. Autonomous existence.

Self-aware (*pratyātma-adhigama*) Direct experience of reality wherein the cognizer, the content of cognition and the cognition are identical due to the absence of any dualistic split into subject and objects.

Seven Limbs of Enlightenment (*bodhy-aṅga*) The Seven Limbs of Enlightenment are mindfulness, awareness, strenuousness, joy, relaxation of body and mind, concentration, and equanimity.

Siddhi The attainments accomplished through engaging in the various *sādhanas* described in the MVT. There are two types of *siddhis*: mundane and supramundane. The mundane *siddhis* are of the type described at length in Ch 6, such as invisibility, sky-walking, eternal youth, and other magical powers. Also Cf. Ch 13.49 *et al.* The supramundane *siddhi* is Enlightenment itself.

Sins (*pāpa*) Unwholesome deeds in general. Needless to say, the word "sin" in Buddhism does not imply transgression of the commandments of a creator deity as in Christianity.

Six streams of existence The six modes of being – the Hells, Hungry Ghosts, Animals, Humans, Asuras and Gods, which make up samsaric existence.

Space (*ākāśa*) The image of space is used as an simile for and sometimes directly equated to the mind in its natural state. The unlimited expanse of space which is nothing in itself is characterized by purity, immutability and emptiness, and yet it acts as the "container" or support for all phenomena without distinction. It shares these characteristics with the mind in its natural state and Enlightenment, so the MVT says that these three are identical and cannot be separated.

Śrāvaka "Listener", the name given to the original followers of Śākyamuni. It is also used to refer to the first of the Three Ways, (q.v.) whose teachings and practices were thought to be limited in comparison with those of the Mahāyāna.

Śrīvatsa A curl of hair or a mark in the shape of a *svāstika* on the Buddha's chest.

Stream of mind (*citta-santāna*) The general term used in Buddhism to indicate the continuity of the personality core of an individual in the absence of a permanently abiding "self".

Subduing The third of the four rites a *mantrin* can undertake to facilitate the practice of the Dharma by himself and others.

Suchness (*tathatā*) The way things are in reality, in the absence of the dualistic split into perceiving subject and perceived objects. Hence *tathatā-jñāna* is both the Awareness of suchness, and the Awareness which *is* suchness.

Supra-mundane (*lokottara*) i) Whatever leads directly to liberation from Saṃsāra. ii) In the case of the mandalas and so forth, it refers to those without perceptual forms.

Tathāgata A common title for a perfectly Enlightened Buddha.

Ten directions North, south, east, west, north-east, south-east, south-west, north-west, up and down.
Ten Masteries (*bodhisattva-vaśitā*) These are mastery and freedom with regards life, mind, possessions, actions, birth, fervent conviction, the Dharma, aspirations, magical powers and Awareness.
Ten mundane wholesome actions (*laukika-kuśala-karma*) The basic moral code common to most religions: to act without taking or harming life, stealing, engaging in improper sexual behaviour, lying, abuse, slander, covetousness, malice and perverse opinions. However, valuable though this morality is, it cannot by itself lead to liberation, hence it is said to be "mundane". This only happens when accompanied by expedient means and insight.
Ten Strengths (*bala*) Ten types of knowledge (*jñāna*) a Tathāgata possesses with respect to i) distinguishing the possible and the impossible, ii) the results of actions, iii) the various interests of beings, iv) the various realms, v) superior and inferior faculties in beings, vi) all outcomes of practice, vii) all states of meditation, *samādhi*, equipoise and their defilement, purification and withdrawal from them, viii) recollection of the past lives of beings, ix) the future deaths and rebirths of beings, and x) the cessation of inflations.
Thirty Two Marks of a Great Being The characteristic physical signs of a Buddha or a Universal Monarch (*cakravartin*), which include the *ūrṇā* and *uṣṇīṣa* (q.v.). See *Mahāpadāna Sutta* (DN II) and *Lakkhana Sutta* (DN III) for full list.
Three Families An early classification of Buddhas and Bodhisattvas with their associated qualities comprising the Tathāgata, Vajra and Lotus Families, epitomized by Śākyamuni, Vajrapāṇi and Avalokiteśvara. This classification is also related to the Mind, Speech and Body aspects of Vairocana, and to the *dharmakāya*, *saṃbhoga-kāya* and *nirmāṇa-kāya*. In the later tantras from the *Tattva-saṃgraha* onwards, this set is supplanted by the Five Family system formed by the addition of the Ratna (Jewel) and Karma Families.
Three Jewels Buddha, Dharma and Sangha.
Three Realms The Realms of Desire, Form and Formlessness which make up *saṃsāra*.
Three Ways (*yāna*) The theoretical and practical aspects of the paths of the Śrāvakas, the Pratyekabuddhas and the Bodhisattvas.
Transformation, transformational power (*adhiṣṭhāna*) An aspect of the power inherent in Vairocana's compassion by which he communicates and reveals the qualities of his Body, Speech and Mind in the form of mandalas, mantras and *mudrās* throughout the universe to beings of lesser ability. The presence of this power also guarantees that such beings may participate in the being of Vairocana through their body, speech and mind when they engage in the practices associated with those transformations.
Tri-kāya According to the general Mahāyāna view, a Buddha has three modes of being or embodiment: the *dharmakāya*, the *saṃbogha-kāya* and the *nirmāṇa-kaya*. The *dharmakāya* which forms the ground for the other two is Perfect Enlightenment itself, primordially existent and is equivalent to Vairocana's Mind. It transcends all perceptual forms and so cannot be directly manifested or perceived. Its qualities (*guṇa*) are authentic unchanging consummacy, freedom from all conceptualization, liberation from all emotional afflictions, and the intrinsic ability to perform all activities. From the *dharmakāya*, two other modes of embodiment arise, the *saṃbhoga-kāya* and the *nirmāṇa-kāya* which are equivalent to Vairocana's Speech and Body respectively. According to the MVT, these two modes of embodiment form the intrinsically existent mandala, and are called the Inexhaustible Adornments of Body, Speech and Mind, which are manifestations of the qualities of Perfect Enlightenment. Being Vairocana's Speech, the *saṃbhoga-kāya* is especially concerned with communication of the Dharma and appears in the form of various Buddhas and Bodhisattvas, though these are beyond the perceptual range of ordinary beings. To cater for their needs and abilities, Vairocana further creates various *nirmāṇa-kāyas*, a lower order of manifestation, in the physical form of such teachers as Śākyamuni.
Two extremes Usually signifies the extremes of nihilism and eternalism as causal explanations, but sometimes used here to mean the polarity of perceiving subject and perceived objects.

Ubhaya "Dual", the term used by Buddhaguhya to classify the MVT, signifying that it has qualities of both Kriyā and Yoga Tantras -external ritual and internal yoga.
Unwholesome deeds (*akuśala-karma*) To engage in actions which involve the taking or harming of life, stealing, engaging in improper sexual behaviour, lying, abuse, slander, covetousness, malice and perverse opinions.
Ūrṇā The circle of hair between a Buddha's eyebrows, also personified as a Goddess.
Uṣṇīṣa The swelling of flesh or the top-knot of hair on a Buddha's head, also personified as the Uṣṇīṣa goddesses.
Utpala The blue lotus, *Nymphaea caerula.*
Vajradhara "Vajra-holder", a title given to accomplished beings who engage in tantric practice, in contrast to that of Bodhisattva which is especially given to those who follow the Perfections, though some Vajradharas may also be called Bodhisattvas. Also an alternative name for Vajrapāṇi.
Vidyā Though literally meaning "knowledge", *vidyās* include a wide range of various skills, crafts, sciences and magical powers. The term basically implies the knowledge of something and hence the power to utilize and control it often by the use of "spells". While this basic popular meaning is often present in the MVT, the Buddhist usage of *vidyā*, according to Buddhaguhya, especially refers to the Awareness of Suchness and to the mantras and mudras which emerge from it, as well as the embodiments of its qualities which are usually in female form.
Vidyādhara A class of powerful beings who live in the snowy mountains of North India and have various supernatural powers derived from their mastery of *vidyās* such as longevity, the ability to fly or to change shape. According to some sources they were thought to have been guardians of tantric lore, hence early tantric corpus of texts is was called the "*Vidyādhara-piṭaka*" in contrast to the Sūtra and Vinaya Piṭakas. By extension *vidyādhara* is used as a title for people who have completed the tantric training and who are endowed with various magical powers.
Vikalpa i) The process which sets up the false dualistic split that is imposed upon reality, and involves belief in the existence of a perceiving subject and perceived objects. ii) The products of this process which can be called concepts, judgmental thoughts, reflective selection or selective concepts.
Vinaya The part of the Buddhist canon which stipulates the rules for all aspects of life as a monk.
Visarga The sign written as two dots or circles used in Sanskrit writing to indicate aspiration after a vowel. It is normally transcribed as *ḥ*.
Wish-fulfilling Gem (*cintā-maṇi*) A legendary magical jewel which spontaneously provides whatever you wish for.
Yakṣa Generally thought to be malevolent flesh-eating demons in later Buddhism, the *yakṣa* and their female counterparts, the *yakṣinī*, were originally more or less benevolent local nature divinities who if correctly propitiated would protect the community. If not treated with due respect they wreaked their vengeance upon the populace in the form of sickness and natural catastrophes. They were also believed to have many magical powers, especially that of shape-shifting. *Yakṣinī* were particularly associated with trees, and are frequently depicted in Indian art as sinuous young women with great sexual grace, though with undertones of menace.
Yoga Here simply implies the intensive technique or method of application to a particular practice.
Yoga Tantra One of the two classes of tantras described by Buddhaguhya in his preamble to the Commentary, which concentrates on internal yogic practices. The later division of this class of tantras into Yoga Tantra proper and Anuttarayoga Tantra seems to have been unknown to Buddhaguhya.

9 780700 71183

CPSIA information can be obtained
at www.ICGtesting.com
Printed in the USA
BVHW03s0136230518
517063BV00011B/54/P

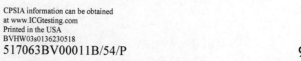